Dictionary of Literary Biography
Yearbook: 1986

Dictionary of Literary Biography

Documentary Series

Yearbooks

Concise Series

Dictionary of Literary Biography
Yearbook: 1986

Edited by
J. M. Brook

685a

A Bruccoli Clark Layman Book
Gale Research Company • Book Tower • Detroit, Michigan 48226

Advisory Board for
DICTIONARY OF LITERARY BIOGRAPHY

Copyright © 1987
GALE RESEARCH COMPANY

Manufactured by Edwards Brothers, Inc.
Ann Arbor, Michigan
Printed in the United States of America

Library of Congress Catalog Card Number 82-645187
ISSN 0731-7867
ISBN 0-8103-2094-0

Contents

Obituaries

Plan of the Series

The advisory board, the editors, and the publisher of the *Dictionary of Literary Biography* are joined in endorsing Mark Twain's declaration. The literature of a nation provides an inexhaustible resource of permanent worth. It is our expectation that this endeavor will make literature and its creators better understood and more accessible to students and the literate public, while satisfying the standards of teachers and scholars.

To meet these requirements, *literary biography* has been construed in terms of the author's achievement. The most important thing about a writer is his writing. Accordingly, the entries in *DLB* are career biographies, tracing the development of the author's canon and the evolution of his reputation.

The publication plan for *DLB* resulted from two years of preparation. The project was proposed to Bruccoli Clark by Frederick G. Ruffner, president of the Gale Research Company, in November 1975. After specimen entries were prepared and typeset, an advisory board was formed to refine the entry format and develop the series rationale. In meetings held during 1976, the publisher, series editors, and advisory board approved the scheme for a comprehensive biographical dictionary of persons who contributed to North American literature. Editorial work on the first volume began in January 1977, and it was published in 1978.

In order to make *DLB* more than a reference tool and to compile volumes that individually have claim to status as literary history, it was decided to organize volumes by topic or period or genre. Each of these freestanding volumes provides a biographical-bibliographical guide and overview for a particular area of literature. We are convinced that this organization—as opposed to a single alphabet method—constitutes a valuable innovation in the

presentation of reference material. The volume plan necessarily requires many decisions for the placement and treatment of authors who might properly be included in two or three volumes. In some instances a major figure will be included in separate volumes, but with different entries emphasizing the aspect of his career appropriate to each volume. Ernest Hemingway, for example, is represented in *American Writers in Paris, 1920-1939* by an entry focusing on his expatriate apprenticeship; he is also in *American Novelists, 1910-1945* with an entry surveying his entire career. Each volume includes a cumulative index of subject authors and articles. The final *DLB* volume will be a comprehensive index to the entire series.

With volume ten in 1982 it was decided to enlarge the scope of *DLB*. By the end of 1986 twenty-one volumes treating British literature had been published, and volumes for Commonwealth and Modern European literature were in progress. The series has been further augmented by the *DLB Yearbooks* (since 1981) which update published entries and add new entries to keep the *DLB* current with contemporary activity. There have also been occasional *DLB Documentary Series* volumes which provide biographical and critical background source materials for figures whose work is judged to have particular interest for students. One of these companion volumes is entirely devoted to Tennessee Williams.

The purpose of *DLB* is not only to provide reliable information in a convenient format but also to place the figures in the larger perspective of literary history and to offer appraisals of their accomplishments by qualified scholars.

We define literature as the *intellectual commerce of a nation:* not merely as belles lettres but as that ample and complex process by which ideas are generated, shaped, and transmitted. *DLB* entries are not limited to "creative writers" but extend to other figures who in this time and in this way influenced the mind of a people. Thus the series encompasses historians, journalists, publishers, and screenwriters. By this means readers of *DLB* may be aided to perceive literature not as cult scripture in the keeping of cultural high priests but as at the center of a nation's life.

DLB includes the major writers appropriate to

each volume and those standing in the ranks immediately behind them. Scholarly and critical counsel has been sought in deciding which minor figures to include and how full their entries should be. Wherever possible, useful references are made to figures who do not warrant separate entries.

Each *DLB* volume has a volume editor responsible for planning the volume, selecting the figures for inclusion, and assigning the entries. Volume editors are also responsible for preparing, where appropriate, appendices surveying the major periodicals and literary and intellectual movements for their volumes, as well as lists of further readings. Work on the series as a whole is coordinated at the Bruccoli Clark Layman editorial center in Columbia, South Carolina, where the editorial staff is responsible for the accuracy of the published volumes.

One feature that distinguishes *DLB* is the illustration policy—its concern with the iconography of literature. Just as an author is influenced by his surroundings, so is the reader's understanding of the author enhanced by a knowledge of his environment. Therefore *DLB* volumes include not only drawings, paintings, and photographs of authors, often depicting them at various stages in their careers, but also illustrations of their families and places where they lived. Title pages are regularly reproduced in facsimile along with dust jackets for modern authors. The dust jackets are a special feature of *DLB* because they often document better than anything else the way in which an author's work was launched in its own time. Specimens of the writers' manuscripts are included when feasible.

A supplement to *DLB*—tentatively titled *A Guide, Chronology, and Glossary for American Literature*—will outline the history of literature in North America and trace the influences that shaped it. This volume will provide a framework for the study of American literature by means of chronological tables, literary affiliation charts, glossarial entries, and concise surveys of the major movements. It has been planned to stand on its own as a vade mecum, providing a ready-reference guide to the study of American literature as well as a companion to the *DLB* volumes for American literature.

Samuel Johnson rightly decreed that "The chief glory of every people arises from its authors." The purpose of the *Dictionary of Literary Biography* is to compile literary history in the surest way available to us—by accurate and comprehensive treatment of the lives and work of those who contributed to it.

The *DLB* Advisory Board

Foreword

The *Dictionary of Literary Biography Yearbook* is guided by the same principles that have provided the basic rationale for the entire *DLB* series: 1) the literature of a nation represents an inexhaustible resource of permanent worth; 2) the surest way to trace the outlines of literary history is by a comprehensive treatment of the lives and works of those who contributed to it; and 3) the greatest service the series can provide is to make literary achievement better understood and more accessible to students and the literate public, while serving the needs of scholars. In keeping with those principles, the *Yearbook* has been planned to augment *DLB* by reflecting the vitality of contemporary literature and summarizing current literary activity. The librarian, scholar, or student attempting to stay informed of literary developments is faced with an endless task. The purpose of *DLB Yearbook* is to serve these readers while at the same time enlarging the scope of *DLB*.

DLB Yearbook is divided into four sections: articles about the past year's literary events or topics; obituaries and tributes; updates of published *DLB* entries; and new author entries. The articles section features essays which discuss the year's work in literary biography, fiction, poetry, and, this year, book publishing. The *Yearbook* also endeavors to cover major awards and prizes. This volume covers the 1986 Nobel Prize in Literature and the 1986 Nobel Peace Prize (including Wole Soyinka's and Elie Wiesel's Nobel Lectures). There is also an entry on Great Britain's prestigious Booker Prize. Each year a literary research archive is described; the 1986 *Yearbook*'s subject is Kent State University's Special Collections. In "Literary Documents," the *Yearbook* presents letters and questionnaires from the People-to-People Program, which was supervised by William Faulkner. Literary topics of current interest are explored: in this *Yearbook* there are reports on the creation of the United States Poet Laureateship; the publication of the complete works of George Orwell; the discovery of a John Webster manuscript; and the posthumous publication of Ernest Hemingway's *The Garden of Eden*.

There are also entries on the University of Iowa Writers' Workshop Golden Jubilee and the Randall Jarrell Symposium held at the University of South Carolina. A special feature of the first section is an interview with a distinguished practicing biographer—this year Justin Kaplan.

The death of a literary figure prompts an assessment of his achievement and reputation. The Obituaries section marks the passing of eight authors in 1986.

The third section, Updated Entries, is designed to supplement the *DLB* series with current information about the literary activities of authors who have entries in previously published *DLB* volumes. An Updated Entry takes as its point of departure an already published *DLB* entry, augmenting primary and secondary bibliographical information, providing descriptions and assessments of new works, and, when necessary, reassessing an author's reputation. The form of entry is similar to that in the standard *DLB* series, and an Updated Entry is preceded by a reference to the *DLB* volume in which the basic entry on the subject appears. Readers seeking information about an author's entire career should consult the basic entry along with the Updated Entry for complete biographical and bibliographical information.

The fourth section is devoted to New Entries on figures not previously included in *DLB*. These entries follow the established format for the series: emphasis is placed on biography and summaries of the critical reception of the author's works; primary bibliographies precede each entry, and a list of references follows the entry.

Each *Yearbook* includes a list of literary prizes and awards, a necrology, and a checklist of books about literary history and biography published during the year.

From the outset, the *DLB* series has undertaken to compile literary history as it is revealed in the lives and works of authors. The *Yearbook* supports that commitment, providing a useful and necessary current record. The march of literature does not halt.

Acknowledgments

This book was produced by Bruccoli Clark Layman, Inc. Karen L. Rood is senior editor for the *Dictionary of Literary Biography* series.

Art supervisor is Pamela Haynes. Copyediting supervisor is Patricia Coate. Production coordinator is Kimberly Casey. Typesetting supervisor is Laura Ingram. Lucia Tarbox is editorial assistant. The production staff includes Rowena Betts, David R. Bowdler, Mary S. Dye, Charles Egleston, Kathleen M. Flanagan, Joyce Fowler, Karen Fritz, Judith K. Ingle, Judith E. McCray, Janet Phelps, and Joycelyn R. Smith. Jean W. Ross is permissions editor. Joseph Caldwell, photography editor, and Joseph Matthew Bruccoli did photographic copy work for the volume.

Walter W. Ross and Rhonda Marshall did the library research with the assistance of the staff at the Thomas Cooper Library of the University of South Carolina: Lynn Barron, Daniel Boice, Connie Crider, Kathy Eckman, Michael Freeman, Gary Geer, David L. Haggard, Jens Holley, Marcia Martin, Dana Rabon, Jean Rhyne, Jan Squire, Ellen Tillett, and Virginia Weathers.

Special thanks are due to the University of Virginia Library for permission to publish documents from the William Faulkner collection.

Dictionary of Literary Biography
Yearbook: 1986

Dictionary of Literary Biography

The 1986 Nobel Prize In Literature

WOLE SOYINKA
(13 July 1934-   )

Thomas Hayes
University of South Carolina

SELECTED BOOKS: *A Dance of the Forests* (London
& Ibadan: Oxford University Press, 1963);
The Lion and the Jewel (London & Ibadan: Oxford
University Press, 1963);
Three Plays (Ibadan: Mbari, 1963)—includes *The
Swamp Dwellers, The Trials of Brother Jero,* and
The Strong Breed;
Five Plays (London & Ibadan: Oxford University
Press, 1964)—includes *A Dance of the Forests,
The Lion and the Jewel, The Swamp Dwellers, The
Trials of Brother Jero,* and *The Strong Breed*;
The Interpreters (London: Deutsch, 1965; New York:
Collier, 1970);
The Road (London & Ibadan: Oxford University
Press, 1965);
Idanre and Other Poems (London: Methuen, 1967;
New York: Hill & Wang, 1968);
Kongi's Harvest (London, Ibadan & Nairobi: Oxford
University Press, 1967);
Poems from Prison (London: Collings, 1969);
Before the Blackout (Ibadan: Orisun Publications,
1971);
Madmen and Specialists (London: Methuen, 1971;
New York: Farrar, Straus & Giroux, 1971);
A Shuttle in the Crypt (London: Collings/Methuen,
1972; New York: Hill & Wang, 1972);
The Man Died: Prison Notes of Wole Soyinka (London:
Collings, 1972; New York: Harper & Row,
1972);
The Bacchae of Euripides (London: Methuen, 1973;
New York: Norton, 1974);
Camwood on the Leaves (London: Methuen, 1973);
republished in *Camwood on the Leaves and Be-*
fore the Blackout (New York: Third Press,
1974);
The Jero Plays (London: Methuen, 1973)—includes
The Trials of Brother Jero and *Jero's Metamor-
phosis*;
Season of Anomy (London: Collings, 1973; New
York: Third Press, 1974);
Death and the King's Horseman (London: Methuen,
1975; New York: Norton, 1975);
Myth, Literature, and the African World (Cambridge
& New York: Cambridge University Press,
1976);
Ogun Abibiman (London & Ibadan: Collings, 1976);
Aké: The Years of Childhood (London: Collings, 1981;
New York: Random House, 1981);
Opera Wonyosi (London: Collings, 1981; Blooming-
ton: Indiana University Press, 1981);
A Play of Giants (London: Methuen, 1984);
Requiem for a Futurologist (London: Collings, 1985).

SCREENPLAY: *Kongi's Harvest,* Calpenny-Nige-
rian Films, 1970.

OTHER: *Poems of Black Africa,* edited by Soyinka
(London: Secker & Warburg, 1975; New
York: Hill & Wang, 1975).

TRANSLATION: D. O. Fagunwa, *The Forest of a
Thousand Daemons: A Hunter's Saga,* translated
by Soyinka (London: Nelson, 1968).

This year's Nobel Prize for Literature to Nigeria's Wole Soyinka (born Akinwande Oluwole
Soyinka) is the first to a black African. In bestowing

Wole Soyinka, 1986 Nobel Laureate in Literature (courtesy of the Swedish Academy)

the award upon Soyinka the Academy chose to honor a man who has led the search for an authentic set of African values. For nearly three decades Soyinka's life and work have mirrored the dramatic political and social transitions of a vast and troubled continent, and by recognizing Soyinka the Swedish Academy honors not only a playwright, translator, actor, producer, poet, novelist, set designer, and political activist but also the struggle by peoples everywhere to define and celebrate their indigenous cultures. More than any other African writer, Soyinka has universalized the art, theater, language, and folklore of Africa. His drama and fiction have challenged the West to broaden its aesthetic and accept African standards of art and literature. His personal and political life have challenged Africa to embrace the truly democratic values of the African tribe and reject the tyranny of power practiced on the continent by its colonizers and by many of its modern rulers.

Self-sacrifice, the search for truth, the struggle between the individual and his society, and the desire for continuity against the need for change are major concerns in Soyinka's Africa, a continent torn by the demands of a complex, technological present and the fractured remnants of a remembered past. "I have one abiding religion—human liberty," Soyinka says. "Conditioned to the truth that life is meaningless, insulting, without this fullest liberty, and in spite of the despairing knowledge that words alone seem unable to guarantee its possession, my writing grows more and more preoccupied with this theme of the oppressive boot, the irrelevance of the colour of the foot that wears it and the struggle for individuality."

Soyinka was born 13 July 1934 in Abeokuta, in western Nigeria, and attended University College in Ibadan from 1952 to 1954, where he was a member of the class that included Chinua Achebe, John Pepper Clark, and Christopher Okigbo. His literary career began with the publication of poems and short stories that appeared in the Nigerian literary magazine *Black Orpheus.* From 1954 to 1960 he studied English literature under George Wilson Knight at the University of Leeds (where he took a doctorate in 1973) and was a reader for the Royal Court Theatre, where his first dramatic effort, *The Invention,* was produced in 1955. The unpublished play wryly explores the difficulties the South African government encounters when the accidental explosion of a United States missile, launched on the 200th anniversary of the Declaration of Independence, destroys all skin pigments in the black population. Unable to distinguish black from white, the government employs the nation's scientists to restore the familiar basis of apartheid. The play is Soyinka's sole direct dramatic treatment of the political situation in South Africa.

In 1960 Soyinka returned to Nigeria as a research fellow at Ibadan University and presented *The Swamp Dwellers* (published in *Three Plays,* 1963) and *The Lion and the Jewel* (1963) at the Arts Theatre in Ibadan. While teaching at Ibadan University Soyinka researched Nigerian folk drama for a year under a Rockefeller Foundation award. During this period he also taught at the Universities of Lagos and Ife. In 1960 he founded The 1960 Masks, a group of professional and semiprofessional Nigerian actors and playwrights dedicated to the formation of a new Nigerian drama written in English but very much in touch with the folkways of the nation. Soyinka was intensely busy during this period, shuttling back and forth between Lagos and Ibadan in a Land Rover he used for his research, organizing and raising funds for the Masks, and sometimes leading rehearsals by telephone. In October 1960 the Masks gave their first production, Soyinka's *A Dance of the Forests* (1963), at the Nigerian independence celebration. In 1965 the troupe was disbanded and largely reformed as the Orisun Players.

The first hints that Soyinka's life would parallel his works in their dignified and uncompromising criticism of tyranny and oppression came in 1963, when he left a position at the University of Ife for political reasons. He devoted the next two years to the theater, but in 1965 he was implicated in an illegal radio broadcast of antigovernment statements over a Nigerian Broadcasting Corporation station. After his arrest writers in the West, such as Norman Mailer and William Styron, issued protests. Soyinka was charged with theft and with threatening to use violence against an NBC official. The government, faced with evidence that Soyinka had not been near the NBC radio station, acquitted him of charges a month later.

In 1967 Soyinka was appointed chairman of the department of theater arts at the University of Ibadan. The same year he was imprisoned and charged with assisting the Biafran independence movement. Soyinka admitted visiting the Ibo revolutionary leader, Colonel Ojukwa, to discuss a peaceful end to the conflict but was never brought to trial. In 1969 Soyinka was released after more than two years in jail, much of it spent in solitary confinement. After his release from prison critics noticed a change in Soyinka's writings, which were becoming more brooding and less optimistic. *The Man Died: Prison Notes of Wole Soyinka* (1972) is the playwright's autobiographical prose account of his incarceration and expresses his contempt for his captors and their regime.

In 1971 Soyinka resigned from his post at the University of Ibadan and accepted a fellowship at Churchill College, Cambridge, for 1972 and then moved on to Ghana to edit *Transition*, a magazine of African culture. In 1975 he returned to the University of Ife as a professor of comparative literature, a position he retains, though he has served as a visiting lecturer at several institutions.

Soyinka is a member of the Yoruba tribe, and the mythology, the folklore, the song and dance and literature of the daily life of his tribe pervade much of his work. In his second autobiographical work, *Ake: The Years of Childhood* (1981), Soyinka relives the village life and early education of his childhood. Highly anecdotal and detailed, the account is lively, humorous, and personal. James Olney, writing in the *New York Times Book Review* (10 October 1982), said, "Through recollection, restoration and re-creation, [Soyinka] conveys a personal vision that was formed by the childhood

world that he now returns to evoke and exalt in his autobiography. This is the ideal circle of autobiography at its best. It is what makes 'Aké,' in addition to its other great virtues, the best available introduction to the work of one of the liveliest, most exciting writers in the world today."

Yoruba proverbs and lore provide a link to the past which lends the power of tradition to Soyinka's criticism of the present and, in a continent where the artist is often at odds with the government, allows him to speak in images rather than polemic. As an artist Soyinka identifies himself with the Yoruba god Ogun, the god of metal and the forge, of creation and destruction, who, as Eldred Jones, an African critic, says, "has always lived a life amidst the challenges and the risks of wrong choices." To understand Soyinka's life and work is to understand his concern that man have the freedom to exercise these choices, even if he is often misguided.

The freedom to choose, and the question of what to choose—the modern or the traditional—is the central theme of three of Soyinka's plays. *The Swamp Dwellers*, Soyinka's first major dramatic production, suggests that certain African traditions must be rejected. Produced for the University of London Drama Festival in 1958, the play is a tragedy of two brothers who reject the domination of their community by a local snake god and his corrupt priests. In *The Lion and the Jewel* traditional Africa triumphs over the forces of modernism. Soyinka suggests that essential African values should be maintained and that progress should come to Africa as it suits the interests of African society. *The Lion and the Jewel*, written in a mixture of prose and loose, unrhymed verse, is the witty, lusty, and satirical story of the seduction of Sidi, a village beauty. Her seducer is the village strong man; his rival, the schoolteacher Lakunle, is weak, ineffectual, and pretentiously modern.

Though disturbing to Western audiences, who are accustomed to taking the benefits of the modern world for granted, the victory of the village strong man over Lakunle is not vindictive. Lakunle rejects tradition partly because he cannot succeed within it (he cannot afford Sidi's bride price). Lakunle is a fine, sad character, as out of place in the world he embraces as in the world he rejects.

A Dance of the Forests was commissioned for the Nigerian independence celebrations, and in it Soyinka cautions Nigerians not to take a romantic view of the past and so ignore present-day concerns. Set in a forest which serves much the same function as the groves of *A Midsummer Night's*

Dream, the play follows a group of bickering humans who have invoked the spirits of the gods for a festival. But the heroes of the past are petty and mean, much like the ordinary people of the day. Critic John F. Povey, in *Tri-Quarterly* (December 1965), has stated that "humour and poetry exist side by side in this play in ways that might be disastrous but never are. *A Dance of the Forests* is pertinent not only to Africa and to newly independent countries there, but also to any and every man's relationship with his past, with his gods and with the concealed parts of his own heart."

The self-sacrifices the African, and all humans, must make as they struggle to understand themselves and their traditions in a conflicting, contradictory world are the subjects of *The Strong Breed* (published in *Three Plays,* 1963) and *Death and the King's Horseman* (1975). In both plays the protagonist is unable to escape the responsibilities of the past. In *The Strong Breed* a young, educated Nigerian, unwilling to inherit his father's role as symbolic "carrier" of the sins of his community but unable to deny his involvement with his people, offers himself as a blood sacrifice to his more traditional villagers. The play centers on his slaughter but ends with the hint that such practices, whether ritual or real, may come to an end. *Death and the King's Horseman* is based partly on the interruption of a ritual suicide that took place in Nigeria in 1946. After the death of a Yoruba king his horseman is expected to commit suicide. The local district commissioner intervenes, and the horseman's son, who has received a Western education, kills himself in his father's place. The play, written after Soyinka's imprisonment, is not an attack against the effects of colonialism on traditional Africa as much as a beautiful tribute to the strength of Yoruba tradition.

Two of Soyinka's plays are parables of the search for truth amid the rubble men have made of the world and of themselves. *The Road* (1965) is a masterful sketch of the curious blend of the prophets, the impoverished, the unemployed, and the insane who haunt the highways of an African nation. The road itself symbolizes Ogun, lusting for blood and sacrifice. Roaming the road is the Professor, a high priest of highway carnage, who seeks The Word amid the accidents he helps create by moving road signs. The search for meaning amid the horrors of wars is the subject of *Madmen and Specialists* (1971). Written soon after Soyinka's release from prison, the play is a sere, brutal examination of tyranny and dogma and the corruption they reap on the dignity of man's professions.

References to Africa are few, and what little action there is could take place anywhere. A young doctor, returning from the wars that have made him a specialist in torture, confronts the seemingly mad old man who is his father. The old man commands a group of cripples and mendicants—the worshippers of "As," or the principle of things as they are, the acceptance of meaninglessness. The son sets out to force the secrets of As from his father. A previous lesson, in which the father exposed the inevitable outcome of all oppression and inhumanity by tricking his son into eating human flesh, was lost on the son. The war has dehumanized the son, and his father is his last contact with life. The final confrontation between the two, a logical development of their characters, is far from hopeful.

In the characters of the Professor and the Madman Soyinka borrows heavily from both Christian and Yoruba traditions. The religious symbolism in Soyinka's plays is rarely subtle, and in three satirical plays—*The Trials of Brother Jero* (published in *Three Plays,* 1963), *Jero's Metamorphosis* (published in *The Jero Plays,* 1973), and *Requiem for a Futurologist* (1985)—Soyinka's targets are religious charlatans and their disciples. *The Trials of Brother Jero,* performed in 1960 at the Arts Theatre in Ibadan, was presented by Radio Nigeria the same year and is in many ways a companion play to *The Lion and the Jewel. The Trials of Brother Jero* is a broad, comic farce about the adventures of a professional huckster, the false prophet Jero. Lagos's Bar Beach, a favorite stomping ground for spiritualists and evangelicals, is the setting, and from the opening monologue Soyinka invites the audience to share in Jero's adventures as he ingeniously handles his congregation, at times quite literally.

Jero appears again in *Jero's Metamorphosis,* a satirical look at the machinations between church and state. Bar Beach is now the sight of Nigeria's public executions, and Jero schemes for the privilege of administering last rites to the condemned. In *Requiem for a Futurologist* Soyinka broadsides the media-hyped brand of evangelical prophets who head the so-called New Age of modern religious expression.

As Soyinka has matured he has hardened his criticism of all that restricts the individual's ability to choose, think, and act free from external oppression. Though he has not limited his concerns to Africa, *Kongi's Harvest* (1967) and *A Play of Giants* (1984) are unambiguously critical of African politics. *Kongi's Harvest* attacks the breed of tyrannical leaders Soyinka sees emerging in Africa. *A Play of Giants,* Soyinka's latest dramatic work, is his harsh-

PLAYBILL

LINCOLN CENTER THEATER AT THE VIVIAN BEAUMONT

Death and the King's Horseman

Cover for Playbill *(March 1987) featuring the revival of Soyinka's 1975 play*

est attack against modern Africa, a blunt, venomous assault on four African leaders and the powers who support them. In this play Soyinka does not adapt African traditions to contemporary concerns. There is no African setting, no African protagonist. The play is set in New York, where African heads of state, representing Jean Bedel Bokassa, Sese Seko Mobutu, Macias Ngeuma, and Idi Amin, have gathered at the United Nations to have their likenesses sculpted. Their conversation reflects the corruption and cruelty of their regimes and the casual, brutal flavor of their rule.

It is in the novel, however, that Soyinka has found the clearest means of expressing his most virulent opinions about modern Africa and Africans. His first novel, *The Interpreters* (1965), was hailed by Bernth Lindfors in *Africa Report* (June 1966) as "the most complex narrative work yet written by an African." It is the story of a group of young Nigerians who meet from time to time to discuss, and attempt to interpret, their lives and the future of their country. The old versus the new and the difficulties of understanding oneself in the

world while continuing to adjust to change are explicit in the young men's discussions and in Soyinka's development of their rather ordinary lives.

Stylistically the novel borrows from Faulkner and Joyce. There is virtually no plot and no conflict. Charles Larson writes in his *The Emergence of African Fiction* (1971), "the movement of the narrative instead of being temporal is figural, through space, and the pattern within the novel itself is based on a montage-like repetition of images, piled up on top of one another."

Season of Anomy (1973), Soyinka's second novel, is relentless, almost savage, in its portrayal of modern Africa. His view of postwar society and of new governments that offer promise after periods of national trial is pessimistic and bitter. John Mellors, in a review for *London Magazine* (April/May 1974), wrote of *Season of Anomy*, "Wole Soyinka appears to have written much of *Season of Anomy* in a blazing fury. . . . The plot charges along, dragging the reader . . . through forest, mortuary and prison camp in nightmare visions of tyranny, torture, slaughter and putrefaction. . . . Soyinka hammers at the point that the liberal has to deal with violence in the world however much he would wish he could ignore it; the scenes of murder and mutilation, while sickeningly explicit . . . are justified by . . . the author's anger and compassion and insistence that bad will not become better by our refusal to examine it."

Soyinka's attacks against certain African traditions and nations have earned him the enmity of many of his countrymen and of several critics from Africa and the West (*Blues for a Prodigal*, a film project that was to premier in 1985, was seized by Nigeria's Buhari government). But he is not controversial for his political views alone. Though Soyinka believes that Swahili should be made the lingua franca of African literature, he writes in English, and when not speaking in pidgin English or reciting Yoruba proverbs his characters often speak an elevated, formal English. Consequently the dialogue in his plays can seem curiously un-African, for of course his characters in reality would more likely speak their own less-formal African vernaculars.

Soyinka's reliance on English, his use of both Yoruba and Christian mythology, and his considerable debt to the Greek theater and to Western dramatic techniques represent not a retreat from African tradition but an embrace of the human experience and a deep awareness of the characteristics that define him apart from his society or his time. At the same time, Soyinka has fought for the uniqueness of African literature, arguing that it must be viewed as a tradition that exists simultaneously with, and not subservient to, Western literature. As Elaine Jahner points out in "African Culture Today" (*Book Forum,* 3, no. 1 [1977]), Soyinka "assumes that his readers are willing to understand that the most insidious and prevalent form of racism is that which forces African concerns into a non-African frame of reference and then judges the African lacking. As sui generis, African literature must be evaluated by the reference points within African culture itself, not by the externally imposed standards of Western civilization."

But African and Western literature are not entirely separate in Soyinka's drama. For *The Bacchae of Euripides* (1973) and *Opera Wonyosi* (1981) Soyinka rewrote two European plays, Euripedes' *Bacchae* and Bertold Brecht's *The Three Penny Opera,* and stamped each firmly with African characters and values. The structure of the earlier plays is infused in Soyinka's versions with African dynamics that broaden their scope to include veiled but specific criticisms of contemporary Africa. *Opera Wonyosi* satirizes the military rule and economic prosperity of Nigeria in the 1970s and is the more critically acclaimed of the two plays.

It is in Soyinka's poetry, however, that he is most universal. "Telephone Conversation," which Soyinka read at London's Royal Court Theatre in 1959, is his most famous early poem. The subject is racism, yet Soyinka handles the topic satirically, revealing the underlying absurdity essential to maintaining the color line. *Idanre and Other Poems* (1967) is Soyinka's first collection of poetry. The central image of the title poem is the road, and the collection reads as a single hymn sung to Ogun. Martin Tucker, in his review for the *Nation* (10 November 1969), saw in this collection a Soyinka who is "meditative and understated, willing to contemplate himself as well as grant others their expressions. This quiet dignity is a new center to Soyinka's work."

The poems published after 1967, however, when Soyinka was imprisoned, are not so balanced. During his incarceration Soyinka wrote several poems which appeared in *Poems from Prison* (1969). A later volume, *A Shuttle in the Crypt* (1972), gives a fuller account of his imprisonment. These poems are solemn, personal, and reflective accounts of the loss of and longing for freedom. *Ogun Abibiman,* a long poem published in 1976, is dedicated to the victims of Soweto, killed the same year, though the poem is a tribute to Mozambique's decision to close its borders to and declare war on Rhodesia.

It is, of course, impossible to predict what effect the Nobel Prize will have on Soyinka's writing, or whether he will continue to publish drama, fiction, autobiography, and poetry, or instead focus on play writing, which has brought him the most recognition. In the 5 August 1977 *Times Literary Supplement,* Soyinka defined his role of playwright thus: "Let me say first of all that I think that my prime duty as a playwright is to provide excellent theatre; in other words, I think that I have only one commitment to the public, and that is to my audience and that is to make sure they do not leave the theatre bored. I don't believe that I have any obligation to enlighten, to instruct, to teach: I don't possess that sense of duty or didacticism." However, one must balance this statement against a more recent assertion quoted in the 23 June 1985 *New York Times Book Review:* "I think the moment I stop criticizing the African situation then you can take it that I have become totally pessimistic about Africa."

Bibliography:

James Gibbs, Ketu H. Katrak, and Henry Louis Gates, Jr., comps., *Wole Soyinka: A Bibliography of Primary and Secondary Sources* (Westport, Conn. & London: Greenwood Press, 1986).

References:

James Gibbs, comp., *Critical Perspectives on Wole Soyinka* (Washington, D.C.: Three Continents Press, 1980);

Eldred Jones, *The Writings of Wole Soyinka* (London: Heinemann, 1973); republished as *Wole Soyinka* (New York: Twayne, 1973);

Gerald Moore, *Wole Soyinka* (London: Evans, 1977; New York: Africana, 1971);

Ogin Ogunba, *The Movement of Transition: A Study of the Plays of Wole Soyinka* (Ibadan: Ibadan University Press, 1975).

NOBEL LECTURE 1986
Delivered by Wole Soyinka

This Past Must Address Its Present
Dedicated to: Nelson Mandela

A rather curious scene, unscripted, once took place in the wings of a London theatre at the same time as the scheduled performance was being presented on the actual stage, before an audience. What happened was this: an actor refused to come on stage for his allocated role. Action was suspended. A fellow actor tried to persuade him to emerge, but he stubbornly shook his head. Then a struggle ensued. The second actor had hoped that, by suddenly exposing the reluctant actor to the audience in full glare of the spotlight, he would have no choice but to rejoin the cast. And so he tried to take the delinquent actor by surprise, pulling him suddenly towards the stage. He did not fully succeed, so a brief but untidy struggle began. The unwilling actor was completely taken aback and deeply embarrassed—some of that tussle was quite visible to a part of the audience.

The performance itself, it should be explained, was an improvisation around an incident. This meant that the actors were free, within the convention of the performance—to stop, re-work any part they wished, invite members of the audience on stage, assign roles and change costumes in full view of the audience. They therefore could also dramatize their wish to have that uncooperative actor join them—which they did with gusto. That actor had indeed left the stage before the contentious scene began. He had served notice during rehearsals that he would not participate in it. In the end, he had his way but, the incident proved very troubling to him for weeks afterwards. He found himself compelled to puzzle out this clash in attitudes between himself and his fellow writers and performers. He experienced, on the one hand, an intense rage that he had been made to appear incapable of confronting a stark reality, made to appear to suffer from interpretative coyness, to seem inhibited by a cruel reality or perhaps to carry his emotional involvement with an event so far as to interfere with his professional will. Of course, he knew that it was none of these things. The truth was far simpler. Unlike his colleagues together with whom he shared, unquestionably, the same political attitude towards the event which was being represented, he found the mode of presentation at war with the ugliness it tried to convey, creating an intense disquiet about his very presence on that stage, in that place, before an audience whom he considered collectively responsible for that dehumanizing actuality.

And now let us remove some of the mystery and make that incident a little more concrete. The scene was the Royal Court Theatre, London, 1958. It was one of those Sunday nights which were given to experimentation, an innovation of that remarkable theatre manager-director, George Devine, whose creative nurturing radicalised British theatre of that period and produced later icons like John Osborne, N. F. Simpson, Edward Bond, Ar-

nold Wesker, Harold Pinter, John Arden etc., and even forced the then conservative British palate to sample stylistic and ideological pariahs like Samuel Beckett and Bertolt Brecht. On this particular occasion, the evening was devoted to a form of "living" theatre, and the main fare was titled ELEVEN MEN DEAD AT HOLA. The actors were not all professional actors; indeed they were mostly writers who jointly created and performed these dramatic pieces. Those with a long political memory may recall what took place at Hola Camp, Kenya, during the Mau-Mau Liberation struggle. The British Colonial power believed that the Mau-Mau could be smashed by herding Kenyans into special camps, trying to separate the hard cases, the mere suspects and the potential recruits—oh, they had it all neatly worked out. One such camp was Hola Camp and the incident involved the death of eleven of the detainees who were simply beaten to death by camp officers and warders. The usual enquiry set up, and it was indeed the Report which provided the main text on which the performance was based.

We need now only identify the reluctant actor and, if you have not guessed that by now—it was none other than this speaker. I recall the occasion as vividly as actors are wont to recollect for ever and ever the frightening moment of a blackout, when the lines are not only forgotten but even the moment in the play. The role which I had been assigned was that of a camp guard, one of the killers. We were equipped with huge night-sticks and, while a narrator read the testimony of one of the guards, our task was to raise the cudgels slowly and, almost ritualistically, bring them down on the necks and shoulders of the prisoners, under orders of the white camp officers. A surreal scene. Even in rehearsals, it was clear that the end product would be a surrealist tableau. The Narrator at a lectern under a spot; a dispassionate reading, deliberately clinical, letting the stark facts reveal the states of mind of torturers and victims. A small ring of white officers, armed. One seizes a cudgel from one of the warders to demonstrate how to beat a human being without leaving visible marks. Then the innermost clump of detainees, their only weapon—non-violence. They had taken their decision to go on strike, refused to go to work unless they obtained better camp conditions. So they squatted on the ground and refused to move, locked their hands behind their knees in silent defiance. Orders were given. The inner ring of guards, the blacks, moved in, lifted the bodies by hooking their hands underneath the armpits of the detainees, carried them like toads in a state of petrification to one side, divided them in groups.

The faces of the victims are impassive; they are resolved to offer no resistance. The beatings begin: one to the left side, then the back, the arms—right, left, front, back. Rhythmically. The cudgels swing in unison. The faces of the white guards glow with professional satisfaction, their arms gesture languidly from time to time, suggesting it is time to shift to the next batch, or beat a little more severely on the neglected side. In terms of images, a fluid, near balletic scene.

Then the contrast, the earlier official version, enacting how the prisoners were supposed to have died. This claimed that the prisoners had collapsed, that they died after drinking from a poisoned water supply. So we staged that also. The prisoners filed to the water wagon, gasping with thirst. After the first two or three had drunk and commenced writhing with pain, these humane guards rushed to stop the others but no, they were already wild with thirst, fought their way past salvation and drank greedily from the same source. The groans spread from one to the other, the writhing, the collapse—then agonized deaths. That was the version of the camp governors.

The motif was simple enough, the theatrical format a tried and tested one, faithful to a particular convention. What then was the problem? It was one, I believe, that affects most writers. When is playacting rebuked by reality? When is fictionalizing presumptuous? What happens after playacting? One of the remarkable properties of the particular theatrical convention I have just described is that it gives off a strong odour of perenniality, that feeling of "I have been here before." I have been witness to this." "The past enacts its presence." In such an instance, that sense of perenniality can serve both as exorcism, a certificate of release or indeed—especially for the audience, a soporific. We must bear in mind that at the time of presentation, and to the major part of that audience, every death of a freedom fighter was a notch on a gun, the death of a fiend, an animal, a bestial mutant, not the martyrdom of a patriot.

We know also, however, that such efforts can provoke changes, that an actualization of the statistical, journalistic footnote can arouse revulsion in the complacent mind, leading to the beginning of a commitment to change, redress. And on this occasion, angry questions had been raised in the Houses of Parliament. Liberals, humanitarians and reformists had taken up the cause of justice for the victims. Some had even travelled to Kenya to obtain

details which exposed the official lie. This profound unease which paralysed my creative will, therefore reached beyond the audience and, finally, I traced its roots to my own feelings of assaulted humanity, and its clamour for a different form of response. It provoked a feeling of indecency about that presentation, rather like the deformed arm of a leper which is thrust at the healthy to provoke a charitable sentiment. This, I believe was the cause of that intangible, but totally visceral rejection which thwarted the demands of my calling, rendered it inadequate and mocked the empathy of my colleagues. It was as if the inhuman totality, of which that scene was a mere fragment, was saying to us: Kindly keep your comfortable sentiment to yourselves.

Of course, I utilize that episode only as illustration of the far deeper internalised processes of

Cover for Soyinka's 1976 poem commemorating Mozambique's declaration of war on Rhodesia

the creative mind, a process that endangers the writer in two ways: he either freezes up completely or, he abandons the pen for far more direct means of contesting unacceptable reality. And again, Hola Camp provides a convenient means of approaching that aspect of my continent's reality which, for us whom it directly affronts, constitutes the greatest threat to global peace in our actual existence. For there is a gruesome appropriateness in the fact that an African, a black man should stand here today, in the same year that the progressive Prime Minister of this host country was murdered, in the same year as Samora Machel was brought down on the territory of the desperate last-ditch guardians of the theory of racial superiority which has brought so much misery to our common humanity. Whatever the facts are about Olof Palme's death, there can be no question about his life. To the racial oppression of a large sector of humanity, Olof Palme pronounced, and acted, a decisive No! Perhaps it was those who were outraged by this act of racial "treachery" who were myopic enough to imagine that the death of an individual would arrest the march of his convictions; perhaps it was simply yet another instance of the Terror Epidemic that feeds today on shock, not reason. It does not matter; an authentic conscience of the white tribe has been stilled, and the loss is both yours and mine. Samora Machel, the leader who once placed his country on a war footing against South Africa went down in as yet mysterious circumstances. True, we are all still haunted by the Nkomati Accord which negated that earlier triumphant moment of the African collective will; nevertheless, his foes across the border have good reason to rejoice over his demise and, in that sense, his death is, ironically, a form of triumph for the black race.

Is that perhaps too stark a paradox? Then let me take you back to Hola Camp. It is cattle which are objects of the stick, or whip. So are horses, goats, donkeys etc. Their definition therefore involves being occasionally beaten to death. If, thirty years after Hola Camp, it is at all thinkable that it takes the ingenuity of the most sophisticated electronic interference to kill an African resistance fighter, the champions of racism are already admitting to themselves what they continue to deny to the world: that they, white supremacist breed, have indeed come a long way in their definition of their chosen enemy since Hola Camp. They have come an incredibly long way since Sharpeville when they shot unarmed, fleeing Africans in the back. They have come very far since 1930 when, at the first organized incident of the burning of passes,

the South African blacks decided to turn Dingaan's Day, named for the defeat of the Zulu leader Dingaan, into a symbol of affirmative resistance by publicly destroying their obnoxious passes. In response to those thousands of passes burnt on Cartright Flats, the Durban police descended on the unarmed protesters killing some half dozen and wounding hundreds. They backed it up with a scorched earth campaign which dispersed thousands of Africans from their normal environment, victims of imprisonment and deportation. And even that 1930 repression was a quantum leap from that earlier, spontaneous protest against the Native Pass law in 1919, when the police merely rode down the protesters on horseback, whipped and sjamboked them, chased and harried them, like stray goats and wayward cattle, from street corner to shanty lodge. Every act of racial terror, with its vastly increasing sophistication of style and escalation in human loss, is itself an acknowledgement of improved knowledge and respect for the potential of what is feared, an acknowledgement of the sharpening tempo of triumph by the victimized.

For there was this aspect which struck me most forcibly in that attempt to recreate the crime at Hola Camp: in the various testimonies of the white officers, it stuck out, whether overtly stated or simply through their efficient detachment from the ongoing massacre. It was this: at no time did these white overseers actually experience the human "otherness" of their victims. They clearly did not experience the reality of the victims as human beings. Animals perhaps, a noxious form of vegetable life maybe, but certainly not human. I do not speak here of their colonial overlords, the ones who formulated and sustained the policy of settler colonialism, the ones who dispatched the Maxim guns and tuned the imperial bugle. They knew very well that empires existed which had to be broken, that civilizations had endured for centuries which had to be destroyed. The "sub-human" denigration for which their "civilizing mission" became the altruistic remedy, was the mere rationalizing icing on the cake of imperial greed. But yes indeed, there were the agents, those who carried out orders (like Eichmann, to draw parallels from the white continent); they—whether as bureaucrats, technicians or camp governors had no conceptual space in their heads which could be filled—except very rarely and exceptionally—by "the black as *also* human." It would be correct to say that this has remained the pathology of the average South African white since the turn of the last century to this moment. Here, for example is one frank admission by an enlightened, even radical mind of that country:

> It was not until my last year in school that it
> had occurred to me that these black people,
> these voteless masses, were in any way con-
> cerned with the socialism which I professed
> or that they had any role to play in the great
> social revolution which in these days seemed
> to be imminent. The "workers" who were
> destined to inherit the new world were nat-
> urally the white carpenters and bricklayers,
> the tramworkers and miners who were or-
> ganized in their trade unions and who voted
> for the Labour Party. I would no more have
> thought of discussing politics with a native
> youth than of inviting him home to play with
> me or to a meal or asking him to join the
> Carnarvon Football Club. The African was
> on a different plane, hardly human, part of
> the scene as were dogs and trees and, more
> remotely cows. I had no special feelings
> about him, not interest nor hate nor love. He
> just did not come into my social picture. So
> completely had I accepted the traditional at-
> titudes of the time.

Yes, I believe that this self-analysis by Eddie Roux,
the Afrikaaner political rebel and scientist, remains
today the flat, unvarnished truth for the majority
of Afrikaaners. "No special feelings, not interest
nor hate nor love," the result of a complete acceptance of "traditional attitudes." That passage
captures a mind's racial tabula rasa, if you like—in
the first decade of this century—about the time, in
short, when the Nobel series of prizes was inaugurated. But a slate, no matter how clean, cannot
avoid receiving impressions once it is exposed to
air—fresh or polluted. And we are now in the year
1986, that is after an entire century of direct, intimate exposure, since that confrontation, that first
rejection of the dehumanizing label implicit in the
Native Pass Laws.

Eddie Roux, like hundreds, even thousands
of his countrymen soon made rapid strides. His
race has produced its list of martyrs in the cause
of non-racialism—one remembers, still with a tinge
of pain, Ruth First, destroyed by a letter bomb delivered by the long arm of Apartheid. There are
others—André Brink, Abram Fischer, Helen Suz-
man—Breyten Breytenbach, with the scars of martyrdom still seared into their souls. Intellectuals,
writers, scientists, plain working men, politicians—
they come to that point where a social reality can
no longer be observed as a culture on a slide beneath the microscope, nor turned into aesthetic
variations on pages, canvas or the stage. The blacks

of course are locked into an unambiguous condition: on this occasion I do not need to address *us*.
We know, and we embrace our mission. It is the
other that this precedent seizes the opportunity to
address, and not merely those who are trapped
within the confines of that doomed camp, but those
who live outside, on the fringes of conscience.
Those specifically, who with shameless smugness
invent arcane moral propositions that enable them
to plead inaction in a language of unparalleled political flatulence; "Personally, I find sanctions morally repugnant." Or what shall we say of another
leader for whom economic sanctions which work
against an Eastern European country will not work
in the Apartheid enclave of South Africa, that master of histrionics who takes to the world's airwaves
to sing, "Let Poland be" but turns off his hearing
aid when the world shouts: "Let Nicaragua be." But
enough of these world leaders of double-talk and
multiple moralities.

It is baffling to any mind that pretends to the
slightest claim to rationality, it is truly and formida-
bly baffling. Can the same terrain of phenomenal
assimilation—that is, one which produced evidence
of a capacity to translate empirical observations into
implications of rational human conduct—can this
same terrain which, over half a century ago, fifty
entire years, two, three generations ago produced
the Buntings, the Roux, the Douglas Woltons, Solly
Sachs, the Gideon Bothas—can that same terrain,
fifty, sixty, even seventy years later, be peopled by
a species of humanity so ahistorical that the declaration, so clearly spelt out in 1919 at the burning
of the passes, remains only a troublesome event of
no enduring significance?

Some atavistic bug is at work here which defies
all scientific explanation, an arrest in time within
the evolutionary mandate of nature, which puts all
human experience of learning to serious question!
We have to ask ourselves then, what event can
speak to such a breed of people? How do we reac-
tivate that petrified cell which houses historic apprehension and development? Is it possible
perhaps that events, gatherings such as this might
help? Dare we skirt the edge of hubris to say to
them: Take a good look. Provide your response.
In your anxiety to prove that this moment is not
possible, you have killed, maimed, silenced, tortured, exiled, debased and dehumanized hundreds
of thousands encased in this very skin, crowned
with such hair, proudly content with their very
being? How many potential partners in the science
of heart transplant have you wasted? How do we
know how many black South African scientists and

writers would have stood here, by now, if you had had the vision to educate the rest of the world in the value of a great multi-racial society.

Jack Cope surely sums it up in his Foreword to THE ADVERSARY WITHIN, a study of dissidence in Afrikaaner literature, when he states:

> Looking back from the perspective of the present, I think it can justly be said that, at the core of the matter, the Afrikaaner leaders in 1924 took the wrong turning. Themselves the victims of imperialism in its most evil aspect, all their sufferings and enormous loss of life nevertheless failed to convey to them the obvious historical lesson. They became themselves the new imperialists. They took over from Britain the mantle of empire and colonialism. They could well have set their faces against annexation, aggression, colonial exploitation and oppression, racial arrogance and barefaced hypocrisy, of which they had been themselves the victims. They could have opened the doors to humane ideas and civilizing processes and transformed the great territory with its incalculable resources into another New World.

> Instead they deliberately set the clock back wherever they could. Taking over ten million indigenous subjects from British colonial rule, they stripped them of what limited rights they had gained over a century and tightened the screws on their subjection.

Well, perhaps the wars against Chaka and Dingaan and Diginswayo, even the Great Trek were then too fresh in your *laager* memory. But we are saying that over a century has passed since then, a century in which the world has leapt, in comparative tempo with the past, at least three centuries. And we have seen the potential of man and woman—of all races—contend with the most jealously guarded sovereignty of Nature and the Cosmos. In every field, both in the Humanities and Sciences, we have seen that human creativity has confronted and tempered the hostility of his environment, adapting, moderating, converting, harmonizing and even subjugating. Triumphing over errors and resuming the surrendered fields, when man has had time to lick his wounds and listen again to the urgings of his spirit. History—distorted, opportunistic renderings of history have been cleansed and restored to truthful reality, because the traducers of the history of others have discovered that the further they advanced, the more their very progress was checked and vitiated by the lacunae they had pur-

posefully inserted in the history of others. Self-interest dictated yet another round of revisionism—slight, niggardly concessions to begin with. But a breach had been made in the dam and an avalanche proved the logical progression. From the heart of jungles, even before the aid of high-precision cameras mounted on orbiting satellites, civilizations have resurrected, documenting their own existence with unassailable iconography and art. More amazing still, the records of the ancient voyagers, the merchant adventurers of the age when Europe did not yet require to dominate territories in order to feed its industrial mills—those objective recitals of mariners and adventurers from antiquity confirmed what the archeological remains affirmed so loudly. They spoke of living communities which regulated their own lives, which had evolved a working relationship with Nature, which ministered to their own wants and secured their future with their own genius. These narratives, uncluttered by the impure motives which needed to mystify the plain self-serving rush to dismantle independent societies for easy plundering—pointed accusing fingers unerringly in the direction of European savants, philosophers, scientists and theorists of human evolution. Gobineau is a notorious name, but how many students of European thought today, even among us Africans recall that several of the most revered names in European philosophy—Hegel, Locke, Montesquieu, Hume, Voltaire—an endless list—were unabashed theorists of racial superiority and denigrators of the African history and being. As for the more prominent names among the theorists of revolution and class struggle—we will draw the curtain of extenuation on their own intellectual aberration, forgiving them a little for their vision of an end to human exploitation.

In any case, the purpose is not really to indict the past, but to summon it to the attention of a suicidal, anachronistic present. To say to that mutant present: you are a child of these centuries of lies, distortion and opportunism in high places, even among the holy of holies of intellectual objectivity. But the world is growing up, while you wilfully remain a child, a stubborn, self-destructive child, with certain destructive powers, but a child nevertheless. And to say to the world, to call attention to its own historic passage of lies—as yet unabandoned by some—which sustains the evil precosity of this child. Wherein then lies the surprise that we, the victims of that intellectual dishonesty of others, demand from that world that is finally coming to itself, a measure of expiation?

Demand that it rescue itself, by concrete acts, from the stigma of being the wilful parent of a monstrosity, especially as that monstrous child still draws material nourishment, breath and human recognition from the strengths and devises of that world, with an umbilical cord which stretches across oceans, even across the cosmos via so-called programmes of technological co-operation. We are saying very simply but urgently: Sever that cord. By any name, be it Total Sanction, Boycott, Disinvestment or whatever, sever this umbilical cord and leave this monster of a birth to atrophy and die or to rebuild itself on long-denied humane foundations. Let it collapse, shorn of its external sustenance, let it collapse of its own social disequilibrium, its economic lopsidedness, its war of attrition on its most productive labour. Let it wither like an aborted foetus of the human family if it persists in smothering the minds and sinews which constitute its authentic being.

This pariah society that is Apartheid South Africa plays many games on human intelligence. Listen to this for example. When the whole world escalated its appeal for the release of Nelson Mandela, the South African Government blandly declared that it continued to hold Nelson Mandela for the same reasons that the Allied powers continued to hold Rudolf Hess! Now a statement like that is an obvious appeal to the love of the ridiculous in everyone. Certainly it wrung a kind of satiric poem out of me—Rudolf Hess as Nelson Mandela in blackface! What else can a writer do to protect his humanity against such egregious assaults! But yet again to equate Nelson Mandela to the arch-criminal Rudolf Hess is a macabre improvement on the attitude of regarding him as sub-human. It belongs on that same scale of Apartheid's self-improvement as the ratio between Sharpeville and Von Brandis Square, that near-kind, near-considerate, almost benevolent dispersal of the first Native Press rebellion.

That world which is so conveniently traduced by Apartheid thought is of course that which I so wholeheartedly embrace—and this is my choice—among several options—of the significance of my presence here. It is a world that nourishes my being, one which is so self-sufficient, so replete in all aspects of its productivity, so confident in itself and in its destiny that it experiences no fear in reaching out to others and in responding to the reach of others. It is the heartstone of our creative existence. It constitutes the prism of our world perception and this means that our sight need not be and has never been permanently turned inwards.

If it were, we could not so easily understand the enemy on our doorstep, nor understand how to obtain the means to disarm it. When this society which is Apartheid South Africa indulges from time to time in appeals to the outside world that it represents the last bastion of civilization against the hordes of barbarism from its North, we can even afford an indulgent smile. It is sufficient, imagines this state, to raise the spectre of a few renegade African leaders, psychopaths and robber barons who we ourselves are victims of—whom we denounce before the world and overthrow when we are able—this Apartheid society insists to the world that its picture of the future is the reality which only its policies can erase. This is a continent which only destroys, it proclaims, it is peopled by a race which has never contributed anything positive to the world's pool of knowledge. A vacuum, that will suck into its insatiable maw the entire fruits of centuries of European civilization, then spew out the resulting mush with contempt. How strange that a society which claims to represent this endangered face of progress should itself be locked in centuries-old fantasies, blithely unaware of, or indifferent to the fact that it is the last, institutionally functioning product of archaic articles of faith in Euro-Judaic thought.

Take God and Law for example, especially the former. The black race has more than sufficient historic justification to be a little paranoid about the intrusion of alien deities into its destiny. For even today, Apartheid's mentality of the pre-ordained rests—according to its own unabashed claims, on what I can only describe as incidents in a testamentary Godism—I dare not call it christianity. The sons of Ham on the one hand; the descendants of Shem on the other. The once pronounced, utterly immutable curse. As for Law, these supremacists base their refusal to concede the right of equal political participation to blacks on a claim that Africans have neither respect for, nor the slightest proclivity for Law—that is, for any arbitrating concept between the individual and the collective.

Even the mildest, liberal, somewhat regretful but contented apologists for Apartheid, for at least some form of Apartheid which is not Apartheid but ensures the *status quo*—even this ambivalent breed bases its case on this lack of the idea of Law in the black mind. I need only refer to a recent contribution to this literature in the form of an autobiography by a famous heart transplant surgeon, one who in his own scientific right has probably been a candidate for a Nobel Prize in the

The Bookseller *(7 November 1986)*

Sciences. Despite constant intellectual encounters on diverse levels, the sad phenomenon persists of Afrikaaner minds which, in the words of Eddie Roux, is a product of that complete acceptance of the "traditional attitudes of the time."

They have, as already acknowledged, quite "respectable" intellectual ancestors. Friedrich Wilhelm Hegel, to cite just my favourite example, found it convenient to pretend that the African had not yet developed to the level where he

> attained that realization of any substantial objective existence—as for example, God, or Law—in which the interest of man's volition is involved and in which he realizes his own being.

He continues:

> This distinction between himself as an individual and the universality of his essential being, the African in the uniform, undeveloped oneness of his existence has not yet attained: so that the knowledge of absolute Being, an Other and a Higher than his individual self, is entirely wanting.

Futile to waste a moment refuting the banal untruthfulness of this claim, I content myself with extracting from it only a lesson which escapes, even today, those who insist that the pinnacle of man's intellectual thirst is the capacity to project his universality in the direction of a Super-Other. There is, I believe a very healthy school of thought which not only opposes this materially, but has produced effectively structured societies which operate independently of this seductive, even productively inspiring but extravagant fable.

Once we thus overcome the temptation to contest the denial of this feat of imaginative projection to the African, we find ourselves left only with the dispassionate exercise of examining in what areas we encounter differences between the histories of societies which, according to Hegel and company, never conceived of this Omnipotent Extrusion into Infinite Space, and those who did—be these differences in the areas of economic or artistic life, social relations or scientific attainment—in short, in all those activities which are empirically verifiable, quite different from the racial consequences of imprecations arising from that post Adam-and-Eve nudist escapade in the Old Testament.

When we do this, we come upon a curious fact. The pre-colonial history of African societies—and I refer to both Euro-christian and Arab-Islamic colonization—indicates very clearly that African societies never at any time of their existence went to war with another over the issue of *their* religion. That is, at no time did the black race attempt to subjugate or forcibly convert others with any holier-than-thou evangelizing zeal. Economic and political motives, yes. But not religion. Perhaps this unnatural fact was responsible for the conclusions of Hegel—we do not know. Certainly the bloody histories of the world's major religions, localized skirmishes of which extend even to the present, lead to a sneaking suspicion that religion, as defined by these eminent philosophers, comes to self-knowledge only through the activity of war.

When, therefore, towards the close of the twentieth century, that is, centuries after the Crusades and Jihads that laid waste other and one another's civilizations, fragmented ancient cohesive social relations and trampled upon the spirituality of entire peoples, smashing their cultures in obedience to the strictures of unseen gods, when today, we encounter nations whose social reasoning is guided by canonical, theological claims, we believe,

15

on our part, that the era of darkness has never truly left the world. A state whose justification for the continuing suppression of its indigenes, indigenes who constitute the majority on that land, rests on claims to divine selection is a menace to secure global relationships in a world that thrives on nationalism as common denominator. Such a society does not, in other words, belong to this modern world. We also have our myths, but we have never employed them as a base for the subjugation of others. We also inhabit a realistic world, however, and, for the recovery of the fullness of that world, the black race has no choice but to prepare itself and volunteer the supreme sacrifice.

In speaking of that world—both myth and reality—it is our duty, perhaps our very last peaceful duty to a doomed enemy—to remind it, and its supporters outside its boundaries, that the phenomenon of ambivalence induced by the African world has a very long history, but that most proponents of the slanderous aspects have long ago learnt to abandon the untenable. Indeed it is probably even more pertinent to remind this racist society that our African world, its cultural hoards and philosophical thought have had concrete impacts on the racists' own forebears, have proved seminal to a number of movements and even created tributaries, both pure and polluted among the white indigenes in their own homelands.

Such a variety of encounters and responses have been due, naturally, to profound searches for new directions in their cultural adventures, seeking solaces to counter the remorseless mechanization of their existence, indeed seeking new meanings for the mystery of life and attempting to overcome the social malaise created by the very triumphs of their own civilization. It has led to a profound respect for the African contribution to world knowledge, which did not however end the habitual denigration of the African world. It has created in places a near-deification of the African person— that phase in which every African had to be a prince—which yet again, was coupled with a primitive fear and loathing for the person of the African. To these paradoxical responses, the essentiality of our black being remains untouched. For the black race knows, and is content simply to know itself. It is the European world that has sought, with the utmost zeal, to re-define itself through these encounters, even when it does appear that he is endeavouring to grant meaning to an experience of the African world.

We can make use of the example of that period of European Expressionism, a movement which saw African art, music and dramatic rituals share the same sphere of influence as the most disparate, astonishingly incompatible collection of ideas, ideologies and social tendencies—Freud, Karl Marx, Bakunin, Nietzsche, cocaine and free love. What wonder then, that the spiritual and plastic presences of the Bakota, Nimba, the Yoruba, Dogon, Dan etc. should find themselves at once the inspiration and the anathematized of a delirium that was most peculiarly European, mostly Teutonic and Gallic, spanning at least four decades across the last and the present centuries. Yet the vibrant goal remained the complete liberation of man, that freeing of his yet untapped potential that would carve marble blocks for the constructing of a new world, debourgeoisify existing constrictions of European thought and light the flame to forge a new fraternity throughout this brave new world. Yes, within this single movement that covered the vast spectrum of outright fascism, anarchism and revolutionary communism, the reality that was Africa was, as always, sniffed at, delicately tested, swallowed entire, regurgitated, appropriated, extolled and damned in the revelatory frenzy of a continent's recreative energies.

Oscar Kokoschska for instance: for this dramatist and painter African ritualism led mainly in the direction of sadism, sexual perversion, general self-gratification. It flowed naturally into a Nietzschean apocalyptic summons, full of self-induced, ecstatic rage against society, indeed, against the world. Vassily Kadinsky on his part, responded to the principles of African art by foreseeing:

> a science of art erected on a broad foundation which must be international in character,

insisting that

> It is interesting, but certainly not sufficient, to create an exclusively European art theory.

The science of art would then lead, according to him, to

> a comprehensive synthesis which will extend far beyond the confines of art into the realm of the oneness of the human and the "divine."

This same movement, whose centenary will be due for celebrations in European artistic capitals in the next decade or two—among several paradoxes the phenomenon of European artists of later acknowledged giant stature—Modigliani, Matisse, Gauguin, Picasso, Brancusi etc. worshipping with varying degrees of fervour, at the shrine of African and Polynesian artistic revelations, even as Johannes Becher, in his Expressionist delirium, swore to build a new world on the eradication of all plagues, including—

> Negro tribes, fever, tuberculosis, venereal epidemics, intellectual psychic defects—I'll fight them, vanquish them.

And was it by coincidence that contemporaneously with this stirring manifesto, yet another German enthusiast, Leo Frobenius—with no claims whatever to being part of, or indeed having the least interest in the Expressionist movement, was able to visit Ile-Ife, the heartland and cradle of the Yoruba race and be profoundly stirred by an object of beauty, the product of the Yoruba mind and hand, a classic expression of that serene portion of the world resolution of that race. In his own words:

> Before us stood a head of marvellous beauty, wonderfully cast in antique bronze, true to the life, incrusted with a patina of glorious dark green. This was, in very deed, the Olokun, Atlantic Africa's Poseidon.

Yet listen to what he had to write about the very people whose handiwork had lifted him into these realms of universal sublimity:

> Profoundly stirred, I stood for many minutes before the remnant of the erstwhile Lord and Ruler of the Empire of Atlantis. My companions were no less astounded. As though we have agreed to do so, we held our peace. Then I looked around and saw—the blacks—the circle of the sons of the "venerable priest," his Holiness the Oni's friends, and his intelligent officials. I was moved to silent melancholy at the thought that this assembly of degenerate and feeble-minded posterity should be the legitimate guardians of so much loveliness.

A direct invitation to a free-for-all race for dispossession, justified on the grounds of the keeper's unworthiness, it recalls other schizophrenic conditions which are mother to, for instance, the far more lethal, dark mythopoeia of Van Lvyck Louw. For though this erstwhile Nazi sympathizer would later rain maledictions on the heads of the more extreme racists of his countrymen:

> Lord, teach us to think what "own" is, Lord let us think! and then: over hate against blacks, browns, whites: over this and its cause I dare to call down judgement.

Van Lvyck's powerful epic RAKA was guaranteed to churn up the white cesspools of these primordial fears. A work of searing, visceral impact operating on racial memory, it would feed the Afrikaaner Credo on the looming spectre of a universal barbaric recession, bearing southwards on the cloven hooves of the Fifth Horseman of the Apocalypse, the black.

There is a deep lesson for the world in the black races' capacity to forgive, one which, I often think, has much to do with ethical precepts which spring from their world view and authentic religions, none of which is ever totally eradicated by the accretions of foreign faiths and their implicit ethnocentricisms. For, not content with being a racial slanderer, one who did not hesitate to denigrate, in such uncompromisingly nihilistic terms, the ancestral fount of the black races—a belief which this ethnologist himself observed—Frobenius was also a notorious plunderer, one of a long line of European archeological raiders. The museums of Europe testify to this insatiable lust of Europe; the frustrations of the Ministries of Culture of the Third World and, of organizations like UNESCO are a continuing testimony to the tenacity, even recidivist nature of your routine receiver of stolen goods. Yet, is it not amazing that Frobenius is today still honoured by black institutions, black leaders and scholars? That his anniversaries provide ready excuse for intellectual gatherings and symposia on the black continent, that his racist condescensions, assaults have not been permitted to obscure his contribution to the knowledge of Africa, or the role which he has played in the understanding of the phenomenon of human culture and society, even in spite of the frequent patchiness of his scholarship?

It is the same largeness of spirit which has informed the relationship today of erstwhile colonial nations, some of whom have undergone the most cruel forms of settler or plantation colonialism, where the human degradation that goes with greed and exploitation attained such levels of perversion that human ears, hands and noses served to atone for failures in production quota. Nations which underwent the agony of wars of liberation, whose earth freshly teems with the bodies of innocent victims and unsung martyrs, live side by side today with their recent enslavers, even sharing the control of their destiny with those who, barely four or five years ago compelled them to witness the massacre of their kith and kin. Over and, above Christian charity, they are content to rebuild, and share. This spirit of collaboration is easy to dismiss as the treacherous ploy of that special breed of leaders who settle for early compromises in order to safeguard, for their own use, the polished shoes of the departing oppressors. In many cases, the truth of this must be conceded. But we also have examples of regimes, allied to the aspirations of their masses on the black continent, which have adopted this same political philosophy. And, in any case, the final arbiters are the people themselves, from whose relationships any observations such as this obtain any validity. Let us simply content ourselves with remarking that it is a phenomenon worthy of note. There are, after all, European nations today whose memory of domination by other races remains so vivid more than two centuries after liberation, that a terrible vengeance culturally, socially and politically is still exacted, even at this very moment, from the descendants of those erstwhile conquerors. I have visited such nations whose cruel histories under foreign domination are enshrined as icons to daily consciousness in monuments, parks, in museums and churches, in documentation, woodcuts and photogravures displayed under bullet-proof glass-cases but, most telling of all, in the reduction of the remnants of the conquering hordes to the degraded status of aliens on sufferance, with reduced civic rights, privileges and social status, a barely tolerated marginality that expresses itself in the pathos of downcast faces, dropped shoulders and apologetic encounters in those rare times when intercourse with the latterly assertive race is unavoidable. Yes, all this I have seen, and much of it has been written about and debated in international gatherings. And even while acknowledging the poetic justice of it in the abstract, one cannot help but wonder if a physical pound of flesh, excised at birth, is not a kinder act than a lifelong visitation of the sins of the father on the sons even to the tenth and twelfth generations.

Confronted with such traditions of attenuating the racial and cultural pride of these marginalized or minority peoples, the mind travels back to our own societies where such causative histories are far fresher in the memory, where the ruins of formerly thriving communities still speak eloquent accusations and the fumes still rise from the scorched earth strategies of colonial and racist myopia. Yet the streets bear the names of former oppressors, their statues and other symbols of subjugation are left to decorate their squares, the consciousness of a fully confident people have relegated them to mere decorations and roosting-places for bats and pigeons. And the libraries remain unpurged, so that new generations freely browse through the works of Frobenius, of Hume, Hegel or Montesquieu and others without first encountering, freshly stamped on the fly-leaf: WARNING! THIS WORK IS DANGEROUS FOR YOUR RACIAL SELF-ESTEEM.

Yet these proofs of accommodation, on the grand or miniscule scale, collective, institutional or individual, must not be taken as proof of an infinite, uncritical capacity of black patience. They constitute in their own nature, a body of tests, an accumulation of debt, an implicit offer that must be matched by concrete returns. They are the blocks in a suspended bridge begun from one end of a chasm which, whether the builders will it or not, must obey the law of matter and crash down beyond a certain point, settling definitively into the widening chasm of suspicion, frustration, and redoubled hate. On that testing ground which, for us, is Southern Africa, that medieval camp of biblical terrors, primitive suspicions, a choice must be made by all lovers of peace: either to bring it into the modern world, into a rational state of being within that spirit of human partnership, a capacity for which has been so amply demonstrated by every liberated black nation on our continent or—to bring it abjectly to its knees by ejecting it, in every aspect, from humane recognition, so that it cave in internally, through the strategies of its embattled majority. Whatever the choice, this inhuman affront cannot be allowed to pursue our twentieth century conscience into the twenty-first, that symbolic coming-of-age which peoples of all cultures appear to celebrate with rites of passage. That calendar, we know, is not universal, but time is, and so are the imperatives of time. And of those imperatives that challenge our being, our presence and humane definition at this time, none can be considered more pervasive than the end of racism, the eradication of human inequality and the dismantling of all their structures. The Prize is the consequent enthronement of its complement: universal suffrage, and peace.

The 1986 Nobel Peace Prize

ELIE WIESEL
(30 September 1928-   )

Stuart S. Elenko
Holocaust Studies Center
Bronx High School of Science

BOOKS: *Un di Velt Hot Geshvign* (Buenos Aires: Central Farbond Fun Poylishe Yidn in Argentina, 1956); revised and abridged as *La Nuit* (Paris: Editions de Minuit, 1958); *La Nuit*, translated by Stella Rodway as *Night* (New York: Hill & Wang, 1960; London: MacGibbon & Kee, 1960);

L'Aube (Paris: Editions du Seuil, 1960); translated by Anne Borchardt as *Dawn* (New York: Hill & Wang, 1961); translated by Frances Frenaye (London: MacGibbon & Kee, 1961);

Le Jour (Paris: Editions du Seuil, 1961); translated by Borchardt as *The Accident* (New York: Hill & Wang, 1962);

La Ville de la chance (Paris: Editions du Seuil, 1964); translated by Stephen Becker as *The Town Beyond the Wall* (New York: Atheneum, 1964; London: Robson, 1975);

Les Portes de la forêt (Paris: Editions du Seuil, 1966); translated by Frenaye as *Gates of the Forest* (New York: Holt, Rinehart & Winston, 1966; London: Heinemann, 1967);

Le Chants des morts (Paris: Editions du Seuil, 1966); translated by Steven Donadio as *Legends of Our Time* (New York: Holt, Rinehart & Winston, 1968);

Les Juifs de silence (Paris: Editions du Seuil, 1966); translated from the original Hebrew by Neal Kozoddy as *Jews of Silence: A Personal Report on Soviet Jewry* (New York: Holt, Rinehart & Winston, 1966; London: Valentine Mitchell, 1968);

Zalmen ou La folie de Dieu (Paris: Editions du Seuil, 1968); translated by Nathan Edelman as *Zalmen, or the Folly of God* and adapted for the stage by Marion Wiesel (New York: Random House, 1975);

Le Mendiant de Jérusalem (Paris: Editions du Seuil, 1968); translated by Lily Edelman and Wiesel as *The Beggar in Jerusalem* (New York: Random House, 1970; London: Weidenfeld & Nicolson, 1970);

Entre deux soleils (Paris: Editions du Seuil, 1970); translated by Lily Edelman and Wiesel as *One Generation After* (New York: Random House, 1970; London: Weidenfeld & Nicolson, 1971);

Célébration hassidique: Portraits et Légendes (Paris: Editions du Seuil, 1972); translated by Marion Wiesel as *Souls on Fire: Portraits and Legends of Hasidic Masters* (New York: Random House, 1972; London: Weidenfeld & Nicolson, 1972);

Le Serment de Kolvillág (Paris: Editions du Seuil, 1973); translated by Marion Wiesel as *The Oath* (New York: Random House, 1973);

Ani Maamin: A Song Lost and Found Again (New York: Random House, 1974);

Célébration biblique: portraits et légendes (Paris: Editions du Seuil, 1975); translated by Marion Wiesel as *Messengers of God: Biblical Portraits and Legends* (New York: Random House, 1976);

Un Juif aujourd'hui (Paris: Editions du Seuil, 1977); translated by Marion Wiesel as *A Jew Today* (New York: Random House, 1978);

Four Hasidic Masters and Their Struggle Against Melancholy (South Bend, Ind.: University of Notre Dame Press, 1978);

Le procès de Shamgorad tel qu'il se déroula le 25 février 1649: pièce en trois actes (Paris: Editions du Seuil, 1979); translated by Marion Wiesel as *The Trial of God (as it was held on February 25, 1649 in Shamgorod): A Play in Three Acts* (New York: Random House, 1979);

Le Testament d'un poète juif assassiné: roman (Paris: Editions du Seuil, 1980); translated by Marion Wiesel as *The Testament: A Novel* (New York: Summit, 1981; London: Allen Lane, 1981);

Five Biblical Portraits (South Bend, Ind.: University of Notre Dame Press, 1981);

Somewhere a Master: Further Hasidic Portraits and Legends (New York: Summit, 1982);
The Golem: The Story of a Legend as Told By Elie Wiesel (New York: Summit, 1983);
Le Cinquième Fils (Paris: Editions Grasset, 1983); translated by Marion Wiesel as *The Fifth Son* (New York: Summit, 1985);
Against Silence: The Voice and Visions of Elie Wiesel, 3 volumes, edited by Irving Abrahamson (New York: Holocaust Library, 1985);
Signes d'Exode (Paris: Editions Grasset, 1986).

Elie Wiesel has taken one of the most remarkable journeys in twentieth-century history. His pilgrimage took him from the hills of rustic Sighet, Romania, to Auschwitz (tattoo #A-7713) and Buchenwald, and then to the podium at Oslo, Norway, on 10 December 1986, to receive the Nobel Peace Prize. This notable journey can be summed up in large part by the three words etched into the Congressional Gold Medal presented to Wiesel by President Reagan on 19 April 1985: "Author, Teacher, Witness." The two key words missing from this medal are activist and humanitarian.

In announcing Professor Wiesel's prize, Egil Aarvik, chairman of the Nobel Committee, stated: "Wiesel is a messenger of mankind. His message is one of peace, atonement and human dignity. . . . Wiesel's commitment, which originated in the sufferings of the Jewish people, has been widened to embrace all oppressed people and races."

It is fitting that Professor Elie Wiesel of Boston University join the ranks of such other luminaries as Dr. Martin Luther King, Jr., Andrei Sakharov, Bishop Tutu, and Mother Teresa. In word and deed, Elie Wiesel, "the conscience of the Holocaust," has personified the highest virtues that this award has traditionally honored. It is ironic that the awarding of this honor to Wiesel comes as a result of one of the most wrenching moments in world civilization. Hitler's execution of the "Final Solution" destroyed Wiesel's former life and plans and set him on a lifelong mission to give voice to the martyred millions.

Eliezer Wiesel, the son of Sarah and Shlomo Wiesel, was born on 30 September 1928 in Sighet, Romania, near the Hungarian border. The only son of middle-class parents—his father a successful shopkeeper and his mother a teacher—Wiesel was the center of attention in his home. His grandfather nurtured him with the tales of the great Hasidic masters; and his mother quoted to him, from memory, sections of the works of Goethe and Schiller. He felt destined to become a scholar and teacher, as did many other gifted Jewish young men in Eastern Europe.

On Passover 1944 the Nazis rounded up the entire Jewish community of Sighet, including all six members of the Wiesel family, and shipped them to Auschwitz. Wiesel records, in his moving memoir *La Nuit* (1958; translated as *Night*, 1960), the deaths of his mother, his youngest sister, Tziporah, and later that of his father, which he witnessed at Buchenwald. This horror became the central theme of his lifework. Pivotal to Wiesel's development was the growth of two conflicting ideas: "to remain silent" and "to bear witness." This conflict was fundamental to much of the creative energy and motivation in Wiesel's life. The need

Elie Wiesel, New York State Senator Abraham Bernstein, and Director Stuart Elenko at the Holocaust Studies Center, the Bronx High School of Science, in 1984 (courtesy of the Bronx High School of Science)

to remain silent, coming during Wiesel's earlier years, was explained by him as a "desire not to speak or touch upon the essentials for at least ten years, long enough to unite the language of humanity with the silence of the dead." Later the need to bear witness was to prevail, coming out of the urgent desire to give voice to the martyred millions, so callously ignored by the world at large.

Auschwitz changed his life in yet another way: by introducing him to writing as a means of expressing his thoughts. Late in his stay there, his block leader, a Czech Jew, offered the precious prize of two bowls of soup to anyone who could write the best tale. Wiesel states: "My first royalties were two bowls of soup. . . . The taste of that soup still lingers today."

As the war neared its end, Wiesel's ordeal was far from over. When the Allied armies approached Auschwitz, Wiesel and his father, along with countless others, were moved to Buchenwald, separating Wiesel from his sisters Hilda and Batya (whom he was not to see again until the end of the war). When the Allies captured Buchenwald on 10 April 1945, a photographer for the American Eightieth Division captured the essence of the Holocaust in a famous portrayal of twenty-five inmates living in their cubicles, with Wiesel in the right corner.

Liberated at age sixteen, stateless and an orphan, Wiesel found his way to France with 400 other orphans. In Paris he mastered French, and he worked as a Bible teacher and choir director while attending the Sorbonne from 1948 to 1951. There he studied philosophy and fell under the influence of Albert Camus and André Malraux. He continues to write in French, and his wife, Marion, translates his manuscripts into English. He states in *Against Silence* (1985), a three-volume collection of his thoughts published by the Holocaust Library: "Why do I write in French? I write in French because it was the language I learned at sixteen, and it is valuable to me. Except for non-fiction, I don't try to write in English. A language is like a person, it doesn't like infidelity."

In 1948 he traveled to Palestine to report on Israel's independence from Britain for a French newspaper. He stayed in Israel for one year. Later he became the chief correspondent for the Tel Aviv daily *Yedioth Ahronot* and was stationed in Paris.

Elie Wiesel (extreme right corner) in Buchenwald concentration camp, 1945 (AP/Wide World Photos)

Wiesel commented in 1977: "Don't ask me how I became a journalist. I don't know. I needed to do something so I became a reporter and managed to fool everybody. I wrote about politics but understood nothing about politics. I still don't. I wrote about anything under the sun because I had to."

According to Wiesel, one of the major turning points of his life was an interview in 1954 with François Mauriac, winner of the 1952 Nobel Prize in Literature and a noted Roman Catholic thinker. "He spoke so much about Christ and his suffering," says Wiesel. "I was timid, but finally I said, 'You speak about Christ's suffering. What about the children who suffered not 2,000 years ago, but yesterday?'" Mauriac was moved and encouraged Wiesel to write about his experiences. Two years later, Wiesel's book, based on 800 pages of handwritten notes, was published in Yiddish in Buenos Aires, as *Un di Velt Hot Geshvign* (And the World Remained Silent).

In 1958 an abridged version, *La Nuit*, with a foreword by Mauriac, was published in Paris. Wiesel had finally broken the silence and had become an articulate witness. According to *Time*, "This work set Wiesel's style: austere, tense phrases, articulating the unreasonable."

Georges Borchardt, Wiesel's literary agent, spent the next year trying to get this "controversial" work published in America but was refused by twenty major publishing houses that felt the world was ill prepared for this horrifying tale. Finally, in July 1959, Hill and Wang advanced Wiesel the sum of $100 and agreed to print the work, translated as *Night*. In the first eighteen months after its publication in 1960 it sold only 1,046 copies.

Wiesel's writings required courage, for he was aware that several major Holocaust writers—such as Tadeusz Borowski, Paul Celan, and Joseph Wulf—had purged their memories by committing suicide. Wiesel vividly recalls that he thought of it at least twice during the early 1950s. "My imagination was tired. How could I go on speaking? And awakening? And altering? To lie down, it felt so easy. What saved my life was the obsession to write and thereby testify."

In a 1983 interview with the *New York Times*, Elie Wiesel stated that he sees himself "not as an essayist or novelist in the accepted contemporary vein, but as a vehicle, a conduit, a messenger." Wiesel presents an effective and universal message of morality. His themes are intended for a large audience. "In fact," Robert McAfee Brown comments in *Christian Century*, "writing out of his own Jewishness . . . is how [Wiesel] touches universal cords. . . .

Correction, in writing about the Jewish Condition, he thereby writes about the human condition." Daniel Stern, commenting about Wiesel in the *Washington Post Book World*, states that "Wiesel has taken the Jew as his metaphor—and his reality—in order to unite a moral aesthetic vision of all men."

His determination to survive, to live, and to love in the post-Holocaust period is comparable to Camus's optimistic vision in the *Plague*. "This is what I demand from literature: a moral dimension," Wiesel stated in 1983 in the *New York Times Magazine;* "Art for art's sake is gone. . . . Just to write a novel, that's why I survived?" Wiesel's novels and essays are designed to teach and to effectively reach people, particularly the young. Few readers will ever forget the smoke of Auschwitz from *Night*. His message reaches far beyond the mere recording of events to the larger role of raising major issues of the most fundamental nature. By his questioning, Wiesel is reverting to his youthful training in Hasidic lore and following in the best traditions of the Eastern European teacher-rabbi.

Two good examples of Wiesel's "teachings" are *La Ville de la chance* (1964; translated as *The Town Beyond the Wall*, 1964) and *L'Aube* (1960; translated as *Dawn*, 1961). In *Town Beyond the Wall*, his main character, Michael, a survivor, returns home after ten years to find the answer to the question, "Why did so many people do nothing?" He is left with unresolved feelings and incomprehension. In *Dawn*, the main character, Elisha, also a survivor, assumes the role of victim turned executioner when ordered by his anti-British group to kill a British officer in revenge for the slaying of a Jew. Here, Wiesel is at his best, as Elisha, trying to understand his situation, questions himself and the act. Finally, he does what he was ordered to do, but with serious reservations and moral trepidation. This is as universal a moral question as might be found anywhere and demonstrates Wiesel's ability to use the novel as a teaching tool.

Elie Wiesel, Andrew W. Mellon Professor in the Humanities at Boston University for the past ten years, enjoys his role as a teacher. In an interview for *Time* magazine in 1985, Wiesel stated: "Had there been no war, . . . I would by now be the head of a small school, instructing the young, unlocking the lessons of the great texts."

In 1984 Elie Wiesel was honored by the Holocaust Studies Center at the Bronx High School of Science for his lifelong work and his efforts as its honorary chairman. He stated:

Why did I accept the invitation to become chairman of this Center? I cannot say no when children are involved. Why? Because we have lost so many children. With every child is created a sense of value, so fragile, so sensitive, so uplifting. Secondly, I believe in teaching. That is my passion: to teach . . . I believe you should remember everybody. I believe you should have compassion for every victim. What is it we are teaching and learning if not to respect every human being for what he or she is?

The human language is rich enough to have words for everything, including catastrophes and tragedies that must move us all to action. Let's leave the word holocaust to mean the unique experiences that the Jews went through.

Elie Wiesel chides and bristles at the often superficial way in which the word *holocaust* is used in the media, ranging from descriptions of soccer games to large forest fires. He is also keenly aware of the problems in trying to teach about the unspeakable events of the Holocaust. In *Against Silence* (volume 1), he states:

After the event, we tried to teach, we felt we had to do something with our knowledge. We had to communicate, to share, but it was not easy. Behind every word we said, a hundred remained unsaid. For every tear, a thousand remained unshed. For every Jewish child we saw, a hundred remained unseen. . . .

When I teach these matters, I teach of children. When one thinks of children or reads of them, one usually sees images of innocence, sunshine, happiness, play, laughter, teasing, dreaming, simple chants, so much promise. But not for us because to us childhood meant something else. It meant death, the death of childhood. . . .

What can I tell you as a teacher who teaches young people? It is more than a matter of communicating knowledge. Whoever emerges in the field of teaching the Holocaust becomes a missionary, a messenger.

It was a natural and logical progression for Elie Wiesel to move from his roles as writer, witness, and teacher to moral activist. "How does a religious Jew respond to Planet Auschwitz. . . . Pious Jews always dreamed of a time when wickedness would vanish like smoke." For Wiesel there is no answer to this question and only one response: "To forget Auschwitz is to justify Hiroshima—the next Hiro-

shima. . . . For the sake of our children and yours, we invoke the past so as to save the future. We recall ultimate violence in order to prevent its recurrence. Ours is a twofold commitment: to life and to truth" (*Against Silence*, volume 2).

In his speech commemorating Remembrance Day at the White House, on 30 April 1981, Wiesel reaffirmed this pivotal belief. "We must tell the tale, Mr. President, not to divide the people, but, on the contrary, to bring them together; not to inflict more suffering, but, on the contrary, to diminish it; not to humiliate anyone, but, on the contrary, to teach others not to humiliate anyone. . . . We speak for mankind" (*Against Silence*, volume 3). In *Célébration biblique: portraits et légendes* (1975; translated as *Messengers of God: Biblical Portraits and Legends,* 1976), Elie Wiesel, by using the prophets of the Old Testament as a vehicle, carries his message most effectively: "the task—for Jews, Christians, Americans, and for every concerned man and woman— is to transform divine justice into human justice and compassion."

"If I have any moral message, this is it: try to save one person," Elie Wiesel stated in a 1979 article for the Anti-Defamation League. In *Un Juif aujourd'hui* (1977; translated as *A Jew Today,* 1978), Wiesel not only focuses attention on Jewish issues and problems but also addresses himself to the issues of the exploitation of blacks in South Africa, the plight of Biafrans, and the problem of Palestinian Arabs.

Beginning with his 1965 visit to the Soviet Union, Elie Wiesel has been a consistent voice of alarm over the plight of Soviet Jewry. Wiesel's despair centers not so much on what is directly happening to Jews in the Soviet Union but on the inability, "the silence," of the rest of the world to come to their aid and support.

Wiesel's first play, *Zalmen ou La folie de Dieu* (1968; translated as *Zalmen, or the Folly of God,* 1975), opened Off-Broadway on 10 May 1974. This rendering of the plight of a small Russian village rabbi speaking out against Russian abuse focused vivid attention on the plight of Soviet Jewry. In his speeches and interviews, Wiesel maintained his criticism of the Soviet government's policies against innocent Jews. His crusade for justice was highlighted in October 1986, shortly after winning the Nobel Peace Prize, by another visit to the Soviet Union. He addressed a crowd of 2,000 in a Moscow synagogue, promising that they would not be forgotten.

Elie Wiesel has effectively spoken out against the apartheid policies of the Republic of South Af-

New York Times Book Review *(2 November 1986)*

rica. In speeches in Durban, Capetown, and Johannesburg, he has spoken out as forcibly before South African white audiences as he has ever done in his writings. He has given much of his time and energies to organizations throughout the United States. He has served on numerous advisory boards, including that of the Holocaust Library since its inception in 1977, and has worked with the Anti-Defamation League in its efforts on behalf of all people's rights.

It was thus fitting that shortly after establishing the President's Commission on the Holocaust, President Jimmy Carter named Elie Wiesel the chairman in November 1978. He was reappointed by President Reagan on 4 May 1986 as head of the United States Memorial Council, formerly the President's Commission on the Holocaust. Wiesel's reappointment to this body had not been ensured because of his courageous remarks to the president on the Bitburg issue, on the occasion of his receiving the Congressional Gold Medal.

Nathan Perlmutter, the national director of the Anti-Defamation League of B'nai B'rith, was one of the people who nominated Wiesel for the Nobel Peace Prize. In his letter to the Nobel Committee, he wrote: "I ask you to consider him for the Nobel Peace Prize because it is peace, the presence of justice, that he has served so well. He has never sought to narrow his message to one of parochial relevance; rather, he has embraced the suffering and the troubled—no matter from what country, what race, what heritage, or what religion—in his message. He has worked to stimulate our awareness, at the same time as he has touched our hearts. . . . He has taken the highest, not the easiest, road to peace." When informed that he had been awarded the Nobel Peace Prize, Elie Wiesel stated: "I don't think that prizes validate work; they give stature, texture, the possibility to reach more people. There's a mystique about the Nobel. It gives you a better loudspeaker."

References:

Yehuda Bauer, *The Holocaust in Historical Perspective* (Seattle: University of Washington Press, 1978);

Harry J. Cargas, ed., *Responses to Elie Wiesel* (New York: Persea Books, 1978);

Samuel G. Friedman, "Bearing Witness," *Time*, 125 (18 March 1985): 81-82;

Alvin H. Rosenfeld and Irving Greenberg, eds., *Confronting the Holocaust, The Impact of Elie Wiesel* (Bloomington & London: University of Indiana Press, 1978).

NOBEL LECTURE 1986
Delivered by Elie Wiesel

Hope, Despair and Memory

A Hasidic legend tells us that the great Rabbi Baal Shem Tov, Master of the Good Name, also known as the Besht, undertook an urgent and perilous mission: to hasten the coming of the Messiah. The Jewish people, all humanity were suffering too much, beset by too many evils. They had to be saved, and swiftly. For having tried to meddle with history, the Besht was punished; banished along with his faithful servant to a distant island. In despair, the servant implored his master to exercise his mysterious powers in order to bring them both home. "Impossible," the Besht replied. "My powers have been taken from me." "Then, please, say a prayer, recite a litany, work a miracle." "Impossible," the Besht replied, "I have forgotten everything." They both fell to weeping.

Suddenly the Master turned to his servant and asked: "Remind me of a prayer—any prayer." "If only I could," said the servant. "I too have forgotten everything." "Everything—absolutely everything?" "Yes, except. . . ." "Except what?" "Except the alphabet." At that the Besht cried out joyfully: "Then what are you waiting for? Begin reciting the alphabet and I shall repeat after you. . . ." And together the two exiled men began to recite, at first in whispers, then more loudly: "*Aleph, beth, gimel, daleth. . . .*" And over again, each time more vigorously, more fervently; until, ultimately, the Besht regained his powers, having regained his memory.

I love this story, for it illustrates the messianic expectation—which remains my own. And the importance of friendship to man's ability to transcend his condition. I love it most of all because it emphasizes the mystical power of memory. Without memory, our existence would be barren and opaque, like a prison cell into which no light penetrates; like a tomb which rejects the living. Memory saved the Besht, and if anything can, it is memory that will save humanity. For me, hope without memory is like memory without hope.

Just as man cannot live without dreams, he cannot live without hope. If dreams reflect the past, hope summons the future. Does this mean that our future can be built on a rejection of the past? Surely such a choice is not necessary. The two are not incompatible. The opposite of the past is not the future but the absence of future; the opposite of the future is not the past but the absence of past. The loss of one is equivalent to the sacrifice of the other.

A recollection. The time: After the war. The place: Paris. A young man struggles to readjust to life. His mother, his father, his small sister are gone. He is alone. On the verge of despair. And yet he does not give up. On the contrary, he strives to find a place among the living. He acquires a new language. He makes a few friends who, like himself, believe that the memory of evil will serve as a shield against evil; that the memory of death will serve as a shield against death.

This he must believe in order to go on. For he has just returned from a universe where God, betrayed by His creatures, covered His face in order not to see. Mankind, jewel of his creation, had succeeded in building an inverted Tower of Babel, reaching not toward heaven but toward an anti-heaven, there to create a parallel society, a new "creation" with its own princes and gods, laws and principles, jailers and prisoners. A world where the past no longer counted—no longer meant anything.

Stripped of possessions, all human ties severed, the prisoners found themselves in a social and cultural void. "Forget," they were told. "Forget where you came from; forget who you were. Only the present matters." But the present was only a blink of the Lord's eye. The Almighty himself was a slaughterer: it was He who decided who would live and who would die; who would be tortured, and who would be rewarded. Night after night, seemingly endless processions vanished into the flames, lighting up the sky. Fear dominated the universe. Indeed this was another universe; the very laws of nature had been transformed. Children looked like old men, old men whimpered like children. Men and women from every corner of Europe were suddenly reduced to nameless and faceless creatures desperate for the same ration of bread or soup, dreading the same end. Even their silence was the same for it resounded with the memory of those who were gone. Life in this accursed universe was so distorted, so unnatural that a new species had evolved. Waking among the dead, one wondered if one were still alive.

And yet real despair only seized us later. Afterwards. As we emerged from the nightmare and began to search for meaning. All those doctors of law or medicine or theology, all those lovers of art and poetry, of Bach and Goethe, who coldly, deliberately ordered the massacres and participated in them. What did their metamorphosis signify? Could anything explain their loss of ethical, cultural and religious memory? How could we ever understand the passivity of the onlookers and—yes—the silence of the Allies? And question of questions: Where was God in all this? It seemed as impossible to conceive of Auschwitz with God as to conceive of Auschwitz without God. Therefore, everything had to be reassessed because everything had changed. With one stroke, mankind's achievements seemed to have been erased. Was Auschwitz a consequence or an aberration of "civilization"? All we know is that Auschwitz called that civilization into question as it called into question everything that had preceded Auschwitz. Scientific abstraction, social and economic contention, nationalism, xenophobia, religious fanaticism, racism, mass hysteria. All found their ultimate expression in Auschwitz.

The next question had to be, why go on? If memory continually brought us back to this, why build a home? Why bring children into a world in which God and man betrayed their trust in one another?

Of course we could try to forget the past. Why not? Is it not natural for a human being to repress what causes him pain, what causes him shame? Like the body, memory protects its wounds. When day breaks after a sleepless night, one's ghosts must withdraw; the dead are ordered back to their graves. But for the first time in history, we could not bury our dead. We bear their graves within ourselves.

For us, forgetting was never an option.

Remembering is a noble and necessary act. The call of memory, the call *to* memory, reaches us from the very dawn of history. No commandment figures so frequently, so insistently, in the Bible. It is incumbent upon us to remember the good we have received, and the evil we have suffered. New Year's Day, *Rosh Hashanah*, is also called *Yom Hazikaron*, the day of memory. On that day, the day of universal judgment, man appeals to God to remember: our salvation depends on it. If God wishes to remember our suffering, all will be well; if He refuses, all will be lost. Thus, the rejection of memory becomes a divine curse, one that would doom us to repeat past disasters, past wars.

Nothing provokes so much horror and opposition within the Jewish tradition as war. Our abhorrence of war is reflected in the paucity of our literature of warfare. After all, God created the Torah to do away with iniquity, to do away with war. Warriors fare poorly in the Talmud: Judas

Maccabeus is not even mentioned; Bar-Kockba is cited, but negatively. David, a great warrior and conqueror, is not permitted to build the Temple; it is his son Solomon, a man of peace, who constructs God's dwelling-place. Of course some wars may have been necessary or inevitable, but none was ever regarded as holy. For us, a holy war is a contradiction in terms. War dehumanizes, war diminishes, war debases all those who wage it. The Talmud says, *"Talmidei hakhamin shemarbin shalom baolam"* (It is the wise men who will bring about peace). Perhaps, because wise men remember best.

And yet it is surely human to forget, even to want to forget. The Ancients saw it as a divine gift. Indeed if memory helps us to survive, forgetting allows us to go on living. How could we go on with our daily lives, if we remained constantly aware of the dangers and ghosts surrounding us? The Talmud tells us that without the ability to forget, man would soon cease to learn. Without the ability to forget, man would live in a permanent, paralyzing fear of death. Only God and God alone can and must remember everything.

How are we to reconcile our supreme duty towards memory with the need to forget that is essential to life? No generation has had to confront this paradox with such urgency. The survivors wanted to communicate everything to the living: the victims' solitude and sorrow, the tears of mothers driven to madness, the prayers of the doomed beneath a fiery sky.

They needed to tell of the child who, in hiding with his mother, asked softly, very softly: "Can I cry now?" They needed to tell of the sick beggar who, in a sealed cattle-car, began to sing as an offering to his companions. And of the little girl who, hugging her grandmother, whispered: "Don't be afraid, don't be sorry to die. . . . I'm not." She was seven, that little girl who went to her death without fear, without regret.

Each one of us felt compelled to record every story, every encounter. Each one of us felt compelled to bear witness. Such were the wishes of the dying, the testament of the dead. Since the so-called civilized world had no use for their lives, then let it be inhabited by their deaths.

The great historian Shimon Dubnov served as our guide and inspiration. Until the moment of his death he said over and over again to his companions in the Riga ghetto: *"Yidden, shreibt un fershreibt"* (Jews, write it all down). His words were heeded. Overnight, countless victims became chroniclers and historians in the ghettos, even in the death camps. Even members of the *Sonderkom-*

mandos, those inmates forced to burn their fellow inmates' corpses before being burned in turn, left behind extraordinary documents. To testify became an obsession. They left us poems and letters, diaries and fragments of novels, some known throughout the world, others still unpublished.

After the war we reassured ourselves that it would be enough to relate a single night in Treblinka, to tell of the cruelty, the senselessness of murder, and the outrage born of indifference: it would be enough to find the right word and the propitious moment to say it, to shake humanity out of its indifference and keep the torturer from torturing ever again. We thought it would be enough to read the world a poem written by a child in the Theresienstadt ghetto to ensure that no child anywhere would ever again have to endure hunger or fear. It would be enough to describe a death-camp "Selection," to prevent the human right to dignity from ever being violated again.

We thought it would be enough to tell of the tidal wave of hatred which broke over the Jewish people for men everywhere to decide once and for all to put an end to hatred of anyone who is "different"—whether black or white, Jew or Arab, Christian or Moslem—anyone whose orientation differs politically, philosophically, sexually. A naive undertaking? Of course. But not without a certain logic.

We tried. It was not easy. At first, because of the language; language failed us. We would have to invent a new vocabulary, for our own words were inadequate, anemic.

And then too, the people around us refused to listen; and even those who listened refused to believe; and even those who believed could not comprehend. Of course they could not. Nobody could. The experience of the camps defies comprehension.

Have we failed? I often think we have.

If someone had told us in 1945 that in our lifetime religious wars would rage on virtually every continent, that thousands of children would once again be dying of starvation, we would not have believed it. Or that racism and fanaticism would flourish once again, we would not have believed it. Nor would we have believed that there would be governments that would deprive a man like Lech Walesa of his freedom to travel merely because he dares to dissent. And he is not alone. Governments of the right and of the left go much further, subjecting those who dissent, writers, scientists, intellectuals, to torture and persecution. How to explain this defeat of memory?

How to explain any of it: the outrage of Apartheid which continues unabated. Racism itself is dreadful, but when it pretends to be legal, and therefore just, when a man like Nelson Mandela is imprisoned, it becomes even more repugnant. Without comparing Apartheid to Nazism and to its "final solution"—for that defies all comparison—one cannot help but assign the two systems, in their supposed legality, to the same camp. And the outrage of terrorism: of the hostages in Iran, the cold-blooded massacre in the synagogue in Istanbul, the senseless deaths in the streets of Paris. Terrorism must be outlawed by all civilized nations—not explained or rationalized, but fought and eradicated. Nothing can, nothing will, justify the murder of innocent people and helpless children. And the outrage of preventing men and women like Andrei Sakharov, Vladimir and Masha Slepak, Ida Nudel, Josif Biegun, Victor Brailowski, Zakhar Zonshein, and all the others known and unknown from leaving their country. And then there is Israel, which after two thousand years of exile and thirty-eight years of sovereignty still does not have peace. I would like to see this people, which is my own, able to establish the foundation for a constructive relationship with all its Arab neighbors, as it has done with Egypt. We must exert pressure on all those in power to come to terms.

And here we come back to memory. We must remember the suffering of my people, as we must remember that of the Ethiopians, the Cambodians, the boat people, the Palestinians, the Mesquite Indians, the Argentinian *desaparecidos*—the list seems endless.

Let us remember Job who, having lost everything—his children, his friends, his possessions, and even his argument with God—still found the strength to begin again, to rebuild his life. Job was determined not to repudiate the creation, however imperfect, that God had entrusted to him.

Job, our ancestor. Job, our contemporary. His ordeal concerns all humanity. Did he ever lose his faith? If so, he rediscovered it within his rebellion. He demonstrated that faith is essential to rebellion, and that hope is possible beyond despair. The source of his hope was memory, as it must be ours. Because I remember, I despair. Because I remember, I have the duty to reject despair.

I remember the killers, I remember the victims, even as I struggle to invent a thousand and one reasons to hope.

There may be times when we are powerless to prevent injustice, but there must never be a time when we fail to protest. The Talmud tells us that by saving a single human being, men can save the world. We may be powerless to open all the jails and free all the prisoners, but by declaring our solidarity with one prisoner, we indict all jailers. None of us is in a position to eliminate war, but it is our obligation to denounce it and expose it in all its hideousness. War leaves no victors, only victims. I began with the story of the Besht. And, like the Besht, mankind needs to remember more than ever. Mankind needs peace more than ever, for our entire planet, threatened by nuclear war, is in danger of total destruction. A destruction only man can provoke, only man can prevent.

Mankind must remember that peace is not God's gift to his creatures, it is our gift to each other.

A TRIBUTE

from ABRAHAM BERNSTEIN
New York State Senator

Elie Wiesel, for many years, was a voice in the wilderness bringing the message of the martyred millions to an indifferent and forgetting world. He devoted his time and energy to teach us that which affects the rights of one man affects us all. His work also for Soviet Jewry, against racial Apartheid in South Africa, and for the starving in Ethiopia is a testament to how well he deserves this most prestigious award.

A TRIBUTE

from NORMAN LAMM
President of Yeshiva University

I have always considered Elie Wiesel's role as preeminently that of an educator. A superb literary craftsman, a world-class writer, a fascinating lecturer, a heroic public figure, a success in his every undertaking. . . .

He has endeavored to communicate the incommunicable, to express the inexpressible, to speak the unspeakable, to make us grasp the ineffable and think the unthinkable.

A TRIBUTE

from JOHN R. SILBER
President of Boston University

The work for which Elie Wiesel was named the Nobel Laureate for Peace began over forty years ago when he was a prisoner at Auschwitz. Thereafter, he endured a long period of silence before he recognized that unless he gave poetic voice to the crimes and to the sufferings that occurred during the Holocaust, the permanent record of those crimes might be lost.

Since then, Elie Wiesel has become one of the greatest teachers of his generation, as novel after novel, book after book has appeared to articulate those crimes, those sufferings, the victims and the acts of humanity that were bright alternatives to degradation. His concern for human rights is not limited to the Holocaust, but has been shown in his compassionate and articulate concern for the boat people of Laos and Cambodia; about the people of Israel; for the people of the Arab nations around Israel who have also suffered; for the people of Angola, Ethiopia, Afghanistan; for the plight of the Miskito Indians in Nicaragua and the victims in Argentina. There is no area of the world in which his concern for the preservation of human rights has not been expressed.

As Mellon Professor of the Humanities at Boston University, Elie Wiesel has brought to his students a compelling and transforming effort to explore the central religious texts of our culture and clarify their ethical demands. All of my colleagues at Boston University—students, staff, and Trustees—are deeply proud of and continually inspired by his presence.

The Poet Laureate of the United States

John C. Broderick
Library of Congress

In February 1986 Daniel J. Boorstin, the Librarian of Congress, appointed Robert Penn Warren as the first Poet Laureate of the United States. The position had been authorized by Public Law 99-194, enacted 20 December 1985 (99 Stat. 1332). The precise, though cumbersome, title of the position to which Warren was appointed is Poet Laureate Consultant in Poetry. The awkward title and appointment by the Librarian of Congress were the result of the kind of legislative compromise common in a democratic society. However long and tortuous the road to the first American poet laureate, the appointment of Robert Penn Warren was widely regarded as the appropriate one. If there had to be a poet laureate, he was the best first choice.

Was this position necessary? For decades, the answer seemed to be no. When it finally came about, it did so abruptly and almost casually, through an amendment to a routine reauthorization bill before the Senate Committee on Labor and Human Resources.

Four major influences shaped the position as it exists today: 1) the tradition of the English poet laureate; 2) the growing number of state poets laureate; 3) the Consultantship in Poetry at the Library of Congress; and 4) the dedication and persistence of Senator Spark Matsunaga (Democrat, Hawaii) in behalf of the laureateship.

Although several of England's most well known poets have been honored with its laureateship (Wordsworth, Tennyson, John Masefield, for example), the origins of the position are nevertheless obscure, and there is no unanimous agreement on who was the first English laureate. The first to bear the title of laureate (and historiographer royal) seems to have been John Dryden, appointed in 1670 with a stipend of £200 per annum, increased seven years later to £300. Earlier court poets such as Samuel Daniel, Ben Jonson, and William Davenant, all identified as poets laureate in some reference works, can be disqualified because they lacked the precise designation bestowed on Dryden.

The laureateship has not been especially good to English poets. Wordsworth's acceptance of the position in 1843 so disillusioned the young Robert Browning that he wrote his famous lament, "The Lost Leader." The most significant occupant of the laureateship was undoubtedly Alfred, Lord Tennyson. His transition from a delicate lyric poet to a public poet and spokesman for an age might have occurred without the laureateship, but that undoubtedly helped. Tennyson's "Ode on the Death of the Duke of Wellington" typifies public, ceremonial poetry at its best.

What Tennyson accomplished in a positive way for the English laureateship, his successor, Alfred Austin, did much to erase. Austin, author of the infamous line "He is no better, and is much the same," was almost universally (and deservedly) ridiculed in the British press. The respectable twentieth-century laureates, Masefield, C. Day Lewis, Sir John Betjeman, and Ted Hughes, have escaped such ridicule but not charges of irrelevance. Thus, despite the three-hundred-year history of the position in England, the 1980s would not appear to have been the propitious moment for an American imitation of the English model.

But there were other models closer to home. More than half the American states currently have poets laureate, and other states are preparing to institute such an office. Most states are satisfied with a single incumbent, but Kentucky has nine poets laureate, each of whom is appointed by the Kentucky legislature to a lifetime term. Robert Frost's tenure as poet laureate of Vermont, on the other hand, has extended nearly twenty-five years beyond his lifetime since no living poet has been appointed to succeed him, and Frost continues to hold the title posthumously. Although a number of state laureates are little known, several poets of distinction are now serving their states as laureate, including James Merrill (Connecticut), Gwendolyn Brooks (Illinois), Reed Whittemore (Maryland), Donald Hall (New Hampshire), and William Stafford (Oregon). Ironically, Hawaii, the home state of Senator Matsunaga, is one of the few states without a poet laureate.

The earliest state laureateship was in California, which in 1915 established the position. In 1933 John Steven McGroarty (1862-1944) was named poet laureate of California. McGroarty, born in Pennsylvania, had moved to Los Angeles in 1901 and, although trained as a lawyer, had become a journalist. He had also edited or written several books of poetry, including *Poets and Poetry of the Wyoming Valley* (1885) and *Wander Songs* (1908). In 1934, a year after his elevation to the laureateship of California, McGroarty was elected to the first of two terms in the U.S. Congress, representing California's eleventh district. On 27 March 1936, House of Representatives Joint Resolution 549 was introduced to designate freshman Congressman McGroarty "honorary poet laureate of the United States of America." Although the resolution was not enacted, this was apparently the first serious legislative initiative toward naming a poet laureate of the United States.

At the time, only a handful of mostly southern and western states had poets laureate. The number was to grow, as were congressional initiatives for a national poet laureate. Representatives W. Sterling Cole of Pennsylvania, Thomas J. Lane of Massachusetts (who favored Robert Frost), and Senator Everett Dirksen of Illinois were a few of the legislators interested in the laureateship, some in behalf of constituent inquiries. Since many national legislators come to Washington via state legislatures, the growing number of state laureateships probably predisposed some members of Congress to accept the idea of a national laureate.

In 1936, the year John Steven McGroarty failed to become "honorary poet laureate of the United States," a much more positive development for American poetry was the establishment of the position of Consultant in Poetry in the Library of Congress, through an endowment fund presented by Archer M. Huntington, son of railroad magnate Collis P. Huntington, and already a generous benefactor of the Library's Hispanic programs.

The first appointment was made in 1937, of Joseph Auslander, an acquaintance of the Huntingtons and then poetry editor of the *North American Review*. Initially, no term was set for the appointment, and Auslander was in the position four years. In the meantime, in 1939 Archibald MacLeish had succeeded Herbert Putnam as Librarian of Congress. An established poet himself, MacLeish was not lacking in opinions about other poets. Auslander was definitely not his idea of who should occupy the highly visible, though not yet prestigious, position of Consultant in Poetry to the Library of Congress.

MacLeish terminated Auslander's appointment, intending to use the position to bring distinguished American poets to the Library for one-year terms. The first poet appointed under the new dispensation was Allen Tate, who served 1943-1944, followed by Robert Penn Warren, 1944-1945. Warren had barely arrived at the Library when MacLeish left to become Assistant Secretary of State. The MacLeish pattern was nevertheless continued by his successor, Luther Evans, and the 1940s roster of Consultants (Tate, Warren, Louise Bogan, Karl Shapiro, Robert Lowell, Léonie Adams, and Elizabeth Bishop) compares favorably with any like period in the history of the position. Evans was guided in his appointments by the Library's Fellows in American Letters, of whom Tate was the acknowledged leader, *primus inter pares*.

When Conrad Aiken, appointed in 1950, was asked to stay a second year, the pattern of one-year appointments was permanently broken. Thereafter, two-year terms were commonplace. About the same time, the choice of Ezra Pound for the first Bollingen Prize created a furor which ultimately affected the Consultantship. The award was made by the Library on the recommendation of the Fellows. At the conclusion of Aiken's term, William Carlos Williams was chosen, but through a series of misunderstandings, mischances, and misfortunes, never assumed his position. There followed a four-year hiatus (1952-1956) before the appointment of Randall Jarrell. As a result of the turmoil of the early 1950s, the Fellows were gradually phased out, and the Library administration took a more decisive role in managing the literary program, including the Consultantship, with a single Library official responsible. The gifts of Gertrude Clarke Whittall about this time to permit an active schedule of literary programming provided something substantial to manage and to enlist the interest of succeeding Consultants.

Robert Frost used his term as Consultant (1958-1959) to purvey the notion that the Library's poet was a national resource, to be resorted to by members of Congress and the administration. He sought and received national attention as no other Consultant before or since, and national awareness followed, especially when Frost was called back to take his well-known part in the inauguration of John F. Kennedy. This public trend was continued by his popular successors Richard Eberhart and Louis Untermeyer and later poets such as James Dickey. In time the public roles became institu-

Robert Penn Warren (right), first Poet Laureate of the United States, with Librarian of Congress Daniel J. Boorstin, October 1986
(Library of Congress)

tionalized, and several of the Library's Consultants (including William Jay Smith, William Meredith, and Gwendolyn Brooks) undertook special projects under the aegis of USIA or other government agencies. It became customary in the public media to refer to the Consultant in Poetry as "the nation's unofficial poet laureate." This tendency received added impetus from the role played by former Consultant James Dickey at the time of the inauguration of Jimmy Carter. Although he did not take part in the official inaugural ceremony, Dickey made several public appearances in Washington as the new president's favorite poet. Dickey's poem "The Strength of Fields," occasioned by Carter's election and inauguration, is laureatelike in inspiration and character.

The impulse toward an official laureateship had meanwhile acquired a tireless congressional advocate in Spark Matsunaga. Twenty years after entering Congress, during which time another thir-

teen Consultants had been appointed, he achieved his goal.

Spark M. Matsunaga, a decorated hero of World War II, after serving in the Hawaii House of Representatives in the 1950s, was elected to the House of Representatives in 1964 and to the Senate in 1976. He made known his interest in a Poet Laureateship almost immediately by introducing legislation leading to its establishment. His remarks on the floor of the House on 27 February 1968 are instructive. The House was considering H.R. 11308, amending the National Foundation on the Arts and Humanities Act of 1965. Mr. Matsunaga, as he had announced he would do, offered an amendment to create the position of Poet Laureate of the United States, appointed by the President after consideration of recommendations by the National Council on the Arts, with a term of office of five years and an annual stipend of $25,000. The manager of the principal bill, Frank Thompson (Democrat, New Jersey), challenged the amendment on a point of order as "not germane to the bill." The point of order, however, was reserved to permit Mr. Matsunaga to make a statement on the amendment, which he regarded as "the encouragement of man's creative imagination" and therefore related to the legislative initiative which had created the national endowments on the arts and humanities. After speaking to his amendment, Mr. Matsunaga yielded on the point of order and withdrew the amendment. It was to be a parallel amendment in 1985 which was to establish the laureateship.

He continued in succeeding Congresses to introduce bills on the laureateship in virtually the same language as his original amendment, differing only in the compensation proposed, which in later versions was "not to exceed 60 per centum of the salary of a Federal District Court Judge."

The last (and successful) attempt began with S. 313, introduced 29 January 1985, which Senator Matsunaga described in the *Congressional Record* of that date as "identical to one which I first introduced in the 88th Congress and, most recently, in the 98th Congress." Before the year was out, Senator Matsunaga was to have his poet laureate.

The Library of Congress, when offered the opportunity to comment on proposed legislation establishing a Poet Laureateship, had invariably opposed the idea. The opposition was based on three factors: 1) the inappropriateness of such a position in a democratic society; 2) the politicization of such a position if filled by Presidential appointment; and 3) the confusion with and detraction from the Library's Consultant in Poetry. In discussions that took place in 1985 between the Librarian of Congress and Senator Matsunaga and others, a Presidentially appointed position was replaced by one appointed by the Librarian, and, rather than authorize a separate poetry position, the final form of the legislation recognized that the Library's Consultantship in Poetry "is equivalent to that of Poet Laureate of the United States," not merely an unofficial poet laureate, as the press had learned to say. Since the Library did not wish to abandon its traditional title on the eve of the fiftieth anniversary of its establishment and since Senator Matsunaga was committed to the designation "poet laureate," the title settled upon was "Poet Laureate Consultant in Poetry." The only authorized stipend beyond that which the Library customarily offered out of its Huntington Fund, was $10,000 for a poetry program under the auspices of the National Endowment for the Arts. In 1987 the Endowment and the Library agreed to cosponsor the poetry program authorized by Public Law 99-194.

In other respects the Consultant's position is unchanged, but passage of the law changed perceptions, and the national media greeted the appointment of Robert Penn Warren with coverage unmatched since the days of Robert Frost. If Senator Matsunaga wanted to increase the visibility of the national poetry position he succeeded immeasurably.

Mr. Boorstin's selection of Robert Penn Warren was almost universally applauded. To some, the selection seemed "obvious," even "too obvious." The only American to receive Pulitzer Prizes in both poetry (twice) and fiction, Warren has been the recipient of many honors and, although in his eighties, is still very much a practicing poet, whose later poetry has seemed to some observers among his best. He has been, in addition, long associated with the Library of Congress, the second Consultant appointed by MacLeish, and a frequent visitor to the Library over the past forty years. When he received the National Medal for Literature in 1970, he chose to have the ceremony take place in the Library.

In a real sense the test of the laureateship will be in the *second* appointment and those that come after. Having fought to maintain the appointing authority for the principal position in American poetry, the Library of Congress is obliged to vindicate its role with each new appointment. Its record in the past, although generally applauded, has not been without occasional critics. The most telling criticism, purely from the standpoint of poetry and not extraneous considerations, has been that there has been too much reliance on an eastern/southern establishment, tame and mannered, and too little venturesomeness in seeking untraditional poets. In the past twenty years only William Stafford and Gwendolyn Brooks have significant western or midwestern roots. Because the Librarian and his principal internal advisors also have relied on suggestions from former Consultants, there is some risk of a self-perpetuating elite.

To these criticisms the Library traditionally directs attention to the roster of Consultants, which ostensibly speaks for itself. The laureateship, however, in addition to making the Consultant's position more visible, has probably made it seem more attractive to poets and their sponsors, many of limited merit except in their own eyes. Hence, although Public Law 99-194 changed little about the Consultant's position, it drastically changed perceptions. There will be added scrutiny of succeeding appointments, for better or worse. Another complication is the announced retirement of Daniel Boorstin as Librarian of Congress, effective 15 June 1987. Mr. Boorstin will have appointed Warren's successor by then, but a new Librarian will appoint those that follow.

"An American Bard at last!," Walt Whitman chanted. He sought to fill the role of national laureate more than one hundred years before such a position officially existed. In doing so he self-consciously sought to embrace the multifarious geographical, societal, and linguistic features of an immense continental nation. If the aspiration eluded Whitman in the nineteenth-century—and it did, barely—how much less successful have been later aspirants, Hart Crane, Carl Sandburg, Allen Ginsberg, to name a few? That is the major philosophical objection leveled at the laureateship. America is not a homogeneous society susceptible to comprehensive poetic embrace, not even to the extent that an individual state may be thought to be. (In this respect the prospect of a succession of laureates may be a virtue.)

The first laureate, Robert Penn Warren, has eschewed the attempt to fashion laureatelike poetry. Although his negations are expressed in terms of parallels to British royal trappings ("I would not serve if I had been required to compose an ode on the death of someone's kitten"), it is clear that he, and others who may succeed him, are not likely to find the same imperatives in a laureateship that Tennyson or even Alfred Austin did. Nevertheless, the Poet Laureate seems to be here to stay, and since the Library of Congress intends to maintain its one- and/or two-year pattern of appointment, by the year 2000 the United States is likely to have as many laureates and former laureates as the state of Kentucky has now.

Participants in the 1978 reunion of former Poetry Consultants. Standing, left to right: Reed Whittemore, Richard Eberhart, Robert Hayden, William Jay Smith, Stephen Spender, Stanley Kunitz, Karl Shapiro, and Howard Nemerov. Seated, left to right: William Stafford, James Dickey, Josephine Jacobsen, Elizabeth Bishop, and Daniel Hoffman (Library of Congress).

The full text of the relevant legislation is as follows:

TITLE VI—POET LAUREATE CONSULTANT IN POETRY

Sec. 601. Authority for Poet Laureate Consultant in Poetry.

(a) Recognition of the Consultant in Poetry.—The Congress recognizes that the Consultant in Poetry to the Library of Congress has for some time occupied a position of prominence in the life of the Nation, has spoken effectively for literary causes, and has occasionally performed duties and functions sometimes associated with the position of poet laureate in other nations and societies. Individuals are appointed to the position of Consultant in Poetry by the Librarian of Congress for one- or two-year terms solely on the basis of literary merit, and are compensated from endowment funds administered by the Library of Congress Trust Fund Board. The Congress further recognizes this position is equivalent to that of Poet Laureate of the United States.

(b) Poet Laureate Consultant in Poetry Established.—(1) There is established in the Library of Congress the position of Poet Laureate Consultant in Poetry. The Poet Laureate Consultant in Poetry shall be appointed by the Librarian of Congress pursuant to the same procedures of appointment as established on the date of enactment of this section for the Consultant in Poetry to the Library of Congress.

(2) Each department and office of the Federal Government is encouraged to make use of the services of the Poet Laureate Consultant in Poetry for ceremonial and other occasions of celebration under such procedures as the Librarian of Congress shall approve designed to assure that participation under this paragraph does not impair the continuation of the work of the individual chosen to fill the position of Poet Laureate Consultant in Poetry.

(c) Poetry Program.—(1) The Chairperson of the National Endowment for the Arts, with the advice of the National Council on the Arts, shall annually sponsor a program at which the Poet Laureate Consultant in Poetry will present a major work or the work of other distinguished poets.

(2) There are authorized to be appropriated to the National Endowment for the Arts $10,000 for the fiscal year 1987 and for each succeeding fiscal year ending prior to October 1, 1990, for the purpose of carrying out this subsection.

References:

Roy P. Basler, *The Muse and the Librarian* (Westport, Conn. & London: Greenwood, 1974);

Edmund Kemper Broadus, *The Laureateship: A Study of the Office of Poet Laureate in England, with Some Account of the Poets* (Oxford: Clarendon Press, 1921);

Richard Helgerson, *Self-Crowned Laureates* (Berkeley: University of California Press, 1983);

Kenneth Hopkins, *The Poets Laureate* (London: Bodley Head, 1954);

William McGuire, *A History of the Consultantship in Poetry in the Library of Congress* (Washington: Library of Congress, forthcoming 1988);

Nick Russel, *Poets by Appointment: Britain's Laureates* (Poole, Dorset: Blandford, 1981).

AN INTERVIEW ———————————
with the POET LAUREATE

DLB: Since you have previously served as the consultant in poetry to the Library of Congress, how do you perceive the significance of the title "poet laureate"; that is, how do you think appending the designation of poet laureate to the position of consultant in poetry improves or enhances the appointment?

RPW: I perceive the title of poet laureate as simply a *title* attached to the old consultantship of poetry at the Library of Congress. I think that this is, roughly, the legal definition.

DLB: Why do you think it took so long to create the poet laureateship? Is there a reason why it is now deemed appropriate?

RPW: I have no notion of what goes on backstage in the matter. The notion of "appropriateness": As defined, the post of consultantship seems to have some utility.

DLB: The Poet Laureate of England is expected to write occasional poems. Do you intend to do the same as Poet Laureate of the United States?

RPW: As I understand the matter from consultation with the Librarian of Congress, the Poet Laureate of the United States has no obligation to write even a word as Poet Laureate of the United States.

I may add that my understanding is that the appointment is made by the Library of Congress, not the Government.

STATEMENTS FROM FORMER CONSULTANTS IN POETRY

JAMES DICKEY

The appointment of Robert Penn Warren as the first Poet Laureate ever designated by the United States is a fortunate occasion, and a fortunate choice. Warren's talents are various, and all are impressive. He is a poet of great vigor and philosophical depth, and a fiction writer unsparing in his search for large and difficult truths. He is also one of the finest literary critics this country has ever produced, and as a teacher has had an incalculable influence for good, and this will certainly continue to exert itself as long as there are serious readers. Warren's appointment is an affirmation of creative intelligence in this country, as his work is an example of it.

RICHARD EBERHART

My Consultantship in Poetry at the Library of Congress constituted two of the best years of my life. I enjoyed the work so much that I wanted to stay on to make it five years but the Library refused, two was supposed to be the limit. My wife and our two children, Dikkon, 13, and Gretchen, 8, lived in Georgetown and I used to take the trolley to the Capitol and walk to the Library. The tracks were taken up some years later than my 1959-1961 service. Betty and I stood on the sidewalk once and watched Eisenhower and Krushchev standing side by side cheering the crowds as they went by. My first year was under Ike and second under Kennedy. For Kennedy's inauguration I had to do with inviting poets to come for it. I remember before one of the balls that in our house were Auden, Tate, Lowell, the originator of social security, Frances Perkins, and the author of *The Ship of Fools*, who, since the weather was so wet, refused to go to the dance because she had only "her little red slippers." Auden stayed at our house rather than get wet.

The hall was very wet twenty feet into it. We had free champagne, danced, and way after midnight Robert Frost, whom I had succeeded as Consultant, walked across the floor and ascended a few steps to sit among dignitaries.

The day after the inauguration we went to a cocktail party near our house. I spied old Frost, went over to say hello (we knew him well) and said, "I hear you went to the White House to see the President in the oval office this morning, what did he say?," I spoke enthusiastically. He answered immediately, "I did all the talking." That is all he said.

At the Library office I recall Frost dozing in the afternoon in the room looking out over the capitol. One was supposed to give a reading in the fall and a lecture in the spring. One was encouraged to do something one wanted particularly to do. I made six recordings of dead poets whose work I admired. I held two seminars in the Woodrow Wilson Room, one for black poets or professors from Howard and one for Catholic nuns. There were poets for readings and lectures in the Coolidge Auditorium. The Librarian held Thursday luncheons for the staff. Once Carl Sandburg appeared unexpectedly in the Library and was invited. He and Frost were known to be at odds with one another. Early in Frost's career he thought Sandburg was ahead of him. He resented it and this was decades later. Frost went up to Sandburg and took out a small comb and handed it to him saying get the forelock out of your face or something to that effect. Taken aback, Sandburg hesitated but came up with some quip which I have forgotten. Frost sat on the right of the Librarian, Sandburg on the left. They kept up a somewhat acerbic banter across the face of the Librarian. I was on Frost's right. My friend Oscar Williams was directly across the table. But it all ended amicably enough.

JOSEPHINE JACOBSEN

As of the spring of 1986, the position of Poetry Consultant to the Library of Congress has come to be known, for the first time in its fifty years of existence, as the position of Poet Laureate Consultant in Poetry. However much some of us may regret this, what remains important is the significance of the change. I feel that significance will largely be lacking.

Relations between politics and poetry have been almost always destructive to poetry. What we had in the Consultantship, and what we will, I trust and believe, continue to have, was a support of and tribute to poetry; an honor and national prestige offered to poets, without strings, which was duplicated nowhere else. The office of Poetry Consultant seems to me to have been an almost idyllic bridge between formal national recognition of a great art, and the total freedom of its practitioners. I am so confident in the force and justice of the Library's guardians that I do not for a minute believe that bridge will be undermined.

In addition to the importance I attributed to increasing the Library's collection of poets reading their own work—which seems to me for the future perhaps the most valuable of all the Poetry Consultant-Poets Laureate's activities—I felt during my own tenure constantly reinforced in my belief that the actual physical presence of the poet in the Poetry Office was crucial. I had visitors from all over the world, famous, obscure, young, old, but all appreciative of the resident poet's time and interest. A personal, kinetic thing took place, which I believe no programming or information service can replace. This was a time-consuming, rewarding process.

The only part of the British Laureateship which could be described as a job was the dubious and unhappy part of which it has now almost completely divested itself—what we may call the Tommy Tucker syndrome. The original purpose of the position was to put the gifts of the poet so chosen in the service of such public events as seemed important to the Sovereign. Though that no longer obtains to any appreciable degree, there is neither a place, nor a working term; most important, it is a lifetime appointment and no new blood or differing creative impulse can impinge. There has never been a woman in the long and in general lusterless lists of British Poets Laureate.

Chosen entirely on the basis of the quality of accumulated work, our office says, in effect, that the poet designated can be considered for a limited period, the representative of what is valuable nationally in his or her work. The limited tenure of our poetry Consultant-Poet Laureate is important. We all know the sad and not infrequent history of poets who after years of distinguished work, in later years dry up, or more sadly continue by putting out weakened or inferior work. The United States is far too rich in genuinely distinguished poets to have one poet isolated in the stasis of a lifetime appointment.

Poetry is paid badly, published sparsely, and a stepchild of the endowments. But it retains its magic and power, and in the Library of Congress I found that it has strong and healthy and far-

reaching roots. Its embodiment in an available poet reaches out all over the country, and all of us are nurtured by what it offers and what it stands for. There are a dozen ways in which the regular and actual presence of the poet can, and does, affect the position. That human contact is the blood and bone of the concept of position; its variety is life-giving; its independence is what I treasure.

WILLIAM STAFFORD

The Consultant in Poetry at the Library of Congress serves the literary community—and through them the larger community—in an odd and special way. The job is a rotating one, and though each person who holds it enjoys some advantages through location and connections, no lasting or heavy eminence hovers over the encounters and acquaintancing that occur. No institution dictates the attitudes and policies that surface and get talked over and disappear in the Consultant's office.

People who come by, or who correspond, get a sense of being connected with each other on their own terms. Person to person, writers meet. They have much to share. And meeting in the center of national events, where power throbs all around, helps literary people know themselves as apart from what is around them. They come to an enhanced realization of their distinctness: they are not coercive; they are not powerful. But they sense the need to be immensely aware and understanding. A sense of the literary community as apart from profit, from fame, from competitiveness is present—has a presence—partly because writers have one of their own in an office in Washington.

REED WHITTEMORE

In the midst of Washington's political culture the position of Poetry Consultant at the Library of Congress has been, for fifty years, a strange and wonderful national phenomenon. I am honored to have been a part of it.

CONSULTANTS IN POETRY

Joseph Auslander	1937-1941
Allen Tate	1943-1944
Robert Penn Warren	1944-1945
Louise Bogan	1945-1946

Karl Shapiro	1946-1947	William Jay Smith	1968-1970
Robert Lowell	1947-1948	William Stafford	1970-1971
Léonie Adams	1948-1949	Josephine Jacobson	1971-1973
Elizabeth Bishop	1949-1950	Daniel Hoffman	1973-1974
Conrad Aiken	1950-1952	Stanley Kunitz	1974-1976
William Carlos Williams		Robert Hayden	1976-1978
(Appointed in 1952		William Meredith	1978-1980
but did not serve)		Maxine Kumin	1981-1982
Randall Jarrell	1956-1958	Anthony Hecht	1982-1984
Robert Frost	1958-1959	Robert Fitzgerald	1984-1985
Richard Eberhart	1959-1961	(Appointed but did not	
Louis Untermeyer	1961-1963	serve because of illness)	
Howard Nemerov	1963-1964	Reed Whittemore	1984-1985
Reed Whittemore	1964-1965	(Interim Consultant)	
Stephen Spender	1965-1966	Gwendolyn Brooks	1985-1986
James Dickey	1966-1968		

Literary Documents: William Faulkner and the People-to-People Program

William Faulkner accepted President Eisenhower's June 1956 invitation to head the writers' section of the People-to-People Program, an endeavor to bring about better international understanding—especially behind the iron curtain. Faulkner's activities as a public figure and administrator—duties for which he had no aptitude—are chronicled in Joseph Blotner's *Faulkner: A Biography* (New York: Random House, 1974).

In September 1956 Faulkner wrote to a list of American writers soliciting their ideas for projects to be sponsored by People-to-People. On the basis of their replies he distributed a questionnaire on 11 October. After an inconclusive and disorganized 29 November meeting with writers at the home of Harvey Breit—who served as cochairman—Faulkner lost interest in the undertaking. On 4 February 1957 he left a People-to-People meeting, terminating his official participation in the program.

The documents reproduced here are from the William Faulkner Collections (#7258-1), University of Virginia Library, and are published with the library's permission.

[late Sept. 1956]

Dear ——

The President has asked me to organize American writers to see what we can do to give a true picture of our country to other people.

Will you join such an organization?

Pending a convenient meeting, will you send to me in a sentence, or a paragraph, or a page, or as many more as you like, your private idea of what might further this project?

I am enclosing my own ideas as a sample.

1. Anesthetize, for one year, American vocal chords.

2. Abolish, for one year, American passports.

3. Commandeer every American automobile. Secrete Johnson grass seed in the cushions and every other available place. Fill the tanks with gasoline. Leave the switch key in the switch and push the car across the iron curtain.

4. Ask the Government to establish a fund. Choose 10,000 people between 18 and 30, preferably Communists. Bring them to this country and let them see America as it is. Let them buy an automobile on the installment plan, if that's what they want. Find them jobs in labor as we run our labor unions. Let them enjoy the right to say whatever they wish about anyone they wish, to go to the corner drug store for ice cream and all the other privileges of this country which we take for granted. At the end of the year they must go home. Any installment plan automobiles or gadgets which they have undertaken would be impounded. They can have them again if and when they return or their equity in them will go as a down payment on a new model. This is to be done each year at the rate of 10,000 new people.

Will you please communicate either with me or Harvey Breit who has accepted the chore of being a co-chairman?

Yours very truly,
William Faulkner*

P.S. In a more serious vein, please read the enclosed one-page description of Mr. Eisenhower's purpose.

Selected Letters of William Faulkner, edited by Joseph Blotner (New York: Random House, 1976).

260 CUMBERLAND STREET, BROOKLYN 5, NEW YORK

September 26,   1956

I shall do it, Mr. Faulkner - join in - with a
very unprepossessing proviso, that I participate by
mail and that I need not receive letters special
delivery, or telegrams.   (I may not be worth
your trouble). .... but I am all for this needful effort.

Marchette Chute and Bruce Catton during National Book
Week, one year, advocated over the radio - lures in
libraries - Placards drawing-attention-to advocating
a sane international and inter-community attitude.

Foreigners delight to explore our department-stores.
Manufacturing plants achieve great contagion, expositing
methods and progress, to stockholders, e.g. "You have no
idea how plumbers like our steel soil-pipe"; United Fruit:
"the banaba - "Nature's dust-proof wrapper; Union Carbide
and Carbon, Dupont, Bethlehem Steel. Why could not these
masters of their business exposit their feats to groups
of young visitors?

Julien Bryan's documentaries were electric in their
power of persuasion.

Above all, push-button features in cars, raising the
windo, raising the top, etc. The Ford Company likes to
exhibit their novelties (at Dearborn, Michigan.

Borden's rotolactor, showing cows milked on a turntable;
dog-training; ball-bearing and photoelectric-cell
demonstrations such as the Museum of Science and Invention
once set up. These exhibits swarmed with visitors.
(No Museum of S and I here now).

Sincerely yours,

Marianne Moore

*Sorry about this inconsiderately small sheet of paper.
Am leaving for California, shall be back after middle of October.
Am very prompt, as a rule. In attending to letters.*

RANDOM HOUSE INC. 457 MADISON AVENUE · NEW YORK 22

THE MODERN LIBRARY
LANDMARK BOOKS
AMERICAN COLLEGE DICTIONARY

October 11, 1956

Miss Marianne Craig Moore
260 Cumberland Street
Brooklyn, N. Y.

Dear Miss Moore:

It has been suggested that you cannot deal people-to-
people through the Iron Curtain, but must deal with a government.

I think we are all agreed that this is a self-evident fact.

The whole purpose of this committee is that this is a self-
evident fact.

Which do you think the more important?

1. The aim of this project, even though unattainable? *Yes*

2. The risk that the project itself might be used as *This kind of*
   a political catspaw? *timidity takes the heart*

Our correspondents have sent in the following suggestions.
Will you rate these suggestions as follows: 1) Excellent
2) Good 3) Poor 4) No. Please check the attached list and send *of one*
it back to me.

I think we are all of one mind that there is no need in calling
a meeting until we are agreed on what we are going to do in it.

Sincerely,

William Faulkner

William Faulkner

Please return to:
William Faulkner
c/o Jean Ennis
Random House, Inc.
457 Madison Avenue
New York 22, N. Y.

*Very sorry to be late
with this —
M. Moore
Nov. 1 1956*

Suggestions	1	2	3	No

No / Contemptible — Suggests program be dropped; thinks it's unworkable. As you say, "anesthetize, for one year, American vocal chords." — *Craven suggestion*

No / very poor — Afraid of left-wing past; writers can't work through institutions; won't be associated with anything sponsored by Republican Party. — *If it's true & stop scapegoating on... "Party"... Parties... we have a man we can really work with*

Poor — Futile. We are barbarians anyway. — *Not*

Excellent — Free and untampered exchange of books. — *Yes*

? — Suggests working through PEN Club. — *Is it equal to such a dynamic...*

Poor / possible — Program should be free of government; suggests letter-writing between authors of the world; interchange via National Institute, American Academy and PEN Club. — *al-though Marchette Chute is an expert (and as conscientious as John Bunyan). Not letters between authors I would say. National Institute, I think. (Feiling ...)*

Yes / Good — Person-to-person communication through lectures, travel, writing; postpone first meeting until after election (too?) because of differing political views among authors.

POOR — Shocked by your letter; will come to meeting out of curiosity; writers shouldn't be organized- must be free. — *Pathetic - trivial - and ... of effrontery, are no help (Curiosity!)*

Poor — Suggests examining discrepancy between what President says he wants and State Department's refusal to grant passports for cultural missions to such places as China. — *Wasteful. We haven't vitality for everything*

Poor — Exchange intelligent men; reform America first. *how? Cliché, vague*

Counteract dark picture of America given by books now available to foreigners by distributing translations of books that show a happier side of American life. — *Yes*

Understand ourselves first. *No* — *Casuistry*

Be honest about ourselves with other peoples. *Certainly*

Good / Poor — Exchange scholarships, professorships; quiet meetings without oratory; personal friendships between authors of various nationalities. — *Yes. No meetings ; no friendships*

adult / good — Suggests some of our corporations invite groups of young foreigners to visit American manufacturing plants. — *Yes*

Such an organization would be automatically suspect as being government-sponsored. *What of it?* — *Depends on how it's done*

taken for granted — Believes in example rather than preachment. Deeds are enduring propaganda. American ideology must be defined. Films should be considered to further understanding. *Films! Good* — *Preaching our theories? No; except if they unmistakably stand out in pronouncements...*

Suggestions	1	2	3	No

Poor — Expedient political device. Besides, she's a Democrat.

Very impatient of egotism like this

insincere / *Ignore him* — Doesn't understand intention of program. Wants to know if it's to help re-elect Eisenhower. He's for Stevenson!

Wants articulate form for cultural exchange.

Poor — Abolish literary agents; satirize America in our writings; send articles on American authors abroad for publication; establish worthy literary prizes; exempt authors from income tax; etc. etc.

Undergrown phase of paranoia

Poor — If first meeting is held after election he will join, since then Eisenhower will perhaps have four years to follow through with it.

bad logic

Good — Convey ourselves to others through our writing.

Certainly

Poor — Stop all propaganda. *very weak attitude*

good — FREE EZRA POUND!! *YES*

Self-evident — Authors' works are best propaganda. *Certainly but why stop there?*

Writers should stay at home, unorganized, and work. *and sally out as well —*

good — Have our works properly translated and distributed abroad, without special frills or official commentary.

Yes — but pretty complex.

good — Circulate books and magazines more widely in other countries; soften up the rigid political barriers that are the real reason why people have very little "friendly contact;" plug European federation along the lines suggested by Dr. Adenauer; and elect Stevenson.

I wouldn't any boltroomery Translated, few of these answers are part.

Suggests a series of small conferences of Europeans, Asiatics, etc., to be held in Washington, over a period of about two years.

Character matters. A man who quotes another may out of context to sink him, is no mouthpiece for me. A shabby American in the White House would not help international reciprocity.

It isn't practical. Bigwig-to-bigwig can hardly be achieved

Marianne Moore
Nov. 1st 1956

THE-PEOPLE-TO-PEOPLE PROGRAM

November 20, 1956

Miss Marianne Moore
260 Cumberland Street
Brooklyn, N. Y.

Dear Miss Moore:

   With regard to the President's proposal for a People-to-People
Program, we have now gone over the material--both letters and filled-in
questionnaires--that fifty-seven writers have been cooperative enough to
send in. The suggestions are, of course, varied, but we believe that most
of them fall into one of the following categories:

   1. The idea of exchange--of books, periodicals and people.

   2. The relaxation of governmental controls--such as the
      McCarran Act, passport and visa regulations, etc.

   3. Miscellaneous--ranging from the freeing of Ezra Pound
      to a sounder foreign policy.

   Now we would all agree that any exchange of books and ideas
is to be encouraged and improved and intensified. But that is part of
an old pattern. There are already government agencies busily doing that,
not to mention the fact that all of us writers spend our lives doing that
very thing, and so we can't very well do more than we have done.

   We are looking for a new pattern, which should be not to
export America, but to import representatives of the people who don't
like us into America--to bring their families and children and live
and work as American families do; let them and their children see how
we live and what it is in our country which makes us, anyway, prefer it.

   We would like to discuss this idea and ways and means of
implementing it. Would you be willing to devote, say, one hour of a
two-hour meeting to this main topic? We would then reserve the second
hour for a discussion of other ideas. We are calling such a meeting
for Thursday, November 29, from 4 to 6 p.m., at Harvey Breit's home,
116 East 64th Street, New York City.

   Will you let us know if you would like to come, and whether
you can?

[handwritten marginal notes: Yes. Shall plan to come 4-5 Nov. 29 116 E 64th]

[handwritten: (If I am well enough, + expect to be of) though am at present helpless (ill)) M. Moore]

                                          Sincerely yours,

                                          [signature] William Faulkner
                                          William Faulkner

William Faulkner
c/o Jean Ennis
Random House
457 Madison Avenue
New York 22, N. Y.

PEOPLE to PEOPLE PROGRAM

Dear Mr. Faulkner: I agree to this, indeed I do; but do you not think Washington might do better for us if we were a little more neatly explicit in Section III ?also I
Please disregard the query if I am unprofitably meticulous. (I am not touchy; never need an answer or an explanation.)

Marianne Moore January 5, 1957
Marianne Moore   260 Cumberland Street
BROOKLYN 5, N Y

EZRA POUND freed, - by all means.

A representative group of American writers led by William Faulkner, after free and open discussion, have come to the following conclusions:

We in America tend to overestimate our enemies. For example, we have believed that the Soviet state has been able to condition their people so that they are impervious to the outside world. In recent months this has been proved completely untrue in Hungary and Poland. The human animal is not conditionable to the extent that we've been led to believe. Therefore, we are convinced that free, and honest communication will not fall on deaf ears.

Our failure to qualify in the cold war ~~is the result of our~~ failure to communicate. The first step of a dictator is to cut off communication of ideas, of people, of arts, to close borders and to stop the interchange of messages. This being so, it is to our advantage to enter into communication upon any or all levels: person-to-person, the written and spoken word, by example, and the arts which communicate without words.

The people of the world have been trained to detect ~~means of~~ propaganda. The only antidote to propaganda is ~~simple~~ honesty and ~~the widest~~ dissemination of truth, undirected and uncensored-- especially uncensored. When communication becomes propaganda, it ceases to communicate.

In order to achieve better communication, ~~these things should be done:~~

I.   To reduce visa requirements to a minimum and abrogate red tape for the Hungarian people and ~~any other people who may or will suffer the same~~ crisis or threatened.

II. ~~To try to bring people from all over the world who do not agree with us to this country for a duration of at least two years to live a normal American life, to~~ see and experience what we have here that makes us like ~~it.~~ This ~~will necessarily~~ require a revision of the McCarran Act.

III. ~~To~~ disseminate books, plays, and moving pictures ~~through our Government, at least to match what the Russians are doing.~~

~~These are the basic three points~~ we feel ~~are necessary in order~~ for us ~~to engage~~ in the world-wide struggle for democracy against totalitarianism. ~~There are~~ other steps to be taken.

-2-

For example, we should free Ezra Pound. While the Chairman of this Committee, appointed by the President, was awarded a prize for literature by the Swedish Government and was given a decoration by the French Government, the American Government locks up one of its best poets.

To accomplish these proposals will require a liberalization of passport regulations for people coming and going, and adequate government subsidy.

William Faulkner
John Steinbeck
Donald Hall

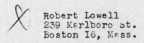

Robert Lowell
239 Marlboro St.
Boston 16, Mass.

September 25, 1956

Dear Mr. Faulkner:

Of course I would like to join any organization that you are giving your time to organizing.

I have few ideas on how writers might
help in a program for people-to-people partnership. I do,
however, flinch at the President's seeming suggestion
that writers might go on missions for the promotion of
American ideology. I think that most of us are too dumb
and too serious to do anything of the sort. Life is too
short; we are too deeply saturated with our country. If
we can only meet writers from other countries naturally,
humorously, with curiosity and humility; then they might
see that we were human. Then the crusade for people to
people partnership would take care of itself.

Our world position, so different from
most other countries, fills Europeans with fear and envy
as we go bouncing among them and shine like a white-washed
lighthouse on them in all our optimism, wealth and shining
ideology. We have such an air of hurry, power and bouyant
vacancy. They find us exhilarating and rather monstrous.

As a writer, I am much interested in
making friends with writers from other countries. As a
teacher, I am interested in teaching the writing of other
countries. I particularly want to know what I am doing

when I try to read French, German, and Italian poetry. How can we read at all if we are unable to learn from other literatures, see that they are different from ours?

I am all for exchange scholarships, professorships, etc., quiet meetings without oratory, and above all personal friendships.

Of course you can see deeper into us and our country than I can. Long ago, I wrote you a long fan letter. I never dared to mail it, but I think I said (as the Democrats say of themselves) that you were our writer with style and a heart. You are. What a joy that this business has allowed me to say so.

Yours sincerely,

Robert Lowell

Suggestions	1	2	3	No
Suggests program be dropped; thinks it's unworkable. As you say, "anesthetize, for one year, American vocal chords,"				X
Afraid of left-wing past; writers can't work through institutions; won't be associated with anything sponsored by Republican Party.			X	
Futile. We are barbarians anyway.				X
Free and untampered exchange of books.	X			
Suggests working through PEN Club.				
Program should be free of government; suggests letter-writing between authors of the world; interchange via National Institute, American Academy and PEN Club.				
Person-to-person communication through lectures, travel, writing; postpone first meeting until after election because of differing political views among authors.		X		
Shocked by your letter; will come to meeting out of curiosity; writers shouldn't be organized- must be free.				
Suggests examining discrepancy between what President says he wants and State Department's refusal to grant passports for cultural missions to such places as China.		X		
Exchange intelligent men; reform America first.				
Counteract dark picture of America given by books now available to foreigners by distributing translations of books that show a happier side of American life.				X
Understand ourselves first.				
Be honest about ourselves with other peoples.		X		
Exchange scholarships, professorships; quiet meetings without oratory; personal friendships between authors of various nationalities.	X			
Suggests some of our corporations invite groups of young foreigners to visit American manufacturing plants.				
Such an organization would be automatically suspect as being government-sponsored.			X	
Believes in example rather than preachment. Deeds are enduring propaganda. American ideology must be defined. Films should be considered to further understanding.				

Suggestions	1	2	3	No
Expedient political device. Besides, she's a Democrat.				
Doesn't understand intention of program. Wants to know if it's to help re-elect Eisenhower. He's for Stevenson!				
Wants articulate form for cultural exchange.	X			
Abolish literary agents; satirize America in our writings; send articles on American authors abroad for publication; establish worthy literary prizes; exempt authors from income tax; etc. etc.		X		
If first meeting is held after election he will join, since then Eisenhower will perhaps have four years to follow through with it.				
Convey ourselves to others through our writing.				
Stop all propaganda.				
FREE EZRA POUND!!	X			
Authors' works are best propaganda.				
Writers should stay at home, unorganized, and work.				
Have our works properly translated and distributed abroad, without special frills or official commentary.	X			
Circulate books and magazines more widely in other countries; soften up the rigid political barriers that are the real reason why people have very little "friendly contact;" plug European federation along the lines suggested by Dr. Adenauer; and elect Stevenson.	X			
Suggests a series of small conferences of Europeans, Asiatics, etc., to be held in Washington, over a period of about two years.	X			

Dear Mr. Faulkner:

        I have answered a few of the questions that interested me. Ofcourse many of them are foolish, random or commonplace. We all have moods when nothing seems serious, when we only want to cultivate our own gardens. At such times the rest of the globe seems of place for readers of the 100 best books, and we would like to spit on governments and our own above all. Thank God for these feelings! Yet it is imbecile not to want to know other countries, stand with our government, and tell the truth about ourselves. I'm not Malvoglio or the new Time Magazine intectual who wants to give a happy picture. Of course your committee can do good work.

                    Yours sincerely,
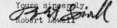
                    Robert Lowell

EDMUND WILSON
WELLFLEET, CAPE COD
MASSACHUSETTS

September 25, 1956

Dear Mr. Faulkner:

I don't believe in these national propaganda
schemes and have always refused to take part in
them. I was surprised to hear that you were involved
in this. I have just come back from Europe and
found your books being sold in London, Paris and
Munich. How can you, or any other writer, make any
better propaganda than by books that get themselves
translated because they have something to say to
people in other countries. There is a lot of anti-
American feeling in Germany, England and France,
and propaganda can do nothing to improve relations.
In fact, my impression is that our own - which is
often puerile - has, if anything, contributed to
making them worse. But the Kammerspiele in Munich,
for example, the serious theater there, now does
practically nothing but American plays: Wilder,
Miller, Wolfe, Faulkner and others. No committee
with a "program" sent them these. The Germans made
an effort to get them. These authors do not, as
a rule, glorify "the American way of life," but they
make people respect America.

The President is well-intentioned, but his
talk about "our American ideology" and "the great
struggle being waged between the two opposing ways
of life" is, in my opinion, nonsense. The American
ideology is not to have any ideology, and the Soviets
and the States, for good or ill, have all along had
a good deal in common, more perhaps than either now
has with Europe, and have in various ways been
imitating one another. The Russians have been
learning, and will learn, from us, not what we want to
tell them, but what they find is valuable to them.

Make any use of this you please.

Sincerely,

Edmund Wilson

Roxbury Road, Southbury Connecticut 26 September 1956

Mr. William Faulkner
Care Miss Jean Ennis:

Dear Mr. Faulkner:

      I shall not make this the occasion for a fan letter. I believe you should not have lent your great name and prestige to this purely expedient political device of a Presidential election campaign. This with no hint of adverse criticism of President Eisenhower, who is a man of good faith, but who cannot in this noise and confusion, look closely into every scheme presented to him by his advisers.

      I believe this is a completely artificial issue manufactured out of campaign smoke and cinders; there is no clause in this plan that the Democrats have not believed in for years, and have worked hard and practically to bring about International peace and understanding by every means within their power; and have been consistently and bitterly opposed by the Reublicans at every step. IF it could happen that the Republicans might actually try to carry out this plan if they stay in power, I can go along cheeffully with them without changing my vote or a single idea- it is only what the Democrats have been saying and for years;   I am voting for Adlai Stevenson. Sincerely yours

Katherine Anne Porter

John Steinbeck

206 East 72nd Street, New York 21, N. Y.

October 3, 1956

Dear Mr. Faulkner:

Of course I must applaud the President's high purpose in his People-To-People Partnerships. To my mind there is no more important project in the world and surely I would do anything in my power to help with it.

You have asked for suggestions and I must make one in all seriousness. In view of the Calm & Slime inroads, the closing of libraries and film units, the literary and art censorship of the State Department, the shrivelled and despairing activities of the U.S.I.S., none of them inspired by the President but also not inhibited by him, I suggest that the group he has asked you and Harvey Breit to assemble hold its

first meeting immediately after, not before the
election – otherwise there might be a strong
"I shall go to Korea" overtone in the program.
But if this project should follow the election,
Mr. Eisenhower will perhaps have four years
to follow through with it. and in such a
case I would surely be available in any
capacity.

Thank you for asking me –

Yours very sincerely

John Steinbeck

J. Berryman.

Suggestions	1	2	3	No
Suggests program be dropped; thinks it's unworkable. As you say, "anesthetize, for one year, American vocal chords." *good idea, but* →				✓
Afraid of left-wing past; writers can't work through institutions; won't be associated with anything sponsored by Republican Party.			✓	
Futile. We are barbarians anyway.			✓	
Free and untampered exchange of books.	✓			
Suggests working through PEN Club.		*poss.*	*poss.*	
Program should be free of government; suggests letter-writing between authors of the world; interchange via National Institute, American Academy and PEN Club.			*inadeq.; fel guess*	
Person-to-person communication through lectures, travel, writing; postpone first meeting until after election because of differing political views among authors.	✓✓			
Shocked by your letter; will come to meeting out of curiosity; writers shouldn't be organized- must be free.	*not shockt; will try to come; agree freedom shd not be interfered with*			
Suggests examining discrepancy between what President says he wants and State Department's refusal to grant passports for cultural missions to such places as China.		✓		
Exchange intelligent men; reform America first.		✓		
Counteract dark picture of America given by books now available to foreigners by distributing translations of books that show a happier side of American life.				✓
Understand ourselves first.		✓ *but impractical*		
Be honest about ourselves with other peoples.	✓			
Exchange scholarships, professorships; quiet meetings without oratory; personal friendships between authors of various nationalities.	✓			
Suggests some of our corporations invite groups of young foreigners to visit American manufacturing plants.		✓		
Such an organization would be automatically suspect as being government-sponsored.		*probably; but by whom? and if it's useful, so what!*		
Believes in example rather than preachment. Deeds are enduring propaganda. American ideology must be defined. Films should be considered to further understanding.		✓		

Suggestions	1	2	3	No
Expedient political device. Besides, she's a Democrat.		*Quite possible.*		
Doesn't understand intention of program. Wants to know if it's to help re-elect Eisenhower. He's for Stevenson!				
Wants articulate form for cultural exchange.	*"✓" (whatever this means)* *"artic. form"*			
Abolish literary agents; satirize America in our writings; send articles on American authors abroad for publication; establish worthy literary prizes; exempt authors from income tax; etc. etc.	✓✓✓✓			
If first meeting is held after election he will join, since then Eisenhower will perhaps have four years to follow through with it.		✓		
Convey ourselves to others through our writing.	?			
Stop all propaganda.	✓			✓
FREE EZRA POUND!!	✓			
Authors' works are best propaganda.	?			
Writers should stay at home, unorganized, and work.		*of course, in general.*		
Have our works properly translated and distributed abroad, without special frills or official commentary.	✓			
Circulate books and magazines more widely in other countries; soften up the rigid political barriers that are the real reason why people have very little "friendly contact;" plug European federation along the lines suggested by Dr. Adenauer; and elect Stevenson.	✓			
Suggests a series of small conferences of Europeans, Asiatics, etc., to be held in Washington, over a period of about two years.	*yes*			

John Berryman

Suggestions	1	2	3	No
Suggests program be dropped; thinks it's unworkable. As you say, "anesthetize, for one year, American vocal chords."				
Afraid of left-wing past; writers can't work through institutions; won't be associated with anything sponsored by Republican Party.				
Futile. We are barbarians anyway.	good			
Free and untampered exchange of books.	good			
Suggests working through PEN Club.	good			
Program should be free of government; suggests letter-writing between authors of the world; interchange via National Institute, American Academy and PEN Club.	good			
Person-to-person communication through lectures, travel, writing; postpone first meeting until after election because of differing political views among authors.	good			
Shocked by your letter; will come to meeting out of curiosity; writers shouldn't be organized- must be free.	good			
Suggests examining discrepancy between what President says he wants and State Department's refusal to grant passports for cultural missions to such places as China.				
Exchange intelligent men; reform America first.	good			
Counteract dark picture of America given by books now available to foreigners by distributing translations of books that show a happier side of American life.				No
Understand ourselves first.	good			
Be honest about ourselves with other peoples.	good			
Exchange scholarships, professorships; quiet meetings without oratory; personal friendships between authors of various nationalities.	good			
Suggests some of our corporations invite groups of young foreigners to visit American manufacturing plants.	good			
Such an organization would be automatically suspect as being government-sponsored.				No
Believes in example rather than preachment. Deeds are enduring propaganda. American ideology must be defined. Films should be considered to further understanding.	good			

John Dos Passos

Suggestions	1	2	3	No
Expedient political device. Besides, she's a Democrat.				
Doesn't understand intention of program. Wants to know if it's to help re-elect Eisenhower. He's for Stevenson!				
Wants articulate form for cultural exchange.	*Gmd*			
Abolish literary agents; satirize America in our writings; send articles on American authors abroad for publication; establish worthy literary prizes; exempt authors from income tax; etc. etc.	*Why not?*			
If first meeting is held after election he will join, since then Eisenhower will perhaps have four years to follow through with it.	*?*			
Convey ourselves to others through our writing.	*good*			
Stop all propaganda.				
FREE EZRA POUND!!	*find?*			
Authors' works are best propaganda.				
Writers should stay at home, unorganized, and work.				
Have our works properly translated and distributed abroad, without special frills or official commentary.	*good*			
Circulate books and magazines more widely in other countries; soften up the rigid political barriers that are the real reason why people have very little "friendly contact;" plug European federation along the lines suggested by Dr. Adenauer; and elect Stevenson.				
Suggests a series of small conferences of Europeans, Asiatics, etc., to be held in Washington, over a period of about two years.	*good*			

Frankly I cant find anything very new in all these suggestions. Why isnt it possible to step up work already being done through the Pen Club, Congress for Cultural freedom etc?

J.D.P.

The Randall Jarrell Symposium: A Small Collection of Randall Jarrells

Thorne Compton
University of South Carolina

On 30 September 1986 a group of scholars, writers, and artists gathered in Columbia, South Carolina, to discuss, explore, argue, and perform the works of Randall Jarrell. Jarrell's accomplishments as poet, critic, novelist, translator, and writer for children made him a major figure in American intellectual and literary life from the early 1940s until his tragic death in 1965. Only fifty-one years old, and in the midst of an enormously productive period when he died, Jarrell left behind with his large body of work the legacy of his deep and sometimes combative commitment to the importance of the arts and intellectual life in an increasingly sterile, shallow, and cynical postwar America.

The Institute for Southern Studies of the University of South Carolina planned this symposium on Jarrell's work, and the conference was notable for its interdisciplinary focus: along with the critical discussion of Jarrell's poetry, fiction, and criticism, there was an examination of the remarkable cooperation between Jarrell and Maurice Sendak on three of Jarrell's children's books, a consideration of the sources in his own life for these children's books, and the world premieres of two song cycles using Jarrell poems by two very different contemporary composers. On the final day of the conference there was an opportunity for the participants to sit down together for a wide-ranging and sometimes intensely personal discussion of Jarrell's life and work.

The participants in the conference, which included poets Heather Ross Miller and Fred Chappell, critics William Pritchard and Gerald Griswold, and composers Paul Alan Levi and Ed Johnson, were brought together both by their strong commitment to Jarrell's work and by Mary Jarrell, his widow and editor of the acclaimed *Randall Jarrell's Letters: An Autobiographical and Literary Selection* (1985). As the keynote speaker and endlessly patient resource for the symposium organizers, Mary Jarrell was responsible for much of the success of the conference. In addition to those who made presentations, there were several special guests invited to be a part of the roundtable. Poet and novelist James Dickey, critics Sr. Bernetta Quinn, Charlotte Beck, Richard Flinn of George Washington University, Richard Calhoun of Clemson University, and Ashley Brown of the University of South Carolina contributed to a thoughtful discussion of the life and work of Randall Jarrell.

The Jarrell symposium was the third in a series of interdisciplinary public programs sponsored by the Institute of Southern Studies and the University of South Carolina on the lives and work of prominent contemporary southern writers. This series has focused on writers who have not only been extremely important in the development of our national as well as regional culture but who were also linked personally and artistically to each other. Robert Penn Warren, James Dickey, and Randall Jarrell were not from fully separate generations, but they do link the flowering of the southern literary renaissance in the national consciousness from the early Fugitive movement to the present moment. These three were also close personally, sharing in addition to their commitment to art, an active sensibility and of course an alma mater, Vanderbilt University.

Robert Penn Warren was a natural beginning point for this series, as much because of his broad influence in a variety of areas of American cultural life as for his historical significance in southern literature. The Warren symposium, held 26-27 February 1982, was distinguished by such participants as critics Harold Bloom and Louis Rubin, and novelist Madison Jones, as well as historian Thomas Connelly and composer Carlisle Floyd, whose opera, *Willie Stark*, had its world premiere shortly before the conference opened. Warren, unable to be present, participated via an hour-long videotaped interview made for the occasion.

The second program (held on 1-4 February 1983), a celebration of poet, critic, and novelist James Dickey's sixtieth birthday, was suggested by Warren and Harold Bloom and attracted an array of guests which included Bloom and John Simon, film scholar Benjamin Dunlap, poets Richard Howard and Susan Ludvigson, and novelist Ben Greer.

The man Dickey often called his mentor, the distinguished critic and teacher of southern writers, Monroe Spears, presented an acute and admiring tribute to Dickey, which opened with a poem composed for the occasion. Like many things involving James Dickey, the event had a measure of flamboyance and unexpected drama. After a black tie dinner with Richard Riley, the governor of South Carolina, at which tributes were read from friends as varied as Jimmy Carter and Norman Mailer, Dickey presented a reading of new work to a standing-room-only audience in the university's largest auditorium. In the midst of this event, the hall was invaded by a belly dancer and a large man in a gorilla suit hired by some unfortunately anonymous well-wisher to greet the poet on his birthday. The poet was amused, the audience amazed, and the program's organizers left yearning for deliverance.

Both Warren and Dickey were southern writers who seemed to transcend regionalism but never lost touch with their cultural heritage. The decision to focus next on Randall Jarrell was an obvious one. Jarrell's accomplishments as poet, critic, novelist, translator, teacher, and writer for children make him a figure of the highest significance in our time. But there is something more. For those who came to literary study in the 1950s and 1960s in the south, Randall Jarrell had a very special meaning. As the star pupil of the last generation of Fugitives, he confirmed that poetry, the affirmation of culture, is not just about the family farm or agrarian values, and while accepting our literary heritage, we could go far beyond it and step directly from the Confederate graveyard to one in Salzburg or Buchenwald. As "Mr. Ransom's" student, who accompanied him to Kenyon, Jarrell bridged the gap and emphasized the link between the poetry of Ransom, Tate, and Davison, and the work of Lowell, James Wright, and James Dickey.

Randall Jarrell was born in Nashville, Tennessee, on 6 May 1914. He died at the height of his powers, when struck by a car in Chapel Hill, North Carolina, on 14 October 1965. Between these two dates was a life of remarkable achievement. By the time of his graduation from Vanderbilt in 1936, he was already a kind of legend among men like Warren, Tate, and Ransom, who were becoming legendary themselves. In that year he won the *Southern Review* poetry contest prize, and it was the first of many prizes and awards, including the John Peale Bishop Memorial prize, the Levinson Prize, the National Institute of Arts and Letters Award (1951), the Oscar Blumenthal Prize (1951), the National Book Award (1961), and election to the National Institute of Arts and Letters (1961).

While his earliest poems were highly praised, his war poems won him wide renown and are still the most often anthologized of all his work. His critical work began early too, and he established a reputation in the New York literary world through his witty and often acerbic reviews for the *New Republic* and the *Nation*. He published essays, poems, and a novel in the 1950s, almost all of which had enthusiastic critical reception. The novel *Pictures from an Institution* (1954) arose from that other vital part of his creative being, teaching.

In the 1960s Jarrell produced some of his most significant work, beginning with *The Woman at the Washington Zoo* (1960), a book of poems and translations which won the National Book Award in 1961; *A Sad Heart at the Supermarket* (1962), a book of essays and "fables"; and *The Lost World* (1965), in which Jarrell risked much in exploring childhood and aging, and which capped a remarkably productive period which ended with his death a few months after its publication. Another means of exploring childhood and the discovery of mortality emerged in his children's books, *The Gingerbread Rabbit* (1964), *The Bat-Poet* (1964), and *The Animal Family* (1967), which have never been long out of print. *Fly by Night*, his last children's book, was finally published in 1976, and, as a kind of Freudian evocation of childhood dreaming, it remains as popular with children as it is puzzling and troubling to adults.

As one participant in the symposium put it, "all of us have brought our own Randall Jarrells to be celebrated here." This was apparent in both the formal presentations and in the informal discussions which took place throughout the conference week in classrooms, offices, and at a local barbecue restaurant. From Mary Jarrell's keynote address on the sources of children's books in his own life, through Paul Alan Levi's stunningly powerful and dramatic setting of "The Woman at the Washington Zoo," which closed the conference, a remarkable collection of Randall Jarrells emerged, from boy genius to realistic war poet, from political cynic to literary moralist, from sentimental social poet to the chronicler of painful self-analysis, both Freudian fabulist and "natural lyricist." For all of the participants there was a curiously personal commitment to Jarrell. His work had made an impact which was intensely intimate on all of them. One explanation for this is surely the highly personal style which is as present in the criticism as it is in

Mary Jarrell (Photography Staff, Instructional Services, University of South Carolina)

the poetry and fiction. Jarrell's criticism, even at its most "cruel and destructive," works because the reader feels that Jarrell takes for granted the high intelligence and elevated taste that Jarrell had and feels included in the critic's outraged conspiracy against bad taste, phony art, and creation without conviction. Another explanation may be that the Randall Jarrell who emerges from the letters and memoirs was loved and admired by those who knew him because the best qualities of his writing, the commitment to art, the human concern and passion, were as present in the real Jarrell as they were in the literary persona. James Dickey, whose famous essay on Jarrell outlined twenty years ago the strongly divided feelings many sensitive readers have about Jarrell's poetry, spoke of him as "a fine kind older brother I never had," while another participant, barely in high school at the time of Jarrell's death, spoke of the "deep human commitment in his work which haunts me, forces me to be my very best artistic self."

From the beginning of the planning for the symposium there was a commitment to explore the

variety of Randall Jarrells. When the planners discovered that Paul Alan Levi had done a musical setting of Jarrell's powerful poem "The Truth," they immediately contacted Levi in New York, who informed them that he had just finished a new work, a song cycle based on Jarrell works which he would like to premiere at the conference. They were of course excited, and when they learned that Ed Johnson in Los Angeles had also set one of the poems to music, there was great curiosity to see what kind of treatment Johnson had done. When he was contacted for information, it seemed that he too had recently completed a cycle which he would like to premiere at the symposium with the renowned soprano Helen Boatwright. The result was a unique experience of not only hearing two radically different musical approaches to the same poet but also hearing the composers discuss their work.

William Pritchard's critical work on Jarrell and the research he had done on a Jarrell biography made him an obvious and very enthusiastic choice for the program. Pritchard seized the opportunity to present a balanced and incisive examination of Jarrell's poetry, which answered the implied criticism of Helen Vendler's statement that Jarrell's talent went into his poetry and his genius went into his criticism. Poet and novelist Fred Chappell took a different tact and explored Jarrell's critical and poetic exploration of the poet in the world. This question is of course a major preoccupation of Jarrell's work in poetry and prose (indeed it informs his novel as well), and Chappell as a fellow artist and as long time friend of the poet found this to be the clearest lens through which to view his Randall Jarrell.

Equally involved in Jarrell's myth of the poet in the world was Heather Ross Miller, whose development as novelist and poet was as profoundly influenced by having Randall Jarrell as her teacher as it was by having Peter and Eleanor Ross Taylor in her family. Her powerful and poignant memoir of Randall Jarrell was both dramatically and intellectually satisfying, as she examined complicated creative complicity of the writer/teacher.

Jerry Griswold of the University of California at San Diego brought a wholly different perspective—he explored the relationship of Jarrell and the illustrators of his children's books, Garth Williams and especially Maurice Sendak. Jarrell was, according to Sendak, an absolutely unique writer to work with because he had a very clear sense of what the book—from type style through illustration even to the binding and shape of the boards— would look like. He had a real sense of the book as an art object and thus was able to communicate remarkably well to illustrators trying to both illuminate the text and express their own artistic ideas.

James Dickey's enthusiasm for the Jarrell symposium was a major influence on its development at its early stages. Dickey's 1956 essay on Randall Jarrell in which he divides himself into two voices and argues the case for and against the poetry probably remains the single most influential piece of criticism about Jarrell, as it is quoted both by Jarrell's attackers and defenders. Dickey's ambiguity about Jarrell's poetry does not detract from (and indeed perhaps intensifies) his commitment to Jarrell as a critic and as an artist carrying on guerrilla war with a culture lacking both a center and the knowledge that one is necessary. Dickey's agreement to be the catalyst for a broad-ranging discussion with all of the participants and invited guests made possible a program rich in insight which seemed to energize everyone present.

In a week of vivid images, perhaps the most remarkable for many participants came during the

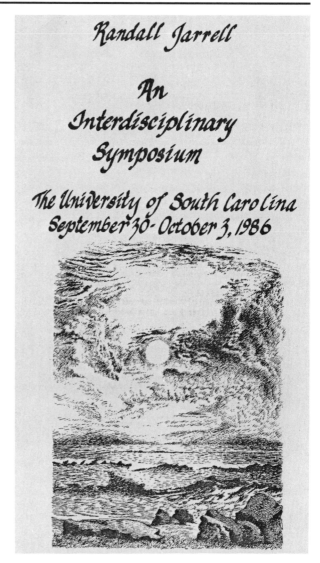

Front cover of the program for the symposium honoring the memory and work of Randall Jarrell

performances of the song cycles which informed Jarrell's work with a different and powerful vocabulary. Jarrell of course was deeply interested in music, writing about it constantly in his letters, though he seemed to feel unqualified to function as a music critic. He used music often as a metaphor, and in "The Player Piano," one of his last fully realized poems, it becomes a principal symbol of the realization of the distance between aspiration and being.

The two works presented certainly seemed to represent very different Randall Jarrells. Ed Johnson's *Anachronisms* is a setting which is highly melodic, and while it does have a certain American folk quality, it seems more like the best of Kurt

Weill, darkly ironic, musically witty, and bitter. The music never covers the text but allows it to reverberate in a haunting melody. Three of the four poems in the cycle were unpublished in Jarrell's lifetime and are certainly among his least known. The final song is a brilliant setting of "The Player Piano," which stresses the lyrical elements of the poem with a consciously beautiful melody and a grandiose piano part, which of course is the ironic counterpoint of the poem. The overall effect at first seems to suggest all of those qualities Jarrell is most often attacked for—a song heavy with sentiment and nostalgia—but this suddenly darkens into a bitter and ironic image of the uncreated life. The piano goes on playing an empty melody after the voice, in plain resignation, is silenced. Soprano Helen Boatwright, as one of America's supreme interpreters of modern (and other) vocal music, has had a vast experience with settings of poems by American writers, from Dickinson to Ives, and she brought an understanding of the poetic tradition to this work, which was an enormous success.

Paul Alan Levi's *Black Wings* is a very different kind of work. A song cycle focusing on the loneliness and isolation of Jarrell's characters, the work uses poems as varied as "The Owl's Bedtime Story," "The Mockingbird," and "The Woman at the Washington Zoo." The music, less concerned with traditional melody, is enormously challenging and dramatic. Soprano Margaret Ahrens, who has a strong interest in poetry, was a brilliant interpreter of the poems. With a voice as rich and powerful as the text, she embodied the Jarrell "heroine" in "The Woman at the Washington Zoo" in a wholly new way, and the "quiet desperation" became an electrifying catharsis of anger and emptiness.

The symposium did not close with a scholarly voice earnestly placing the poet into his proper place in the accepted pantheon. Rather it closed with a soprano voice full of frustration and pain, crying, with the poet's words "change me!, change me!," and fading into the discordant, wrenching harmonies of Paul Alan Levi's music. It somehow seemed a peculiarly appropriate echo of a poet, who kept as holy words Rilke's biblical injunction: "you must change your life." It seemed the one point at which all of the various Randall Jarrells met.

Excerpts From Papers Delivered at the Randall Jarrell Symposium

from "Some Sources in Jarrell's Writings for Children: A Memoir," by Mary Jarrell

Mary Jarrell's opening presentation explored Jarrell's presence in his own work, not as a "confessional poet" but as a fantasist and psychological writer for children. Randall Jarrell's books for children were composed during the enormously difficult and creative period at the end of his life (between 1962 and his death in 1965), which also produced The Lost World, *his most personal and controversial book of poetry. Mary Jarrell believes that the sources, the seeds for these enormously successful books, lie in Jarrell's own childhood and in his attempt at mid-life to understand and come to a reconciliation with his own history.* The Lost World *is another part of that same attempt.*

At age forty-eight Randall had written only for grown-ups and this work took the form of an academic novel, extensive literary criticism, and many poems about soldiers, death, women, loss, dreams, and yes, childhood. In the childhood poems, like "Lady Bates," "Moving," "A Quilt Pattern," "The Truth," "A Child of Courts," and others, Randall drew to some extent on the case histories of troubled children in Piaget, Anna Freud, Bettelheim, and others: children in abnormal stress and loneliness crying out against poverty, war, divorce, death, and blame. Adding to these he also drew on the case history he knew so well, his own. He made many poems around the nightmares that trapped these children and would not go away when they woke up. Such is not the case in his stories for children.

In Randall's late autobiographical poem "Children's Arms," he says, through the boy in it, "I'll never forget what it was like when I'm grown-up!," and what he remembered from his childhood about his aloneness-in-the-world got into those poems, and they are haunted by the anxiety for approval, fear of desertion, and the guilt that tears us all apart when Good Me loves Mother and Bad Me hates her.

That is what came of writing about children. In the stories he was writing *for* children, and he wrote for them in the old-fashioned way—for fun, we have the same sunny mind and man but what a difference when he is remembering the sunny side of his childhood . . . , especially the love and security he felt as a child in his grandparents' home in Los Angeles. . . .

. . .

One motif from his grown-up writing which does steal into this story [*The Gingerbread Rabbit*] unchanged is the adoption device that gives the story its happy ending. The fantasy of stepping into someone else's life and being adopted had great appeal for Randall. . . . In the novel *Pictures from an Institution* the girl student Constance is invited to live with the childless Professor Rosenbaum and his wife. And there near the end of the book, the author (Randall, of course) actually intrudes himself on the printed page, asking Professor Rosenbaum, "Aren't you going to adopt me too?"

The autobiographical source of these adoptions is surely the well-known incident with Randall and the Schultzes in Nashville when he was about thirteen. The Schultzes were the sculptors for the Parthenon Frieze in Centennial Park, and they had encountered Randall as a sidewalk spectator who was quite knowledgeably informed on the Greek gods. Charmed with their young friend they got him to pose for Ganymede . . . and when their work was finished and they were about to leave Nashville, they expressed a half-serious wish to his mother to adopt Randall. According to her she did not tell him at the time for fear he would have taken them up: Randall told me later, "And she was right," he said. "I'd have gone with them like that!" Likewise he would have stayed on with his grandparents in California.

. . .

The Bat-Poet has been called a parody of the artist's needs and the world's misunderstanding of them. . . . Seen in that light it does show us how necessary it is for the artist to detach himself: detach from family, at times, friends, institutions, geo-graphical locations, etc., when one or all of these interfere with the artist's perception of and dedication to his work of art. . . . Another point *The Bat-Poet* makes is the dependency but more than that, the enormous need the artist has for a devoted follower whose judgment he can trust . . . : the little bat says, "The trouble isn't making poems. It's finding someone to listen to them." The chipmunk listened. The chipmunk encouraged . . . Michael di Capua, Randall's young, new editor and I easily recognized Randall as the bat-poet and saw ourselves, with pleasure, as the chipmunks. . . .

Finally the allegory tries to make the world understand that the artist's art is not at his command. When the bat-poet cannot do the cardinal's portrait in verse as the chipmunk suggested, and as he himself very much wanted to do, Randall had harked back to his own experience with a small book on the poet Hart Crane that Holt and Company commissioned and paid him for it in advance. As Randall wrote Lowell, he piled up notes and threw away notes and got absolutely nowhere with Hart Crane. . . . In the story, the bat tells the chipmunk sadly, "I can't make up a poem about the cardinal . . . I would if I could, but I can't. I don't know why I can't. . . . He's just beautiful, he'd make a beautiful poem. But I can't think of a thing." In the case of Hart Crane, Randall wrote Holt a letter of heart-felt apology and spent the next year scraping up the money to repay that advance.

from "Randall Jarrell's Poetry: An Evaluation," by William Pritchard

Critic William Pritchard began his reevaluation of Jarrell's poetry by recalling James Dickey's influential essay on Jarrell which expressed Dickey's stridently ambiguous feelings about Jarrell's poetry. Pritchard agrees with Dickey's negative voice, that Jarrell was sometimes prolix, sentimental, and self-indulgent, but argues that these qualities were not typical of Jarrell's best work. The poems that really count are marked by a "unique combination of pathos and wit" which make them continue to live. "Fully realized" poems like "Nestus Gurley" and "The Player Piano" transcend "sentimentalism," if indeed that term has meaning, and embody memory with power, imagination, and veracity.

Just over thirty-five years ago, when Randall Jarrell's *Selected Poems* was published, James Dickey found himself either unable or unwilling to write about it in the usual reviewer's style of measured praise or blame. Rather Mr. Dickey created two fictive speakers, gave them the bland but unprejudicial names of A and B, then set them loose at each other.... Both speakers set down positions which they scarcely alter over the course of their argument: A called the *Selected Poems* a "Triumph," "the work of an honest, witty, intelligent, and deeply gifted man, a man who knows more about poetry, and knows it in better, more human ways than any other of our time." To which B responds that he finds the book "dull beyond all dullness of stupefaction or petrification," and that Jarrell's poems seem to him "the most untalentedly sentimental, self-indulgent, and insensitive writings that I can remember." . . . This dispute about the value of Jarrell's poetry does not of course take into account the two best volumes of it he was to publish in the last ten years of his life. The first of these, *The Woman at the Washington Zoo*, won the National Book Award for 1960, while *The Lost World* seems for many readers, including this one, Jarrell's best, most original book of poems. Even so, Dickey's criticism of the poetry remains the most inventively probing of any Jarrell received during his life or after his death. Much of that interest has to do with its form as a dialogue of opposing voices, a form Dickey made no use of in his many other reviews of contemporary poets. Could it be that the form was due less to his momentary impulse toward something out of the ordinary, than it was a response dictated by the special problems for the reader that Jarrell's work presents?

. . .

First published in 1954, the year Jarrell turned forty, "Aging" shows us how, once more, the child is father to the man, and it does so without any strongly individuated "character being created through a distinctive, idiosyncratic speech rhythm." Rather the voice in the poem aspires to speak for us all, insofar as we have experienced those (endless) Pleasure Drives and Study Hours that now, viewed from the long perspective of these days, make us think that in those days everything was better, or at least shapeable—just by being imaginable. . . .

This is the sort of poem that distinguishes Jarrell from other contemporary poets of the self, like Lowell or Berryman or Roethke or Plath. The language of "Aging" is ordinary language; the posture of its dramatic speaker is not eccentric or overwhelming or lurid or farcical; the tone stays fairly steady; the prosody isn't something which asks to be noticed or commented on. In fact, maybe "Aging" isn't even a very good poem. I have never come across mention of it in published criticism of Jar-

rell's poetry. . . . Could it be merely the subject matter—getting older, the approach of death—that makes a sucker out of one, especially as one who is middle-aging? It is probably the sort of poem one of my students was thinking of when she said to me that, oh yes, Jarrell was sentimental, but she loved sentimentality. Yet no one who grew up with New Criticism can love sentimentality unless he rejects his past, and besides, one says finally, "Aging" is not a sentimental poem. It is *not* that we are tricked by the subject matter into soft-headedness; it is rather that the poem is as humorous as it is plangent. For surely what Jarrell has created here is a grim joke, with those ironic capital letters and that speaker whose own argument does itself and himself in. "I am never more serious than when I'm being humorous," Robert Frost liked to say. "Aging" exemplifies a similar unity of purpose and mood.

. . .

His own expressed willingness to sound limp and prosaic, rather than rhetorical and false, was surely abetted by the second world war. When he entered the service and began, in the spring of 1943 about six months after he had enlisted, to write poetry every night. . . . He began also to explore a subject matter that felt too large, too serious and grave, too *something* for it ever to be well-served by nicely turned formal effects, certainly by a regular, insistent pattern of rhyme and stanza. Jarrell's war poems have perhaps been respected more than read. They lack the poignant expressiveness of the voice he would find in the late domestic narratives. But generally they have been admired. . . .

R. W. Flint speaks of Jarrell's career as containing two peaks in which the full quality of the man was present. The first, in those narratives of war; the second . . . surely to be found in those narratives of the lost world recaptured which he wrote near the end of his life. These latter poems can be seen as an answer, though not exactly a triumphant one, to a recurrent complaint in the few poems Jarrell wrote in the 1950s—the complaint of the self grown old. "The world goes by my cage and never sees me," laments the woman at the Washington Zoo, and she ends by crying out to the vulture, a predatory and threateningly desirable figure: "You know what I was? You see what I am: change me, change me!" But ironically another sort of change has already occurred from "was" to "am" in which the Grown One has been made out of the childish heart of "Aging."

Critic William Pritchard presents an evaluation of Jarrell's poetic work (Photography Staff, Instructional Services, University of South Carolina)

. . .

Nothing is more surprising to me than the terza rima Jarrell employed so effortlessly in "The Lost World" (the worksheets of this poem show how much effort he expended in trying out list after list of rhyming words) to create a pace of movement and a brilliance he had never previously commanded. It was an answer to or vindication of what, years before in reviewing his earlier volumes, his poet contemporaries said about him, as, when Robert Lowell compared him both to Pope and Matthew Arnold—the satirist and the lyricist merged. Or an answer to Delmore Schwartz who in reviewing *Little Friend, Little Friend*, wished that the "wit of Jarrell's prose essays might become part of his verse." What a "modernist Pope" we would then have, wrote Schwartz. Or to prove Karl Shapiro's seemingly overpartial claim that Jarrell was the only poet of his generation "who made an art out of American speech as it is, who advanced beyond Frost in using not only a contemporary idiom . . . but the actual rhythm of our speech."

from " 'Stone Axes': Randall Jarrell's Vision of the Poet's Place," by Fred Chappell

Poet and novelist Fred Chappell used Jarrell's concern for role of the poet in society, a frequent theme in his poetry and prose, as an opening to a discussion of his work and life. Chappell indicts his own generation of writers for ignoring some of the problems of the artist, art, and society which Jarrell confronted and examines Jarrell's attempts to work through these concerns in poems like "A Conversation with the Devil," in his essays, and in the novel Pictures from an Institution.

Some questions that are real, problems that Randall Jarrell recognized and dealt with many times, are, "What is the place of contemporary literature in the world?" and its concomitant, "What is the place of the poet in the contemporary world?"

These issues are difficult. For Jarrell they became urgent and maybe, in the end, overpowering.

He is hardly the only poet of his generation to be deviled by them. Theodore Roethke, Karl Shapiro, John Berryman, Delmore Schwartz—these poets and many others found the issues urgent and disturbing, and their concern with them is one of the things that marks them as belonging to their generation. Later generations of poets—my own, for example—have found the questions to be unanswerable and therefore irrelevant. We do just as the physicists do when they find some glaring anomaly in particle theory—we put the matter aside with the vague hope that it will be satisfactorily explained at some later date or will die a natural death from irrelevancy.

Yet, as important as the question was for him, as finally unanswerable as it was, he did manage often to see it with some sense of proportion and with some nettled amusement. The unnamed narrator of his novel, *Pictures from an Institution*, is a poet who finds that even at the fictional Benton, that most absurdly broad-minded of all liberal universities, and that even in the eyes of his creative writing colleague, the novelist Gertrude Johnson (a woman who gives the word *redoubtable* its final

Poet and novelist Fred Chappell (Photography Staff, Instructional Services, University of South Carolina)

and utmost authority), his vocation is a subject of uncomprehending astonishment. The novel informs us that the narrator could never have become a confidant of Gertrude if he had been a novelist; there would be too much competition for the local material. "But I was only a poet—that is to say, a maker of stone axes—and she felt a real pity for me because of it . . . , it puzzled her; finally she dismissed it from her mind, saying to herself—as you do about someone who won't go on relief or mind the doctor—'Well, he has only himself to blame!' "

. . .

The voice in "The Intellectual in America" is "like the voice of God." Jarrell says, but it must issue from an iron and vengeful God, for this is what it says: "You highbrows, you longhairs, you eggheads, are the way you are because there's something wrong with you. You sit there in your ivory tower pretending you're so different from other people, wasting your time on all these books nobody buys, and all these pictures my six-year-old boy can draw better, and all those equations it takes another egghead like yourself to make heads or tails of—why don't you get wise to yourself and do what I do, and say what I say, and think like I think, and then maybe I'd have some respect for you?". . . It is surprising that the tone of the whole essays is not bitter but rather gaily resigned. If "plain Americans" don't like the intellectual, still "he likes them: he no longer despairs and flees to Europe, but stays home and suffers fairly willingly—is fairly thankful for—his native fate. Living among them as he does, he can hardly avoid realizing that Americans are a likable, even a lovable people, possessing virtues some of which are rare in our time and some of which are rare in any time. . ."

. . .

That is one sort of courage, and I have my own anecdote about Jarrell's courage. On that dreadful night in October 1965, when we received news of his death, Robert Watson, Peter Taylor, and I waited at a funeral home in Greensboro for the poet's body to be transported from Chapel Hill. . . . Peter fell to reminiscing—it was inevitable—about happier hours and about finer parts of the man as he knew him. He spoke of parties, of European journeys, of a green hat his friend had given him in celebration of one of Peter's short stories he especially admired. Then he spoke of a local television interview with Jarrell just after he had received the National Book Award. "At the end of the interview," Peter said, "the reporter asked him in that condescending tone they put on, 'Are you an intellectual, Mr. Jarrell?,' and Randall said, 'Yes, of course I am.' " Peter wagged his head and his voice took on a defiant melancholy quality. "That was the sort of fiber he had," he said. "He didn't bat an eye. . . ."

The most famous of his formulations of this dilemma (the artist or intellectual in contemporary society) is his poem "A Girl in a Library," which personifies the unthinking profane public as a college student dozing over her books. The exasperating blameless girl is his best embodiment of that obtuse Voice because she is ambiguous: she is lovable, and she is—perhaps has been made—uneducable. Is it possible that she is lovable *because* she is uneducable, this never-to-be-possessed Lorelei who lures her poet-professors to metaphysical despair? She represents the facts of the case: "For nineteen years she's faced reality:/They look alike already." She resists education as easily as a catfish resists the effort of learning human speech, because in neither case is there the least temptation. Herself absolutely lacking in imagination, she is impervious to the attempts of the imagination to absorb, to transform, or even to understand her. As always for Jarrell, the brutal unblinking facts are inaccessible to the imagination. "Poor senseless Life. . . ."

Yet facts are products of the imagination and in the very act of imagining her as inaccessible the poet has made her accessible. He has found it a difficult task, but at last the speaker of the poem places her in the realm of the mythical, places her in the basic matrix of myth itself. . . .

He sometimes saw the greater number of Americans as in his novel he saw his fictional university. "You felt about the people of Benton: *If only they weren't so complacent! If only they weren't so—* then you stopped yourself, unwilling to waste an afternoon on *if only's,* and mumbled a summary *If only we were all dead or better!* Though this was unjust to the great mass of people, normal in-between people with nothing much wrong with them, people like you and me; well, not us exactly, but us if we were different."

Jarrell put great store in Rilke's message from his archaic Apollonian torso: *You must change your life.* The missionary impulse is strong in his work. But, after all, if we were different, we wouldn't be us. If the world were enlightened, the struggle for enlightenment would disappear, and when it did, much of the world's poetry would disappear, and the furious tragic impulse toward poetry.

from "Randall Jarrell : The Gift of True Pitch," by Heather Ross Miller

Poet and novelist Heather Ross Miller studied creative writing and literature with Randall Jarrell at the Women's College of North Carolina (now UNC-Greensboro). In her recollection of that experience, she examined the qualities Jarrell brought to his teaching and his legacy as teacher, mentor, and catalyst in the creative process.

Alfred Kazin, in his essay found in *Randall Jarrell, 1914-1965,* tells us "Randall was as full of quotations as a Unitarian minister—they were his theology. . . ." "Probably there was no better teacher of literature in the country," wrote Robert Lowell in the same book, "and yet he was curiously unworldly about it and welcomed teaching for almost twenty years in the shade or heat of his little-known Southern college for girls in Greensboro, North Carolina. There his own community gave him a compact, tangible, personal reverence that was incomparably more substantial and poignant than the empty numerical long-distance blaze of national publicity. . . . He gloried in being a teacher, never apologized for it, and related it to his most serious criticism."

. . .

Pasternak also wrote that biography belongs to heroes and that poets cannot be presented in such a way. The recorded life of a poet does not lie down in a straight line with easy, predictable facts. It has to be made up from seeming unessentials, from subconscious things that are hard to measure, and "composed of all that is happening to his readers and which he does not know."

Those seeming unessentials and subconscious things, hard to measure, were part of the gift of true pitch, the touchstone—the ability to talk about anything—that Randall Jarrell had as a teacher. They were the unselfconscious minglings of the sublime with the ordinary that marked his accessibility, his willingness to share and teach.

. . .

I first heard the name *Randall Jarrell* travel through my family's conversations. It had a nice tone, the accents falling on the two final sets of long wavering *l*'s. The name sounded like a rhyme, a couplet given to some character in Mother Goose or Grimms. The double *l*'s resonated in my mind as the family talked and I imagined what he really was, what sort of phenomenon could be called Randall Jarrell.

The family never described what Randall looked like, never gave me a book of his to read. They exchanged lively stories with equal delight and horror about "wicked Randall" and "splendid Randall," and I let their stories decorate the Phenomenon I imagined.

Years later when I left the family and went to the Women's College of the University of North Carolina in Greensboro . . . the Phenomenon looked much as I thought he might: slender, heavily bearded, with quick dark eyes that never rested long on anything. His mannerisms jarred me: his squeaky, stuttering voice; the jerky gestures of enthusiasms; the quick burst into laughter. And his habits and tastes surprised me. He drove sports cars, sometimes with the top down and in the rain (himself properly covered in raincoat and hat). He played tennis and touch football. He lived in a cottage in the country . . . adorned with Dutch doors, live Christmas trees still living inside far past Groundhog Day, hunting horns . . . and a ship's figurehead. . . . He read the funny papers and *Road and Track*.

. . .

When I think of Randall in the classroom, I think of the Duchess Browning described:

> "She had
> A heart—how shall I say?—too soon made glad,
> Too easily impressed; she liked whate'r
> She looked on, and her looks went everywhere. . . ."

To sit and listen to Randall talk about books, to watch him soon made glad as he looked at all these books, to see and delight in how easily his looks went everywhere—from Tolstoy to Elizabeth Bishop to the Court of King Harold Bluetooth to "The Rat and Mouse in Partnership" back out to Shakespeare and Robert Frost and Gogol and Little Nemo in Dreamland—was to be *impressed;* was to want to run yourself right out and read those things that so impressed him; was to understand very clearly that books were yours to be impressed and made glad *by.*

All you had to do was turn the page.

All you had to do was make the page yourself. He was not so good with exactly how to make the page—he inspired you to make it, but Randall wasn't interested in giving you a practical "exactly why" or "exactly how" the page went together. He took off with the skyrocket. He didn't bother much with the fueling and designing of the skyrocket. The design and the choice of fuel were taken for granted, maybe.

It worked, or it didn't work, with Randall.

He was immediately honest with student writers. He told you at once if he liked it or not—if it worked or not. But he would not say immediately, or perhaps ever, "This is what you need to do to get it right."

He taught us to become better writers by becoming better readers. The excitement of discovery was essential in his lesson. Somebody else might show you how to assemble the rocket. Randall showed you the thrill of flight. . . .

. . .

Randall himself said, "There is no work so dear as teaching. Teaching is something I would pay to do. . . ." We agree with the multitude of quotations, what a teacher, a master, a touchstone, what a gift of true pitch.

from Paul Alan Levi's remarks on "Black Wings: Three Songs to Poems of Randall Jarrell"

Composer Paul Alan Levi's brief discussion of the genesis of his settings of Jarrell poems explains what drew him to Jarrell's work and some of the musical problems posed by these particular poems. . . .

I am a musician and I did not start out as much of a reader of poetry. I first encountered Randall Jarrell in his poem "The Truth," which I read in a magazine in a dentist's office in the early 1970s, and I knew immediately that I had to set this poem. . . .

"The Truth" is a kind of litmus paper poem among those who read Jarrell's poetry. . . . It took me some years to get the opportunity to write the music, which finally happened when I got a commission from Chamber Music Northwest in Portland, Oregon. When I asked what instruments were available, there were a lot of strings and woodwinds and a harpsichord and voice and the whole combination just sort of hit me right, especially the harpsichord.

"The Truth" is about a small boy who has been caught in the London firebombings and whose father and sister and dog have all been killed. His mother is unable to tell him the truth about these deaths and he begins acting strangely and is sent to a mental institution in the country. There he tricks his mother into admitting that his father is dead. So it is a very powerful and dramatic poem. The harpsichord is the thing which interested me most in this ensemble because harpsichords sound very powerful by themselves but are very easily drowned out by any other instruments playing along with them. . . . It seemed that it happened unconsciously as I was writing it that the harpsichord would stand for the voice of the boy. Although there was a soprano singing the words, of course, the harpsichord would appear in the most intimate moments as the boy and would gradually get overwhelmed by the other instruments just as the boy himself was overwhelmed by the adult events which blew his life apart. I felt that in setting "The Truth" I first found my own voice, my own "true pitch." It required such integrity from me and, basically an abandonment of cleverness, I couldn't just write it, I had to bring as much integrity to it as Jarrell did.

The appeal of it for me is, of course, the powerful emotional impact with this very reticent means—Jarrell doesn't talk about his own feelings—it's all spoken in the voice of this one small child. Technically what appealed to me in that poem and in the other four I have set is the simple clear diction. In "The Truth" the words seem to be almost all of one syllable, and in all of the poems I have set, the diction is very clear. In all of them it is easy to hear whether spoken or sung, even on the first hearing what is supposed to be happening.

The other thing that appeals to me in "The Truth" and in the other poems I have set is the identification that Jarrell has with children, which is remarkable. Having spent three quarters of my life either being a child or raising one—not an untypical story for someone my age—I still think it is rare to find someone else to whom childhood is so important.

As a composer I have written vocal music for a wide variety of ensembles: as a pianist I have spent most of my time as an accompanist for singers. I like the literature so much better than the piano literature (and also the company). I finally decided that it was time to write a song cycle just for soprano and piano. When I chose these three poems ("The Owl's Bedtime Story," "The Mockingbird's Song," and "The Woman at the Washington Zoo"), I had a problem—how to make a unified song cycle out of these three poems which of course Jarrell did not see as a cycle or a single statement. I thought it would work, but I did not really know why. If anybody asked me I said they all had birds in common ("The Mockingbird's Song" has a list of birds, "The Owl's Bedtime Story" is about an owl, the woman cries out to the vulture at the climax of "The Woman at the Washington Zoo"), and there

were musical things I would do to make it seem that the three songs were a part of the same work of art. Still, it wasn't until I had finished the cycle that a friend of mine pointed out to me that the theme they have in common is isolation and loneliness. Which is also what they have in common with "The Truth." In "The Truth" you have the isolation of the child who has lost almost all his family and who has been abandoned, in effect, by his mother. The mockingbird chases all the other birds away and imitates their songs all night alone. He triumphs, but alone. As some others have pointed out this week, this might stand for Jarrell the Poet or any poet or artist that imitates the world so well that one wonders which is the mockingbird, which one the world. The observer who narrates "The Mockingbird's Song" is also isolated from the scene somehow. I cannot really explain how that is, I just smell it. The baby owl is lonesome and goes out to find company, and the woman at the Washington Zoo is mortally lonely.

The other problem of setting these poems is the length of "The Owl's Bedtime Story" . . . , it takes much longer to sing this poem than it does to read it. I had to find the equivalent of Jarrell's terza rima, which is basically an "and then" form which seems to invite you further and further into the story . . . and then the secondary rhyme becomes the main one and keeps on introducing something new gradually—in effect the way you would tell a story to a child—"and then this happened and then that happened, and then 'what happened next?' " The musical equivalent of that is a steady running rhythm which runs through much of the song which allows me to eat up lots of verse in a fairly short amount of time. . . . I was also asked by friends "why are you setting a children's poem in a work that is certainly not for children?" On the other hand, in "The Owl's Bedtime Story" there is loneliness, and longing for love, and dreaming of the supernatural and courage in the face of danger, and facing one's own inadequacy and facing up to death and glory and reunion, and resting after dangerous exertions. This does not seem so childish to me anymore.

The other thing which makes the cycle is the progression in which each song seems to contain more emotional depth than the one before. That occurs very literally in the piano part as each song uses more of the bass register of the piano and more and more of the upper register of the soprano, that is, more and more of the power and brilliance of the soprano.

Siegfried Loraine Sassoon: A Centenary Essay

Dame Felicitas Corrigan, O.S.B.
Stanbrook Abbey

See also the Sassoon entry in *DLB 20: British Poets, 1914-1945*.

Siegfried Loraine Sassoon was born on 8 September 1886 at Weirleigh in the quiet countryside of the Kentish Weald. He died on 1 September 1967 at Heytesbury House, Wiltshire, and was brought for burial to the tiny Somerset village of Mells within the shadow of the Mendip Hills, where he rests in a simple grave a few yards away from Ronald A. Knox, his spiritual mentor and friend. The eight decades of his life span some of the most momentous years in the history of the whole human race: two world wars, a social revolution, the splitting of the atom, and the threat of nuclear destruction.

No fashion is so dead as that of the day before yesterday, and Yesterday is essentially that seemingly golden age preceding 1914—a gap between Then and Now impossible to bridge. Yet it is precisely these yesterdays of Sassoon's life, from youth to maturity, roughly no more than twenty-eight of his eighty years, which have created a legend that obfuscates the truth. The legend portrays the perfect English gentleman, educated at Marlborough and Clare College, Cambridge, aspiring young poet, musician, cricketer, golfer, horseman, fox hunter, who, on the outbreak of war in 1914, filled with noble patriotism, at once donned khaki and cheerfully exchanged the cherry orchards, point-to-point races, opera, ballet, and London clubs for brown rats, sludge, bullet-riddled corpses, and the hell of trench warfare. Twice wounded, he achieved fame first as "Mad Jack," a soldier of almost incredible courage, and then as the Angry Young Man who flung his beribboned Military Cross into the river Mersey and sent eyebrows up and temperatures soaring with a public protest against the continuance of a war that had degenerated into a crime against humanity, a protest reinforced by his savage satires:

Goodbye, old lad! Remember me to God,
    And tell Him that our Politicians swear
They won't give in till Prussian Rule's been trod

Siegfried Sassoon, 1961, sitting in the chair in which he said he "wrote and revised most of my three vols of autobiography" (photo by Maurice Wiggin, Sunday Times)

Under the heel of England . . . Are you there? . . .
Yes . . . and the War won't end for at least two years;
But we've got stacks of men . . . I'm blind with tears,
    Staring into the dark. Cheero!
I wish they'd killed you in a decent show.

No one is going to deny the power of poetry like that, yet, strange to stay, no biography has so far been attempted of the man who wrote it, who, with his sharp contradictions and many-sidedness, is one of the most arresting literary figures of the twentieth century. The first and only full-length study of Sassoon's writings, Michael Thorpe's *Siegfried Sassoon: A Critical Study* (London & Oxford University Press, 1967), the authoritative work of an able academic, while not neglecting the poetry (especially that of the war years), concentrates on Sassoon's prose, that memorable achievement of his middle years. In no sense is the book biographical, and the image remains unchanged, fixed once and for all by "those clever people up in London," as Thomas Hardy called the critics. Sassoon is a divided hero whose selves fall into three distinct parts: the fox hunter, mindless, time-wasting, and ideally happy; the soldier, brave, compassionate, rebellious, and bitter; and the disillusioned pacifist-hermit of Heytesbury, where for almost half a century, be it noted, in the immortal phrase of Joseph Cohen's *The Three Roles of Siegfried Sassoon* (the title is significant), "like a decommissioned man-of-war, he rests quietly at anchor in poetry's mothball fleet." These three disconnected segments of the continuous human life so subtly depicted in Sassoon's own narratives are mirrored clearly in the modest centenary celebrations. They have been drawn almost exclusively from his childhood and from the trenches of the Somme—those four years that for today's youth have become almost as dim historically as Napoleon and the First Empire.

It may be well at this point to preface the list of Sassoon's publications with his own incontrovertible assertion: "My real biography is my poetry. All the sequence of my development is there. For me, it is the only thing that matters, and was my only path in the bewilderments and inconsistencies of existence. And all my best poems expressed an element of experience. The art of poetry belongs to *life*. It is one's earthly home, and the other poets, dead or living, when masters of the art, are one's housemates." All Sassoon's work, whether prose or poetry, is autobiographical: whereas he wrote poetry from the age of ten and a half until he was seventy-eight, his prose-writing was confined to no more than two decades. His three volumes of fictional autobiography, *Memoirs of a Fox-Hunting Man* (1928), *Memoirs of an Infantry Officer* (1930), and *Sherston's Progress* (1936) were followed by three straight autobiographies, which cover precisely the same field, occasionally deal with the same episodes, yet complement and never overlap: *The Old Century and Seven More Years* (1938), *The Weald of Youth* (1942), and *Siegfried's Journey, 1916-1920* (1945). No one of the six could be jettisoned without serious loss.

Since material written in so memorable a style lends itself readily to public reading and monologue, the centenary programs have drawn largely on Sassoon's own work in his own words. The village community of his birthplace rose to the occasion magnificently. Mr. Dennis Silk, Somerset

cricketer and Old Marlburian, whose frequent visits to Heytesbury with his wife Diana and baby daughter Katharine brought human warmth and deep enjoyment to Sassoon in the closing years of his life, has written: "My wife and I went to Brenchley for the Centenary celebrations and were very touched and moved by all we saw. There was a delightful play written by a local lady, called 'Watercress Well.' It was most tastefully done and, as the title suggests, dealt mainly with the early period of *The Old Century*. There was a commentator on one side of the stage, and S. S. on the other, making sensible statements about his life and times interspersed with Tableau Vivant, highlighting certain events in S. S.'s life. For a village production it was remarkable, and was a tribute to the sort of talent which lies undetected in most good English villages."

That was not all. Next day, Silk himself went into action in a replay of "The Flower Show Match"—that incomparable account in the *Fox-Hunting Man* of Butley village yokels under Bill Sutler, the one-legged cobbler, a "grossly partisan umpire," playing the Rotherden Eleven, a superior team that included the Rector, Parson Yalden, who was not only a member of the M.C.C. but also Lord Chatwynd's first cousin once removed:

> The clock struck three, and the Reverend Yalden's leg-stump had just been knocked out of the ground by a vicious yorker from Frank Peckham. "Hundred and seventeen. Five. Nought," shouted the Butley scorer, popping his head out of the little flat-roofed shanty which was known as "the pavilion." The battered tin number-plates were rattled on to their nails on the scoring-board by a zealous young hobbledehoy who had undertaken the job for the day.
> "*Wodger* say last man made?" he bawled . . .
> "Last man, *Blob*."
> The parson was unbuckling his pads on a bench near by, and I was close enough to observe the unevangelical expression on his face as he looked from under the brim of his panama hat with the M.C.C. ribbon round it. Mr. Yalden was not a popular character on the Butley ground, and the hobbledehoy had made the most of a heaven-sent opportunity.

It cannot be too often repeated that Sassoon changed but little over the years. In 1966 with major surgery in prospect, he saw life's ending in terms of cricket. Death had nothing morbid or macabre about it: it was filled with gladness and a life more intense than cricket or even poetry could express. "Like the late lamented Cleopatra I have immortal longings in me," he wrote. "I just go on being told that I am a war poet, when all I want is to be told that I am only a pilgrim and a stranger, utterly dependent on the idea of God's providence to my spiritual being. But the game goes on, so I must put my pads on and make my way to the wicket. The wicket— O please, dear St. Peter, don't delay too long in opening it to me!" One fervently hopes that Simon-Peter the gatekeeper summoned Sassoon to his side to peer over heaven's ramparts and enjoy the sight of his dear Dennis going in first and making forty-three not out in the centenary celebration of the Butley Flower Show Match. "The spirit of S. S. was very much in the air," Dennis himself commented, "and I found a delightful picture of him in the pavilion acting as scorer in a village match around the turn of the century."

Silk was also interviewed by Julian O'Halloran of the BBC in a program shared by Peter Barkworth, a well-known actor, who illustrated the talk. Barkworth had given several one-man shows to crowded and appreciative audiences—in the Salisbury Playhouse, Winchester Theatre Royal, and the Truro Cathedral. "Peter Barkworth's portrayal of Siegfried, entirely in his own words, was brilliant," Vivien Clarke, a lifelong friend of the poet has written. "Tender, sensitive, embattled—and at the end, almost at peace. Perhaps entirely. . . . 'Everyone suddenly burst out singing;/And I was filled with such delight. . . .' Hackneyed? In all the anthologies? But triumphant. And P. B. finished with those lines, which showed how S. S. had come through hell and somehow survived. Hearing him as a child at Brenchley set the scene: his papa such a sad disappointment to him, but so dearly loved and longed-for—his abiding love of the Kent countryside—his genuine love for people and his agony over the deaths of friends, and indeed all deaths, was made very clear in the second half of the program: after his happy childhood, his desire to die for his country and his disillusionment. . . . Yet triumph. He brought out S's sense of humor but, above all, his deep goodness and sincerity."

Sassoon's own interpretation of "Everyone Sang"—its popularity irritated him—was anything but triumphant. A tape recording of his reading the poem in the Stanbrook Abbey parlor is done in a very quiet unemphatic voice, completely free from any dramatic effect, and is all the more powerful for that. As a child, Sassoon used to stand in the garden of Weirleigh, send his voice ringing over the Weald to God, who lived across the valley, an infinite space of twenty miles away, and then stand listening intently to the silence, waiting for the divine reply. That was how he read poetry: his "Everyone Sang" can find a parallel in many others, but especially in his own favorite poem, "A Chord." He was a good musician, and the internal imagery of the lines, he told me, is that of "striking a rich chord on the piano and then letting it vibrate on and on into silence—a trick of mine which produces a vision of a great dark church with a lit altar":

> On stillness came a chord,
> While I, the instrument,
> Knew long-withheld reward:
> Gradual the glory went;
> Vibrating on and on,
> Toward harmony unheard,
> Till dark where sanctus shone;
> Lost, once a living word.

"Words don't like being run off their legs," he said, and his calm, matter-of-fact reading of a deeply felt experience drew his listeners into his own silence, and the silence became a prayer:

> Eternal, to this momentary thing—
> This mind—Thy sanctuary of stillness bring.

It is a lesson that the young of the present day are avid to learn: as in so much else, Sassoon is the mouthpiece of the common man of the twentieth century.

By way of public acclamation of the centenary, only two more items are known to me. Readings from the *Memoirs of a Fox-Hunting Man* have been given by Stephen MacDonald, an actor-writer, on BBC Radio 4 in a weekly program of seven fifteen-minute renditions. The last of the readings fittingly marked the eve of Armistice Sunday. MacDonald's play, *Not About Heroes*, heard on Radio 4, was recently staged by the National Theatre. Its two main characters are Sassoon and Wilfred Owen, but it was Sassoon and not Owen who became a kind of obsession with the author, so he confesses, for he spoke out of lived experience in direct and immediate utterance. As such, it bears the stamp of authenticity. Finally, in the autumn number of *This England*, Elizabeth Saintsbury, granddaughter of the famous critic, has written the first of a series of articles: "Salute to the Soldier Poets: Siegfried Sassoon." Always "the soldier poet." Small wonder that Sassoon dismissed a journalist eager to record the "soldier poet's views" on the consequences of the Great War fifty years ago, with the curt reply: "One word suffices, RATS!"

Far more substantial and impressive than the passing show of the media are the publications over the last three years issued by Faber & Faber under the editorship of Rupert Hart-Davis. One can discount the reissue of *The War Poems of Siegfried Sassoon.* Sir Alan Lascelles, Sassoon's exact contemporary, like him an Old Marlburian, soldier in World War I with a Military Cross to his credit, Private Secretary to three kings, whose journals under the editorship of Sir Rupert's son, Duff Hart-Davis, are being published by Hamish Hamilton (1986), said of Sassoon's war poems: "Nothing will make me, who have had two wars and lost two generations, read Siegfried's war poems any more. I told him so, and he commended me." Of far greater interest are the three diaries so far published, covering the periods 1915-1918; 1920-1922; and 1923-1925. The centenary year has also seen a delightful but disappointingly lightweight production of Sassoon's letters to Max Beerbohm together with a few of Beerbohm's replies, eked out by extracts from the Sassoon diaries of the mid 1940s.

The diaries are the raw material of the three fictional volumes of George Sherston's memoirs, but they are something more. On 14 February 1918 as he was in the train returning to the Front, Sassoon scribbled in his diary: "Funny mixture of reality and crude circumstance with inner flame-like spiritual experience. . . . In the 'awful brevity' of human life I seek truth." This may explain why he did not erase, but left the diaries to the judgment of posterity: "I have formed an inflexible resolve to reveal myself; my inner self; the self that never sees the light of day." The evocation of Oscar Wilde and the "Naughty Nineties" is obvious. For if, like dark-eyed handsome Jowett and thick-set grey-eyed Stiffy Phillips, his comrades, Sassoon passed out of soldiering "brave and tender-hearted and clean-souled," things changed. Like so many others left with heavy-laden hearts, whom death had made "wise and bitter and strong," there was a backlash. After demobilization, his existence became "distracted, chaotic, experimental and confused. I was all over the place," he told Sydney Cockerell, Director of the Fitzwilliam Museum at Cambridge.

To judge from Harold Owen's (Wilfred Owen's brother) authentic but unflattering portrait in *Aftermath,* the Sassoon of the 1920s, in sandy-coloured tweeds, yellow waistcoat and pink shirt, whom Wilfred Owen in 1917 had regarded as Keats plus Christ plus Elijah plus his colonel plus

his father confessor plus Amenophis IV in profile, was not an overattractive figure. Outwardly sophisticated and sardonic, he was busily identifying himself in loud-voiced satires with unemployed miners while himself frequenting the fashionable salons of London's most brilliant hostesses. Yet with it all, he was writing lyrics of white-hot intensity; in this, as in so many other ways, he was Everyman:

> In me the cave-man clasps the seer,
> And garlanded Apollo goes
> Chanting to Abraham's deaf ear.
> In me the tiger sniffs the rose.
>   Look in my heart, kind friends, and tremble,
>   Since there your elements assemble.

This "bundle of blundering animal unblessedness that I have been," to quote his own self-description of the postwar homosexual phase—already in 1972 brought to public notice in Sam Behrman's *Tribulations and Laughter*—has been highlighted in the 1920-1922 diary. On 17 December 1915 of his diary of that year, he had found it "nice to look back on my childhood which lasted so long (until I was twenty-three anyhow)." His adolescence seems to have been equally protracted. Our whole life, Shelley said, is an education of errors, and Sassoon would be the last man to deny his:

> This making is a mystery. Me He made
>   And left to build my being as best I could:
>   A child afraid who for protection prayed,
>   Worsted by wrong, but wanting to grow good.

The world at large, ever ready to seize upon human failings frequently chooses to ignore the sorrow and amendment that follow. There is a passage in *The Old Century and Seven More Years* which cost him as much to write, he told me, as any one of his finest poems:

> Ringing the bell and asking to be allowed to
> walk in and have a look at one's past! All the
> world would like to do that, for the sense of
> the past is strong in us—as strong as our
> awareness of the irremediable errors in it.
> In mind-sight we return: but even if in more
> than mind-sight we could somehow be there
> in the actuality of outlived experience, we
> should be strangers, invisible, and powerless
> to avert so much as the overwinding of a
> clock.
> "Don't do it; don't do it!" we should cry, discerning in some blindly enacted blunder the
> first step taken on some very wrong road.
> But the warning would be like dumb shout-

ff

faber and faber

SIEGFRIED SASSOON

centenary
8 September 1986

Publisher's announcement marking the one-hundredth anniversary of Sassoon's birth

ings in a dream. Not by one faintest whisper could we safeguard our vanished self while he gaily or sullenly created the sorrow and bitterness of after days. Those eyes of youth would look past us even as they look past the troubled faces of those who try to help them.

The Old Century is no mere gentle revisitation of a vanished world of childhood: it is a subtle study of the evolution, growth, vicissitudes of a sensitive human being with a capacity for glorious deeds and inglorious misdeeds. The conscience that afflicted the eight-year-old child who had falsely maligned his nurse, Mrs. Mitchell, may have seemed to him a contrivance attached to him like the lamp of a safety bicycle, to be used in the dark. To the end of his life it continued to cast its bright beam into the dark places of his soul. In 1951 he was to write in *A Dream:*

> I met a stranger on the brink of sleep:
> Hooded he stood, whose eyes acknowledged
>   sorrow . . .
> "Stranger," I said, "since you and I are one,
> Let us go back. Let us undo what's done."

One cannot call back yesterday and, after half a century, Sassoon's postwar deviations have become a time-deodorized dump of Dead Sea fruit by the roadside of his life's course, unlovely but negligible, its sole function to feed what medieval man called "compunction of heart"—or, as Sassoon himself has put it:

> Bring no assurance of redeemèd rest
> No intimation of awarded grace
> Only contrition, cleavingly confessed
> To Thy forgiving face.

In 1933 Sassoon married Hester Gatty, niece of Juliana Ewing, the well-known writer of children's books. He invited only four of his friends to the wedding (Edmund Blunden, perhaps his greatest friend, was abroad): Rex Whistler, the artist who was to join the Welsh Guards and meet his death in 1944; Glen Byam Shaw, the theatrical producer; T. E. Lawrence; and Geoffrey Keynes, surgeon, bibliophile, and Blake scholar. For ten years all went happily, but then the marriage came under strain when each parent vied with the other for the affection of their only child, George. They finally agreed on friendly separation, Sassoon securing the solitude he craved by remaining in his manor house at Heytesbury, Hester taking possession of her country house in Mull, their unfortunate off-

spring shuttling between the two for the rest of his school days.

The next twenty years were to be productive of poetry at least as fine as anything Sassoon had written so far:

> Allow me now much musing-space
> To shape my secrecies alone.

Having written very little during World War II, when his predictions of chemical and biological warfare were proved only too true and, like one in purgatory, he learned the loss of hope, he resumed publication in 1950 with the eighteen poems of *Common Chords,* the twenty of *Emblems of Experience* (1951), and the twenty-four of *The Tasking* (1954), combined into the sixty-two poems of *Sequences,* published by Faber & Faber in 1956. For the most part, the author met with the stolid silence of nonrecognition. Yet one could indict the whole of the twentieth century out of Sassoon's mouth and, what is more important, out of Sassoon's own experience. Acutely aware of the problems of his time, he had no ready answers: he had to face them in his own person and so become the parable of twentieth-century man. This is a Sassoon unknown to the media: he never once appeared in any centenary celebrations, yet this is the poet of whom Robert Nye, a fellow-poet, has written: "It might not be excessive to suggest that histories of poetry in English in this century are going to have to be rewritten when the full scope and significance of Sassoon's journey begins to be realized." We live in a world of men whose deepest need is unsatisfied because God seems to have become a dead language. Who is He anyway? Our contemporary existential approach claims that certainties, if they exist at all, are to be found solely within man himself. Sassoon never applied his mind to philosophy or dogma or metaphysics: he arrived at conclusions by means of his own perceptions accompanied by felt experience. Step by step, often groping in darkness, he moved forward, until on 18 November 1955, he entered in his diary:

> Last thing at night, in solitude serene,
> I am unpossessed of all that I have been.
> It is as though I were about to go
> Some journeying far beyond what I now know:
> It is as though the microcosm of Me
> By mercy were made free—
> Of troubling past uncluttered and washed clean.

It was not a sudden conversion: it was the movement of a straight line from the age of eight to seventy, it was the small boy arms outstretched calling to God across the Weald, it was George Sherston, the infantry officer, adding to his memoirs the curious epigraph: "I told him that I was a pilgrim going to the Celestial City." In 1957 Siegfried Sassoon was received into the Catholic Church at Downside Abbey in Somerset:

> While you were in your purgatorial time, you used to say
> That though Creation's God remained so lost, such aeons away,
> Somehow He would reveal Himself to you—some day!
> For Him, the living God, your soul and flesh could only cry aloud.
> In watches of the night, when world event with dev-ildom went dark,
> You implored illumination.

She could never afterwards explain why, but it was the Superior of the Assumption Convent in Kensington Square, London, Mother Margaret Mary, who wrote to the poet after reading *Sequences,* and by her letters lit a candle in his darkness. When I was brought into contact with Siegfried Sassoon in 1959, it was on literary grounds: in a letter to Sydney Cockerell I had analyzed a few of the lovely prose cadences of *Siegfried's Journey*— notably his apostrophe to the dead Wilfred Owen, and his last meeting with Wilfrid Blunt. My letter had been forwarded to Sassoon and as a happy result, he became a regular visitor to Stanbrook Abbey and a dear friend. As a consequence of getting to know him well, I felt an urge to chart his journey from beginning to end, the true inner biography revealed only in his poetry. He entered into the project with complete trust in whatever treatment would be meted out to him, and lent me diaries to use as I chose, often himself copying out passages he considered relevant. The study, *Poet's Pilgrimage,* was published after his death. Two letters from men who in no way shared Sassoon's religious faith, seem worth quoting. One wishes that something of the sort could have marked a centenary celebration. Sir Alan Lascelles wrote on 30 July 1973: "The book is not only a vivid picture of an exceptional personality; it is a very valuable literary document, and I believe a unique one. I can't think of any other book, in any language, which records so authentically the development from childhood of a man's poetic instinct and poetic accomplishment— and records them *concurrently,* almost from day to

day, in the words of the poet himself. John Keats' letters to his brothers are the only near-parallel that occurs to me, but they cover all too short a period and that not very intimately. What makes your story of S's pilgrimage so enthralling is that it is not a retrospective old-age autobiography (such as Goethe might have written, and possibly did write—I don't know) but a contemporary account of the constant changes in the poet's mind and heart, revealed to us at the very moment of their genesis."

The other letter came from Sir Geoffrey Keynes whom Sassoon had initially appointed to be his literary executor. From 1933 onwards Keynes had been responsible for the design of almost all Sassoon's privately printed work; he was, in addition, the compiler of *A Bibliography of Siegfried Sassoon* (London: Hart-Davis, 1962), so that no one knew better than he the value and extent of the library at Heytesbury House. In the event, however, Sassoon made his son George sole executor with Sir Rupert Hart-Davis, a friend from the 1960s as "literary adviser." Upon Sassoon's death in 1967, Sir Rupert at once carried away the poet's massive diaries of more than a million words, now transcribed, edited, and, in the course of publication by Faber & Faber, under his general editorship. In chapter nineteen of his autobiography, *The Gates of Memory: No Life is Long Enough* (London: Oxford University Press, 1981), Geoffrey Keynes has described what he terms "the Rape of Heytesbury," when irreplaceable treasures, the garnering of a lifetime, went into the van from Christie's which, by order of the poet's son, "carried off the whole Sassoon archive remaining at Heytesbury House, to be thrown to the wolves at auction." Had Keynes been in command as literary executor, would things have taken a different course? Brother of the famous economist, Maynard Keynes, Geoffrey was an agnostic married to a Darwin, yet his letters show his astonishing sympathy and insight. In August 1973 he wrote: "I have just finished *Poet's Pilgrimage. . . .* I have enjoyed every part of it to a high degree, and felt that within its intended limits the picture of S. S. is a very just and moving one. I was, as you know, responsible for the design of several of his later volumes, and have always resented the general neglect of him as a contemplative and religious poet. . . . I had always recognized his spiritual leanings, so well brought out in your survey of his pilgrimage from early youth. One did not have to forgive his patent ego-centricity, in fact I enjoyed it. I had the same interest in his personality as himself and admired it as well—more than he did! He was a wonderful friend and letter-writer. His to you are, as always, enchanting, I have some 250 of them."

This letter makes reference to Sassoon's "patent egocentricity." The phrase is a just one. There was a time when Sassoon bade fair to become a reincarnation of Sir Willoughby Patterne, to read deeply into the eyes of others in order to find the man he sought there, squeeze him passionately and let them go. In 1946 Otto Kyllman, chairman of Constable's, asked Sassoon to write a study of Meredith. Its publication the following year gave its author great satisfaction because, he told Sir Sydney Cockerell, "it has shown me that I can write about someone else in addition to my unworthy self." But could he? The writing of it brought him into close contact with Helen Waddell, who at once saw subject and biographer as kindred spirits—the anemone-shrinking sensitiveness allied to self-torture and the demand of the ego to publish its one thing of genius, or otherwise run the risk of burying the talent which 'twere death to hide. Indeed, were I to recast *Poet's Pilgrimage*, I should probably interpret the course of Siegfried Sassoon's life of eighty years as the breaking down of an immense egocentricity by the continuous hammer-blows of human affliction and failure into something very like Christian holiness and humility. But of this, nothing has appeared in the 1986 celebrations. One hundred years have not sufficed to erase from the public mind the fictitious image of the Young War Hero. I should like to conclude by putting upon Sassoon's lips the last words of a poet whose first poems were one of the glories of the boy Siegfried's collection. "I have respected posterity," Patmore wrote, "and should there be a posterity which cares for letters, I dare to hope that it will respect me."

"Mocker," I said, "of mortal wit,
Me you shall not mock. I can wait."

A TRIBUTE

from VIVIEN F. CLARKE

I knew Siegfried best during the forties, and quite apart from appreciating his talent as a writer I found that he was a kind & generous man. It was he who gave me strength to carry on when I went to him with the news that my young son had been killed in action, just before V.E. Day. With his knowledge of the horrors of war, he was able to

project himself into one's grief; not sentimentaly but sensitively.

A TRIBUTE

from MICHAEL THORPE

Siegfried Sassoon's reputation has not suffered the common writer's fate of abrupt decline in the almost twenty years since his death; it has, rather, strengthened. This can be explained in several ways. In a period of sustained interest in the First World War, kept alive by such diverse agents as academic criticism and television series, his poetry and prose of the war have continued to attract fresh readers. His major work, *The Memoirs of George Sherston*, has been kept in print by his publishers, Faber & Faber, who have indeed served all his writings well. Both the semi-fictional Sherston memoirs and the fuller, if still somewhat oblique, autobiographical companion trilogy, *The Old Century, The Weald of Youth* and *Siegfried's Progress*, the first two volumes especially, have fed the nostalgic appeal that clings to the "golden afternoon" version of the late Victorian and Edwardian period during which Sassoon reached his mid-twenties. This appeal persists, under the shadow of another dark future, as was the case in 1938, when *The Old Century* was first published. Sassoon admitted then to having shaped a deliberately seductive picture of an age which, for most of his fellow countrymen, was far from idyllic: "All human beings desire to be glad. I prefer to remember my own gladness and good luck," and he later added (in a letter to me): "I wrote [in the winters of 1936-37] deliberately to afford people nostalgic escape in those years of imminent catastrophe." A handsome paperback reissue of *The Old Century*, for which I contributed an introduction in 1967, has been reprinted in this centenary year.

Another source of Siegfried Sassoon's still growing reputation is the posthumous publication, since 1981, of his diaries, edited by Rupert Hart-Davis. Three volumes have so far appeared, *Diaries 1920-1922* (1981), *1915-1918* (1983) and *1923-1925* (1985), making the beginnings of a third essay in autobiography, overlapping, supplementing and, in some respects, contrasting with the trilogies. A marked contrast in subject-matter and tone stems from Sassoon's open avowal of his homosexuality (sexual experience has been edited out of the trilogies). Like E. M. Forster, whose unpublished stories he had read in the 1920s, he had hoped that publication of writing he had felt obliged to suppress in the less tolerant climate prevailing in his lifetime might "help others with similar literary, social and sexual difficulties." The diaries are also intriguing source material for the memoirs and autobiographies, providing a rare insight into the transmutation of experience into art and into the relation between the complex self and the simplified Sherston *persona.*

It now seems clear that, while his war poems will hold their place as the most forceful English satire since Byron, it is not chiefly as a poet that he will be remembered (though his later poetry, especially that which traces, from the 1920s on, his spiritual quest, culminating in a Roman Catholic conversion, has illuminated moments). His autobiographical prose is his major artistic achievement. In that a troubled, anxious investigation of the baffling self seeking, in a transitional time, a sure foothold in a volatile world that threatens the very survival of individuality, is a central modern concern, pursued with signal integrity.

Packaging Papa: *The Garden of Eden*

Ernest Hemingway began writing the work now published as *The Garden of Eden* in the early months of 1946. It dealt with two couples: Catherine and writer David Bourne in the south of France, and Barbara and painter Nick Sheldon in Paris. By mid July 1946, after at most five months, Hemingway claimed to have written 1,000 manuscript pages. He then appears to have abandoned this novel for a decade, while he wrote *Across the River and Into the Trees* (1950), *The Old Man and the Sea* (1952), and the posthumously published *Islands in the Stream* (1970). Late in 1957 or early in 1958 Hemingway returned to *The Garden of Eden* project and rewrote or revised twenty-eight chapters by the end of June. At some undetermined time or times he extended the narrative to forty-eight chapters of between 150,000 and 200,000 words—which Carlos Baker has described as "repetitious" and "interminable."

Several editors at Charles Scribner's Sons worked on this material after Hemingway's death before Tom Jenks produced a reading text that was approved by Charles Scribner, Jr. The published version of *The Garden of Eden* has thirty chapters and some 70,000 words.

The Garden of Eden was published on 28 May 1986 to a predominantly favorable reception. It was a Book-of-the-Month selection, excerpts appeared in *Life* and *Sports Illustrated*, and 300,000 copies were sold. Of the initial reviews in mass-circulation periodicals that have been seen, only the *Los Angeles Times* challenged the editorial procedure. Other reviewers praised the conversion of an unpublishable manuscript into a readable novel—although they knew nothing about the nature of the manuscript. Two noteworthy reviews were written by respected novelists. E. L. Doctorow's front-page *New York Times Book Review* (18 May 1986) piece is particularly instructive because he was formerly head editor at Dial Press and so approached the book with a double perspective—as novelist and as a member of the publishing trade. This long review expends little space on textual considerations: "But the truth about editing the work of a dead writer in such circumstances is that you can only cut to affirm his strengths, to reiterate the strategies of style for which he is known; whereas he himself may have been writing to transcend them. This cannot have been the book Hemingway envisioned at the most ambitious moments of his struggle to realize it. . . . And it should have been published for what it is, a part of the design."

John Updike's *New Yorker* (30 June 1986) review evades the problem of how to judge a work in which the author's words have been drastically cut and re-ordered. He describes the published version of *The Garden of Eden* as "something of a miracle" that "falls just short of the satisfaction that a fully intended and achieved work gives us. The miracle . . . does not seem to be Hemingway's alone but is shared with workers unnamed. . . ." The closest Updike comes to addressing the editorial question is: "A chastening, almost mechanically rhythmic order has been imposed, and though an edition with a scholarly conscience would have provided some clues to the mammoth amounts of manuscript that were discarded, this remnant does give the reader a text wherein he, unlike the author in his travails long ago, never feels lost. Endearingly, many of Hemingway's eccentricities have been defended from copy editors. . . ."

Hemingway's will named his widow as sole executrix. In consultation with Charles Scribner, Jr., and Alfred Rice, Hemingway's attorney, Mrs. Hemingway initiated a program of publishing her husband's work-in-progress, commencing with *A Moveable Feast* (1964). Mary Hemingway had typed his manuscripts and read some of the unpublished material while it was being written. She apparently assumed editorial responsibility for *A Moveable Feast* and *Islands in the Stream;* but her failing health prevented her from taking any role in the publication of *The Dangerous Summer* (1985) and *The Garden of Eden.*

When *Islands* appeared in 1970 there was mild debate about the propriety of salvaging Hemingway's literary remains. What might be called the loyalist faction took the position that, given Hemingway's fierce concern for his reputation and his angry reaction to the reprinting of his apprentice writings, it was a clear violation of his standards and policies to publish his unfinished work. These partisans felt that finance had overwhelmed literary judgment. Another faction argued that Hemingway's stature was too great to be diminished by the posthumous publications and that everything he wrote would be published sooner or later, anyhow.

Outside of a few English departments there was no concern about *how* the posthumously published work had been or should have been edited. Inside English departments the concern was mainly restricted to talk, although the manuscripts may be consulted at the Kennedy Library. *Feast* has been the subject of two textual articles: Gary Brenner's "Are We Going to Hemingway's *Feast*" (1982) and Jacqueline Tavernier-Corbin's "The Manuscripts of *A Moveable Feast*" (1981). It is not yet known how trustworthy the texts of *Islands* or any of the subsequent posthumously published volumes are. It was possible to rationalize that *Feast* and *Islands* had Hemingway's indirect approval through Mary Hemingway. *The Dangerous Summer* did not merit much concern, although James Michener's defense of the editorial process in his introduction was puzzling because he had not examined the unedited manuscript.

The editing of *The Garden of Eden* raises—or ought to raise—serious concern about the packaging—or repackaging—of Papa. Just what has been printed? Can the published work be truly credited to Hemingway? Is the seventy-four-word "Publisher's Note" merely inadequate; or is it deliberately misleading? This unsigned statement reads: "As was also the case with Hemingway's earlier posthumous work *Islands in the Stream,* this novel was not in finished form at the time of the author's death. In preparing the book for publication we made some cuts in the manuscript and some routine copyediting corrections. Beyond a very small number of minor interpolations for clarity and consistency, nothing has been added. In every significant respect the work is all the author's." Since the latest Hemingway version with which editor Jenks worked has at least 150,000 words, "some cuts" means in the range of 80,000 words." "Some cuts" also involved the total excision of the Sheldons.

The *New York Times* (17 December 1985) article announcing the forthcoming publication of *The Garden of Eden* included Jenk's declaration that "there's nothing in the book that is not Hemingway. The book is identical to the structure—scene by scene, chapter by chapter, line by line." He provided his editorial rationale as follows: "When you go into something like this, you go totally under the law established by the writer—in this case the law of an ancient god." Jenks subsequently identified this deity as Hemingway himself. It is clear from Jenks's other explanations that his fealty to the ancient god necessitated more than cutting. In a *New York* magazine (28 April 1986) article he is quoted as explaining about one of the many gustatory passages: "That last part came from another place in the manuscript altogether. I had to remove the two characters they met in the cafe, so I healed the gap by taking narrative from a different eating scene that I didn't have room to use."

Apart from the ballyhoo that accompanies any Hemingway resurrection, of instruction here is what the treatment of *The Garden of Eden* reveals about the publisher's attitude toward textual fidelity. Trade publishers generally hold that dead authors and living authors deserve the same treatment, and that the departed are best served by editing an unfinished work into what is known in the business as "a publishable manuscript." This policy is founded on a presumed knowledge of the author's intentions and a desire to fulfill his wishes. In the case of *The Garden of Eden,* the argument runs that Hemingway would not have wanted his

Publishers Weekly *(24 January 1986)*

work in progress to be published as work in progress to be "used against" his other work, as he expressed it. But it does not follow that he would have approved of a stranger cutting and shuffling it for publication. In 1941 he wrote Maxwell Perkins about the posthumous publication of *The Last Tycoon:* "It is damned hard on Scott to publish something unfinished any way you look at it but I suppose the worms won't mind."

All authors are not equal. Hemingway is not another dead author. To patch and rearrange his work is more than disrespectful to one of the greatest writers who ever lived: it diminishes the value of literature as the expression of genius, which is always singular. Scribners has been salvaging Hemingway's unfinished work for twenty-five years, during which scholars have not troubled to investigate the trustworthiness of the posthumously published texts. It is unlikely that such investigation would result in a reformation. Yet it is difficult—perhaps unfair—to denounce Scribners when Hemingway scholars have failed in their duty.

—*M. J. B.*

An Interview with Tom Jenks

DLB: Who made the decision to edit or salvage *The Garden of Eden* material for publication? Were you in on that?

JENKS: In the spring of 1985, when I was first preparing to come to Scribners, the president and publisher, Mildred Marmur mentioned to me that this material did exist and asked me if I might have an interest in looking at it with some thought of finding a book. I said no. What I really wanted to do was publish good, young new American writers. Then, after I fully arrived at Scribners in July, Mrs. Marmur again suggested that *The Garden of Eden* was here and I might look at it, and I again said no. But a little later on, Charles Scribner, Jr., who had known and published Hemingway in his lifetime, asked me to come to his office and there, during a long conversation, he told me the history of the manuscript, his own thoughts on it, and ended by putting it in my lap and asking me just to read it and to venture an opinion on whether or not there might be a book in it all and would I be interested in making an edit. So I went home that night with two shopping bags of manuscript. Four versions, one of which turned out to be a previous editor's attempt at making an edit, a version that I threw out eventually.

I started reading *The Garden of Eden* with the utmost skepticism. In recent years, there had been a lot of biographical attention to Hemingway, much of it second rate. There had been the publication of *The Dangerous Summer.* Soon *Dateline: Toronto* would come out, as well as further biographies and reminiscences of Hemingway. I felt there had been enough published by and about him, and I had no real hope or excitement about *The Garden of Eden.* I maintained a skeptical distance through most of the reading, though I was seeing awfully good material. By the time I had read all four manuscripts, compared them, eliminated one, I knew that *The Garden of Eden* not only could be edited but absolutely had to be published—not for scholars but for general readers, because the novel presented a terrific story in David and Catherine Bourne. So you could say the decision to edit was mine, while the final decision *to publish* was made by the Hemingway family on the basis of my edit and with the approval of Charles Scribner, Jr., and Mildred Marmur.

DLB: One of the four versions you were given in the shopping bags represented another editor's attempt?

JENKS: Several editors since Hemingway's death had looked at this material, and one had performed an edit. Also, on many manuscript pages were editorial markings by two or three previous editors. I had mentally to erase all of that and go back to the point at which the material was untouched.

DLB: What was wrong with the one completed edit?

Tom Jenks (© Jim Kalett)

JENKS: It was an accordion job, a case of an editor looking at a volume of work and thinking: Well, this needs to be shorter. The editor had made cuts without any true understanding of the author's vision.

DLB: Of the three versions which were Hemingway's, was it clear which version was which, or did you have to reconstruct the versions?

JENKS: The versions were not radically different from each other. There was one of some 500 pages, one of about 1,200, and another of some 1,500 pages.

DLB: So the longer the version, the later the version?

JENKS: Each longer version appeared to me to be an extension of the last. Each version had the same trajectory, some of the exact same material, some revised material, and some entirely new material.

I could see many instances of Hemingway's own editing and those examples were a guide to my work. But much of the book as published has very little work from me.

DLB: Which version did you work from?

JENKS: From the longest with some recourse to the other two.

DLB: When you began the job, were you given any instructions by anyone at Scribners telling you, advising you, what kind of book to produce? Or were you given a completely free hand?

JENKS: I was not given any instructions on what kind of book to produce. I did consult with Charles Scribner, Jr., in the course of the editing. That is, I showed him edited sections of 100 to 200 pages at a time, which means that he saw my edit in three sections. He read each section and was enthusiastic. In each section he made several copyediting corrections. But the only instruction I was given is the one that has applied to all of the posthumous Hemingway material: You can cut but you can't add.

DLB: How did you go about preparing for this assignment? Did you re-read Hemingway? Did you look at any of the standard works on scholarly editing?

JENKS: Absolutely not. That would have been no help. I did not approach *The Garden of Eden* as a scholar. I'm a fiction editor, and once having read and compared the ms. versions, in the process of deciding to undertake an edit, I was faced with an alternative—to edit in a scholarly fashion, or to edit as though working with material from a living writer and from a point of view of storytelling. Would I leave material in the book that would be in there primarily because it was Hemingway, because it would be of scholarly interest? Or would I leave in material that could only be justified from the point of view of storytelling, material that advances a story in a narrative way? The latter is what I chose to do. It's one reason there is no introduction to the book; I felt that if in fact there were a worthwhile book to be published, it should speak to the reader without anyone standing between the story and the reader. I'm satisfied that that was accomplished, that the book was complete enough from Hemingway's hand to stand as a trade book, even for a reader with no prior acquaintance with the author's life or work. I gave *The Garden of Eden* the same sort of editing that I have given to the best work of the living writers that I have known so far. And when I was finished with the edit, while I was still the only one with the edited version in hand, and before the edit was shown to the Hemingway family, I did something that from a publishing company standpoint I was not supposed to do. I secretly showed the edited manuscript to two well-known, established writers, who are familiar with all of Hemingway, who themselves write in the language that men use, who had nothing to gain or lose by the book's trade publication, whose integrity and literary knowledge I trust. As a check against what I call *publishing vanity*, I asked these two writers—Raymond Carver and Tobias Wolff—for their opinions, and had they come back negative, I was prepared to destroy the work I'd done. Wolff felt the edited version of *The Garden of Eden* was a gift to literature, and Carver felt its strengths outweighed its weaknesses and that it should be published. So then, the edited version was shown to the Hemingway family.

DLB: Was it clearly impossible to do a cosmetic job on that 1,500-page last version—copyediting job—and print it as it was?

JENKS: I suppose some kind of a scholarly publication of the manuscript might have been possible. I don't really know. But from a trade editor's point of view I don't see any virtue in the argument that because a man is dead you don't give him a good edit. There was a subplot that Hemingway undertook at some point in the composition of the book—I don't know whether it was conceived initially or conceived in process—but it went nowhere.

DLB: This would have been the Nick and Barbara story?

JENKS: Yes, if you'd published the book as in the full manuscript you would have had that subplot and a lot of other incidentals that didn't connect to much of anything. The reader would have been wandering all over the place. The story in the book was the story of David and Catherine Bourne. All I did was to let that story show.

DLB: Did Nick and Barbara appear only in a later version, or were they there from the beginning?

JENKS: They and another character named Andrew, who was the link between the two couples, had been in evidence from the shortest version, but in the longer versions they were just chunked in. Hemingway had taken ten or sometimes a hundred pages in very rough draft and just sandwiched it in with—and I'm speculating—the intention to come back later and integrate it. In the shortest version of the book Nick and Barbara were integrated into the narrative. In the longer versions Nick and Barbara were integrated into the narrative. In the longer versions Nick and Barbara were not integrated at all. And it was not a case of good storytelling by alternation of characters or points of view. But Hemingway was working in a manner that is not unusual for any writer—which is to turn to the material that you can work on and then reconstruct it, refine it, and fuse it with already crafted work.

DLB: As you know, the Nick and Barbara material is of great curiosity to the reviewers.

JENKS: Well, I don't know that it is. I've not read very many reviews that have expressed much curiosity about them at all. I've encountered reviews that have expressed sensational impulses about them. But honest curiosity about them, no, I haven't encountered much of that. Two or three people.

DLB: For the record, can you tell me something about the Nick and Barbara plot? I gather they are in Paris and Nick is an artist. Is that correct?

JENKS: Nick is an artist.

DLB: What is the connection between Nick and Barbara? Between the Sheldons and the Bournes?

JENKS: They all knew each other in Paris at a time that predates the opening of the story. The Sheldons enter the manuscript fairly early, in passages strictly about them and a little later when David and Catherine have gone on an extended driving tour, and are at the Hendaye, a beach town, and run into these two sitting at a cafe. The Sheldons and Bournes spend time together at Hendaye and then they part. Later on there were other rough draft passages about the Sheldons, in one case narrated by Andrew, telling a story quite apart from David and Catherine. I think these passages were written by Hemingway as he began to get some of the language and atmosphere for the Sheldons' story. But if you want to get a really accurate idea of the Sheldons, you'll have to go up to the Kennedy Library and read those parts of the ms.

DLB: Are you saying that if Hemingway's intention was to get counterpoint, he never developed the meshing?

JENKS: I believe that if he had lived and kept his clarity and strength, he might have found ways to weave further dimension into an already complex novel.

DLB: Will you explain for the readers of the *Yearbook* how you actually went about physically editing. Did you make a Xerox and mark it up? Did you get scissors and paste? Did you cut and patch. Can you tell the interested amateur how you actually proceeded day by day and week by week? How did you take a shopping bag full of manuscripts by an author you can't work with and carve a book out of it.

JENKS: Very, very slowly. You do make a Xerox of the manuscript you're editing. You do all of the things you mentioned. You work with a pencil. You work with scissors and tape and a stapler. I worked at the office and at a desk in my house. I carried pages back and forth so that I could be working on it continuously day and night.

But what's more interesting in a case like this is how careful an editor must be not to damage what the writer is doing. You must be sensitive to rhythm and meaning and go over and over and over everything—every word, every line, every paragraph, every chapter, every passage, the punctuation, the spellings again, again, and again. By the time you're finished, you're exhausted. The characters have lived for you. I know David, Catherine, and Maurita thoroughly.

DLB: Did you construct for yourself as you went along, a table of rules such as you would correct spellings, but you would not alter punctuation unless absolutely necessary. Did you end up with ten commandments that you tried to abide by?

JENKS: No, not really. You go a lot by ear.

DLB: John Updike's review in *The New Yorker* mentioned that the published text of *The Garden of Eden* had retained Hemingway's idiosyncratic punctuation when there was a string of adjectives.

JENKS: I didn't want to change anything I didn't have to, obviously, and if there was ever any doubt about changing anything—Is this change going to create some harm?—well, you don't do it. There is an interesting thing that goes on here. Hemingway's style is of course very well known, and *The Garden of Eden* is a book he began writing in 1946, and now stands published in 1986, forty years later. The subject of the book, its atmosphere are amazingly modern. Yet its style in many ways seems very old-fashioned. So there's a tension, and you don't want to disturb that tension. It was very easy to maintain and honor it by allowing Hemingway to speak for himself, by not doing anything to disturb what is his.

Yet the work I did is really the weakest part of the book. For instance, *The Garden of Eden* has many more line spaces than other Hemingway books. Most of those spaces are ellipses where I made cuts. If you look at *A Farewell to Arms* or *The Sun Also Rises* you'll find very few line spaces. In *The Garden of Eden* the line spaces create a little bit of a cinematic feel, which is not Hemingway. The line spaces are the mark of the editor, not the writer.

DLB: Peter Prescott's *Newsweek* review states that in order to remove three unsalvageable characters you had to *rewrite*—that's his word—rewrite scenes of dialogue involving several characters so that only two remain.

JENKS: Hemingway wrote a lot of dialogue for *The Garden of Eden*, pages and pages that I cut. In some scenes, early in the book there had been as many as five characters sitting around a table talking, and when I pulled out three characters I was left with gaps into which I brought dialogue from pages I had cut, or, in a few instances, I reconstructed the dialogue already in place.

DLB: I'm particularly interested in the word *rewrite*. Is that an accurate statement, that you rewrote scenes rather than cut and pruned?

JENKS: No, that's not accurate in the way you seem to want to imply, nor is it what Prescott meant. I spoke with him for his article and I think he understands the kind of editing I did. When I began to cut Nick, Barbara, and Andrew out and move dialogue from other places or rearrange existing bits of dialogue within a scene I thought that the work would be good enough that readers would not mind that it showed, even very careful readers like Prescott. However, by the time I completed the edit, I realized that most of the work I had done would not show at all. My final answer on this question and all similar ones is that if there is any editorial magic involved in the publication of a book like *The Garden of Eden* it works on the page, and I have no obligation to reveal it to anybody. On the other hand, nothing is hidden. The manuscripts are at the Kennedy Library.

DLB: In the first announcement of the forthcoming publication of *The Garden of Eden*, December 1985 in the *New York Times*, you are quoted as saying the book is actually "identical to the structure, scene by scene, chapter by chapter, line by line." But according to Carlos Baker's biography of Hemingway the last, longest version of *The Garden of Eden* had forty-eight chapters; and the published version has thirty, leaving a difference of eighteen chapters. Is it true, then, that the published text is identical to the structure of the manuscript?

JENKS: Much of what's gone is the Nick and Barbara and Andrew material. Also, I cut a large number of redundant scenes of eating, drinking, sleeping, and of extraneous discussions of art, travel, and politics. I also cut pages and pages of repetitious dialogue. Chapter one in the published book appears virtually unchanged from the ms. except that in the original the chapter went on a little bit longer. There was another love scene in the middle of the night before the chapter ended. I took that love scene off the end of chapter one and moved it into chapter two as a memory when David is sitting on the beach beginning to experience the first twinges of remorse over what he and Catherine are beginning to be up to in bed. I moved it because the first chapter went on too long and had a double or false ending. And the revision in chapter two, as David sat with Catherine laid out in the sun on the beach, gave David's doubts more immediacy and weight. There are other, similar revisions throughout the book. Yet, the time line, the character development, the flow of the dialogue and where it led as Hemingway told the story—the architecture that he had always used in his books, the relative proportions of dialogue, narration, reflection—are, as published, exactly what he had laid out for *The Garden of Eden.* He wrote by extension. He would sit down and let his characters start talking. They might talk for forty pages. They would cover the same ground three and four and five times. Later on he would go back, select, revise, organize, rewrite until he honed it. What had been forty pages might be four pages; it might be ten pages. The same was true for the narrative work

he did. Much of this book he had already gone back over and honed. The elephant hunting story within the novel needed virtually no editing. Many chapters and long passages needed little or no editing.

DLB: In the same *New York Times* article MacDowell quotes you saying, "When you go into something like this, you go totally under the law established by the writer. In this case, the law of an ancient god." May I impose upon you to explicate that phrase: "the law of an ancient god."

JENKS: Richard Ford wrote an article for an issue of *Esquire* that appeared on the magazine's fiftieth anniversary. The article was titled "The Three Kings," and in it Richard reflected on Faulkner, Fitzgerald, and Hemingway. For any modern writer Hemingway is a primary influence. His power is still overwhelming. It was like sitting under a mountain to work with him. Make no mistake—he was very present and exacted a tribute from me. I had never imagined sacrificing myself to anyone the way I wound up having to sacrifice myself to him. The authority for a work must always rest with the writer.

DLB: So the ancient god you're referring to was not Hemingway, but rather the god of literature?

JENKS: No, Hemingway. Quite literally. Literature is embodied in Hemingway. The man is immortal. There's no question.

DLB: The publisher's note that proceeds the volume, did you write that?

JENKS: No, I didn't.

DLB: Let me read it into the record, into the interview. "Publisher's Note: As was also the case with Hemingway's earlier posthumous work, *Islands in the Stream*, this novel was not in finished form at the time of the author's death. In preparing the book for publication, we have made some cuts in the manuscript and some routine copyediting corrections. Beyond a very small number of minor interpolations for clarity and consistency, nothing has been added. In every significant respect the work is all the author's." You just said you didn't write that. Do you stand behind it?

JENKS: Charles Scribner, Jr., wrote the note, and I'm told it's basically the same note that's in the front of *Islands in the Stream.* E. L. Doctorow in the *New York Times Book Review* singled out the words *some cuts.* The published book is approximately one-third the length of the longest manuscript, and Doctorow felt that the words *some cuts* were disingenuous.

The note, I think you would have to agree, is written in something of an almost nineteenth-century manner. Not quite, but almost. It does not represent my style nor my thoughts exactly. But throughout his lifetime, and ever since his death, Hemingway has been published by Charles Scribner's Sons, with the exception of the first book, which was published by Boni and Liveright. And all of Hemingway's work has stayed in print constantly with Scribners. It is an outstanding publishing record, one of faithfulness between a writer and a publisher, of a publisher's long-standing commitment to honor a writer. Charles Scribner, Jr., has spent—as far as I can tell from my very short historical view—perhaps half his publishing life maintaining the Hemingway publications. So here I come, a very young editor, new to the house, not looking for this kind of project, finding myself into it in spite of many other interests, in spite of wanting to do an entirely different kind of thing. I feel that the work absolutely has to be done, and I do it very much under the good graces of Charles Scribner who feels definite about the appropriateness of the note. I'm not going to say don't put that note on there. I'm not going to say I'm the one who should write the note. Here I've done the editing; I'm going to be the one who is doing most of the talking with the press, who in many ways is getting attention that (a) I didn't look for and (b) is entirely disproportionate to what an editor should receive. And then I'm going to say to Mr. Scribner, "Bow out of here, buddy, I'm going to write this note the way it should really be written?" No, that would not have been right. And I do think it's accurate to say that beyond a small number of minor interpolations nothing has been added to *The Garden of Eden* and that in every significant respect the work is all the author's.

DLB: Could you give us an example of a minor interpolation?

JENKS: If you took all of the words that I added to the book and typed them out single-spaced, they would probably fill up a half-page 8 x 11. Most of those words would be *but, and, we, he said,* and so on.

But the fact remains that Hemingway has the reputation of always having been his own editor. So of course there will be years and years, and page upon page of speculation now that *The Garden of Eden* is out in the world to speak for itself.

The Practice of Biography V

AN INTERVIEW

with JUSTIN KAPLAN

Before becoming a full-time writer in 1959, Justin Kaplan did free-lance work for several New York publishers and was an editor for Simon and Schuster. His first biography, *Mr. Clemens and Mark Twain* (1966), won both a National Book Award and a Pulitzer Prize in 1967. *Walt Whitman: A Life* (1980) was awarded the American Book Award. Kaplan's other books include *Mark Twain: A Profile* (1967), *Lincoln Steffens, A Biography* (1974), and *Mark Twain and His World* (1974).

DLB: When you left editing and moved to Cambridge, Mass., to write your own books, did you already know that it was biography you wanted to do?

KAPLAN: Yes. I had been in publishing in New York for a long time and done a fair amount of free-lance writing. I realized that I really wanted to write rather than be an editor. The problem was what form my writing should take. I was only interested in narrative, and I thought of making various approaches to history, but I could never find a shape I felt comfortable with. Then, quite accidentally (or providentially), a friend in publishing said, "Why don't you write a biography of Mark Twain?" Suddenly it all came together.

DLB: Before that suggestion was made, had you been particularly interested in Mark Twain?

KAPLAN: I'd been an admirer, but nothing much beyond that. My background at Harvard, in college and graduate school, had been almost exclusively in English literature. It was only in my last year or two in graduate school that I began to realize that there was such a thing as American literature. I left graduate school because I had no interest in teaching, went into publishing, and sure enough, ended up being pushed into a project that involved nineteenth-century American literature. It was a valuable experience. I was asked by Simon and Schuster, for whom I eventually worked as an in-house editor, to prepare an edition of Thoreau. I spent half a year doing nothing but reading Thoreau, his biographers, and his critics.

Then I was farmed out to Louis Untermeyer, the anthologist, who was by then preparing a quite considerable edition of Walt Whitman for Simon and Schuster. I was his researcher and errand boy, and he tried his best to teach me how to work as a writer. He would say, "We're writing this introduction together. Now it's your turn to write a section." I would say, "I really don't feel like it." And he'd say, "It's not a matter of whether you feel like it or not. If you're going to do it, you do it." I wish that lesson had burned itself in earlier.

DLB: For *Mr. Clemens and Mark Twain,* you've noted that you were able to get access to materials that hadn't been available to earlier biographers. How did that come about?

KAPLAN: It was through luck and timing, not any skill of my own. The Mark Twain Papers had long been under various kinds of control. Mark Twain's original literary executor, who was also his official biographer, Albert Bigelow Paine, refused to allow access to them. He was afraid free access by others would jeopardize the image of Twain that had been passed down through Harper and Brothers. Paine died and was succeeded by people who progressively liberalized this policy. Bernard De Voto was one of the editors, and then Dixon Wecter. The final editor, in my experience, was a wonderful man, Henry Nash Smith, who died in 1986. He was willing to open up the Papers to anyone moderately qualified.

It was a wonderful experience, because there were thousands and thousands of Mark Twain documents at the General Library in Berkeley. They were then in the process of being organized and were in rough form, so that when you went through the Mark Twain correspondence, for example, you simply dumped out on the table a huge folder marked 1874 or whatever it was, and you went through it as if no one had ever gone through it before. Part of the exercise, of course, was comparing some of that material with published versions. Then you discovered that the published versions had been heavily edited by people like Albert Bigelow Paine. I spent three months at the

Mark Twain Papers in Berkeley, was absolutely ec-static, and worked harder than I'd ever worked in my life. I also did some of the same sorts of things at the Berg Collection at the New York Public Library and at the Library of Congress.

DLB: Did the new materials in particular bolster the idea that you expressed in the book's title, the dichotomy between the man and the persona?

KAPLAN: Yes, they did. The image you formed of Mark Twain from the official editions and the official biographies was quite different from the one you got if you looked at the Papers. When I saw how preoccupied this man was with business, with status, reputation, and money affairs, I began to feel that Mark Twain was a secular character. But I also saw in him a dark, private, and tormented sensibility that he shared with Poe or Hawthorne. I was especially intrigued by a cycle of unfinished stories that Mark Twain worked on during the 1890s, stories about nightmare dreams and voyages, about radical dislocation in time and scale. Then I began to feel more strongly than ever how haunted a character he was. This was a very anxiety- and guilt-ridden Mark Twain that I produced; you could say, a Mark Twain of the post-Freudian generation. Somebody else might come out with a much cheerier version, but I don't believe that version would be true to the facts. One of his contemporaries described him as spending the greater part of his life on his knees begging forgiveness, and I thought, if someone in the 1870s could see that, there's no reason why I should ignore it.

DLB: The risky move from editing to writing, from New York to Cambridge, worked exceedingly well for you, as it turned out. What was it like making such a major transition?

KAPLAN: I left a terrific job in publishing: I was a senior editor, I was assistant to the chairman of the board, I had an office with windows over the skating rink at Rockefeller Plaza and a private bathroom. But I was bored. My family then consisted of my wife and two children, and the change meant asking them to move out of New York and move to Cambridge, buying a house in Cambridge, dislocation, and then a great deal of anxiety. For several years, I would wake up at two or three in the morning, terrified, and ask myself, What have I done? I had written little things, but I had never written a full-length book before, and I'd certainly never written a biography. This anxiety became

considerable. I had never shown any of the book to anyone other than my wife, but toward the end of one draft I sent a chapter to Joseph Barnes, my editor at Simon and Schuster and also a close friend, and got such an extravagant response that I knew the book was going to work out.

DLB: Winning a National Book Award and a Pulitzer for the first biography had to be a heady experience. Did it, though, make proceeding with the second book scarier in a way—the business of living up to the initial success?

KAPLAN: It did. Those two prizes, along with good reviews and good sales, were gratifying, of course. But I'm deep down superstitious and primitive. If you are like me, you begin to feel that you should not have had such a great success with a first book, that you're letting yourself in for trouble—a lightning bolt is going to hit you, or something like that. And then, when I was still feeling good about the book, someone in the school parking lot where I delivered my children came up to me and said, "It's absolutely wonderful what you've done, but what are you going to do for an encore?" That was reality knocking.

It *was* a hard act to follow, and I agonized about what to do next. But the one thing that I did not have when I finally began my second book was the kind of terror that I had when I was writing my first. I used to come to my desk then trembling with fright, and after two or three hours I'd be exhausted. I would also spend a lot of time looking out the window and just feeling anxious. I lost that with my second book and the others. I no longer have an irrelevant anxiety. I've got, let's say, a healthy professional anxiety. My standards have become higher.

DLB: With Lincoln Steffens as a biographical subject, you were again dealing with a man in whom there were deep contradictions. Did you find him a hard character to get a grip on?

KAPLAN: I found when I was halfway into the Lincoln Steffens book that I was dealing with a rather different kind of character from Mark Twain. I discovered that Steffens's internal life was not so interesting to me as the history that he was a witness to. So there had to be a very deliberate shift in narrative strategy and focus. I was not primarily interested in Lincoln Steffens's fantasies or dreams or internal conflicts; I was interested in the events that he saw and how he interpreted them:

Dust jacket for Justin Kaplan's most recent biographical volume

the Russian Revolution, for example, the Versailles peace conference, and America's move to the left during the 1920s and 1930s. I think I took up Lincoln Steffens as a subject not because he interested me intrinsically but because I felt his experience could teach me about an entire era of history. I was guilty about my ignorance. Since then I've learned that there are easier ways to get an education than to write a book. You can *read* one instead.

DLB: You've spoken of the grief you felt when you finished the first Mark Twain book. I suppose there wasn't anything of the sort with Steffens, but what about Walt Whitman after you'd written your Whitman biography?

KAPLAN: With Steffens, I was relieved to be done. With Whitman, it was quite different. I did not have the profound sense of bereavement that I had with Mark Twain—but only because I was prepared for it. When I felt grief-stricken at the end of the Mark Twain book, it was because I hadn't realized what went on in biography. That is, I hadn't realized how much I actually loved the man. There's a question I don't think the biographer can afford to ask: Do you like the person you're writing about? It's much more important to be utterly fascinated and

compelled. Otherwise, how are you going to write a biography of Genghis Khan or Stalin or Hitler? I did feel a great deal of emotion about Whitman when I'd finished with him, and I'm still very attached to him.

DLB: You said before in our talk that you'd worked with Louis Untermeyer on Whitman. Did you come to doing the biography through an earlier love of the poetry?

KAPLAN: Oh yes. I remember my first exposure to *Leaves of Grass* when I was a student at the Horace Mann School in New York City. I memorized a great deal. This was in an era of literary education—in private education, anyhow—when part of the discipline was memorization. It's an absolutely terrific way for a writer to develop unconscious allusions and unconscious verbal rhythms.

DLB: According to some accounts, you'd begun the Walt Whitman biography before the Lincoln Steffens one and stopped because of frustrations with the research. Did that have to do with Whitman's practice of editing and sometimes destroying his papers?

KAPLAN: No, it concerned what I consider the central challenge in biography: storytelling. When I gave up on Whitman and took up Lincoln Steffens instead, it was because I did not see any way then of telling his story in a way that I found satisfactory. I had found most of the Whitman biographies quite unsatisfactory. They start off with a rather shadowy infant and young man who, in a mysterious and miraculous way, develops, writes *Leaves of Grass*, and then becomes famous, notorious, and "official," so that by the end of his life there's been so much written about him that the real man disappears. In his place you have the guru of Camden, New Jersey. I found that pattern, which is basically the pattern of a disappearing act, unsatisfactory for narrative biography. Most of the Whitman biographies trail off at the end because the biographers are bored with him; he talks too much, poses too much, and generates too much material.

It was only after I finished the Lincoln Steffens book that my simpleminded solution came to me: To turn the whole story around, to start at the end and go back to the beginning. I thought, since Whitman in old age was so elaborately documented, if you started off with a highly articulated portrait of him then, rendered in detail, you could use that as a baseline or scaffold in dealing with a reconstructed Whitman, a speculative Whitman. When I started telling the story of Whitman as a boy and young man, at least I would have something to refer to, some feeling of conviction. What that device also did was to turn the whole direction of the narrative around and give it the kind of impellence that I wanted, namely, to suggest that one book, *Leaves of Grass*, was the center of Whitman's life, his heart's companion, his reason for living. The whole of Whitman's life seen from old age can be told as the story of a rather lonely man, writing and rewriting, publicizing and battling for his sacred book, *Leaves of Grass*. That was the momentum I wanted.

DLB: Were there other things you wanted to do in the Whitman biography that you felt previous writers hadn't done?

KAPLAN: Writing this book in the 1970s, I found it easier to deal with the previously much vexed question of Whitman's homosexuality. For any moderately sophisticated person, there's no longer anything terribly newsy about the fact that he defined himself as homosexual. I was interested in, let's say, an existential approach. That is, regardless of what he did and with whom, if you have the feeling that he thought of himself as homosexual, that should be quite enough. I thought this was a sane and sensitive way of approaching a subject that used to frighten Whitman biographers and make them gibber with embarrassment.

DLB: You've said that, in dealing with the lives of Twain and Whitman, you consciously created a tension between yourself and them. Could you tell me about how that process worked, and whether you used it as a means of distancing yourself in order to become more objective?

KAPLAN: I'm very mistrustful of the word *objective*. I don't think you can be really objective. Biography is not an objective exercise; it's a literary exercise which involves imagination, empathy, and intuition, a great deal of speculation and selection. I started writing biography with an unconsciously articulated policy; I was not interested in writing judgmental biography. I *was* interested—and this is the exercise in the historical imagination—in finding out what it was like for another person to do what the person did at that time, what it felt like, what the density, feel, and texture of that experience were. To do that, I thought it was necessary to maintain what Lytton Strachey called freedom of spirit. Distance doesn't mean objectivity or coldness or removal. It means a certain kind of fierce independence in the exercise of imagination and literary judgment. You want to say, I'm not getting myself confused with the person I'm writing about.

There are ways of maintaining independence. One, of course, is stylistic. I think the worst possible thing one could do would be to try to write an overtly rather than subtextually humorous biography of Mark Twain. It's too much *like*. Or to write a biography of Whitman in the dithyrambic, vaporous prose that Whitman sometimes favored. The narrative would simply get too fuzzy, too murky. Part of the job is to find a satisfactory counterstyle, something that will be harmonious with the person I'm writing about but at the same time set up some tensions. These stylistic considerations take a lot more time and thought than most readers know. They think biography is largely a matter of getting the information and putting it down on paper in an orderly fashion. I think that's the least part of it.

DLB: What about the business of empathy with the subject? Can it undo the biographer's critical capacity?

KAPLAN: You've got to be able to put yourself in the other person's position. I'll give you an example of how this sort of thing works. In practically every book about Whitman, the biographers have had to apologize for something he did in 1855. Having published *Leaves of Grass* privately and sent it out into a largely indifferent world, he received a private letter from Ralph Waldo Emerson hailing it as the greatest piece of wit and wisdom an American had produced. Without receiving or even asking Emerson's permission, Whitman released this private letter to the newspapers and used it to advertise the second edition of his book. All the biographies say, What a terribly rude thing that was to do; we'll have to make allowances for Walt. I thought what he did was absolutely wonderful. Here's a man who believes so deeply in his book that he'll do anything to give it a breathing space in the world, who will be indifferent to normal codes of conduct, who will be as arrogant as saints and martyrs and will do exactly what he must do to advance his book. I didn't feel the least need to apologize or qualify.

DLB: You're known as a careful and thorough researcher. In addition to the work you'd done with Untermeyer, were you already quite experienced in research before you became a writer?

KAPLAN: I was pretty well trained in college and graduate school. Harvard was a very exacting place. And of course when you're an editor, as I was, you have to be exacting. But I don't really think of myself as a very good researcher. I'm appalled at the number of things that I've ignored or not known about. I'm impatient to get out of the research and into the writing. When I first started, I tried to come up with some analogies. Using baseball imagery, I thought research is the equivalent of fielding and writing is the equivalent of hitting. That was all very cute, but it doesn't hold up well. A wonderful fielding team can be a winner, but of course you've got to do some hitting too. Sometimes I turn to football metaphors such as running and passing.

DLB: Some writers have the opposite problem. They have to pull themselves out of the library to get on with the writing.

KAPLAN: They think the hard work is the writing. Writing *is* the hard work, of course, but that's the work I look forward to. I love library work, but after a while you begin to have the sneaky feeling that it's not the work you should be doing; it's writing you should be doing.

DLB: Do you try to finish all the research—as much as that's possible—before you start to write?

KAPLAN: I suppose ideally, but it's not always possible. One thing I've learned is that it's not possible to make any distinction between research and writing. Imagine that the very first day that you were at work on a biography, you went to a standard biographical entry, in *Who's Who,* for example. In your note-taking on that information you would already have started making certain writerly decisions, because obviously certain things would appear to be especially significant. You note some things and ignore others. That rather simple act of note-taking is inseparable from writing. At that very moment you are interpreting and shaping your story.

DLB: What techniques do you think biography can fairly take from fiction?

KAPLAN: Biography can take from fiction just about everything short of inventing dialogues and things that never happened. I see no reason biography should not be as compelling a narrative as the novel. As a matter of fact, the whole distinction between the novel and nonfiction prose tends to break down. There are species of fictions that are not novels. According to Northrop Frye, fiction is a genus and the novel is a species of fiction. So is autobiography; so is the confessional form. And so, I think, is biography.

DLB: Autobiography is bound to be fiction in part because our memories change with time; we tend to reshape events in our minds as we get farther from them.

KAPLAN: It's Wright Morris who says that anything that's processed through memory is automatically fiction. You can't help it. And the moment you begin shaping a biography into narrative you're also writing fiction.

DLB: Have you taught the writing of biography?

KAPLAN: I've taught a little, but mainly literary history and criticism. But I have written a fair amount about the writing of biography. In the past ten or fifteen years many biographers have become conscious of biography as a literary form with its own "poetics," if one has to use that pretentious word. We've also become outspoken, even irrepressibly so, about what we do and how we go about it. I've counted some two dozen relatively current books on the subject—I don't believe there's been a comparable proliferation of craft statements by practicing novelists or poets. Sometimes it seems as if everyone who writes biography also takes part in lectures and symposia on the subject—and interviews. The common ground of these declarations is that biography is no longer an orphan or a poor relative but an autonomous literary genre. We're proud of what we do, and we want to do it better.

DLB: Who were your own models or inspirations?

KAPLAN: I've been reading biographies ever since I learned to read. Some have been crucially important in suggesting what life-writing can do and be. Lytton Strachey's *Queen Victoria* and *Eminent Victorians,* for example, are classics of narrative clarity and stylistic elegance. A little book by Geoffrey Scott, *The Portrait of Zélide,* published in 1925, told the story of an eighteenth-century bluestocking and salonière in a way that recalled for me Madame de la Fayette's spare and elegant novel *The Princess of Cleves.* Two historical narratives, multiple biographies in effect, helped open my eyes to the nineteenth century: Cecil Woodham-Smith's *The Reason Why* (about the Crimean War) and Margaret Leech's *Reveille in Washington* (about the American Civil War). Francis Steegmuller's *Flaubert and Madame Bovary* served as a direct model for me in writing *Mr. Clemens and Mark Twain.* Henri Troyat's biography of Tolstoy reads like *Anna Karenina.* For many of us, the highest praise we can receive is to be told that our books "read like novels."

DLB: Do you have any quibbles with present biographers or with trends in current biography?

KAPLAN: There are many books that represent undigested research, that are basically information storage-and-retrieval systems, biographical monoliths. I think they're compendia rather than biographies. That's one direction that doesn't make

me very happy. Another direction is so-called psychobiography. Except in the hands of brilliant practitioners like Erik Erikson, it's a disaster. What is the point of telling a story in order to demonstrate clinically preconceived conclusions? There's no discovery here, no narrative suspense.

DLB: Your wife, Anne Bernays, is also a writer. Do you act as first readers for each other, or in any other way help each other through the process?

KAPLAN: We're first readers for each other, though on somewhat different schedules. Annie prefers quicker feedback; she shows me her material at a relatively early stage. I don't show anyone, including Annie, anything until I'm pretty well satisfied with it—that is, until it's been polished and worked over a great deal.

DLB: One can feel so very vulnerable where his own writing is concerned.

KAPLAN: Inviting criticism can be a dangerous and tricky thing. If you start showing your work to more than one person, you may be inviting confusing and conflicting opinions. On the other hand, if you show your work only to your wife or husband or lover, you create certain problems of tact. What do you say if you *don't* think it's very good? Are you doing the other person a favor by being gentle and evasive, or would you be more helpful simply by being brutal and apparently tactless? There are middle grounds, of course.

DLB: At the time *Lincoln Steffens* was published, you told John F. Baker for *Publishers Weekly,* "I write evenings, weekends; I find I become addicted, and I feel guilty when I'm not at work." Is your writing schedule still the same?

KAPLAN: Somewhat the same. It's a little hard to generalize in the summer, when I'm living on Cape Cod in sight of the water and it's so easy to go swimming at 10:30 in the morning. But, yes. You get into a certain fighting trim. Or, to put it another way, you develop addictive patterns of behavior, so that when you're not writing, you feel guilty and anxious.

—Jean W. Ross

An Interview with Peter S. Prescott

Peter S. Prescott is a senior writer and book critic at *Newsweek* magazine. He also teaches a seminar, "Writing with Style," at Columbia's Graduate School of Journalism; this course will presently be metamorphosed into a book of the same name. He received the George Polk Award for Criticism for pieces collected in his most recent book, *Never in Doubt: Critical Essays on American Books, 1972-1985* (New York: Arbor House, 1986). Mr. Prescott's previous book, *The Child Savers: Juvenile Justice Observed* (1981), won first prize in the Robert F. Kennedy Book Awards.

A director of the Authors Guild and President of the Authors Guild Foundation, Mr. Prescott has lectured under the auspices of the U.S. State Department in Syria, Egypt, and Ireland. He was an editor at Dutton and has been, at various times, a columnist for *Look* magazine and a syndicated book columnist at *Women's Wear Daily.*

His earlier books include: *A World of Our Own: Notes on Life and Learning in a Boys' Preparatory School* (1970); *Soundings: Encounters with Contemporary Books* (1972); and *A Darkening Green: Notes from the Silent Generation* (1974). He has also edited *The Norton Book of the American Short Story*, which will be published in 1988, and is at work on a biography of Alfred A. Knopf.

DLB: Do you think of yourself as a reviewer or a critic, and is there a difference?

PRESCOTT: I tried to make a distinction in the introduction to my last collection, *Never in Doubt*, between three breeds of beasts. One is the academic literary critic who is accustomed to applying great labors to narrow areas; he examines the past—old and relatively recent books—and retrieves from it that which is of use to the present. But the book reviewer, who is often called a "mere reviewer," lives entirely in the present. He is content to describe a new book's contents and, if he remembers, to indicate whether he approves of it. Somewhere in between is the fellow that I call a book critic. He is working in a journalistic way; he is concerned with the present, but he brings to it some sense of the past. He puts the new books he considers into some kind of context, perhaps the condition of history today, or biography today, or the novelist's

Peter S. Prescott (photo by Martha Kaplan)

past work, or the genre to which the book belongs—if it's a western, science fiction, English mystery, or that kind of thing. And what the book critic has to do is to show how the book works. He mustn't be simply content to describe what's in the book and say, well, it's good or it's bad. He has to show how it works, as a man explaining a magic act would show how the trick is done. He has to turn the glove inside out so the reader can see the seams. And this is the aspect of being a book critic that most reviewers forget about, or don't know how to do.

DLB: Do you adhere to any critical school?

PRESCOTT: No, absolutely not. I don't think a journalistic critic can afford to.

DLB: Who are the critics living or dead you most admire?

PRESCOTT: Speaking only of journalistic critics, first and in a class by himself is G. B. Shaw. Shaw invented modern reviewing as we know it today. He started out as a music critic, and he remains the best critic in music that we've had ever since. He then switched to become a theater critic, and he remains the best theater critic we've ever had. So he would be the first. Others whom I admire are H. L. Mencken, Max Beerbohm, Edmund Wilson, Michael Arlen in television. For style, not for content, I admire what Dorothy Parker did. Currently, John Updike in books.

DLB: How much formal literary criticism do you read?

PRESCOTT: Nowadays very little. I did a great deal of that in college—enough, perhaps, for a lifetime. If an interesting-looking book comes out which purports to describe in 200 pages what structuralism is all about or what the Marxist critics have been trying to do, I'll read through it. Terry Eagleton's books, for instance.

DLB: Do you claim credit for having spotted any significant writers before any of your colleagues did?

PRESCOTT: I've been told that I have. By that I mean that sometimes a publisher, more often an author, will write to me or call me and say that without my favorable review the book would have sunk unnoticed. This is pleasing, I guess, but it isn't what we try to do.

DLB: Do you feel that it is any part of your kind of critic's proper job to try to encourage young talent?

PRESCOTT: Yes, if I can. It's difficult for good writers to get noticed at all. Editors reliably turn down the best books: John Kennedy Toole's *A Confederacy of Dunces*, Bill Kennedy's *Ironweed*—the list is endless. Publishers' salesmen treat good books with indifference and occasionally contempt. Bookstores won't order good books, or if they do, they cart them out the service door almost as soon as they come in. Newspapers and magazines—yes, even the *New Yorker*—aren't much interested in reviewing good books. Editors of journals don't think the arts matter; few ever have. Shaw used to boast about how he awed his editors, but you can't awe editors today. They really don't think the reviewing job is worth doing. But the best journalistic critics are authors themselves and know just how hard it is for a writer to make his voice heard, never mind

make a living from what he writes.

So, yes, we want to encourage young talent. But it's not one of our major jobs. The hardest thing to explain to an author, or his editor, is that we journalistic critics are not writing for literary magazines. We are not primarily responsible to the republic of letters. We are responsible to our readership, and their interests are not quite necessarily what mine would be as an explorer in the republic of letters. So when we have satisfied our obligations to the readers, then we have time to play around to see what interests us, what we can find and promote that perhaps other people don't know about. Yes, at that point I would rather find a new writer of fiction than almost anything else.

DLB: Your current collection is titled *Never in Doubt*, but if you were not in doubt at the time you wrote your pieces are there any books or writers you have reappraised up or down since the time you wrote about them?

PRESCOTT: The title is meant to be somewhat self-mocking. I once heard Leslie Fiedler refer to himself as "often wrong, but never in doubt." As for revising my evaluations, I can remember when a periodical called *New American Review* ran an early passage from Philip Roth's *Portnoy's Complaint*. I gave it a pretty bad review at the time. I changed my mind when the book was completed, and I saw the whole thing in place. I can think of a number of writers who have gone downhill in recent years— it would be unkind to name them—and none, I'm afraid, who have become better. I think I tend not to reassess the good books that a writer once wrote because like so many writers they tend to go on and write bad ones after the appearance of the first good one. It's the career of the writer taken as a whole that gets reassessed as the bad books continue to come. In my earlier years, there were probably a few books that I was too kind to. I would now either not review them or be a bit harder on them. Beyond that I'll pretty much stay with what I wrote.

DLB: I'd like to talk about the clout a mass-circulation critic has. A prominent novelist has said that all he cares about is four reviews: *New York Times Daily*, *New York Times Sunday*, *Newsweek*, and *Time*. He said if he gets reviews in those four publications, good or bad—it doesn't matter—his book will be a success in terms of sales.

PRESCOTT: That would be true of certain writers. I suspect most people who are familiar with the book reviewing media in this country would probably agree with your novelist on the top four. Fairly close after these come the *Washington Post* and maybe the *Los Angeles Times* and then you go into more specialized periodicals like the *New York Review of Books*. Those I guess are the top four, yet I am reasonably certain that you can write a book, even a good book, and get noticed by all four of these publications and still not have any success. I know, for instance, that I've had this kind of coverage for my books—with the exception of *Time*, which I hope will someday see the light. So I've had three out of the top four review my books, and it hasn't made a big commerical success out of them.

Again, we are not in the business of trying to make or break a writer commercially. We are trying to assess his achievement book by book and to suggest to our readers whether this individual book is worth their attention. Clout is a hard thing to define. People will sometimes come to you and refer

Dust jacket with caricature of Prescott by Gerry Gersten

to your power. Beware of your power, they will say. I like to claim that I don't have power. Editors have power; editors can get things done. They can make people do what they want them to do. Writers at best have influence, and there is quite a distinction between those two forces. I would like to think that what I say about a book will cause people either to be attracted to it or to shun it. But I have no illusions that anything I say about a really bad book by Harold Robbins or James Clavell or James Michener, for instance. . . . there's nothing I can do to prevent such authors from becoming immensely successful.

DLB: I think what this fellow was really thinking about was that a handful of publications that print book reviews have the ability to give a book exposure and visibility—which may or may not translate into sales—but most Americans may very well go through their lives never seeing a book review. Do you feel that book reviewing is really a private occupation, and that although there are lots of book buyers in America there are really very few book review readers.

PRESCOTT: It depends on what you mean by "few." When I was a kid growing up I never thought that I would be writing for an audience of perhaps twenty-four million people. Now that is not the number of people who read the book reviews in each issue of *Newsweek;* it is supposed to be about the number of people who read the magazine. How many of those people read the book reviews I couldn't tell you. But even if you were to take a conservative percent, say ten percent of the twenty-four million as readers of *Newsweek*'s book reviews, that is still a huge audience. It's the kind of audience that a sports team would be delighted to play for. I'm pleased because I think that probably the ratio between what we are trying to do, the people who take this job seriously—it's a peculiar job—and try to do it as well as we can, and the size of the audience is just about right. I find that I am allowed by my editors to write just as well as I can and with just as much of an intellectual spin on what I write as I'm capable of putting on it without anyone objecting and saying, "You're too highbrow," or "You're trying to clobber a readership that isn't equipped to read what you write." So if I can write as best as I can and get an audience of over two and a half million, perhaps considerably over, I'm pleased: that seems to me to be a sizable number of readers.

DLB: Do you feel there is a need for a national American book review such as the *Times Literary Supplement* in England?

PRESCOTT: A national publication may work in England, in a country that is as small as England, and a country with the class and educational systems constructed as they are in England. I don't think anything that's based on the English experience is going to have a similar success in this country. Probably the *New York Review of Books* is the closest attempt we've ever made to make a national publication based on the *TLS*, and it works to a degree. I'm not one of the world's greatest admirers of the *TLS*. I think it works very well for serious non-fiction. If you want to undertake volume eight of Bonar Law's official correspondence, and give it a 10,000-word review, no one is going to do that job better than the *TLS*. But if you want to review a batch of novels, the *TLS* generally turns in a pretty poor performance. So the question is, what kind of emphasis would you want in your national publication? I certainly would not want to have anything that so embraces the American intelligentsia as the *TLS* does in England, that performs as the *TLS* does. That would not be a useful service.

DLB: Each day hundreds of books get delivered to *Newsweek* for review. Probably you have as many as 1,000 possible books that you could review in a given week. How do you decide what your book of the week is?

PRESCOTT: This is done at a weekly book conference in which the editor of the arts sections meets with as many of the book reviewers as are available at the time, and sometimes we have others on long distance conference hook-ups talking with us. We go over lists that have been prepared by ourselves and by an assistant whose job it is to keep an eye out for upcoming books of importance; and we try to assess, sometimes for several weeks in advance, those books which ought to lead the section—the ones that will get the longest reviews and perhaps be the most important books—as well as the other books that will be noticed. Leaving at the same time whenever we can opportunity for space for individual enthusiasms and preferences of the reviewers themselves. This is not easily done, but it is perhaps more of a mechanical aspect of the book reviewing trade than any other part of it is. It simply means keeping in touch with the professional magazines that announce the forthcoming books, keeping abreast of the publishers' catalogues, keep-

ing an ear open to rumors. Once you convince yourself that you are on top of what is coming, then you have to think of what the magazine's editors want. The idea of what books we should be emphasizing changes from time to time as we change editors. We also try to bring to bear whatever understanding we have as to what our readers would prefer to read about. At the same time we try to keep a mix—we would like, if we can, in each section to have a mix of nonfiction and fiction, serious books and light books, with the occasional odd book that you would hardly expect to see reviewed in *Newsweek* at all. For instance, I once gave a very short review to a book called *An Encyclopedia of London.* It was a great big fat book and it had under individual entries everything you ever heard about London, every building, river, shop, the names of the people who were known to have lived in London, and so on. It was a gigantic thing and it would suit an Anglophile just down to the ground. Not the kind of book that *Newsweek* would normally review, but we just had the time and the space, and I was very pleased to see it there. So were our readers.

DLB: What is the size of the book review staff at *Newsweek*?

PRESCOTT: It fluctuates. At the moment we have two full-time reviewers who have been there for ages—myself and Walter Clemens. I've been there over sixteen years, Walter about fourteen. Then we have several part-time people. We have a woman who divides her time between dance and the book section. We have a man who divides his time between pop music and the book section. We have a free-lance writer we draw upon frequently, and we have one assistant.

DLB: Apprenticeship. You're an extraordinary case. You're the only son of a book reviewer I know of who became a book reviewer. Was it that when you were growing up and you saw your father—Orville Prescott of the *New York Times*—sitting around reading books and getting paid for it you said, "Gee, this is a pretty good way to live."

PRESCOTT: I think I once said exactly that at about the age of eight, and I said it in front of a party my parents were giving and there was much merriment about this. In fact, I never intended to grow up to be a book reviewer at all. I like to think that the fact that I followed in my father's profession is simply the way the world worked until just about our century. If you shoed horses for a living you expected your son to shoe horses when he grew up.

DLB: Were you encouraged by your father?

PRESCOTT: Absolutely. He was a great support, still is. Even though he disagrees with my approach and my taste from time to time, he manages nevertheless to be extremely supportive. I started out as an editor at a book publishing firm, and I spent most of my time writing reports on books for file drawers and for editorial conferences. I thought, what the heck, you enjoy doing this kind of thing and apparently you have some flair for it, why do it for a file drawer, why not do it for public consumption? So it was an easy shift for me from editorial work to being a book reviewer.

DLB: It just occurred to me what a crapshoot it is trying to be a full-time professional book reviewer. There are so few slots. You've got a better chance of being a professional baseball player.

PRESCOTT: Well, I didn't. Still, if you figure it out, there are three book critics on the *Times;* on *Time* and *Newsweek* combined full-time there are four of us, that's seven; then there's at least one on the *Washington Post,* that's eight; one on the *Los Angeles Times,* that's nine. Say there are fifteen of us in the country who make a full-time living doing book reviews, excluding the editors on the *New York Times Book Review.* I mean the people who actually do the writing of the reviews. I would be surprised if there were fifteen, possibly twenty, of us who do it full-time for a living. Part of this condition is the result of the contempt with which the book-reviewing craft is held by the editors of the journals across the country. Book reviewing is not considered by most editors an enterprise that they want to encourage. They tolerate it to a certain extent because they know that it is wanted by a certain percentage of their readers. Probably the average editor still thinks it is the housewife who is interested in this thing because real men don't read books. The result of this is that all too often the editor assigns a book for review to his wife or to a guy on the sports desk who isn't busy today. The job is not very well paid. Except for a few places at the top, where the pay is very decent, you find people getting twenty-five to one hundred bucks for a book review. I started out doing it for free for two years, and then I was promoted, or I promoted myself, to a freelance slot where I was being paid twenty-five dollars

a book review. You can't live like that.

DLB: Is part of the reason for editors' reluctance to waste space on book reviews that advertising budgets from publishers don't stretch to most papers, so that the editor says running book reviews doesn't bring us a nickel in revenue.

PRESCOTT: That's quite true and is an extremely important consideration. But it is their own bias, really, because sports don't bring in advertising either, and editorial pages don't bring it in. But try to find a newspaper that doesn't have a sports section and some kind of editorial section. It's a discontent that spreads over to the arts as a whole and the reason is very simple: the kind of man who runs the newspaper, his whole training, his frame of reference, the things that interest him have nothing to do with what's called soft news, the arts. He's interested in foreign news, domestic news, violence, politics, scandals, corruption, sex. If that concerns you all of your professional life, it's going to be very hard to persuade you that a new novel by a "lady writer" is worth anybody's space in the newspaper.

DLB: You said that the obvious solution probably won't work: book review publications. So is there any possible cure? Is there any way to convince some midwestern newspaper in a city of half a million population that it ought to have a Saturday book page or a Sunday book page?

PRESCOTT: I would say there must be because a number of these newspapers do have a Saturday book page or an arts page or culture page.

DLB: But the books coverage tends to be one review.

PRESCOTT: That's right. We won't get better coverage because the space isn't there. The editors don't want to pay people to do it. Perhaps they sense what they're getting isn't very good anyway.

DLB: Maybe they are right. Maybe their readership doesn't want it. It could be that they know exactly what they are doing.

PRESCOTT: Yet I know from the reception of my books that you get sometimes scores of reviews from little newspapers. I got two reviews from Bartlesville, Oklahoma, for my last book, but then it was not reviewed in some places I rather thought might review it. I find that a book of mine will bring in half a dozen reviews from South Carolina. I don't know what the answer is. These things are not done very well, but they're usually enthusiastic, so that takes the curse off the incompetence. Please understand I'm glad to have these reviews. I like the discourse about books around the nation. It doesn't have to be very well done.

DLB: If you were given a huge bankroll and told there's as much money as you need to do something about the state of book reviewing, book readership, book publishing, bookselling in America, what would be your first move?

PRESCOTT: If I had unlimited funds, really, I would conduct a study about book distribution. It seems to me from what I read that the worst part of the problem is that books simply are not made available. It's one thing for a reader of a newspaper or a magazine not to know about the existence of a book because it's not being reviewed. But it's quite another thing for that same reader who is kept in ignorance by the stuff he subscribes to, to be kept still in ignorance when he goes to his local bookstore because the books are not there. There is a total blackout on a large proportion of the books that come out in this country today simply because they do not get to the point where anybody can buy them even if they were to know about them. You hear from the publishers all the time how the books are moved from jobbers to warehouses to bookstore chains to the independent bookseller and so on. There is corruption involved; apparently books are purposely damaged. I would love to see that straightened out. The book publishers claim that they can't do it themselves, that they haven't got a clue as to how to get this thing done properly. Common sense tells the American businessman that yes, it can be done if you just knew how to start. If I had all the money in the world to figure it out, I ought to be able to hire the people who could do it.

Literary Research Archives V:
Kent State Special Collections

Alex Gildzen
Curator of Special Collections
Kent State University Libraries

It began modestly. A Romanian princess came to Kent State University in 1951 to dedicate a collection of materials about her mother, Queen Marie, which had been donated to the library by Ray Baker Harris of Washington, D.C. The next year university librarian John B. Nicholson acquired Kent's first major book collection, the library of Cleveland businessman Paul Louis Feiss. Among the 5,000 titles were 450 rare books, including Holinshed's *Chronicles* (1587), Walt Whitman's *Two Rivulets* (1876), the Kelmscott Chaucer (1896), and several incunabula.

The same year the Elizabeth Clark Tyler Miller collection of 35,000 bookplates was purchased. These and the Feiss rarities were kept in the librarian's office until 1958 when an addition to the library included a rare book room. In 1969 a department of special collections was established with founding curator Dean H. Keller responsible for moving the collection to the top floor of the twelve-story university library which opened in the fall of 1970.

Today the rare book and manuscript division of Kent State University Library's Department of Special Collections houses more than 15,000 catalogued books and 50,000 manuscripts with particular strengths in nineteenth- and twentieth-century American and British literature and history, as well as noteworthy holdings in bookplates, children's literature, comic books and books on the cinema, cryptography, graphic design, history of printing, parapsychology, theater, and Western Americana.

At first the collection grew slowly but deliberately based on the Feiss foundation. "Significant additions in 19th and 20th century English and American literature were made," remembers Keller, currently associate director for collection development and management, "including some of Dickens' novels in their original parts, books and manuscripts by Constance Holme, Logan Pearsall Smith and James Stephens, a group of first editions of James Fenimore Cooper and Samuel L. Clem-

ens, and a fine collection of the works of William Faulkner including first editions of most of his books, foreign editions, first periodical appearances and a large quantity of critical material."

When the university began offering doctoral programs in 1962, the fledgling collection began a period of serious growth. With the support of President Robert I. White, university librarian Hyman

Poet Robert Duncan reviews the manuscript of his "Medieval Scenes" with the founding curator of special collections, Dean H. Keller (Special Collections, Kent State University Library)

W. Kritzer made two major purchases in 1968 which shaped the collection.

First he acquired the complete stock—some 16,000 items—of the Charles S. Boesen bookstore in Detroit. From individual pieces, such as James Boswell's *Life of Johnson* (1791) and the sketchbooks of Miner Kellogg, to subject collections, including 3,500 titles by and about the Beat generation, this addition built on existing strengths while moving collections policy toward contemporary writers.

Then came what many believe was the largest library purchase ever made, the entire stock of Gilman's, the Crompond, New York, bookstore. Over a quarter million volumes, weighing 325 tons, came to Kent in seven over-the-road trailers. Although the majority of the purchase went into the main collection, curator Keller gleaned hundreds of items for Special Collections. Among them were the two-volume *History of the Expedition under the command of Captains Lewis and Clark to the sources of the Missouri* (1814) and four different editions of the Paris publication of James Joyce's *Ulysses* (first edition published in 1922).

At the same time Matthew J. Bruccoli presented his Raymond Chandler collection and later added collections of Ring Lardner, John O'Hara, and Nelson Algren.

The final blocks in the department's foundation were laid in 1969 with the purchase of the B. George Ulizio collection and establishment of the Robert L. Baumgardner, Jr. Memorial Collection of Contemporary Poetry. Ulizio was a prominent businessman in Philadelphia where he began collecting with his friends A. Edward Newton and Morris L. Parrish. He built and sold two distinguished collections before amassing the 1,500 volumes that would come to Kent. This was highlighted by fifty-six copyright deposit copies traded from the Library of Congress, including Ralph Waldo Emerson's *Nature* (1836) and Edward Bellamy's *Looking Backward* (1888). Other Ulizio high spots include the dedication copies of Edgar Allan Poe's *Tales of the Grotesque and Arabesque* (1840), John Galsworthy's *In Chancery* (1920), and presentation copies of Robert Frost's *A Boy's Will* (1913) and Joseph Conrad's *Chance* (1914). Also in his collection were letters from Henry W. Longfellow, Samuel Clemens, Theodore Dreiser, and Carl Sandburg.

Also in 1969 university trustee Robert L. Baumgardner and his wife began a contemporary poetry collection in memory of their son who had been a K.S.U. student. The establishing gift was a William Carlos Williams collection that included the manuscript of *Paterson, Book I* (1946) and his letters to David Ignatow. Early additions to this collection were Gary Snyder's letters to Will Petersen and the manuscript of his *Myths & Texts* (1956).

The next phase of growth for the department began with the move into elegant new quarters on the top floor of the new library in fall 1970. A wood-paneled reading room featured exhibition space for both the traditional (the Ulizio collection) and the avant-garde (the concrete poetry of Michael McCafferty). Additionally there was a workroom, curator's office, and closed shelves. During the initial decade in its first real home the department continued building on strengths, especially in modern poetry, while establishing itself as a serious research center in the theatrical arts and film.

In 1970 playwright Jean-Claude van Itallie began depositing the record of a career which had blossomed the decade before Off-Broadway. Resident writer at the beginning of the Open Theater, he went on to achieve international fame with his controversial *America Hurrah* (produced in 1966). In addition to donating the manuscripts of all his plays and his adaptations of Chekhov, van Itallie gives his correspondence and ongoing files on a regular basis. Before the Open Theater disbanded in 1973 members of the group voted to maintain its archives at Kent State. That collection consists of manuscripts, photographs, posters, business files, clippings, props, and costumes. Visiting scholars from around the world have called it one of the most complete archives of any avant-garde company available to the public. To these rich interlocking collections actor-director Joseph Chaikin, founder of the Open Theater, added his papers which include the manuscript of *The Presence of the Actor* (1972) and his correspondence with Samuel Beckett, Eric Bentley, Peter Brook, Adrienne Kennedy, and Sam Shepard. The Open Theater's administrative assistant Marianne de Pury-Thompson, who also composed the music for *Viet Rock* (1966), donated her papers to the collection. Playwright Susan Yankowitz gave her working papers for *Terminal* (produced in 1969), company member Rhea Gaisner supplied photographs, programs, and other support material, and critic Eileen Blumenthal donated the manuscript of *Joseph Chaikin: Exploring at the Boundaries of Theater* (1984). To mark the twentieth anniversary of the Open Theater's founding, the library, in conjunction with the university's school of theater, sponsored a conference which brought Chaikin, van Itallie, Pury-Thompson, Gaisner, Yankowitz, and Blumenthal to campus for a reunion with other members of the legendary company whose productions of *The Serpent* (1968), *Mutation Show* (1971), and *Nightwalk* (1972) were examined.

The Collection of Motion Picture & Television Performing Arts was founded in 1971 by Lois Wilson, who played Daisy Buchanan in the silent film version of *The Great Gatsby* (1926). Her collection of rare silent film stills and memorabilia from a career that spanned sixty years serve as a core. To this was added the personal reference library and newsreel collection of two-time Academy Award-winning producer Robert Youngson. Supplementing these are collections by several prominent film historians: the papers of Gerald Mast, author of *A Short History of the Movies* (1971); the reference library of James Robert Parish, author of *The MGM Stock Company* (1973); the press book and still collections of Alvin H. Marill, author of *Movies Made for Television* (1980); and the clipping

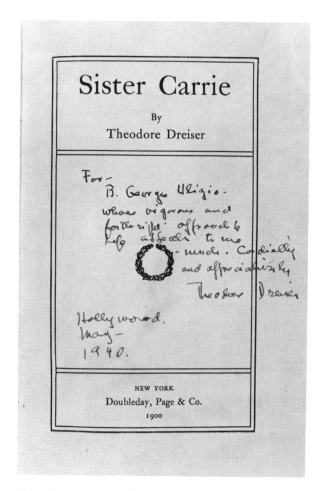

One of many presentation copies in the library of B. George Ulizio which came to Kent shortly before his death in 1969 (Special Collections, Kent State University Library)

files of Jim Meyer, former film critic of the *Miami Herald.*

The department's holdings in children's literature were bolstered by two major acquisitions. The archives of Akron's Saalfield Publishing Company were purchased in 1977 and the Roy Van-Devier collection in 1985. For sixty years Saalfield was a major imprint of children's books. Their archives include manuscripts by Frances Trego Montgomery from the Billy Whiskers series and by James Ball Naylor, as well as Shirley Temple paper-dolls, original artwork, business files, coloring books, sewing cards, dot books, and activity boxes. VanDevier, author of *A Son of Michigan: or a Short Biography of Byron A. Dunn* (1949), was an Akron collector and book dealer specializing in juveniles. His collection of thousands of entries in such popular series as the Rover Boys, the Young Kentuckians, and the Frank Merriwell dime novels occupies ninety-three shelves. Recently the library became the depository for the papers of two contemporary writers for children, Virginia Hamilton, winner of the Newbery Medal for *M. C. Higgins, the Great* (1975), and Cynthia Rylant, a Newbery Honor winner for *A Fine White Dust* (1986).

A major manuscript collection which has been coming to the department over the past decade are the papers of poet-filmmaker James Broughton, whose seventy-fifth birthday next year will be celebrated by Paragon House with the publication of a Broughton reader. His collection includes journals, working prints of his films, drafts, and correspondence with Helen Adam, Stan Brakhage, Robert Duncan, Willard Maas, Frank O'Hara, Robert Peters, and Eve Triem.

The papers of Charles Wesley Slack (1825-1885), editor of the *Boston Commonwealth* and a Massachusetts legislator, were donated by his great-grandson Paul C. Kitchin, emeritus professor of political science. Among the 750 items are letters from Henry David Thoreau, Ralph Waldo Emerson, Frederick Douglass, Edward Everett Hale, and Henry Ward Beecher. In 1978 Stephen R. Donaldson, who earned a Master of Arts in English from Kent seven years earlier, began depositing his manuscripts which now include the first and second *Chronicles of Thomas Covenant: The Unbeliever* (1977) and a pair of detective novels published under the pseudonym Reed Stephens.

One of the most significant manuscript collections to be donated to Special Collections came in 1985. Professor Vivian H. Pemberton of Kent's Trumbull campus discovered a cache of more than a hundred letters to and from Hart Crane. The letters, which had been in the possession of the poet's cousin, Betty Crane Madden, were written between 1917 and 1932, the year of Crane's death. Of particular interest is the correspondence between the poet and his father and Crane's carbon of his 1930 letter to Yvor Winters defending *The Bridge* (1930). Although the gist of the contents had been surmised by critics, the original was destroyed by Winters. "Kent State's acquisition of the letters includes it in the very limited number of public institutions where indispensable Crane materials are located," noted John Unterecker, author of *Voyager* (1969), the definitive biography of the poet.

Among the little magazines with archives at Kent are Cid Corman's *Origin* (third and fourth series), John Perreault's *Elephant,* and Coburn H. Britton's *Prose.* The department houses the manuscripts of several contemporary novels, including Robert Lowry's *Casualty* (1946), Leo Rosten's *Captain Newman, M.D.* (1961), Max Weatherly's *The Mantis and the Moth* (1964), Robert Kelly's *The Scorpions* (1966), and Thomas McMenamin's *Call Me Manneschewitz* (1971).

Key author holdings include the Walter and Virginia Wojno collection of Joseph Conrad, the Josiah Q. Bennett collection of Flannery O'Connor, and in-depth collections of Charles Brockden Brown, Stephen Crane, Sherwood Anderson, Djuna Barnes, Anaïs Nin, and Paul Metcalf.

The library of the American Cryptogram Association was deposited at Kent in 1971. More recently Special Collections acquired the archives of the Broadcast Designers Association and the University and College Designers Association.

The Virginia Glenn Memorial Collection of Readings in Human Potential was established by Stanley Krippner, author of *Song of the Siren* (1975). One of the most respected names in parapsychol-ogy, Krippner later donated his papers, including letters from Timothy Leary, Gardner Murphy, J. B. Rhine, and Alan Watts.

Other collections include the library of William E. Warner, a pioneer in technology education, the G. Harry Wright showboat collection, the diaries of naturalist George Jason Streator, the Lillian Zevin collection of World Publishing Company imprints, the papers of poet Collister Hutchison, memorabilia of local vaudevillian Andy Purman, the Frank B. Queen collection of Western Americana, *The Gestalt Journal* collection of Frederick Perls tapes, and the papers of poet-playwright Marc Kaminsky.

In addition to the traditional tasks of uncovering, processing, and interpreting research materials, the department from its beginnings has been active in publishing. Dean Keller edited *The Serif: Quarterly of the Kent State University Libraries* (1964-1975) and inaugurated a series of *Occasional Papers* (1968-1972) which included *The Cataloguing Requirements of the Book Division of a Rare Book Library* and *A Festschrift for Djuna Barnes on Her 80th Birthday.* His successor has begun a second series of *Occasional Papers* which includes Stephen R. Donaldson's well-received *Epic Fantasy in the Modern World.* Special Collections also issues broadsides, such as James Broughton's *Packing Up for Paradise* (1977) and William Bronk's *Sizes* (1980), and catalogs which have included introductions by Paul Metcalf and Jonathan Williams.

From modest beginnings the department of special collections looks forward to its twentieth anniversary knowing it supports not only the research needs of Kent State University's students and faculty but the international community of scholars who acknowledge use of its holdings in a growing number of books and articles.

The Booker Prize

Martyn Goff

The Booker Prize was first announced in 1969. Booker McConnell, now Booker PLC, is a conglomerate whose interests include health foods, supermarkets, and authors. The authors' division arose through a tax loophole whereby writers like Ian Fleming, Agatha Christie, Denis Wheatley, and Harold Pinter sold their copyrights to Booker who then paid them salaries and expenses. The Chancellor of the Exchequer soon put a stop to this tax dodge, but the division remained and has been profitable since its establishment. Whether it was this that led Bookers to listen sympathetically when approached by Tom Maschler of Jonathan Cape and the Publishers Association about setting up a prize is not firmly established. But set one up they did with the prize being worth at the outset £5,000.

The prize has always had two objectives, to reward the writer of the best novel of the year and to increase the public's awareness and appreciation of serious fiction. It has certainly done the second. The first is arguable and has been argued over, as soon as the result is known, every year. What must be emphasized, however, is that the prize is not for a body of work, but for the best novel of the year. Iris Murdoch may have written a string of excellent novels; but if in any given year hers is not the best, then the prize should not be awarded to her.

For the first two years, 1969 and 1970, the prize was run by the Publishers Association. In 1971 it was transferred to the National Book League for administration and publicity. The NBL was (it changed its name in September 1986 to Book Trust) an independent charitable trust whose remit was and is to promote reading and books. In 1970 a new Director, Martyn Goff, was appointed. He had a special interest in book prizes, which is shown by the fact that the NBL was then running one prize and now runs fifteen, with the Booker as the jewel in the crown.

Soon after the NBL took over, a basic structure and plan were worked out which have operated until today with very little change. Bookers appoint a management committee which consists of a hardback and paperback publisher, a bookseller, a librarian, an author, the chairman, and one other director of Bookers and the Director of the National Book League. This committee has two tasks, to appoint the judges and to review the rules and amend as necessary. Normally, three meetings are held each year. The first, in February, is to appoint the judges for the current year; the second is to meet the chairman of the judges whom they have appointed; and the third is to consider the success (or otherwise) of the year's prize and so is held just after the dinner at which the award is made.

In 1978 the amount of the prize was upped to £10,000 for the winner, though Bookers were still against the idea of rewarding the runners-up. The prize was still only making mild progress in the public's consciousness, even though there was a scandal connected with the 1972 award. John Berger, who won the prize for his book *G*, discovered that Bookers had sugar plantations. So, on being given the prize, he promised to hand half of it to the Black Power movement. Unfortunately he was misinformed: Bookers had long since been dispossessed of their sugar plantations, and the Black Power movement no longer existed.

In 1980 the prize really came into its own when there was a much-publicized finish between William Golding, who won for *Rites of Passage*, and Anthony Burgess for his *Earthly Powers*. As a result the 1981 prize was lifted on to an altogether different plane. To begin with it was the subject of an hour-long live television program. It was also won by a previously unknown novelist, Salman Rushdie, for his book, *Midnight's Children*.

Nineteen eighty and 1981 marked the emergence of the prize in a way that saw it achieve international status. Serious national newspapers began to feature not just the winning announcement but even the shortlist on their front pages. In 1983 the prize was won by the South African novelist J. M. Coetzee, and the 1985 prize was claimed by a New Zealander, Keri Hulme, for a first novel, *The Bone People*.

Nineteen eighty-four saw a surprise win since all the advance speculation had designated J. G. Ballard as the winner; however, Anita Brookner

Kingsley Amis (photo ©Jerry Bauer)

committing the publishers to entering the books in question for Booker.

In sum the prize has achieved its aim. Huge extra copies of serious novels have been bought and borrowed (from public libraries); and many of the authors who have won have become worldwide figures overnight. The prize has, too, given a fillip to the literary scene that it much needed. It has also, clearly, fulfilled the expectations of its sponsors.

Address by Anthony Thwaite, Chairman of The Booker Prize Judges

received the prize for *Hotel du Lac*. This speculation was not confined to the press, radio, and television. One of Britain's most famous bookmaking firms began to run a "book" on the Prize. Brookner's novel sold 85,000 copies against the 4,000 to 5,000 that she had habitually sold until then. However, *The Bone People*, a serious and somewhat experimental book by a new writer, sold only about 35,000 copies. Shortlisted books began to add a minimum of 10,000 copies to their hardback sales. But mention of such figures does not take into account the enormous financial and other advantages both of being shortlisted and above all of winning. Today students do theses on Booker; fifty British Council libraries round the world are running Booker Display competitions as are many United Kingdom libraries; seminars and conferences are held on the shortlisted books (and even on those that some think should have been shortlisted).

In 1984 the prize went up to £15,000, but its reputation has now grown to a point where the actual amount is no longer important. In Britain both the Whitbread and Trask prizes are worth more than Booker but fail to get a tithe of the publicity. Book Trust produces a large amount of publicity, including posters, showcards, bookmarks, and tapes for local radio stations; publishers band "Booker Winner" or "Booker Shortlist" round their books; and booksellers order automatic scale-outs of the shortlisted books months in advance. It is not all smooth sailing. There were over 120 entries in 1986, which makes the judges' task unenviable. Publishers have started to keep all their aces for middle autumn publication, distorting fiction releases throughout the year. Literary agents have begun demanding clauses in contracts

Now that the announcement has been made, and all the excitement has evaporated as the television cameras move away, and all the postmortems are being carried out, and all of us have had a lot to eat and drink, and all of us are tired, it's hard to know quite what it's appropriate to say. I promise you I shan't go on for long.

It seems to have become customary for Booker Prize chairpersons to make general remarks about The Novel. I don't intend to do so. We all know what a novel is. True, my fellow judges and I have spent an intensive five months exploring the thing; and perhaps *what* we've found out is that it is an extraordinarily resilient as well as various form. It can be something Homer (whoever he or she was) would be able to recognise in 1986, and, again, something which might even have surprised James Joyce. It can be as apparently straightforward as *David Copperfield*, and as apparently devious as *Tristram Shandy*. In judging the novels this year, we have not tried to achieve "balance," or looked deliberately for "novelty," or for "tradition." We've tried to avoid any sense of playing the market—whatever the market may be.

What I think we've all emerged with, after our hours and days and months of reading and rereading, is a strong feeling that there are very many novels being written today, in English, within the terms of reference of the Booker Prize, which can stand comparison with all but the best novels of the past 200 or so years. We are *not* living in a dead period of fiction, for all the rubbish that's published, including some submitted for the Booker, and indeed for all the rubbish that sells. In the house of fiction there are many mansions, and most of them are inhabited.

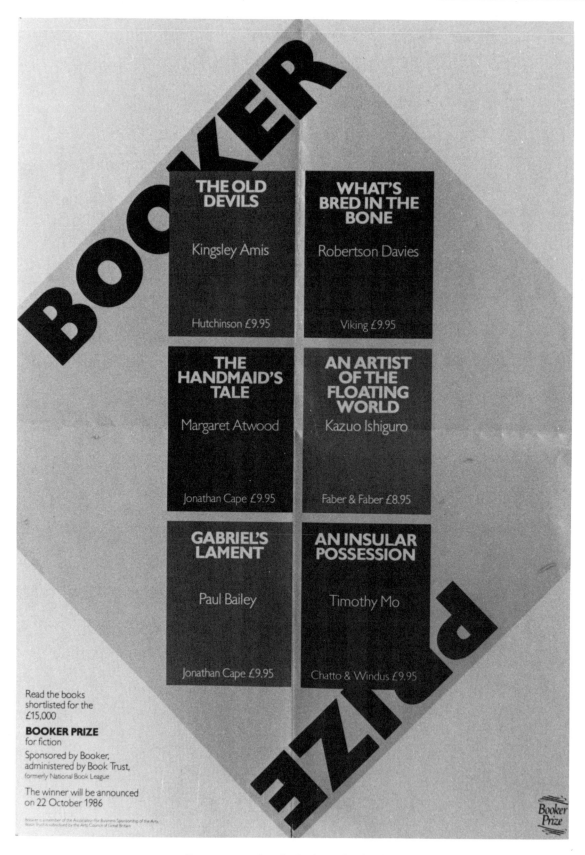

Poster announcing the Booker Prize shortlist

I want now to indulge in an act of whimsy which isn't just whimsy. I ask you to cast your minds back to the Booker Prize presentation, 1886—an occasion remembered by surprisingly few people. But for those who do remember, that the chairman of the judges was Mr. Edmund Gosse. His fellow judges were Mr. Austin Dobson, Mr. Andrew Lang, Professor J. E. Thorold Rogers (representing both economies and the man in the street), and Mrs. Gladstone.

They were faced with a formidable task. A lot of novels were published in 1886—though not nearly as many as in 1986. The judges had, by the end of September, arrived at a shortlist. In their private conclaves, some of them had pressed hard for an especial favourite: Mrs. Frances Hodgson Burnett's *Little Lord Fauntleroy.* Mrs. Gladstone had made particular protestations for this. But it was finally felt that it had to be considered as a book primarily suitable for children, and therefore—perhaps—not quite eligible; though Mrs. Gladstone continued to say that Mrs. Burnett's book had done more than anything else in the history of literature to strengthen the bond between Britain and the United States of America.

Some apparent candidates excluded themselves quite quickly, through being ineligible through nationality. For example, there was a novel by Mr. Henry James, called *The Bostonians;* well-written, civilised, it was judged to be of merit by Mr. Gosse and Mr. Dobson—but it turned out that Mr. James was an American citizen, and therefore disqualified.

But these exclusions still left six strong contenders. There was Miss Marie Correlli's *A Romance of Two Worlds,* which made up in sentiment what it perhaps lacked in finesse and high seriousness. There were *two* novels by the young Mr. George Gissing—infinitely depressing, but truly serious. A more popular contender was Mr. Rider Haggard: his *King Solomon's Mines* followed the frequent Booker Prize penchant for fictions set in exotic places. And finally there was a duel between what emerged as the favourites: Mr. Robert Louis Stevenson's *Dr. Jekyll and Mr. Hyde,* and Mr. Thomas Hardy's *The Mayor of Casterbridge.* Mr. Stevenson had the edge when it came to Youth (a criterion about which several of the judges were concerned). Mr. Hardy, on the other hand, had both the High Seriousness and the Rural vote.

There are gaps in the record here, I'm sorry to say. No one seems to remember who won. The main thing, it seems, was the shortlist; and it's true to say that at any rate half the books on that 1886

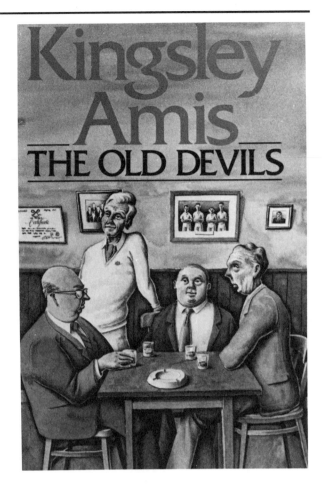

Dust jacket for the Hutchinson edition of the 1986 Booker Prize novel

shortlist remain with us. I hope it will be true that the 1986 shortlist will still remain in the year 2086, to be read and enjoyed.

And that, I think, is the point, or part of the point. We were asked by the Booker Prize Management Committee to pick novels which we considered would still be read in twenty years time. My whimsy about 1886 puts the problem even more sharply into perspective. How can we presume, now, to choose six novels—indeed, a winning novel too—which will be read and enjoyed *twenty* years from now, let alone a century from now? The present-day critic, or judge, or reader, isn't *always* wrong, it's true. His contemporaries knew that Dickens was great, and he still is. You just can't predict. What we do know is that we've settled on six novels which we believe in, which we hope and trust will still be read in twenty years time, and which—if there is still a world for such things—have a strong chance of being read in a hundred years time. To the Booker sponsors and organisers, our thanks; to the novelists on the shortlist—and in particular to the winner—our congratulations. And now your chairman, after the curious and not entirely pleasing experience of having been famous for five minutes, can go back to his more congenial obscurity.

A COMMENT

from PENELOPE FITZGERALD

It's a business-sponsored prize which, like many institutions over here, seems to have grown in importance as though it had a life of its own. In 1977 I remember my asking my (then) publisher what the Booker was, & he told me that there was a dinner where the runners-up were presented with copies of their books bound in leather, & the winner got a cheque, & everyone had to wear evening dress: he himself had had to borrow a dinner jacket from a cousin, who was fortunately the same size as himself. (I'd like to add that this publisher has done so well since that he could buy any number of dinner jackets.) My first novel (apart from a mystery story), *The Bookshop*, was on the Booker List of 1978 (the prize that year was won by Iris Murdoch), and although the dinner wasn't very good, I enjoyed it. I queued up behind Kingsley Amis, like children on Speech Day, to receive my leather-bound *Bookshop*.

In 1979 Collins published my novel *Offshore*, which was a reflection, as true as I could make it, of life in the barges moored along the River Thames, the feeling of belonging neither to land or water, & of our emotional struggle which ran parallel with that. This novel won the Booker (the judges, of course, are different every year); however, I hadn't been expected to win it, & had already been asked to appear on a BBC programme for the runners-up. When I arrived at the studio as a winner I could see that the organisers were disconcerted, not to say irritated. Things are better adjusted now, & the element of surprise is one of the greatest assets of the Booker award.

I felt proud (and still do) that the judges had liked my book and had appreciated the true point of what I had written. The award made a very great difference to my career & to my confidence as a writer. From a general point of view, I am sure the Booker has succeeded, as it set out to do, in increasing public interest in the novel and novelists—who, in Britain, are a very lowly class of human being.

A COMMENT

from NADINE GORDIMER

When I received the Booker Prize in the mid-Seventies it did not have the apparently great influence on sales that it has now. I was already an established writer and it made very little difference to the sales of my books; other factors, over the years, have widened my readership. I would say that other literary awards I've received, in other countries, have had a greater effect in bringing me new readers. As for any effect the Booker or any other prize might have on the actual direction of my work, the answer is: none. I have gone my own way without consideration of prizes.

A COMMENT

from P. H. NEWBY

I was the first recipient of the Booker Prize (1969) and it made little difference to my sales and certainly none to my career. The fact is that the prize had not yet established itself with the reading public who, in this country (unlike France and possibly the USA) did not *at that time* take literary prizes at all seriously. As time went by, however, and well-known writers like Iris Murdoch and William Golding received the prize it really took off. The most recent winner, Kingsley Amis, received an enormous amount of publicity and must have sold thousands of extra copies as a result. Mind you, he is a popular writer anyway and I daresay he would have been in the best-seller list even if he had not won the prize. But I think the Booker has achieved what its promoters initially intended—to publicize quality fiction and promote sales. The novel is enjoying a comeback here and Booker must have played a large part in that.

A COMMENT

from BERNICE RUBENS

Winning the Booker Prize had a dramatic effect on my writing career. Quite simply, it made the difference between earning and not earning a living as a writer. Since *The Elected Member* (10 books ago), I have lived entirely off my work as a novelist. It was the first book that I was able to publish in

America. The others have followed. The prize also opened doors to paperback and foreign rights.

This year when the prize was awarded (wrongly I thought) to Kingsley Amis, I was on the judges' panel so I have seen the prize from both corners. It's very much a "Miss World" business. The prize is conditioned by personal taste. All the jurors this year were over 50, nudging old age, so it was obvious that their choice would be *The Old Devils*. When I won it, I think the jury was into drug addiction! It's important for a winner to be aware of the fact that he has not necessarily written the best book of the year. They have simply taken the judges' fancy. Still, I'm not complaining. It paid for my little hideaway on Majorca.

WINNERS OF THE BOOKER PRIZE: 1969-1986

1969—P. H. Newby, *Something to Answer For*

1970—Bernice Rubens, *The Elected Member*

1971—V. S. Naipaul, *In A Free State*

1972—John Berger, *G*

1973—J. G. Farrell, *The Siege of Krishnapur*

1974—Nadine Gordimer, *The Conservationist*

1975—Ruth Prawer Jhabvala, *Heat and Dust*

1976—David Storey, *Saville*

1977—Paul Scott, *Staying On*

1978—Iris Murdoch, *The Sea, The Sea*

1979—Penelope Fitzgerald, *Offshore*

1980—William Golding, *Rites of Passage*

1981—Salman Rushdie, *Midnight's Children*

1982—Thomas Keneally, *Schindler's Ark*

1983—J. M. Coetzee, *Life & Times of Michael K.*

1984—Anita Brookner, *Hotel du Lac*

1985—Keri Hulme, *The Bone People*

1986—Kingsley Amis, *The Old Devils*

The University of Iowa Writers' Workshop Golden Jubilee

23-25 May 1986

Lewis Turco

On Friday, 23 May the Writers' Workshop of the University of Iowa began its three-day Golden Jubilee celebration of the fiftieth anniversary of the founding of the oldest and most influential writing arts program in the world. A chartered bus took some of the early arrivals to Iowa City from the Cedar Rapids airport, among them Eugene Cantalupe, of the generation of John Berryman; the younger David Lunde from SUNY College at Fredonia; and Scott Heller, a young journalist who had attended Iowa, but not the Workshop—he was back to cover the story.

Registration began at 4:00 P.M. at the Iowa Memorial Union. John Gilgun from St. Joseph, Missouri, was among the first to put his name on the sign-up sheet for the Marathon Reading that was to take place that night. Joe Nigg, a Coloradan and editor of company publications for Re/Max in Englewood, and Sam Hamod from Washington, D.C.—both graduates of the Workshop, but at different times—got into a conversation. This would be the pattern for the whole Jubilee, which was at once a reunion of classmates, a convention of writers, a meeting of correspondents and of friends from various places other than Iowa, a gathering of people who had shared publishing space for years and sometimes decades but who had not previously come face-to-face, and a mob of total strangers. It was a peculiarly exhilarating atmosphere that began to build early.

Before things got going officially some of the Jubileers found their way downtown to the Prairie Lights Bookstore, where there was a table full of recent books by Iowa writers. The store was much larger and more prosperous than the original Iowa City paperback store, The Paper Place, which had been tacked together in 1959 by graduate students including Mike and Marlene Fine, who had returned for the Jubilee. An often-recollected scene involved the Fines, who were putting up shelves prior to the opening of their shop: they had the frames for the bookcases up; one person would lift a shelf to the frame, and someone else would scribe it about a half-foot in at each end. After a while an onlooker said, "Can I ask you a question, Mike?"

"Sure," he replied.

"Instead of cutting six inches off each end of the board, why don't you just cut twelve off one end?" There was an abashed silence for a while and everyone began to blush.

"That sounds like something I'd do," Mike said when he was reminded of the episode at the cocktail party in the evening. But the shelves stood until The Paper Place burned down a decade or so later, long after the Fines had left town to return to Manhattan, where Mike became involved in publishing with Simon and Schuster.

Upstairs over the bookstore a coffeehouse called The Renaissance II had been the scene of poetry readings by students in the Iowa program. Though there had always been readings by eminent visiting writers, and sometimes Iowa faculty as well, student readings were something of an innovation in the early 1960s. The coffeehouse was the scene also of many other activities, such as organizing the new anti-establishment student paper, the *Iowa Defender*, which was intended to stand against the philistinism of the establishment paper, the *Daily Iowan*. The "I.D." became a lively and interesting underground venture while it lasted. It would be replicated often nationwide during the '60s.

The next stop after Prairie Lights was across the Iowa River, which flows through the center of campus. The opening cocktail party and buffet was held at the Iowa Museum of Art at 6:00 P.M. It was here that writers began to meet the other writers they'd come to see. Scott Heller was circulating and interviewing people. Paul Engle, the earliest director of the Workshop, was present and continually surrounded by a changing crowd of friends and former students. With Paul was his wife Hualing, currently director of the Translation Workshop, which Paul had founded and with which he had been affiliated until his retirement.

There seemed to be a large contingent of writers from the SUNY system: besides Lunde, Donald Petersen was present from Oneonta, as was Gregory Fitz Gerald, recently retired from the faculty at Brockport. Donald Justice, who had spent two lengthy terms at Iowa first as a graduate student and then as a faculty member, arrived and was soon almost as mobbed as Paul Engle. Among those with whom he was reunited were the poet Mark Strand, currently living in Salt Lake City, who had taken his M.A. in 1962; Kim Merker, poet and fine editions printer for the University; Nick Crome from Colorado.

It was at the cocktail party that a division among the participants became noticeable: there was an older "Engle crowd" and a younger "post-Engle group." Although the two intermingled physically, there was remarkably little interaction between them. The two groups remained spiritually and conversationally discrete. This situation was formalized later at the "Decade Parties" that took place beginning at 9:00 P.M. in a tent in the field across from the entrance to the Iowa House, the hotel and conference center that had been built as a wing of the Memorial Union.

John Leggett, soon to retire as director of the Workshop for the past sixteen years, was circulating among the post-Engle students, but Vance Bourjaily, his immediate predecessor, did not attend. As one searched among the faces for old friends, it became evident that there were quite a few people missing. Of these, a considerable percentage had evidently boycotted the Jubilee on principle. As one person put it when asked whether he would attend, "I didn't see my name or the names of any of my friends on the program, so I guess I'll pass." Another, who did attend, later wrote in a letter, "this is the same point I made in 1959—that the clique system, the star system is nonsense." Others were discussing the haves and have-nots as well, and the word began to circulate that the Workshop was not to blame; rather, it appeared that the Iowa Foundation had made the final decisions about everything, including the program, without a great deal of consultation with Leggett and his faculty.

Many others didn't attend owing to circumstances of various sorts. The novelist Hortense Calisher, who had been a staff member in 1959-1960,

and her husband Curtis Harnack, the outgoing director of Yaddo, were among these. So was John Irving, who was back in Vienna, scene of episodes in several of his novels. David Duer, a young man who edits a little magazine called *Luna Tack* in West Branch, a town fifteen miles distant, was perhaps overfamiliar with the Iowa City scene, and he had family responsibilities that prevented his attendance as well. John Gilgun said of Duer, "He's the kind of person this Jubilee is all about," the unsung laborer in the literary vineyards.

Leigh Allison Wilson, a recent Iowa M.F.A. and post-graduate James A. Michener Fellow, now a fiction teacher at SUNY Oswego, felt that she'd not been away from Iowa long enough to feel nostalgic about it. Leggett and James McPherson, of the Iowa staff, asked about Wilson, and so did the novelist and National Public Radio columnist Doris Grumbach—"Tell her to write, call, or *something*," she said later. Such frustration was typical among many of the attendees who, though they were enjoying themselves, would have liked it much better if *everyone* had been present. Though not everyone was, the final tally was 457 registrants; about 300 had originally been expected.

Nor were only writers and journalists present—Arthur Small, a state legislator from Iowa City, currently running for Lieutenant Governor of Iowa, was among those circulating on the plaza of the Art Museum. Magazine editors, publishers, and agents made their opening contacts, socialized, and toured the museum.

In the Union at the same time the Marathon Reading was taking place. It was mostly the young people who were participating, not the older crowd such as Phil Levine, Melvin Walker LaFollette, and Henri Coulette; but Gilgun and Harold Bond from Melrose, Massachusetts, enlisted and closed the show.

Back at the decade parties a young woman was overheard to say, "The poets of the older generation do that formal sort of thing so well, but we've never learned how." While she was being told by a member of that older generation of the return to formalism that was currently going on in American poetic letters, the recently published neoformalist anthology *Strong Measures: Contemporary American Poetry in Traditional Forms*, edited by Philip Dacey and David Jauss, was mentioned. At that moment Dacey walked up and introduced himself—he said he'd heard somebody talking about his book and came over to see who it was.

The next morning, C. Michael Curtis of the *Atlantic*, Dan Menaker of the *New Yorker*, and Theo-

Paul Engle (former Workshop director), Hualing Nieh Engle (Director of the University of Iowa International Writing Program), University of Iowa President James O. Freedman and Mrs. Freedman, visiting Czechoslovakian translator Igor Navratil, and writer James McPherson (photo by Rodney White)

dore Solotaroff participated in the 9:30 panel on the "Care & Nurture of New Writers." One of the many writing teachers present took the microphone during the question period of that session to say that he felt the Iowa Workshop had spawned too many replications in the form of graduate programs over the years, and that undergraduate programs that trained young people for jobs other than those few available in college-level writing arts faculties would have been of greater service. For every college-level teaching job in writing now there are scores of applicants, and the average income of free-lance writers in the U.S. is still under $5000 per annum. Joe Nigg, who had tried it both ways, agreed. "I got tired of starving and hopping around," he said, "so I got a job in industry. I've never regretted it."

Edwin C. Cohen, Frank Conroy, Gerald Freund, and Kenneth Hope gave a panel on "Grants & Arts Colonies" at 10:35, and at 11:40 there was one on the "University as Patron" with

the President of the University of Iowa, James Freedman, Doris Grumbach, the poet Michael Harper, John Leggett, and Paul Engle. It wasn't, however, much of a panel, for the opening statements of each participant took up all the time allotted. When he took the stand at last, Engle was reborn. No longer a seventy-eight-year-old retiree, he suddenly was transformed into the old, feisty, funny, slippery-tongued pepperpot he used to be. He was absolutely at the top of his form. Most of the people present were transported, amazed, and delighted. It was certainly the high spot of the conference to that point.

In the afternoon, pursued by the omnipresent photographers and a television crew, Paul Engle went over to talk with Justice and his coterie of poets including Henri Coulette, Philip Levine, Melvin Walker LaFollette, and several others lunching at a table near an open tent flap where there was a bit of warm air moving. One cameraman wanted to get Engle in a "candid" shot walking down the street with his friends and tried to recruit a large group of people including the poets Jane Cooper, Donald Petersen, Michael Harper and the Justice group who were playing word-games; but the photo session turned into a free-for-all snapfest and it was many minutes before everyone was walking down the street talking and laughing self-consciously while the lenses blinked and the sound crew dangled the boom-mike overhead.

At 2:00 P.M. there was a panel on "The Writing of the 80's" with Russell Banks, Tess Gallagher, Levine, Mark Strand, Charles Simic, and Hilma Wolitzer. One listener summed it up this way: "I guess you're supposed to get on the trend wagon or be left behind, but if you do, you have to despise yourself because you've sold out." The 3:05 panel was "Renaissance in the Short Story" with T. Coraghessan Boyle, Ray Carver, James McPherson, Bob Schacochis, and Stephanie Vaughn. It appeared that Syracuse University, where Carver and Tobias Wolff teach, is the trendsetter, or at least this was the impression left by some of the panel.

The 4:10 panel was "Trends in Poetry: New Directions for the 90's." James Tate, the moderator, wasn't serious and did a fair amount of clowning. Most of the rest of the panelists—Marvin Bell, Daniel Halpern, Michael Palmer, and Charles Wright—seemed not to agree on where the literary scene was going. Jorie Graham was the only one who mentioned neoformalism, but she did so in the specific context of feminist writing.

The President's reception took place at Dr. Freedman's house at 102 Church Street at 6:00 P.M. The house was crammed to overflowing, and a TV crew held sway in the sunporch where they were interviewing Paul Engle among others. George Keithley, whose poetry book *The Donner Party* was a best-selling phenomenon in 1972, fought for elbow room with Tess Gallagher and her escort Ray Carver. Robley Wilson, Jr., editor of the *North American Review*, Robert Patrick Dana, James Baker Hall, and William Dickey from San Francisco State helped themselves to hors d'oeuvres and exchanged pleasantries. Doris Grumbach expressed her regret over the recent death of her N.P.R. colleague John Ciardi. Jorie Graham held her small daughter tightly by the hand as they inched their way through the crowd.

At the 7:30 Jubilee Dinner the tables were reserved by decades. The Fines, Gilgun, Nigg, Kent Baker, and Keithley sat together at a '60s table where they found waiting at their places copies of *Seems Like Old Times*, an anthology of reminiscences of the Workshop edited evidently at breakneck speed by Ed Dinger. Masters-of-ceremony were John Leggett, Doris Grumbach, and Galway Kinnell. President Freedman gave the welcome.

The members of John Berryman's class read poems: Jane Cooper, Coulette, Dana, Dickey, Ronald DiLorenzo, Shirley Eliason, Justice, LaFollette, Levine, Petersen, Paul Petrie. Henri read a poem sent by Pulitzer Prize-winner W. D. Snodgrass, who, when he tried to come from his Mexico vacation, was stopped at the border because of an irregularity in his visa. By the time the State Department straightened things out he had driven 600 miles back to his vacation spot, but he'd managed to get the poem into the mail and it had arrived in time.

There were also "A Half-Century of Reminiscences" given aloud: Deborah Digges for the '80s, Allan Gurganus for the '70s; John Irving's for the '60s (read by Carver). James Baker Hall and Oakley Hall covered the '50s, and Kay Burford read Ray West's for the '40s. Paul Engle was presented with a chair with a plaque on it by John Leggett, who also announced that there would be fellowships and a faculty chair established by the Iowa Foundation in Engle's name.

Engle rose to speak, and he went on at great length. The younger people at the tables in the far end of the Iowa Memorial Ballroom became rather noisy, and Engle's partisans were by turn annoyed with them and embarrassed. The event would have had to be anticlimactic at any rate, for it would have been unreasonable to expect Engle to transcend, or even reach again, the peak of performance he'd attained at the morning panel. Before Engle had stopped speaking, some of the younger people began to leave. One, standing in the hall, was heard to say to a photographer, "Yes, take my picture, please. No one's paying attention to us."

At last it was over, however, and everyone drifted off, many to the Jubilee Ball across the river again at the new Theatre Building, where two bands, the Max Lyon Quartet and The Rhythm Rockers, were playing. Others went to walk the streets of Iowa City into the dark hours, searching for their past. They managed to find Iowa Book and Supply, which was still on its corner of Clinton Street, though it was a totally new shop. Nearby was a familiar bar, The Airliner, exactly as it had been left a quarter-century ago, even to the old neon sign. The next corner, where Whetstone's Drugstore had been, is a hair-styling salon. There is a new brick mall next to the spot where The Paper Place had stood and later burned, and across the street where Kenney's Fine Beers had stood, there is a shoe store named, only too ironically, Kinney's.

Sunday brunch was scheduled at 10:30 A.M. Afterwards, at the Prairie Lights Bookstore people found stacks of the Sunday edition of the *New York Times*. In the old days the *Times* arrived on Tuesday. Back in their rooms readers of the magazine section discovered an article on the Jubilee they were at that moment attending.

A fair number of people went to the final panel, "Regional and Fine Press Publishing" with Edwina Evers, David Hamilton, Kim Merker, and Robley Wilson, Jr. Paul Zimmer, director of the University of Iowa Press, was also listed, but for some reason he did not appear.

Some Iowa English department professors not associated with the Workshop in particular, such as Sven Armens and his wife Kathleen, were present and being reunited with their former students on this final day. People were all saying their last farewells, taking their last pictures, buying their last copies of the special issue of the *Iowa Review*, buying their final T-shirts and Workshop cookbooks, picking up their copies of the free posters. Paul Engle was inviting some of "the old crowd" to his house at 4:00 P.M., but many had made arrangements to leave, including Donald Justice, and they had to decline regretfully.

The Jubilee, however, had incredibly been a marvel of success. That was more than remarkable; it was a bona fide miracle. When would one again see the day when nearly one hundred percent of the writers at a literary gathering would claim, against all likelihood and all hope, that they'd had, one and all, the time of their life in celebrating the best and the worst times of their lives when they were students in that Camelot in the cornfields, the Writers' Workshop of the University of Iowa?

A Field Guide to Recent Schools
of American Poetry

Ronald Baughman
University of South Carolina

In "Tradition and the Individual Talent" (1919), T. S. Eliot stated that "Poetry is not a turning loose of emotion, but an escape from emotion; it is not the expression of personality, but an escape from personality." Eliot's statement typified what Donald Hall called, in his influential preface to *Contemporary American Poetry* (1962), the "orthodoxy of Eliot and Pound" that demanded poets write "a poetry of symmetry, intellect, irony, and wit," the so-called "well-made poem" advocated by the New Criticism. The New Criticism held that each literary work should be considered without reference to its social milieu, its author's biographical information, or its historical context. Instead of evaluating the work on its moral or philosophical questions, the work should be judged by matters of technique—style, language, meter, metaphor, structure. Avoiding autobiographical revelations, the poet often employed a persona, or what William Butler Yeats called an "anti-Self" mask. Well-made poems used traditional metrics and forms to insure that, as

James Dickey notes in a comment on Yeats, the poem "should end like the click of a closed box."

After World War II, most American poets rebelled against the requirements for poetry established by Eliot and the New Criticism and instead placed emphasis on the writer's personality, the writer's self. This reversal is perhaps the single most important occurrence in the poetry of the postwar decades. The autobiographical emphasis granted poets the opportunity to explore the inner workings of the mind and heart in relation to the outer reality beyond the self. Some writers attempted to unify these two worlds—the inner and the outer—while others examined the alienating inability to find such connections.

In his essay "Creation's Very Self" in *Cry of the Human: Essays on Contemporary American Poetry* (1975), Ralph J. Mills, Jr., asserts that post-World War II poets achieved the "kind of poetic breakthrough James Dickey calls 'The Second Birth'—an intense imaginative liberation, achieved at great personal cost, in which the poet, like a snake shedding his skin, frees himself of the weight of imposed styles and current critical criteria to come into the place of his own authentic speech. The secret of this renewal, Dickey observes, 'does not, of course, reside in complete originality, which does not and could not exist. It dwells, rather, in the development of the personality, with its unique weight of experience and memory, as a writing instrument, and in the ability to give literary influence a new dimension which has the quality of this personality as informing principle.'"

As Mills notes, such a change in subject matter and in poetic conventions puts new demands on the reader and critic. Working with what Alan Williamson in *Introspection and Contemporary Poetry* (1984) has labeled the "energy of original vision," the post-World War II poets must be read and evaluated not through the Modernist criteria established by earlier masters of prosody but through their own poetic theories and practices. One method of approaching these writers is through placing them in the "schools" of poetry with which they are associated. Such an effort cannot, of course, penetrate the secrets of individual genius; but it can yield valuable information about the traditions fueling this genius.

The Academic poets, among them Richard Wilbur, Howard Nemerov, James Merrill, Elizabeth Bishop, William Meredith, and Karl Shapiro, continued and extended the traditions they inherited from Eliot and the New Critics. Rather than turning inward, as did most of their contemporaries, the Academic Poets shared the belief that through an adherence to the traditional controls of the well-made poem, the writer's imagination could gain a control over the confusions in the outside world. Form and craftsmanship, therefore, became extensions of a philosophical belief that a decorous, reasonable, restrained stance led to civility and to strength in poetry and life. The voices of these writers are not those of change or rebellion; rather, they offer complex philosophical explorations of their worlds without exclusively focusing on their own self-revelations.

Wilbur's poetry fulfills the Eliotic prescription for "symmetry, intellect, irony, and wit" while retaining its emotional effect. Wilbur often writes in rhyme, using complex conventional forms. He, like Eliot, often relies on mythological references and allusions to give metaphysical dimensions to his poetry. Because his language is polished to find the exact word, his knowledge of the history of individual words is important. In his poem "Mind" (1956), for example, Wilbur compares the workings of the mind to a bat's flying about a cave:

Mind in its purest play is like some bat
That beats about in caverns all alone,
Contriving by a kind of senseless wit
Not to conclude against a wall of stone.

He borrows his comparison from Plato's earlier image of man entrapped in a cave, and although Wilbur's poetry can be understood on a variety of levels, grasping the allusion enriches the content of the work. However, this writer's carefully honed craftsmanship, erudition, and control are often seen as his greatest weakness. M. L. Rosenthal states in *The Modern Poets* (1960) that Wilbur's poetry reminds readers "only of what we have already been taught to value: elegance, grace, precision, quiet intensity of phrasing." Yet Wilbur achieves moving poetry that is authentic and convincing in such works as "The Pardon" (1950), in which a boy discovers that his pet dog has been killed by a car, or in "Boy at the Window" (1956), in which a small child watches at his window as the snowman he had built slowly dissolves. Both poems treat life's transience but avoid sentimentality through their creator's technical control over his subject matter.

Howard Nemerov, another poet noted for his control, elegance, and wit, actually employs three voices: that satirizing the dehumanizing activities and institutions man confronts in his day-to-day existence, that celebrating nature which rises above the everydayness of life, and that defining true artists who connect the world and the spirit. A contemplative, philosophical poet capable of incorporating sophisticated scientific, mythological, and religious allusions into his speculations, Nemerov distinguishes between reflexive and reflective imagery: reflexive imagery mirrors an object as well as acts upon itself, while reflective imagery conveys the "stillness in moving things" in which "running and standing still at once/is the whole truth." Thus, in "By Al Lebowitz's Pool" (1980), Nemerov states that "by law/Any three things in the wide world/Triangulate: the wasp, and Betelgeuse/And Our Lady of Liberty in the harbor; if/It's any comfort to us, and it is." What comfort is achieved by such connections is primarily that of design—or art—over the disparate, apparently disordered chaotic details of life. Through the designs created in his art, Nemerov is able to achieve a balance of opposites and a perception of the natural designs that "the watching mind" observes. In the final stanza of the poem, the speaker returns to an empty swimming pool in the early autumn and states: "Reflections and reflexion, lovely words/I shall be sorry to let go when I let go:/ . . . For things reflected are more solemn and still/Than in themselves they are." Nemerov's key theme is the order art gives to the randomness of life, and he captures this theme through elegance, wit, and emotionally moving reflection.

James Merrill's poetry in one sense combines the skillful craftsmanship and elegance of the Academic School with the exploration of the self associated with other post-World War II schools of poetry. As David Kalstone comments in *Five Temperaments* (1977), "Many of Merrill's poems return to fictions believed in childhood, later fleshed out in life"; yet the writer is "suspicious of the straightforward first-person present indicative active: 'this addictive self-centered immediacy, harder to break oneself of than cigarettes. . . .' Merrill prefers poems in the first-person present which begin 'with a veil drawn.'" To help draw that veil, Merrill sometimes employs a persona named Charles, a narrative surrogate who allows the poet his belief that "life was fiction in disguise," particularly in terms of childhood and early adolescent years. In one of his best-known works, "Laboratory Poem" (1958), Merrill uses a high school science project to comment on larger topics, thereby illustrating his handling of persona, his verbal wit, his formal stanzaic craft, and his emotional depth beneath the surface humor:

Charles used to watch Naomi, taking heart
And a steel saw, open up turtles, live.
While she swore they felt nothing, he would gag
At blood, at the blind twitching, even after
The murky dawn of entrails cleared.

While Naomi, "taking heart," charts the contents of the dead turtle's heart, Charles thinks "of certain human hearts, their climb/Through violence into exquisite disciplines/Of which, as it now appeared/they all expired." Thus, Merrill, like the best of the Academic poets, moves artfully and movingly toward the universal implications that his work promises.

The Concretist movement—which has numbered among its participants such American poets as Emmett Williams, May Swenson, Mary Ellen Solt, Richard Kostelanetz, Aram Saroyan, Edwin Morgan, and John Hollander—announced itself with the 1952 publication of Concrete verse in the Brazilian magazine *Noigandres*. According to Douglas Thompson in his 1977 *Paideuma* article, "Pound

and Brazilian Concretism," the magazine's title was drawn from Ezra Pound's "Canto XX" and was a "term whose meaning . . . was taken as a synonym for poetry in progress as a motto meaning experimentation and concerted inquiry." The Concretists wanted the poem on the page to be a visual design that contained its meaning. Their poetry merged words, shapes, and spaces to create a work of art. Experience was therefore not interpreted but rather created.

May Swenson's poem "Women" (1968) illustrates the relationship between method and meaning presented on the page:

Women   Or they
    should be   should be
       pedestals   little horses
         moving   those wooden
           pedestals   sweet
             moving   oldfashioned
               to the   painted
                 motions   rocking
                   of men   horses
the gladdest things in the toyroom. . . .

As the poem continues, the two vertical lines of the poem weave back and forth, as if on an unsteady pedestal or rocking horse's legs—or on the uncertain rocking of the narrator's overtly conventional but inwardly rebellious perceptions ironically suggested by the feminist theme and language (*pedestals, toyroom, sweet, oldfashioned, painted*) of the poem. The form, language, and subject matter merge to create a graphic design and the poem's meaning. Daniel Hoffman states in his *Harvard Guide to Contemporary American Writing* (1979) that Swenson's "sensibility shares with Marianne Moore and Elizabeth Bishop a close and loving attention to the particulars of experience, the actualities of how things look, sound, or, if animate, act; above all, how it feels to perceive and understand them."

In the introduction to her anthology *Concrete Poetry: A World View* (1969), Mary Ellen Solt declares that a concrete poem can be identified by its "concentration upon the physical material from which the poem or text is made." "Sunflower" (1968), Solt's best-known work, repeats the word *Sunflower* to re-create the stem and bloom of the flower. Richard Kostelanetz's "Disintegration" (1970) prints the title in large black capitals as its first line and repeats the word in progressively smaller type in six succeeding lines until it gradually fades to a few indistinguishable marks in the final line. John Hollander's "Swan and Shadow"

(1969) provides a complex meditation on seeing the swan and its shadow, a meditation which physically represents swan, waterline, and swan shadow on the page. Edwin Morgan's "Siesta of a Hungarian Snake" (1968) must be regarded as a sample of linguistic and visual humor of a Concretist sort:

s sz sz SZ sz SZ sz ZS zs Zs zs zs z

Kostelanetz, in his introduction to *Imaged Words and Worded Images* (1970), provides perhaps the most evocative label—"word-imagery"—for Concretist poetry, a label that emphasizes the close proximity for this school of the literary to the visual in art.

Among the most important groups of writers emerging during the postwar period were the Confessional poets, so labeled by M. L. Rosenthal. As Jon Rosenblatt states in his 1976 *Genre* essay, "The Limits of the 'Confessional Mode' in Recent American Poetry," "While he did not at all conceive of confessional poetry as a religious poetry, Rosenthal was obviously thinking of the kind of revelation that a Catholic might make before his priest in the confessional: the torments of individual guilt and sin, of psychological disturbance and family dislocation." Yet instead of turning toward a system of belief beyond the self, toward reliance on a traditional relationship between God and man, as had Eliot, the Confessionalists in a sense celebrated their separation from all systems except individual, private ones.

In *The Confessional Poets* (1973), Robert Phillips lists key characteristics of this kind of poem:

It is highly subjective.
It is an expression of personality, not an escape from it.
It is therapeutic and/or purgative.
Its emotional content is personal rather than impersonal.
It is most often narrative.
It portrays unbalanced, afflicted, or alienated protagonists.
It employs irony and understatement for detachment.
It uses the self as a poetic symbol around which is woven a personal mythology.
There are no barriers of subject matter.
There are no barriers between the reader and the poet.
The poetry is written in the open language of ordinary speech.
It is written in open forms.
It displays moral courage.
It is antiestablishment in content, with alienation a common theme.

Personal failure is also a favorite theme, as is mental illness.
The poet strives for personalization rather than for universalization. (If totally successful, the personal is expressed so intimately we can all identify and empathize.)

As Phillips indicates, the chief characteristic of Confessional poetry is its concentration on highly intimate feelings and experiences. At its best this kind of poetry illuminates the workings of the writer's psyche both for himself and for his reader; at its worst, as Hall states in *Contemporary American Poetry*, a "series of excruciating self-discoveries . . . dissipates in an orgy of exhibitionism."

Perhaps the most important and respected of the Confessional poets was Robert Lowell, whose *Life Studies* (1959), along with W. D. Snodgrass's *Heart's Needle* (1959), broke ground for this movement. As Hoffman states, "*Life Studies* is the fulcrum of American poetry after the war, the turning point not only in Lowell's own career but also in the work of many younger poets. What he had accomplished here—the break-through from received to provisional rhythms and forms—corresponded to a widely sensed change in feeling, in the expectations of readers of poetry. Lowell's new subjects placed the poet's personality at the center of his art and at the center of his audience's interest in his work."

Life Studies focuses on Lowell's family and frequently dramatizes his childhood awarenesses of and apprehensions about their deaths ("My Last Afternoon with Uncle Devereux Winslow"). His emotional crises seemingly are brought on by the emptiness of his society, its Godless and corrupted values that cause him in "Skunk Hour" to state directly, "My mind's not right. . . . I myself am hell." "Skunk Hour" depicts Lowell's depression—he was frequently hospitalized for psychiatric difficulties—and is perhaps his best-known dramatization of his own dark night of the soul. The poem ends with a qualified affirmation: just as a mother skunk and her kittens ravaging the speaker's garbage pails in the predawn hours will not be scared away, neither, it is implied, will the narrator; yet what he has seen in the daylight—the depravity of his own society—is a source of his fears, and that vision, too, will not be driven away.

While teaching poetry at the University of Iowa Writers' Workshop, Lowell was influenced, as he acknowledged, by one of his students, W. D. Snodgrass. Snodgrass's ten-poem cycle *Heart's Needle*, which won the Pulitzer Prize in 1960, dra-

James Dickey (courtesy of the University of South Carolina Information Services)

matizes the emotional anguish its speaker feels because of his separation from his wife and his growing estrangement from his daughter. Though more formal than *Life Studies, Heart's Needle* is equally honest in confronting the poet's pain and the anguish he creates in others. Still another of Lowell's students who emerged in the early 1960s was Anne Sexton, whose writing actually began as a form of therapy for her. That her two daughters were separated from her while she was hospitalized for her emotional disorders became one of the central sources of the guilt permeating her work. Her first book, *To Bedlam and Part Way Back* (1960), like her subsequent ones, illustrates the painful events she endured in her life. About the work of Sexton, who committed suicide in 1974, Phillips writes, her "poetry of misfortune reaches some sort of apogee. So many are her afflictions, we recognize in the poet a female Job. . . . Her books, as she herself says, 'read like a fever chart for a bad case of melancholy.' "

Another student of Lowell, a close friend of Sexton, and an important member of the Confessional movement, Sylvia Plath also suffered from emotional disturbances. In such volumes as *Ariel* (1965) and *Crossing the Water* (1971), she was consumed by her sense of failure as wife, mother, and writer. Dominated by a fascination with death, by a vision of life as ungovernable, Plath's work, like that of Sexton, presents few opportunities for hope; and she, too, was ultimately driven to suicide.

John Berryman is usually recognized, with Lowell, as one of the major writers in the Confessional school. His *77 Dream Songs* appeared in 1964 and *His Toy, His Dream, His Rest*, containing "Dream Songs 78-385," in 1968. Collected as *The Dream Songs* in 1969, these works convey the poet's sense of longing that ultimately is thwarted. Berryman, who like Sexton and Plath committed suicide, created for himself a complex, multiple-voiced persona, Henry, who confronts in *The Dream Songs* the poet's own despair concerning his alcoholism, difficulties within his love-marriage relationships, and his father's suicide. At times Berryman provides Henry with an adversarial counterpart, Mr. Bones, a minstrel figure who affects black slang and whose name suggests a skeleton figure of death; the dialogues between Henry and Mr. Bones convey the constancy of death that haunted the poet, and one can read many of his works, like those of Plath and Sexton, as parts of an extended suicide note. Although Berryman's poems also have a bitterly comic thrust, they more emphatically chronicle the breakdown, the sense of alienation of the individual, which is so frequently explored by the Confessional poets.

In the early 1950s Charles Olson, as rector of Black Mountain College in western North Carolina, attracted a group of poets, dancers, and musicians to the small, unaccredited school and formed in the process the literary movement called the Black Mountain School, or The Projectivists, the latter label taken from the title of Olson's 1950 essay "Projective Verse." Robert Duncan and Robert Creeley were Olson's two major disciples, although Edward Dorn, Denise Levertov, John Weiners, Larry Eigner, and Paul Blackburn were among the other poets who have been identified with this group. They published most of their early poetry in the seven issues of the *Black Mountain Review* edited by Creeley. The college itself closed in 1956 for lack of students.

As an aesthetic theorist, Olson turned to Ezra Pound and William Carlos Williams for direction. In *Pavannes and Visions* (1918), Pound had stated that the Imagist movement relied on three principles: "(1) Direct treatment of the 'thing' whether subjective or objective; (2) To use absolutely no word that does not contribute to the presentation; (3) As regarding rhythm: to compose in the sequence of the musical phrase, not in sequence of a metronome." Pound's concern with the "thing" about which the poem is written, with economy of language and with freeing of rhythm patterns, became particular interests of Olson's. Williams's description of the poem as a machine in his "Introduction" to *The Wedge* (1944) also proved instructive to Olson. Williams stated: "Let the metaphysical take care of itself, the arts have nothing to do with it. They will concern themselves with it if they please, among other things. To make two bald statements: There's nothing sentimental about a machine, and: A poem is a small (or large) machine made of words. When I say there's nothing sentimental about a poem I mean that there can be no part, as in any other machine, that is redundant."

In his effort to gain new forms and subjects, Olson sought to rid poetry of its traditional conventions of language and of metrics in an attempt to remove barriers between poet and poem and reader. He viewed the head and heart as the source of the poem and the vehicle for conveying his world. The typewriter became an extension of the body in that it graphically indicated line length, line arrangement, and breath patterns. The poem, Olson believed, should be a "high-energy construct" connecting the heart—the nonconscious element of writing—with an almost prelogical reason. Thus, in "Projective Verse" (1950), he provided a formula for combining the mind and the heart to create a poem:

> the HEAD, by way of the EAR, to the SYLLABLE
> the HEART, by way of the BREATH, to the LINE.

Using this formula, Olson hoped to "project" his poem from poet to reader. By using breath patterns to determine the length of the line, the poet instructed his reader how to read each line. Through these various means, Olson felt that form and content became inseparable, each determining the other. As Charles Altieri states in *Enlarging the Temple: New Directions in American Poetry During the 1960s* (1979), "Meaning, Olson is fond of repeating, is 'that which exists thru itself.' "

Through his theoretical essays and his own poetry, particularly the *Maximus* poems, on which he worked from 1953 until his death in 1970, Olson attempted to convey his vision through concrete "things" in his environment and his thought. Set in Gloucester, Massachusetts, Olson's hometown, the works composing the *Maximus* poems praise the labors of working men—carpenters and fishermen—while expressing contempt for political, eco-

nomic, and social systems that dehumanize and devalue men's lives. "In place of society's dead values," Karl Malkoff contends in *Escape from the Self* (1977), "Olson presents a vision that . . . reality is accurately perceived only by those who can penetrate the world's tangle, or those who have not yet been enmeshed in it." Such people are primarily the makers—the artists, whether poet or painter or carpenter—of society.

Although the works of Robert Duncan, Robert Creeley, and Denise Levertov differ vastly, all three writers have shared and advanced certain of Olson's theories. Roberta Berke, in her book *Bounds Out of Bounds* (1981), calls Duncan "the most adventurous, splendid and underestimated of the Black Mountain group. . . . He is poised between passion and form, like a dancer." Retaining the Projectivist interest in the thing itself, Duncan tends to be more metaphysical in his concerns than most members of the school. In his "Poetry, a Natural Thing" (1960), Duncan illustrates not only his graceful treatment of ideas but also his views of poetry in terms of projective verse.

> The poem
> feeds upon thought, feeling, impulse,
>   to breed itself,
> a spiritual urgency . . .
>
> This beauty is an inner persistence
>   toward the source . . .
> a call we heard and answer
>   in the lateness of the world
> primordial bellowings. . . .

Robert Creeley, unlike Duncan, tends to focus upon the more earthbound particulars of human relationships, especially those of marriage and child rearing. He often uses the typographical shorthand advocated by Olson, as in these lines from "I Know a Man" (1962):

> As I sd to my
> friend, because I am
> always talking,—John, I
> sd, which was not his
> name, the darkness sur-
> rounds us, what
> can we do against
> it, or else, shall we &
> why not, buy a goddamn big car. . . .

In other poems, such as "Ballad of the Despairing Husband" (1959), Creeley's concerns seem conventional if not maudlin, though a comic tone is intended to undercut this weakness:

> My wife and I lived all alone,
> contention was our only bone.
> I fought with her, she fought with me,
> and things went on right merrily.
>
> But now I live here by myself
> with hardly a damn thing on the shelf,
> and pass my days with little cheer
> since I have parted from my dear.

Denise Levertov, who was born and raised in England but became an American citizen in 1956, was highly influenced by the experimental verse of the Projectivists, whose tendencies are particularly reflected in her second volume, *Here and Now* (1957). Probably the most respected and accomplished poet of the group, Levertov attempts to render observable reality in her poems while using the objects of this reality to manifest her own inner feelings and, frequently, to convey a moral and a political theme. During the 1960s and 1970s she raised her voice against the Vietnam War and for women's rights. Lines from her poem "Advent 1966" (1971) exemplify her expression on the Southeast Asian conflict:

> Because in Vietnam the vision of a Burning Babe
>   is multiplied, multiplied,
>   the flesh on fire
> not Christ's, as Southwell saw it . . .
> but wholly human and repeated, repeated,
> infant after infant, their names forgotten. . . .

This fragment from "A Day Begins" (1967)—"A headless squirrel, some blood/oozing from the un-evenly/chewed-off neck"—places her more squarely in the Projectivist tradition of concern with the "thing," with economy of language, with the freeing of metrical patterns. At the same time, like the other members of the Black Mountain school, Levertov has evolved her own distinctive voice as a poet.

In 1958 Robert Bly established, edited, and contributed to a journal that used as its titles the decades in which it appeared, *The Fifties, The Sixties,* and finally *The Seventies*. Through this journal a literary school called the Deep Imagists developed; the group included Bly, James Wright, and James Dickey and eventually attracted Galway Kinnell, Louis Simpson, William Duffy, and Donald Hall to its ranks.

In his preface to *The Lion's Tale and Eye: Poems Written Out of Laziness and Silence* (1962), Bly announced his break with the confessional mode, which tended to recount the particulars of a poet's alienation from his world, and offered instead a poetry that attempted to prove the pre- or non-rational response of the poet. Bly believed that by exploring one's imaginative response, the writer could arrange a series of intuitive responses into an *image*, his word for the poem created. The poem then would transcend the restrictions of reason and exact reality in the "outer world" producing in their stead a "deep image" borne out of one's inner self. In his 1978 *American Poetry Review* essay "Chapter and Verse," poet Stanley Plumly noted that "the Deep Imagism of the 60s was intended as an alternative to the rhetoric of cause and effect." The convergence of nonlogical intuitive associations often produced the sudden burst of image that tends to summarize, in the best of the Deep Imagist poetry, the currents in a specific work.

In his poem "Melancholia" (1967), for example, Bly provides a series of details that hauntingly suggest emptiness, silence, and despair:

> A light seen suddenly in the storm, snow
> Coming from all sides, like flakes
> Of sleep, and myself
> On the road to the dark barn,
> Halfway there . . .

In the last stanza, however, a surprising final observation occurs:

> There is a wound on the trunk,
> Where the branch was torn off.
> A wind comes out of it,
> Rising, swelling,
> Swirling over everything alive.

The wind rising from inside the tree is analogous to the vision coming from within the poet. But instead of producing melancholia leading to further details of darkness and despair, these particulars suddenly and surprisingly connect to a rising, swelling, swirling of "everything alive."

Wright's frequently anthologized poem "A Blessing" (1963) provides still another example of the sudden flowering of image—of the capacity to call up, as Alan Williamson says in *Introspection and Contemporary Poetry* (1984), "not the thing itself, but a quality or value it has for the poet"—that characterizes the best of Deep Imagist poetry. As the speaker and his companion travel a side road outside Rochester, Minnesota, they stop to admire a pair of Indian ponies. The narrator is moved by a black and white mare:

> Her mane falls wild on her forehead
> And the light breeze moves me to caress her long ear
> That is delicate as the skin over a girl's wrist,
> Suddenly I realize
> That if I stepped out of my body I would break
> Into blossom.

Perhaps Wright's poem more than any other single work from this school dramatizes how the poet's reaction to an event or object in the outer world generates a highly emotional image to be brought forth from the poet's inner self. In the easy flow of simple details, the poem moves to a nonlogical but intensely lyrical conclusion, showing the reader exactly what the speaker feels. Such revelations emerge quietly, effortlessly, and—perhaps most importantly—without the constraints of reason.

Although he shares Bly's and Wright's interest in connecting the inner and outer worlds through emotional connections, Dickey differs from the other Deep Imagists in emphasizing the narrative over the lyrical elements in his poetry. Yet once again a sudden flowering of image, a surprising but intuitively powerful vision, is effected, in part because Dickey gains the perspective of what he calls "the Other." As H. L. Weatherby explains in his 1966 *Sewanee Review* essay "The Way of Exchange in James Dickey's Poetry," the poet adopts the point of view of whatever he encounters outside the self—the living and the dead, the animate and the inanimate—and thus frees himself from the limitations of human thought or feeling. For example, in "Approaching Prayer" (1964), the protagonist ceremoniously puts on the head of a boar he, as a hunter, killed with a bow and arrow. Adopting this mask, the speaker records both his emotions as he drew the arrow to kill the boar and the boar's response as he watches the man prepare to kill him. From this exchange of identities, Dickey is able to provide highly original, complex poetry that offers the kind of startling, nonrational, but profound insight most valued by the Deep Imagist school.

The two most notable poets of the New York School, Frank O'Hara and John Ashbery, met while students at Harvard University. Later, upon graduation, they worked in New York City as critics of contemporary painting and gravitated toward the innovative group called the "action painters"—William de Kooning, Larry Rivers, Mark Rothko, Jack-

son Pollock, and Franz Kline—and became friends with such composers as John Cage, Anton von Webern, and Ferruccio Busoni. Just as the action painters attempted to reach the unconscious with their experiments in Surrealism, so too did the New York School poets wish to create a poetry that abandoned the traditional conventions of the well-made poem in favor of explorations of the individual psyche. O'Hara and Ashbery, along with poets Kenneth Koch, Barbara Guest, and James Schuyler, made New York salons, cafés, and nightclubs their headquarters for exchanging ideas with these painters and musicians, gaining in the process the aesthetic framework for their literary approaches.

In *Bounds Out of Bounds* Roberta Berke identifies three principal concerns shared by the New York School of poets:

> The first of these concepts is Surrealism . . . , an attempt to reproduce in art the processes of the unconscious mind. . . . Automatic writing is the aspect of Surrealism most relevant to the New York poets. The second concept which characterized the New York poets is the importance of the Present Moment. Just as dreams often seem to take place in an enormous present time, so the poems of the New York poets were concerned with what was happening in the immediate moment. History on a grand scale and myths were ignored, except for the mock-epics of Koch and Ashbery's dream-landscapes, both of which are too private to be universal myths. . . . Present actions preoccupied the New York poets, just as the action painters . . . used automatic painting to reach the unconscious. . . . The third concept . . . is the importance of the Ordinary: everyday events and speech.

In addition to these three concepts, the New York poets shared a strong affection for and identification with the New York City setting; this locale, especially for O'Hara, was the center of excitement, companionability, and love, rather than the urban Hell filled with crime and alienated, despairing people so often portrayed by such other poets as Allen Ginsberg. O'Hara's lines in "Walking" (1969)—"the country is no good for us/there's nothing/to bump into/or fall apart glassily/there's not enough/poured concrete"—reflect the attitude shared by the New York School.

The poetry of both O'Hara and Ashbery attempts to capture the protean, disparate associations that occur in each present moment as it is

Amiri Baraka (courtesy of Lordly & Dame, Inc.)

registered in and reflected by the poet's mind. Each line denotes a single present moment, until the final, culminating emotional or intellectual response occurs. In the best of the poetry of O'Hara and others of his school, the reader is required to participate in the poet's process of observation. In *Frank O'Hara: Poet Among Painters* (1977), Marjorie Perloff emphasizes this aspect of O'Hara's art.

> *The esethetic of culmination rather than examination*—this formulation applies nicely to O'Hara's own poetry. . . . O'Hara's poems reject the dense network of symbolic images one finds in, say, Richard Wilbur's "Love Calls Us To The Things Of This World." . . . Rather, the reader's eye and ear must "travel over the complicated surface exhaustively," participating in the ongoing process of discovery and continually revising his sense of what the poem is "saying." The observer can no longer be detached. . . . If the art work has *presence* and if the beholder is as *attentive* as possible, the process of identification thus becomes complete.

In his essay "Personism: A Manifesto" (*Yūgen #7,* 1961) O'Hara offers a mock-serious manifesto about his methods and purposes. Though he

adopts a comic voice in this essay, O'Hara succeeds in providing valuable insights into his artistic intent:

> Personism has nothing to do with philosophy, it's all art. It does not have to do with personality or intimacy, far from it! . . , one of its minimal aspects is to address itself to one person (other than the poet himself), thus evoking overtones of love without destroying love's life-giving vulgarity, and sustaining the poet's feelings toward the poem while preventing love from distracting him into feeling about the person. That's part of Personism. It was founded by me after lunch with LeRoi Jones on August 27, 1959, a day in which I was in love with someone (not Roy, by the way, a blond). I went back to work and wrote a poem for this person. While I was writing it I was realizing that if I wanted to I could use the telephone instead of writing the poem, and so Personism was born. . . . It puts the poem squarely between the poet and the person, Lucky Pierre style, and the poem is correspondingly gratified. The poem is at last between two persons instead of two pages.

Perloff comments, "What he means is that the poet does not use the poem as a vehicle to lay bare his soul, to reveal his secret anxieties or provide autobiographical information. . . . Rather, Personism means the 'illusion' of intimate talk between an 'I' and a 'you' giving us the sense that we are eavesdropping on an ongoing conversation, that we are present." Significantly, it is the poem, rather than its reader, that is primarily "gratified"—or enriched—by coming between poet and reader, yet all three benefit from the tensions of the relationship.

Lines from O'Hara's best-known poem, "The Day Lady Died" (1959), illustrate his method of layering seemingly random thoughts as he strolls down a New York City street; this process reproduces the unplanned, almost prelogical juxtapositions of the poet's stream-of-consciousness:

> It is 12:20 in New York a Friday
> three days after Bastille day, yes
> it is 1959 and I go get a shoeshine
> because I will get off the 4:19 in Easthampton
> at 7:15 and then go straight to dinner
> and I don't know the people who will feed me

These apparently random associations provide both the reality of the poet's immediate environment and his emotional responses to that environment. The tone and list of present moments continue for three more stanzas until he reads, again seemingly by chance, a newspaper headline and sees a photo announcing that blues singer Billie Holliday ("Lady" or "Lady Day") has died:

> then I go back . . . and
> . . .
> casually ask for a carton of Gauloises and a carton
> of Picayunes, and a NEW YORK POST with her face
>   on it
>
> and I am sweating a lot by now and thinking of
> leaning on the john door in the 5 SPOT
> while she whispered a song along the keyboard
> to Mal Waldron and everyone and I stopped breathing

The details remain disparate and the connections between action and emotion unexplained, yet the writer's feeling, his unique sensibility, is cryptically but powerfully conveyed.

Although John Ashbery is a generally more complex, less accessible poet than O'Hara, he shares O'Hara's—and the New York School's—concern with the workings of the unconscious mind, with the present moment, and with the ordinary. In *Five Temperaments*, David Kalstone comments on Ashbery's poetic practice through reference to one of the poet's interview statements:

> Ashbery writes autobiography only inasmuch as he writes about the widening sense of what it is like to gain—or to try to gain—access to his experience. The present is the poem. "I think that any one of my poems might be considered a snapshot of whatever is going on in my mind at the time—first of all the desire to write a poem, after that wondering if I've left the oven on or thinking about where I must be in the next hour. . . ." Like Penelope's web, the doing and undoing of Ashbery's poems is often their subject: fresh starts, repeated collisions of plain talk with the tantalizing and frustrating promises of "poetry."

This marriage of the present moment, the ordinary experience or object, the workings of the unconscious conveys what Harold Bloom in *Figures of Capable Imagination* (1976) has called a "profound self-revelation" growing out of extreme and highly individual "subjectivity." That such verse is often difficult is hardly surprising. Berke comments on the "formal, hermetic, secretive" elements of Ash-

bery's poetry: "he often slides a deliberate barrier between himself and his readers. . . . Often these secrets are conveyed in code, secret messages hidden in the everyday. Code is a metaphor for the special language of poetry, into which Ashbery ciphers his secrets. He outlines two of his main methods of coding: 'I thought if I could put it all down, that would be one way. And next the thought came to me that to leave it all out would be another, and truer, way.' " In a 1974 *Confrontation* interview with Louis A. Osti, Ashbery himself addresses the issue of "secrecy" in his verse: "It seems to me that my poetry sometimes proceeds as though an argument were suddenly derailed and something that started out clearly suddenly becomes opaque. . . . What I am probably trying to do is illustrate opacity and how it can suddenly descend over us, rather than trying to be willfully obscure."

Lines from a 1981 poem, "Paradoxes and Oxymorons," which treats the nature of poetry, illustrate some elements of Ashbery's complexity:

> This poem is concerned with language on a very plain
>   level.
> . . . .
> The poem is sad because it wants to be yours, and
>   cannot.
> What's a plain level? It is that and other things,
> Bringing a system of them into play. Play?
> Well, actually, yes, but I consider play to be
>
> A deeper outside thing, a dream role-pattern,
> As in the division of grace these long August days
> Without proof. Open-ended. . . .

The language may, in fact, be "on a very plain level," but the juxtapositions it sets up, the undefined connections it implies, involve Ashbery and his reader in a playful but highly demanding relationship. This relationship is one that the best of the poets in the New York School explore and depend upon.

About the same time the New York School was being established in Manhattan, the Beat Generation poets were coming together in New York and California. The label "Beat" was applied to this gathering of social and/or literary revolutionaries by novelist Jack Kerouac, who, with William S. Burroughs, is commonly regarded as the most enduring of the Beat fiction writers. According to Berke, "The term 'beat' was first used widely by Jack Kerouac, who said it was short for 'beatific.' 'Beat' also meant broken down, weary, oppressed, and referred to the syncopated beat of jazz." Gravitating to San Francisco, where the cultural climate seemed hospitable to the Beats' desire for a variety of experimentation, these poets announced their arrival through the October 1955 reading, at the city's Six Gallery, of five poets—Allen Ginsberg, Michael McClure, Gary Snyder, Philip Whalen, and Philip Lamantia. Other poets identified with this school included Gregory Corso, Brother Antoninus, and Lawrence Ferlinghetti.

The Beats were—and have continued to be—essentially romantic rebels against conventional middle-class values and proprieties. Issuing no specific manifesto to announce their views, they instead presented their ideas as much through their dress and behavior as through their writings, becoming in the process social predecessors of the more sharply political but nonliterary counterculture movement that developed during the 1960s and 1970s. The Beats saw themselves as intentional outcasts—and frequently as unconventional holymen—who embraced modern jazz, sexual freedom, drugs, and general spontaneity as stimuli for both their lives and their work.

Like the members of the New York School, the Beats focused on urban settings; however, their version of the city setting is filled with corruption, danger, and repression. Eschewing conventional forms, subjects, and language, they proclaimed their preference for first-draft manuscripts as marks of intellectual and spiritual honesty. They concentrated on forbidden subjects in a conscious attempt to shock their audiences and often employed vulgar language as another indication of their freedom from repressive conventions. References to Judaism, Hinduism, and Buddhism appear through the works of these writers, positing a quasi-religious/philosophical view of themselves as "holy barbarians," as Kerouac once labeled the group.

Among the most highly regarded of the Beat poets are Ginsberg, Ferlinghetti, and Snyder, whose works represent different faces of the generation with which they are identified. When Ginsberg's poem "Howl" (1956) was first published, it prompted a lawsuit charging that the work was obscene. The opening lines from "Howl" became a kind of anthem for the movement:

I saw the best minds of my generation destroyed by
    madness, starving hysterical naked,
dragging themselves through the negro street at dawn
    looking for an angry fix,
angelheaded hipsters burning for the ancient heav-
    enly connection to the starry dynamo in the ma-
    chinery of night. . . .

The most obvious features of these lines are the concrete details drawn from mean streets and assembled in long, metrically irregular lines, and the tone of fiery denunciation coupled with the assertion that the "angelheaded hipsters" are, in fact, holy men seeking "the ancient heavenly connection." Here, as in much of his work, Ginsberg portrays himself as a visionary.

Ferlinghetti, whose City Lights Bookstore became a central gathering place and publishing outlet for many of the Beat writers, is perhaps best known for his poem "Coney Island of the Mind" (1958), a popular antinuclear war statement. In another of his works, "Tentative Description of a Dinner to Promote the Impeachment of President Eisenhower" (1959), Ferlinghetti not only parodies conventional gatherings of poetry audiences but also wittily recalls Ginsberg's lines in "Howl":

We have seen the best minds of our generation
destroyed by boredom at poetry readings.
Poetry isn't a secret society,
It isn't a temple either.
Secret words & chants won't do any longer.

Snyder is, in many respects, the most accomplished poet of this group. Removing himself from the San Francisco scene, he spent several years in Japan and ultimately settled in the rural Pacific Northwest, where he has continued his longtime interest in Far Eastern religions, particularly Zen Buddhism. His poetry often manifests the elliptical lyricism of a Zen haiku. In one of his best-known poems, "Milton by Firelight" (1959), Snyder's characteristic subject matter and tone are illustrated:

In ten thousand years the Sierras
Will be dry and dead, home of the scorpion.
Ice-scratched slabs and bent trees.
No paradise, no fall,
Only the weathering land
The wheeling sky,
Man, with his Satan
Scouring the chaos of the mind.
Oh Hell!

Here the poet contrasts the gradual evolution of nature ("the weathering land/The wheeling sky") with the Western religious conception of man's abrupt fall from Paradise (described as "chaos of the mind" and earlier called "a silly story"). Through his imagery Snyder conveys his Buddhist vision that nature impassively endures in one form or another and that human concerns and activities are insignificant but frenzied when measured against the processes of the natural landscape. Thus, like Ginsberg, Snyder has a distinctly religious flavor to his work, though his background in Eastern philosophies and the natural scene makes his expressions seem more reflective, judicious, and calm than those of his contemporary. Ginsberg's poetry is engaging and colorful, and Ferlinghetti's is thoughtful and acerbically witty; but Snyder's works may prove most enduring.

Such writers as Gwendolyn Brooks, Lucille Clifton, Robert Hayden, LeRoi Jones (Imamu Amiri Baraka), and Nikki Giovanni reflect in their works the black experience in America. Because theirs is the poetry of a group that has suffered social and political oppression, much of the emphasis on this work is on the personal dislocation perceived by the self. Generally the poems defining the New Black Aesthetic are set in urban locations and dramatize the horrors of ghetto life; yet while the writers of this movement voice their outrage at such conditions, they also celebrate the pride and strength growing out of their cultural heritage and present circumstances. The language and rhythms of the poetry are often but not always those of contemporary black English, although these writers avoid the kind of duplication of black dialect found in the works of such earlier Afro-American authors as Paul Dunbar, whose poem "A Death Song" (1905) contains the characteristic line "Lay me down beneaf de willers in the grass."

Brooks, who has spent much of her life in Chicago, was the first black writer to receive a Pulitzer Prize, which she won for her second book of poems, *Annie Allen* (1949). Her "We Real Cool" (1960), a poem which both analyzes and attacks the black street-gang mentality, illustrates her terse, biting oral quality:

We real cool. We
Left school. We

Lurk late. We
Strike straight. . . .

Early in her writing career, she focused most frequently on the difficulties of long-suffering black women, but during the 1960s and 1970s, her poetry widened to treat other segments of her community outraged or ostracized by the white world. She wrote, for example, of "The Blackstone Rangers" (1968), a Chicago street gang, as well as of civil rights disturbances. Whatever her subject, she

brings a precise authenticity of imagery and character to her work.

Although not as well known as some other black writers, Clifton is nonetheless an accomplished poet. Her pride in being black and being a woman serves as a thematic affirmation over difficult conditions. In her poem "Miss Rosie," appearing in her first book, *Good Times* (1969), she employs startling imagery to dramatize her central figure's loss of beauty and youth through years of oppression; at the same time she offers a quiet but profound tribute to Miss Rosie's life:

When I watch you
wrapped up like garbage
sitting surrounded by the smell
of too old potato peels
. . . .
you wet brown bag of a woman
who used to be the best looking gal in Georgia
. . . .
I stand up
through your destruction
I stand up.

Like the best of the writers of the New Black Aesthetic, Hayden in his work transcends definition by race alone. His poetry is philosophically complex yet emotionally powerful. His most anthologized poem, "Those Winter Sundays" (1962), dramatizes in clear, concise, but lyrically evocative form a portrait of his father and the tangled crosscurrents resulting from his son's early rejection but mature affection expressed too late:

Sundays too my father got up early
. . . .
then with cracked hands that ached
from labor in the weekday weather made
banked fires blaze. No one ever thanked him.
. . . .
Speaking indifferently to him,
. . . .
What did I know, what did I know
of love's austere and lonely offices?

The most successful writers of the New Black Aesthetic, exemplified by the three poets referred to here, will endure not only because they capture the content, feeling, and rhythms of the black experience but also because they attain what all great poets have always offered to their readers—vision, honesty, and a mastery of an appropriate and evocative language and form.

This survey of various schools of recent American poetry indicates at once the vast diversity and the great similarities that exist among the poets classified in these groups. What can be said generally about these writers is that they share a reliance on the self as a source for and subject of poetry. Though they differ in terms of how to express what the self knows or feels, they invariably return to and trust in that self's knowledge and feeling. Most poets no longer subscribe to traditional methods for conveying what they see, yet all employ considerable craftsmanship and conviction in setting forth their particular vision.

References:

Charles Altieri, *Enlarging the Temple: New Directions in American Poetry During the 1960s* (Lewisburg, Pa.: Bucknell University Press/London: Associated University Presses, 1979);

W. C. Barnwell, "James Dickey on Yeats: An Interview," *Southern Review*, 13 (Spring 1977): 311-316;

Roberta Berke, *Bounds Out of Bounds: A Compass for Recent American and British Poetry* (New York: Oxford University Press, 1981);

Harold Bloom, *Figures of Capable Imagination* (New York: Seabury Press, 1976);

James E. B. Breslin, *From Modern to Contemporary: American Poetry: 1945-1965* (Chicago & London: University of Chicago Press, 1984);

The Distinctive Voice, edited by William J. Martz (Glenview, Ill.: Scott, Foresman, 1966);

Donald Hall, *Contemporary American Poetry* (Baltimore: Penguin, 1962);

Harvard Guide to Contemporary American Writing, edited by Daniel Hoffman (Cambridge & London: Belknap Press of Harvard University Press, 1979);

David Kalstone, *Five Temperaments* (New York: Oxford University Press, 1977);

Anthony Libby, *Mythologies of Nothing: Mystical Death in American Poetry 1940-1970* (Urbana & Chicago: University of Illinois Press, 1984);

Karl Malkoff, *Escape from the Self: A Study in Contemporary American Poetry and Poetics* (New York: Columbia University Press, 1977);

Jerome Mazzaro, *Postmodern American Poetry* (Urbana, Chicago & London: University of Illinois Press, 1980);

Ralph J. Mills, Jr., *Cry of the Human: Essays on Contemporary American Poetry* (Urbana, Chicago & London: University of Illinois Press, 1975);

Charles Molesworth, *The Fierce Embrace: A Study of Contemporary American Poetry* (Columbia & London: University of Missouri Press, 1979);

Louis A. Osti, "The Craft of John Ashbery: An Interview," *Confrontation*, 9 (Fall 1974): 84-96;

Marjorie Perloff, *Frank O'Hara: Poet Among Painters* (New York: Braziller, 1977);

Robert Phillips, *The Confessional Poets* (Carbondale: Southern Illinois University Press, 1973);

Jon Rosenblatt, "The Limits of the 'Confessional Mode' in Recent American Poetry," *Genre*, 9 (1976): 153-159;

M. L. Rosenthal, *The Modern Poets: A Critical Introduction* (London, Oxford & New York: Oxford University Press, 1960);

Stephen Stepanchev, *American Poetry Since 1945: A Critical Survey* (New York: Harper & Row, 1965);

Douglas Thompson, "Pound and Brazilian Concretism," *Paideuma*, 6 (1977): 279-294;

Alan Williamson, *Introspection and Contemporary Poetry* (Cambridge & London: Harvard University Press, 1984).

(Re-)Publishing Orwell

Peter Davison

In September 1981 I was asked by Tom Rosenthal, then chairman of Secker and Warburg, whether I would check through the texts of George Orwell's nine "books" which that house intended to publish in a deluxe edition to mark 1984. The idea of a deluxe edition might seem a trifle ironic for such titles as *Down and Out in Paris and London* and *The Road to Wigan Pier*, not to mention *Homage to Catalonia*, but Rosenthal's intention was businesslike. The deluxe edition would carry the setting costs, enabling the trade edition, which would follow a year or so later, to be sold at a reasonable price. It was known that there were a few textual errors—Ian Angus and Ian Willison had noted some in the course of their work on the Orwell bibliography—and McDonald Emslie and P. G. Scott had listed some variants in their description of a set of page proofs for *Down and Out* which had been published in *The Library*, 5, no. 32 (1977): 372-376.

It was proposed to publish all nine volumes in March 1984, and, because of the importance of that date, I had to promise to have all volumes checked by July 1982. I could not start work until October 1981. I was teaching full-time at the University of Kent and also editing *The Library* single-handedly, so I knew I should have to work fast to complete the checking of a book each month. The University of Kent Library had a few early editions—heavily taped-over with "Overnight Loan" and "Three-Day Loan" stickers and embellished with undergraduates' notes; the Orwell Archive at University College London was not only a treasure house but had immensely helpful (and overworked) staff—Janet Percival and Gill Furlong; and Ian Angus put at my disposal his collection of Orwell editions so that I was not restricted to the archive's hours of opening on the one day a week I could afford to devote to this work in term-time.

There were upwards of fifty editions and sets of proofs to be collated. In addition, and particularly valuable, were publishers' files (especially those of Victor Gollancz, which Ian Angus and I searched with the help of the founder's daughter, Miss Livia Gollancz). Emendations were also found

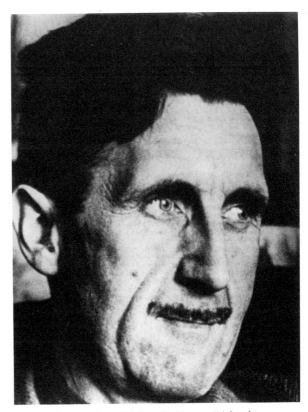

George Orwell (photo by Vernon Richards)

in correspondence—in letters by Eileen Blair and in those exchanged by Orwell and his first French translator, Yvonne Davet. Orwell's letters to Madame Davet showed he took an intimate interest in the process of translation, and it was partly on the basis of this newfound cache that I was later to incorporate into the new edition footnotes in French found in the translations of *Down and Out* (1935) and *Homage to Catalonia* (published in 1955, five years after Orwell's death). Finally, there were two signed and witnessed documents in which Orwell gave instructions to his literary executors. These included instructions about reprinting—that he did not wish, amongst other things, *Keep the Aspidistra Flying* and *A Clergyman's Daughter* to be reprinted—and details of certain textual changes which he did want made. It might be useful if I here interpolate a comment about my (and the publishers') disregard for the first instruction but my following the second.

One change Orwell required was that the two "political" chapters of *Homage to Catalonia* (five and eleven) should be extracted and printed at the end of the text as appendices. He also wanted certain facts corrected and others checked. One reviewer of the new edition's first three volumes thought that as Orwell's wish that two of his novels should not be reprinted had been disregarded, so should the instruction about these chapters. Another, Michael Foot, former editor of *Tribune* and one-time prime minister, was marvelously enthusiastic about the change. Why follow one instruction and not the other? As I see it, the two novels Orwell rejected, though certainly not without weaknesses, have already entered the public domain (though not in the copyright sense) and are no longer simply their author's possession: they are a part—a small part—of the history of the novel, of our culture. Thus, we, the readers, also have "rights" to them. I think one can go a little further and say that when the history of the first publication of these novels is understood (as this new edition makes clear), it can be seen *why* Orwell rejected them, and for the same reason that he rejected the first English edition of *Burmese Days.* All three were, to use his word, "garbled." An editor should, therefore, ignore Orwell's wish about the republication of these two novels and endeavor to perfect them so far as he is able and, in doing so, throw light on a small corner of the history of publishing in the 1930s and what Orwell was trying to do in these novels, but which censorship hindered.

Whether one critic likes the extraction of the chapters from *Homage to Catalonia* and another does not seems to me immaterial. I am delighted at Mr. Foot's enthusiasm—what editor would not be?—but the editor's duty is quite simple here: to bring out the text, to emend the text, as its author wished. Incidentally, the French edition, almost (even entirely) unnoticed in the Anglo-Saxon world, follows that change in chapter order, and Orwell was in direct correspondence with Madame Davet when she was making her translation. The author may be wrong, as Orwell surely was in wishing to have *Coming Up For Air* published without any semicolons, as an experiment, which Secker's persisted in undermining (until the new edition), but he is entitled to be wrong and must be judged according to his expressed wishes. A literary editor may dicker about with his author's text, perhaps; an analytical editor must surely try to realize his author's intentions even if he wishes they were other than they are.

The publishers—and for Orwell there are two, Secker and Warburg in England and Harcourt Brace Jovanovich in the United States—had not expected there to be very much that needed altering from the texts in print. Most scholarly editors would take a less sanguine view and in this case that was fully justified, but even my suspicious nature was surprised. One tiny difference *has* hit the headlines. Never did I think the day would come when I should waste hours on the transatlantic telephone being interviewed by journalists in New York and Los Angeles, or answering questions for a phone-in program in Australia, or splashed all over newspapers in Germany, and even appear on television in England and Canada, and talk on radio, all about a textual variant. All English editions of *Nineteen Eighty-Four* after the first give the famous formula, 2+2=5, as 2+2= . The "5" dropped out of the type form. A printer-friend thinks the reason is that in Monotype, quad spacing is infinitessimally undersize and, if used to pack round that formula, with spacing above and below, as happens at the bottom of a page in that first English edition, it would have facilitated the "5" working loose. The implications are important for a proper reading of the novel. In editions with the "5"—all American editions, for example, set, incidentally, from a carbon copy of the typescript and not from page proofs, such was the rush to get the book into print—Winston Smith is shown to have accepted O'Brien's logic totally. By implication, there is nothing to be hoped for from the intelligentsia; if there is any hope, it lies, as Orwell says, in the proles. But if the "5" is missing, then Smith has retained a little of his independence of thought, of his integrity. Perhaps lurking deep within him and those like him there is hope.

When it was realized how extensive were the changes necessary, it was agreed that I should contribute an introduction to the first volume and that each volume would be provided with a textual note and lists of the more significant variants. No footnotes were to be allowed, but even that requirement was modified for *Down and Out* and *Homage to Catalonia* (which already have Orwell's footnotes), to permit some additional notes, using Orwell's own words, to clarify changes in the text and additions from the French translation (translated back into English). I wished to include footnotes in *A Clergyman's Daughter* in order to indicate, on the page, just where extensive modifications had taken place but where the text could not be restored, but here

Secker's wishes prevailed. Their argument, a not unreasonable one, was that these are reading texts for the general reader and they feared such readers would be put off by editorial comment at the foot of pages. Although I regret the decision, I must stress that both Secker's and Harcourt Brace Jovanovich have been most generous in allowing what was intended to be a straight, but corrected, trade reprint to become, if not "the total scholarly edition-cum-apparatus," an edition that gives the interested reader a very clear idea of the genesis of each book. For the textual notes and readings I have adopted the plan devised by the late Terence Spencer for the New Penguin Shakespeare, which, from my experience in preparing two editions, seems to marry scholarly requirements with the needs of the general reader intelligently and honestly.

One or two of the volumes have additional appendices. Victor Gollancz's foreword to the Left Book Club Edition of *The Road to Wigan Pier* is being reprinted; Orwell's would-be introduction to *Animal Farm* is being included in that volume; most intriguingly, *Burmese Days* will be provided with a frontispiece reproducing Orwell's sketch map of the village of Kyauktada, drawn to help him in the process of delocalizing the area for the English edition in order to forestall possible libel actions. (Gollancz's lawyers regularly required delocalization, and it occurs in *A Clergyman's Daughter* and *Keep the Aspidistra Flying;* the new editions restore the original·locations.) In an appendix I have identified most of the points of interest in Orwell's sketch map—Flory's, Macgregor's and the Lackersteens' bungalows, the Club, Dr. Veeraswami's house, and so on. The new edition also reproduces, for the first time since *The Road to Wigan Pier* was published in England and America, the thirty-two pages of plates illustrating depressed areas of England, Scotland, and Wales and conditions of the poor.

It would be otiose to repeat here what I have already described in some detail in each of the nine volumes and more generally in "Editing Orwell: Eight Problems" (in *The Library*, 6, no. 6, 1984) and in "What Orwell Really Wrote," in *George Orwell & Nineteen Eighty-Four: The Man and the Book* (Washington, D.C.: Library of Congress, 1985). It will suffice to say that each book shows changes and that some will suggest a different reading though others are really quite insignificant in interpreting and assessing Orwell and his work. What does stand out is that, even when he didn't quite succeed, Orwell was a better craftsman than he has sometimes been allowed to be—in *A Clergyman's Daughter* in particular.

The new readings also show plainly the border between fiction and actuality which Orwell trod. This is most notable in *Keep the Aspidistra Flying,* in which Orwell had wished to use genuine advertising slogans and a real "advertising character" but was prevented at page-proof stage from so doing. Deeply upset, he made the changes required—the more agonizing because he was asked to do them the very day he had been down the Crippen Pit near Wigan, about which he wrote so graphically in his diary entry for 24 February 1936 (and reprinted in the *Collected Essays, Journalism and Letters*). After half a century the original slogans can be restored. Two days later Orwell wrote to his agent, Leonard Moore, showing bitter resentment at what he had been required to do. He had wished to link the "garbage" of advertisements promising miracle cures (advertisements which would now be illegal in Britain) with the "garbage" written by such popular novelists as Ethel M. Dell and Warwick Deeping. The libel lawyers feared action from the medical-claim advertisers; but, significantly, Orwell was allowed to attack popular literature. Had he been advised earlier, he wrote, he would "have entirely rewritten the first chapter and modified several others" of *Keep the Aspidistra Flying*. And he went on: "In general a passage of prose or even a whole chapter revolves round one or two key phrases, and to remove these, as was done in this case, knocks the whole thing to pieces." No wonder he rejected these two "garbled" novels! The full correspondence is to be included in the complete essays, letters, journalism, broadcasts, and reviews, now in the course of preparation.

I completed preparing the texts of the nine books on time and that chimed in well with the change in my academic life. The British government's cuts in university finance led to my university (among others) seeking volunteers for what was politely called "early retirement" but what was, in effect, voluntary redundancy. I agreed to go provided I could first take up a British Academy Award to spend four months at the Folger Shakespeare Library and I then took on what was, in theory if not in practice, a part-time job, looking after a historic building in London, and writing.

It seemed to my publishers and to me an ideal opportunity to revise also the four volumes prepared by Sonia Orwell and Ian Angus of Orwell's essays, journalism, and letters. Having ascertained *a*) that Ian Angus had no wish to do this; and *b*) that he was very willing to help and guide me—as

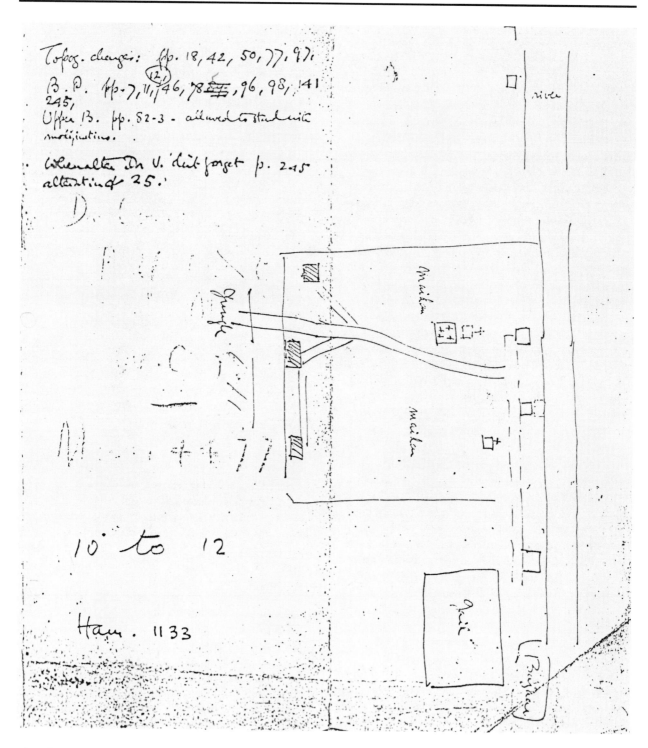

Orwell's map for the village of Kyauktada in Burmese Days *(by permission of the Orwell Archive, University College, London)*

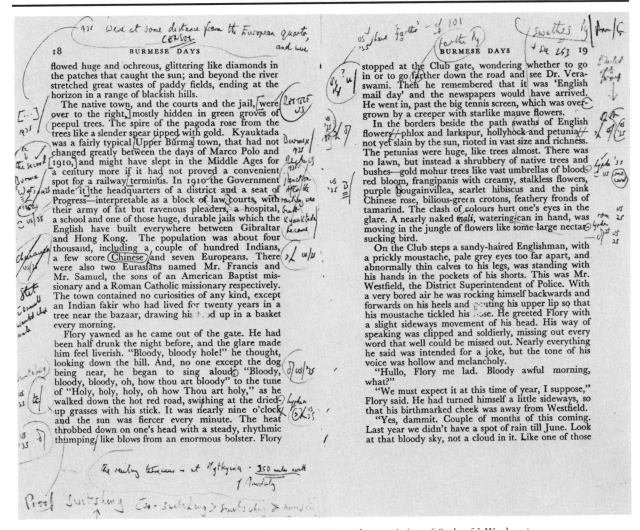

Peter Davison's working copy of Burmese Days *(by permission of Secker & Warburg)*

he most certainly has done—I agreed with some enthusiasm. So far I have prepared about 5,000 pages of text, taking the edition up to the beginning of 1944. While at the Folger I sought an opportunity to meet Dan Siegel, owner of the surviving leaves of the manuscript of *Nineteen Eighty-Four*. His kindness and cooperation permitted me to prepare that for publication, and the facsimile appeared in England, America, Germany, Holland, Italy, and Spain in 1984.

Among the items destined for inclusion in the complete essays, reviews, letters, etc., are the talks, news commentaries, and correspondence written by Orwell while working for the BBC during World War II and the plays he wrote for radio after leaving its service. (One of the latter, his adaptation of *Animal Farm*, broadcast on 14 and 15 January 1947, will be included as an appendix to the new edition

of that novel.) In 1985 two volumes of war broadcasts and war commentaries, edited by W. J. West, were published in a totally different enterprise from that which I am undertaking. The preface to the first volume announced this material as a "sudden discovery," and certainly Mr. West turned up some material which Ian Angus and I—engaged in the totality of Orwell's oeuvre over some forty years—had not then come to. However, that such material existed was well known to us; much had been in the possession of the Orwell and BBC Archives for a considerable time. Before Mr. West began his work and since the publication of his volumes we have collected more material. In any case, some of Mr. West's discovery had been, unknown to him, published some forty years earlier. Thus, the talks on Bernard Shaw and Jack London and extracts from the news commentaries were published, under Orwell's editorship, in India during the war.

Production of the original nine volumes was, alas, very slow. There were problems with the printing; proofs and text were mislaid and lost; 1984 came and went; only toward the end of 1985 did the English publishers decide to get the books out, no longer as a deluxe edition—the market of 1984 had been missed—and no longer all nine together, but three at a time in April 1986 (to mark Frederick Warburg's taking over Secker's fifty years before), September 1986, and spring 1987. Because of the long delay I asked to read all the proofs again to ensure nothing had gone amiss. Eventually the first three volumes appeared on the due date, 4 April 1986.

Reviews were rather good, though the critics reacted, perhaps understandably, to overenthusiastic hyping in the announcement of the edition. My whales, frowned D. J. Enright, were mere minnows. It depends, I suppose, whether you think an author's words and accidentals matter. Poets, I have noted, seem singularly uninterested in such matters, at least insofar as other authors' words are concerned. It was a professor of poetry at Oxford, Thomas Wharton, who wrote, "The faithful representation of texts is a matter of very subordinate importance." But then he wrote such lines as, "All pensive from her osier bowers, Cherwell arose."

But more worrying, Enright noted misprints—and misprints where my wife (a far better proofreader than am I) and I felt positive there should be none. Sure enough, the text was wrong. Laser wobble, said the printers. "Interference from radios of passing taxis," they offered. Then—and one has to appreciate to the full the depth of depression in the northeast of England to realize the hollow significance of this excuse: "Interference from ships' radar on the River Tyne." Would that the Tyne *had* ships passing along its narrow ways.

There probably is laser wobble—or radio interference—or even radar. But most of the errors come from something more fundamental. The errors are, in the main, those of an earlier setting of the text. They had been corrected and it would *seem*, though I am not a computer expert, that an uncorrected back-up disc has been resuscitated from limbo and used in printing this new edition. Only the review copies have been released; the rest have been pulped, I understand; and my wife and I have reread all the proofs of a second edition. A nice problem for a future enumerative bibliographer here! The frustration for publishers and editor may be imagined. Fortunately, only one reviewer seems to have noticed anything amiss. When the new "editions" appear, no one will be able to claim that the production of these new texts has been undertaken without straining every effort. But, oh for the days of hot metal printing. At least one knew one had dropped a form.

John Webster: The Melbourne Manuscript

Felix Pryor

The so-called Melbourne Manuscript (named after the house where it was found) was discovered on Good Friday 1985. It is a rough draft for part of a play, dating from the early years of the seventeenth century, and is written in a mixture of verse and prose. Its author has been identified as being John Webster (1580?-1634). If it is by him, it is the only manuscript in his handwriting to have survived. Not even a signature otherwise is known. Webster left a small body of work, two tragedies (*The White Devil* and *The Duchess of Malfi*) and one relatively minor tragicomedy (*The Devil's Law-Case*). Nevertheless, on the strength of these two tragedies, he is the most performed Elizabethan playwright after Shakespeare. William Hazlitt, who played a major part in re-establishing Webster's reputation in the early nineteenth century, declared that his tragedies came "the nearest to Shakespeare of anything we have upon record." Not even Ben Jonson is read or performed so often. Indeed in England, while five paperback editions of *The White Devil* and *The Duchess of Malfi* are available, there are no such editions of Jonson's two tragedies, *Sejanus* and *Catiline*, currently in print. Authorship apart, the Melbourne Manuscript is of indisputable importance as it is the only working draft (or "foul paper") by a playwright from Shakespeare's time to have come down to us.

The handwriting combines elements of the native Secretary forms and the modern Italic—an intermediate style highly characteristic of the first two decades of the century. From the revisions, overwritings, and crossings-out it is clearly autograph, in the hand of the author rather than dictated or copied. The manuscript covers four folio pages, made up from one large sheet folded in two.

It was found among the papers of Sir John Coke, who was at one time Principal Secretary of State to Charles I and founder of the dynasty that lives at Melbourne Hall to this day (among his descendants was the Viscount Melbourne after whom the Australian city is named, who did not live at the house himself but used it as a sort of penitential retreat for his erring wife, Lady Caroline Lamb). Coke's papers are preserved at Melbourne in their entirety. Among them are to be found family correspondence, official accounts, bills, reports, estimates—documents which testify to the meticulous habits of a distinguished public servant. Although Coke had for a while been secretary to the poet and politician Fulke Greville, it did not seem likely that the archive would yield up any further material of literary importance. The Fulke Greville papers had already been thoroughly catalogued in the three-volume report published by the Royal Commission on Historical Manuscripts in 1888. The transcript of an unrecorded seventeenth-century play had, it is true, been found there in the early 1870s. This had probably found its way into the archive because of the family's connections with the Inns of Court and had every appearance of being an isolated phenomenon. (The play, attributed to Thomas Heywood, is at present being edited for the Malone Society by Richard Proudfoot.)

Although the present manuscript was found among Coke's papers, it was never, properly speaking, part of them. This is perhaps why the Historical Manuscripts Commission catalogue makes no mention of it. Nevertheless the cataloguer did take care to docket it in pencil, and thus preserve a record of its original context within the archive. It is marked "Packet 3." From this it seems that when he first came across it, it was being used as wrapping for a bundle of documents. It had, in other words, been thrown away by its original owner and had subsequently found new employment in this humble capacity. This is borne out by the manner in which it has been folded and, in one section, dust-stained. According to the annotated catalogue at Melbourne Hall, two sets of Fulke Greville's household accounts for 1602-1603 were originally contained in the packet, along with other documents of the 1620s and 1630s.

Archaeological material that has come down to us is often retrieved from ancient rubbish pits. But it is unusual for the literary archaeologist to find things in this way. In the days before modern university archives, literary wastepaper was not usually preserved. This probably explains one of the salient features of the Melbourne Manuscript.

It is a unique survival. No other "foul paper" for a play of this period has come down to us. The fact that it had itself been thrown away provides a graphic illustration of the fate that must have befallen other examples.

The term "foul papers" means simply a rough or working draft. Thus in *The Devil's Law-Case*, Webster pokes fun at a lawyer whose brief has been torn up and instead has to "make shift with the foul copy" (and goes on to boast, having just been given twenty double ducats, "be the hand never so foul, Somewhat will be pick'd out on't"). The term is now used only in a bibliographical context. A foul paper has been defined by Sir Walter Greg as being any manuscript which retains "recognizable evidence of free composition"; or, as Harold Jenkins in his New Arden edition of *Hamlet* puts it, "any manuscript in a condition that presupposes that it will be succeeded by a fair copy"—a manuscript too messy for use in the theater. Foul papers have their origin therefore in the author's study rather than the playhouse. It is of them that Shakespeare's first editors wrote when they said that they had "scarce received from him a blot in his papers."

Their bibliographical importance derives from the fact that it is from them, rather than the playhouse prompt books, that a great many Elizabethan plays seem to have been printed. No doubt the prompt copy was deemed too valuable for the theater to part with. It contained, apart from anything else, the certification of the Master of the Revels without which the play could not be performed (making it very much the master copy). So not only does the Melbourne Manuscript allow us to see an Elizabethan dramatist at work, but it provides an important source of bibliographical data.

But even in the absence of any known examples, a good deal was already known about the nature and format of Elizabethan foul papers. One knew what to expect. For example, in his correspondence with the theatrical manager Philip Henslowe, the playwright Robert Daborne makes several references to his foul papers which he has promised to copy out. Commenting on this, Greg writes that "when he speaks of sheets he means, not leaves or pages (as a modern author might), but four page foolscap sheets, the unit of numbering in many playhouse Books." The Melbourne Manuscript is just such a four-page foolscap sheet, the first page being numbered "2" (as Richard Proudfoot was first to notice), presumably indicating that it was the second unit of the complete draft. It has also been established that writing paper was sold by Elizabethan stationers ready folded,

trimmed of some of its deckle, and measuring $12'' \times 7\ 3/4''$. This again conforms exactly to the format and dimensions of our manuscript.

The Melbourne Manuscript contains, more or less, a complete scene from an otherwise lost play. Two pieces of evidence allow one to reconstruct a surprising amount about the lost work—not least the fact that it was cast as a tragedy. A reference in the fragment to Lorenzo de' Medici makes it clear that the plot is based on the history of Alessandro de' Medici, first Duke of Florence, who was murdered by his boon companion and kinsman Lorenzo, known as Lorenzino. In our scene, laid early in the play (as the number "2" indicates), Alessandro is shown a letter accusing Lorenzo of treachery. He is thrown into a welter of anxiety. This earns him the scorn of his favorite (who has come to him with the news that he has procured for him his sister). When the letter is produced, Lorenzo grumbles that it must be the complaint of a tailor, an innkeeper, or a pregnant mistress, and expresses the opinion that a favorite should not be subjected to such petty harassment. He is given it to read, the prince—like Hamlet at the play—"attentively marking him" (as the stage direction states). He remains unmoved, and the prince concludes that he must be innocent. Whereupon Lorenzo confesses his guilt. The prince is horrified. His favorite then assures him that he has only been consorting with enemies of the state so as to discover their secrets.

This outline can only give an inkling of the scene's complexity and dramatic momentum. The richness of the plotting is matched by the language. For example, news of his favorite's treachery forces from the Prince the anguished reflection: "can there be a happy state Before man meets with his last state?" Recognizing this as a well-worn cliché (the last couplet of *Oedipus Rex*), his murderer to be—the person who is going to grant him such happiness—compliments him on his learning: "well, it is a commendable thing in a prince, I hope you will in time write books, that the whole world may laugh at you." When Lorenzo comes to account for his activities, he gives a chilling justification of the spy's trade: "are not all your statesmen great intelligencers, and without this intelligence can there be anything done in this commonwealth; why it is the spectacles wise men put on to read other lines and how they should direct their own acts. Some with infinite sums corrupt those who are able to inform them; Consalves the Grand Capitan, put in Ferdinand's reckoning a million of Crowns given to spies. Others with an easier way, and sweeter know their enemies' secrets namely by lying with their wives or mistresses. . . ."

This "Websterian" tone is of course by no means conclusive proof that Webster wrote the piece. But, at any rate, it gives us a starting point. Not all imagined literary discoveries sound typical of their putative authors (or for that matter have the merit of being well written). And if Webster is indeed author of the piece, there can be no doubt from the manuscript's "foulness" that it is in his handwriting (of which no other examples are known).

Two of the most Websterian passages (including the one quoted above) contain echoes of *The White Devil* and *The Duchess of Malfi*. In any other writer, this might be seen as having only a limited significance. After all, an echo is a common enough thing. But Webster used echoes (or "borrowings") of phrases and vivid images as a compositional technique: a practice that Muriel Bradbrook likens to the collage technique of *The Wasteland*. Images, which in themselves are far from commonplace, are found both in *The White Devil* and *The Duchess of Malfi*. In the Melbourne Manuscript a bizarre parallel is drawn between a courtier's staff and a surveying instrument called a Jacob's Staff, which Lorenzo thinks would be ideal for measuring a cuckold's horns (the prince's). The same thought had occurred to Flamineo in *The White Devil*. Similarly, Lorenzo's use of a startlingly concrete image (a pair of spectacles) in conjunction with an abstract notion (intelligence gathering) echoes Bosola's complaint (made in response to Ferdinand's query, "How thrives our intelligence?") that he needs spectacles to read what is hidden in the stars.

One of Webster's favorite quarries for "borrowing" images was Jonson's *Sejanus*. This, with the later *Catiline*, was the only contemporary stage work that he used in the thoroughgoing manner that characterizes his use of more academically "respectable" sources, such as Continental works in translation and Sidney's *Arcadia* (a compliment to Jonson made explicit by the ranking accorded him in the introduction to *The White Devil*). Since Lorenzo is made to compare himself to Sejanus, the seducer of Livia, it seems that, when writing this scene, Webster's mind was running on Jonson's play. So it is surely more than a coincidence that in it he "borrows" an image from *Sejanus*.

On the subject of *Sejanus*—it has, from time to time, been conjectured that its preface alludes to Shakespeare: "this book, in all numbers, is not the same with that which was acted on the public

stage, wherein a second pen had good share: in place of which I have rather chosen, to put weaker (and no doubt less pleasing) of mine own, than to defraud so happy a genius of his right, by my loathed usurpation." Webster had at about this time been responsible for adapting Marston's play *The Malcontent* for performance at the Globe. He makes perhaps a slightly less improbable candidate than Shakespeare.

The second piece of evidence from which we can reconstruct at least a hypothetical outline of the lost play is *The Traitor* by James Shirley (who is known to have adapted elements from *The Duchess of Malfi* in his most successful play, *The Cardinal*). *The Traitor* also tells the story of Alessandro's murder by Lorenzo, and tells it in the manner of *The White Devil*, *The Duchess of Malfi*, and *The Revenger's Tragedy*, complete with a revenger's masque and the heroine's corpse made-up to masquerade as the real thing. The corresponding scene in Shirley's play (I.ii) is clearly a reworking of the Melbourne play, preserving a general outline and some verbal echoes (none reflecting Webster's distinctive style). Shirley's version is the work of an inferior playwright. In it we are no longer confronted by the malcontent's mockery or the prince's foolish attempts at erudition, nor with the unexpected reversals of the plot which give the scene its dramatic power and purpose. We are given merely accusation and denial, delivered straight and with gusto, without the humor or the complex and disturbing modulations that characterize the original.

John Russell Brown has observed that *The White Devil* and *The Duchess of Malfi* share many of the characteristics of a diptych—"two great tragedies, both set at court" and "in important ways two versions of a single subject." If Shirley's play preserves at least the outline of the original, the lost play might well have formed the third part of a triptych. Like them, it is based on what was then a relatively recent occurrence in Italian Renaissance history, and like them it hinges on the relationship between a sister and her brother (or brothers). Its plot is drawn from the same source as *The Duchess of Malfi*, Painter's *Palace of Pleasure*. The subplot of Shirley's play is based on the same translation of Machiavelli's history as had been used by Webster in *The White Devil*. The Melbourne fragment shows the same painstaking manner of using source materials (analyzed in great detail by Gunnar Bocklund) as the other two plays, *The White Devil* especially. The scene is taken from Bernardo Segni's *Istorie Fiorentine*, where Lorenzo's double bluff is described. In missing this, Shirley's version can

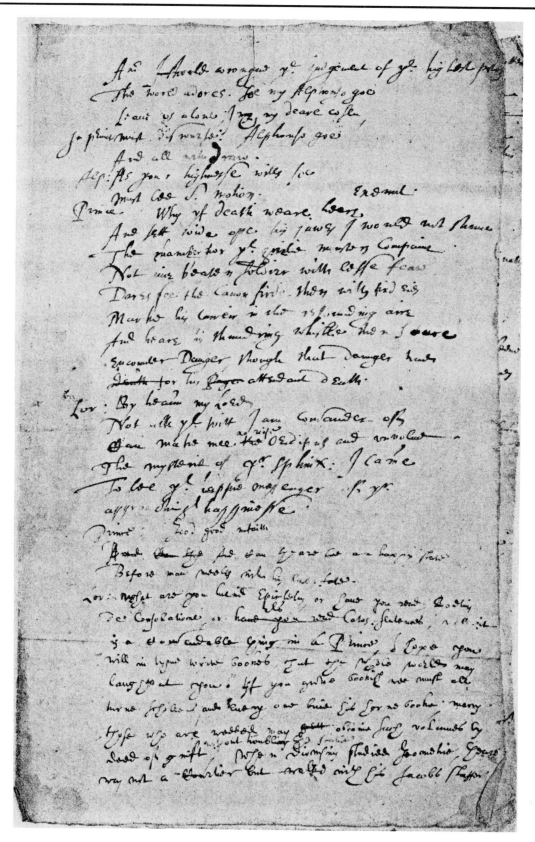

Manuscript page from John Webster's The Duke of Florence, *with a transcription of the page (Trustees of the Melbourne Garden Charities/Bloomsbury Book Auctions, 20 June 1986)*

And wrongue y^e judgement of y^e highest policy
The world adores. Goe my Aphonso goe
Leave us alone I w[ith] my deare cosen,
In privie must discourse: Alphonso goe
And all withdraw.
Alp: As your highnesse wills soe
must bee o^r motion: Exeunt.
Prince. Why yf death weare heare
And sett wide ope his jawes I would not shune
The chamber for ye grizlie monsters Companie.
Nor [. . .] beaten soldire with lesse feare
Dares see the Canon firde, then with fixd eie
Marke his Carreir in the resounding aire
And heare his thundring whistle then I [?] dare
Encounter Danger, though that danger had
For his attendant death.
Lor: By heav'n my Lord
Not alle, ye witt I am com[m]ander of
Can make mee a wise Oedipus and unvolve
The mysterie of y^r sphinx: I came
To bee ye happie messenger of y^r
approaching happinesse.
Prince: Good good infaith
And can there bee an happy state
Before man meetes with his last fate.
Lor What are you [?] learnd Epictetus; or have you read Boetius
de Consolatione; or els Catos sentences; well: it
is a Com[m]endable thing in a Prince, I hope you
will in tyme write bookes, that the whole world may
laugh at you. Yf you quote bookes wee must all
turne scholers, and every one buie his horne booke; marry
those who are wedded, may obtaine such volumes by
deed of guift/ without troubling the stationer/; when Dionisius studied Geometrie theare
was not a Courtier but walkd with his Jacobs staffe

be said to have less historical, as well as dramatic, validity. Lorenzo's mocking erudition, a characteristic which he shares with that other malcontent, Bosola, is also rooted in the historical record, but finds no place in Shirley's version. It is possible also that Lorenzo's machinations were suggested by episodes in *The Fawn* and *The Malcontent* by John Marston—a playwright who had a considerable influence on Webster.

One of the most intriguing aspects of the whole business lies in the relationship of the Alessandro-Lorenzino plot to the source material of *The White Devil*. None of the known sources for *The White Devil* explains why Webster should have given his heroine, Vittoria, a Moorish serving maid. Nor do they explain why Zanche, the serving maid, should become violently infatuated with Francesco de' Medici, Duke of Florence. The Duke of Florence, in his turn (and in defiance of historical probability), adopts the disguise of a Moor in order to accomplish his revenge on Vittoria. This Moorish element is the only one for which Professor Bocklund can find no source; a factor which he believes to be "of considerable significance for our understanding of the art and dramatic workmanship of John Webster." The Duke of Florence who appears in *The White Devil* was successor to Cosimo, the second Duke and avenger of the subject of the Melbourne fragment. In real life, Alessandro's mother

was believed to have been, like Zanche, a Moorish serving maid and his father the Medici Pope, Urban VII. Certainly his portrait by Bronzino shows readily enough why Alessandro de' Medici, Duke of Florence, should have been nicknamed "il Moro."

James Shirley's adaptation held the stage for many years and was much admired by Samuel Pepys (who didn't think much of *The White Devil*). Shirley's play in its turn was subjected to adaptation. This last metamorphosis is the rumbustious melodrama *Evadne: or the Statue* by Richard Sheil (1791-1851), later member of Parliament for Milborne Port and a distinguished supporter of Daniel O'Connell. *Evadne* played thirty times at Covent Garden during the season of 1818-1819. It was also performed with great success in St. Louis and Philadelphia, and its last recorded performance was in New York on 13 December 1881. It is strange to think of the attenuated ghost of Webster's lost tragedy stalking the New York stage little more than a hundred years ago.

The manuscript was put up for sale by Bloomsbury Book Auctions in London on 20 June 1986, with a presale estimate of £200,000-£400,000 (approximately $300,000-$600,000). However, it failed to find a buyer, remaining unsold at £170,000.

The Cult of Biography

John Letts
Managing Director, The Folio Society

The Folio Society is an unusual organization, which has no exact parallel anywhere in the world. It was founded in 1947. It celebrates, therefore, its fortieth birthday this year. It sells unlikely books (by which I mean not obviously popular books) all over the world from its headquarters in Southwark, London, England, close to the boundary wall of the old Marshalsea Debtors Prison, where Charles Dickens's father was once imprisoned. Name any country in the world (almost) and the Folio Society will have members there. It will have members in Moscow, in Peking, in Mexico City. (It even has at least one member in Peculiar, Ohio, which to the English sounds as near as Timbuktu.) It sells books to the humble and the grand, impartially. Recently, Her Majesty's ambassador in Washington (a member of long standing) presented a copy of a Folio Society book to the president of the United States, by way of celebrating the bicentennial of the signing of the Treaty of Paris. The society therefore treasures a charming letter of thanks from the forty-seventh president of the United States. But it has also a formidable army of humbler supporters all over the English-speaking world, who will occasionally recognize each other by some hint, some remark, some quotation, as part of what sometimes seems a highly intriguing underground cultural freemasonry.

Biography, history, and memoirs have long been a major part of the range of books the Folio Society has been selling. But before describing the society's interest in biography, perhaps one should give a broader description. The intention of the founders was "to produce editions of the world's greatest literature in a format worthy of the contents, at a price within the reach of everyman." In the preface to his famous 1758 edition of Milton, the great printer and type founder John Baskerville was aspiring to similar objectives when he wrote: "It is not my desire to print many books; but such only as are *books of consequence, or intrinsic merit, or established Reputation;* and which the public may be pleased to see in an elegant dress, and to purchase at such a price as will pay the extraor-

Front cover for texts of the debate on literary biography

dinary care and expense that must necessarily be bestowed upon them."

In practice, this has meant publishing one new book a month (with a few extras) for forty years. It has also meant publishing in a curious half world, which has no exact parallels in normal trade publishing. It has always seemed to me that future researchers in the history of publishing will find one small group of enterprises, all started in the second quarter of the twentieth century, which will be impossible to classify except in a little group of their own. Clearly they were not private presses, as antiquarian booksellers understand the term. Nor were they exactly commercial publishers, in the normal sense of the word, because they did not distribute books in the customary way through bookshops: they sold direct to their customers by post. That should perhaps suggest a classification as book clubs. Yet that title hardly suits either, because, unlike the commercial book clubs (which were first conjured up by marketing men in the United States in the 1920s), this group generally chose or commissioned their own editorial material rather than buying it from the originating publishers, and, in particular, always designed their own editions, and never took sheets from other publishers.

Doubtless those historians and archaeologists of the book trade will argue at length about the membership of this specialized group. By my personal definitions, it would include just three enterprises which have continued to publish in their idiosyncratic way for a longish period. These are the Limited Editions Club of New York (whose life span started in 1929 and is not yet quite complete); the English Nonesuch Press, whose heyday ran from 1923 to 1934; and the Folio Society, founded in 1947 and still apparently at the peak of its orbit in 1987. Purists, or the disputatious, might suggest adding the short-lived Imprint Society of Boston to the list, or the strangely erratic Fortune Press of London. But for me, as I said, this biological subclassification would contain a mere three members, and each so unlike the others as almost to cast doubt on the validity of this genus.

That splendid eccentric of line and vision, Saul Steinberg, once published a drawing which illustrated a dialogue between a sturdy and rather stupid-looking art student and an irritated professor of drawing. The girl was saying, defiantly: "But you said half horse and half man. . . ." What she had drawn on her canvas was a pantomime horse rather than a centaur. What the members of my genus have in common is that all were centaurs of the publishing world: half publisher, and half book club, in different mixtures. But, as Steinberg observed, there are more ways than one of constructing a centaur.

The bias of the Limited Editions Club at its best was toward the artist. The late George Macey even persuaded such eminent names as Picasso and Matisse to join his cast list, although these were in their eminence very much the exceptions among the four or five hundred artists employed by the LEC in half a century. Typographical expertise was

always present, of course, but perhaps less pervasively than in the Nonesuch list where the household god, if there was one, was probably Aldus Manutius, and the glories of type were worshiped above all else. In both these lists, editorial consideration was manifest: deployed in ways sometimes capricious or esoteric, as at Nonesuch, or sometimes distinctly perfunctory in the later LEC. In the Folio list, it seemed to perform a different and more prominent role, which is in the end (together with the fact that Folio books have set themselves the added task of being relatively inexpensive) mainly responsible for the highly characteristic and individual Folio flavor.

In Folio 21, Charles Ede had this to say about the development of the society's editorial policy:

> In building each year's programme, the first aim has always been to achieve a balance between the different categories of literature— novels, short stories, memoirs, belles-lettres, poetry and drama. . . . To begin with our policy was frankly unadventurous and largely based on the established classics, partly because we felt that only books which had stood the test of time justified a comparatively expensive "suit of clothes" and partly because we were in no state to take the commercial gamble of publishing the lesser known. Gradually, we began to "rescue" minor classics which we felt had been unjustifiably neglected. Over the last decade, and under the influence of our present editorial director, Brian Rawson, we have published an increasing number of non-fiction titles which fall broadly into the category of "eyewitness history!" These range from the first English translation of the verbatim report of Joan of Arc's trial to Sherman's own account of the famous "March to the Sea!"

Brian Rawson, editorial director from 1956 until his death in 1975, made an outstanding personal contribution to the editorial output of the society for nineteen years. His influence is most easily to be found in the length and strength of the vast number of interesting—and often half-forgotten—books to be found under the heading of History and Memoirs. The great classic diaries, autobiographies, personal memoirs of extraordinary travels or adventures at which the writer was present—all have been grist to our mill. Since I share his enthusiasm for the genre, it has not proved a difficult example to follow. However, my guess is that whichever style of Folio books one prefers— classical fiction, fiction in translation, poetry, history and memoir, essays, or belles-lettres—this un-usual collection holds together simply because it is a balance of opposites.

In the first decade, 1947-1957, it is certainly true that most of the popular books were fiction, but then the early lists contained few titles which were not either novels or poetry. Perhaps the pub-lication of that compelling piece of literary detec-tion by A. J. A. Symons, *The Quest for Corvo*, in 1952, gave members a taste for the biographical and his-torical, because a translation of Saint-Simon's vivid memoirs headed the list in 1953 and from then on history and biography never lagged far behind.

It was in the 1960s that the historical strain in our output came to the surface. *The Twelve Cae-sars, Scott's Last Expedition,* and *The Life of Muhammad* led the list in 1964, and from 1968 until 1971 all the most popular titles were history. The storm troops of this palace revolution were *The Travels of Marco Polo* and *The Hammer of Witchcraft,* Geoffrey of Monmouth's *History of the Kings of Britain, The Tudor Venturers* (an astute compilation from Rich-ard Hakluyt), Brian Rawson's new and revised edi-tion of *A Memoir of the 'Forty-five* by the Chevalier de Johnstone, and George Bull's translation of Va-sari's *Life of Michelangelo.*

Perhaps some readers can plot the move-ments within this enigmatic tideswell and draw con-clusions which escape me. For my part, I can see none, except that members of the Folio Society en-joy the advantages of a well-stocked bookcase (or library), where the roving eye will find much that is familiar, and much that is surprising, too. This feature was neatly expressed by Kingsley Amis, who, in reviewing the society's list in 1979, wrote:

The section of the list I will call non-fiction gave me most of my surprises. Bernal Diaz was a soldier with Cortes' expedition to Mex-ico; he saw it all, remembered it in astound-ing detail, and dictated the story to his children at the age of 84, when almost blind. J M Cohen made what is evidently the first modern translation—title, *The Conquest of New Spain.* In *The Mutiny and Piratical Seizure of HMS Bounty,* by Sir John Barrow (Navy Secretary in the 1800s), the accounts of Bligh's immense open-boat voyage and of the disaster-racked pursuit of the mutineers fas-cinated me even more than the mutiny itself. *The Narrative of the Voyage of HMS Beagle* (compiled from contemporary sources and illustrations) is a very different but no less extraordinary sea-story.

Of course the boundaries between history, memoir, biography, and autobiography are vaguer than one imagines. The society's taste in recent years has been pretty catholic in this area. It has ranged from Anna Leonowens (*A Governess at the Court of the King of Siam*) to Harriet Wilson (of "Pub-lish and be damned" fame). It has included Hes-keth Pearson's incomparable *The Smith of Smiths* and Michael Kelly's musical reminiscences. It has in-cluded Benjamin Constant and T. E. Lawrence; Boswell and Pepys; Fanny Burney and Flora Tris-tan. A recital of our publishing in this area looks like a set of campaign honors from some Hundred Years War of Biography. It may explain how, when the Folio Society set about choosing a subject for its second public debate, it felt entitled to choose biography as a subject, having served so many years in its service. In opening this debate, the current managing director justified his choice in these terms:

I remember Malcolm Muggeridge once opened a review of a biography in these words: "Searching around for a new subject for his busy pen, Lord Beaverbrook has hit upon Christ." In that industrious and cath-olic spirit, we have hit on the subject of bi-ography. Let me say why.

The Folio Society, for many years, has divided its favours, more or less equally, be-tween fiction and history, with a little—per-haps too little—poetry thrown in. The history side has included all sorts: memoirs, gossip, autobiographies, eye-witness narra-tives, even a certain amount of real history; and some biography. So we do have a de-clared interest.

In our list today, for instance, I am proud to say members can find the first great classic of English biography . . . the moving life of Sir Thomas More, set down shortly before his death, by his son-in-law William Roper. Roper knew his place. His opening words were brief: "For as much as Sir Thomas More, sometime Lord Chancellor of England, a man of singular virtue, and of pure unspotted conscience, was in his day accounted a man worthy of perpetual fa-mous memory . . . I, William Roper, though most unworthy, thought it my part to set forth such matters touching his life as I could at present call to remembrance."

Such humility is perhaps less common today. One modern writer, revealing in a re-cent symposium that he had published full length biographies in 1977, 1978, 1980, 1981 and 1983, also disclosed that he normally does hardly any research before writing a first draft, and yet claims "to know his subject better than I know any of my friends." Some writers present tonight might envy such Stakhanovite productivity.

However, apart from such classics as Iris Origo's marvelous *The Merchant of Prato*, and Michael Sadleir's fine double biography *Blessington D'Orsay*, most Folio editions in this area are in fact autobiographies. And autobiography, it was once wisely said, " . . . presents an unrivalled vehicle for telling the truth about other people."

Today the boot is somewhat on the other foot. Last year I found a branch library in which biographies were on the shelves classed as fiction—and who would say the librarian was wholly wrong?

But I must not leave the idea that I am taking sides in this motion. Some of my best friends are biographers. To them we are indebted for most of those glimpses of the great that make them seem a little smaller and more human as one approaches more closely. I treasure the thought of Ruskin, seen crossing the Channel on a stormy day, advocating jumping as a cure for seasickness. Or Admiral Collingwood saying testily: "I do wish Nelson would stop signalling. We all know what to do." And I think of the immortal John Aubrey, fixed forever in this one short paragraph by his quarrelsome friend Anthony Wood: "He was a shiftless person, roving and magotty-headed, and sometimes little better than crazed. And being exceedingly credulous would stuff his many letters sent to A. W. with fooleries and misinformations, which sometimes would guide him into paths of error."

Let us hope none of today's biographers do that. Otherwise, the practice of biography would certainly add a new terror to death. . . .

The brief outline I have given here of the society's interest in biography is, of course, strictly a view from the inside. For a view from the outside, looking in, let me turn to a perhaps unlikely source, *The British Medical Journal*. In its issue of 5 January 1980, it carried an article called *Anything but Science* by M. H. Lader. He wrote:

Intrigued by the descriptions of the forthcoming year's offerings (for one must buy at least four volumes a year, in advance), I have ordered books that I would normally have considered of little interest. And I have rarely been disappointed. In my fifteen years

or so of membership, I have stormed Quebec with Wolfe, braved the prairie Indians with Parkman, been sickened at Cortez's treatment of the Aztecs, seen the rivers of blood at the sack of Jerusalem in AD 70, been revolted at the barbarities of the Caribbean pirates, travelled Asia with Marco Polo, and shivered with Napoleon in the Russian wastes. I have sniggered at Aubrey's *Brief Lives*, and studied Machiavelli's *The Prince* for helpful hints with administrative duties. I have read Tolstoy and Tolkien, Manzoni and Monmouth, Plato and Pliny, Stendhal and Saki, Aksakov and Zola, and *The Bible*, in a version meant for reading not quoting or intoning. More offbeat offerings have included *Malleus Maleficarum*, a sort of witch-catchers *vade-mecum*, and *The Ship of Fools* by Sebastian Brant with its vision of the world overrun by fools of every description. . . .

Such praise, of course, seems an almost unbelievable reward for one's labors. We, working at the coal-face of book production, are aware, only too aware, of the product itself, its waywardness and imperfections. So it is pleasant to be reminded so graphically that the end product, on the occasions when we plan correctly, can give such genuine and lasting pleasure.

The Second Folio Society Debate (excerpts)

Resolved: "Biographers are generally a disease of English Literature"

From Germaine Greer's speech for the motion:

Literary biographers are not like the benign inhabitants of the bowel that enable the processes of digestion to be completed, but like *Shigella* and *Salmonella*, weaken and debilitate their host, feeding on him to make a product of their own. Of all the biography organisms, literary biography is the most predatory, the laziest and the least enterprising, for its subject is the most accessible and the most vulnerable. Since the microbe came to its full development in Boswell, it has grown steadily more resistant and more impassive.

From Victoria Glendinning's speech against the motion:

Whatever the "English Disease" is, it is not biography. The biographical impulse, together with the lyric impulse, is in fact the source of all literature, of mankind's entire body of writing. Biography, in its origins and as it has developed in our own lifetimes, is inextricable from history, from fiction and from poetry. The biographer has a secure place in the literary tradition. What were the bards who celebrated the feats of chieftains in preliterate days, but poetic biographers? What were the heroic epics and the romances out of which European and English literature grew, but biographies? What are the four gospels, the glory of the English language in the King James Bible, but four biographies of the same mysterious person?

From Auberon Waugh's speech for the motion:

So let us categorise the gossip tradition of literary biography as a disease in the sense of a benign growth. The nineteenth century saw an altogether more assertive form of biography bedevilled by a claim to seriousness, respectability and above all comprehensiveness. My objection to this approach is the same as my objection to most history and all serious journalism. Anybody who has been present at an incident and later seen it reported, with the best will in the world, in the newspaper the next day—at a time when the incident is fresh in everyone's mind—will be aware of innumerable inaccuracies in the report. It seems to me an absurdity which is implicit in serious biography that any outsider can possibly describe the life of anyone else; further, that it is an insult to all human intelligence to suppose that by studying a person's public actions or by rooting around for his private ones, anything but a partial and prejudiced portrait can result. To the extent that biography relies upon other people's testimony it has the same virtues and vices as the gossip column where truth is generally acknowledged to be partial and probably prejudiced. It is for this reason that I often maintain that greater truth is to be found in the gossip columns than in the news columns of newspapers.

From Richard Holmes's speech against the motion:

Yet for all this, biography—good biography—is never complacent. Its very nature is to be experimental, enquiring, relentlessly question-

ing. It is never satisfied with human affairs, it always wishes to know more, and to tell the story differently. In this aspect it seems to me that it frequently goes beyond the novel, and asks the kinds of questions that fiction cannot really formulate. As a working biographer I am continually coming across questions of the following kind:

(a) How is the human character formed, and can a person act "out" of character? And if so, what does this mean? Now a novelist cannot really pose this question—he can only pretend to—because he is in the end the absolute arbiter of everything that happens to his people.

(b) What is the inter-play between family inheritance, social circumstance, personality, historic events, and "sheer chance" in the shaping of a human life? In what sense are we the pawns of destiny?

(c) How far can we ever really know another human being? Are conversations, letters, even intimate diaries and journals a true guide to someone's inner life? Or are they in a sense themselves fictions—metafictions—of that life? And what lies in that innermost sanctum—religious or sexual experience perhaps? Or childhood memories? Or something beyond these, a kind of private poetry of the self ?

(d) Then what, morally speaking, makes a human life worthwhile or "fulfilled"? What, indeed, is the nature of human worth, which surely must be distinguished from such modern shibboleths as "success" or "fame"?

(e) Finally, what is the nature of artistic or scientific creativity? Is it entirely a mystery, or can we have some insight into its workings and inspirations?

Biography addresses itself to all of these questions.

[Postscript]
After some speeches from the floor, the motion was put to the vote and defeated by a majority of approximately two to one.

The American Poets' Corner:
The First Three Years (1983-1986)

Daniel Haberman

The American Poets' Corner was formally dedicated on 7 May 1984 in the Cathedral Church of St. John the Divine, New York City. Similar in concept to the English Poets' Corner in Westminster Abbey, which since 1599 has served to remind all peoples of that nation's literary heritage, the American Poets' Corner is housed in the arts bay on the north side of the cathedral's nave. Twenty-three words had been cut into the stone of the back wall: "THE POETS' CORNER Dedicated To American Literature *My heart is inditing a good matter; my tongue is the pen of a ready writer.*'" [Psalm 45].

The first writers to be elected for induction into the Poets' Corner were Emily Dickinson and Walt Whitman; Washington Irving was inducted at the same time, having been previously selected by the dean of the cathedral to commemorate the bicentennial of Irving's birth. Subsequently, Herman Melville and Edgar Allan Poe were elected (1985); then, Robert Frost and Nathaniel Hawthorne (1986); and, Ralph Waldo Emerson and Mark Twain (1987).

The service of dedication linked 385 years, recalling a time when Ben Jonson, Michael Drayton, and others dropped their quills into the grave of Edmund Spenser and began the original Poets' Corner. The greeting of the current dean of Westminster, the Very Reverend Edward Carpenter, began, "It gives me great pleasure—indeed I regard it as a privilege—to send the greetings of the Dean and Chapter of Westminster to you on the day when you are formally dedicating your American Poets' Corner, . . . " and concluded, "I therefore greet you most warmly on this significant day and I can assure you that it gives satisfaction here that a great nation which speaks 'the tongue that Shakespeare spake' and is linked up with us in a common literary heritage should have the means, in a Cathedral Church, of honouring those who have used this language with felicity, grace and genius. I know I am right when I say that you will not lack such worthies to honour in the coming years."

The history of the Poets' Corner is an American one, indeed. In December 1982 the novelist Howard Fast had introduced Daniel Haberman to the Very Reverend James Parks Morton, the Dean of the Cathedral Church of St. John the Divine. None of them then knew of the quest of the Reverend William D. Eddy, rector of Christ Episcopal Church, Tarrytown, New York—the church in which Washington Irving had served as a vestryman; unable to place Irving in Westminster Abbey's Poets' Corner, Father Eddy had been trying to convince the National Cathedral in Washington, D.C. to commence an American Poets' Corner, with Washington Irving. On 1 March 1983 Dean Morton attended a poetry reading by Daniel Haberman; the next day, Father Eddy was in the dean's office; the following day, he wrote to Dean Morton: "To have the idea of Washington Irving's Bicentennial launching the Poets' Corner pondered, accepted and, in a trice, set up for Nov. 27, 1983 at 4 P.M. after Evensong—what has ever been done with more dispatch!"

In mid October Daniel Haberman was presented with the dean's request that he become the first cathedral poet-in-residence and create an American Poets' Corner. The position was subsequently accepted upon the following conditions: (1) the entire arts bay of the cathedral would be exclusively reserved for writers, though not limited to poets; (2) the Poets' Corner would be created outside the cathedral and the poet-in-residence would have the freedom to assemble a group of writers who would function as consultants (electors) and, in addition, choose the candidates for induction; (3) the dean's authority over the Poets' Corner would be limited to that of a veto and the poet-in-residence would report directly to the dean; and (4) the service of dedication would be in May, rather than November, and at that time three writers would be inducted into the Poets' Corner.

From its inception the Poets' Corner was "its own institution," and it would have to earn the respect of its nation's writers and other artists, its academies and academics, as well as that of the press and general public. It would have to establish guidelines and consult with writers representing different regions of America, with different styles of writing, with a reputation for integrity. They would be called electors, to make it clear that they do the electing of the deceased American writers to be inducted into the Poets' Corner, rather than follow the English method, which has the dean of Westminster do the selecting.

The first telephone call made was to Anthony Hecht, who was then the consultant in poetry to the Library of Congress. Other calls produced the following thirteen original electors: Daniel Aaron, Edgar Bowers, Joseph Brodsky, the late J. V. Cunningham, Guy Davenport, Daniel Haberman, Anthony Hecht, John Hollander, the late Josephine Miles, Ann Stanford, Robert Penn Warren, Eudora Welty, and Richard Wilbur. From then on all decisions were made in consultation with various electors, and not one was vetoed by the cathedral's dean. Never did an elector decline a telephone call, or say, "I'll have to call you back"; all stopped and gave their full attention to the Poets' Corner.

Upon the acceptance by the original electors, a call was placed to the Academy of American Poets. The late Marie (Mrs. Hugh) Bullock, founder/president of the academy, subsequently accepted the position of honorary chairman; Lyn (Mrs. Edward T.) Chase, a vice-president of the academy and a trustee of the cathedral, became an elector ex officio.

The Poets' Corner would, during its formative years, restrict itself to three activities: (1) an annual election and memorialization of two deceased American writers; (2) an annual Poets' Corner Cathedral Lecture, which would be an original lecture on a writer who had been elected to the Poets' Corner, and which would be given by a poet who previously need not have done extensive work on the elected writer; and (3) a Muriel Rukeyser Poetry Wall, which would be an interior wall of the Cathedral dedicated to deceased American poets who are today not well known, that is, "poets' poets," and which would for a period of time display poems, letters, and biographical material for one poet.

Eighteen months later, the "Guidelines for the American Poets' Corner" had been agreed upon, accepted by the cathedral's dean, and sent to the *New York Times*. These guidelines recognize that the Poets' Corner is dealing with an infinite period of time and operating within a religious institution. They attempt to provide a proper tension of checks and balances. For example, the terms of both the electors and the poet-in-residence must be limited, and they must not appoint their own successors; the dean of the cathedral must consult with writers before choosing a new poet-in-residence. These guidelines are:

1) *THE ELECTORS*

There shall be thirteen Electors. Twelve of these Electors shall serve on a constantly rotating committee and the thirteenth Elector shall be the Poet-in-Residence. The rotational cycle shall be achieved by having four Electors serve for a five-year term, a four-year term, and a three-year term. No Elector shall serve for more than two consecutive terms.

The Electors shall vote annually by written ballot to admit two deceased American writers into The Poets' Corner. The Electors shall keep voting until two valid candidates have each received eight votes. There is no limitation with regard to the style of writing or to the writer's date of death.

The Electors shall be American writers and should represent different regions of America, though all of them need not be poets, nor should they represent only one or two schools of literature. The Electors shall be persons of personal ability and professional integrity.

2) *THE CATHEDRAL POET-IN-RESIDENCE*

The Poet-in-Residence shall serve at the pleasure of the Dean of The Cathedral Church of St. John the Divine, and without compensation (except for out-of-pocket expenses). He shall report directly to the Dean and he shall not serve for a period in excess of five years. The Poet-in-Residence shall submit all proposed appointments to the Dean for his possible veto.

The Poet-in-Residence shall appoint the Electors, the annual Lecturer for the Poets' Corner Cathedral Lecture, and the deceased American writer for the semi-annual display on the Muriel Rukeyser Poetry Wall. He shall choose the inscriptions for the memorial stones, and he shall be responsible for all poetry activities within the Cathedral Church.

The Poet-in-Residence shall consult in writing with the Electors on the choice of future Electors, the annual Lecturer, and the memorial inscriptions.

Guests at the first induction ceremony in 1984: Front, Marie Bullock; left to right, Zubin Mehta, Michael Tree, Dean Morton, Daniel Haberman, Edgar Bowers, Marcus Haddock, aide to Mrs. Bullock, Walter Cronkite, Rosalyn Tureck, and Barbara Nissman (photo ©1984 by Susie Maeder)

3) *THE DEAN OF THE CATHEDRAL CHURCH*

The Dean shall choose a Poet-in-Residence who is a person of serious literary ability, though he or she need not be a "recognized" poet.

Prior to making this appointment, the Dean shall request at least one book of poetry written by the poet and, in addition, some written comments by other writers on the poet's literary merits. The Dean shall then check these with the literary members of the American Academy of Arts and Letters. The Dean shall also make inquiries with four poets, though two of these may be among the then-sitting members of the Academy, and two of these may be among the then-sitting Electors to The Poets' Corner.

The Dean reserves the right to veto any activity of The Poets' Corner.

The rotational cycle of electors began in November 1983 with the following five-, four-, and three-year terms: five years—Edgar Bowers, J. V. Cunningham, Guy Davenport, Daniel Haberman, Richard Wilbur; four years—Anthony Hecht, John Hollander, Josephine Miles, Robert Penn Warren; three years—Daniel Aaron, Joseph Brodsky, Ann Stanford, Eudora Welty. The Honorary Chairman

and the member ex officio do not vote.

In late December the electors were informed of the results of the first balloting: Emily Dickinson was the first writer to be elected to the American Poets' Corner, having received twelve of the thirteen votes. No other writer was elected on the initial balloting, since none received the requisite minimum of eight votes. Three writers received more than one vote: Walt Whitman, four; Anne Bradstreet, two; Herman Melville, two. Six writers each received one vote: Ralph Waldo Emerson, Robert Frost, Nathaniel Hawthorne, Henry James, Henry Wadsworth Longfellow, and Edgar Allan Poe. The second balloting did not produce an election, since Walt Whitman received six votes and Herman Melville received four votes, while Anne Bradstreet and Ralph Waldo Emerson each received one vote. (One of the electors was unavailable.) Walt Whitman was elected on the third balloting, having received eight votes; Herman Melville received five votes.

"Captivity is Consciousness—/So's Liberty" (the last two lines from "No Rack can torture me—") became the inscription for Dickinson's memorial stone. "I stop somewhere waiting for you" (the last line from "Song of Myself") became the inscription for Whitman's memorial stone. "Pioneering man of letters" was selected for Irving's memorial stone.

With the exception of Irving's inscription, it has been the policy of the Poets' Corner to request suggested memorial inscriptions from all the electors. The inscriptions for both Dickinson and Whitman were suggested by Richard Wilbur.

The calligraphy and stonecutting for the Poets' Corner have been done by John Benson, whose family members have been stonecutters since the Revolutionary War. Working in Rhode Island, at the John Stevens Shop, John Benson achieves ninety-degree "v-cut" handcarved letters for the memorial stones, which are 1 1/4" smooth-rubbed Buckingham Virginia slate (measuring 2′ 9″× 1′ 3 1/4″).

The freedom to plan the service of dedication was great, given the Poets' Corner's initial insistence that it would be its own institution and Dean Morton's willingness to limit his authority to that of a veto. Immediately, however, this very freedom was circumscribed by the appreciation of an American tension: the difference in the perceptions of this nation's writers, who have always been anxious about their literary tradition and suspicious of the general press and clergy, and the perceptions of the American public. Could the Poets' Corner reach for the public's imagination and sense of our extraordinary literary heritage without offending American writers? And could this be done without a budget? Throughout America many would be asked to give their thoughts and their time; many would be asked to donate their performance and their travel expenses. Only one person, a musician, did not respond to the poet-in-residence's telephone calls or letters.

At the service of dedication Walter Cronkite, the master of ceremonies, stated: "It is rare that we can say with truth that we are present at the making of history." The greeting from the Poets' Corner in Westminster Abbey was read by the cathedral's dean. Endorsements of the new national shrine by the president of the United States, the governor of New York, and the mayor of New York City, which were read by Mr. Cronkite, followed his speech. Endorsements by the American Academy and Institute of Arts and Letters, the American Academy of Arts and Sciences, the Academy of American Poets, the American Philosophical Society, the PEN American Center, were read by the poet-in-residence. Brief musical interludes separated the endorsements.

Robert Penn Warren, later to become America's first poet laureate, began the memorial readings with the first five sections from "Memories of President Lincoln" by Walt Whitman: "When lilacs last in the dooryard bloom'd" through "Night and day journeys a coffin." Pianist Barbara Nissman followed the Whitman reading with the "Nocturne" by Samuel Barber. Gregory Peck read the "headless horseman" scene from *The Legend of Sleepy Hollow* by Washington Irving. Michael Tree, violist with the Guarneri Quartet, followed the Irving reading with a saraband by Bach. Edgar Bowers concluded the memorial readings with four poems by Emily Dickinson: "There's a certain Slant of light," "The difference between Despair," "These are the days when Birds come back," and "The last Night that She lived."

Following Edgar Bowers, Rosalyn Tureck performed a chorale prelude by Bach at the cathedral's organ. As the last chord echoed within the huge cathedral the dean ascended the pulpit. He began: "We are pleased to announce the commencement of The Poets' Corner Cathedral Lectures—to be given annually—on the evening after each year's memorial service. . . . The first Cathedral Lecturer—on Emily Dickinson—will be J. V. Cunningham, the poet, essayist, and scholar. . . . The Muriel Rukeyser Poetry Wall will be expanded and dedicated. . . . We will begin with Frederick Goddard Tuckerman, . . . whose work was admired by Emerson, Hawthorne, and Longfellow. After visiting Tennyson in 1855, Tuckerman wrote to his brother: 'I should tell you that at parting Mr. Tennyson gave me the original ms. of *Locksley Hall,* a favour of which I may be justly proud, as he says he has never done such a thing in his life before, for anybody.' "

Marcus Haddock sang and Barbara Nissman played the Schubert song "Du bist die Ruh'." Then began the procession to the unveiling of the Poets' Corner—Robert Penn Warren and Gregory Peck; Rosalyn Tureck and Marcus Haddock; Marie Bullock and Walter Cronkite; Barbara Nissman and Michael Tree; Edgar Bowers and Daniel Haberman; Dean Morton and sub-Dean Canon West; acolytes and the cathedral choir; John Chatfield (Emily Dickinson's cousin), his daughter, and granddaughter; and Zubin Mehta of the New York Philharmonic, who had lent his support as honorary conductor.

At the arts bay the Cathedral Choristers sang a plainchant from Psalm 45 ("my heart is inditing a good matter . . . "). Walter Cronkite introduced Marie Bullock, who then unveiled the American Poets' Corner; the dean inducted the first three writers into the corner; and all ended with roses being placed upon Emily Dickinson's memorial inscription by her ten-year-old cousin. As the audi-

The Poets' Corner at the Cathedral of St. John the Divine
(photo ©1986 by Mary Bloom)

ence left their seats, Paul Winter leaned against a wall of the corner, quite alone, and played his soprano saxophone. Outside the cathedral Japanese lanterns and a quintet were waiting.

News of the American Poets' Corner traveled throughout this nation, and to other nations. It was covered in England's *Guardian* and *Times,* Puerto Rico's *El Mundo,* and *Newsweek International.* The *Christian Science Monitor* devoted a page and a half to Emily Dickinson, Washington Irving, and Walt Whitman. News stories on the dedication of the corner appeared in the *New York Times* and the *Washington Post,* on the *MacNeil/Lehrer Report* and other television programs.

Of equal importance, the news arrived in the smaller cities of America. In Greensboro, North Carolina, in a lead editorial, the *News & Record* stated: "America is now trying to make amends for its literary neglect. . . . " In Wichita, Kansas, the *Eagle & Beacon* thought: "It is only fitting, then, that America finally would celebrate those who have celebrated America by their literary achieve-

ments. . . ." In Lima, Ohio, *The News* commented: "Nearly 100 years after her death, Emily Dickinson has achieved a permanent measure of fame. . . ." In Red Wing, Minnesota, the *Republican Eagle* stated: "GOOD for St. John the Divine Cathedral in New York, launching America's own Poets' Corner. . . ." And so it was in Excelsior Springs, Missouri; Walnut Creek, California; Greeneville, Tennessee; Lock Haven, Pennsylvania; and Beaumont, Texas.

Surely, six months after its inception, the Poets' Corner had reached the imagination of the American public. And, it was hoped, reached the imagination of American writers. Certainly the endorsements of the academies had been ample. John Kenneth Galbraith, president of the American Academy and Institute of Arts and Letters, applauded "the proposal for a Poets' Corner at the Cathedral of St. John the Divine and not less the initial suggestion as to those who should be so honored." Galway Kinnell, president of PEN American Center, stated: "We at PEN are honored to have this permanent memorial to American poets."

Over one million people a year visit the Poets' Corner. Their responses would have been understood by our pioneering man of letters, who had visited Westminster Abbey early in the nineteenth century. Washington Irving wrote of this visit in *The Sketch-Book of Geoffry Crayon, Gent.:*

> I passed some time in Poets' Corner, which occupies an end of one of the transepts or cross aisles of the abbey. The monuments are generally simple, for the lives of literary men afford no striking themes for the sculptor. . . . Notwithstanding the simplicity of these memorials, I have always observed that the visitors to the abbey remain longest about them. A kinder and fonder feeling takes the place of that cold curiosity or vague admiration with which they gaze on the splendid monuments of the great and the heroic. They linger about these as about the tombs of friends and companions; for indeed there is something of companionship between the author and the reader. Other men are known to posterity only through the medium of history, which is continually growing faint and obscure; but the intercourse between the author and his fellowmen is ever new, active, and immediate. He has lived for them more than for himself; he has sacrificed surrounding enjoyments, and shut himself up from the delights of social life, that he might the more intimately commune with distant minds and distant ages. Well may the world

cherish his renown; for it has been purchased not by deeds of violence and blood, but by the diligent dispensation of pleasure. Well may posterity be grateful to his memory; for he has left it an inheritance not of empty names and sounding actions, but whole treasures of wisdom, bright gems of thought, and golden veins of language.

In late August the electors were informed of the results of the first balloting for 1985: Herman Melville had been elected to the Poets' Corner, having received eight votes. Two writers received more than one vote: Edgar Allan Poe, five; Robert Frost, three. And ten writers each received one vote: Ann Bradstreet, Willa Cather, Hart Crane, T. S. Eliot, Ralph Waldo Emerson, Nathaniel Hawthorne, Henry James, Robert Lowell, Marianne Moore, and Edwin Arlington Robinson. The second balloting did not produce an election, since Poe received seven votes: Emerson and Hawthorne each received two votes, and Frost and James each received one vote. Poe was elected on the third balloting, having received nine votes. Emerson, Frost, Hawthorne, and James each received one vote.

"The running battle of the star and clod" (the sixteenth line from the "Epilogue" of *Clarel: A Poem and Pilgrimage in the Holy Land*) became the inscription for Melville's memorial stone. "Out of Space— out of Time" (the last line of the first stanza from the poem "Dream-Land") became the inscription for Poe's memorial stone.

The spring announcement of the 1985 memorial service and lecture had been mailed to the members of PEN American Center, Poetry Society of America, and other organizations for writers. It included these lines: " John Hollander will introduce J. V. Cunningham, who will give the first of the annual 'Poets' Corner Cathedral Lectures.' Mr. Cunningham's lecture, 'IF FAME BELONGED TO ME: DICKINSON,' begins what is hoped will be a long-followed tradition. . . ." Then news arrived of Jim Cunningham's death.

The memorial service for Herman Melville and Edgar Allan Poe on 12 May 1985 was different from the previous year's service of dedication. The audience was seated in the much smaller great choir and the anthems that separated the readings were sung by the Cathedral Choristers and Singers. An anthem by Samuel Barber preceded Daniel Hoffman, who began the memorial readings with four poems by Edgar Allan Poe: "Alone," "Romance," "To One in Paradise," and "Israfel." Carl Rakosi continued the Poe readings with four poems

and one prose excerpt: "To Helen," "To _____" ("I heed not that my earthly lot"), "To Science," "Silence," and the first two paragraphs from "The Cask of Amontillado."

Stanley Kunitz read excerpts from two of Herman Melville's letters to Nathaniel Hawthorne, Melville's poem "The Portent," and an excerpt from *Moby-Dick*, beginning "His motions plainly denoted his extreme exhaustion," from chapter eighty-one. Josephine Jacobsen continued the Melville readings with the poem "Lone Founts" and excerpts from *Moby-Dick* beginning "—But oh! shipmates! on the starboard hand of every woe" from chapter nine and "But this august dignity I treat of " from chapter twenty-six.

Daniel Hoffman returned to read words spoken by Walt Whitman on the occasion of the dedication of Poe's tomb in Baltimore and the poem "At the Tomb of Poe" by Stéphane Mallarmé (translated by Mr. Hoffman). Daniel Haberman concluded the memorial readings with the poem "At Melville's Tomb" by Hart Crane and the "Epilogue" from *Clarel*. After an anthem by Abraham Wood, the poet-in-residence spoke briefly about the late J. V. Cunningham. None knew that Josephine Miles—another elector—had died that day.

The procession to the Poets' Corner included Dean Morton, who had not participated in the memorial readings or announcements, since these were now to be literary events, while the coming induction of the memorialized writers would remain the province of the cathedral's dean. Dean Morton gave the following prayer: "Bless, O Lord, our induction into the American Poets' Corner in this Cathedral Church of Herman Melville and Edgar Allan Poe. Grant that even as we record and honor their names, so their words may continue to live in the hearts of our people. . . . Amen." Now there were five memorial inscriptions on the floor of the corner.

In late June the electors were informed of the results of the first balloting for 1986: no one had been elected. (Due to the deaths of two electors, the eleven electors had agreed that the minimum number of votes for election would be reduced to six.) Emerson and Frost each received five votes and Hawthorne received three votes, while Henry James and Mark Twain each received two votes. Five writers each received one vote: Ann Bradstreet, Sarah Orne Jewett, Henry Wadsworth Longfellow, Edwin Arlington Robinson, and Louis Zukofsky. The second balloting produced two elections: Robert Frost and Nathaniel Hawthorne each received six votes. Three other writers received

Memorial markers in the Poets' Corner (photo by John Benson)

votes: Emerson, five; James, three; Twain, two. "ON A FIELD, SABLE, THE LETTER A, GULES" (the last line from *The Scarlet Letter*) became the inscription for Hawthorne's memorial stone. "I had a lover's quarrel with the world" (the last line from "The Lesson for Today") became the inscription for Frost's memorial stone.

It was decided that the next five Poets' Corner cathedral lectures should now be scheduled. Among the speakers would be John Heath-Stubbs (1986) and Joseph Brodsky (1987). A collection of these lectures will be published every six years; the first collection is to be dedicated to the memory of J. V. Cunningham and published in 1991. A financial pledge by Eugene Power (founder of University Microfilms International) has helped to make these lectures possible.

Daniel Haberman, having completed the task of establishing an American Poets' Corner, ex-pressed the wish to once again devote all his energies to the writing of poetry. William Jay Smith was appointed poet-in-residence as of May 1986. He is a former consultant in poetry to the Library of Congress.

As of the end of May 1986, the rotational cycle of electors would be the following: five years (ending in 1991)—William Jay Smith; three years (1989)—Josephine Jacobsen, Stanley Kunitz, Walker Percy, Reynolds Price; five years (1988)—Edgar Bowers, Guy Davenport, Daniel Haberman, Richard Wilbur; four years (1987)—Anthony Hecht, Daniel Hoffman, John Hollander, Robert Penn Warren. Daniel Aaron (Harvard University) and R. W. B. Lewis (Yale University) were named electors ex officio, in addition to Lyn Chase. Marie Bullock continued to be the honorary chairman.

By September 1986 three years had passed. The transition had been completed: William Jay Smith was planning the memorial service for Robert Frost and Nathaniel Hawthorne and the following evening's Edgar Allan Poe lecture.

The induction of Frost and Hawthorne into the Poets' Corner took place in the great choir on 19 October 1986. John Hollander, Eudora Welty, and William J. Smith conducted the program, which included Miss Welty's reading of Hawthorne's "The Birthmark" and Mr. Hollander's and Mr. Smith's readings of works by Robert Frost.

The following evening in the Chapel of St. James, the annual Poets' Corner cathedral lecture was delivered by British poet John Heath-Stubbs, who spoke on "The Nightmare of Edgar Allan Poe." Heath-Stubbs discussed the uniquely American quality of Poe's work, which projects with unusual power his intense nightmarish visions extending to the depths of his subconscious.

The events of these two days served to demonstrate the significance of the Poets' Corner: Great living writers paying homage to the great writers of the past in celebration of an enduring literary tradition.

The Year in Fiction

George Garrett
University of Virginia

The year 1986 in fiction, with its slightly more than 5,000 new titles, is part of the larger publishing business; in fact, a little over 10% of the hardcover business. According to the Fall 1986 edition of the *Authors Guild Bulletin*, in its annual "State of the Industry" roundup, it was on the whole "a good year for American publishing." Sales for the first time rose to $5 billion, an 8.8% increase. And the sales of adult hardcover books were up by 22.7%. But fiction's piece of the pie, shrinking gradually since 1981, represented a falling off of 10.2% from the year before.

Writers of fiction therefore received mixed signals from the publishing industry. As if to add to the confusion, there was a sudden upsurge in the trend toward mergers, the buying and selling and assimilation of publishing houses, what the *Bulletin* called a "frenzy" in the latter part of 1986, in part a result of the new tax law which significantly increases capital gains taxes beginning in 1987. Similarly publishers changed hands, sometimes with significant changes. For example, Carl Navarre, a thirty-four-year-old Chattanooga entrepreneur, purchased Atlantic Monthly Press and promptly installed as his new editorial director, thirty-two-year-old Gary Fisketjohn, editor of the lively Vintage Contemporaries line of trade paperbacks and chiefly celebrated as the discoverer and publisher of *Bright Lights, Big City* (1984), by Jay McInerney, his former Williams College classmate and old friend. Fisketjohn was chosen and featured, in the year-end issue of *New York* magazine for its "The Powers That Will Be" section, as the best of the best and brightest in American publishing and celebrated for his "sharp eye for emerging talent and a brash, aggressive style in marketing it." His chief success of 1986 was the third novel by Richard Ford, *The Sportswriter,* which, published in the trade paperback form of Vintage Contemporaries and strongly promoted, sold better than his first two novels put together. Ford, also selected by *New York* among "The Powers That Will Be," will follow Fisketjohn to Atlantic Monthly Press.

The story is exemplary of the times: publishing houses changing hands, editors moving freely from one place to another and, often, writers following them. It also illustrates another odd recent development. In such a fluid and shifting situation, reputations, for both publishers and writers, can be made out of fairly small, if emblematic events and limited achievements. Similarly, that Fisketjohn should have made his way by means of a new and vigorous trade paperback line is illustrative of the increasing importance of trade paperback publication, both original and reprints. Penguin has made its mark in the bookstores with several lines, including the large-scale Contemporary American Fiction series. Other series which were much in evidence during the year include Norton's Shoreline Books, Morrow's Quill Books, and Scribners' Signature Editions, this latter edited by another Wunderkind of American publishing—Tom Jenks. The extent to which the trade paperbacks will capture the fiction market and thrive remains to be seen.

Other new developments in 1986 included a considerable expansion, evidently marked by some success, of the audio, books-on-tape market. And just at the turn of the year *Newsweek* critic David Lehman reviewed the first two "serious" interactive, electronic novels, designed as computer programs and published as formatted discs. It is interesting that these electronic books—"Mindwheel" by Robert Pinsky and "Amnesia" by Tom Disch—were created by poets. Nobody has a clue how this form of fiction will do in the future. At a cost of, give or take, forty dollars, they are more expensive than most books, but maybe twice as much fun as most.

If the year was in flux in many ways, the bestseller lists conservatively held the line. By and large the 1985 best-sellers moved over to dominate the paperback best-seller list. The names on the 1986 lists were mostly familiar and, once aboard, stayed put, shifting position slightly at most: Stephen King, Danielle Steel, Harold Robbins, Irving Wallace, Len Deighton, Robert Ludlum, Judith Krantz, Jeffrey Archer, Barbara Taylor Bradford, Isaac Asimov, and Louis L'Amour. Still there were some literary types who appeared on the lists briefly or

George Garrett in a publicity photo for Poison Pen *(photo by Cathy Hankla)*

a little longer—John Updike, Louise Erdrich, Peter Taylor, Pat Conroy, and the surprising first novelist, Sue Miller. Also John D. MacDonald early in the year and P. D. James and Elmore Leonard at its end. John Le Carré rode the lists high and long; and even longer in a major position was *Red Storm Rising* (Putnam), another first-rate military entertainment by the amazing Tom Clancy, whose *The Hunt For Red October* came from nowhere the previous year to be a major best-seller. Probably the only real equivalent surprise on the 1986 lists was *Flight of the Intruder,* a Vietnam naval story by Stephen Coonts, published by the same Naval Institute Press which originally published Tom Clancy.

Using the fairly reliable indices of review attention and advertising space, it is clear that there were any number of books, both serious and lightweight, aimed at the best-seller lists. Among the more obvious examples of "big" books which somehow missed the mark were James Carroll, *Supply of Heroes* (Dutton); Wilbur Smith, *Power of the Sword* (Little, Brown); Lynn V. Andrews, *Star Woman* (Warner); Barbara Michaels, *Shattered Silk* (Atheneum); Thomas Tryon, *All That Glitters* (Knopf);

Will Weaver, *Red Earth White Earth* (Simon and Schuster); Victoria Holt, *Secret For A Nightingale* (Doubleday); Leona Blair, *Privilege* (Bantam); Freddie Gershon, *Sweetie Baby Cookie Honey* (Arbor House); and Morris West, *Cassidy* (Doubleday).

It is hard to imagine what went wrong for Richard Condon's *Prizzi's Family* (Putnam), where both author and subject have very high visibility. A classic example of the "blockbuster" *manqué* was Doubleday's *The Agent,* "A Novel Created by Bill Adler and Written by David R. Slavitt." Well-executed by the adroit Slavitt, who as "Henry Sutton" was often on the best-seller lists and, because Adler, like the central character, Leonard Castle, is both best-selling author and glitzy agent, with more than a hint of the roman à clef, should have done well, but did not.

Nineteen eighty-six was a year of names, in fact, the marketing of names as much as books, most often public names from other fields. Thus Sally Quinn produced a best-selling novel about "Washington's fast lane," *Regrets Only* (Simon and Schuster). Other novels by public figures from our nation's capital include: *One Woman Lost* by Jane

Gray Muskie and Abigail McCarthy (Atheneum); *The Landing* by Haynes Johnson and Howard Simons (Villard); *The China Card* by John Ehrlichman (Simon and Schuster); and Gary Hart's *The Strategies of Zeus* (Morrow). We have also witnessed the publication of fiction by athletes—Ilie Nastase's *Break Point* (St. Martin's). There was a second novel by Judith Martin ("Miss Manners"), *Style and Substance* (Atheneum). Novels appeared and disappeared by the whole range of celebrities, from Johnny Cash to Thomas Hoving to the late Simone Signoret. Everybody was getting into the act. Even writers appeared as . . . *other writers;* see *Belinda* (Arbor House), described as "A Novel by Anne Rice Writing As Anne Rampling." So much for pen names. In all fairness it ought to be noted that some public figures who began writing careers as celebrity curiosities have gone on to earn reputations as writers. William Buckley's latest, *High Jinx* (Doubleday), was generally well received. And Jimmy Breslin's *Table Money* (Ticknor and Fields) not only sold well but was chosen by the *Washington Post Book World* as one of the "Best Books of 1986."

Among the more serious literary works, some which were heavily promoted appeared very briefly on the lists: Iris Murdoch's *The Good Apprentice* (Viking), Margaret Atwood's *The Handmaid's Tale* (Houghton Mifflin), Thomas Williams's *The Moon Pinnace* (Doubleday). Others, widely reviewed and advertised, and well promoted, failed to move much in the marketplace. Among these books by writers of literary reputation were Ken Kesey's *Demon Box* (Viking), Paul Theroux's *Ozone* (Putnam), Maureen Howard's *Expensive Habits* (Summit), David Leavitt's *The Lost Language of Cranes* (Knopf), and Denis Johnson's third novel, this one a timely view of things in Nicaragua—*The Stars At Noon* (Knopf). Perhaps surprisingly, Rita Mae Brown's story of transvestitism and gender confusion in the Confederate cavalry, *High Hearts* (Bantam), failed to catch on. And Anthony Burgess's latest (his twenty-ninth) novel, *The Pianoplayers* (Arbor House), vanished from sight in spite of an intriguing advertising campaign featuring the writhing body of a nude woman and simple and challenging statement: "A woman's body is like a keyboard. Unfortunately, men are born tone deaf."

It appears that these days, more than ever, the fate of a mid-list author with a literary novel depends very much on the chancy prospect of good reviews in key places. *The Pianoplayers* was roughly handled by Gene Lyons in the *New York Times Book Review.* And James Purdy's latest novel, *In The Hollow of His Hand* (Weidenfeld and Nicolson), re-

ceived its coup de grace at the hands of novelist Lee Smith in the *New York Times.* On the other hand, as if to disprove any possible generalizations, good reviews and sufficient advertising and promotion, though they may not contribute to significant sales, can, at least, save a literary book (and sometimes its author) from oblivion. Carolyn See's apocalyptic novel *Golden Days* (McGraw-Hill) is an excellent example of this. With considerable attention already, it may yet prove to be a "breakthrough" book for its talented author. Books like Updike's and Erdrich's and Sue Miller's required more than ordinary effort at promotion to arrive safely on the best-seller lists; and Pat Conroy's *The Prince of Tides* may well have been the most massively promoted and advertised work of fiction in 1986.

One book which appeared just at the end of 1986 and looks like a shoo-in to be a large-scale best-seller is Philip Roth's latest version of the Nathan Zuckerman saga, *The Counterlife* (Farrar, Straus and Giroux), which has already received the most prominent and extensive coverage in the papers and magazines. In this novel Roth indulges in the postmodernist fictional device of *possible* lives; that is, principal characters, including Nathan, die in one chapter to live in the next, exchange identities, pasts, and futures. The extent to which the general readership is ready for this kind of fun and games, even from an honored and favorite writer, will be tested.

The good news is that, in response to careful attention and powerful promotion, books of literary quality can (apparently) be sold in satisfactory numbers. The bad news is that the effort required by the publisher is so great and disproportionate as to eliminate many other worthy books from the process altogether.

But, serious or popular, all this, all of the above, is concerned with business. And, finally, we are here concerned with art, the art of fiction, which, like publishing itself, may or may not be good business. And judging by the many excellent works of fiction published in 1986 it was a good year for fiction. There are works which will last and be remembered, always a cause for celebration.

It was a year which witnessed additions, revisions, and editions of the work of old masters. Putnam brought out a translation of Vladimir Nabokov's *The Enchanter,* an overlooked early version of the Lolita theme. Random House published the latest version of James Joyce's *Ulysses,* extensively revised and corrected by German bibliographer Hans Walter Gabler. But the new edition had scarcely appeared, backed by fanfare, before it was faced with serious questions and some bibliographical controversy. Even if these things are answered and settled favorably, it seems likely that the book will have to settle for being somewhat less than the definitive text. Condensing, arranging, and rearranging the materials from several drafts of a huge and uncompleted Hemingway manuscript, Scribners' Tom Jenks magically produced a brand new Hemingway novel—*The Garden of Eden*. Soon enough—indeed the process has begun already—Hemingway scholars will test the validity of the book against the manuscript; but meanwhile Jenks, using only the master's own words, successfully put together a Hemingway novel which aroused much critical interest and discussion and, happily, found a place for itself on the best-seller lists. The old magic is there in the evocation of places (France and Spain), time (the immediate post-World War I years), weathers and seasons and fishing, swimming, eating and drinking well. What interested contemporary reviewers most was the depiction of androgynous sexuality, including a certain amount of what is now called gender role reversal. Reviewers were also fascinated by the parallels between the life of the protagonist, David Bourne, a recently married young writer, and Hemingway. Most (maybe beginning with Jenks himself) failed to make anything at all out of the significant background fact that Bourne, young and innocent as he is, is also a former wartime aviator and shown to be inwardly wounded by that exceptional experience. Even John Updike, whose piece "The Sinister Sex," in the 30 June 1986 *New Yorker,* is the best critical account so far, failed to notice the long shadows of World War I which fall across Bourne and his story.

Another remarkable and adept editorial job was performed by novelist Nicholas Delbanco to produce two posthumous novels in one volume, *Stillness and Shadows* (Knopf) by the late John Gardner. This book did not receive widespread critical attention by any means, but it is there now for Gardner's admirers who are more than just a few. Under the guidance of poet Gerry Costanzo, Carnegie-Mellon University Press continued its interesting reprint series, bringing out this year a new edition of Richard Hallas's (Eric Knight) *You Play The Black and The Red Comes Up* (1938). They also produced a trade paperback of James M. Cain's *The Magician's Wife*.

If 1986 ended with the first echoing salvos of a journalistic twenty-one-gun salute for Philip Roth, it began with just as much excitement, sound,

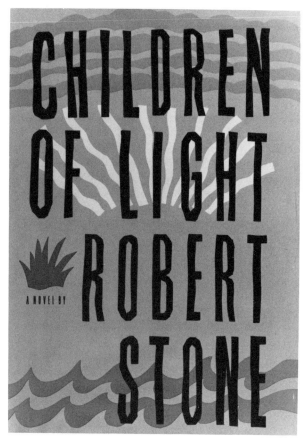

Dust jacket for Robert Stone's novel about the effects of drugs and alcohol on the lives of his protagonists, actors Gordon Walker and Lee Verger

and fury celebrating the arrival of Robert Stone's flashy new novel, *Children of Light* (Knopf). This time Stone offered up a "Hollywood" novel which, besides being an up-to-date, state-of-the-art accounting of the movie business, presented a couple of new wrinkles—the protagonist, Gordon Walker, an actor and a writer, is a heavy dope addict. His lover, screen actress Lee Verger, is married and a chronic schizophrenic, haunted (when she neglects her medication) by hallucinatory "Long Friends." It was all, as it should be, glamorous and sad.

In between *Children of Light* and *The Counterlife*, some of our most accomplished active novelists produced outstanding, memorable work. In spite of its mildly off-putting title, *Diary of a Yuppie* (Houghton Mifflin), Louis Auchincloss's thirty-eighth book (his twenty-ninth book of fiction), proved to be one of his finest and most complex, yet altogether accessible, works. This is an accounting of the decline and degeneration of our ethical system seen from the point of view of a ruthlessly rational and ambitious young corporate lawyer. It is a tight, quick-moving story with resonance. Eleanor Clark's fifth novel, though equally swiftly paced, is denser in both style and substance and seems to have confused some reviewers and readers. *Camping Out* (Putnam) is best described by critic Malcolm Cowley, on the book jacket, as an independent vision of "the new American age." He writes: "With utter conviction she tells how a short camping trip by a Vermont lake, planned by two women as a casual excursion, is transformed into a nightmare of violence, terror, and unmotivated evil."

As indicated earlier, some of the distinctly literary novels by prominent writers managed in 1986 to achieve some measure of both fame and good fortune. John Updike's *Roger's Version* (Knopf) is, in part, a playful rewrite and updating of *The Scarlet Letter*. Since its central character, Roger Lambert, is a theologian and a divinity professor, it allows Updike to explore and exploit his own long-standing theological interests and at the same time to offer ironic observations of the sexual high jinks and confusions of our times. Pat Conroy's *The Prince of Tides* (Houghton Mifflin) is large enough and long enough (567 pages) to be called *major*. Bringing together some elements familiar to readers of *The Great Santini* and *The Lords of Discipline*, he presents the recent chronicle of the Wingo family to the best advantage of what the jacket calls his "lyric gifts, abundant good humor, and compelling story telling. . . ." In *The Beet Queen* (Holt), "a tale of abandonment and sexual obsession," Louise Erdrich continues the lyrical accounting of rural North Dakota which began with the prizewinning *Love Medicine*. Here the story is at once more complex and daring than the earlier book. Perhaps the most interesting result of the full spotlight of publicity focused on Ms. Erdrich and her novel was the revelation (see the *New York Times*, 13 October 1986, C13) that her novels are in fact a collaboration with her husband, Michael Dorris, professor of Anthropology and Native American Studies at Dartmouth. Joyce Carol Oates's *Marya: A Life* (Dutton), a "portrait of a modern woman in search of self-understanding and fulfillment" and, in many details, her most overtly autobiographical novel to date, received mixed reviews, but nonetheless earned its author considerable and respectful attention. Herbert Gold's latest, *A Girl of Forty* (Donald I. Fine), was a light and lively novel (with some shadowy overtones) of contemporary San Francisco life, featuring Suki Read, "A Holly Golightly of the 80's." *Cold Spring Harbor* (Delacorte/Law-

rence) was the highly respected Richard Yates's ninth book, an unusually slim, quick-paced story set on Long Island during the early World War II years. Yates continues to grow and develop and to be honored by critics; but, for perhaps inexplicable reasons, he does not catch on with many readers.

Another writer of roughly the same age, whose career has also been marked by hits and misses, is Vance Bourjaily whose eleventh novel, *The Great Fake Book*, appeared just at year's end. (A fake book is a book of simplified arrangements which allow a musician to "fake it.") A son, living here and now, searches for the past of his dead and gone father, Mike Mizzourin, some thirty years earlier during World War II, following his father by means of his journal and his fake book. Told "through letters, phone conversations, tape transcripts and firsthand documents," it is an odd and daring book for Bourjaily, which has (so far) earned mixed notices, uniform only in their agreement that its best parts are the scenes set in wartime America.

Any year graced with a new Peter De Vries book ought to be officially declared a good year; but, at least in terms of public attention, his newest, *Peckham's Marbles* (Putnam), did not do very well. Perhaps that is because it is a "literary" novel, wild and woolly and wacko as can be, built around the quest of Earl Peckham, author of the "relentlessly highbrow novel, *The Sorry Scheme of Things Entire*," to seek and find the three Americans who bought his book. De Vries fans may rest assured it's as funny and on the mark as it ought to be.

Moving very close to *genre* fiction—perhaps not close enough, not offering quite enough of the unpretentious qualities of an "entertainment"— was Geoffrey Wolff's *Providence* (Viking). It is a fast-moving, well-told crime story, maybe not "blazing and unforgettable" as the publisher claims, but, anyway, alive with good stylish sentences. Maybe the problem here is *Providence* itself, which, except for a precious few fans, cannot live up to Wolff's claims for its being "an ensemble production, a society of quid pro quo, want and grab, crimes and punishments." Paul Theroux and Margaret Atwood, quite separately, arrived at stories set in the future, fantasy stories. Atwood's *The Handmaid's Tale* (Houghton Mifflin), part feminist tract and part political allegory, has moments of power and light but suffers (somewhat) from the uncertainty of Ms. Atwood's grasp of political facts and possibilities in America and, as well, from some internal inconsistencies which weaken the credibility of her surface story. That is, the inward and spiritual doctrine is probably acceptable to many readers, but it is sometimes hard to take the details of the outward and visible characters and events. Paul Theroux's *Ozone* (Putnam) has an opposite problem. Its surfaces are well realized and exciting. He is always an energetic storyteller. What it all adds up to, if anything, is another matter. Never mind, *Ozone* is a big (527 pages) adventure in futuristic fiction and will make a fine movie.

Three of the best novels of the year, measured by any standards, came from contemporary southern masters. Reynolds Price gave us his finest work in years, *Kate Vaiden* (Atheneum), a beautifully created, first-person narration of the life and times of Kate, "born in 1927, white, and reared in the upper South." It is a rich, resonant, mature story, and it has been justly selected by the National Book Critics Circle as their selection for the best novel of 1986. Another book, widely praised and nominated, a finalist, for several national awards, is Peter Taylor's novel, *A Summons to Memphis* (Knopf), his first

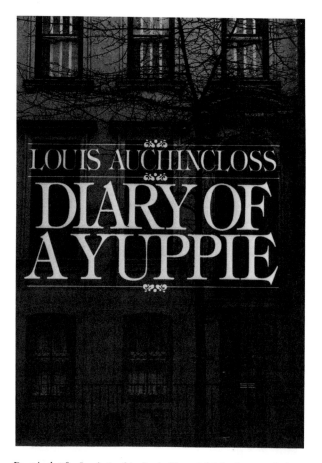

Dust jacket for Louis Auchincloss's thirty-eighth book, a novel about modern mores and life in a big New York law firm

novel in almost forty years, years which have been given to the short story, the form which won him the PEN/Faulkner award for 1985. Jamesian in ways and means, but, even at its most serious, lighthearted, funnier than James, it, basically, is a family story, played out, as the publisher quite precisely describes it, in "the fascinating world he has made his own: the complex and privileged society of wellborn Tennesseans, adapting (or not) to the exigencies of modern life." It was briefly on the *New York Times* best-seller list, considerably longer elsewhere, including the *Washington Post Book World*.

Another book by a distinguished and prizewinning southern writer (and, in fact, she, like Peter Taylor, lives in Charlottesville, Virginia) was Mary Lee Settle's *Celebration* (Farrar, Straus and Giroux). Not directly related to any of the books of her Beulah Quintet, it is closest in feeling and spirit, though at once deeper and more joyously mature, to *Blood Ties*, which won her a National Book Award some years ago. Set in London in 1969, it brings together a cast of survivors ranging from Teresa Cerruti, a young American woman recovering from the death of her husband and a close encounter with cancer, to Pius, a six-foot-nine Jesuit out of Africa and the Sudan's Dinka tribe. All have strong, well-realized stories, allowing the overall story to move easily to Africa, Hong Kong, and Turkey. It ends with a sad funeral immediately following a happy wedding, all ending in celebration of life and love. After rave advance notices *Celebration* had to settle for mixed reviews in the major journals. This reviewer agrees with novelist Richard Bausch, who wrote in the *Philadelphia Inquirer* (14 December 1986): "*Celebration* is the strongest kind of proof that her energy and her gifts are undiminished. It is as good as anything that precedes it in a long and distinguished career."

Outstanding books by mid-career, mid-list writers, of various ages, were, it seems, fewer than usual. A few of these survive to earn mention. *Making Believe* (Houghton Mifflin), by John Leggett, tells the story, set in the 1960s and 1970s, of a liberal Episcopal priest and bishop, Roy Train, a complex story of spiritual crisis. Laura Furman's not completely original strategy in *Tuxedo Park* (Summit) is to bring together in marriage and family (for a while) Jewish Sadie Ash and a stereotypical WASP named Willard Weaver; but she succeeds in giving her story a freshness by writing very well and by, improbably but audaciously, setting it firmly in that classic WASP haven, the real Tuxedo Park. National Public Radio book critic Alan Cheuse turned, in his third book, *The Grandmother's*

Club (Peregrine Smith), to a retelling of the immigrant story in an original way which yields very interesting results. A story of power and empathy. Stephen Koch established himself as a novelist of skill and originality with his earlier *Night Watch*. With *The Bachelor's Bride* (Marion Boyars) Koch takes us deep into the New York pop art scene of the 1960s, a period and a scene he knows by heart. The result is lively, intelligent, and interesting, though perhaps not quite as exciting as the book jacket asserts: "Sex, stimulants and The Supremes—the sixties!" Doris Grumbach's latest, *The Magician's Girl*, (Macmillan) is a highly intellectual and well-wrought version (one hopes maybe the *last* version) of *The Group*. This time it is three girls from Barnard—Minna Grant, who becomes a history professor; Liz Becker, photographer; and Maud Noon, poet—and what became of their lives. Its greatest success is more a matter of style than substance, presenting a quality which Cynthia Ozick describes as "the clear focus—and eerie serene spirit—of a Diane Arbus photograph. . . ."

Elly Welt's *Berlin Wild* (Viking) and Scott Spencer's *Waking The Dead* (Knopf) were highly touted and well hyped and both were offered as Featured Alternates by the Book-of-the-Month Club. Spencer's novel, mixing politics and social themes with a ghostly love story, suffered in comparison with his earlier success—*Endless Love*. Welt's remarkable (and authentic) story of Josef Bernhardt, a half-Jewish boy genius in the Third Reich's Kaiser Wilhelm Institute fared better at the hands of the reviewers but sold less than had been hoped. Wonderfully imaginative and engaging is fantasist Steven Millhauser's latest, *From The Realm of Morpheus* (Morrow), which is a very literal excursion in that realm, guided and presided over by a fully realized character named Morpheus. Some sense of its direction can be gained from the initial predicament in which the central character "chases a foul ball into a thicket and discovers an opening into the underworld."

Another adventure in a different kind of Never-never Land is Donald Barthelme's *Paradise* (Putnam), in which a fifty-three-year-old married man, Simon, settles in, for fun and games, with three beautiful young women whom he finds modeling lingerie in a bar. They bring him plenty of joy and more trouble. His basic problem, stated by Barthelme, is that he "wanted very much to be a hearty, optimistic American, like the President, but on the other hand did not trust hearty, optimistic Americans, like the President." Get it? Having dealt most seriously with the world of big time tennis in

his recent nonfiction book, *Short Circuit*, the productive and talented Michael Mewshaw brings the same world to life in fiction, and the result is a deeply funny dark comedy, dealing with the fate and fortune of Latif Fluss, a Taureg tribesman and tennis great. *Blackballed* (Atheneum) is first-rate comedy.

Another younger writer who does not repeat himself is Ben Greer. His *Time Loves A Hero* (Doubleday) is at once a description and a satire of life among the very rich as seen by young Cody Walker, a southerner with endless ambition and everything to learn. Plenty of culture shock. Jim Shephard, whose first novel, *Flights*, earned him high praise, turns, in *Paper Doll* (Knopf), to a story of American flyers stationed in England in World War II. It is fully imagined and adroitly executed. And a genuine surprise. T. R. Pearson's *Off for the Sweet Hereafter* (Linden/Simon and Schuster) follows last year's highly praised first novel, *A Short History of a Small Place*, and precedes next year's *The Last of How It Was*, as the middle book in a Tar Heel trilogy of smalltown, New South fictions. Steven G. Kellman, who reviewed it for *Saturday Review* (September 1986), was typical and right on the money when he called it "above all a vocal performance" made up of "obsessive, digressive ruminations."

Nineteen eighty-six was not a year for major work by the major black fiction writers. Ishmael Reed gave us *Reckless Eyeballing* (St. Martin's); Clarence Major came on with *My Amputations* (Fiction Collective); and Charles Johnson received a good deal of attention for the eight stories in his slender volume—*The Sorcerer's Apprentice* (Atheneum). Essentially more interesting than any of the above were two first-rate books by black writers who, for whatever reasons, have been somewhat ignored all around. It is hard to see how anybody could have missed young Percival Everett, whose third novel, *Cutting Lisa* (Ticknor and Fields), is daring, tough-minded, and written in a lean, strictly controlled prose. Everett is rapidly turning into a major novelist, with or without attention and support. Don Belton is a first novelist whose *Almost Midnight* (Morrow) somehow and inexcusably slipped through the cracks. (One would think and hope that with a whole growth industry of Afro-American Studies that couldn't happen, but. . . .) Belton tells a wonderful tale of Daddy Poole, who was once a millionaire preacher with thousands of followers, and of the handful of women who stayed with him to the end, damning and praising him in, accurately called, "a spellbinding song of redemption."

It was a busy year for the first novel, especially for first novels by young women. Kaylie Jones, daughter of the late James Jones, produced her first book, the very professional semiautobiographical *As Soon As It Rains* (Doubleday), a fine, auspicious beginning. Candace Denning's *Adventures With Julia* (North Point) is slender, bright, and clever, possessed of magic and yet relentlessly minimal. Cut from the same bolt of cloth is Lorrie Moore's first novel, following *Self-Help,* her well-praised collection of stories last year: *Anagrams* (Knopf); but this joke-riddled story of the *possible* lives of Benna Carpenter is more ambitious and is firmly based on a concealed foundation of real sorrow. She truly has, as the Los Angeles *Herald Examiner* has written, "a gift for going to the heart of heartache." Another Knopf story writer who produced a good first novel in 1986 was Janet Kaufman, *Collaborators.* Her stories *Places in the World a Woman Could Walk* won awards. This tightly laced, poetic novel did not receive the attention it deserves. And neither did (in spite of a lengthy blurb full of highest praise, by John Irving) Elizabeth Hyde's *Native Colors* (Delacorte), a complex and dramatic story of the friendship of two grown women. Gladys Swan, whose earlier collection of stories, *On the Edge of the Desert,* appeared in the University of Illinois Short Fiction series, published her first novel with Gary Fisketjohn's Vintage Contemporaries series. It is more fable than story, dealing with a down-at-the-heels carnival in the American Southwest.

Two first novels which earned more than usual attention were Susan Minot's *Monkeys* (Dutton) and Sue Miller's *The Good Mother* (Harper and Row), which vaguely have in common the general fact that both are domestic, family stories set in contemporary New England. Miller's book became that very rare item, a first novel of literary quality which was also a best-seller.

Some of it may have to do with last year's remarkable success of *The Beans of Egypt, Maine,* by Carolyn Chute; but, in any case, the hard life of upper New England, town and country, was the source and essence of three first novels: Cathie Pelletier's *The Funeral Makers* (Macmillan), Dorothy Casey's *Leaving Locke Horn* (Algonquin), and Lucy Honig's *Picking Up* (Dog Ear Press), which won the 1986 Maine novel award.

Alike in their regional strengths (and limitations) are the following: *The Calling* (Peachtree), by Stirling Watson, a very lightly, indeed transparently, veiled novel about Gainesville novelist and teacher Harry Crews, here called Eldon Odom; *The*

Vigil and *Agatite* (St. Martin's), the first and second novels respectively of Clay Reynolds, a Texas writer of power, energy, and imagination; and *The Great Pretender* (Atheneum), by James Atlas. This last calls for a word or two. Regional? Though it begins in Illinois, the milieu is urban and Eastern, with a dash of the mid Atlantic. Atlas, author of *Delmore Schwartz: The Life of an American Poet* (1977), formerly an editor at *Atlantic* and the *New York Times Book Review,* now with *Vanity Fair,* had been expected to produce an autobiographical memoir. Instead came this autobiographical fiction, one which greatly pleased some reviewers and deeply annoyed others. Not regional, exactly, but distinctly *ethnic* was Stephen Fleming's Vietnam novel, *The Exile of Sergeant Nen* (Algonquin), the imaginative story of a veteran of that war who is Vietnamese.

Three excellent first novels by women of the contemporary South are Kathleen Ford's *Jeffrey County* (St. Martin's), a novel of rural Virginia; Valerie Sayer's *Due East* (Dolphin/Doubleday), a South Carolina story; and (probably my favorite among novels of the New South, new or old) *Bobby Rex's Greatest Hit* (Atheneum) by Marianne Gingher. Lee Smith's praise for it—"You'll never forget it."—expresses my feelings exactly.

Finally, among first novels, this one, published just at the end of December, Mona Simpson's *Anywhere But Here* (Knopf), received immediate and respectful attention and is clearly a large, moving, mother-daughter story of ambition and amplitude. It also, as it happens, takes the blurb prize for 1986, offering extraordinary praise from Walker Percy, Jayne Anne Phillips, Louise Erdrich, Alice Munro, Mary Robison, John Ashbery, David Bradley, and Jay McInerney. For the edification of creative writing students, who are ever and always looking for means of support, here are the acknowledgments on the copyright page of *Anywhere But Here:* "The author wishes to thank the Corporation of Yaddo, the MacDowell Colony, VCCA, the Transatlantic Henfield Foundation, The Beard's Fund, the Kellogg Foundation, and *The Paris Review* for their support during the writing of this book. Also, the author would like to thank Allan Gurganus, Elizabeth Hardwick, Robert Asahina, Robert Cohen, Lionel Shriver, and George Plimpton for multiple and generous readings." The jacket further informs us that: "She is the recipient of a number of awards, including a National Endowment of the Arts Fellowship, a Kellogg National Fellowship, and a Whiting Writers' Award." Unquestionably it is the best-supported first novel of our time, perhaps ever. Nowhere does the publisher mention that Ms. Simpson is employed as senior editor of *The Paris Review*.

The reader who has come this far has already noticed (and will notice, considering short fiction) how much involved small presses have become in publishing fiction. This is good news; though, in general, the sales figures and the review space are not what they might be. A few of the other good novels published by small presses would have to include: Marianne Hauser, *The Memoirs of the Late Mr. Ashley* (Sun and Moon Press); Jack Butler, *Jujitsu For Christ* (August House); James Lee Burke, *The Lost Get-Back Boogie* (Louisiana State University Press); Rochelle Ratner, *Bobby's Girl* (Coffee House Press); Frederick Ted Castle, *Gilbert Green: The Real Right Way to Dress for Spring* (McPherson). And if I may here take a more personal stance, I ought to say that George Garrett's latest novel was published in 1986 by a small publisher—*Poison Pen; Or, Live Now & Pay Later* (Stuart Wright). Although the edition was very small and distribution was a serious problem, the shelf life of *Poison Pen* has been longer than any of my commercially published books.

Dust jacket for Reynolds Price's sixth novel, selected by the National Book Critics Circle as best novel of 1986

And, ironically I suppose, it has been more widely and extensively reviewed than most of my other work.

At this writing I have no valid statistics and am forced to depend on personal observation and anecdotal evidence, but it certainly seems that 1986 was not an especially noteworthy year for fiction in translations. In a sense the year began and ended with Mario Vargas Llosa, the handsome and highly regarded Peruvian. His novel, *The Real Life of Alejandro Mayta* (Farrar, Straus and Giroux) was well and attentively received early in the year; and in December the same publisher brought out his highly personal, nonfiction study of Flaubert and Madame Bovary—*The Perpetual Orgy*. Patrick Suskind's odd, highly sensual, and allegorical fantasy, *Perfume* (Knopf), found a place on some best-seller lists. Other outstanding works in translation which received a full share of critical attention include: *Across* (Farrar, Straus and Giroux), by Peter Hanke; *The Monkey's Wrench* (Summit), by Primo Levi; *To The Land of the Cattails* (Weidenfeld and Nicolson), by Aharon Appelfeld; *Vienna Girl* (Norton), by Ingeborg Lauterstein; and Francesca Duranti's haunting venture into "magic realism," *The House on Moon Lake* (Random House). Less well known, perhaps, is *Other Fires: Short Fiction By Latin American Women* (Clarkson Potter), which, if nothing else, reminds North American readers how little we have known about the women writers of Latin America.

It is seldom in any given year that we are given the cheerful and clear-cut example of a genuine, unmanipulated *discovery*. But 1986 offered such an example. *Mrs. Caliban* (Harvard Common Press) by Rachel Ingalls was, in its British edition, chosen by the British Book Marketing Council as one of the twenty best postwar American novels. Ms. Ingalls, whose other works have been published in England, but not here, is likely to be heard from here as well.

For perhaps mysterious reasons genre fiction in general, and especially the whole range of detective stories, spy stories, suspense tales, etc., loosely catalogued as "thrillers," though it is widely popular and read, remains separated from "serious" fiction. The thriller is not often given serious attention in the literary press. Yet a number of sufficiently dead writers have earned considerable posthumous attention. And several among the living experts of the genre have managed to earn Class-A treatment from critics and reviewers as well as readers. Several of these contributed to the literary year, both early and late. John Le Carré's latest, and largest, spy novel, *A Perfect Spy* (Knopf), received unusual attention and extraordinary promotion and advertising and sat comfortably on the various best-seller lists, among much distinguished company, for months. This one is his densest, most self-reflexive work and, it was widely announced, his most personal and autobiographical novel, the sad and complex story of Magnus Pym, double agent and classical con man. It took years of the Smiley books (and films) to prepare a public for a work of this weight and substance. Other British writers who have moved upward from strict genre are P. D. James, whose *A Taste for Death* (Knopf) brought back Detective Adam Dalgliesh; and the prolific Ruth Rendell, whose *Live Flesh* (Pantheon) proved to be as much a psychological study as a thriller but, in any case, proved to be an engrossing and altogether satisfactory novel.

Three old-timers who have earned their places on the literary A-list are George V. Higgins, John D. MacDonald (who is, alas, at this writing, the *late* John D. MacDonald), and Elmore Leonard; all three produced thrillers which were at once serious and successful in 1986. Higgins's *Impostors* (Holt) is his most thoroughly complex story in quite a while, adding the media people, hustlers in "communications," to his familiar gallery of criminals and lawyers and sleazy politicians. Strong stuff. "Theirs is a world where scruples are a sham and sex is the ultimate weapon," the publisher writes with what turns out to be more accuracy than overstatement. MacDonald's *Barrier Island* (Knopf) is more a straight novel than conventional thriller, retelling the story of an up-to-date multimillion-dollar land swindle; though there are plenty of (what else?) dead bodies to be found in its pages. Late in the year came Elmore Leonard's latest, *Bandits* (Arbor House), a fast-moving story, set in New Orleans, and dealing, with magic timeliness, with the hanky-panky of raising funds for the Contras. Members in good standing with the Left took some comfort in Leonard's apparent political stance, which they hope may be "mainstream." Something of the power and growing literary respectability of the thriller is indicated by the latest books by two younger writers whose reputations are built on serious fiction. Speer Morgan's fourth book, *The Assemblers* (Dutton), takes us deep into the worlds and words of computers and computer crime. Timely in other ways as well, it features "a tough-minded female security cop." The amazing Madison Smartt Bell, still not thirty, may have surprised some of the admirers of his first two novels with a classic "entertainment," a hard-driving, deftly written *ca-*

per novel—*Straight Cut* (Ticknor and Fields).

Not surprisingly, Louis L'Amour's latest, *Last of the Breed* (Bantam), found its place high on the best-seller lists even though it is not a Western. On the other hand two writers of distinction, well outside the barbwire limits of genre, took familiar materials from the Western and treated them with unusual seriousness. Oakley Hall, author of fourteen well-regarded novels over thirty-five years, completed a trilogy of Westerns with *Apaches* (Simon and Schuster), a novel of New Mexico in the 1880s, which is exactly the same decade used by essayist and ecologist Edward Hoagland in *Seven Rivers West* (Summit). Both are well-executed stories, but, different as they are, they share some of the same strengths and weaknesses. The scenes and dialogue are always crisp and lively, and both writers handle scenic description, the evocation of landscape with grace. But, on the whole, authentic narrative history and memoir have an edge over imaginary events in the Old West.

There seems to have been a mild resurgence in the serious historical novel. Tudor England re-

Dust jacket for Peter Taylor's first novel in thirty-six years

ceived more than its share of the attention of novelists, ranging from Susan Kay's prizewinning (Georgette Heyer Prize and Betty Trask Prize) *Legacy* (Crown), a near-romance concerned chiefly with Elizabeth I and Leicester and Essex, to Margaret George's massive and impressively researched *The Autobiography of Henry VIII With Notes by His Fool, Will Somers* (St. Martin's). Probably the most elegantly successful, though it is often wildly speculative, is Robert York's lean and taut *My Lord The Fox* (Vanguard). An excellent work of nonfiction popular history, Mary Luke's *The Nine Days Queen: A Portrait of Lady Jane Grey* (Morrow) found itself in the fiction sections of most bookstores. Perhaps the whole period has become a fiction to readers. Another serious novel of the Renaissance, this one with the full flourishes and ruffles of a full-scale Knopf production was Dorothy Dunnet's *Niccolo Rising*, announced as the first in a series of fifteenth- and sixteenth-century novels as *The House of Niccolo*, an account of Renaissance business and adventure.

Nineteen eighty-six seems to have been another good year for the short story and for story writers. Raymond Carver worked with regular co-editor Shannon Ravenel to select the material for *The Best American Short Stories 1986* (Houghton Mifflin) and came up with a nicely balanced mixture of tried and true voices—Donald Barthelme, Ann Beattie, Frank Conroy, Richard Ford, Tess Gallagher, Thomas McGuane, Grace Paley, Alice Munro, Joy Williams, etc., these "names" personally chosen, as he admits in his "Introduction," as much for their cumulative individual reputations as for the particular stories—together with a good selection from among the fine newer writers beginning to build careers as story writers, people like Tobias Wolff, Mona Simpson, Charles Baxter, Amy Hempel, and the greatly gifted Kent Nelson. Carver's "Introduction" is, in and of itself, one of the more interesting and provocative of its kind since, in 1978, *The Best American Short Stories* assumed the habit of using annual guest editors.

Theoretically (and somewhat at odds with his actual choices of stories and authors) he outlines a bias toward "realistic, 'life-like' characters" acting "in realistically detailed situations." He adds that he is most strongly attracted by the "traditional" means of telling stories. Carver goes on to describe his own editorial process very candidly and arrives at the conclusion that what his choices have in common deeply is that all the writers are dealing with "things that count." "What Counts?" He asks and gives his own answer. "Love, death, dreams, am-

bition, growing up, coming to terms with your own and other people's limitations." And finally Carver deals directly with the problem of success (though he chooses not to use that word): "But once in a great while lightning strikes, and occasionally it strikes early in the writer's life. Sometimes it comes later, after years of work. And sometimes, most often, of course, it never happens at all." It is not clear in context, perhaps not clear to Carver, whether he means the aesthetic lightning of brilliant accomplishment or the more conventional shock and flash of recognition. Since Carver is, himself, a gifted and honored story writer, even this kind of intellectual confusion is at once interesting and challenging.

It is also interesting that this year, unlike previous years, there is no overlap between *Best American Short Stories* and William Abrahams's *Prize Stories 1986: The O. Henry Award* (Doubleday). Abrahams, having edited the annual anthology for twenty years, is at once more sure of himself and his duty (his "Introduction" this time is a brisk three pages) and, perhaps paradoxically, more flexible, willing to change and to take chances, than guest editors seem to be. On the whole, though, he used to favor the more commercial magazines as his sources, Abrahams has clearly, this time, ranged wider and deeper in the literary magazines than his rival. In comparison Carver seems more the servant of the literary establishment; though Abrahams, too, has his own galaxy of stars—Alice Walker, Ward Just, Bobbie Ann Mason, Alice Adams, Irvin Faust, Elizabeth Spencer, and Joyce Carol Oates. Both anthologies are lively and of uniformly high quality, though neither seems to me fully representative of the vigorous plurality, the energetic diversity of the American short story, out there in its fields of play, the literary magazines. Even Shannon Ravenel's extensive annual appendix to *Best American Short Stories*, "100 Other Distinguished Short Stories of the Year 1986," seems limited and incomplete. In any case, both these prize anthologies testify to the quality and vitality of the short story at this time. Even their limitations make that point—that the story is doing well, being done well, and with growing appreciation in this country.

Other excellent anthologies of 1986 make the same point from slightly different angles. Two prominent entrepreneurs of the literary scene produced large scale, inclusive works aimed to please the readers, old and young, of the short story. The indefatigable Clifton Fadiman selected the sixty-two stories of *The World of the Short Story: A Twentieth*

Century Collection (Houghton Mifflin), a solid gathering of modern and contemporary masterpieces, some familiar and some, fewer, not well known, covering three distinct generations of writers from all over the world, from Colette to Ann Beattie. Similarly inclusive, though somewhat more limited in the time covered, is Daniel Halpern's, *The Art of the Tale: An International Anthology of Short Stories 1945-1985* (Viking). Halpern has judiciously chosen a fairly wide range of aesthetic diversity, and his international selections offer some special pleasures like the work of Chinua Achebe (Nigeria), Abdeslam Boulaich and Mohammed Mrabet (Morocco), together with stories by Yukio Mishima, Amos Oz, Mercé Rodoreda, Naguib Mahfouz, Yasunari Kawabata, Luisa Valenzuela, and others. The French, Italians, Germans, and especially the Latin Americans, are well represented; and the Americans cover a variety of aesthetic persuasions from the worlds of Robert Coover to Richard Yates, from Guy Davenport to T. Coraghessan Boyle.

Some of the other outstanding anthologies are more strictly limited in scope and design. *20 Under 30: Best Stories By America's New Young Writers*, edited by Debra Spark, appears in the handsome new trade paperback series created by Scribners' Tom Jenks—the Signature Editions. Twenty good stories by writers who are (or were at the time of publication) not yet thirty years old. Some names already familiar in the literary press—David Leavitt, David Updike, Lorrie Moore, Mona Simpson, and Susan Minot. Others not well known at all, at least out of some limited literary circles. Most people who try to keep up with the new and young talents will, of course, be annoyed by what seem to be serious omissions. Certainly there is nothing here which is superior in quality to the work of other equally young and younger writers whose stories have been appearing prominently in literary magazines over the past several years, writers like Alyson Hagy, Madison Smartt Bell, Pinckney Benedict, and Darcey Steinke. Still, the idea is honorable and it illustrates dramatically the fact that the form of the short story is widely attractive to bright new writers.

In *New American Short Stories*, a Plume Contemporary Fiction trade paperback, edited by writer Gloria Norris, twenty prominent American story writers (the oldest are John Updike and Gail Godwin; the youngest must be Amy Hempel) have each selected their own "favorite" story and written a short afterword explaining how he or she came to write that story and why it is, for the time being at least, a personal favorite. Again this is an all-star

cast, inevitably; but it is not without interest that some of the stars (for example, Robert Taylor, Jr., Robley Wilson, Jr., Mary Hood, and John E. Wideman) are different from most in other anthologies. Meaning? There are many stars out there, more than can be contained in any anthology.

Other gatherings are regional in spirit. Two of the best are Shannon Ravenel's *New Stories From the South: The Year's Best 1986,* announced as the first of a new series by Algonquin Books, and *From Timberline to Tidepool: Contemporary Fiction from the Northwest,* edited by Rich Ives for the Owl Creek Press. Note that small presses and publishers outside of the New York-Boston axis are beginning, more and more, to make the kind of mark with the publication of short fiction that they have already done with poetry. Two first-rate examples: *Fiction 86,* edited by Richard Peabody and Gretchen Johnsen for Paycock Press, and *Sudden Fiction: American Short-Short Stories,* edited by Robert Shapard and James Thomas, for Peregrine Smith Books of Salt Lake City, a press which is not "small" by any means but whose ventures into the publication of fiction have only just begun. *Fiction 86* is made up, mostly, of more experimental fiction by lesser-known writers, but most of it is of excellent quality. Especially noteworthy are stories by Elizabeth Moore, both Cathryn and Susan Hankla, and the 1983 winner of the Iowa School of Letters Award for Short Fiction, *Heart Failure,* by the highly praised Ivy Goodman. *Sudden Fiction,* on the other hand, is united by *form.* All of the stories are less than five pages long. The short-short offers, then, an opportunity to include more writers of short fiction than usual in the boundaries of a simple anthology. Shapard and Thomas have chosen a surprising variety of writers who have worked within the fences of this form. The result is, ironically, that precisely because of its self-imposed limitations, *Sudden Fiction* turns out to be the anthology which most accurately suggests (if it does not fully represent) the complexity, variety, and excitement of American short fiction here and now. There are acknowledged masters—Grace Paley, John Cheever, John Updike, Joyce Carol Oates, Peter Taylor, Tennessee Williams, Ernest Hemingway, Ray Bradbury, Bernard Malamud. . . . There are justly fashionable and influential mid-career celebrities like Barry Hannah, Mary Robison, Max Apple, Elizabeth Tallent, Raymond Carver, Tobias Wolff, and Jayne Anne Phillips, people whom you would, reflexively, expect to grace any 1986 anthology. But then there are others, superb writers really, equally gifted with any of their better-known colleagues, who, for one reason and another and most often because they do not fit easily into any familiar label or category, are too seldom found in conventional anthologies. I, for one, rejoice to find work here by Arturo Vivante, Jack Matthews, Fred Chappell, Tom Whalen, James B. Hall, Gary Gildner, Fielding Dawson, and Philip F. O'Connor. As a kind of lengthy appendix, "Afterwords," the book offers statements by most of these writers and by others who, though not included among the short-short stories, clearly are fascinated by the form.

If it was a good year for anthologies, 1986 was also a fine year for individual collections. There were valuable posthumous collections. Knopf brought out, handsomely as usual, *The Stories of Heinrich Böll* (translated by Leila Vennewitz), sixty-three stories by the Nobel Prize winner, some twenty-two of them previously uncollected in book form. And this is only a selection from a much larger canon. Not without modesty, Knopf claims that "this collection allows us at least to see complete the development of one of the greatest writers of our age." Fourteen years after his death Viking published *Nights in the Gardens of Brooklyn: The Collected Stories of Harvey Swados*. There are twenty-one stories collected here, taken from the three volumes of stories published in his lifetime and a few others, including (the publisher says) "nearly every story Swados published during his lifetime." The publisher makes as much as possible of Swados's "Unwavering commitment to the socialist cause in America." The author's son, Robin Swados, in a bright "Introduction," makes more of the contrast between the stories of Harvey Swados and the "alienated sensibilities" of the most celebrated writers of this decade. He celebrates his father's success in creating stories of amplitude and characters "whose common bond lies in their resolute refusal to capitulate to emptiness." It is a good thing to have the work of Harvey Swados available again. Though he did not live to be old, Swados started young. And, in fact, he was seventeen years old when his first story was included in the *Best Short Stories of 1938*.

Not posthumous, thank heavens, is the *Collected Stories 1948-1986* (Harper and Row) by Wright Morris. With nineteen novels and a batch of other books, including only one collection of short stories, *Real Losses, Imaginary Gains,* Morris has sometimes been ignored or forgotten as a story writer. But he has been writing stories regularly, beginning in 1942. And, like his novels, they are like nobody else's. Nobody could confuse the translucent simplicity of the prose style, the odd, quirky

angles of clear vision, or the subtlety of text and subtext with the work of anybody else. Morris's stories cannot be divorced from his novels or, indeed, from his essays, memoirs, or books of phototext; but neither can those things be wholly appreciated without an awareness of his short fiction. Morris is a master artist, and everything he wrote or writes matters.

Other masters, though not so old or established or complete, yet, as Morris, produced important collections of stories in 1986. Three outstanding collections of selected stories, taken from a lifetime's work, so far, deserve mention. *Out of India: Selected Stories* (Morrow) by Ruth Prawer Jhabvala, offers fifteen stories chosen by the author from four previous collections published over a thirty-year period. Much honored, Mrs. Jhabvala offers the singular perspective of a European woman married to an Indian and, since 1951, living in India. Penelope Gilliatt's *22 Stories* (Dodd, Mead) presents work taken from five previous books of stories published from 1965 on. Most of the stories,

Dust jacket for Michael Mewshaw's novel that exposes corruption in the men's professional tennis circuit

all but four by my count, appeared in the *New Yorker* and are marked by wit and, as her publisher (Dodd, Mead) asserts, by "subtle irony, scrupulous eye for detail, and impeccable ear for speech." Herbert Gold's *Twenty-Seven Stories: Lovers & Cohorts,* coming from the new Donald I. Fine, Inc., is an impressive and coherent selection from stories published over forty years. It is the coherence of all the work, old and new, which astonished Gold in his "Introduction: Four Decades A Young Writer," where he discovers that not as much has changed for and about him as he might have imagined. He writes that "I am still a Young Writer and will probably remain so when my great-grandchildren are gathered dutifully about my running shoes to ask what it's like to be the oldest young writer in the retirement home."

Perhaps as a part of this brief mention of selected stories we should factor in a most curious volume which received a good deal more journalistic attention than any of the above books or, indeed, all of them put together. Ken Kesey's *Demon Box* (Viking) appeared and was widely treated (plenty of space though mixed reviews) as a work of fiction by the reviewers. In part the attention is attributable to Kesey's extraliterary status as a public figure. But the acceptance of the book as a collection of fiction is mildly odd. Almost all of the individual pieces had appeared, over some years, as essays and articles, works of nonfiction, in the magazines. Changing a few names, including calling himself Devlin Deboree, he rehearses his life and the 1960s as well as what happened afterward. Critic Campbell Geeslin, writing (appropriately) in *People,* accurately describes the mixed signals of the book: "Everything is funny and sad, tainted with memories of some kind of glorious past that just wasn't as wonderful as some people think."

(Another amusing fusion of fact and fiction in 1986, though not by choice of the author was Auberon Waugh's collection of essays and commentary, *Brideshead Benighted* [Little Brown], which the majority of American booksellers must have assumed to be a sequel to his father's famous novel.)

There were a good number of individual story collections by prominent writers during the year. Margaret Atwood, whose novel *The Handmaid's Tale,* had appeared early in 1986, was represented by *Bluebeard's Egg* (Houghton Mifflin), her second collection of stories. Russell Banks, who had received considerable acclaim for his recent novel, *Continental Drift,* produced *Success Stories* (Harper and Row), a dozen emphatically ideological stories, mostly concerned with "blue collar" life in America

and dealing with, as his publisher openly announces, "the economic nihilism of our time and place." Following the critical success of her novel *Nights at the Circus,* the "original and disturbing" British writer Angela Carter (who had been teaching at the University of Texas) brought out *Saints and Strangers* (Viking), eight fanciful, sometimes fabulous tales, several of which are set, historically and geographically, in America. Ann Beattie's *Where You'll Find Me* (Linden/Simon and Schuster) arrived with a full share of advance praise and earned mixed reviews. The favorable notices pointed out a deepening, darkening sense of maturity, coming appropriately, as her baby-boomer characters begin to reach middle age. The negative reviews called attention to the interchangeability of characters and to characteristics of the writer's ways and means which have become habits. True, Ms. Beattie has some habitual ways and means, technical obsessions; but this reviewer found the collection to be her best, her most dimensional to date.

Another highly regarded *New Yorker* writer, Laurie Colwin, created a group of closely linked stories with the same central characters in all, very close to being a novel in concept and strategy, with *Another Marvelous Thing* (Knopf). Bittersweet, funny, and clever in the best contemporary manner, this one received more negative response than her earlier work. Andre Dubus, who has been steadily producing short and long stories appearing regularly from the same small publishing house (David R. Godine), has arrived at last as "one of the authentic voices of his generation", and his latest, *The Last Worthless Evening: Four Novellas and Two Stories,* is his most accomplished work so far, justly described (and praised) by John Updike as "life's gallant, battered ongoingness, with its complicated fuelling by sex, religion, and liquor, constitutes his sturdy central subject, which is rendered with a luminous delicacy. . . ." In *Drunk With Love* (Little, Brown), Ellen Gilchrist gives us more of her same (including some of the same characters) spunky, idiomatic, funny, liberated southern woman's point of view which won her the 1984 American Book Award. It is addressed directly to her existing fans, those whom the publisher describes as "devoted readers of Gilchrist short stories."

Thirty years after the appearance of her brilliant first collection of stories, *The Black Prince,* and a dozen years since her last published book of stories, Shirley Ann Grau is strongly represented by her *Nine Women* (Knopf). These stories seem almost old-fashioned in their fullness, amplitude, and power. Coming early in 1986, the book did not receive the appreciative attention it honestly deserved. Another writer of distinction and reputation, poet, critic, and story writer Josephine Jacobsen, brought out her second collection of stories, *Adios, Mr. Moxley* (Jackpine Press), complex and carefully crafted stories whose density is increased by the earned and elegant simplicity of style. These are, as Joyce Carol Oates has written, "small, perfect, gemlike stories." Well known for his novels and screenplays, Thomas McGuane's short stories, published in a variety of magazines, from 1981 to the present, are collected in *To Skin A Cat* (Dutton). Wide attention and mixed reviews greeted these stories which are a little "slick" in execution for the contemporary taste. Canadian Alice Munro, who has published a novel and four celebrated collections of stories, is solidly successful in her fifth, *The Progress of Love* (Knopf); certainly one of the finest books of the year. Oates, who, like Margaret Atwood, began 1986 with the publication of a novel, *Marya: A Life*, later brought out her (by my count) fourteenth collection of stories—*Raven's Wing* (Dutton). Once the immutable fact of her amazing productivity has been put aside, it is clear that she has continued to grow, develop, and deepen as a story writer while maintaining a certain highly charged, electric innocence. This book may well be remembered for her first fictional venture into the world of boxing, the surprising story "Golden Gloves."

Also wonderfully productive, a good deal more various, and (unjustly) not nearly so well known as she ought to be is novelist Kit Reed. She has done it all before, and in this case, *The Revenge of the Senior Citizens**Plus* (Doubleday) returns to the combination of self-reflexive science fiction and fantasy she developed for *Other Stories and: The Attack of the Giant Baby* (1981), a highly original method which her publisher aptly defines as a "savage blend of off-the-wall humor and unfettered imagination." It is too bad that so far no one has seen fit to publish a collection of Kit Reed's "serious" stories, which appear regularly in first-rate magazines. Any year which includes a collection by William Trevor would be at least memorable, and this latest collection, *The News From Ireland* (Viking), is his finest work to date. Free ranging in historical time and contemporary places, the dozen stories are models of what his publisher names as "his three great qualities: Subtlety, honesty, and humanity."

Collections by younger and newer writers, many of them first collections, continued to appear in spite of some gloom and sense of doom in the

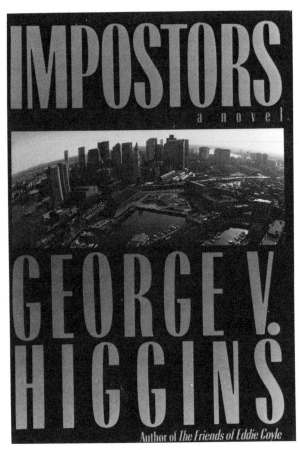

Dust jacket for George V. Higgins's novel about the manipulations of people attempting to protect the secret of a twenty-year-old scandal

publishing industry. One of the most widely publicized books—by all means, press, T.V., and even a music video—of any kind was Tama Janowitz's campy, moderately wacko (without being in the least "experimental") collection called *Slaves of New York* (Crown). An overt and major promotional attempt to make the young author a bona fide Public Figure appears to have been successful, although best evidence is that, nevertheless, the book did not sell well or widely, especially beyond the borders of New York City. Other collections which received considerable, and considerably more serious, attention include Mary Ward Brown's *Tongues of Flame* (Dutton/Seymour Lawrence), Lydia Davis's adventure in lyrical minimalism, *Break It Down* (Farrar, Straus and Giroux), and the flashy and funny pyrotechnics of Deborah Eisenberg's *Transactions In A Foreign Currency* (Knopf). Some other collections by commercial publishers which deserve mention include: *I am Having an Adventure*, by Perri

Klass (Putnam); *Naked to Naked Goes*, by Robert Flanagan (Scribners); *Small Claims*, by Jill Ciment (Weidenfeld and Nicolson); *One Way or Another*, by Peter Cameron (Harper and Row); Linda Collins's *Going to See The Leaves* (Viking); and two genuinely excellent collections—Ron Carlson's *The News of the World* (Norton) and *The Girl Who Would Be Russian* (Harcourt) by Willis Johnson. In my opinion the finest collection of stories by a newer writer and published by a commercial publisher was Mary Hood's *And Venus Is Blue* (Ticknor and Fields). Ms. Hood's previous collection, *How Far She Went*, won the 1984 Flannery O'Connor Award for Short Fiction and was published by the University of Georgia Press.

And the plain truth remains that some of the very best and most interesting short fiction is coming to us from the university presses and the small and regional publishers. It can be argued that the success and the competition of these publishers has helped inspire the commercial houses to seek and find story collections. Certainly there are many more commercially published collections now than there were before small and university presses were as active as they are. There are far too many even to list the more obvious examples; but, allowing for that, it would be unjust and unfair not to mention at least those books (most of them, in every way, of equal quality to any of the commercial volumes) which have captured my attention. The two latest winners of the Flannery O'Connor Award, both handsomely published by Georgia, are poet Peter Meinke's *The Piano Tuner* and Tony Ardizzone's *The Evening News*. Ardizzone, like a number of other writers mentioned here (Oates, Atwood, and Herbert Gold), also published a novel during 1986. His is a baseball novel, adroitly told in the "magic realism" manner—*Heart of The Order* (Holt). The fourth volume in the Bright Leaf Short Fiction series Algonquin Books, and the author's second collection, is Gary Gildner's *A Week in South Dakota*, composed of a variety of stories published in leading literary magazines since 1971. Another second collection, and an outstanding one which arrived with an impressive chorus of advance praise, was David Huddle's *Only The Little Bone* (Godine), a cycle of six stories and a novella, linked by place, rural southwest Virginia, and a central consciousness—Reed Bryant. Two excellent collections from Stuart Wright Publisher would be noteworthy in any year. Early in 1986 came Hilary Masters's *Hammertown Tales*. Masters, who has already established himself as a novelist of distinction and who enjoyed considerable success with his memoir *Last Stands*

(1982) here demonstrates the highest skills as a story writer.

Late in the year, in mid December, came an exciting first collection of short stories—Alyson Carol Hagy's *Madonna On Her Back*. Stuart Wright books are among the most beautifully designed and made trade books being published in America. Two other exemplary works from very small presses are Jack Pulaski's *The St. Veronica Gig Stories* (Zephyr Press) and Rebecca Cummings's *Turnip Pie* (Puckerbrush Press). The latter is a sequence dealing with the early twentieth-century Finnish immigrants in Maine and is at once authentic and deeply moving. Until now these reticent people had found no literary voice. Rebecca Cummings, a lineal descendant, gives them new life.

It has been often said that American publishing has less memory than a mayfly, and there is enough truth in the cliché to sustain it. A world without much past, then, and not much present, either; for, as things go, with a short season of shelf space allotted to all new books, except the fortunate and few best-sellers, in the stores, a period conservatively estimated as including a maximum of four months, the fate of a new trade book, fiction or nonfiction, has most likely been more or less determined before that book ever appears on any shelf. That is, the book clubs have had their looksee and voted yea or nay, certainly by the time the book is in proof and probably in manuscript. Similarly, the chain bookstores Dalton, Walden, and some others have made an early, prepublication choice as to whether or not to carry a particular title in their stock and, if so, then how many copies to order and offer for sale. Paperback sale, if any, of the new books often takes place prior to publication date; though in the case of a literary work of undetermined status and unknown potential value, the hardcover publisher may well gamble on good reviews and good coverage and wait at least part of the sixteen-week season of an American book to seek a paperback publisher.

Anybody with only the most casual experience of business can see that the only sensible thing for a publisher to do with a "property" which arrives at its publication date with, as is inevitably the case for the overwhelming number of hardcover trade books published nowadays, no book club sale, no advance sale or very small sales to the chain bookstores, which account for a very large percentage of all the trade books sold in contemporary America, with no likely paperback sale in the offing, and with uncertain prospects of major reviews, anybody can see the business necessity of the publisher to cut losses to a minimum and to back the few books on a given list, those which have some real promise of sales and profit, with all available resources. It is true, and has been proved any number of times by well-meaning publishers, that a good book, strongly supported in spite of its apparent destiny, can become a break-even "property" or, indeed, can turn a modest profit in the short run.

Recent literary history also tells us that the publisher able to maintain a backlist may turn very large profits in the long run on books whose immediate success was modest at most. Witness the sales of books by Faulkner, Hemingway, F. Scott Fitzgerald, and others of our first generation of twentieth-century masters. Whether such a sea change could happen now, for any book or author, in a world of changed habits, changed business practices, means of distribution, and even new and different tax laws, remains to be seen. Meantime book publishers struggle to stay in business, more and more as a not especially profitable part of larger business conglomerates. Cash flow is a huge problem; for the distributors and bookstores do not, cannot really, pay promptly. And the policy of returns, whereby the bookstore may return to the publisher any unsold copies of a given title, at once greatly complicates the whole picture and certainly delays any clear and present evidence of profit or loss. Good, accurate figures are hard to come by, but individual editors and publishers confirm that returns represent at least one third and often one half of the number of apparent sales. Give or take. Moreover the money market, capital, is especially complex in the publishing business. The ingrained practice of supporting the creation of books through advances against future royalties means that most publishers are heavily in debt, depending on credit lines and interest rates, usually running behind, if only on paper, even during a profitable year.

What all these factors, together with others, add up to is that contemporary publishing is, like the commodity market, a game of futures. Everything looks forward. It is generally agreed now that the chief busywork of editors is not editing but acquisitions. In these circumstances looking back is a luxury. Under these circumstances history is whatever can be recalled or remembered or, perhaps more precisely, whatever has not already been forgotten. Thus all the recent history of American publishing is subject to manipulation, to distortion, to constant revisionism. And fragmented. To be accurate and inclusive at all it must be personal, must represent, ideally, the integrity and point of

view of an individual observer, someone whose self-interest is at least held in check by commitment to other ends not only than profit and loss or repute within the book world but also by the temptation, in journalistic terms, to shape the past into patterns which confirm the prejudices of the present: Thus the professional reviewer in the major and conventional media is, in fact and even at best, part of the problem for the rest of us. For one thing the professional book critic is really part of the publishing industry, albeit a variable and fringe part. (This is true, as well, of many more serious academic critics.) All have a serious investment in the status quo. Such conflict as may arise is mostly in the family, within the literary establishment. Under the circumstances it is no wonder that, amid the clamor for attention and the obligation to support both the industry which feeds them and the art they profess to admire, most professional critics have precious little time for deviation from the official programs laid out in advance by the major publishers and next to no time for "discovery." The working literary press has, of course, institutional obligations and affiliations; but, perhaps more pertinent, they are likewise committed to the concepts and ethics of journalism. To an extent their criticism must present itself as "news." In which case any yesterday is hardly ever as important or as interesting as any tomorrow.

On the other hand the academicians, who have more influence than is generally realized, are supposed to take long views of the past and to make intelligent projections for the future. And to an extent their point of view is longer and longer. But, nevertheless, and especially since the study of contemporary literature became a respectable part of the curriculum, they, too, like the journalists, have a vested interest in the status quo, in preserving received opinions and judgment not merely in the history of our times but also for the future.

All of which means that essays, such as this one, rare as they are and limited as they must be, by the tastes, knowledge, and capability of one individual critic (though he or she must surely be alert to the work of others, journalists and academics alike, if only to know what is happening, must know the official history even as it unfolds), are important as checks against the loss of so much of the past and, alas, the present. The system of publishing, distribution, and criticism of contemporary literature is enormously wasteful. In spite of all the best intentions so much that is wonderfully and worthy is lost to us.

And now the future is already upon us. The Philip Roth novel, appearing just at the end of December 1986, has already in early 1987 received massive media attention and looks likely, at this writing, to be a best-selling success. Robert Coover's latest postmodern japes and pasquils, in *A Night At The Movies* (Linden/Simon and Schuster), although bearing a 1987 copyright and scheduled for a January publication date, had likewise appeared in bookstores and had already received some major reviews in late 1986. And in early January a new book by D. M. Thomas, *Sphinx* (Viking), and Harry Crews's first novel in more than ten years, *All We Need of Hell* (Harper), commanded attention. Word is already traveling around literary circles about a new Walker Percy novel, Tom Wolfe's first novel, and a long-awaited novel by Stephen Becker—*A Rendezvous in Haiti*. Short story collections are coming from John Updike (*Trust Me*) and Mary Gordon (*Temporary Shelter*).

In the spirit of publishing futures I should end this report with a list of new books for 1987, which I have read in advance proof in 1986, and can enthusiastically recommend to good readers of good books. Some of these books may be well known soon enough; others may remain unknown except here and in the homes of the authors. Time and luck will tell the answer to that problem. Meantime their excellence is demonstrable. Some good novels: Denise Giardino, *Storming Heaven* (Norton); Alice McDermott, *That Night* (Farrar, Straus and Giroux); Cathryn Hankla, *Blue Moon in Poorwater* (Ticknor and Fields); G. F. Borden, *Easter Day, 1941* (Beech Tree/Morrow); Sharon Sheehe Stark's first novel, *A Wrestling Season* (Morrow); Hilary Masters's latest, the brightly original and moving *Cooper*. Among the new collections of stories the best I have seen include: Madison Smartt Bell, *Zero db* (Ticknor and Fields); Pinckney Benedict, *Town Smokes* (Ontario Review); Cathryn Hankla, *Learning The Mother Tongue* (Missouri); Richard Ford, *Rock Springs* (Atlantic Monthly Press); Richard Bausch, *Spirits And Other Stories* (Linden/Simon and Schuster).

The Year in Poetry

Lewis Turco

Nineteen eighty-six was a considerable year for what critics and readers have begun to call "Neoformalism" or "The New Formalism" in American poetry. For the past three years the onset of the movement has been chronicled in these annual survey reviews. Early in 1986 Harper and Row published the first anthology of formal poetry in many years, Philip Dacey and David Jauss's *Strong Measures: Contemporary American Poetry in Traditional Forms*.

In his review "Six Poets" in the spring 1986 issue of the *Sewanee Review*, Thomas Swiss wrote, "New poems by young writers like Molly Peacock, Baron Wormser, Mary Jo Salter, and Richard Kenney exhibit meter and rhyme. Some of these poets have been dubbed New Formalists, but how does one tell the 'new' formalists from the 'old' if all these writers are mining the same traditions, exhibiting the same manners?"

The answer lies in that qualifier, "if," for of course all these poets do not "exhibit the same manners," though they must perforce "mine the same traditions," which are the traditions of literature in English: one can tell the Neoformalists from the old by getting to know the names of the people who wrote formally twenty-five years ago, and the names of those who are currently struggling to throw off the anti-intellectual egocentrism of these last two decades and more.

The most astonishing manifestation of the onset of Neoformalism appeared in the May-June 1986 issue of the *American Book Review* where Diane Wakoski, in an essay titled "The New Conservatism in American Poetry," launched an ad hominem attack on "John Hollander as Satan" and on Robert Pinsky, "a nice man, even a good writer, but NOT one of the searchers for a new American voice." These two poets, Wakoski maintained, are representative of conservative, literary legions who are making an assault upon "the free verse revolution, denouncing the poetry which is the fulfillment of the Whitman heritage, making defensive jokes about the ill-educated, slovenly writers of poetry who have been teaching college poetry classes for the past decade, allowing their students to write drivel and go out into the world, illiterate of poetry."

The last time critics attacked what was then called "academic poetry" and equated it with "Fascism" and the "military-industrial complex" (a phrase invented by Dwight Eisenhower), the ploy worked. Rather than be perceived by their students as members of the American Nazi Party or the Ku Klux Klan, poets on college faculties everywhere during the activist 1960s abdicated their responsibility to provide their pupils with substance and became a caste of "nurturers" rather than teachers. Now, a quarter-century later, Wakoski is shocked to discover that she and her generation are the conservatives, and the consideration of craft and structure is new, perhaps even revolutionary, to younger poets.

Whether one is an innovator or a traditionalist in poetry, however, has nothing to do with one's politics. Wakoski was so intent upon scoring rhetorical points that she equated T. S. Eliot with Robert Frost. If Eliot was a conservative in politics and religion, he was one of the most innovative and experimental poets of the twentieth century like his friend Ezra Pound, who was in many ways responsible for the revival of the "Whitman heritage." Pound—wild man of the Modernist literary world, first to cry "make it new!" and to make it stick— far from being a liberal of any kind was, in fact, a Mussolini Fascist. If Frost was a New England conservative, Edwin Markham, author of "The Man with the Hoe," was twice as formalist in his poetics and a hundred times more liberal in his politics. International socialist poetry is as "formal," "traditional," and "rhetorical" as any.

Regarding "American" as opposed to "European-style" poetry: the work of Robert Frost is as American and as American-sounding as anything William Carlos Williams ever wrote. No perceptive American or European reader would or could confuse Frost's voice with that of Wordsworth or Elizabeth Barrett Browning or Keats or Dickinson or anyone else Wakoski might invoke. As though any of this had any importance at all. What is the difference whether a poem is American or English or Canadian or Australian if it is a good poem? What is the difference whether it is a

rhymed and metered poem or a prose poem, so long as it is well done? None whatever, except that if people know how to handle the language well in every way possible, perhaps they will stand a better chance of writing a good poem, and that surely is what John Hollander and the other teachers of craft and technique are attempting to give their students. Wakoski is a college teacher herself, though to read her essay one would never suspect it.

Case in point: a full-page review by Michael Heller in the *New York Times Book Review* for 26 January looked at *From This Condenserie: The Complete Poems* of the late Lorine Niedecker, edited by Robert Bertholf (Jargon Society). Niedecker was a member in good standing of the long-established antiestablishment who wrote a cryptic, "condensed" material inspired by Bashō and, one assumes, other Oriental poetry. (Her work has been described in *Contemporary Literary Criticism* as a substitution of the clipped top of an evergreen for a cultivated and trained bonsai tree.) Heller used as his last quotation what he called "this brief [auto]biographical summation" of her life:

> What horror to awake at night
> and in the dimness see the light.
>   Time is white
>   mosquitoes bite
> I've spent my life on nothing.

This, at least, is not poetry or any other form of "condensation"; it is doggerel in the traditional form of an inept limerick that unbuilds to an anticlimax.

Heller, Niedecker, and Wakoski are members of the conspiracy that has existed in this country since Walt Whitman to glorify nonwriting or bad writing as quintessentially "American" literature. American it may be, but it isn't necessarily literature. Because the United States is a democracy, it is decided that everybody ought to be able to write, and when it is discovered that not everyone can, a corpus of bad writing is developed and praised so that those who can't write won't feel bad. Unfortunately, those people who do know how to write or who enjoy reading literature feel worse than bad when they read such material.

Rather than stemming the tide of the New Formalism, the Heller/Niedecker/Wakoski product merely displays the poverty and bankruptcy of the old antiformalism. Wakoski's own new book, *The Rings of Saturn* (Black Sparrow Press), will stand as an example. Here is the beginning of a perfectly representative "poem" titled "Braised Leeks & Framboise": "The ocean/this morning/has tossed someone's garbage/over its surface,/half oranges/ that make my mouth pucker for/fresh juice,/lettuce leaves/looking fragile, decorative, like scarves/for the white curling locks/of old water."

If something said well is something well said, and something said superbly is a poem, then what is this? And what does one call Charles Bukowski's *You Get So Alone at Times That It Just Makes Sense* (Black Sparrow)? Here is a Bukowski offering, "some suggestions": "in addition to the envy and the rancor of/some of my peers/there is the other thing, it comes by telephone and/letters: 'you are the world's greatest living/writer.'//this doesn't please me either because somehow/I believe that to be the world's greatest living/writer/there must be something/terribly wrong with you."

Both these examples are at best merely unappetizing prose without a sense of rhythm or line.

In the spring the University of Arkansas Press brought out Lewis Turco's first book of literary criticism, *Visions and Revisions of American Poetry*, integrated essays that cover the period from the seventeenth century to the present from a formalist perspective. Two other critical books that take a historical perspective of American poetry were published this year, one of them covering the American Colonial period, and the other addressing contemporary poetry.

A collection of essays edited by Peter White, *Puritan Poets and Poetics: Seventeenth-Century American Poetry in Theory and Practice* (Pennsylvania State University Press), addresses three aspects of early American poetry, "Puritan Aesthetics and Society," "Individual Achievements: Selected Poets," and "Genres: Selected Poetic Forms." It is tonic to have this book and rediscover in it a viable heritage of writing in the United States that antedates the "Whitman tradition" by two centuries. It has been pointed out by historians that Americans try desperately to ignore their past and to pretend that everything of importance has happened only recently. One can even, in White's anthology, discover an essay titled "Baroque Free Verse in New England and Pennsylvania" by Jeffrey Walker, a piece that gives data to show that Walt Whitman was not the first poet to write prose poems.

The second book, too, addresses a problem of discovery, in this case the search for a tradition of American Jewish poetry. *Apocalyptic Messianism and Contemporary Jewish-American Poetry* by R. Barbara Gitenstein first locates the beginnings of the tradition in nineteenth-century American-Se-

phardic literature, and then in later Ashkenazic, Eastern European immigrant work. In the rest of this fascinating and very readable academic treatise, Gitenstein examines the effect that Jewish mystical traditions have had on recent and current poetry in the United States.

In August the Louisiana State University Press published Miller Williams's *Patterns of Poetry: An Encyclopedia of Forms*, which differs from the Dacey-Jauss book in that it is more specifically focused upon traditional structures of poetry and includes work by poets ranging back to the Middle Ages. The same press issued Miller Williams's latest collection of poetry as well, *Imperfect Love*. As always, these formal lyrics and short narratives consider the human condition in such a way as to provide the reader with both insight and delight, as in "A Little Poem":

for Jack Marr

We say that some are mad. In fact
if we have all the words and we
make madness mean the way they act
then they as all of us can see

are surely mad. And then again
if they have all the words and call
madness something else, well then—
well then, they are not mad at all.

In November the University Press of New England brought out *The New Book of Forms: A Handbook of Poetics*, an expansion and updating of Lewis Turco's *The Book of Forms* (1968). Thus formalist penury, which had lasted since the 1950s, is suddenly a plenitude. But of course these events have been in the works in most cases for years, and it is largely a coincidence that what has in fact been a slow swing of the pendulum appears to be a revolution in poetic practice. There are more books to come in the next two years—one hopes that this luxury won't prove in the end to be a surfeit.

Last year we reported on the movement called L=A=N=G=U=A=G=E poetry and traced its beginnings in the abstract poetry of Wallace Stevens, through the New York School of John Ashbery, and thence to the West Coast. It now seems to be spreading in chapbooks into the South and New England as well. Two collections this year are of particular interest. George Butterick's *The Three Percent Stranger* (Zelot Press/Asphodel Book Shop) is a curious blending of surrealism and abstraction. Here is the opening of his title poem:

Front cover for the expanded and revised edition

The snore in the nose cone. I pass my son
mining in the caves of sleep. The house,
warped without sound, hangs. Where there
was unpolished floor a carpet of lilies arises
and tries to gnaw my unslippered feet

Butterick, a librarian at the University of Connecticut, in the past has been associated with the "neo-Black Mountain" school of State University of New York (S.U.N.Y) at Buffalo and elsewhere—he edited *The Maximus Poems* of Charles Olson, discussed in "The Year in Poetry 1983." But West Coast members of that persuasion, including Robert Duncan have been feuding with the L=A=N=G=U=A=G=E people, and one of that argument's chroniclers is another poet who has flirted with Olsonism, De Villo Sloan, an instructor at Auburn University. Sloan's chapbook *Ourang-Outang* (published by "bomb shelter propaganda" of Tempe, Arizona) is a combination of concrete poems and another sort he describes in a foreword: "The other

more conventional linguistic 'poems' are also dislocated language—machines of language. They have been described as 'da-da,' 'surreal,' 'constructivist,' even 'L=A=N=G=U=A=G=E.' Ultimately, these designations are useless."

One must pause to demur, for of course designations are not useless, they are elementary and seminal. We know things by their names or we do not know them at all. Sloan continues, "In this writing I seek to represent the flow of pure language found in the hypnogogic state, the state of consciousness between waking and sleep. It is, I believe, a language of nonsense and great possibility." Here is Sloan's "Neither":

Airglow places uproar dynamism. Unknowing islands
  raven
unicorn sustain lightyears, galaxies, the anchor.
Pilgrims thinking
Pilgrims cosmology

Mammoth vault discarding air.

Such work appears to be at the opposite end of the spectrum from Neoformalism, but it is equally distant from the work of the Established Antiestablishment, or so it would appear. However, if Sloan and others want to try (again) to capture in words the "hypnogogic state," then they share a goal with one of the more absurd movements currently thriving in America—Anthropoesy.

It appears that it is the desire of certain poetically inclined social scientists to throw over their profession of anthropology and usurp, instead, the position of shaman, which has been left empty since Western societies forsook the cave, the forest, and the system of sympathetic magic. The first major attempt to fill this vacancy is an anthology of anthropoesy titled *Reflections: The Anthropological Muse*, edited by J. Iain Prattis and published by the American Anthropological Association. Unfortunately, none of the bards included write poetry any better than Loren Eiseley did (though Eiseley was one of the great scientific essayists of his day), and most of them write it a great deal worse. It is an amazing thing to read some of these attempts to forsake science—which has achieved everything that the shamans never could through their magic mushroom trances—and reachieve ignorance. It is exactly as though a college of chemists had reverted to searching for the Philosophers' Stone, or the people on Mount Palomar had discovered dragons in the sky.

One felt fortunate indeed to be physically present last year at S.U.N.Y. at Oswego to see and hear the editor of this anthropoetical anthology achieve the self-hypnogogic state. On that occasion he asserted that, after a peace conference which he was sponsoring in Canada, where he works, he would be elected prime minister of some country—he did not at that moment know which one precisely—and soon thereafter the world would take peace seriously. Having spent some time oneself in the hypnogogic state leafing with dismay through *The Anthropological Muse,* one was constrained at last to harken to the voice of Polyhymnia, who whispered in his ear,

> Shame on you, loresman!
> Go be a shaman,
> A guru or fakir—
> You won't be a *makir.*

It's nice to know that some things never change, that there is a fixed star in one's universe by which one can steer and judge. In 1973 the scholar and critic Richard Londraville distilled what he called "The Rod McKuen Formula": "1) [The speaker is a] *male persona with female fantasies.* He pines for a woman who has left him, and he is powerless in his love for her. 2) *A lonely setting, emphasizing the separateness of the persona.* He is either physically removed from others, strolling down a deserted strand at low tide, for example; or he may be 'alone in a crowd,' surrounded by people who are insensitive to him. 3) *Nostalgic tone.* The present for the persona is a time to be endured. The really good times of his life are gone, never to return. 4) *One contrived, 'pretty' image,* usually having to do directly with the sensuous appreciation of a woman or the warmth of remembered love; it is often clever and 'cute' rather than appropriate to the situation. [McKuen's] use of syllepsis in 'A Cat Named Sloopy'—'my arms full of canned liver and Love'—is a fair example. 5) *Brevity.* The poem should not exceed twenty lines. Half that length is better. 6) *'Free verse'* [that is, line-phrased prose]. Rhyme may be used, of course, but lack of craft may be more easily concealed where there are fewer rules to follow."

One of these following poems is by Rod McKuen, taken from his new collection *Valentines* (Harper and Row); the other is by Richard Londraville:

AT THE SUPERMARKET

The decision for peanut butter
jarred long rows of memories
and sent them scattering across the aisles.

I saw the back of your head
through the maze of pushcarts
and was stabbed, again,
by that succulent, cloudy mane
that always used to mingle
with our kisses.

Has it only been a year?

BAGGAGE

The year was only
one long noisy day
that never knew a quiet night.
                Your grin
(once strong as any shoulder),
disappearing in so many crowded rooms
each time I thought I'd found your face again,
hardly helped at all.

I suppose it was a glad adventure
              however quickly gone.
Still, leave me your address
so I won't have to stand in line
             at American express.

Londraville, who teaches at S.U.N.Y. at Potsdam, claims to be able to write a "Rod McKuen poem" in under three minutes. The difference is that McKuen will earn a great deal more from these poems than Londraville will from teaching poetry.

Elsewhere one has discussed the differences between the two traditional views of poetry, the "classical" and the "romantic," or the Aristotelian and the Platonic. The former is "art poetry," and it derives from the social practices of mankind—storytelling, word games, work songs, and suchlike activities. The latter is "priest poetry"; its derivation is from the system of sympathetic magic, which obtained in the world at large before the age of science. The object of priest poetry is to control the environment of mankind through "words of power," incantations, prayers, charms—liturgics of various kinds.

Art poets tend to define *poetry* as "language art," but priest poets, depending on their particular religious set of mind, define poetry in more circumscribed ways, as "vision" or "prophecy" or "revelation" or "ecstasy," and these writers consider language not as their primary focus, not as the substance of their product, poetry, but rather as merely the vehicle for their religious experience, whatever it may be. The reason that priest poets tend to despise art poets is that social poetry is seen as to a degree frivolous, for wordplay does not have a deeply serious and significant point. Art poets, on the other hand, can appreciate the work of priest poets, because priest poetry may utilize language as well as art poetry can.

But if the art poet's definition of poetry is broad enough to encompass the narrower definitions of the priest poet, nevertheless the art poet will perceive the priest poet as an "amateur," one who uses language for special, not for "professional" purposes. A third sort of poet, however, is the "agonist"—a professional who is as committed to language art as any other poet, but who is more interested in theoretics than in performance. Sometimes such poets—as for instance Wallace Stevens—will embody their theories in poetry rather than in essays. William Carlos Williams was in his own way a propagandist, one who made great claims for a liberal America in his poetry; he was not an agonist, however, but a true professional because it wasn't in his poetry that he did his agonizing; rather, it was in his letters to young poets and in what little prose he wrote, sometimes in his long poem *Paterson* and in *In the American Grain*. He was, in most of his poems, very much interested in the dance of language. He maintained that he wasn't interested so much in sound, but in image: Williams was one of the prime members of the school of poets called Imagists which gave rise subsequently to Charles Olson's Black Mountain "projective verse" theories, Charles Reznikoff's cadre of "Objectivists," and Robert Bly's "deep imagism" among other movements. Yet Williams in fact was also interested in the sonic dance of language. He invented a prosody which would do rhythmically for him what he wanted the language to do. One can see the beginning and much of the development of these ideas as they were put into practice in *The Collected Poems of William Carlos Williams: Volume I, 1909-1939*, edited by A. Walton Litz and Christopher McGowan (New Directions). This is the first of two new, fully revised and expanded volumes planned as the definitive presentation of Williams's poetry.

Jerome Rothenberg is one of those poets who are not so much interested in the way language works as they are in various kinds of "religious" experience. Rothenberg, whose *New Selected Poems* was also published in 1986 by New Directions, is one of the poets whom Barbara Gitenstein discusses in her book *Apocalyptic Poetry*. Gitenstein seems to have little trouble understanding Rothenberg, but that is because she brings with her a ready-made context of Jewish kabbalism, something not available to most readers. Here is Rothenberg's "A Poem in Yellow after Tristan Tzara":

angel slide your hand
into my basket   eat my yellow fruit
my eye is craving it
my yellow tires screech
o dizzy human heart
my yellow dingdong

This "poem" may or may not be "apocalyptic," "messianic," or "kabbalistic"; it may be a poem written in "abstract syntax" or merely in obscure sym-

Front cover for a selection of verse by the publisher and poet James Laughlin

bology. It may be "deep" or "superficial." Most of us will never know because it is not written for us, it is written for the Initiates, whoever they may be. It is written in a private priest-language. Other poets whom Gitenstein discusses, such as John Hollander, write in a public language. In the landscape of their minds they provide landmarks one can follow, by which one can steer a course through the words.

Now here is the paradox: Hollander, who is an art poet and a formalist, is accused by Wakoski, who speaks for the Whitman/Williams people, of being elitist, whereas she and Rothenberg think of themselves as democratic to a fault. Yet it is art poetry, not priest poetry, that is accessible to most readers, because it is written for *all* of the literate, not merely the caste of shamans and priests, not the minority of the already-convinced and baptized. And here is the paradox within a paradox: Williams was *not* a priest poet, he was an art poet. Nor did he have anything in common with Whitman except his desire to write for the common man, and to that end he attempted to invent a system of poetry writing, a "prosody," that the common man could understand. What Rothenberg and the other priest-poets have done is to pervert Williams, making of his language experiments an excuse for writing experimental poetry that is accessible only to members of a kabbala.

The man who has done most to further this progression from democracy to cabal, perhaps, is James Laughlin, publisher of New Directions, whose own *Selected Poems, 1935-1985* was published this year by Lawrence Ferlinghetti's City Lights Press. Here is a poem, "Dream Not of Other Worlds," that restates Williams's Imagist dictum about ideas:

this one we're in will have to
do for us there is no other ni-

hil in intellectu quod non prius
in sensu no ideas but in things

we must live on what we see and
touch and love with what we give

each other heav'n is too high
for us so let us try to find

our heaven in what concerns us
being together and lowly wise.

What, one wonders, would Williams have thought of a poet using Latin in a poem?

Black Sparrow is another press that issues work by the *Demokratik Kabbal,* and here is a selection of quotations from some 1986 releases. First, a few lines from "The Excavation of Artaud" in Clayton Eshleman's *The Name Encanyoned River, Selected Poems 1960-1985:* "Shaman of obsession—I said at his tomb—/excavated in electricity, opened between/anus and sex. In the Australian outback of the soul,/3 dead men are fingering your anesthetized root support/shining like a chain of sputtering lights, for the key to creation,/between the bone they've drawn out and your bone they so desire. ***O shaman, from having been so masterfully plundered!/O priest, from having been fixed in antithesis!/O pariah, from having been so desired by the dead!"

Next, "By the Five Dollar Bill" in John Wieners's *Selected Poems 1958-1984:* "Oh Bo-Bo/what are you up to now,/I'm in the deserted hotel ballroom/and afternoon neighbor-hood cafe;//painful love is never pleasant/after the distance and death/ poetry is the only way we/can keep in touch though not enough//love, as you know it in fame and politic's [*sic*]/success has not been mine/[this slash is part of the poem] on the toilet/as now you rise from it,/in Hindu yoga and Tibetan LSD."

Robert Bly also brought out a *Selected Poems* this year, from Harper and Row. Here is the whole quarter-century range of "politically sensitive" work by the founder of the senescent school of "Deep Imagism."

John Allman's *Scenarios for a Mixed Landscape* is an anomaly in that it is a formalist collection issued by New Directions, but perhaps one ought to remember that this publisher also gave American readers the poems of Dylan Thomas—that sweet-tongued, bell-eared Welsh archformalist—back in the dim ages of the 1950s. Allman is a real writer, interested in everything about people, their lives and language. Whether he chooses to write decasyllabic stanzas, as in "Flower," a sestina, as in "The Rising," or a sequence of poems in the form of a calendar bestiary, as in "Creatures of Heaven and Earth," Allman keeps his eye on the reader's delight as well as on his subject, and often he succeeds in writing poems that speak deeply and brilliantly at the same time.

Ode to the Chinaberry Tree and Other Poems by James Applewhite (Louisiana State University Press) is about the nostalgia of a region—the South. The formal range of these poems is from line-phrased prose to loose traditional forms such as terza rima. The meters are conversational; echo, where it is used, is often consonance rather than true rhyme. The effect is pleasant in a brooding, moody way.

Maggie Anderson's *Cold Comfort* (University of Pittsburgh Press) is about a region also, in this case West Virginia. Anderson is a less formal poet than Applewhite, and some might describe her metric as free verse, but it is really variable iambics that usually come back to the pentameter norm. These portraits of people and places are beautifully controlled and evocative. Here is the beginning of strophe two of "Palimpsest":

What if you were to live somewhere far from here?
Somewhere, perhaps, like Alliance, Ohio, where
you would lay your whole life down on the brick
    streets
under the big maples with their yellow leaves in au-
    tumn?
Somewhere where you would suddenly remember
    how blue
the sky opens out, how the cornstalks shamble for
    miles,
how the highway's straight all the way to Wyoming?

Christianne Balk won the 1985 Walt Whitman Award of the Academy of American Poets for her first book of poems, *Bindweed* (Macmillan, 1986). Anthony Hecht, who judged the contest, writes that "Grief and loss have rarely been given more poignant utterance than in this brilliant volume ... which unites dream, imagination, nightmare and fantasy with an authority that incontrovertibly persuades because it is grounded in a dense physical reality." That is a great deal to claim for a first collection, but this is a good book, one of the better productions of the year.

Jared Carter was praised in these pages when his two 1984 pamphlets, *Pincushion's Strawberry* and *Fuque State*, were reviewed here; there is more to praise in a third, *Millenial Harbinger* from Slash and Burn Press of Philadelphia. Carter has a special feeling for this fragile form of publication, the fine editions press chapbook. He writes an annual review of chapbooks for the *Georgia Review* that is well worth the aficionado's attention.

The 1985 George Elliston Poetry Prize selection is *Cracking the Code* by David Bergman (Ohio State University Press, 1986), a collection of poems that tell stories. The emphasis is always upon character. The poet turns himself into other people— the first voice in the book is that of a woman in "Elective Surgery"—and skillfully draws the reader out of his or her life into the lives of others. The technical approaches are always formal but never stiff.

The winning volume in the 1985 Yale Series of Younger Poets competition is George Bradley's *Terms To Be Met* (Yale University Press, 1986). James Merrill, who judged the competition, writes that "George Bradley belongs to a tradition of philosophical poets that includes Lucretius and Wallace Stevens. His lines are long, unfreighted, the easier to lift us to high and distant places, and teach us to listen for 'the sound of the sun.' " Despite Merrill's overstatement and the irrelevance of long lines to high and distant places, this is a respectable first book. The long lines *are* a fit (and traditional) vehicle for elegiac poems, and Bradley's "Leaving Kansas City," an ode, is extraordinarily fine, for it captures perfectly the essentially plains, plain personality of a western metropolis.

Turner Cassity in *Hurricane Lamp* (University of Chicago Press) approaches his themes always in formal, often in traditional structures. There is usually a satirical, if not a sardonic wit in evidence in these poems on many subjects, and a hint of brimstone. But perhaps the clever mind eventually overimpinges upon the reader's perception of the poem, and the reader becomes a bit too aware of the poet manipulating his lines and rhymes, his themes and audience. This is, however, a good book, best taken in small doses.

In 1983 David Citino's *The Appassionata Poems* was praised lavishly here. That edition sold out and now the publisher, the Cleveland State University Poetry Center, has issued a version expanded by thirty-six poems—a doubling of the first collection—in *The Appassionata Doctrines*. Citino, reading his poems in October at "A Jubilation of Poets," the twenty-fifth anniversary celebration of the Center's founding, said that the essential characteristic of Sister Mary Appassionata, the speaker of these monologues, prayers, and declamations, is that "she believes in absolutely everything." The reader does likewise while engaged with this amazing persona.

Citino's *The Gift of Fire* (University of Arkansas Press), the poet's second collection of the year, begins with myths of the Creation and works its way through Cleveland and the poet's family, ending at last, after turning the complete circle, in the caves of Lescaux. Citino has great range of subject matter and depth of feeling. His style is always recognizably his own—nothing fancy about it, but capable of doing everything he wants to do, which is considerable.

The Marble Queen by Henri Cole (Atheneum) is a first book, published by a major publisher, that hasn't won a prize! One has no idea why it won no award, for it's a good book full of good poems. Another paradox: the poems are usually about nature carefully observed and carefully depicted, by a poet who lives in New York City.

Living Gloves (Dutton) by Lynn Doyle, on the other hand, is a winner of the National Poetry Series competition, selected by Cynthia Macdonald who, however, provided no blurb for the book. Annie Dillard praises Doyle for her heartfulness; Albert Goldbarth does likewise for her "tenderness and wit," but others might find it a bit difficult to stay interested in these talky, prosy pieces.

Another winner in the National Poetry Series is *Saints* by Reginald Gibbons (Persea Books), selected by Ronald Flint. Flat-out prose effusions alternate frequently with somewhat strophically inclined pieces, but all of them are more or less ego poems in the style of the late Confessional school. A bit more art and a bit less wearing of the heart on the sleeve would have helped turn these sighs and gasps into poems, perhaps.

Cornelius Eady's *Victims of the Latest Dance Craze* (Ommation Press) was the 1985 Lamont Poetry Selection of the Academy of American Poets for a first collection of poems. The judges were Louise Glück, Charles Simic, and Philip Booth. The book begins with an epigraph from Paul Laurence Dunbar's "A Negro Love Song" which is rhythmic, lyric, ethnic, and colloquial, but no poem in the book combines all these elements again. The line-phrased prose poems are too stiff and formal—in the social sense, not the technical.

Dana Gioia is one of those rare poets who establish reputations before they ever publish a collection of poetry. Such people run the risk of disappointing the book's eventual readers, but *Daily Horoscope* (Graywolf Press) is far from being a disappointment. Here is another first book that has won no prize, and one begins to suspect that it is more of a distinction to miss an award than to snag one these days. Nor is Graywolf a major publisher, though it is distinguished. Gioia is among the best of the Neoformalists, one who works outside the closed world of academe. It is a great pleasure to read and savor the work of one who knows how to write well. (Parenthetically one might note that Gioia's outraged response to Diane Wakoski was one of five published under the overall title "Picketing the Zeitgeist Picket" in the November-December number of the *American Book Review*.)

Reviewing Albert Goldbarth's last collection of poems in these pages four years ago, it was pointed out that reading his work is like sitting around listening to a garrulous and humorous un-

Dust jacket for the first volume of verse by Cornelius Eady

cle rattling cleverly away about everything in the world. There have been no changes from that book to *Arts & Sciences* (Ontario Review Press), but perhaps it's time for an example. This is from an interminable sequence titled "Knees/Dura-Europos": "It was Dura first, an Assyrian name, at its founding./When it fell to the Seleucids in 323 BC, they/named it: Europos./Then it fell to the Parthians: Dura./Then the Roman emperor Trajan took and/successive Roman rule renamed, it: Europos./Then the Sassanians won it: Dura. Archeologists/simply call it Dura-Europas, to avoid confusion. No wonder, though, a man is confused./No wonder a man runs circles."

R. S. Gwynn's two previous publications of poetry included the hilarious satirical tour de force *The Narcissiad*, which appeared as a chapbook from Cedar Rock Press in 1981. Now a third has been published: *The Drive-In* (University of Missouri Press), a nonprizewinner and yet another example to support the observation that, of the year's crop of first books, those that come unlaureled tend to be among the best.

Gwynn, in a long review he wrote for the fall issue of the *NER/BLQ*, objected to the label "New Formalist" being applied to such young formal poets as Timothy Steele. Gwynn suggested that such a designation at best ought to be applied to faddists who use formal structures to write society verse, a kind of "Yuppy poetry." If that definition is to be accepted, then Gwynn himself is no neoformalist. He is certainly, however, one of the new generation of formal poets who can make the language dance and go deep. As X. J. Kennedy says in his blurb, "Verse so strictly crafted is rare, yet Gwynn is no mere tinkering formalist: his work has equal parts of passion, energy, and outrageousness. Poem after poem reads like a tightly corked explosion.—Here is a mature, slowly perfected voice with its own distinctive power and resonance." Here is an epigram and a credo:

ARS POETICA

Sweet music makes the same old story new.
That is a lie, but it will have to do.

An Alternative to Speech (Princeton University Press) is not David Lehman's first book but it is the first substantial collection of his own poems. Like Gioia and Gwynn, Lehman arrives with a reputation already in evidence, and he is an active member of the generation of Neoformalists. His work appears in *Strong Measures,* and he is editor of the forthcoming *Ecstatic Occasions/Expedient Forms* (Macmillan), an anthology of poems and prose commentary by sixty-five contemporary poets that was previewed in New York City in a program sponsored at the Modern Language Association convention by the Poetry Society of America at the end of 1986. Lehman's own poems, like the title of his anthology, combine traditional and experimental elements in sometimes stunning, always intelligent, ways and forms.

One cannot fault Audre Lorde's range of life experience. The jacket copy reads, "As Marilyn Hacker has written, 'Black, lesbian, mother, cancer survivor, urban woman: none of Lorde's selves has ever silenced the others; . . .'" But in *Our Dead Behind Us* (W. W. Norton) the rendition of many of these states leaves something to be desired. Perhaps everyone might be a poet if all that counts is experience and artistic performance means nothing. Too many of these pieces are prose chopped up into lines that fall flat on the ear, the eye, and the page. Here is the first strophe of "For Jose and Regina":

Children of war
learn
to grow up alone
and   silently
hoping
no one will notice
somebody's life could depend on it.

Michael McClure's *Selected Poems* (New Directions) is the first major retrospective collection of a poet and innovative playwright who has been associated with the San Francisco/Beat schools since the 1950s. The poems are distinctive in style, offbeat, often whimsical, and usually weird. They can be fun to read, but one needs to pause between them.

Another retrospective is Robert Phillips's *Personal Accounts: New & Selected Poems 1966-1986* (Ontario Review Press), which reprints poems from three earlier books going back to 1966. One-third of the book is comprised of poems hitherto uncollected. It is interesting to see how consistent Phillips has been over the years, both in his voice and in his performance. From the beginning he has been a meditative poet—an elegist and an odist with a sense of humor—and he continues to write thoughtful, semiformal poems that can make the reader smile.

Long ago Adrienne Rich forsook her excellent formal poetry to write programmatic feminist poems in "open" prose forms imitating the compositions of such male models as Whitman and Robert Lowell. She writes now in the jacket copy of *Your Native Land, Your Life* (W. W. Norton), "In these poems I have been trying to speak from, and of, and to, my country. To speak a different claim from those staked by the patriots of the sword; to speak of the land itself, the cities, and of the imaginations that have dwelt here, at risk, unfree, assaulted, erased. I believe more than ever that the search for justice and compassion is the great wellspring for poetry in our time, throughout the world, though the theme of despair has been canonized in this century. I draw strength from the traditions of all those who, with every reason to despair, have refused to do so." In other words, she has switched her focus slightly, but she is still writing confessional propaganda rather than literature. That is her prerogative, but it is ours not to be bored.

One had good things to say about some of the poems reprinted in Timothy Steele's *Sapphics Against Anger and Other Poems* (Random House) when his chapbook *The Prudent Heart* was discussed in these pages in an earlier review. Now, in this second full-length collection—after *Uncertainties and Rest* (1979)—readers are treated to the full range of talents that have been granted to and developed by the poet X. J. Kennedy describes as standing "clearly preeminent" among "those young poets still working in time-tested forms." Richard Wilbur and Thom Gunn agree. Rather than merely stick another leaf into the laurel wreath, one might quote the first stanza of "Old Letters":

> Old letters are reproaches, mute petitions
>   Unlosable in some desk drawer
> Or attic box. Bunched in brown folders, or
> In packets tied with ribbon, they speak of
>   Now-jettisoned ambitions
> And insecurities which passed for love,
> And document not times when we were stronger,
> But rather climates favorable to
> Illusions not illusions any longer.

Not far behind in the Neoformalist lists, though, rides Leon Stokesbury. Not quite so much a contemporary Yvor Wintersian as Steele is, in *Drifting Away* (University of Arkansas Press), Stokesbury is more lyrical than classical, more colloquially humorous than sharp-witted, and he has quite a wide range of subjects.

The poems of Thomas Swiss, whose review was quoted in the beginning of this essay, flirt with traditionally formal verse structures, but in *Measure* (University of Alabama Press) tradition is a benchmark, not a touchstone. This is yet another distinguished first book that has been denied a prize for its excellence. The individual pieces are thoughtful and clear-eyed, concrete in detail and anchored in the real world.

Lot's Wife by Janice Thaddeus (Saturday Press) won the Eileen W. Barnes Award for 1985; the series editor is Charlotte Mandel and the contest coeditor was Rachel Hadas. About as close to formalism as Swiss, Thaddeus is more a narrator than an elegist. Her stories are solidly grounded in human nature. The language she uses in her depictions of convincing characters in realistic situations is well equal to the task of relating her incidents and keeping the reader's interest.

The 1986 George Elliston Poetry Prize was won this year by David Weiss for his collection *The Fourth Part of the World* (Ohio State University Press). This is the one that justifies all the other prizes. Weiss is one of those rare poets, like Howard Nemerov (though their styles are none of the same), who think philosophically, on a great scale, yet who have the ability to anchor their metaphysics in the world of fact and feature. One example will have to do: in "Hell's Kitchen" one boy has beaten another until the left side of his face is caved in. The narrator says, "I lifted/him, after, out of his blood/and held him until he stood without/touching the ground. Then he looked up,/leaving my arms, and pirouetted/slowly like a blind figure skater/or a planet far from the sun./And he said softly, *O my God, O my God, O my God,* his arms spreading/ wider as he turned. He was still/smiling when the two cops hurried him/into the back seat and sped off./This was near dawn near Field's/bakery where two thousand loaves or so/of wheat and rye were rising, moist." The overtone of this passage, the implication, what is left unsaid, is of far greater weight than the literal statement of the poem. Such a thing is hard to do, impossible, perhaps, for most writers to accomplish, yet it is what poetry *is*, essentially. The burden of meaning *behind* the words is what one looks for in the best art.

This year's essay will end with a consideration of three books that attempt something longer than the lyric or the short narrative. The first is *The New World: An Epic Poem* by Frederick Turner. Having read the introductory note; having been fascinated with the thought and planning that went into the architectonics and prosodics of the piece, one turns with a good will, predisposed to give every consideration to this futurist heroic narrative, only to find that the execution of the design is fatally flawed by some extremely ugly writing:

> Kingfish has set in the blind socket a new
> miraculous eye, with its own brain, and spliced
> its output not only across the chiasmus to the visual
> cortex but also into the olfactory bulb,
> with a bleed into the midbrain, and a feedback loop
> through the auditory cortices on both sides of the
>   brain.

This is not poetry. It isn't even good narrative. This "epic" turns out to be a science-fiction soap opera afflicted with the disease of unreadability.

The Blizzard Voices by Ted Kooser (Bieler Press), on the other hand, cannot be put down once the reader dips into it. It is a series of monologues by characters who have survived the prairie blizzard of 1888. This is the second poem in this historical series, "A Man's Voice":

> Father and I had pulled the pump up
> out of the well to put
> new leathers in the cylinders.

Front cover for the first major retrospective collection of Michael McClure's verse

I looked toward the house and saw
that our cats were spinning around
and around on the steps
as if they were drunk. Then the air
was suddenly full of snow,
weeds, dust and fodder, blowing
out of the northwest. We ran in
and pulled the door shut, snapping
the bottom hinge in the wind.
A wall of snow hit the house
and shook it hard, and it grew dark
as night. We had plenty of coal
to burn, for Father had bought a load
the week before. Through the night,
the house rocked like a cradle,
cracking much of the plaster loose.
In the morning we found
the wind had packed the snow so hard
our horses could walk on it

without breaking the crust.
The drifts were there till June.

The piling up of concrete detail in lines of spare, clear verse; the accumulation of lives and deaths as each of these small dramas unfolds, eventually builds to such power that, when the series is finished, the reader for a moment cannot believe he has not himself lived through this harrowing experience with these simple, heroic survivors. And, as usual, Bieler Press has presented this work in a package that is a tribute to the printer's and book designer's art.

Carole Oles has done something similar in *Night Watches: Inventions on the Life of Maria Mitchell* (Alice James Books). Mitchell was America's earliest female astronomer, born in 1818, and these pieces are a sort of fictive biography of her, as Kooser's book is a fictive dramatization of a real event. Both are based on historical documents, and both make absorbing reading.

Thus, 1986 was a year in which the long poem attempted a comeback, but narrative found its most compelling voices in two series of poems rather than in an epic. The Neoformalist revolution came to a boil, and steam began to rise about the poets on both sides of the ancient American rift between verse craftsmen and prose shamans. The argument had lain dormant but smoldering subterraneously this past quarter-century; the priest-poets had apparently won a preemptive victory, but what few critics and readers realized was that, evidently, young poets have been hovering over their own desks, turning the pages of books of forms and teaching themselves what their instructors were not giving them in the classroom. Now, suddenly, they are entering their maturity and publishing books of work manifestly different in structure, style, and approach from the hitherto prevailing poetry. It is a much more interesting literary scene than that which existed four years ago.

Editor's Note. Besides his book of criticism, *Visions and Revisions of American Poetry,* and his *The New Book of Forms: A Handbook of Poetics,* in 1986 Lewis Turco issued a collection of poems, *A Maze of Monsters,* a bestiary of mythical creatures which is the first publication from the Livingston University Press. *Visions and Revisions* won the 1986 Melville Cane Award of the Poetry Society of America.

The Year in Literary Biography

Gay Sibley
University of Hawaii

In the "Year in Literary Biography" essay for 1984, Professor Anthony M. Friedson considered the question of "literary genius as social pariah"; then went on to demonstrate that, if the biographies appearing in that year were indicative, those writers having literary genius would indeed seem to be denied any sort of wide personal popularity. With one notable exception, the biographies of 1986 are not much different. However, as a corollary to this pervasive stereotype, it seems that literary genius also is likely to have a capacity for unusually intense personal relationships. Though few, the friendships settled on by the exceptional literary figure are extreme, containing both loyalty and betrayal beyond normal social custom. Life would appear to allow the person judged to possess "genius" no more than a handful of affiliations that buoy above the tumult when the friendship is working and dash to the rocks when it fails. Such intense alliances mediate between the soul of the artist and those elements which indict the artist himself as a "social pariah." It is as though the genius and his notable associates occupy a stage upon which their loves and converse hates battle for a vibrant existence against the nudgings and needlings of an unremitting, smug, and slightly boring chorus. Literary biographies are nothing if not studies, first, of the proportion of genius to fame, and second, of the degree to which genius is successful in securing alliances willing enough and powerful enough to filter out those lifelong conservative chantings that are mercilessly fatal to art.

In the case of Henry David Thoreau, the subject of *Henry Thoreau: A Life of the Mind*, a critical biography by Robert D. Richardson, Jr. (University of California Press), not only did the genius warrant the fame, but the intensity and quality of Thoreau's friendship with Ralph Waldo Emerson aided the younger genius in driving the chorus offstage with a vengeance. Thoreau and Emerson gave the subject of friendship more attention even than Aristotle, thinking about it, talking about it, writing about it, and acting as best they could on what they believed. The focus began with Emerson, who in his essay on friendship argued for two important ingredients: truth (even when it hurts) and tenderness. The journals of Thoreau echo Emerson on the subject, summarized by the biographer Richardson as "what is wanted in a friend is not a double but a complement, friends should seek out the distances between them."

Both men worked hard at their relationship. The Richardson biography eloquently recaptures a winter during which Thoreau was down with bronchitis and Emerson blue with " 'parsing and spelling and punctuating, and repairing rotten metaphors and bringing tropes safe into port.' " During this lengthy bout of Concord cold, Emerson visited Thoreau often, and one particular visit, as Richardson documents, "left Thoreau with the unutterable security and exaltation that comes when someone the world loves loves us." Thoreau did not mind the subsidiary role he held as Emerson's younger disciple, because Emerson's motives were so obviously clean. With Emerson as friend, Thoreau could grow with the guidance and self-esteem that accompany being chosen by one of the chosen.

During that same winter, Thoreau's journals are centered on this topic of friendship, and, predictably, both the tone and the intensity of Thoreau's entries were mirrored in the actual friendship between the two men. Notably absent from the Emerson/Thoreau alliance is any sort of petty competition, yet it is clear that the relationship itself, along with the pinnacle upon which it perched, was exclusive. Though invited to join Brook Farm with Hawthorne and others, Thoreau chose to move to Emerson's house instead, and, according to Richardson, "both felt that their own world and immediate community were improved and reformed by the new arrangement."

This is not to say that the friendship was flawless. As Richardson points out, both "made such demands as to make it all but unattainable." When Thoreau was on the fourth draft of *Walden* (1854), for example, he went into a tunnel of personal isolation, taking long walks by himself and consulting no one. Emerson, living up to his own belief that truth (though tempered by tenderness) was the main ingredient of an ideal friendship, called him a "cold intellectual skeptic." Though hurt by the criticism, Thoreau acknowledged to himself that if it were indeed true, he hoped that the indictment would "wither and dry up those sources of my life."

In most of his other relationships, Thoreau could indeed be considered an alien, but the alienation was self-imposed and, to his more intimate relations, admirable. In the initial letter from Harrison Gray Otis Blake, with whom Thoreau was to carry on an extended correspondence, Blake compliments Thoreau on his goal of removing himself "from society, from the spell of institutions, customs, conventions." Such a determined absence on Thoreau's part is a far cry from the passive absence of the social outcast.

The obverse of the intensely positive friendship shared by Emerson and Thoreau was the inevitable souring, as Thoreau grew famous and Emerson older. But whereas Emerson regarded Thoreau as his best friend until Thoreau's death, even after, with the onset of senility he had forgotten Thoreau's name. Thoreau grew impatient with his mentor, claiming he "talked to the wind." For Emerson's part, documents Richardson, he "felt and tried to fight what he perceived as Thoreau's increasing, unreachable, provincial isolation and loneliness. Of an evening's talk with Thoreau in October 1851 he wrote, 'we stated over again, to sadness, almost, the eternal loneliness . . . how insular and pathetically solitary, are all the people we know!' "

So the famous friendship, hard wrought, carefully analyzed, did not sustain itself forever. Nevertheless, the coming together of these two greatnesses in a particularly intense bond contributed to a veering in American literary history. Though Thoreau (and the transcendental movement) had other important friends—William Ellery Channing, whose closest tie to Thoreau (according to Channing's biographer) consisted of their both liking walks and their both being thought of by the town as unemployed idlers; and Bronson Alcott, whom Thoreau called "the man of the most faith of any alive"—Emerson was the one who made the difference.

Some famous people have been less successful in their alliances with others, which may or may not have something to do with their level of "genius." Take, for example, Colley Cibber, the subject of *Colley Cibber: A Biography*, by Helene Koon (University Press of Kentucky). A contemporary of Swift, Addison, Steele, Fielding, and Pope, in comparison Cibber has become known as the second-class artist most famous for his onstage performances as Lord Touchwood, Fondlewife, Sir Novelty Fashion, Lord Foppington (both in John Vanbrugh's *The Relapse*, 1697, and in his own *The Careless Husband*, 1705), as Sir Fopling Flutter in Sir George Etherege's *The Man of Mode* (1676), and in nearly a hundred other such parts. His acting assignments in portrayals not meant for ridicule (such as Richard III in 1699 and as Iago in 1709) were rare in a career on the stage that spanned fifty-five years. Accordingly, it has been difficult to separate the roles from the man, so much that it is a temptation to pronounce "Colley Cibber" with the hint of a lisp and an inflective flourish.

Cibber's major literary contribution was as the author of what has come to be judged "the first sentimental comedy," *Love's Last Shift; or The Fool in Fashion* (1696). Following the wild ribaldries of the Restoration, with its joyful acceptance of infidelity, betrayal, and hypocrisy as not only inevitable but worthy of appreciative chuckles, sentimental comedy overall appears more utilitarian than artistic. Colley Cibber's close association with the move to sentiment, to a belief in, and a comic affirmation of, all those values the Restoration found unbelievable and boring, marks him as a scapegoat—someone who did a job that somebody, maybe anybody, sooner or later had to do.

Also smacking of the middle-class utilitarianism of the times was Cibber's other major contribution, as manager of Drury Lane Theater. It was not that the plays Cibber voted for were consistently successful—some were disasters—but that his judgment enabled the theater to compete, however erratically, with Lincoln's Inn Fields as arranged by Christopher Rich. The competition was as political as it was aesthetic, and the preservation of two theaters mirrored the healthy preservation of a two-party system, as the Whigs and Tories sustained their tug-of-war, and as actors and playwrights often chose their theaters according to political patronage and affiliation.

In Cibber's case, in other words, "genius," as the term is commonly defined, appears to have had very little to do with the successes he had. Correspondingly, and perhaps predictably, Colley Cibber was anything but a social pariah. As Helene Koon's biography documents, he had many "highly placed friends," and he "listened to their troubles, never burdened them with his own, and his good humor was contagious." And it was these friends, in fact, who were largely responsible for his being named poet laureate of England in 1730. Yet that special intensity of friendship that seems somehow crucial to the triumph of the great was denied him, and the alliances which might have enriched his contribution have had a hefty, lasting, and a decidedly negative impact. Koon delineates these alliances with finesse and clarity; through such delineations, a reader can see at least some of the reasons why Cibber, in spite of his varied achievements, has ended up as a name that often inspires scorn. His associations with famous actors—Thomas Betterton, Barton Booth, Robert Wilkes—appear to history to be as ephemeral as the roles they all played.

But Cibber's most intense associations were negative ones, and instead of sustaining him, they had quite the opposite effect. First appeared *The Laureat; or, The Right Side of Colley Cibber* (1740), a scathing personal satire charting gossipy anecdotes as fact, and assumed by almost everyone, both then and now, as having been written by Henry Fielding, who also had listed as author of his *An Apology for the Life of Mrs. Shamela Andrews* (1741) one "Conny Keyber." The other, and finally the most damning, intense association was with Alexander Pope, who in his *Dunciad* (1743) put a caricature of Foppington on the "Throne of Dulness" and labeled the image "Cibber."

Cibber retaliated by telling and retelling an unflattering story of Pope's visit to a whorehouse, but predictably (perhaps because genius is what it is) Pope's attack shaped history's view of Colley Cibber, whereas Cibber's counterattack remains as little more than an amusing footnote to the life of Pope. Included as an appendix in the Koon biography and appearing here in its entirety for the first time is "A Second Letter from Mr. Cibber to Mr. Pope. In Reply to Some Additional Verses in His Dunciad, Which He Has not yet Published." It is a brave but pathetic letter; David attacks Goliath with a marshmallow and with only a broken arm to throw it with.

The details of the rancor between Cibber and Pope, as well as the impact of this relationship on literary history, are amply illustrated in Maynard Mack's *Alexander Pope* (Norton), which is probably the most important biography of 1986. "As court sycophant," documents Professor Mack, "[Cibber] demeaned what Pope believed was the proper dignity of a subject and the proper role of a poet." However, Cibber was not alone in eliciting Pope's scorn. John Dennis, a critic in formidable standing before the arrival of the young Pope, was viewed by Pope as a critical tyrant, and "it is the tyrannical spirit of Dennis . . . that the entire third part of the *Essay on Criticism* implicitly seeks to exorcise." In

other words, Alexander Pope went after those in public life who weren't up to his own very high and very classical standards regarding talent, judgment, and both social and professional decorum. And his judgments, though some were made when he was in his early twenties, have mostly turned out to be correct over time.

By the end of Maynard Mack's biography of Pope, the reader has a vivid sense of the man who was undoubtedly one of the most complex and fascinating of English poets. Pope's personal and professional paradoxes—his humility/presumption, Whiggism/Toryism, narrowness/expansiveness—all get equal treatment in this biography; and what results merits (as most biographies do not) the praise of "definitive."

Through his refusal, as a public person, to ally himself politically to any particular party, Pope was able to establish in his works that artistically necessary absence of such polemics as crush the

Dust jacket for the first complete biography of Alexander Pope since 1900

art. Yet there was nobody more polemic than Pope; but he let the focus lie on the art and the excellence, and on the obligation that he saw the talented as having an obligation not only to preserve and protect a cultural heritage (which some of his critics have observed as a limitation) but also to add to and modify it with decorum.

As a Roman Catholic growing up at a time when people of such religious persuasion were required to live at least ten miles from London, and as a victim of a tuberculosis of the bone which condemned him "for life to the stature of a twelve-year-old boy," Pope made an easy target for anyone who did not think as he did, and there were many. Dennis, as a particularly vicious example, placed into print a detailed ridicule of Pope's shrunken body. How Pope managed to turn it all around, to have it so that even his contemporaries would view Cibber and Dennis as "sycophantic" and "tyrannical" and view the much younger Pope's judgment as undeniably accurate is part of the secret of Pope's success and an indicator of his genius.

Though Pope has been accused of cultivating friendships exclusively for personal gain, what the Mack biography documents is that he gained from his friendships, yes, but gained secondarily. He respected only those whom he esteemed to be particularly good at what they did; his judgment, even as a youngster, was excellent; and he liked only those who liked him. Naturally, opportunity would follow the resulting friendships.

In terms of the stereotype of "genius as social pariah," Alexander Pope breaks the mold. He had many friends, took the topic of friendship seriously, and kept most of the friendships intact for the duration of his life. As Maynard Mack observes, "One wonders where among the poets (that *genus irritabile!*) another may be found who succeeded so happily over periods of many years in binding to himself and in binding himself to, such a diversity of men and women, young and old, literary and otherwise: Atterbury, Arbuthnot, Congreve, Jervas, Gay, Parnell, and Swift; Peterborow, Bathhurst, Bolingbroke, Oxford, Orrery, the Burlingtons; Martha Blount, Ann Craggs, Anastasia Robinson, Henrietta Howard, even finally the old duchess of Marlborough; Mallet, Harte, Savage, Spence; Cornbury, Lyttelton, Wyndham, Marchmont, Murray; Garth, Wycherley, Trumbull, Betterton, Walsh; Blount, Bethel, Caryll, Fortescue, Richardson, Allen, and Warburton."

An impressive list, even though, as Mack points out, the "record has its blemishes" (most notably, Lady Mary Wortley Montagu, with whom

Pope had an increasingly rancorous relationship. Overall, though, Pope's intensity toward most friendships, and toward the subject of friendship, seems sincere. Pope confided to John Gay in 1730 that his "one strong desire was to fix and preserve a few lasting, dependable friendships."

Behind it all was what Maynard Mack names a "corporateness: for the responsibility of the individual member, whether a person, idea, work of art, or critical term, to some sort of community or whole." Alexander Pope was in the business of literature and criticism, and he had a firm belief in his product. In order to perfect the product and to know and preserve what was worthy in the products of the past, he chose old friends when he was young and young friends when he was old, like any diligent student of either literature or life. "For Pope, and for his contemporaries in the other arts (architecture, sculpture, painting, but also those arts which produced the furniture, silver, and porcelain that are the envy of the modern world)," says Professor Mack, "the aim is still to work within a known vocabulary of motifs and patterns, extending their reach by the individuality and diversity with which one disposes and applies them but not forgetting (to borrow an image that would have fascinated Pope had he known of it) that like the genetic double helix they contain much encapsulated wisdom, and therefore not neglecting to appropriate their strength."

Pope's friends would always be those who could both tap those "known motifs and patterns" and at least think about and discuss adapting them. Although the friends were "complementary" in personal as well as professional ways (a number of dandies seeming to balance out Pope's physical incapacities for that classification), and although the intensity of the friendships was in varying degrees, Pope's friends almost always contributed to the poet's overall historical goal as poet and critic.

Another factor which also seems to hover around creative genius is madness. Professor Mack quotes Spence in saying even of Pope, that "Little People mistook the excess of his genius for madness." In the case of writers such as Swift or Pound, the madness did not consume and destroy until after the brilliance was on record. In the case of William Cowper, however, the madness is there early, truncating whatever greatness there may or may not have been. James King's lucid and sympathetic *William Cowper: A Biography* (Duke University Press) charts the career of a man who, finally, was more driven by melancholia than by art. After the death of his mother when he was six, Cowper seems to have spent an entire lifetime in search of something he never hoped to find. Part of the problem was his near-fanatic belief in Calvinistic doom and a corresponding conviction that he had been from birth one of the unchosen. Accordingly, everything he did or thought subsequent to this conviction was determined by it, including his choice of friends and the passive role he assumed in their relationships. Armed only with such a fierce presage of failure, he failed at practically everything: at maintaining his health; at furthering a romance with his cousin Theodora; at sustaining a closeness with his family; at warding off frequent and debilitating depressions; and finally, at achieving an art that was not always able to transcend his own therapeutic needs.

Further, the friends he chose seemed to contribute little more than patient nurturing for a morbidly depressive personality; and one of these friends, the evangelical divine John Newton, appears often to have pushed him toward, rather than pulled him from, the edge. Wound in with this relationship was Cowper's involvement with Mary Unwin, the wife of a clergyman who was himself deeply attached to the poet. Although there was much talk of "Improprietys," from all evidence it seems that if a sexual component with Mary existed, it was more on her side than his, his attraction and love being more like that of a son for a mother. And if Mary Unwin played mother to the needy Cowper, John Newton, as King points out in this biography, played the "harsh, domineering father." Newton was a strange character, whose intensities ranged from atheism as a young man to strident evangelicalism during the latter half of his life. Further, he seemed to relish the power he held over Cowper. They collaborated on the *Olney Hymns* (1795), and Cowper's passivity, his "willingness to accept the role of outcast," comes through in his part of the contribution, whereas Newton's tone is always the more (for lack of a more accurate word) pontifical. Newton took a peculiar control in other ways as well. He was instrumental in Cowper's checking in to Dr. Cotton's famed "Collegium Insanorum"; he was jealously reluctant to introduce Cowper to anyone who might usurp his own influence; he wanted to see Cowper's lyrics first and was furious when he discovered that Cowper's *The Task* (1787) was to be published. Whatever Newton's motives, the results do not seem to have been particularly beneficial to the frail recipient of his actions.

Another intense relationship in Cowper's life was John ("Johnny") Johnson, Cowper's second cousin and another clergyman, who was a fraud (claiming that some of his own verse was written by the Duke of Norfolk), a snob (who spent an inordinate amount of time charting his pedigree), and a leech (who drifted from member to member of the extended family, securing sustenance and brief approval where he landed). Nevertheless, the elder Cowper adopted him as a son, and it was Johnny who acted as the poet's confessor at the end of his life, even attempting to ease Cowper's anxiety by drilling a hole in the wall behind his bed, inserting a tin tube, and whispering through it messages that were supposed to be comforting. Unfortunately, by this time, Cowper was paranoid to the extent that what might appear as a positive message to anyone else was to him a stroke of condemnation.

In short, there is no accurate way to measure the depths of Cowper's genius, since whatever there was never stood a real chance. He began with a cringing humility, exacerbated by a chorus of malignant angels hymning to him that his greatest sin was his inability to commit suicide. Added to the Calvinistic gloom were a handful of friends who, however well-meaning, served only to make him less sure of the value of his contribution. Such friendships could provide a list of Emersonian "tenderness" but very little truth. The converse of his sad humility was a presumption that made him see Pope's translation of Homer as inferior to one he might himself write, and he wasted a good deal of time on this futile attempt. Finally, Cowper's contribution to English letters was peripheral: his humble balance in Newton's *Olney Hymns;* his influence on Wordsworth, who, as King points out, acknowledged *The Task* as "the first significant autobiographical poem in the English language"; and as the author of "The Castaway," a short lyric of "Perfect Despair," in which the poet compares his own sense of spiritual abandonment with that of a drowning sailor whose boat cannot retrieve him— a poem that invokes an embarrassed sympathy for its creator and provides a vehicle of self-indulgence for anyone who's ever felt alienated, spiritually or otherwise.

Religion seems to have played a weighty part in another literary relationship, that of Hilaire Belloc and G. K. Chesterton, the subject of *G. K. Chesterton: A Life,* by Michael Ffinch (Weidenfeld and Nicolson). Without question, Chesterton was a bit of an oddball from the beginning, particularly in his infamous aversion to cleanliness. He had a penchant for the evil side of the imagination, to which the only sensible antidote was an intense religion.

Dust jacket for the biography that presents new material on Wells's public career and on his intellectual and creative achievements

His best friends at school, Edmund Bentley and Lucian Oldershaw, went on to Oxford, leaving Chesterton behind as one who, as his biographer notes, "believed in prolonging childhood." Slow to mature physically, slow in learning to read, Chesterton was often considered a personage of paradoxes in that he consistently won prizes for his literary efforts, though left school without a degree. In and out of a variety of political intensities, Chesterton was first in the same room with Belloc at a pro-Boer meeting at the Bedford Park Studio of Archie MacGregor, the artist. Both men spoke at the debate, but it was Chesterton who was dazzled by Belloc's eloquence.

Also held at this studio were mock trials in which Bernard Shaw often played important parts. Although Belloc did not participate in the trial proceedings, he and Chesterton were to meet at a later time in a restaurant, and Belloc was then to compliment Chesterton on his writing. Neither at this time had any idea that they were soon to form what

Bernard Shaw would later call "a formidable monster, Chesterbelloc." Although the "formidable monster" is hard to define, since both men were complex personages, it was vehemently pro-Catholic, and just as vehemently anti-Calvinist.

As might be expected, "Chesterbelloc," with a religious stance that denied the gloom of Calvinism, relied a great deal on humor. Chesterton, in particular, took pleasure in a literary iconoclasm. At one point, as documented by the Ffinch biography, he "dressed as Old King Cole, had run a tobacco stall," for charity, "and sold parodies on the nursery rhyme in the style of five different poets, including Yeats." H. G. Wells commented once that Chesterton "should be restricted to using [the word 'jolly'] only forty times a day."

Shaw felt Belloc to be a damaging influence on Chesterton and portrayed "Chesterbelloc" as a "four-legged pantomine elephant" which, according to Ffinch's summary, was made up of two parts that were ill-matched, and because Belloc was the forelegs Chesterton was obliged to follow. Shaw felt Chesterton should write a play, and in order to see this happen, Shaw desired "to dismantle the monster and free Chesterton from the domination of 'Hilaire Forelegs.'" Shaw's main complaint, it seems, was Belloc's influence on Chesterton in intertwining art with religion and politics. Chesterton, says Ffinch, "had learnt from Belloc what Belloc in his youth had learnt from Cardinal Manning: that all human conflicts ultimately have a theological basis."

As is most often the case, polemics tend to sully art, and of Chesterton's major works, it is the message rather than the media that lingers. Belloc's own commitment to polemics was revealed when the works of Chesterton's he most often referred to were those essays that appeared in Catholic newspapers, a segment of which was quoted by Belloc: "It is enough to say that those who know the Catholic practice find it not only right when everything else is wrong; making the Confessional the very throne of candour where the world outside talks nonsense about it as a sort of conspiracy; upholding humility when everybody is praising pride; charged with sentimental charity when the world is loud and loose with vulgar sentimentalism—as it is today. At the place where the roads meet there is no doubt of the convergence. A man may think of all sorts of things, most of them honest and many of them true, about the right way to turn in the maze at Hampton Court. But he does not think he is in the centre; he knows." And so on. When Bernard Shaw tried to pull Chesterton away from Belloc with "Write a play!," the advice was undoubtedly sound; yet it was advice that Chesterton failed to take seriously.

It is not surprising, then, that the Chesterton/Belloc friendship remained constant and relatively unruffled until Chesterton's death in 1936. Despite their different backgrounds, what was prevalent in the relationship was a persistence in sustaining an affinity of goal and purpose, a lack of "measuring the distances between them." Shaw saw the liability, of course, and his insight is reflected in his caricature of the two as a single monster, with Chesterton unwittingly cast as the "hindlegs," always following and following in directions that prevented the cultivation of genius.

Though Chesterton's career was most influenced by Belloc, the literary nucleus of the era was Henry James, and his influence is seen in one way or another on the biographies of all those writers who got anywhere near him when he lived. Although Leon Edel's definitive biography of James, appearing in five volumes between 1953 and 1972, documents these influences in more depth, a splendid abridgment of that biography, *Henry James: A Life* (Harper and Row), connects so well the lives and contributions of those lesser talents that its mention here is inevitable. Although a critic or two may have found Edel's rendition of James's life "too Freudian," James's life did, after all, cry out for such a reading. For the purpose of evaluating the friendships in biographies coming out this year, Edel's work has been an invaluable resource.

G. K. Chesterton and Henry James were neighbors, but not friends. As recorded in Ffinch's biography of Chesterton, there was one situation which summarized, from Chesterton's point of view, their relationship: it was not that they could not, or neglected to, "measure the distances between them"; it was simply that the distances were too vast. On one occasion, after Chesterton had moved next door to James, the latter made a courtesy call on his new neighbor. James "complimented Chesterton on his writing but expressed surprise that he managed to write so much. Chesterton suspected him of meaning 'why rather than how.'"

During the conversation, a sound like that of "an impatient fog horn" (Chesterton's description) emanated from a distance and turned out to be Hilaire Belloc, having returned from France penniless and unshaven and hollering for "bacon and beer." Chesterton's analysis of the scene is revealing: "Henry James had a name for being subtle; but I think that situation was too subtle for him. I

doubt to this day whether he, of all men, did not miss the irony of the best comedy in which he ever played a part. He left America because he loved Europe, and all that was meant by England and France; the gentry, the gallantry, the traditions of lineage and locality, the life that had been lived beneath the old portraits in oak-panelled rooms. And there, on the other side of the tea-table was Europe, was the old thing that made France and England, the posterity of the English squires and the French soldiers; ragged, unshaven, shouting for beer, shameless above all shades of poverty and wealth; sprawling, indifferent, secure. And what looked across at it was still the Puritan refinement of Boston; and the space it looked across was wider than the Atlantic."

Reading between the lines reveals Chesterton's defensiveness about his own and Belloc's position, as well as a certain ignorance about how rather than why James had achieved his reputation for subtlety. Studying the smudging of European lineage was, after all, one of James's specialties. One only has to look at the character of Maggie Verver's Prince in *The Golden Bowl* (1904) to imagine that, to James, Belloc probably appeared as a transported Prince contaminated by American taste. As is shown in the Edel biography (whose index has only one entry for Chesterton and none for Belloc), James's view of his neighbor was more dismissive than defensive. Miss Theodora Bosanquet, James's secretary, recorded on 27 July 1908 that in "the course of the morning Mr. James made me go and peep through the curtain to see 'the unspeakable Chesterton' pass by—a sort of elephant with a crimson face and oily curls." "James," continued Edel, "thought it 'very tragic that his mind should be imprisoned in such a body.'"

Another biography out this year which touches on this same literary era and circle is *H. G. Wells: Desperately Mortal* (Yale University Press), by David C. Smith. Although the relationship between Wells and Chesterton was not particularly intense or long lasting, one common link they shared at the beginning was the Fabian Society and a commitment to socialism. Although their goals may have been similar, their resolutions were decidedly different, given their polar proclivities. Whereas Chesterton saw religion as the cosmic linchpin, Wells's training in science and evolutionary theory made a meeting of the minds between these two men not at all easy. But both were in alliance against the presence of Bernard Shaw, who, as one of the "Old Gang," was seen by new recruits such as Wells

ARNOLD RAMPERSAD
THE LIFE OF
LANGSTON HUGHES
VOLUME I: 1902-1941
I, TOO, SING AMERICA

Dust jacket for volume one of the first biography of Hughes to be based largely on the Langston Hughes Papers at Yale University's Beinecke Library. The papers were previously unavailable to most scholars.

as being too conservative and by Chesterton as being too profane.

When Shaw argued for cremation, for example, Chesterton countered with "the flesh is a sacred thing." And Shaw appears to have intensely disliked Wells, calling him a "leary, rash egotist." Eventually Wells dropped out of the Society, but Shaw and Sidney Webb, who, as Smith documents, "felt that they could continue to tap Wells's mind, and at the same time keep him under control," sent him a revised "Fabian Basis," which Wells returned completely rewritten. Shaw responded with a letter in which he referred to Wells's "father's career as a professional cricketer in derogatory terms"; then Wells replied by calling Shaw and Sidney Webb "the most intolerable egotists, narrow, suspicious, obstructive, I have ever met," and wrote a letter to Shaw in which he referred to him as "an unmitigated imbecilic Victorian ass."

As is pointed out in the Smith biography, "Shaw and HGW remained childlike especially to each other in their adult years." And although Chesterton and Wells did occasionally team up—most famously in a parodic enactment of the Minority Report on the Poor Law Commission during the summer of 1911—their radically different views precluded any sustained intimacy. Chesterton had indicted Wells in his work *The Heretics* (1905), and Wells's own feelings toward Chesterton remained ambivalent: "I love GKC," wrote Wells, "and I hate the Catholicism of Belloc and Rome."

All in all, the Wells biography is among the most fascinating of the year because the subject of it took so many literary risks, and those risks held important political implications. His work *The Food of the Gods* (1904), though coming after his more famous *The Time Machine* (1895) and *The War of the Worlds* (1898), illustrates how some bungling scientists allow their creation of a miracle food to get out of their control, creating a race of giant children, who are then counteracted by a Tory politician taking the role of Jack the Giant-killer and offering the giant children a reservation in some faraway place such as North America or Africa. But a spokesperson for the giant children, realizing that the "giants and pygmies" cannot coexist in their present forms, sees the giant children and their miraculous food dying out, leaving the pygmies to "attain a sort of pygmy millennium, make an end to war, make an end to over-population, sit down in a world-wide city to practice pygmy arts, worshipping one another till the world begins to freeze. . . ." So the giants decide to make the food (which, as Smith points out, seems a somewhat obvious symbol for socialism) available to everyone, and eventually "it will transform the world of pygmies into a world of giants, the home of the blessed."

G. K. Chesterton was one of the few who violently opposed the tenets held in this book, because, as Wells's biographer shows, Chesterton "realized the threat the Wells vision posed for Edwardian life." He understood clearly that the story of Jack the Giant-killer lay at "the foundation of human mythology—that if the small and insignificant could not have the hope of occasional triumph, then they could not be suppressed. Their anger would lash out, and the inevitable class war would come." Referring back to the criteria for friendship delineated by Emerson and Thoreau, one can see in the biographies of more modern writers that such relationships, those furthering the greatest literary achievements, do not seem to prevail. If truth was one of Emerson's criteria for such friendships, how can there be an alliance in a time when no truth was sure? Nothing illustrates this better than the relationships among Chesterton, Shaw, Wells, and Henry James. Even though one or the other might have liked one or the other, as most of their "truths" were different, and defensibly different, since there was no longer a definable chorus to ally against, intimate alliance leading to the fostering of genius was impossible, and what resulted was cacophony.

H. G. Wells's relationships with Shaw and, later, Joseph Conrad, fizzled out in a sea of different "truths"; and, not surprisingly, Henry James pretty much went on his own, having largely among his coterie "prodigies and disciples," as Edel points out. A good example was the painter John Singer Sargent. Edel comments that, "The two had so much in common that they must have seemed to each other, in certain respects, mirror images." No necessary "complement" here, and, no "truth even when it hurts," no "measuring of distances."

Although James had more respect for Wells than for Chesterton, Wells was presumptuous (and, perhaps, envious) enough to write a parody of James's style, that last resort for most of James's critics. Feeling guilty about it later, he apologized, then tried to measure their differences. "To you," wrote Wells, "literature like painting is an end, to me literature like architecture is a means, it has a use." He then went on to say that his parody of James's style was "just a wastepaper basket." In his response, notes Edel, "James . . . began by saying that he didn't think Wells had made out any sort of case for his bad manners: one simply didn't publish the content of waste-baskets. He went on: 'I live intensely and am fed by life, and my value whatever it be, is in my own kind of expression of that. Art *makes* life, makes interest, makes importance,' adding that he knew of no substitute whatever for 'the force and beauty of its process.' "

Both Chesterton and Wells possessed the limitation that James with his true genius was able to avoid—the substitution of polemics for art. In a world no longer providing any sort of truth, the artist can no longer presume to dictate answers, as both Chesterton and Wells, each from his own throne, tried to do. What makes James the captain of the turn-of-the-century ship was his essential humility (ironic in light of his personality), a humility that asked all the new questions and reconsidered the old ones, and gave his readers the impetus and strength to do the same, by avoiding the fatalism of Calvinism, the panacea of Catholicism, or the resignation of Darwinism as answers in an age when no answer can be demonstrated as true.

Another important 1986 biography is the first volume of Arnold Rampersad's *The Life of Langston Hughes: I, Too, Sing America* (Oxford). Langston Hughes, as the major black writer of his generation and as a leading figure in the Harlem Renaissance of the 1920s, is portrayed vigorously and warmly. Hughes recognized early his "need to find new ways, based on a steadfast loyalty to the forms of black culture, to express black consciousness—and, in so doing, to assist at its passage into the hostile modern world." As is the case with most young writers, Hughes was often lonely and saw himself as an alien. Rampersad documents an incident when Hughes overheard some boys playing in a nearby yard as he was reading: "Boys playing ball in the dusk, running and shouting across the vacant lot on the corner. For the first time the loneliness strikes me, strikes me terribly, settling down in a dull ache round about, in the dusk of the twilight, in the laughter of the playing boys. . . . I am lonely."

As an emerging black writer, at a time when blacks were having trouble surviving, let alone emerging as poets, Hughes did not have the early benefit of a circle of literary benefactors. So he attended countless poetry readings, attempted to make the acquaintance of the poets, and was frequently unsuccessful. At one point, however, knowing that Vachel Lindsay was to read, he caught that poet alone in a hotel dining room, mumbled a few words of appreciation, then dropped a few of his own poems on the table. "That evening," notes Rampersad, "Lindsay startled his large audience by announcing that he had discovered a poet, a bona fide poet, a *Negro* poet no less, working as a busboy in their very midst." But such nods were rare and hard won.

One of Hughes's patrons, Mrs. Charlotte Mason, had a great deal of money and fantasies of African art museums. Rampersad says, in Hughes she saw "a noble young savage." Although Mrs. Mason funded a number of young black talents, Hughes was the one who was genuinely loyal, and it was Hughes who bore the brunt of her anger when the others were manipulative or even fraudulent. His letters begging her forgiveness (for what, is not clear) are embarrassingly pathetic because they are so obviously sincere and just as obviously unwarranted. With much stylistic grace, Rampersad traces this relationship and others and documents in lively detail the lengthy, hard-fought, and ultimately triumphant career of a fine poet and novelist, one whose involvement as a citizen and an artist broke important ground. One looks forward to volume two.

Another ground breaker was Lillian Hellman, the subject of William Wright's *Lillian Hellman: The Image, The Woman* (Simon and Schuster). This woman's life and her biographer's rendition of that life are a feminist's dream. Apparently unabashed by anything at all, a drinker and a pursuer of young men (with some of whom she is known, when quite old, to have had a hilarious marijuana evening), Hellman's participation in life has caused almost as much attention to her as her two most famous plays, *The Children's Hour* (1934) and *The Little Foxes* (1939). The list of her involvements and achievements seems endless, and through reading this biography one gets the sense that here was a woman born with considerably more than the usual component of energy. Most notorious was her thirty-year-long relationship with Dashiell Hammett, the author of *The Maltese Falcon* (1930), who went to jail during the McCarthy scourge, prompting Hellman to write an antiwitchhunt editorial for the Screen Writer's Guild magazine during the time when the political right was seeing red under every Hollywood palm. This biography radiates the strength and character of its subject—a book to be read at a single shot.

Some other items worth mentioning: Gordon Haight's splendid account of the life of George Eliot is out in paperback this year from the Penguin Literary Biographies series; at last professors can guiltlessly make this definitive work required reading. Also, William Griffin has given us a wonderfully entertaining dramatic biography of C. S. Lewis (Harper and Row). And, as additions to the series category this year are several new titles. In the Key Women Writers series (Indiana University; editor, Sue Roe), Angela Leighton's *Elizabeth Barrett Browning*, Kate Fulbrook's *Katherine Mansfield*, Rachel Blau Duplessis's *H. D.: The Career of That Struggle*, and Gillian Beer's *George Eliot* were published in 1986; appearing in the Literature and Life: American Writers series (Ungar) are J. D. Brown's *Henry Miller* and Barbara Ewell's *Kate Chopin;* and in the Lives of Modern Women series (Penguin; editor, Emma Tennant) are Carole Angier's *Jean Rhys*, Fay Weldon's *Rebecca West*, and Allan Massie's *Colette*.

This last volume is a persuasively feminist biography, persuasive because of a reasonable tone that gives the reader credit for some intelligent perception, a credit not granted by some of the more strident champions of feminism. Finally, the most compelling biography of 1986 is a real hybrid, yet another work on Colette. Though in no way definitive and, in fact, largely photographic, Genevieve Dormann's *Colette: A Passion for Life* (Abbeville Press) not only provides intriguing photographs and drawings, but is also a good read.

The Year in Book Publishing

John Tebbel

As 1986 came to an end, the book publishing industry could look back on a year noteworthy for the enormous prices paid for houses bought and sold and for blockbuster manuscripts as well. Though general economic forecasts were favorable for the year ahead, the trend toward mergers and acquisitions begun in the 1950s reached a new high point, with changes that further altered the face of American publishing and which continued to erode its traditional character.

Lee Iacocca's 1984 autobiography, *Iacocca* (Bantam), was a 1986 phenomenon too, reaching a new astronomical figure of 8,000,000 copies sold in the publisher's softcover edition. Among the new candidates for best-sellerdom, James Clavell's *Whirlwind* was acquired by William Morrow for a record $5 million, after an auction for publishing rights. A modern record for hardcover nonfiction was set by *Fit for Life* (Warner), Harvey and Marilyn Diamond's health book, which reached the 1.8 million sales figure in April, nine months after publication. Summer, ordinarily the slowest publishing season, produced two new best-sellers, Bill Cosby's *Fatherhood* (Dolphin/Doubleday) and Sue Miller's novel, *The Good Mother* (Harper and Row).

If there was a literary event of the year, it was the publication by Random House of the first American trade edition of James Joyce's *Ulysses* in its corrected version. In serious nonfiction, there was a plethora of books by distinguished historians, anticipating the bicentennial celebration of the Constitution in 1987. For many writers, the outstanding event of the year was the convention in New York of PEN, the international writers' organization, which produced a major controversy when its president, Norman Mailer, invited Secretary of State George Schultz to give the keynote address, angering many who opposed the Reagan administration's foreign policy. These opponents urged that the invitation be withdrawn, but Mailer argued successfully that a writers' convention, of all places, should be open to opposing points of view.

Publishers were more interested in the economics of the industry. Statistics were, as always, confusing and sometimes contradictory; but on the whole they were encouraging, especially in a business under such continuing pressure from social and technological change. One reason for a brighter outlook, especially at the retail end of the business, was the increased expansion of outlets selling books into such subsidiary areas as video and audio cassettes, as well as magazines and the software for computers. Volume in all these categories continued to grow, and such sidelines were increasingly involving publishers.

Sources in and out of the industry were generally bullish about economic prospects, beginning in January when analysts predicted a four-year rise in trade book sales, always the weakest part of the business. It was forecast that sales in this category would rise by 26.4% between 1984 and 1988, to reach a level of $5.8 billion, a new record if attained. Publicly held companies, which now include most of the major houses, were showing considerable strength in the marketplace. Nine major houses reported that they had experienced growth in the value of their stocks during the first three months of 1986, a trend that continued through the year.

If there was a cloud on the economic horizon, it was the falling off, by 3.7%, of consumer spending for books in the second quarter of the year, following a similar decline in the first quarter. The drop was expected to continue through the year, although analysts believed that spending would maintain a flat level in 1987, followed by a 4.4% rise in 1988. With consumer spending at an annual rate of $7.94 billion for books only, however, there was reason for optimism, particularly when analysts estimated that over the next five years it would increase 91% in dollars and 48% in units.

Most encouraging were the year-end figures estimating total sales at $11.2 billion, a 3.5% increase over the preceding year. Growth was strongest in elementary school textbooks and workbooks. A rise in the unit sales of trade books was attributed to an increase in the number of retail stores. Children's book sales were reported as rising at an annualized rate of 10% over the past five years, even though prices in this category have increased at twice the rate of adult trade books.

Only one segment of the industry produced disappointing figures. Romance novels had been the fastest growing category among paperbacks for several years, creating an industry within an industry which had its own convention, its own league of writers, and even its own magazine. Annual sales in 1985 were nearly $300 million, comprising about 40% of total paperback sales. In 1986, however, a definite decline had begun, with sales barely maintaining their current level in the big retail chains, where they had represented a large part of the business. Apparently, so the analysts said, it was a case of the formula having been worked over once (perhaps twice) too often.

The largest publishing house, Simon and Schuster, got out of the adult romance category altogether, selling its Silhouette line to Torstar, a Toronto-based company, for $10 million, adding to the Canadian firm's Harlequin line, and making the combination the leader in this field. But even if the romance novel was "soft" and getting softer, there were still millions of devotees, and several writers were earning large incomes to supply them.

The industry lost four of its best-known figures during the year. In May came the death of Cass Canfield, who had been head of Harper and Row for nearly forty years until his retirement. A courtly yet outspoken man, with social connections reaching into the White House, he had been responsible for acquiring many of Harper's most successful books on the contemporary scene and was regarded as one of the most notable figures in publishing during the past half-century. In the same month, Peter Heggie, executive secretary of the Authors Guild, a man unknown to the public but widely respected by thousands of writers and publishers, also died. Heggie was a quiet, diffident man who did much for the Guild in his long years of service.

Still another of publishing's elder statesmen, Donald Klopfer, died in May at the age of eighty-four. With Bennett Cerf, he had founded Random House and remained as its head for decades. To Cerf, he was "the saner of us"; to others, he was the last of the great gentleman publishers. Finally, in August, Lyle Kenyon Engle died in semiretirement, having operated for years one of the most prolific mass-market packaging operations in the industry. Through Book Creations, located on his own country estate near Canaan, New York, Engle launched the career of John Jakes, among others.

Looking ahead at the end of 1986, publishers are anticipating future trends as the result of new technologies. The industry, however, remains apprehensive about the results of the tax reform bill passed by Congress, particularly the prospect of drastic reductions in educational spending by the states, added to the already decreased federal funds available for school and library programs.

Apart from these general developments, publishing in 1986 was characterized by further moves toward consolidation through acquisition and by a further advance toward a global ownership of American houses. The major event of the year, one that shocked traditionalists, was the acquisition by Bertelsmann, the German publishing conglomerate, of Doubleday, the last of the privately held major houses. Always a closely held family operation since its founding, the house had lost some of its best editors and authors in recent years. In acquiring Doubleday for a total figure of $500 million (excluding the New York Mets baseball team, owned in partnership by Nelson Doubleday, Jr.), Bertelsmann became the second-largest publisher in the United States. Combining Doubleday with its previous softcover acquisition, Bantam Books, the German firm would have a total of more than $600 million in annual sales, compared with the $920 million recorded by Simon and Schuster, still the leader. However, in trade publishing, Bertelsmann emerged as the world's leader, with $450 million in sales drawn from thirty publishing houses worldwide. Much of Simon and Schuster's total comes from textbooks and from business and professional books, the result of its recent acquisition of Prentice-Hall. By acquiring Dell's $60 million in annual sales as part of the Doubleday deal and adding it to Bantam's more than $200 million, Bertelsmann also became the largest mass paperback owner.

Another notable acquisition of the year, and a further intrusion of foreign capital into American publishing, was the purchase by British Penguin, itself a subsidiary of the British conglomerate, Pearson PLC, of New American Library and its recently acquired E. P. Dutton and Company, a house dating back to 1852. The sale price was not disclosed. While the principal result of this purchase was to strengthen Penguin's extensive softcover lines, the acquiring of Dutton's children's books would give Penguin and its American subsidiary, Viking Press, perhaps the strongest line of such books in American publishing. Besides Dutton, they will include Viking Kestrel editions, Penguin Puffins, and the children's books of Dial, a house recently acquired by NAL.

These British and German moves into the United States market, consistent with the current general trend in American industry, were added to other acquisitions over the past two years which have not only considerably altered the publishing scene in this country but have begun to transform world publishing. This became clear when the trade journal *BP Report* estimated that of the $9.8 billion total sales figure for the American industry in 1986, about 15% (from $1.4 to $1.5 billion) came from foreign owned companies. Two-thirds of these companies are controlled by just three organizations: Bertelsmann, International Thomson (the Canadian-based worldwide conglomerate), and British Penguin.

Moreover, it appeared that a new figure would shortly emerge on the scene. In December, Robert Maxwell, the British printing and publishing entrepreneur, announced that he intended to acquire American publishing and printing companies, for which he was prepared to spend from $2 to $3 billion. Maxwell compared the information industry of today with the oil industry of the past.

A few giant corporations had controlled oil, he recalled, and predicted that "communications is likely to be dominated by ten or a dozen major international corporations. . . ." Maxwell is the publisher of Pergamon Press and chairman of the British Printing and Communication Corporation, as well as the London *Mirror* newspaper group. Maxwell purchased two American printing companies within the past year.

With the British, Dutch, French, Germans, and Italians already in the American market, others may be expected to follow. Generally speaking, this foreign capital is more likely to be invested in small, specialized companies rather than primarily trade houses. What industry observers fear is that foreign buyers may eliminate the trade divisions of larger houses they buy if they are losing money, as most of them are.

American conglomerates were also busy in 1986, adding to their holdings. Time Incorporated seemed ready to challenge Bertelsmann for second place by purchasing the venerable Chicago textbook house Scott, Foresman from SFN Companies for $520 million in cash. Since its founding in 1896 Scott, Foresman had been one of the dominant

Bennett Cerf and Donald Klopfer, 1925

firms in educational publishing, but in the post-World-War-II expansion, it had created SFN Companies as an umbrella for diversification into non-book operations. However, it continued to deal in publishing houses as well and over the past several years had bought and sold such old-line firms as William Morrow, Fleming H. Revell, Silver Burdett, and University Park Press. The decision to sell Scott, Foresman was part of SFN's move to liquidate itself by the close of 1986. To that end, SFN also sold its Southwestern Publishing Company for $270 million in cash to the International Thomson Organization, presently the largest publisher of print media in the United States and the world. Time Incorporated, building from its original base, Time-Life Books, had since acquired Little, Brown, the Book-of-the-Month Club, and Oxmoor House. Adding Scott, Foresman meant a total of $620 million in annual sales.

Current turmoil at CBS Incorporated's broadcasting division was reflected in its book and magazine operations. CBS and Greenwood, the Westport, Connecticut, publisher, acquired Praeger Publishers for an estimated $3 million. Praeger, a publisher of serious nonfiction, had been in an uncertain state since its founder, Frederick Praeger, left the house. The CBS purchase occurred in January, but in November that firm began to divest itself of some of its publishing interests, selling its entire Educational and Professional Publishing Division to Harcourt Brace Jovanovich for $500 million. Since HBJ had already acquired Holt, Rinehart and Winston's textbook division, it was now the largest publisher of elementary-high school textbooks.

There were other changes in the educational field. John Wiley, the oldest American publisher still operating under its original name, sold 300 active college texts in sociology, political science, education, and home economics to Macmillan, adding to that firm's already strong position in that area. Silver Burdett, bought and sold several times in recent years, had still another owner when Gulf and Western, owner of Simon and Schuster, acquired it.

There were several acquisitions in 1986 that could be considered unusual. The managers of Dodd, Mead formed a partnership and acquired the company, another of the old-line houses, from Thomas Nelson and Sons, making it the first major house to be owned by its employees. Still another international figure in the communications field, Rupert Murdoch, the Australian entrepreneur who owns newspaper, broadcasting, and magazine properties in England and America as well as Australia and elsewhere, entered United States book publishing by acquiring Salem House and Merrimack Publishers' Circle, using his Australian publishing subsidiary, Angus and Robertson, to make the deal.

Malcolm Forbes, publisher of the business magazine *Forbes*, bought the American Heritage Publishing Company for a figure estimated at $8 to $10 million. The deal included not only the company's book division, but its magazine, *American Heritage*, which the new owner redesigned and began to promote vigorously. Mortimer Zuckerman, the Boston businessman who bought the Atlantic Monthly Company and became its chairman, and who also owns *U.S. News & World Report*, sold the Atlantic Monthly Press to Carl Navarre, a Tennessee businessman. Paul Feffer, one of the oldest names in book distribution, took over sole ownership of his company, Feffer and Simon, in May after buying Doubleday's interest in the firm, but then in October he sold it to Baker and Taylor, a pioneer book distributor.

Rumblings of change in the bookstore chain business, with rumors of falling sales due in part to intense competition, culminated in November with the announcement that Barnes and Noble, the New York-based firm, had bought the B. Dalton Bookseller national chain of retail shops, itself a subsidiary of the Dayton Hudson Corporation, for a figure estimated by industry analysts at between $250 and $300 million. Again, foreign capital was involved. Vendex International, a Dutch corporation, had recently become a part owner of Barnes and Noble, controlling about 30% of its stock. Vendex, a retail giant in the Netherlands controlling 10% of the retail market in that country, also owns department and other retail stores in this country, Brazil, and Japan. Its American subsidiary, Vendamerica B.V., based in Greenwich, Connecticut, is the operating monitor of the Dutch conglomerate's interests in America and other non-European countries.

Until the merger, Barnes and Noble operated thirty-seven trade bookstores, all selling at discount prices, with 1985 sales of about $225 million, while the much larger 798-outlet Dalton chain reported $538 million in revenues the same year. Together, the two will now be the largest American bookstore chain, surpassing the former leader, Waldenbooks, which had $565 million in 1985 sales. Besides its trade bookstores, Barnes and Noble also has 142 college bookstores, which it leases, and owns Supermart Books, servicing 153 book departments in

Tribute from Robert Penn Warren

drugstores and supermarkets, besides Marboro, a wholesale remainder and mail-order division, and the Missouri Book Company, which deals in used college textbooks.

All told, the new Barnes and Noble/B. Dalton operation will have 973 bookstore outlets, as opposed to Waldenbooks' 1,000, but the other operations described above make it a considerably larger enterprise. B. Dalton has also been expanding its leasing business in the college field and in the Dayton Hudson department stores. Waldenbooks' expansion has been most recently in the direction of servicing book departments in K Mart stores, its parent corporation since 1984, when it was sold by the Carter Hawley Hale corporation.

Waldenbooks remains the industry's largest chain operation, substantially so when K Mart's 2,100 stores are added to its own 1,000 outlets. The company estimates that in five years its sales will be more than $2 billion annually. It operates several book clubs and recently has begun to publish books of its own, which some publishers see as a dangerous trend.

From the standpoint of authors, the Macmillan Company's announcement near the year's end that it would reduce its overall adult hardcover out-

put by about 35% was a matter for concern. Macmillan had only recently purchased Scribners and Atheneum, two of the most distinguished publishers of hardcover trade books, but its announcement said simply that it "really doesn't want to be a major trade publisher," as the firm had been since its founding.

This announcement was followed by a similar declaration from Arbor House, the Hearst Corporation's hardcover imprint, that it would cut its annual trade book output by 50%, from ninety to forty-five titles, spread over three years, presumably to allow for publication of books under contract. Macmillan could count on its substantial backlist to produce future hardcover revenue, but Arbor House, an imprint established originally by Donald Fine, had several recent best-sellers but no backlist of consequence.

A more imminent industry danger is censorship, and in 1986 a survey made by People for the American Way, a public interest group, showed that incidents of censorship had risen 35% over the previous year and 117% over the past four years. Most of these cases were attempts to censor library books and those used in school curricula, and nearly half resulted from efforts by four major con-

Alfred A. Knopf, 1940

servative and evangelical organizations. But there were some censorship attempts by liberals as well, including the NAACP and feminist groups. Publishers could record two victories against censorship forces: the U.S. Supreme Court's ruling as unconstitutional an Indianapolis antipornography law, initiated by feminists, forbidding publication of material depicting the "sexually explicit subordination of women"; and rejection by Maine voters of an antiobscenity law promoted by religious groups, placed on the November ballot by referendum.

In December, Volunteer Lawyers for the Arts, a nonprofit organization of more than 800 lawyers who give free legal assistance to artists and arts organizations, filed a friend-of-the-court brief with the Supreme Court in the *Pope v. Illinois* case, which some consider the most important obscenity issue of the past few years. It involves the case of a Rockford, Illinois, adult bookstore clerk who was found guilty in a jury trial of selling three obscene magazines to a local detective. The case is important because it will test that part of the Court's obscenity ruling in *Miller v. California* which cites "contemporary community standards" as the basis

for finding a work obscene rather than determining on an objective basis whether a work has significant literary, artistic, political, or scientific value. Irwin Karp, then counsel for the Authors Guild, who filed the *amicus* brief, asserted that previous court decisions indicated that the objective basis be applied; the Illinois Appellate Court had used the contemporary community standards test. If that were upheld, Karp said, "creative works of significant value" would be deprived of their First Amendment protection, even though they might be unpopular in the view of a community majority.

The *Pope v. Illinois* case, legal experts said, might be even more important than the results of the report by the President's Commission on Pornography, better known as the Meese Commission report because of Attorney General Edwin Meese's active role in the commission. With California adopting tougher antiobscenity laws in April last year, publishers waited with some apprehension for the Meese report, anticipating that it would go far beyond limitations set by previous Supreme Court decisions. When the commission, in advance of its report, wrote letters to chain stores selling magazines and books warning them that they were risking prosecution for selling such magazines as *Playboy*, industry and civil rights organizations took legal action. *Playboy* sued and so did the American Civil Liberties Union, charging violation of the Freedom of Information Act because of the commission's refusal to allow access to its papers, an action won by the ACLU, which was given complete access.

When the commission released its report, with two dissensions, it contained ninety-two recommendations for action against pornography, including not only proposed legislation but urging that citizens act as individuals in reporting the sale and seeking the removal of materials they considered obscene. The report sought to establish a linkage between pornography and crimes of violence, completely reversing the verdict of the similar Nixon Commission in 1974, which found the opposite.

In November, Meese made it known that he would adopt many of the commission's recommendations and began to set in motion the machinery to bring that about. The attorney general said the Justice Department would seek legislation from congress requiring "producers, retailers, and distributors of sexually explicit visual depictions to maintain records of consent and proof of age by performers and to prohibit the use of performers under age 21." He also announced that a center for obscenity prosecution would be created and that a task force of Justice Department lawyers would be established to work with it.

Meese stopped short of adopting the commission's recommendation that obscenity law violators be given mandatory prison sentences, but he did indicate that he would try to have enacted the

kind of "forfeiture legislation" recommended by the commission which would enable prosecuting agencies to seize the assets of a publishing company accused of violating an obscenity law. The center for obscenity prosecutions would also be asked to "draft model anti-obscenity statutes for use by state and local legislative bodies," an action intended to broaden existing laws to make them more inclusive.

With the American Library Association reporting a steady rise in censorship incidents during the year, publishers appeared ready to join civil rights organizations and others to fight censorship in whatever venues were possible.

Thus the year ended on a distinctly sour note in other aspects than the economic. It was widely believed that consolidations, new ownerships by foreign firms, cutbacks by houses like Macmillan and Arbor House, and bottom-line closeouts of every operation that failed to produce satisfactory returns would shrink publishing in significant ways. Once one of the most stable industries where employment was concerned, publishing was becoming as much of a swinging-door operation as advertising—consistent with mass firings and layoffs in other industries. Hardcover lists reduced to glitzy best-selling novels, the memoirs of celebrities, and other virtually guaranteed best-sellers, with mass-market paperbacks devoted mostly to reprints of these works, would mean that traditional trade publishing might eventually be reduced to insignificant proportions, with the burden possibly taken up by the burgeoning small-press industry. These were the gloomy thoughts of all but the entrepreneurs, foreign and domestic, and the authors of best-sellers as the publishing year ended.

OBITUARIES

Simone de Beauvoir
(9 January 1908-14 April 1986)

Liliane Lazar

Simone de Beauvoir, writer, existential philosopher, memorialist and life companion of Jean-Paul Sartre, fought all her life against injustice and prejudice and for the equality and rights of women. Her work *Le Deuxième Sexe* (1944; translated as *The Second Sex*, 1953) is regarded as the first and most important feminist text of the twentieth century. Beauvoir's life as an independent woman of letters and intellectual has been an inspiration to many. Beauvoir acknowledged that writing had given her more pleasure than any other event or activity, although her life was far from uneventful or restricted. As Jean-Paul Sartre's companion she participated actively, after World War II, in many political and social causes.

Beauvoir is best known for her involvement in the women's movement, but indeed this is the latest manifestation of a long-standing commitment to existentialism. As a member of the intelligentsia of the French Left she criticized the bourgeois society, but her commitment was more ethical and social than political. "Her life and work were a seamless web," said feminist writer Gloria Steinem; "many good works are undone by hypocrisy, but she lived her life according to her beliefs."

Simone de Beauvoir was born on 9 January 1908. She was the first child of an upper-middle-class family. Her father, Georges Bertrand de Beauvoir, was a lawyer at the Court of Appeals in Paris, but his real passion in life was the theater and literature. Her mother, Françoise Brasseur de Beauvoir, a devout Catholic, came from a rich provincial family, and she attempted to pass on her religious principles to Simone and Hélène (nicknamed Poupette), her younger sister born two years after Simone. Beauvoir's childhood was secure and happy. In *Mémoires d'une jeune fille rangée* (1958; translated as *Memoirs of a Dutiful Daughter*, 1959), she confessed that she had violent temper tantrums, but otherwise she felt surrounded by the love of her family and God and accepted, without question, the beliefs and values of her family. When she was six years old, she started to attend a private

girls' school, Cours Desir. There, she met Zaza (Elizabeth Mabille), with whom she had an intense and profound adolescent friendship. She spent her summer vacations at her grandfather's house in the Limousin.

Although her parents censored her reading, she immersed herself in those books that she was allowed to read. At the age of eight, she decided she wanted to become a writer. She soon had the idea of writing stories and reading them to her family. By the age of fourteen she discovered she

Dust jacket for the first American edition of Simone de Beauvoir's 1958 memoir

no longer believed in God. The immortality in which she had believed (at a very early age she had wanted to enter a convent) was replaced by her tenacity in her own plan, an awareness that would permit her to affirm that she was her own cause and her own end. At the same time, she was now obliged to face the consequences of God's absence: anguish, solitude, and the inevitability of death. During her otherwise secure adolescence Beauvoir did suffer a traumatic emotional blow: the death of Elizabeth Mabille (Zaza). Elizabeth was forced by her mother to give up a man she deeply loved. She developed meningitis and died soon after. In *Memoires d'une jeune fille rangée*, Beauvoir writes that she had somehow paid for her newfound freedom with Zaza's death.

The decline of her family economic situation also coincided with Simone's adolescence. Both her father and mother came from wealthy families, and the increasing economic difficulties were hard to bear for Beauvoir's parents. There was no more money for entertaining and elegant clothes. Beauvoir's mother became even more devout, and her father became more careless, indifferent, and absent. Her father, who was first proud and delighted by Simone's early academic success, became increasingly critical of his daughter's achievements in school. He felt guilty that he could not provide his two daughters with a "dowry" to attract wealthy marriage partners and was uncomfortable at the thought that his daughters would have to support themselves. After completing her *baccalauréat* in philosophy and mathematics, Simone left the school to continue studying at the Institute St. Marie in Neuilly and the Institut Catholique. She wanted to go on studying philosophy at the Sorbonne, but to please her parents, she also took courses in literature.

By the age of seventeen Beauvoir had come to despise the bourgeois values she had been brought up to accept. She began to see the emptiness of the standards by which her parents had lived. There was no sudden break between Beauvoir and her parents, but her estrangement from their bourgeois world grew gradually. She developed a strong friendship with her cousin Jacques and thought of marrying him, but she soon realized that Jacques had no real desire, like her, to escape from the bourgeois order she now rejected. Her commitment to become a writer grew stronger as she felt it was the best way to reconcile her need for survival and her desire to serve others. She became absorbed in literature and started to keep a diary in which she expressed her loneliness and

disappointments. She obtained her degree in literature and philosophy and was accepted for postgraduate work at the prestigious school l'Ecole Normale Supérieure, which trains university professors. During her preparation for the *agrégation*, the highest teaching competition in France, she met a group of brilliant students. Among them were Merleau-Ponty, Paul Nizan, Raymond Aron, and Jean-Paul Sartre. Sartre had failed the *agrégation* the first time, and it was his second attempt. Beauvoir was immediately impressed by the way Sartre was interested in everything and by his confidence in becoming a writer. For the first time in her life, she felt intellectually dominated by someone. Sartre had already thought out an original philosophical system and had a clear idea of what he wanted to do. Beauvoir realized she had found in Sartre the companion she had wished for since the age of fifteen, and he would always have a place in her life. This relationship lasted for more than fifty years in spite of vicissitudes, absences, and separation.

Beauvoir and Sartre achieved outstanding results in the philosophy *agrégation*. He was number one and she was number two. At age twenty-one Beauvoir was the youngest ever to pass the *agrégation* for the first time. One of the professors on the jury remarked, "of the two, she is the philosopher." She moved out of her parents' home and gave as much time as possible to her relationship with Sartre. They decided against marriage and parenthood. Sartre suggested that their relationship was the important and necessary one, but they could have other contingent relationships. Her teaching appointment in Marseilles, in the south of France, came as a blow as Sartre was appointed in Le Havre, the opposite end of the country. In his dismay Sartre changed his mind and proposed marriage in order to facilitate teaching appointments in the same town, but Beauvoir refused, feeling that he would be wrong to marry only for the purpose of living in the same place. Beauvoir was also afraid of alienating Sartre by changing a freely chosen relationship into a bond, and she did not want to become overdependent upon him. After one year in Marseilles, Beauvoir was transferred to a position in Rouen, close to Le Havre where Sartre was still teaching.

Like most of their contemporaries, Beauvoir and Sartre failed to see the threat of political events in Germany, even though Sartre was studying in 1933 in Berlin. They were indifferent to political matters and deeply immersed in philosophy and literature. Sartre was profoundly stimulated by the philosophical method of inquiry of Edmund Husserl. In the summer of 1934 Beauvoir came to visit Sartre and together they made a long tour of Germany and Austria convincing themselves that the spread of Nazism was temporary and insignificant. The prewar years were happy ones for Beauvoir and Sartre. She read constantly, discovering Hemingway, Faulkner, Dos Passos, Heidegger, and Husserl. She went to theaters, art galleries and movies and spent hours in the cafés talking with friends. Her teaching duties left her enough time to write. An enthusiastic hiker, she spent hours walking in the surrounding country and loved to take long solitary walks. Her second autobiography, *La Force de l'age* (1960; translated as *The Prime of Life*, 1962), expresses the joy she felt during this period of her life.

Beauvoir recognized that both she and Sartre worshipped youth and feared adulthood. In fact she believed that Sartre suffered a severe depression, expressed in *La Nausee* (1938; translated as *Nausea*, 1949), caused by the approach of adulthood in his thirties. As for her, her indignation against old age and fear of death were obsessions that she expressed constantly in her memoirs. The experience of a triangular relationship between Sartre, herself, and Olga Kosakiewicz, a former student of Beauvoir, was the basis for her first novel, *L'Invitee* (1943; translated as *She Came to Stay*, 1954). Besides being able to use creatively a traumatic experience, it provided Beauvoir with themes of primordial importance in her work: the relationship of self with others and the awareness of the existence of another consciousness.

In 1939, when war was declared, Sartre was drafted into the army. At the beginning of the war Beauvoir and Sartre were hopeful that it might end quickly. When the "phony" war came to an end and Sartre was taken prisoner, Beauvoir left Paris as the German Army entered the capital, but she soon returned as she realized that the German occupation was not going to be temporary. Beauvoir experienced the effects of the German occupation on a personal level: food restrictions, lack of everyday goods, and the curfew. The anti-Semitism of the Germans soon became apparent, and Beauvoir was shocked by the Vichy regime, which she found as odious as the German occupation. She was dismissed from her teaching post by the Nazis, and she began writing a novel about the Resistance, called *Le Sang des autres* (1945; translated as *The Blood of Others*, 1948). When Sartre was released in 1941, they both adopted the notion of commitment and active resistance against the occupiers but felt

unqualified to engage in sabotage and confined their activities to writing. Sartre wrote *Les Mouches* (*The Flies*), a symbolic play about the Resistance, and Beauvoir wrote an essay on ethics, *Pyrrus et Cineas* (1944).

During this time, they became friends with Michel Leiris, Raymond Quenau, Andre Malraux, and Albert Camus. They were all drawn together by the common determination to provide an ideology of commitment and individual responsibility for the postwar period since the Liberation was now near. In July 1944 Beauvoir finished writing her only play, *Les Bouches inutiles* (*The Useless Mouth*), a month before Paris was liberated. After the liberation of Paris, Sartre and Beauvoir were optimistic and believed that the end of fascism would bring a new era of justice and a revision of social structures. They never joined the Communist party but considered themselves fellow travelers anxious to defend the individual rights against Marxist doctrine.

In 1945 Beauvoir, along with Sartre and a group of Leftist intellectuals, founded the review *Les Temps Modernes*. Although editorial work in the journal used much of her time and energy she wrote a long philosophical novel, *Tous les hommes sont mortels* (1946; translated as *All Men are Mortal*, 1955), which was not well received. She also composed an essay, *Pour une morale de l'ambiguite* (1947; translated as *The Ethics of Ambiguity*, 1949), which was to provide a morality for Sartre's *L'etre et le neant* (1943; translated as *Being and Nothingness*, 1956). On Sartre's suggestion, she started working on a massive overview of women's conditions.

During a lecture tour in the United States Beauvoir met Nelson Algren in Chicago and started a relationship of several years with the American writer. Algren offered to marry her, but Beauvoir remained attached to Sartre and could not conceive of exile from France. She transposed and related this romantic relationship in *Les Mandarins* (1954; translated as *The Mandarins*, 1956), which was awarded the celebrated literary prize Le Prix Goncourt (1954).

Les Mandarins is much more than a psychological novel about personal relationships. It recreates the atmosphere of the postwar period and the illusions and growing disillusionment of a group of leftist intellectuals between 1944 and 1947. The two main characters are Anne Dubreuilh, a psychiatrist, and Henri Perron, a journalist and former Resistance fighter. Beauvoir used a technique in *Les Mandarins* she had used in previous novels. She alternated the first-person narrative of Anne Dubreuilh with the third-person narrative of the journalist Henri Perron. Events are seen from two different perspectives and characters are revealed through subjective interpretations. It was the most popular of Simone de Beauvoir's books as it appealed to many readers as a roman à clef. The public interpreted the breakdown of the friendship between the two male characters, Robert Dubreuilh and Henri Perron, as the transposition of the serious rift between Sartre and Camus in 1952. Henri Perron was identified as Camus, Robert Dubreuilh as Sartre, Anne as Beauvoir herself, and Lewis Brogan was Nelson Algren. Beauvoir denied vehemently this interpretation and insisted that *Les Mandarins* was "an evocation" of the problems of leading French intellectuals after World War II and claimed that she put as much of herself in the character of Henri Perron as in Anne. "In Anne," Beauvoir commented, "I saw the negative aspect of objects whose positive side was revealed through Henri" (*Force of Circumstance*, 1965; translation of *La Force des choses*, 1963).

Her four-month visit to the United States resulted in *L'Amerique au jour le jour* (1948; translated as *America Day-by-Day*, 1953). Written in diary form, the book conveys Beauvoir's curiosity about the United States, her excitement at discovering this new country and sense of adventure. Although she lectured at various colleges during her visit, she had much free time to travel. She recognized in the preface of the book that she did not see many important aspects of the American life. She did not visit any factory, did not speak with workers, and met no political figure. Indeed, Beauvoir was critical of certain aspects of American life she observed: racism, conformism, puritan morality, and political apathy among the young. She was especially critical of the French people living in the United States, whom she found "with only a very few exceptions to incarnate all the faults of their country and embody only very fleetingly its qualities." *L'Amerique au jour le jour* remains a perceptive account of the United States, and its observations are still relevant.

Beauvoir finally completed her massive study on the status of women in 1949, and when the two volumes of *Le Deuxième Sexe* were published they created a furor. Beauvoir was attacked as bitterly by writers of the right as by those of the left. Albert Camus told her that "she had insulted the French male." The angry reactions were caused in part by her frank discussion of feminine sexuality and of such issues as marriage and motherhood, but she was comforted by the fact that thousands of women

wrote to her over the years that her book had been a great help and had changed their lives.

Le Deuxième Sexe is as much an anthropological as a sociological study of the condition of women. In both *Le Deuxième Sexe* and *La Vieillese* (1970; translated as *The Coming of Age*, 1970), a sociological study on old age, Beauvoir dealt with themes that are central to all her fiction and essays: bad faith, freedom, responsibility, and the relation of the self with others. Her method is similar in both books. The discrimination against women is even more intensified with old age and accompanied by solitude and economic difficulty.

Le Deuxième Sexe postulates that man conceived of himself as the essential being and has made the woman the unessential being, the other, the second. Beauvoir's other main postulate is that there is no biological law that determines feminine nature and all notions of feminine nature are therefore cultural or artificial: "One is not born, but rather one becomes a woman." Men, Beauvoir declares in *Le Deuxième Sexe*, can assert their will in the world by their actions and decisions. She analyzes the constraints that inhibit women from their full participation in the world. Women, according to Beauvoir, are given few opportunities to act and are judged on the performance of their social roles (wife, mother, mistress). Beauvoir proposes that women reject these traditional roles in order to obtain freedom and assume responsibilities for their lives. *Le Deuxième Sexe* was used as the starting point in the women's movement and was considered the feminist Bible. Its impact and influence on women throughout the world were immense. Today it is criticized by younger feminists as being too pessimistic and too critical, but its historical significance cannot be overlooked.

In 1952 Beauvoir decided to live with Claude Lanzmann, a journalist and film director who was seventeen years her junior. Lanzmann's youth helped Beauvoir lessen her anxiety about aging and their relationship was to last for six years. During this time, Beauvoir's life was filled with travels that she took either with Lanzmann or with Sartre, or sometimes with both. Her relationship with Lanzmann did not weaken her bond with Sartre and her associations with these two men drew her closer to the political issues of the times. She and Sartre spent two months visiting China and in 1957 she published a comprehensive study of that country entitled *La Longue marche; essai sur la Chine* (translated as *The Long March*, 1958).

Both Sartre and Beauvoir were saddened and shocked by the suppression of the revolution in

Dust jacket for the first American edition of Beauvoir's account of her relationship with Jean-Paul Sartre, which comprises a biography of Sartre's last ten years and a long dialogue between Sartre and Beauvoir

Hungary in November 1956. They immediately declared their opposition to the Russian intervention and broke off their ties with the Communist party. The most pressing issue at that time was the Algerian struggle for independence. In 1956 there was little opposition to the war in Algeria, so that Beauvoir and Sartre, who believed in Algerian independence, were in the minority. Beauvoir was horrified to find out that there was total silence in the media about the tortures inflicted by French soldiers on the Algerian population. She was one of the organizers of a meeting to protest French torture of Algerians and she campaigned on behalf of Djamila Boupacha, a young Algerian woman tortured by the French. As a result of their opposition to the French Algerian War Sartre's apartment was bombed. Fearing more attacks, they moved to a secret address under a false name. The new apartment was also bombed. Beauvoir and

Sartre were overwhelmed by their sense of shame about the Algerian War and did not have any hesitation in signing the "Manifesto of the 121" with other intellectuals who supported the right of young French men to resist conscription. Considering France to be more a police state than ever, Beauvoir and Sartre embarked on a two-month visit to Cuba, Brazil, and the United States. During this period she started to publish the first volume of her autobiography, *Memoires d'une jeune fille rangée*. The success of the book encouraged her to continue with a second volume, *La Force de l'age*, which was a critical and commercial success. The third volume of her autobiography, *La Force des choses*, was not as well received.

At the invitation of Soviet writers, Beauvoir and Sartre went to visit the Soviet Union and they managed to visit Czechoslovakia where they both felt there were new possibilities for freedom emerging. Her mother died shortly afterwards and in *Une Mort très douce* (1964; translated as *A Very Easy Death*, 1966) Beauvoir gave a moving account of her mother's fight against cancer. At this time Beauvoir decided to return to the novel. The result was a short novel, *Les Belles Images* (1966; translated, 1968) which evokes the atmosphere of the consumer society in Paris in the 1960s. Her last work of fiction was *Femme rompee* (1967; translated as *Woman Destroyed*, 1969), which is a collection of three novellas. Each novella tells the story of the disintegration of a woman who shows either self-deception, egocentrism, or bad faith. Each story, skillfully constructed and masterfully written, reflects Simone de Beauvoir's preoccupations with the problems of old age, the passage of time, isolation, and failure of communication.

Since 1962 Beauvoir had taken very little interest in the politics of France. However, the student revolt in May 1968 found both Sartre and Beauvoir strongly involved on the side of the students. They hoped that the Gaullist regime might be overthrown and signed a manifesto expressing support for the students and asking support of workers and intellectuals. Sartre and Beauvoir were invited to the Sorbonne, occupied by the students, and Sartre addressed a large crowd of students, but they were greatly disappointed when the government regained control, and there was no change in the structure of the French society.

Beauvoir realized that change for women will not come from a Communist or even a Socialist government. She revised her belief that socialism alone would solve the subordination of women. Recent Socialist examples in Cuba, Russia, and China had shown her that it was not the case. She admitted that before 1970 she saw feminism as only legalistic, but in 1970 she joined the demonstration of the Women's Liberation Movement and signed the "Manifesto of 343" as one of the women admitting to an illegal abortion. Sartre and Beauvoir felt even more committed to help in practical ways the cause of the poor and the oppressed. In 1970 they condemned the arbitrary measures taken against the leftist newspaper *La Cause du Peuple* and to call attention to police harassment they sold the censured newspaper on the streets. They were arrested and later released. Beauvoir continued to be involved in clashes with the government and joined demonstrations protesting crimes against women. She started a feminist section in *Les Temps Modernes* which related examples of sexism or discriminatory statements about women and was named president of the French League of Women Rights. In 1973 she published her last and fourth volume of her autobiography, *Taut compte sait* (translated as *All Said and Done*, 1973).

Beauvoir was awarded the Jerusalem Prize in 1975, the first prize she had agreed to accept since Le Prix Goncourt, and explained that she was totally opposed to any solution of conflicts in the Middle East which might endanger Israel as a nation.

In 1979 Beauvoir agreed to the publication of her first collection of short stories, *Quand Prime Le Spirituel* (1979; translated as *When Things of the Spirit Come First,* 1982), a text that had been rejected by two publishers more than forty years earlier. In the late 1970s much of her time and energy were taken in helping Sartre, who was ill and blind, by reading to him and collaborating with him on his remaining projects. Her last published work was *La Ceremonie des adieux* (1981; translated as *Adieux: Farewell to Sartre,* 1984), an account of Sartre's death and some interviews she did with him a few years earlier. She died 14 April 1986, six years after Sartre's death.

For half a century Simone de Beauvoir lived with Sartre an association of thoughts and ideas. From existentialism to Algerian independence, to the defense of the state of Israel, their commitments were the same. Beauvoir added her struggle for the women's liberation movement and abortion. Their union, based on intellectual exchange and mutual respect, had become legendary. In *La Ceremonie des adieux* she concludes with these words:

> His death separates us. My death will not reunite us. It is so. It is already beautiful that our lives could intertwine for so long a time.

Personal Tribute To
Simone de Beauvoir

Yolanda Astarita Patterson
California State University, Hayward

She is no longer in her apartment on the corner of the rue Schoelcher, ready to scribble off notes of appreciation, advice, support, and encouragement on her endless supply of graph paper. The woman who rejected motherhood for herself and cautioned others about its ramifications, who laughed when I suggested that she had become a mother figure for thousands of women and remarked that the analogy was a false one because daughters don't pay attention to what their mothers tell them, died at the Hôpital Cochin in Paris on Monday, 14 April 1986.

I was more caught up in the drama of her death than I could ever have imagined, because her younger sister Hélène, whose art work I had arranged to have exhibited at Stanford University in April and May 1986, was a houseguest of ours when an early morning telephone call from Paris informed us that Simone de Beauvoir had lost the battle against pulmonary edema. Hélène had been reluctant to make the long awaited trip, her first visit to the San Francisco peninsula, because her sister was in the hospital. With characteristic concern for others, Simone had urged her to come, not to miss the *vernissage* reception scheduled for

10 April at the Office of the President on the Stanford campus and the opportunity to enjoy the beauty of the Bay area. From the time of her arrival, Hélène and I shared a gnawing anxiety about her sister's health, but tried to take events as they came. Our schedule included a visit to a Women's Studies class of mine at Cal State Hayward where Hélène graciously answered questions about *A Very Easy Death*, the deeply personal text Simone had written about their mother and dedicated to her sister, which I had made the first reading assignment of the spring quarter for my course on "Mothers, Daughters, and Sons."

Events happened so quickly after that Monday morning phone call that they still have an unreal quality about them for me. I knew that I had to arrange to have Hélène return to Paris as quickly as possible and was able to enlist the help of the Air France office in San Francisco to change her reservation and get her on a plane that afternoon. When she called on Wednesday morning to tell me about the arrangements that had been made for the funeral, I suddenly knew that I simply had to be there. I had been reading Simone de Beauvoir's works since the 1950s, had taught many courses whose syllabi included one or more of her books, given numerous papers at conferences, and written several articles about her writing. I had interviewed her on two occasions, in June 1978 and again in September 1985, and had been in regular contact with her as secretary and then as president of the American-based Simone de Beauvoir Society.

Funerals are always difficult emotionally because of the necessity of balancing one's sense of loss against the social requirements of the situation. This is particularly true when the funeral takes place in another country. Does one send flowers? Yes. Where? To the hospital. What about viewing the body? This took place in the hospital amphitheater, where someone checked off names of those invited by the family before allowing anyone in. In that amphitheater I found a hushed silence and the grave faces of family members and friends, literary and political figures: former Prime Minister Laurent Fabius and his wife; former Minister of Culture Jack Lang; former Minister of the Rights of Women, Yvette Roudy; Colette Audry, author and colleague of Simone de Beauvoir's in a Rouen lycée in the 1930s; Sylvie Le Bon de Beauvoir, the author's adopted daughter; Claude Lanzmann, friend, collaborator on the political review *Les Temps Modernes,* and producer of the recently released film *Shoah*; American feminist Kate Millett; cousins Madeleine and Jeanne, about whom

Beauvoir writes in *Memoirs of a Dutiful Daughter;* and of course Hélène de Beauvoir and her husband. And in an inner room lay a body which had just so recently had so much life and energy, so much intellectual acumen, that it was painful to see it so inanimate.

The *cortège* proceeded from the hospital along the Boulevard du Montparnasse, on which all traffic had been stopped. It passed by the cafés to which Beauvoir's readers had accompanied her vicariously: La Rotonde, Le Dôme, Le Sélect, la Coupole. During the long walk behind the flower-laden funeral car decorated with a large "B," I saw several French feminists whom I had met the previous April at a colloquium on Simone de Beauvoir held at Columbia University. At the Montparnasse Cemetery, the heavy metal gates clanged shut and most of us waited outside while the brief graveside ceremony took place. Later the crowds made it impossible to approach the grave, so I left the cemetery and joined a gathering at the home of a friend of Hélène de Beauvoir's, where I had the privilege of meeting many of the family members whose names were familiar to me from the autobiography and of whom I already had vivid mental images. Still frustrated at never having come close to the graveside, I returned by métro to the cemetery, only to find it closed. Kate Millett was there too, with a French friend who tried valiantly to persuade the guard to let us in. We eventually came to the conclusion that it would be easier to return the next day than to try to cut through the bureaucratic red tape necessary to open up that entrance.

Sunday, 20 April, was a rainy day in Paris. The floral arrays still made a brilliant display of color in the corner of the Montparnasse Cemetery where Simone de Beauvoir was now buried next to Jean-Paul Sartre. Standing under cover of the guardhouse waiting for the rain to let up a bit, I started to chat with another woman carrying a camera. She confided to me that she had been Beauvoir's official photographer. She was Gisèle Freund, whose photographs had enriched many of the books I had read about Beauvoir.

After I returned home to California and my classes, I was preparing a talk about Beauvoir for a group of secondary and university level foreign language colleagues which meets regularly at Stanford. I had been thinking of beginning by saying that I really knew Hélène de Beauvoir a lot better than I knew Simone. Then I stopped to consider the hundreds of hours I had devoted to reading, rereading, analyzing, and writing about Simone de

Beauvoir and decided that such a statement would not be true. Although I had only spent approximately two hours face to face with the author, the time spent reading and reacting to what she had to say would be more than enough to qualify ours as a long-standing relationship of over thirty years.

For me as for many of her other readers, her disappearance from the fourteenth *arrondissement* has created both a sense of personal loss and of an empty place in the universe that can never be filled again in quite the same way.

Jorge Luis Borges

(24 August 1899-14 June 1986)

Jaime Alazraki
Harvard University

On 14 June of last year, at about 4:30 in the afternoon, I was working on a long essay on Borges for the *Latin American Encyclopedia* (Scribners) in my home in Sarria, Barcelona. The telephone rang. It was Borges's wife, María Kodama. Her voice sounded muffled but firm: "It's over. Borges is dead." I thought of a dozen replies, but none reached my mouth. I mumbled a few broken sentences, but I couldn't bring myself to ask her about funeral or burial arrangements. Borges was too much of a living presence to be thought of as a dead body. Besides, how do you go about sending into the grave a man whose *life* had been a figment of his own literature, the letter of his own spirit? I hung up more confused than disturbed. One of those situations in which you don't know what it is that events expect from you, how you fit into the scheme of things. And then, of course, the regrets for not having found out the details about his burial. While I was pondering these and other questions, I found myself calling the Sants Railroad Station in Barcelona to get information about the first train leaving for Geneva.

I had been with Borges in Geneva only three weeks earlier. His voice sounded husky and punctured with mute or muffled blanks. It was very hard to follow his speech. At times, he had to repeat the same sentence a couple of times before I was able to understand. The last time I had seen Borges was at a symposium at Dickinson College in April of 1983. During the sessions he appeared lively and energetic, vigorous and tireless. The Borges I was sitting next to in Geneva, three years later, was a shadow of the other, a physical ruin. His head was deformed, as if the frontal bone had grown beyond

Jorge Luis Borges (Gale International Portrait Gallery)

proportion and was threatening to tear the skin through. It was not so much the ravages of time as the onslaught of disease, as if his mind kept growing while his body decayed. Publicly, Borges was suffering from a pulmonary emphysema. The cancer of the liver that eventually killed him was a secret known only to himself, his doctor, and María

Kodama. Borges and María left Buenos Aires in November of 1985 after a biopsy revealed the terminal nature of his illness. They spent a short period in Italy and then settled in Geneva. When I visited them, three weeks before the final collapse, María told me that Borges was adamant about not returning to Argentina. Friends and relatives were pressing for his return and María became the target of abuse. Borges's answer was his marriage by proxy in Paraguay to María Kodama.

He received me kindly and with a warning: "No politics, please." "Borges"—I replied—, "I came to see you and wish you well." From then on the conversation was smooth, and at times intimate. Of that exchange, I only have the records of my memory somewhat eroded by the moving circumstances of the encounter. I remember isolated phrases: "Argentine history is a work of fiction, that is, the official version of it." "The military have turned the country into a financial private business." "I am not loved in Argentina." He added details about his break with his closest friend and collaborator, Adolfo Bioy Casares, about his refusal to return to Argentina, about the French edition of his complete works in the series "Bibliothèque de la Pléiade" of Gallimard (Cervantes and García Lorca being the only other Spanish-language authors included in that series). We reminisced about previous encounters in Oklahoma, San Diego, Los Angeles, Buenos Aires, Maine, Chicago, Pennsylvania, and Harvard, where he received an honorary degree in 1981. It was a rambling conversation, digressing from personal comments into literary matters, from food into the ways of the Swiss. But then, that has always been Borges's favorite way of chatting: going wherever the branching and winding corridors of his formidable memory would take him.

By noontime, a nurse showed up to bathe him, help him with daily physical exercises, and feed him lunch. Since Borges needed an afternoon nap, María suggested we go out for lunch. We walked through the town and headed to the John Calvin *collège* where Borges had attended school between 1914 and 1919 while his family was living in Geneva. In that yard we were standing, and under those same arches and galleries, Borges spent a good chunk of his life learning Latin, German, and French, and actually laying the foundations of his legendary erudition. "The city,"—he would say later of Geneva—"where I read all the great books, from Verlaine to Virgil." Of those adolescent years, Borges wrote: "The first fall of 1914 I started school at the College of Geneva founded by John

Calvin. It was a day school. In my class there were some forty of us; a good half were foreigners. The chief subject was Latin, and I soon found out that one could let other studies slide a bit as long as one's Latin was good. . . . We lived in a flat on the southern, or old, side of town."

The memory of those years in Geneva, far from having been erased by time or oblivion, was very much kept alive in Borges's mind and even grew to become the affectionate territory of a second country. In his 1970 "Autobiographical Essay," he wrote: "I still know Geneva far better than I know Buenos Aires, which is easily explained by the fact that in Geneva no two streetcorners are alike and one quickly learns the differences. Every day, I walked along that green and icy river, the Rhone, which runs through the very heart of the city, spanned by seven quite different-looking bridges."

Borges chose to die in Geneva. In his last published book, *Los conjurados* (The Conjurors), a 1985 collection of poems, he called Geneva one of his motherlands, and he defines Switzerland as "a tower of reason and solid faith." Borges came to Geneva searching for a country which, through the years, had become very much his own. Argentina, his own country—he felt—had been lost to him, and Switzerland offered him a peace he could not find in his native land.

Argentina was, for Borges, a handful of friends, a few national and family myths, the Spanish language, intimate corners and wistful streets of Buenos Aires. But Argentina was far more than that: a nation that since Perón in the 1940s went through a period of profound changes in its social and political makeup. Borges refused to acknowledge and come to terms with those changes. Like Leopoldo Lugones, a leading Argentine writer of the 1920s, Borges believed that the military should intervene in the nation's political life and seize power by force. He identified the generals with the fathers of Argentine Independence and believed that the military were "the only gentlemen left capable of saving the country." Those gentlemen are now behind bars, tried by civilian courts and sentenced by Argentine laws. Borges could not find solace, let alone national recognition, in that tormented and soul-searching country. So, he came to die in the country of his adolescence, in that "tower of reason" where life is as private as its aloof citizens and runs as serene as the Rhone waters. That environment was much closer to his intellectual constructs and labyrinthian artifices. Perhaps Borges was mistakenly born in Buenos Aires. He wanted to believe—as he wrote—that "the Argentine tradition is all of Western culture." "And I also believe"—he added—"we have a right to this tradition, greater than that which the inhabitants of one or another Western nation might have."

Of course I could not discuss this with Borges. I came to renew an old acquaintanceship and to pay homage to the artist. And there I was, with María, back from our stroll, standing by his side, taking photographs: Borges hugging María, clinging to her like a child, holding her as in a permanent farewell. The most vivid and moving impression of that last visit happened at the time of saying good-bye. Borges pressed my hand very hard, with a strength most unusual for him.

When my train arrived in Geneva at seven thirty in the morning on 15 June, it was too early to look for María Kodama. I walked from the railroad station to the Hotel L'Arbalète at a slow pace. It was Sunday and the city was deserted. I eventually found an open coffee shop and had breakfast. Only then, I crossed one of the seven bridges that spanned the Rhone and headed for the hotel. María was up, but she was surrounded by journalists and photographers and flooded with telegrams and phone calls. When finally I got to talk to her I learned that there was no date for the funeral. Arrangements were being made to bury him in Plainpalais, the cemetery reserved for the Swiss notables, but that was not an easy undertaking. When finally the Swiss authorities approved the burial in Plainpalais, the funeral was scheduled for Wednesday, 18 June.

A few of us went together to Plainpalais to help María choose the plot for Borges's grave. We were shown the few sites available, and as we walked through we passed Alberto Ginastera's tomb, the only other Latin American buried there. María hesitated until she saw the last plot under a mature and beautiful yew tree, which in French is called *if*, and only a few yards from a very modest grave that turned out to be John Calvin's. The tree, evoking Kipling's poem (Borges was a loyal admirer of Kipling), the closeness to Calvin's shadow, and the quiet peacefulness of that particular corner made the decision for María. Two days later, Borges was buried in that spot where he rests now.

The funeral service was conducted at the Saint Pierre Cathedral, a majestic church located in the highest and oldest part of town. There were two eulogies: one delivered by a Catholic priest and the other by a Protestant minister. The press explained that this was so because Borges's mother was a staunch Catholic whereas his paternal grandmother was Protestant. The press failed to explain, though, that Borges had been a committed agnostic throughout his life. However, the priest disclosed during his eulogy that he had assisted Borges the night before his death, heard his confession, and given him absolution.

Borges's work is a prodigious artifice, an iridescent language, a self-contained form cut off from historic reality. It was forged within the boundaries of that library he never, in his own words, ventured out of. John Ashbery has defined Borges's art as "the work of a metaphysical Fabergé," and in comparing him with Kafka, he added: "We read Kafka from something like necessity; we read Borges for enjoyment, our own indifference taking pleasure in the frightful but robust spectacle of a disinherited cosmos." As Borges, the man, was being dispossessed of the world, the world was merciless in restating the terms of that old divorce he so much believed in, between him and the world. With the exception of María Kodama—his old student and friend, his daughter figure and wife—Borges died in the most absolute solitude. One may say that he chose to die that way, but then the choice was the result of a slow and gradual losing of the world. First, by confining himself within the walls of the library. Then, he lost the Argentine people by siding with the torturers and assassins of his own nation. This led to the loss of his native country. Eventually, for very complicated reasons and bitter feuds, he also lost the remaining part of his family. Finally, he lost his best friends for obscure and controversial motives. All this was somewhat reflected in his funeral. All of Borges's most important publishers were there: Diego Hidalgo from Alianza Editorial, Claude Gallimard who escorted María, Franco María Ricci for whom Borges directed the series "The Library of Babel." There were a couple of official delegations from Spain and Argentina, a few local academicians, a handful of Argentine residents, and dozens of journalists, photographers, and cameramen. Conspicuous in their absence were family members, personal friends, and fellow writers.

John Updike closes his essay "The Author as Librarian" with the following rumination: "We move, with Borges, beyond psychology, beyond the human, and confront in his work, the world atomized and vacant. Perhaps not since Lucretius has a poet so definitely felt men as incidents in space." His funeral at the Saint Pierre Cathedral and his death in Geneva were metaphors for that solipsistic existence: his residence was not so much the world as the chambers of the library where he truly dwelled. His story "The House of Asterion" can be read as Borges's own metaphor. There, the Minotaur *chooses* to stay in the labyrinth where he has been imprisoned. "One afternoon"—he confesses—"I did step into the street; if I returned before night, I did so because of the fear that faces of the common people inspired in me." Confronted with the chaos of the world, Asterion the Minotaur chooses the orderly space he has found in a human construction, Daedalus' labyrinth. Borges made a similar choice: confronted with the chaos of the world, he chose the order of the library, the safety of a decipherable labyrinth. His books grew out of other books. He wrote fiction based on theologies and philosophies, literature founded in literature. He knew that the hard face of reality lurks in every corner of life, but he renounced the world because, he said, of its impenetrable nature. Instead, he anchored his writings in the order of the intellect, in the chartable waters of the library. What he wrote about Paul Valéry is applicable to himself: "In a century that adores idols of blood, earth and passion, he always preferred the lucid pleasures of thought and the secret adventures of order." Any form of knowledge that challenged his skeptical understanding of the world met with his strong disapproval and even condemnation. In the same essay, he wrote: "The meritorious mission that Valéry performed (and continues to perform) is that he proposed lucidity to men in a basely romantic age, in the melancholy age of dialectical materialism, the age of the augurs of Freud's doctrine and

traffickers in surrealism." Borges indicted literary movements (romanticism and surrealism) and forms of thought (Marxism and psychoanalysis) that deal not so much with sheer abstract reasoning (although in a highly abstract fashion), but with questions concerning life: distrust of and revolt against the abuses of rational order, class order, and ego order. Life in its subliminal plane, as struggle or desire, seemed to horrify him. Borges was an intellectual animal, a solipsist locked—like the Minotaur of his story—in a labyrinth of his own construction.

Because he saw writing as rewriting, and because he showed—in theory as well as in practice—that "one literature differs from another, either before or after it, not so much because of the text as for the manner in which it is read," he fascinated structuralists as well as semioticians. Because he concluded in "Pierre Menard, Author of the *Quixote*" that "Cervantes' text and Menard's are verbally identical, but the second is almost infinitely richer," he dazzled the followers of intertextuality. When he wrote, in 1953, that since Homer all metaphors had been recorded, and yet the ways of stating at the terms of a given metaphor are, in fact, endless, he advanced an essential tenet in the theory of the Russian formalists, and prompted John Barth to write his essay "Literature of Exhaustion." Finally, because of his invisible and rigorous style, Borges became, as Carlos Fuentes put it, a sort of father figure of the contemporary Spanish American novel.

The Poetry of Jorge Luis Borges

Stuart Evans

Enchanted (and sometimes mystified) as his admirers are by the labyrinthine subtleties of the stories and tales of Jorge Luis Borges, many of us find his poems more accessible, although they too are many faceted, the focuses giving light to many peripheral insights and reflections. I propose, therefore, since much has been and will be written about Borges's prose to concentrate in this brief essay on Borges the poet.

In the "Author's Foreword" to his *Selected Poems, 1923-1967* (1972) Borges wrote: "All that is personal to me, all that my friends good-naturedly tolerate in me—my likes and dislikes, my hobbies, my habits—are to be found in my verse. In the long run, perhaps, I shall stand or fall by my poems." Norman Thomas di Giovanni, the volume's editor and the supervising translator of much of Borges's work, recorded in his "Introduction" an early exchange in his relationship with the author: " 'What I liked about you, di Giovanni,' Borges confided to me on my arrival in Buenos Aires almost a year after we first met, 'was that there in Harvard you were the only person who took me seriously as a poet.' 'But I see you as a poet, Borges.' 'Yes,' he said, 'I see myself as a poet—that's our link.' "

Borges insisted in various interviews and prefaces on the "fundamental paucity" of his work, asserting that he wrote on very few themes, that he was limited. This will surely come as a most disputable surprise to those readers who are convinced of the richness of Borges's writing.

Admittedly he returned to several important themes time and again and concentrated on recurring, even obsessive images—dreams, tigers, fantasies, weapons, battles, violence, mirrors, labyrinths, but in an index made up some years ago for personal interest of ideas explicit or implicit in those poems of Borges's that I had then read I noted some 109 different perceptions. And I probably missed a few. Any one poem might have multiple implications and, as is proper, might assume this or that meaning according to a particular reader's mood or preoccupation. It is not so with all poetry, which indicates the scope of Borges's intellect, sensibility, and imagination. Borges would not quarrel with the relationship of poem and reader. He believed that once written the poem and its reader work on one another and that the poet's own intentions in writing that particular piece are no longer relevant. Indeed, in later editions of his early work, he has virtually disowned whole collections. In the 1969 preface to *Luna de enfrente— Cuaderno San Martín*, he noted laconically: "The fact is that I feel removed from them: I take no responsibility for their mistakes or for their possible virtues. . . . I have made few changes in these two collections. They are no longer mine."

In spite of my submission that Borges was a poet of abundant, cross-fertilizing ideas, it is necessary here to concentrate on the main themes of his work as he pursued them with abiding, maturing fascination. What moved the young man and Borges, the aspirant writer, still moved the elderly blind librarian and international poet and fictionalist. He was at pains to point out in the short piece "Borges and Myself " that they were different people.

> It is to the other man, to Borges that things happen. . . . I live, I let myself live, so that Borges can weave his tales and poems, and those tales and poems are my justification. Little by little, I have been surrendering everything to him, even though I have evidence of his stubborn habit of falsification and exaggerating. . . . Years ago, I tried ridding myself of him, and I went from myths of the outlying slums of the city to games with time and infinity, but those games are now part of Borges, and I will have to turn to other things. And so my life is running away, and I lose everything and everything is left to oblivion or to the other man.
>
> Which of us is writing this page I don't know.

Otherness is an enigmatic preoccupation for Borges, while oblivion becomes a repeated theme in his later work, where it superseded his earlier obsession with death.

In almost all the poems dealing with death there is a quiet, lasting compassion ("Remorse for Any Death," "Inscription on Any Tomb") which extends to Borges's many poems about his ancestors. In these poems about family pride and the poet's respect for courage on the battlefield and against ferocious political adversaries, his admiration for their feats in arms is tempered by an underlying sadness and understanding. Isidoro Suarez and Isidoro Acevedo were his great-grandfather and grandfather on his mother's side. But perhaps the ancestor he most admired was his paternal grandfather, Colonel Francisco Borges, to whom he addressed several poems. All three men, in their time, favoured a unified Argentinian state and suffered for it at the hands of the *caudillos*, or local war-lords, so-called federalists, in whose interest it was to keep the country divided. Whether fighting for other causes in exile or for Argentina they acquitted themselves with dedication and honor.

Perhaps this tradition explains Borges's interest in men-of-action of all sorts and acts of violence, even when these acts are perpetrated by scoundrels and tyrants. The same contemplation of death occurs in poems addressed to a "Shadow of the Nineties," the knife-fighter Muraña, and to the savage Général Quiroga, even to the hated dictator, Rosas (who confronts Quiroga in one of Borges's stories, "Dialogue of the Dead"). However hostile these poems are, however violent, there is still (even in the poem to Rosas) more than a hint of pity, as there is in the "Milonga of the Two Brothers."

More important are Borges's generalized poems about death. In "The Recoleta" he writes of the Buenos Aires cemetery for the rich and privileged, where he thinks he will one day be buried. He describes the family vaults,

whose rhetoric of shadow and stone
promises or prefigures the coveted
dignity of being dead.

Then later, in the same poem:

We mistake this peace for death
believing we yearn for our end
when we yearn for sleep and oblivion.

Less personal, though profoundly moving, is "Deaths in Buenos Aires." Here Borges contemplates the two major cemeteries of the city: the humble La Chacarita beyond the southside slums, originally opened to house the teeming victims of a yellow fever epidemic; and La Recoleta, graveyard of proud families. In the first poem, he describes the origins of La Chacarita, reflecting:

The frauds of mortality—stained as in childbirth—
still fatten your subsoil; so you muster up souls
for your compounds, for your hidden contingent of
    bones
dropped into holes or buried away in your night
as if drowned in the depths of a sea,
preparing a death without hope of eternity, without
    -honour.

It is in La Chacarita that he is moved by a guitar-player, "one of the dispossessed poor," who sings:

Death is life lived away,
Life is death coming on.

In La Recoleta, "Death is scrupulous. . . ." Here is to be found the "suffrage of marble," the dutiful wreaths:

Here something holds me: I think
of the fatuous flowers that speak out so piously now
    -in your name
the leaf-yellow clay under the fringe of acacia,
memorial wreaths lifted in your family crypts—
why do they stay here in their sleepy and delicate way
side by side with the terrible keepsakes of those whom
    -we loved?

I put the hard question and venture an answer:
our flowers keep perpetual watch on the dead
because we all incomprehensibly know
that their sleepy and delicate presence
is all we can offer the dead to take with them in their
    -dying,

without giving offence through the pride of our living
or seeming more alive than dead.

There are many other poems about death, which, as Borges grew older, became increasingly involved with his perplexities concerning time and a sort of Nietzschean sense of continuity, somewhat at odds with his brooding over loss of identity and his growing preoccupation with oblivion. In the later poems this is a dominant theme, though the "labyrinth" metaphor, in different forms, reappears frequently. "Everness," "Ewigkeit," "Oedipus and the Riddle," and "To a Coin" all contain some direct reference or suggestion of a yearning for a state of final rest. The "Oedipus" poem ends:

It would annihilate us all to see
The huge shape of our being; mercifully
God offers us issue and oblivion.

If what has been written above might suggest that Borges was a gloomy poet, such was emphatically not the case, as his two poems of the "gifts" readily bear witness. He is truly a "literalist of the imagination," who is, if sometimes melancholy, never morbid. Throughout his work there is a powerful element of delight in discovery: his explorations of Buenos Aires, his study of other languages and literatures, his interest in philosophy and metaphysic (often at the gently mocked expense of professional philosophers), his discovery of himself through ancestors, loves, his poetry and fiction, and eventually in his blindness.

Borges's love for Buenos Aires is evident through his work. Di Giovanni has commented on the difficulty of communicating allusions, place references, and street associations in another language. What infallibly comes through to readers who do not know the city and who may have little Spanish is the exuberance of Borges's enthusiasm, as well as his intense feeling for people of all sorts and conditions. An early evocative piece is "Unknown Street":

. . . and only afterward
I realised that the place was strange
that every house is a candelabra
where the lives burn each in its separate flame,
that each of our unthinking footsteps
makes its way over the Golgothas of others.

His love of Buenos Aires and loyalty to Argentina did not prevent wide-ranging discovery elsewhere. Proud of his part-English ancestry (his grandmother, Frances Haslam, hailed from Northumbria), Borges, immensely well-read in several languages, took a special interest in English literature and in Anglo-Saxon and Nordic culture. His massively curious genius missed little and cast nothing aside. Several of his poems focus on Anglo-Saxon subjects and with typical ebullience, he began a study of Old English (upon which he held seminars) after going blind. From "Embarking on the study of Anglo-Saxon Grammar" we have:

> All praise to the inexhaustible
> Labyrinth of cause and effect
> Which before unveiling to me the mirror
> Where I shall see no one or shall see some other self
> Has granted me this perfect contemplation
> Of language at its dawn.

Self-discovery through his metaphysical probings and investigations is an altogether more difficult aspect of the work of Borges. He claims that "The Cyclical Night," "The Golem," and the two "Chess" poems either prefigure one another or are on the same theme. A hint of his later absorption in metaphysical mysteries which are perhaps unlikely ever to be explained occurs in an early poem, "Daybreak":

> Under the spell of the refreshing darkness
> and intimidated by the threat of dawn,
> I felt again that tremendous conjecture
> of Schopenauer and Berkeley
> which declares the world
> an activity of the mind,
> a dream of souls,
> without foundation or purpose or volume.

The poem ends:

> But once more the world comes to its own rescue.
> The light streaks in inventing dirty colours
> and with a tremor or remorse
> for my complicity in the daily rebirth
> I seek my house,
> amazed and icelike in the white glare,
> while a songbird holds the silence back
> and the spent night
> lives on in the eyes of the blind.

In "The Labyrinth," a poem from his later years, Borges struggles with the problem of identity:

> My mind forgets
> The persons I have been along the way
> The hated way of monotonous walls,
> Which is my fate.

Yet again, the poet looks toward oblivion:

> I know that hidden in the shadows there
> Lurks another, whose task is to exhaust
> The loneliness that braids and weaves this hell
> To crave my blood, and to fatten on my death
> We seek each other. Oh, if only this
> Were the last day of our antithesis!

Now at a literal level, this may well be the Minotaur, but it might also be the poet speaking for himself or for any one of us.

"The Golem" is a very difficult poem in which Borges's natural compassion transcends ironic metaphysical curiosity. It is not out of sentimentality that the reader feels pity for the homunculos created by the invocation of words by the Czech Rabbi, it is rather out of awe and fear. As the Rabbi looks with "tender eyes/And terror" at his creation, who can guess at the feelings of God as He "gazed upon His rabbi there in Prague?"

Borges's sensitivity is shown in such a poem, but at a more attainable level in those poems devoted to the suffering of others, such as his friend the poet Merino, who killed himself. His affection extends beyond his family and friends, more generally to the people of Buenos Aires and universally in the fine poem "Luke XXIII," which annotates the brief exchange between Christ and the condemned man alongside him at Calvary who asked:

> *Remember me when thou comest*
> *Into thy kingdom. . . .*

The same compassion is aroused for poets, sometimes real, sometimes imagined, and all who struggle with the art. Apart from the discreet elegy for his friend Merino, there are lines for a minor anonymous Greek poet discovered in an anthology, for a imaginary poet of 1899, and especially for two Saxon poets (the latter the putative author of "The Wanderer"). Borges understood the inherent frustration of poets at any time, in liberty or under tyranny, as they failed to grasp exact meanings, failed to make the precise association, failed to work something that would be perfect in meaning, imagery, diction, and modality. To the earlier Saxon poet, he wrote:

> Of my gods or of the sum of time I ask
> That my days attain oblivion,
> That like Ulysses I may be called No One
> But that some verse of mine survive
> On a night favourable to memory
> Or in the mornings of men.

At the last, Borges is most pleasantly revealed when he chose, however guardedly, to talk for himself without metaphysical or literary embroidery. He does so in "Empty Drawing Room" and, to an extent, in "The Borges" and very much so in the moving dedication to Leonor Alcevedo de Borges, the poet's mother. Then, in the second of two poems written in English, we learn something more about the witty, urbane, cerebral, cautious man behind the ironic mask of Borges. Here is the last passage of that poem:

> I can give you my loneliness, my darkness, the hunger
> of my heart; I am trying to bribe you with uncertainty,
> with danger, with defeat.

Lastly he revealed himself to be a man of surpassing courage and goodwill, as well as Borges the poet of consummate artistry and labyrinthine imagination, in the two poems about gifts. The second of these is a moving recital of events, experiences, and people (some real, some fictional) for whom the poet wishes to give thanks. The first, "Poem of the the Gifts," speaks for itself. Here are three stanzas:

> No one should read self-pity or reproach
> Into this statement of the majesty
> Of God who with such splendid irony
> Granted me books and blindness at one touch.
>   . . . . .
> Something, which certainly is not defined
> By the word *fate,* arranges all these things;
> Another man was given, on other evenings
> Now gone, these many books. He too was blind.
>   . . . . .
> Groussac or Borges, now I look upon
> The dear world losing shape, fading away
> Into a pale uncertain ashy-gray
> That feels like sleep, or else oblivion.

A Definition of Baroque

> . . . that style which deliberately
> exhausts (or tries to exhaust) all
> its possibilities and which borders on its own
>   parody.
>
>   J. L. Borges

> Dread redeemer and implausible impostor,
> The Widow Ching, purveyor of iniquity,
> A disinterested killer, the insulting master
> Of etiquette, the masked dyer, streetcorner
> Man, theologian in death, wizard postponed,
> Generous enemy. . . . .
>   Your definitions define
> The rest of us, especially those who gaze
> Optimistically into mirrors, kempt or bleared,
> Searching the blindness of the velvet iris
> And blank pupil's depth. And retch for ourselves.

> But you are, praise be, always there, before
> A temple the gods will not save; inventing
> Stoic modesty, preparing us for that face
> Disfigured by strange calamities.

>   Drunk or shaving,
> We try to exhaust our potential with grimaces,
> Collapse into decrepitude such lines foretell,
> Strain to outdo Bosch and to outface Freud.

> On the other hand:
> There is the Kapelmeister breaking his step
> As he walks seriously to his duties. And there is
> You, Senor, calmly, meticulously inspecting chickens.

>   Stuart Evans

John Braine

(13 April 1922-28 October 1986)

Judy Simons
Sheffield City Polytechnic

See also the Braine entry in *DLB 15: British Novelists, 1930-1959.*

"None of my novels is autobiographical, but all of my life is in them," John Braine once said. "Whenever I'm writing a novel, I see places in my mind's eye. I must see it. It must be absolutely concrete." These two statements from Braine himself perhaps most acutely summarize, more than any work of objective criticism could have done, the reasons for his continued appeal to readers over a period of almost thirty years. The combination of the personal elements in his writing and his unerring ability to portray a solid realistic world gave to his novels a feeling of immediacy and truthfulness with which his audience could at once identify. Yet, although he was the writer of over a dozen novels, six screenplays, and numerous pieces of journalism, his name will always be associated with his first outstanding success, *Room at the Top* (1957), the book which became a landmark in British writing of the mid-twentieth century and which earned Braine his place as one of the most outspoken "Angry Young Men" of his time.

John Braine was born in Bradford, Yorkshire, in the north of England on 13 April 1922 into a lower-middle-class family. He was always intensely conscious of his background, and it dominated his perceptions of class relations, a recurrent theme of his fiction. At the age of eleven he won a scholarship to the local grammar school, St. Bede's, but he left after five years without taking his final school certificate examinations, and consequently he never went on to a university. This lack of formal education was to determine the tone of his subsequent literary career, which was fiercely anti-intellectual in its thrust. After struggling with a variety of temporary jobs, Braine became more settled when in 1940 he found employment with the public library service in Bingley, a small town close to Bradford, and he was to stay there for the next ten years, apart from a short break for naval service in 1942 and 1943.

He had always had literary ambitions, and in 1951 he decided to leave the north of England and to try his luck in London as a free-lance writer. Disillusionment soon set in. He felt that his regional accent and his attitudes marked him out as unacceptably provincial in a sophisticated metropolitan environment, and although he managed to publish a few left-wing articles in various journals, his initial idealism quickly faded. John Braine never forgot the experience, and the sense of cultural dislocation it produced was to return again and again in the subjects of his novels. Ironically, it was to be this

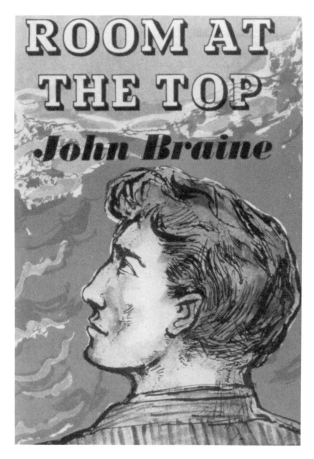

Dust jacket for the first edition of John Braine's first and best-known novel

214

provincialism, the factor to which he had attributed his failure in London, that was ultimately to be the key to his success, and he afterwards regarded it as one of his major achievements that *Room at the Top* put "Northern" novels on the map as serious works of literature.

John Braine returned to the north of England after his mother's death in a road accident in November 1951. Emotionally and physically drained, he was discovered to be once again suffering from tuberculosis—the illness that had caused him to be invalided out of the navy—and had to spend the next eighteen months of his life in a hospital. In later years he was to become one of the most insistently professional of writers, keeping strict office hours and disciplining himself to a rigorous routine, but in the early 1950s John Braine was to discover his métier almost by accident, having virtually given up hope of ever achieving anything in the literary line. It was during his recuperation from his long and debilitating illness, when, bored and lonely in the hospital, he gave vent to his resentment about the way life had treated him, and in allowing release to his frustrations, began work on the novel that was to change both his life and the literary scene in England. On leaving the hospital he got a job as a librarian, married, and in his spare time managed to complete the manuscript he had begun the previous year.

Room at the Top appeared to unanimous popular and critical acclaim, a feat that none of Braine's subsequent novels was ever quite able to duplicate. In the first year it sold 35,000 copies and was serialized in a leading national newspaper, the *Daily Express*, an extraordinary occurrence for a first novel by an unknown writer. It had arrived at a perfect historical moment for a reading public which contained among its ranks the first products of the newly founded welfare state—young men and women who were hungry for a literature that appeared to speak to them directly rather than pander to the avant-garde tastes of a cultivated minority. As Malcolm Bradbury pointed out in *The Twentieth Century Mind*, there seemed at this time to be a whole group of writers, of whom John Braine was one, who were "making over into literary material the new social alterations and new social viewpoints of postwar Britain, often from a lower-middle-class or working-class perspective." *Room at the Top*, together with works by Kingsley Amis, John Osborne, Colin Wilson, and John Wain, seemed to herald a new wave of social realism, articulating a challenge to authority on the part of the young generation.

In telling the story of the rise of the young, aggressive, and upwardly mobile Joe Lampton to what today seems fairly tame bourgeois respectability, John Braine created a myth for his age. His dynamic antihero became regarded as a prototype of the blunt, northern, vigorous male, contemptuous of outmoded establishment values and intent on asserting an individualist ethic that would win him power, money, and sexual satisfaction. Braine approached his subject with a what was then shocking explicitness and imbued his hero with a degree of self-awareness that prevented him from becoming merely a crude stereotype of naked ambition. Joe Lampton *was* the "angry young man," defining his own terms for survival in a world that at first tried to ignore him. Unsophisticated and often inarticulate, Joe, like Braine's subsequent heroes, could see through the hypocrisies and injustices of the privileged world to which he was desperately trying to gain an entrée, and his resulting dilemma of conscience brilliantly encapsulated the current mood of dissatisfaction.

Set in a northern industrial town, a thinly disguised version of Braine's own Bradford, *Room at the Top* offered a realistic gloss on the essentially romantic rags-to-riches scenario that it embodied. Joe Lampton's world was one of brand names, price tags, and easily recognizable artifacts. The materialism of contemporary society was accurately caught and was simultaneously derided and coveted by Braine's hero. Determined to beat the privileged classes at their own game, Joe wins the boss's daughter, displays a remarkable sexual athleticism in the process, and gains the rewards of the capitalist society while recognizing the moral compromise such an achievement costs him. This ironic ambivalence which overshadowed Joe's prowess helped to rescue the novel from banality, but in retrospect *Room at the Top* is still very much a book of its time, and the historical reasons for its contemporary appeal must always form a part of any critical assessment of it.

In 1957, however, it was undeniably exciting. "An extraordinary vitality pulses through *Room at the Top*," noted the *Times Literary Supplement*, responding to Joe Lampton's potent energy, and such appreciation was widespread. The novel was picked out by Kenneth Allsopp in his review of the decade for its compelling mixture of fantasy and realism, for "no-one until John Braine has described the exact kind of urges operating within the post-war specimen." It was both powerful and easy to read. Braine's gifts as a storyteller gained full expression, and it is as a storyteller that he later said he wanted to be remembered. In the public imagination of 1957 Braine himself became indistinguishable from the character he had created and, together with other young writers of his generation, seemed to personify the spirit of rebellious youth currently permeating British institutions. Yet the book had worked a crucial change in him. It was as if, with the publication of his novel, he felt that he now had a license to speak on behalf of the dissident— but up to now largely silent—majority, and he reveled in the publicity that followed in the aftermath of *Room at the Top*'s success, as well as in the financial rewards which allowed him to pursue the career he had always longed for, that of full-time writer.

Braine always wanted to demystify the literary process, to remove from it any sense of elitist experiment, and most of his novels that followed *Room at the Top* relied on the same formulae that had worked so well in that first book. Despite his stance of rebelliousness, John Braine was deeply traditional. His books constantly promoted family stability, security, and links with past values. Similarly his fictional methods revealed his strong debt to the classic realist approach of nineteenth-century English writing. His novels were distinguished by their clear narrative direction and well-defined plot structures. Braine's forte was accurate social observation and uncompromising satiric commentary, and he was a perceptive recorder of his age. He felt strongly that literature should be accessible to all, not a refined specialist interest, and although his political views were to change drastically, this was the artistic credo that was to guide him throughout his life. When *Room at the Top* (and later *Life at the Top*) was made into a highly successful film in 1958, Braine's audience extended even further, and the television series *Man at the Top* (1970 and 1972), based on his work, made him a household name. Such widespread popularity was in some ways critically damaging, for the dramatized versions of his work lacked the moral subtleties and the careful craftsmanship of his novels; and his work, somewhat unfairly, became associated in the public mind with an undiscriminating taste.

His second novel, *The Vodi* (1959; published as *From the Hand of the Hunter* in America), again drew on Braine's own experience of injustice, set in another environment he knew only too well, a tuberculosis hospital. Once again he presented a hero who was struggling to survive, but whose concept of what constituted success was more sensitively probed than in the portrayal of Joe Lampton. The book lacked the dynamism of *Room at the Top*, and its disappointing reception stimulated Braine

to produce a sequel to his first novel. *Life at the Top* appeared in 1962 and featured a more subdued Joe Lampton, reaping the sour harvest of his newly acquired prosperity and power. In the stark opposition the book presented between the crass commercialism of the bourgeoisie and the world of working-class simplicity that Joe had left behind, there was revealed, more sharply than in his earlier works, the sentimental streak that was always at the heart of Braine's writing. In *Life at the Top* working-class values were required to shoulder the burden of the lost innocence and personal integrity that Joe Lampton had forfeited in exchange for worldly success. The force of the argument was somewhat reduced by its oversimplified presentation, but the novel provided a devastating exposé of contemporary mores, a picture of a Britain trapped by its reliance on the current political manifesto of "you've never had it so good"; and it was recognized as being a pertinent reflection of its time.

His next novel, *The Jealous God* (1964), treated a subject that was new to John Braine, the issue of Catholicism. Braine had inherited his religion from his Irish-Catholic mother, and the attendant problems of conscience it produced permeated his work, although *The Jealous God* was the only one to confront these in their explicitly theological dimension. "I'm always aware," Braine had said, "that at the centre of things there's a mystery. Religion is the acknowledgement of this mystery." In the story of the naive Vincent Dungarvin, who has leanings toward the Catholic priesthood but who falls in love with a Protestant divorcée, Braine tried to communicate something of this "mystery" and the tensions it could create in one attempting to live in the modern world. The contrast between spiritual asceticism and sexual urges formed the main source of conflict in the novel, but its real achievement was in Braine's acutely felt portrayal of the repressive environment in which he placed his hero. "The story moves dramatically and fast against a closely observed scene of depressing materialism," said the reviewer in the *Times Literary Supplement*, but as Anthony Burgess recognized in *The Novel Now* (1967), "his hero's ambitions are spiritual, not material. Inevitably such a theme is less popular than that of the fleshly rat-race."

Indeed, after the initial sensation produced by *Room at the Top*, the critics were not, in general, kind to John Braine. "There is absolutely no selection in his work," remarked the *Spectator* of *Stay with me Till Morning* (1970). "Braine puts his words together solidly, bluntly, with no charm and precious little distinction," commented the *New States-*

Dust jacket for the first edition of Braine's sequel to his first novel

man in the same year. An article, "The Boy from Bingley," assessing Braine's work in 1975, concluded that "he is an innocent." Ironically, these were comments that Braine himself would have welcomed. Defiantly anti-intellectual, he consistently maintained his pose of artistic naïveté in a literary world that he felt was becoming increasingly elitist and alienated from popular concerns. "The people who write the reviews of my books are not the people whom I particularly want to read them," he once said, "and therefore I'm not interested in what they think." As for scholarly articles, he had nothing but contempt for their tone and views, refusing to recognize himself or his work in the detached analytic approach they adopted. He despised academic criticism, seeing it as a sterile discipline removed from the genuine responses of what he felt was his true readership, the mass market. Yet he knew that to write artlessly required art: that one had to "have read a great deal and to have thought a great deal about prose," as he put it. He believed that the ideal background for a writer was to be an ordinary working journalist, one "who goes round the police courts, sees accidents and the seamy side of life, and sees human beings under pressure," and he was unhappy about the direction of con-

temporary fiction with its emphasis toward academia.

Like several other of the so-called "angry" writers of the 1950s, John Braine's political opinions underwent a dramatic reversal. He moved from his stance as a Socialist, committed to the view that he expressed in an article for the *Daily Worker* in 1960 that the "main hope for peace lies with the Labour and trade union movement," to ally himself wholeheartedly with the right wing of the Conservative party. This political *volte face* coincided with his move from the north to the south of England in 1966, when he settled with his wife and family in the prosperous stockbroker belt area of Surrey. During this period his novels bore evidence of his changing views. Both *The Crying Game* (1968) and *Stay with me Till Morning* (1970) mounted an attack on liberal values. Artistically they are disappointing novels, failing to develop the potential of Braine's earlier work. Perhaps even more disappointing to Braine's admirers was the apparently undiscriminating manner in which they struck at their targets of the permissive society, the liberal press, the untidy appearance, and bad manners of the younger generation.

But John Braine had not forgotten his origins, and he returned to explore them in his next novel, *The Queen of a Distant Country* (1972). Although he protested that the book was not autobiographical, it dealt centrally with the development of a writer who, successful in middle-age, goes back to the town of his youth to meet again the woman who had been such a startling influence on him. Braine himself said that he needed to move south in order to see the North properly, and certainly *The Queen of a Distant Country* communicates a more detached perspective than his earlier books. It is mostly remarkable for the opportunity it gave Braine to present in fictional form his own artistic beliefs, for above all it offers a telling, if unsophisticated defense of literary realism. The novel was applauded. "John Braine has produced a novel of real unforced style and feeling," said the *Times Literary Supplement*, although not all reviews were complimentary; the *New York Times* for one felt that "Mr. Braine was better when he was an Angry Young Man." Yet John Braine was able to project his ideas most convincingly in imaginative form. He acknowledged that fiction was what he was best at, and when he tried to propose an intellectual argument without the protective fictional covering—as he did in *Writing a Novel* (1974)—he was lost.

Despite his advice to aspiring artists, John Braine firmly believed that writing was a craft impossible to teach to others. During his stay as visiting writer at Purdue University he found his students exhausting in their eagerness for instruction. "People can only teach themselves to be writers," he concluded. "There is no other way. All you need to learn how to write is a pen and paper." The authors he himself most admired were those whose styles lacked any trace of self-consciousness. Although his roots were English, Braine was profoundly influenced by American writing. John O'Hara was an author he greatly admired. Mark Twain was another. *Huckleberry Finn* was a book he could read again and again. For him this represented prose writing at its peak: "perfect because it's not trying to be literary—it's just a human voice talking, and that's what I aim at—the sound of the human voice."

It was this sound of the human voice that determined the shape of *Waiting for Sheila* (1976), based on the recollections of a middle-aged man. Waiting for his wife to return from an adulterous liaison, the hero recalls traumatic incidents in his sexual past which have made him impotent and his marriage a travesty. A psychological study, in the style of *The Vodi*, the book treated its subject with a sensitivity which had been missing from Braine's

more sensational 1960s novels, and although critics still tended to underrate his abilities, it did receive some notice. "The prose occasionally rises to wonderful heights," commented the *Listener*, recognizing Braine's gift of being able to "conjure a scene and an atmosphere from the smallest of effects."

Once he had become a professional writer, John Braine could not afford the luxury of waiting for artistic inspiration to strike. The need to earn a comfortable living made him accept commissions that were often outside his range. His two spy stories, *The Pious Agent* (1975) and *Finger of Fire* (1977), were written, as he frankly acknowledged, for profit. The biography of the Yorkshire writer J. B. Priestley (1979) was undertaken because, as he confessed, "I never turn any offer down." Yet he could write with genuine feeling about Priestley, while conscious that he would rather write about himself than about another, however interesting and celebrated a personality.

So it was that his last two novels, *One and Last Love* (1981) and *These Golden Days* (1985), were admittedly more openly autobiographical than anything that had gone before. Adopting the persona of Tim Harnforth, Braine drew a thinly veiled self-portrait in this middle-aged northern writer who had moved to Surrey and become involved in a blissful love affair, finding ultimate happiness in Hampstead, Braine's own final home. The realism, the precision, and the honesty of presentation in these last two books carried all the conviction of his first. John Braine was aware that time for him was running out, and although in the past he had always felt the need to measure out his experience, to be economical with his material, as he put it, he now wanted, nearly thirty years after *Room at the Top*, to let himself go.

John Braine died on 28 October 1986. He was one of the most widely read authors in Britain, among the twenty who received the maximum annual £5,000 Public Lending Right share, based on the demands of library borrowers—a fact that gave the ex-librarian much pleasure. As a writer he was totally without pretentiousness. His interest in human beings and his belief in the value of personal relations remained a dominant feature of his work, and his ability to communicate the power of feeling never faltered. He retained his deep sense of commitment and his "anger" about injustice, and in his last years he was quite capable of becoming just as impassioned as when he was young. His primary aim in art was to tell the truth about what he knew, and in this he succeeded consummately.

A TRIBUTE

from STAN BARSTOW

It is hard now to convey the importance of John Braine's first novel, *Room at the Top,* for a generation of writers from the north of England; not because it in any way showed the best of his contemporaries how or what to write, but because its huge success in the discouraging literary climate of the 1950s confirmed each in his determination to use as the basis of his art the regional working-class life he knew from the inside, which at the time was far from being the fashionable mine of material it later became. Publishers didn't want to know. Three of them, it turned out, had not wanted to know about *Room at the Top.* The fourth thought differently.

Braine's kindness to me when I first met him, in the summer of 1957, is a part of my personal history. He remained a kindly man, given to generous impulse; a nicer man than most of his characters.

A TRIBUTE

from WILLIAM COOPER

I write briefly yet with fervour in praise of John Braine. He was one of the most generous of writers and of men. After thirty years his first novel, *Room at the Top,* is established as a classic of its period. I write with especial fervour about his generosity as a writer because I am a beneficiary of it: he frequently observed, both in speech and in writing, that he would not have written *Room at the Top* as he did without the example of my own novel, *Scenes From Provincial Life,* before him. He was a good man, and in his last novel, *These Golden Days,* he achieved an unselfconscious mode of self-revelation, both original and appealing, that I greatly value and admire.

John Ciardi

(24 June 1916-30 March 1986)

Miller Williams
University of Arkansas Press

See also the Ciardi entry in *DLB 5: American Poets Since World War Two.*

When John Ciardi died suddenly on Easter Sunday in 1986, a few weeks before his seventieth birthday, he left a library shelf of published work, crates of unpublished manuscripts, and a curiously unsettled place in the world of letters.

Few poets in our time, if any, have had so public a presence or made so much of it. He was on the staff of the Bread Loaf Writers' Conference for a quarter of a century and its director for fifteen years; poetry editor of *Saturday Review* and author of its weekly "Manner of Speaking" column for seventeen years when that magazine represented all that was best in literature, the arts, and opinion; host in 1961 and 1962 of the CBS series *Accent,* where he was a peripatetic interviewer of writers, painters, philosophers, and other men and women of interest to an audience who surely subscribed to *Saturday Review;* and one of the best voices ever on the poetry and lecture circuit.

A man of intensely held beliefs, he was fiercely committed to the principles that art in general—poetry in particular—is a function primarily of an imagination informed by intellect and only secondarily of the sentimental faculties and that skill is the midwife of beauty and is hard earned. An almost compulsive honesty made it impossible for John Ciardi to soften the expression of this commitment in public or private discourse. His dissent, in *Saturday Review,* from the national clamor over the poetry of Anne Morrow Lindbergh brought in the largest and longest-lasting avalanche of letters in the magazine's (possibly any magazine's) history. His open contempt for what he saw as increasingly popular romantic assumptions that, fed by the proper politics and a mystical faith, ignorance naturally gives rise to good poetry and that all people are equal in the arts, and so all art is at heart equal, precipitated the end of his tenure as director of the Bread Loaf Writers' Conference. His candid responses from the platform to questions about the work of his contemporaries undoubtedly resulted in more than a little rancor. His careful, pointed critiques of poems presented in workshops left many a head both bloodied and bowed. The fact that he parlayed his talents as a poet, an essayist, a reader of his poems, a lecturer, an editor, an administrator, and a shrewd investor into a considerable accumulation of this world's goods caused some poets and readers—not a few, I think—to feel that somehow he was therefore less a poet. Among the damage done by his free-swinging ways should probably be counted the two decades without one review of his work in the *New York Times*. For whatever reason, his work was denied much critical attention during the last couple of decades, from about the time—say, 1966—when an adversarial relationship began to be felt and verbalized between two camps, symbolized to some by the names and attitudes of Robert Frost and Charles Olson, to others by poetry clothed and poetry naked, or poetry cooked and poetry raw.

Through it all, countless children read their way into adolescence through his extremely successful books of juvenile verse; went on to learn about grown-up poetry from his widely adopted text, *How Does a Poem Mean?;* as older students, pored over his ingenious translation of Dante's *Divine Comedy;* later drove to work or home listening on some NPR station to the richly textured, deep, assuring voice, "Hello again. This is John Ciardi with a word in your ear . . . ," followed by a brief but dazzling pursuit of a word's hidden roots. These were a large and faithful audience. Many of them knew little of the man's poems, apart from what he called his kinderwork, or that beside the poems he considered everything else only diversion—marvelous diversions though they were (at his death he was awaiting publication of the third *Browser's Dictionary*, the first two of which had established him as a brilliant and impious lexicographer).

So what can be said of the poems? What, especially, can be said by the writer of this piece, Ciardi's coauthor on the second edition of *How Does A Poem Mean?*, author of *The Achievement of John Ciardi*, and his friend for thirty years? If I had been his friend for two years, I might have been likely to see his work through a mist; a perspective of thirty years invites a matter-of-factness that serves truth and the reputation equally.

John Ciardi published sixteen volumes of poetry for adults. Some of his best work is in the final book, *The Birds of Pompeii,* finished in the last year of his life. He was one of the few poets in any time to invent a clearly defined and intricate form. The last poem he finished, "A Trenta-Sei on The Pleasure We Take In The Early Death of Keats," was set in an admirably complex, lyrical, and thoroughly delightful form never before devised. It has already been used by at least two other poets and appeared in national journals; it has the balanced qualities of charm and difficulty that may well make it—the trenta-sei—a standard pattern for poets, like the sestina and the villanelle. Because the posthumous volume in which the poem will appear is not scheduled to be published for some time, and it is the final poem penned by John Ciardi, it may be appropriate to set it down even—or especially—in a reference work as this, noting in passing that "psilanthropic," a typically playful invention of Ciardi's, gives us "merely human" from the Greek *psilos* (mere) and, of course, *anthropos.*

A TRENTA-SEI OF THE PLEASURE WE TAKE IN THE EARLY DEATH OF KEATS

It is old school custom to pretend to be sad
when we think about the early death of Keats.
The species-truth of the matter is we are glad.
Psilanthropic among exegetes,
I am so moved that when the plate comes by
I almost think to pay the God—but why?

When we think about the early death of Keats
we are glad to be spared the bother of dying ourselves.
His poems are a candy store of bitter-sweets.
We munch whole flights of angels from his shelves
drooling a sticky glut, almost enough
to sicken us. But what delicious stuff!

The species-truth of the matter is we are glad
to have a death to munch on. Truth to tell,
we are also glad to pretend it makes us sad.
When it comes to dying, Keats did it so well
we thrill to the performance. Safely here,
this side of the fallen curtain, we stand and cheer.

Psilanthropic among exegetes,
as once in a miles-high turret spitting flame,
I watched boys flower through orange winding sheets
and shammed a mourning because it put a name
to a death I might have taken—which in a way
made me immortal for another day.

I was so moved that when the plate came by
I had my dollar in hand to give to death

John Ciardi at West Point, circa 1978

but changed to a penny—enough for the old guy,
and almost enough saved to sweeten my breath
with a toast I will pledge to the Ape of the Divine
in thanks for every death that spares me mine.

I almost thought of paying the God—but why?
Had the boy lived, he might have grown as dull
as Tennyson. Far better, I say, to die
and leave us a formed feeling. O beautiful,
pale, dying poet, fading as soft as rhyme,
the saddest music keeps the sweetest time.

When a writer is living, we tend to make judgments of the work addressed to some imaginary mean: How good is this poet on the whole? What grade does all this work earn, on the average? By this measure, MacLeish, Robinson, and Tennyson would certainly be ranked much lower than they are. When a writer is dead, we are inclined to look at the best the writer has done and forget what fails to keep our interest engaged. It is, in fact, the good men do that lives after them, and it ought to be so. We say, "What has this poet given us that we are glad to have?" So we gladly live with such masterpieces as MacLeish's "Not Marble Nor the Gilded

Monuments," Robinson's "Mr. Flood's Party," and Tennyson's "Ulysses."

What may not hold our interest well, in the poetry of John Ciardi, are some of the poems in a body of work perhaps best called suburban, in which the poet deals autobiographically with his family, money matters, and crabgrass. All poets write such poems, I suppose, or wander into paths which for the given poet amount to the same thing. Most poets throw those poems away, or let them gather dust and crumble away. Ciardi published what he finished, what seemed to him right at the time, and left it for the anonymous jury of readers to decide what poem was a victory and what poem was not, and deal with him as they will.

All writers, in the years after they die, suffer a change upward or downward in their reputations. For some, like Donne, Blake, and Whitman, the change may come many years after death. For some—Blake and Whitman, for instance—there may be changes over time in both directions. No one can know, but only believe, what the fortunes of any writer's name will be; I do believe that John Ciardi will be among those whose best work, as it rises to the top of the readers' minds, will both

221

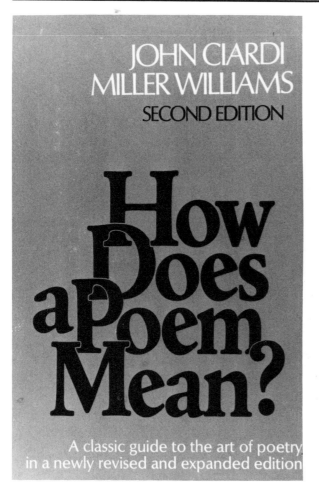

Dust jacket of Ciardi's influential textbook

enhance the already luminous name and focus attention on the poetry, where he greatly wanted it to be focused.

So what has he given us that we are glad to have? If one asks that a reputation rest on certain poems, one ought to be obliged to name some of them. They are small poems, most of them, able to fit on a page, but they enlarged our vision of who we are and enriched the voice by which future readers will know our generations. I think of "Washing Your Feet," a strangely touching piece of blank verse in which each line has a life of its own; "Talking Myself to Sleep at One More Hilton," an *apologia pro vita sua* that is honest, painful, and lovely; "The Evil Eye," the story of a poet's beginning that any poet must envy; "On a Photo of Sgt. Ciardi A Year Later," a verse that stands with the most excellent poems from any time about men at war; "Tree Trimming" ("I could weep by slow waters for my son/who has no history, no

name/he knows long, no ritual from which he came,/and no fathers but the forgotten."); "Men Marry What They Need" and "Most Like An Arch This Marriage," certainly two of the finest poems ever written about the married state—I am tempted to say that there are none finer.

These are a few of many. Among them are some that will be read long after all eyes reading this have closed. That is one of the ways we measure—given that saying this in the poet's own time leaves something to be desired in the way of perspective.

Then let it be a confession of faith, but not one born of friendship; he would not have abided that. It is a faith in the poems themselves.

The friendship, knowing the man, was for those who knew him a mind-altering experience. All those I know who knew John Ciardi will divide their days into those before and those after they met him. He was a blustery man, charming, old-world in many ways, harrumphing, kidding, questioning, praising, criticizing, loving, with a voice none could interrupt nor wanted to and a memory that mocked encyclopedias; impatient with cant and pretense, embarrassed to say love within touching distance, thinking always of connections, origins, implications, and possibilities; vulnerable and generous, opinionated, and as honest as a human is allowed to be.

An anecdote: In a conversation about everything a number of years ago Ciardi said to Isaac Asimov, Sprague de Camp, and Fletcher Pratt, dear friends whose minds and writings he much admired, that science fiction had yet to come into its own as a literary form, that it was a mechanical contrivance with no characterization to speak of or character development and that without characters there is no real story, hence no real literature—and, further, that any intelligent person, with the pattern in hand, could write a publishable science fiction story overnight. Fletcher Pratt turned his words back to him as a challenge and laid money on it. That night the story was written. It began:

> Jarvis held the object cupped in his hand
> while his thumb stroked the small hollow in
> its polished side. "It's really the prize of my
> collection," he said, "but there isn't any real
> name for it. I call it the hypnoglyph."

A short while later the story appeared under the name John Anthony in an anthology called *A Decade of Fantasy and Science Fiction* and subtitled

Out of This World Masterworks by Masterminds of the Near and the Far Out.

There was a poet; there was a man. There was a translator, a writer of children's books, a limericist, an essayist, a critic, an editor, a lexicographer, an anthologist, a textbook author, a host of a television cultural series, a radio commentator on words and the ghosts that move inside them, and the author of a single science fiction story by one of the masterminds. They are all gone now. What remains is what John Ciardi put on paper, and that is what the world has to judge him by. If we are to judge him on his own terms, we will pay most attention to his poetry, for a poet is what he meant to be first, and what he was.

He said at the last that it didn't matter to him how he was judged. "I have outlived ambition," he said. If ambition for prizes and praise from strangers died within him, it was because he didn't let it feed upon him and it starved. He tells us this in one of his late poems:

There comes a season for saying only what's possible.
I ask nothing but to say it right, if I can.

A TRIBUTE

from ISAAC ASIMOV

I met John Ciardi in 1950. He was slim then, craggy-faced, fearsomely outspoken and intelligent, a master storyteller. He was also a great poet, but I thought he had an unfair advantage there. He had a bass-baritone voice that poured out like warm, thick, sweet honey. It seemed to me that when he read his poems with that voice, they *had* to sound wonderful. What if *I* had written those poems and had read them with *my* voice.—Well, maybe they would still have been great.

A TRIBUTE

from X. J. KENNEDY

Let me offer a brief assessment of what John Ciardi has left us with. First, he wrote a hatful of good poems, some of them excellent, including the strong and sustained long autobiographical poem *Lives of X.*

Second, he made Dante vivid, intelligible, and enjoyable to writers and readers of my generation and the generation after it. I have not seen any subsequent translator of the *Divine Comedy* catch so much of the force of the original, nor so much of its music.

Another thing: John Ciardi started writing poetry for children when children's poetry was the prerogative of elderly retired schoolmarms chucking kids under their chins. He brought to it the same bluntness and intelligence that he brought to everything else. Practically singlehandedly, he changed the whole character of American poetry for children, and made it possible for many later writers to take the stuff seriously.

Then, too, Ciardi mastered the informal essay and raised many of his regular columns to the level of literature.

Still another feat: Ciardi put together the most valuable record of American poetry immediately following World War II—the annotated anthology *Mid-Century American Poets* (New York: Twayne, 1950). For me, it remains one of the most revealing anthologies of poetry criticism ever assembled.

Ciardi did a great deal to make his countrymen care about the English language. Besides his services as broadcaster and telecaster, he was a tough and generous teacher, the author of a memorable textbook, a lecturer of wide influence, a fine practical critic, a good poetry editor, a master of the limerick, a wonderful writer about words.

It is no small feat to stick around for nearly half a century as a hardworking, honest poet, faithful to the uncharitable Muse, as a critic unafraid to speak his mind. All this is part of John Ciardi's legacy. We will be collecting the interest on it for a long time.

A TRIBUTE

from LEWIS TURCO

When the news of John's death arrived during the spring of 1986, many of his friends and colleagues were preparing our contributions to a John Ciardi Festschrift volume. Now, in the summer and fall of the year, we are involved in turning these materials into a John Ciardi memorial. It is difficult to bear.

John was a poet, and it was through our common love for poetry that he and I maintained our fellowship and our correspondence for a quarter-century. My instinct, then, is to turn to poetry to express my feelings about him, and to sing my farewell:

DELAY

*In memory of John Ciardi, from lines
in Emily Dickinson's letters.*

I have tried to delay the frosts,
I have coaxed the fading flowers,
I thought I would detain a few
    of the crimson leaves,

but their companions call them—they
cannot stay away. You will find
blue hills with autumnal shadows
    silently sleeping

on them: there will be a glory
lingering round the day. You will know
Autumn has come and gone his way
    through the acorn wood

wrapping his faded cloak about him.

A TRIBUTE

from JOHN UPDIKE

I didn't know John Ciardi well but liked what I knew. Once I was on a commencement stage behind him as he boomed out the address—indeed, for a time it was hard to be in a college auditorium in June without hearing from the tirelessly speechifying Ciardi. Then, at Winchester Country Club, where he had once caddied, we played in a foursome. His game was very rusty, and he had a substantial corporation to maneuver his swing around, but he got a par on one hole by the following vivid method: bad drive, bad second shot, skulled third shot that squarely hit the flagstick as it was trying to rocket across the green, and a nicely executed putt of the twelve-inch distance that remained. Another moment I recall is when, during the Vietnam strife, Lewis Mumford seized the stage of the American Academy and Institute of Arts and Letters with an attack upon the United States and all its works, Ciardi from one of the rows behind him, let out a solid, patriotic "Boo!" His translation of Dante is lovely, and he was the most robust poet I've ever known.

Jean Genet

(19 December 1910-15 April 1986)

Wallace Fowlie
Duke University

Jean Genet's death was announced in the *New York Times*, 16 April 1986. He had died alone the day before in the Paris hotel where he had lived several years. He was seventy-five. A representative from his French publisher, Gallimard, reported that he had been suffering from throat cancer and had been undergoing radiation treatment.

Genet was a private person. His cell-like hotel room had been his home. His possessions were contained in one small suitcase. His mail was delivered, not to his hotel—that address was never given out—but to Gallimard in Paris and to his American publisher, Grove Press, in New York. There were no survivors. Today his books remain, along with a set of striking photographs taken by Henri Cartier-Bresson.

In April 1986, six years after Jean-Paul Sartre's death, Simone de Beauvoir died at seventy-eight of a lung disease. The next day Jean Genet died of throat cancer. The premier ministre of France, Jacques Chirac, called these deaths "the end of an era."

In Simone de Beauvoir's book of conversations with Sartre, she records that after the war the two men with whom Sartre had really cordial bonds were Alberto Giacometti and Jean Genet. Sartre, the controversial philosopher, and Simone de Beauvoir, the controversial feminist, met the controversial criminal and novelist Jean Genet for the first time at the Flore (the café in Saint-Germain-des-Prés). Sartre and Beauvoir had already read Genet's first novel, *Notre-Dame des Fleurs* (1943), and had liked it. "Our conversation was most agreeable," Sartre said. "This was at the end of the war, 1943 or 1944."

Genet asked Sartre for a preface to one of his books. The preface turned into the long book *Saint Genet, comédien et martyr* (1952; translated as *Saint Genet* in 1963 without the subtitle "actor and martyr"). Genet's feelings about the book were mixed. He claimed the things Sartre said were true, but he was irked by it. It may have created a writer's block in Genet, who wrote nothing for the next few years.

Jean Genet (photo ©Jerry Bauer)

Toward the end of the book of conversations, the two friends speak of the theme of freedom in Sartre's writings, and again Sartre refers to Genet and the transformation that took place in him which was "the work of freedom." He calls it "the metamorphosis of Jean Genet, the unhappy homosexual child, into Jean Genet the great writer, and if not happy, then at least sure of himself."

In the 1940s and 1950s Genet's books were clandestine publications. The general story of his life was publicly discussed, and since then has been enriched with all the variations of a legend. His plays are still being performed in the professional and university theaters of several countries. The importance of his art has won him an official widespread recognition justifying the predictions in the 1940s of such prophets as Jean Paulhan, Jean Cocteau, Jean-Paul Sartre, Jouhandeau, Picasso, and even François Mauriac.

These men, with varying degrees of moral reservation, proclaimed Genet's exceptional gifts as a writer at a time when his works were sold in expensive limited editions to a very small public. During the 1950s the Gallimard edition of some of his books appeared, and translations into English of these books were made by the late Bernard Frechtman.

The world of his books is an underworld or a counterworld, which reveals a consistent development of his personal life. He was born 19 December 1910. His unwed mother abandoned him and he was raised as a foundling (*pupille de la nation*). The theme of the humiliated mother as it appears especially in Genet's last play, *Les Paravents* (1961; translated as *The Screens*, 1962), is drawn from his personal drama. At the age of twenty-one, he asked the Administration for the name of his parents. He was informed that he was born at 22, rue d'Assas in Paris. When he went to that address (a street between the Luxembourg Garden and the Observatoire), he found it to be a maternity center of L'Assistance Publique. His mother's name was Gabrielle Genet. As a baby he was given over to a peasant family in Le Morvan, a poor region in central France. He was a well-behaved boy, an altar boy in the church, and a good pupil. There exists a photograph of Jean at the time of his first communion.

He was ten when he was accused of a petty theft. He decided at that time to become a real thief and thus deserve the name attached to him. "I repudiated a world that had repudiated me," is a statement he made about this early event in his life.

Throughout his adolescence he passed from one reformatory to another: Mettray, Fontevrault, Fresnes. These were the sites for young Genet which Combourg was for Chateaubriand, and Balbec for Proust. He escaped at twenty-one and joined the French Foreign Legion, which he subsequently deserted. For ten years he led a nomadic and criminal life in Europe, expelled from five countries on various counts. He sold saccharine illegally in Yugoslavia, stole cattle in Albania, was a pickpocket in Venice, created an early system of black marketing in Berlin. Highways of Poland, the harbors of Anvers, Marseilles, and Brest were stages and halts in his itinerary. Between 1937 and 1943 he was sentenced thirteen times, of which eight were for the theft of books, first editions of Rimbaud and Léon Bloy.

In prison in 1942, Genet wrote the poem "Condamné à mort." This elegy of 260 alexandrine lines was dedicated to his friend Maurice Pilorge,

who had been executed in 1939 in Saint-Brieuc. The text was printed at the time of the German occupation of Paris, without a publisher's name. It was passed around from hand to hand. When Cocteau read the poem, he immediately intervened in order to bring about Genet's liberation. A letter written to the prefect of police in Paris by Henri Mondor, the famous surgeon and biographer of Mallarmé, was instrumental in expediting the release. The letter pleaded that all obstacles which might impede the development of Genet's poetic genius should be removed.

He was accused again of theft in 1948. A petition for his release was signed by Sartre, Cocteau, Gide, and Claudel. Because of the number of times he had been imprisoned, he could have been committed to a penal colony for life, according to French law. The president of France, Vincent Auriol, signed the necessary paper for the writer's release.

In the prison of Fresnes, Genet wrote his first novel, *Notre-Dame des Fleurs*. It was confiscated and destroyed. He began it again. It was published in a limited edition in 1943 and appeared in English in 1949. This novel, called by Genet "an epic of masturbation," was the real genesis of his career.

The harshest terms which the world has used in its indictment of Genet—thief, traitor, homosexual—are used by himself in his own writing as his principal themes, as the subject matter of his novels and plays. He began writing in prison with the avowed purpose of composing a new moral order which would be his. His plan was to discover and construct a moral order that would explain and allow his mode of life.

All of his early commentators spoke, with considerable wonderment, of two matters in particular: the unusual boldness of Genet's themes, and the ease with which this writer, from the very start, wrote in a style and with a profundity of thought which placed him in the category of "great writers." To reach, with so little preparation (he was taken from school at ten), the highest rank in literary art, was almost as shocking to the first readers of Genet as his obvious determination to glorify evil as it appears in those forms which are the most rigorously castigated by society. The question still remains unanswered. Who taught this boy, as he moved from cell to cell, how to compose the sumptuous cadences of his prose?

Genet celebrated those particular manifestations of evil which he knew personally. His books are blatantly or indirectly autobiographical. The central drama is the struggle between the man in authority and the young man to whom he is attracted. The psychological varieties of this struggle are many. Each of the novels and each of the plays is a different world in which the same drama unfolds. *Querelle de Brest* (1953) is the ship: naval officers and sailors. *Pompes Funèbres* (1948) is the Occupation: Nazi officers and young Frenchmen of the capital. *Notre-Dame des Fleurs* is Montmartre, with its world of male prostitutes and pimps. *Miracle de la Rose* (1946) is the prison, with its notorious convicts and their slaves.

The play *Haute Surveillance* (1949; translated as *Deathwatch*, 1954) is also the prison cell with its intricate hierarchy of criminals where those standing under the death sentence exert the greatest power and prestige over those with lesser sentences. *Les Bonnes* (1947; translated as *The Maids*, 1954) is the household, where in the absence of the mistress, one of the maids plays her part. *Les Nègres* (1958) is the world of colonialism: the conflicts between whites and blacks. The oppression from which the blacks of Genet suffer is so hostile, so incomprehensible, as to be easily the oppression of mankind. The hostility which Genet persistently celebrates throughout all of his work, in his opulent language, is the strangely distorted love joining the saint and the criminal, the guard and the prisoner, the policeman and the thief, the master and the slave, the white and the black.

The action of his first play, *Haute Surveillance*, takes place in a prison cell where a very precise and powerful hierarchy of seductiveness exists between three young men. Yeux-Verts (also called Paolo les dents fleuries) is the murderer of a girl. He expects that in two months' time, he will be guillotined. He loses himself in admiration over the magnitude of his own condemnation and fate. He is the *maudit*, but without the romantic halo of rebel and apostle. He is the exalted criminal. By his prestige he dominates a second prisoner, who in his turn dominates a third prisoner, a mere thief.

The heroes of *Haute Surveillance* walk back and forth in their cell and provide a picture of their obsessions. Genet does not move outside of the world of the damned and gives to it the inverted vocation of evil. In the uniform structure of *Haute Surveillance* and *Les Bonnes*, the important male figure is absent: the husband of the house in *Les Bonnes*, and the black criminal, Boule-de-neige, who obsesses the minds of all three prisoners, in the prison play.

There are three visible actors in each play. One of the actors, Madame in *Les Bonnes* and Yeux-Verts, the head criminal in *Haute Surveillance*, serves as an intermediary between the absent actor and the couple: the two maids in *Les Bonnes* and the other two prisoners, Maurice and Lefranc, in *Haute Surveillance*. Genet calls this couple the eternal marriage between the criminal and the saint: "*le couple éternel du criminel et de la sainte*" (*Les Bonnes*).

The hallucinatory beauty with which Jean Genet expressed his system of morality and his philosophy of evil increases the difficulty of defining his tradition. He is the arch romantic, far more the artist than the philosopher. His nature was essentially religious. His was also a nature of extreme passivity. He was the opposite of the revolutionist and the reformer. He was the man living just outside of the normally constituted society. He had no desire to play a part in society, and especially no desire to mount in society, to triumph over it.

The society into which Genet was born, with its laws and institutions, is dominated by the male. This is the kind of society that instinctively will tend to exclude Genet and to crush him. The virile types he exalts are traitors and criminals. At an early age "evil" became synonymous with "virility." (*Mal* and *mâle* have the same sound in French.) Between the ages of sixteen and thirty, he sought in his reformatories and prisons and bars not a series of transitory adventures, but a way of identifying himself with the individuals he met there and whom he admired. Every night the intricate ceremonial of search, far more cerebral than physical, would be performed, until the inevitable failure became part of the ceremonial.

The myth of Arthur Rimbaud, as formulated by his critics and biographers, and exhaustively studied by Etiemble, made the poet into either a supernatural being, god or demon, or into the type of intractable convict. Etiemble believes that this myth, so variously interpreted in the 1930s and 1940s, has today split into four other myths which our contemporary world is trying to understand and explain: the myths of Federico Lorca, T. E. Lawrence, Antonin Artaud, and Jean Genet.

For the formulation of his "myth" Genet had the good fortune to attract the attention of one of the most forceful thinkers of our day, Jean-Paul Sartre. In his 600-page *Saint Genet*, the philosopher elaborately analyzes his belief that Jean Genet incarnated existentialist freedom.

The life story of Genet is cited by Sartre as a case history. He reduces the story to a few words. As a baby, he was abandoned by his mother and raised in a peasant home. He committed a theft and was sent to a reformatory. He escaped and lived by begging, stealing, and by prostitution. In other words, he gave himself over to what the world calls crime and evil. Then he turned to writing and in rapid succession produced books that are apologies of evil and that could not be printed and sold in the usual way. But the time came when his books were permitted, when his plays were produced, and when he reached the status of a recognized writer of importance.

Sartre's thesis becomes clear when he points out that after society determined meticulously and repeatedly what Jean Genet was, after his "case" had been defined and publicized, this criminal became something else. He became a writer and a poet, and hence, according to Sartrian terms, practiced his freedom, chose his life, and defined himself.

This experience of Genet is the basis of Sartre's long investigation into the problem of evil. He does not conceal the shocking elements in the writings of Genet. He uses them in a purely philosophical way in order to describe the human anguish of this man. Sartre never forgets that the subject of his study is a man ostracized from society. He finds in Genet's revindication of evil the only form of dignity vouchsafed to him.

The concept of sovereignty obsessed the imagination of Genet. Sartre believed that Genet chose evil because that was the realm in which he could hope to reach a status of sovereignty. In *Miracle de la Rose*, in those passages where the character Harcamone is meditating in his cell, the ideal of sovereignty is ascribed to the assassin who is about to be executed. The state of evil is the reverse of the state of holiness. Genet plays on the two words because he finds them similar in the sense that the extremes of both are forbidden to an ordinary man, and that both are characterized by danger and violence.

In discussing his sympathy for Genet, Sartre made very clear his conviction that evil is a myth created by the respectable members of society. They tend to call Genet wicked and to use him as a scapegoat who committed the acts which they have been tempted to commit and which they may or may not have committed.

In *Saint Genet*, Sartre demonstrates that he has no respect for theology and that he scorns the attitude of those respectable citizens who allowed Genet to be condemned in the police courts. It is a familiar thought whereby the bourgeois falsely represent the good and certain scapegoat criminals incarnate evil.

The theme of alienation is prevalent in contemporary literature, but it has never been orchestrated so richly, with such tragic and sensual poignancy, as in Jean Genet's books. The existences evoked in his novels and plays, which are obviously the writer's own existence, are unable to find their realization. These characters fully understand how estranged, how alienated they are, and they are both obsessed and fascinated by this state. The anomalies Genet sings of, as if they were the noblest themes for a poet, are all present in *Les Bonnes*. No play in the contemporary French theater is more cruel in its intention, more capable of bewildering, exasperating, and scandalizing an audience.

Roger Blin's production of *Les Nègres* was the outstanding success of the 1959-1960 theater season. The success came from many sources: from the text itself, one of the strongest Genet wrote for the stage; from the mise-en-scène of Blin who showed himself sensitive to the poetry and the dramatic intention of a very difficult text; from the performance of the thirteen blacks who played at being actors, with the seriousness and frenzy of children convinced that their game was real.

Once again, in the history of the theater, a poet had created a play that was totally outside trends and theories of the theater of his day. The rich prose of Genet, interspersed with argot and scatological language, was indeed the art of a poet controlling the action of his play, a text which is the parody of a ritualistic crime.

A clue to the dramaturgy of *Les Nègres* is in a letter by Genet published in the 1958 L'Arbalète edition of *Les Bonnes*, where in six succinct pages, he discusses his total dissatisfaction with the formula of the contemporary theater. The Western play had become a masquerade for Genet. He advocates a theater of ceremony, a return to the conception of the mass, of a theater for initiates, where the high dramatic moment would be comparable to the Elevation in the Catholic mass. Genet suggests that what is needed is a clandestine theater, which the "faithful" would attend in secret.

Les Nègres is a nightly ritual, a kind of mass celebrated before a catafalque. The play, called a *clownerie*, opens with a dance, a Mozart minuet, performed by four black males and four black females. As they whistle and hum, they dance in front of a casket. Five members of the court enter: the queen, her valet, the governor, the judge, and the missionary. These are blacks wearing white masks. The masked members of the court are whites as blacks see them when the whites are in power. The eight black dancers are blacks as they imagine they are seen and judged by whites. They are assembled to enact an imaginary crime (the slaying of a white woman), committed by real blacks in the presence of false whites.

Even before the catafalque turns out to be two chairs covered with a cloth, the spectators sense that this is a ritualistic crime on the nature of love which the man in power feels for the one in his power. The one in power is a queen who demands the love of her black subjects. The subjects are the group of blacks who are uncontrollable, who are constantly moving about, uttering shouts of laughter, parodying themselves and others, expressing anguish and mirth, as if they lived in a world both fictitious and real.

In the original performance, Roger Blin created the dramatic ambiguity which is the central situation of the play, namely, the conflicting relationships between actors and public on the stage, and the public in the audience. He did not neglect a more subtle relationship existing between the desire of the actors to amuse themselves as they act and their desire to amuse us in the audience at the same time.

In the earlier play *Les Bonnes*, Genet studied the curious bond of duplicity between the mistress of the house (Madame) and her two maids. In Sartre's study of the psychology and art of Genet, he analyzes the persistence of this theme in all the writings of Genet. A strangely distorted love joins the saint and the criminal, the guard and the prisoner, the policeman and the thief, the master and the slave, the white and the black. The blacks in *Les Nègres* play the personal drama of Jean Genet, which is the agon between the actor and the martyr.

It is a play of philosophical implication, as Sartre points out: the drama of a man who must play the part of a criminal in the very society that has ostracized him because of his crime.

Six years later, the April-May 1966 performances of Genet's last play, *Les Paravents* (1961; translated as *The Screens*, 1962), became part of theater history in France. Roger Blin directed the play, Genet's longest and most ambitious, in Jean-Louis Barrault's theater of the Odéon-Théâtre de France. Written during the Algerian War, it can hardly be called a political play, although it condemns the French role in Algeria. The Blin production of *Les Paravents*, in the state-subsidized theater of the Odéon, with such actors as Barrault, Maria Casarès, and Madeleine Renaud, was a curious twist to the history of the *poètes maudits* of France: one of them, and the most authentic, writing for the bourgeois public of a national theater.

Genet tells us that we live close beside the worst kind of moral distress, that which creates monsters. His revelations may well confirm the latest suspicion in all of us that literature is not innocent but guilty. His books were not composed as rules for life and conduct. They were creations of his mind. His characters are not himself but the heroes of his mind. His words belong to a literature of delirium and hagiography.

Genet was not a philosopher, and he was not a blasphemer. He was the artist who felt guilty by his very being. He explained his return to France (in *Journal d'un voleur*), after crossing so many frontiers in his search, as a desire to accuse himself in his own language.

Christopher Isherwood

(26 August 1904-4 January 1986)

Carolyn Heilbrun
Columbia University

See also the Isherwood entry in DLB 15: British Novelists, 1930-1959.

Recounted in a novel, the life of Christopher Isherwood, who died in 1986, would be dismissed as an improbable fiction: it is entirely too neat and rounded off. Isherwood himself was impressed with the irony of his life story as long ago as 1971. As explained in Isherwood's *Kathleen and Frank*, "His final ritual act of breaking free from her [Kathleen, his mother] was to become a citizen of the United States, thus separating himself from Mother and Motherland at one stroke. But this was equally a recognition of the fact that the days of his opposition to Kathleen were over. Ironically, his life in the States had involved him more and more in activities which she would be able to approve of, at least partially. By teaching in colleges he had become an academic, even if he had also become a clown. By embracing Vedanta he had joined the ranks of the religious, even while remaining anti-church. By opposing those fellow-citizens whom he regarded as a menace to his adopted country he had turned into a patriot, even though his enemies did all the flag-waving." Somerset Maugham wrote, at the conclusion of his novel *The Razor's Edge* (1944), popularly supposed to be about Isherwood, though Isherwood always denied it: "I looked back with my mind's eye on my long narrative to see if there was any way in which I could devise a more satisfactory ending; and to my intense surprise it dawned upon me that without the least intending to I had written nothing more or less than a success story."

Isherwood, too, in living his apparently counterculture life, had written for himself nothing more or less than a success story: too wise to anticipate the form his destiny would take, he must have known by the time I had met him in July 1975, that his life would be seen, not only as a "success" but as a model for others. As the irony of this was never lost upon him, so the irony of his obituary essay being written by a woman might also have amused him. He once said to me, during the time

Christopher Isherwood and W. H. Auden, 1938 (photo by Louise Dahl-Wolfe)

of his fight for homosexual rights in California, that "middle-aged Jewish women" had been the staunchest in the fight for civil and personal rights in his state. Vedanta, the religion Isherwood practiced for most of his life, teaches that human beings are not to be judged or categorized by their physical presence. God works in mysterious ways, in this religion, as in others, but Vedanta distinguishes itself most sharply from the Christianity Isherwood scorned by not presuming to know divine intentions or the personal characteristics of its agents. I am, as far as I know, the only woman to have written at all extensively on Isherwood, and I find it fitting to write his obituary essay because his life is translatable, not only into the richly comic terms

230

he suggests in the passage I have quoted but also into the lives of many who seem, superficially, most removed from his struggles and achievements.

Loneliness and what Claude Summers calls the lack of community always fascinated Isherwood. While he, declaring himself a camera, was, by definition, a mere observer, his fascination was always with what he called "The Lost." This was to have been the title of his Berlin stories, an account of those excluded from the dominant society and unable to find or create a community of their own outside it.

Isherwood's first two novels, which preceded the Berlin stories, *All the Conspirators* (1928) and *The Memorial: Portrait of a Family* (1932), recounted the particular quality of the English "Lost." They were, for the most part, the "weak" sons of strong and "evil" mothers. Isherwood was far from unique, in those days, in blaming all that he most despised about the British patriarchy—its self-satisfaction, its militarism and flag-waving, its religion compounded of sin and judgment, and its family dominating all lives—on women: wives and mothers. For many in England and more in America, identifying women, the chief victims of middle-class morality, as its advocates, was only logical. Germany was the country which awakened Isherwood from this conviction. When he returned to England to write his early "autobiography," *Lions and Shadows: An Education in the Twenties* (1938), he was able to see English institutions rather than its mothers as the essential source of what to him was to be, quite simply, evil: that is, actions arising from ignorance and fear.

The German books made Isherwood's name, and there are still many who remember him primarily for *Goodbye to Berlin* (1939) and his other accounts of Hitler's coming to power in the 1930s. Isherwood's famous phrase, "I am a camera," which John Van Druten was to take as the title of his successful play based on Isherwood's work, and which eventually became the even more famous musical *Cabaret*, identifies Isherwood's simultaneous attempt to become the recorder of events and to render himself invisible. His analogy was a good one. Margaret Bourke-White, the photographer, wrote: "Whatever facts a person writes have to be colored by his prejudice and bias. With a camera, the shutter opens and closes and the only rays that come in to be registered come directly from the object in front of you." This description of camera work is artistically true of neither photography nor Isherwood's writing, but it does suggest the submersion of personality, the effect which would soon

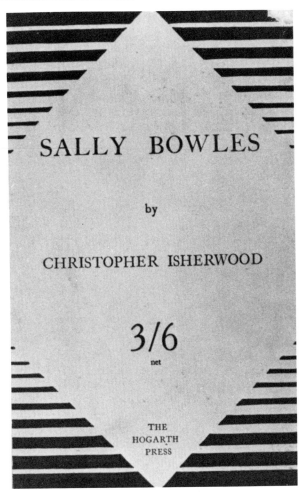

Dust jacket for the 1937 publication of the novella later included as an episode in Goodbye to Berlin *(1939)*

lead Isherwood to Vedanta. He had discovered that one can write of oneself, using one's own name while claiming total objectivity. Thus he began to create fictions more artful than "fiction" itself.

By the end of the prewar period, when Isherwood moved to the United States, he had developed his art to a point of rare maturity, progressing beyond his two early, more conventional novels about the problems of being an artist and gay in dreadful England. *The Memorial's* unconventionality had arisen more from the book's scrambled chronology than from the originality of its theme, which is not to say that *The Memorial* was not a good novel, but that in it Isherwood had not yet found his "voice." The stories about Berlin, which followed within the next seven years, comprise that sort of success often achieved at the final culmination of a writing career. That from this perfection Isherwood would move on to what amounts to another peak of literary development is remarkable. Isherwood, at forty, underwent a transformation that amounted to a rebirth. The seeds of this new vision can be discerned in *Lions and Shadows*, published at the time of the Berlin stories.

Claude Summers has called *Lions and Shadows* "essentially a series of rejections and failures: rejection of old school loyalties, of academic pursuits, of conventional heroism, of aestheticism, and, finally, of England itself "; this is a concise and accurate summary. The work is otherwise memorable for its brilliant portrait of W. H. Auden, Stephen Spender, Edward Upward, and others. After *Lions and Shadows* and the German years, Isherwood would leave for China and the United States, deserting England, Christianity, and all the institutions of propriety which Lytton Strachey had mocked as early as 1914: the army, the public schools, the church. A vital clue about the future in *Lions and Shadows*, apart from what Isherwood had rejected, lies in those writers he admired, even as a young man: Katherine Mansfield and Emily Brontë, as well as Charles Baudelaire and Wilfred Owen. And as Isherwood moved toward his home in California, his model was no one grand or great, but E. M. Forster, the writer who had taught him to "tea-table" it, to play it down, and whose protagonists were women, as trapped by English institutions as Forster himself.

Isherwood's "the lost" are primarily male homosexuals, but he understands how all despised groups learn to discriminate among so-called revolutions. He became disaffected with leftist political causes as early as the 1930s, judging them by their treatment of the homosexual cause. Isherwood determined "never to think of sacrificing himself masochistically on the altar of that false god of the totalitarians, the Greatest Good of the Greatest Number—whose priests are alone empowered to decide what 'good' is."

Wholly in keeping with this vow, he chose a religion which did not claim to identify "sin," or to judge him, a homosexual, differently from others. Isherwood was drawn to Vedanta when his "guru" declared that lust was ill-advised, but no form of lust especially damned. As a pacifist and a homosexual, he found himself isolated from leftist causes, as he had, in youth, been revolted by rightist ideology. He understood the beauty, not of tolerance, which implies superiority, but of indifference, which does not presume to judge. Alan Wilde has identified the essence of Isherwood's achievement: that "as a writer becomes more religious he may also become more humanistic and more hu-

mane." Isherwood lived into a time when "humanistic" was to become a word of hate to those considering themselves "religious," and his books, like his life, became prophetic.

It is merely another irony that as Isherwood continued to write and speak, not so much against the establishment as for his ideals of pacifism and love, he did so in Hollywood. His telephone remained listed, his presence available, his writing and speaking courageous. In December 1975, at the annual convention of the Modern Language Association in New York, he addressed a packed ballroom on the subject of his homosexuality: his talents as a "ham" and as a responder to, he hoped, antagonistic questions were apparent. I see him yet on that platform: his short stocky figure, his red socks, his way of swaying back and forth on his sturdy legs, the wonderful humor of his smile and manner. He looked like a belligerent boxer who has long deserted belligerence.

From the publication of *Prater Violet* in 1945 until the end of his life, his books express what life had taught him: its comedy, its desperation, the importance of indifference. After the translations of Vedanta texts, undertaken with his guru, he produced until 1980 a series of novels and reminiscences embodying his world. He took a trip to South America, but admitted, with characteristic honesty and humility: "the truth is that South America *bored* me, and I am ashamed that it bored me, and I hate it for making me feel ashamed."

His novel *The World in the Evening* (1954) has been much criticized, but remains rewarding and close to unique in its creation of a woman writer as a central character. It is not as good a novel as *Prater Violet*, but dares intermittently to abandon the ironic tone characteristic of his earlier work. *Down There on a Visit* (1962) begins the rewriting of his life, marked both by his newfound faith, dissolving bitterness, and by the revelations about his sexual life. Someone jokes in the book that Isherwood is always merely "down there on a visit," and he leaves the phrase as an apparent condemnation. But in its lack of egoism, it is also a model. *A Single Man*, published in 1964, is close to perfect. I called it a "masterpiece of a comic novel" in 1970 and see no reason to change that judgment. It is, as Summers wrote, "among the most undervalued novels of our time."

Isherwood was given the Common Wealth Award in 1982. A good sum of money, the prize pleased him most because it would go to Don Bachardy, his life's companion since 1954, at Isherwood's death, which I believe he already

CHRISTOPHER
ISHERWOOD
——— 1904-1986 ———

'One of the most powerful writers in Europe or America in his time'
PETER LEVI, *Sunday Telegraph*

'Only now that he is dead can the pattern be seen clearly in a life that
ranged restlessly from Oxbridge sceptic to Hindu disciple, from literary
collaborator with his friend W H Auden to Boswell
of pre-war Berlin and post-war Hollywood....
His novels and non-fiction now seem to be all chapters of one enormous work
in which he is the major character on a spiritual safari'
W J WEATHERBY, *The Guardian*

Since August 1984, coinciding with his eightieth birthday, Methuen have embarked
on a programme of reissuing all Christopher Isherwood's fiction in uniform
paperback editions in the Methuen Modern Fiction series,
together with his major autobiographical books.

Coming on March 13

A SINGLE MAN
413 59630 3   paperback £3.50*
Methuen Modern Fiction Series

(Originally published in 1964)

'A testimony to Isherwood's undiminished
brilliance as a novelist'
ANTHONY BURGESS, *The Listener*

'An absolutely devastating, unnerving, brilliant
book'   STEPHEN SPENDER, *Bookmark*

Already available in the uniform paperback edition

All the Conspirators (1928)
413 56130 5 £2.95
Lions and Shadows (1935)
413 59850 0 £2.95*
Prater Violet (1946)
413 56110 0 £2.50*
The World in the Evening (1954)
413 56100 3 £3.50*

Down There on a Visit (1962)
413 59800 4 £3.50*
Exhumations (1966)
413 56120 8 £4.50*
A Meeting by the River (1967)
417 05910 8 £2.95*
Christopher and his Kind (1977)
413 59620 6 £2.50*

Other books available

My Guru and His Disciple (1980)
417 05590 0 £1.95*
and (with Don Bachardy)
October (1983)
413 50040 3 £12.50

also available in hard cover edition

In preparation for publication in 1987
Mr Norris Changes Trains (1935)   Goodbye to Berlin (1939)

methuen

The Bookseller *(15 February 1986)*

anticipated. The occasion of that award was the last time I saw Isherwood and Bachardy. It seemed to me then, in the elegant hotel dining room, that Isherwood was slipping, gently but undeterrably, out of life. Bachardy watched over him and, what had not happened before, took the major part in the conversation. I remember especially that he spoke of some dreadful building which, against all zoning laws, had been erected, blocking their wonderful view. But they also spoke of the dangers of resentment to the person who holds it. I think I knew I would not see Isherwood again.

I had never known him well. Women were rarely if ever his chosen companions, with the possible exception of Beatrix Lehmann, back in the Berlin days, and certain elegant wives and hostesses in California. And yet I felt, as I had done from the first time I encountered his books many years ago, that his was an exemplary life, not because any self-styled moralist would ever find it so, but because he had guessed at the issues that from now on will lie at the heart of any humane struggle. He wanted the right of individuals to choose their lives, their loves, their sexuality. He wanted peace, and a stop to the destruction of the earth. He wanted comedy, and the chance to laugh at all pomposities, not least his own. The words he wrote about E. M. Forster are Isherwood's best epitaph: "While the others tell their followers to be ready to die, he advises us to live as if we were immortal. And he really does this himself, although he is as anxious and afraid as any of us, and never for an instant pretends not to be."

A TRIBUTE

from ROY FULLER

I admired the early works, particularly *Lions and Shadows;* found the later fiction not up to scratch, even at times disagreeable. But the later books of a personal kind I again enormously admired; *Kathleen and Frank* perhaps never having had its rightful due.

A TRIBUTE

from GRAHAM GREENE

I am proud to be able to claim Christopher Isherwood as a cousin. I think to all writers of my generation *Mr Norris Changes Trains* stands as a permanent landmark in the literature of our time. In its very different way it is a kind of *Ulysses* for us, a book to which we continually refer back.

John D. MacDonald

(24 July 1916-28 December 1986)

Edgar W. Hirshberg
University of South Florida

John D. MacDonald was a true pro. He loved to write, and he respected writing as a craft. After the advent of the Travis McGee books in the 1960s and the resulting fame, he was tempted to participate in activities that would keep him away from his typewriter—overseeing TV and movie productions, making speeches, appearing on talk shows. But he quickly came to the realization that these were not the things he ought to be doing. In 1970, in a letter to Dan Rowan, reprinted in *A Friendship* (1987), he wrote: "There is, in me, a kind of wistful feeling about trying to get involved in things that are not my dish. Now, in the closing years of my second adolescence I might even be getting smart enough to keep myself hauled back from such external idiocies, mostly by remembering that for me—sedentary though it is—this procedure of putting words together is where my action is."

It had taken MacDonald a relatively long time to come to the realization that writing was where the action was for him. He was reared in Utica, in upstate New York, where the family had moved soon after he was born in Sharon, Pennsylvania. His father was an executive with the Savage Arms Company, and MacDonald prepared for a career in business because he apparently did not have anything else in mind that he particularly wanted to do. He graduated from Utica Free Academy in 1932, at sixteen, and waited around for a year of postgraduate work—taking a course in typing, which he enjoyed—because he was too young to go to college. He started at the Wharton School of Finance at the University of Pennsylvania in 1934, did satisfactory but not outstanding work, and unaccountably quit school in the middle of his sophomore year because, he once told me, of a feeling of "disassociation . . . of not knowing where the hell you are or where you're going or why." But after a few months he returned to school, this time to Syracuse University, where he took his B.S. in business administration in 1938. Then he went to the Harvard Graduate School of Business, where he entered an accelerated program that enabled him to get his M.B.A. in June of 1939. Meanwhile he

had married Dorothy Prentiss, a graduate in fine arts from Syracuse, in 1938, and their first and only child, Maynard John Prentiss MacDonald, was born the following year.

In the brief succession of jobs in business—an insurance company, a finance company—that he took during the succeeding year he "did miserably," and in 1940 he was glad to accept an offer of an army commission as a lieutenant in Procurement. He served as Ordnance Officer in Rochester and Schenectady and went overseas in 1943, still in Ordnance, to the China-Burma-India theater of operations. Here he ended up in the Office of Strategic Services—now known as the CIA—as a branch commander in Ceylon with "Detachment 404," an extremely hush-hush operation involved in secret dealings with the Chinese and other espionage activities. The nature of his work was so secret that he was not allowed to write home about it, and this restriction led indirectly to his becoming a writer. In his spare time he wrote a short story called "Interlude in India," which he sent to his wife. Apparently because it was a story and not a letter, it passed the censors. It was about a young American officer's involvement with a Eurasian girl. Dorothy MacDonald sent it to *Esquire*, and the editors returned it with a request that she send them something longer by the same author. She sent "Interlude in India" off to another magazine, *Story*, edited by Whit and Hallie Burnett, who accepted it, sent a check for twenty-five dollars, and eventually published the story in the July-August 1946 issue. When MacDonald got home in 1945 and discovered that she had actually sold something that he had written, "it did something to him." He immediately embarked on a strenuous writing program, producing what he termed "800,000 unsaleable words in four months . . . , the equivalent of ten novels . . . , all in short-story form." He made his first sale in February 1946, to Mike Tilden, the editor of *Dime Detective*, who paid him forty dollars. It was not enough for four months of work, and MacDonald had to take a job in Utica, where he had settled with his wife and son. But he kept on writing, and during 1946 he made about $6,000, which at that time was enough to live on and enabled him to quit his job. He made his living as a professional writer from that time on.

The writing habits that he learned during those early days stayed with him. He regarded writing as his job, and he worked at it eight hours a day—sometimes more—like any other professional. He learned by doing, and the editors of the pulp magazines where he sent his stories taught him about what would sell and what wouldn't. In his comments about these early years at a conference held in his honor at the University of South Florida in 1978, MacDonald said that these editors "were forcing improvements upon me by acting as filtering agents for the great flood of words. The ones which were improved were sold."

Sometimes there would be as many as thirty stories in the mail, aimed at such periodicals as *Doc Savage, Dime Detective,* and *Black Mask,* as well as *Cosmopolitan, Liberty,* and *Esquire.* He would never aim at a particular magazine but would write each story as the spirit moved him and then find a market for it. "My work habits," he observed, "accounted for not only the diversity of plot and structure and societal themes in my early work, but also for the diversity of the places where they were published. . . . When I tried to work exclusively within a specific genre, everything went stale for me. The words died."

This is a key to the understanding of what MacDonald's work has really amounted to. Most of the kudos he has received have been in recognition of his mystery, suspense, and detective stories: the Grand Prix de Littérature Policière for the French version of *A Key to the Suite* in 1964, the Grand Master Award from the Mystery Writers of America in 1972, and the American Booksellers Association's award for the best mystery in 1980, for *The Green Ripper.* But he also won the Ben Franklin Award in 1955 for "The Bear Trap"—which had nothing to do with mystery or detection—as the best short story to appear in a mass-circulation magazine. He received the George Arents Pioneer Medal from Syracuse University in 1971 for his contributions to American literature; and the citation accompanying his honorary Ph.D. from Hobart and William Smith College in Geneva, N.Y., in 1978 praised him for setting "an example to those who seek to paint a contemporary picture of mankind with the medium of the printed word." The citation with his honorary Ph.D. from the University of South Florida, which he received in 1980,

reads in part that the university "takes pride in honoring you as one of our nation's greatest living writers of fiction in an indigenously American mode."

MacDonald should be regarded as one of the foremost fiction writers of this generation, and not specifically as a skilled writer of mystery or detective or suspense fiction. Certainly his work includes these three categories, but, as he pointed out in his last interview, published in the *New Black Mask No. 8,* a sizeable portion of it is mainstream fiction that cannot be so categorized. Before the advent of Travis McGee in 1964 he had written over forty novels and some three hundred short stories. His early work in the short story form, in addition to mystery and suspense, concerned his war experiences, the relationships between home-coming veterans and their postwar environment, and the problems of middle-class Americans in their quest for business success and marital happiness. After 1950 he became interested in longer forms of fiction because of the changing fiction market. His first full-length novel, *The Brass Cupcake* (1950), shows the influence of the Hammett-Chandler hard-boiled detective school of fiction. But as his production increased his choice of subjects widened. He wrote two science-fiction novels, *Wine of the Dreamers* and *Ballroom of the Skies,* and about twenty short stories in the same genre in the early 1950s. Later he wrote another science fiction novel with comic overtones, *The Girl, the Gold Watch & Everything.* His experiences living in Mexico with his family during the mid 1950s formed the background for another comic novel, *Please Write for Details* (1959), and for several more serious books, such as *The Damned* (1952), a morality tale with biblical overtones involving sin and redemption; *Border Town Girl* (1956), a novelette about an American writer who is caught in the crossfire of drug smuggling operations along the Mexican border; and *The Empty Trap* (1957), a violent story about a well-meaning sinner and his encounters with the consequences of revenge.

Although his primary purpose always was to tell a good story, many of MacDonald's novels point toward specific social or moral objectives. *Cry Hard, Cry Fast* (1955) is a straightforward account of the consequences of a fatal auto accident on a crowded highway and makes no attempt to conceal its main point about the hazards of driving. *A Flash of Green* (1962) and *Condominium* (1977) are strong exposés of the dangers to Florida's environment posed by the rapacity and carelessness of builders, developers, and public officials who are spoiling the

Dust jacket for MacDonald's last novel

state's natural beauties. *Barrier Island* (1986) concerns environmental problems in the region bordering the Gulf of Mexico off the coast of Mississippi. Two of the Travis McGee books examine aspects of modern American life that are particularly threatening to young people: *Dress Her in Indigo* (1969) concentrates on drugs and the drug culture, and *The Green Ripper* (1979) is an indictment of radical religious cults. The excesses of religious feeling as it is disseminated over TV and radio is the subject of a subsequent novel, not in the McGee series, *One More Sunday* (1984).

Many of MacDonald's novels written in the 1950s and 1960s come under the general heading of adventure and suspense, but again they are difficult to categorize. Books like *The Crossroads* (1959), *The End of the Night* (1960), and *The Last One Left* (1966) are tautly plotted stories with strong, believable characters, but they are not mystery or detective stories in the usual sense. *You Live Once* (1955), *The Price of Murder* (1957), *Soft Touch* (1958), and *One Monday We Killed Them All* (1961) are heavily dependent on police action in the development of their plots, but they can by no means be considered police procedurals because there are many other elements involved in the action in addition to the police. And novels like *The Brass Cupcake* (1950), *Judge Me Not* (1951), *Dead Low Tide* (1953), *You Live Once* (1956), and *Deadly Welcome* (1959) resemble "private eye" stories but again do not

strictly adhere to the rules pertaining to the genre. The person doing the detecting is not a professional but someone who gets involved in a crime or a series of crimes more or less inadvertently, and detection is only one of several aspects of the story.

Even the Travis McGee novels defy classification. Travis hardly resembles the usual private eye, living on *The Busted Flush,* a luxurious houseboat moored at Bahia Mar in Fort Lauderdale, surrounded by beautiful women of varying ages and sexual proclivities, sipping Plymouth gin and watching the spectacular sunset with his boon companion and confidant, Meyer. There is an obvious and radical contrast between him and such ascetic and single-minded progenitors as Sherlock Holmes, Philip Marlow, and the Continental Op. Travis considers himself a "salvage expert," not a detective, and as such he involves himself in a series of quests in which MacDonald often equates him with a knight in shining—but sometimes not so shining—armor. Emerging fully developed in 1964 in the first novel about him, *The Deep Blue Good-By,* McGee almost immediately captured the imaginations of millions of readers. His popularity increased with the years and, justifiably or not, he became the chief source of MacDonald's fame. Each of the twenty-one episodes resembles a folktale, as MacDonald himself admitted: Travis rides out into an evil world, rights a wrong, rescues a damsel, recovers loot, and sometimes keeps half in order to subsist—which he manages to do, quite adequately.

But in addition to his fascination as a hero, McGee served the important function of being MacDonald's mouthpiece. He and Meyer voice their opinions on all sorts of topics and as such they become modern philosophers and savants. Mac-Donald has said that he felt he was within his rights to "try to move my suspense novels as close as I can get to the 'legitimate' novels of manners and morals, despair and failure, love and joy. . . . I shall continue with my sociologist asides, with McGee and Meyer's dissertations on the condition of medicine, retirement, education, face lifting, ear mites, road construction, white-collar theft, apartment architecture, magazine editing, acid rain, billy rock, low fidelity, and public service in America today." What MacDonald was saying here was that he felt, as a writer, that he could express his opinions on any subject—and indeed he did. Uppermost in his mind, from the very beginning, were the ramifications of the conflict between good and evil that rages in everyone. Even in his earliest books, those that he wrote in the 1950s, this conflict was evident in his characters and in how they handle themselves in the situations he put them into. Though the good guys do not always win, MacDonald made his own sentiments clear. "At the heart of it all," he said, "I am a moralist . . . because I believe people must accept responsibility for all those acts that affect the lives of others." Travis McGee typifies all of MacDonald's heroes, who are always trying to right the few wrongs they can do anything about in a generally evil world.

MacDonald always tried to tell a good story—that was his paramount consideration in writing fiction. But he also had important things to say about moral and social issues. He aimed his most persistent and energetic efforts against men's insistence on destroying their environment because of greed and against their insistence on using force to solve their problems. He considered these two issues to be aspects of the eternal conflict between good and evil, a conflict with which he was constantly concerned. Perhaps, in the end, his fame will depend at least in part on his moral stance, an attitude about what is good and what is bad. Though good does not always conquer evil in his stories, his readers always knew what side John D. MacDonald was on.

A TRIBUTE

from MICHAEL AVALLONE

John D. MacDonald was elected President of Mystery Writers of America in 1962. This is an honorary post (not given lightly) of one year's tenure and he handled the role with aplomb. I cite this Presidency among all the others that have occurred since 1945 because he was the *First* paperback writer to achieve the post. No small potatoes that, for *no other softcover writer has ever earned the crown*—and that's a quarter of a century ago. Yet it serves to show what MWA thought of him as a professional mystery writer despite his absence in hardcover books. A condition he was to shatter irrevocably several years later as he won the respect of the Reading World.

To the rest of us toiling in the Paperback Original vineyards of those dark days, he was a Hero. A Pro's Pro, a Writer's Writer *a la* actor's actor, ballplayer's ballplayer. The ultimate accolade. Putting it even more simply, he was the Writer, in a successful and artistic sense, that the rest of us wanted to be. We reveled in his great reviews, sales and recognition because he was living proof that the category *softcover* concealed at times Writing that was the *equal of* and yes, *better than* a lot of its hardcover relatives. Proving that publishing some books *soft* and some *hard* could simply be a matter of publishing economics and not a *Quality* judgment entirely. As so many Hardcover Purists insisted—"*it's a paperback book because it isn't good enough to be a hardcover one!*" It was a very very old argument.

John Mack, as I always called him to differentiate between him and Ross Mack, the other Macdonald (small "d") Writing Great, was the major weapon in that argument. I used *it* and *him* when I presented MWA with the contention in 1970 that Paperbacks Were Here To Stay, and with the help of some champions (Joe Gores) instituted the yearly Best Paperback Mystery Award which exists in MWA to this writing. I paraphrased W. H. Auden too—"*Let us honor if we can—the paperback man. Though we honor none but the hardcover one.*" John Mack, as was his way, wanted no part of the fight, despite my appeals to him. He was basically a loner, did not mix with groups and merely got on with what he did so well—the writing of solid, splendid, finely crafted novels of Today. Not so much mysteries anymore as genuine chunks of Modern Times rigged out in the clearly flying colors of suspense, reality and excitement.

I have always called him the Greatest Paperback Writer of Us All. I always think of him as the Great Original Novel Writer, in soft covers as he certainly was in the early days of Gold Medal. In the Fifties and the Sixties, no one had written greater, more unforgettable books than *The Brass Cupcake, The Neon Jungle, The Girl, The Gold Watch & Everything,* and *The Only Girl In The Game.* Those were as good as those kind of stories can get. Or ever be. And sadly, they were imitated over and over again. But that's the way it always is with true Writing Greats. How many *Gatsbys* and *Postmans* have you read?

The Travis McGee books were less my cup of MacDonald tea but you could hardly ever quarrel with the writing, no matter the heavy patches of preachment and self-righteousness. For that is the bottom line to the entire career of this American writer who died just before the New Year dawned. He simply, out-and-out, all-the-way-down-the-line, was one of the greatest writers ever. A carbon and ribbon man to rank with the best there ever was.

Nobody ever did it better—not since the end of WWII at least. He has peers, certainly, but no one he has to take a back seat to.

And my favorite MacDonald quote is from a *New York Times* article we both shared on July 9, 1973:

"You realize in the literary establishment, to be prolific, is to be considered, without any further discussion, a commercial hack. Well, let them blunt their teeth on Georges Simenon if they want to go that route."

You see, John Mack who began as a Paperback Man, *without loss of quality,* has written far far many more books than the average Hard-Cover Writer. I like that. I will always like that.

You could look it up.

A TRIBUTE

from ROBERT BLOCH

John D. MacDonald needs no tribute. He left his own memorial—a body of brilliant, perceptive, insightful and entertaining work which will preserve his identity for generations of readers yet to come. May they enjoy and be enriched by him, as we were!

A TRIBUTE

from MICHAEL COLLINS

I never met John D. in person, although through mutual friends and his books it somehow seemed to me that I had, and I did not always like what he wrote in all those hard-nosed books anymore than I always like everything any author writes, but there was an honesty and integrity about John D. that always commanded respect. In particular, more than any other writer in our genre, he was the constant proof that no writer since Homer has ever written "just to tell a story," spin a yarn, entertain. All real writers write because they have seen something about people, the society, the world, the universe they want others to see. Writers have something to say about the world they live in, and no one ever said more clearly or honestly what he had to say than John D.

A TRIBUTE

from JAMES ELLROY

John D. MacDonald was the only writer out there who could stop a hot-blooded narrative to run a discourse on politics, or economics or ecology—and not piss you off. He was not—as some people claim—the great American storyteller; he was a very good storyteller—one with the ability to bend his reader's will to his digressions and have him back into the plot inside of three seconds—knowing he'd learned something.

A TRIBUTE

from EVAN HUNTER

John D. MacDonald was a consummate pro and a good man. That is the highest accolade I can give any writer.

A TRIBUTE

from JOHN JAKES

What Simenon is to France, and the world, John D. MacDonald is to the U.S., and the world. A writer grounded in popular art who time after time transcended his genre. A writer with matchless understanding of his society and human character. A writer who created not merely one good work but a body of work, of enduring interest and worth. John D., with whom I had a warm occasional correspondence . . . whom I always wanted to meet and never did . . . whom I tried to imitate early in my career (always failing—understandable, given his great talent) was and remains a sort of Dickens of our mean streets, which he made all the more stark and shocking and true by flooding them with Florida sunshine. We have lost one of the major literary figures of the century. Increasingly, he will be recognized as such.

from ROBIN W. WINKS

John D. MacDonald wrote acutely: he saw the country and its cultures plain, he knew how to tell a compelling story, and he was a craftsman in words. Over his long record he was surely the best writer in the genre and the most consistently representative of all that is good and almost none of the much that is bad in the field.

Bernard Malamud
(26 April 1914-18 March 1986)

Jeffrey Helterman
University of South Carolina

See also the Malamud entries in *DLB 2: American Novelists Since World War II; DLB 28: Twentieth-Century American-Jewish Fiction Writers;* and *DLB Yearbook: 1980.*

In Bernard Malamud's last novel the hero, who is also the last man on earth, complains to God that the final nuclear holocaust has destroyed the just as well as the unjust. God tries to explain his decision to Calvin Cohn, but when Cohn won't listen, God pelts the earth with a storm of lemons. Cohn sees bitter rejection in the citric rain, but one of his companions, a literate chimp, sees an opportunity to make vast quantities of lemonade. As philosophy, the "if life gives you lemons make lemonade" message may be unreconstituted "Dear Abby," but the wonderfully absurd circumstances—a *kvetching* former Jew whining about a lemon lump on his head, a witty Christian monkey taking rational stock of the situation, and a Creator who plays cosmic practical jokes—are pure Malamud.

Until his death on 18 March 1986, Bernard Malamud was the comic moralist of a universe whose absurdity varied in degree from novel to novel but never disappeared. At the center of his novels is a Chaplinesque hero (some have compared his heroes to Rouault's sad clowns or Giacometti's skeletal human beings), usually a Jew, always Jewish in attitude, who struggles immensely to make lemonade out of the lemons life hands him. Some succeed, some fail, and the lemonade always has a bitter tang, but the key to success is a simple one—love one other person completely. The key is simple, but not easy. In one story the hero can save his father by answering positively the question,

"Do you love your father?," but he avoids the question three times with such circumlocutions as "what I feel is obvious," "you're putting it as a sort of paradox," and "I've answered that." If it is so hard merely to say "I love" how much harder is it to love, and for Malamud to avoid love is to avoid commitment to another, to life, to God. This commitment requires a person to become completely himself, which also means that the person must become someone other than he has been. For this reason, the Jews who become totally Jewish are Christ-like, and Christians are most themselves when they become Jewish.

Such inversions are part of the concept of *narrishkeit,* which informs all of Malamud's novels and most of his short fiction. *Narrishkeit* is folly so complete and unworldly that it confounds the wisdom of worldly wise men. Its greatest practitioners are Jesus and a succession of Fools, like I. M. Singer's Gimpel, in Yiddish literature. In addition to the mockery of the powerful and the successful, what these Fools share is the ability to love for no reason at all. Jesus loves man even though man is unworthy of his love, and Gimpel loves his wife despite the fact that she is an adultress, a scold, a husband beater, and a cheat. This is the point that Malamud makes again and again: love that has to have a worthy object to embrace is not love at all, but a form of self-love. In his story "The Silver Crown," the young man who cannot bring himself even to say he loves his father cannot understand why the rabbi in the story loves his fat, ugly, retarded daughter. But he misses the point, love which asks the reason why is not love at all. Such rationalism in the pursuit of love is true folly, and

Bernard Malamud (photo ©Jerry Bauer)

Malamud names his misguided hero Gans, a "goose" or fool.

Malamud's understanding of folly has made him the wisest of our contemporary novelists, even though he lacks the intellectual complexity of Saul Bellow and the witty grace of Philip Roth. This wisdom has produced eight novels and three original collections of short stories. Among the oeuvre is one great novel, *The Fixer* (1966), which won a Pulitzer Prize and the National Book Award, and one almost as good, *The Assistant* (1957), which won the Rosenthal Award of the National Institute of Letters and the Daroff Award of the Jewish Book Council in 1958, and a luminous collection of short stories, *The Magic Barrel* (1958), which also won the National Book Award. Malamud produced work steadily from the publication of *The Natural* in 1952 until the appearance of *God's Grace* in 1982. A prolific period from 1957 to 1966, which produced five books including the two National Book Award winners, established him as a major force in American fiction. Though a heart bypass in 1981 slowed him down, he continued to publish short fiction and at his death was at work on another novel, purportedly about a Jew in the Old West.

Though much has been made of the small scale and limited geography of Malamud's fiction, his best novel, *The Fixer,* explores a man's relation to himself and his history and shows how even the least among us, through a harrowing confrontation with his friends, his enemies, and his God, can make the mightiest of nations tremble. Most of the novel takes place in a prison and then in a single cell of the prison, but the repercussions of the hero's courage shakes two continents. The Russian government uses force, guile, bribery, and even love to convince Yakov Bok to confess to a ritual murder he did not commit, yet no amount of pressure can change Bok as he grows in strength under each onslaught. At the beginning, Bok's persistence, mostly mere whim and stubbornness, makes no sense even to himself, but as he places himself in relation to everything that would make him change, he comes to understand what he is, what man is, what a Jew is, and almost what God is. Bok becomes a living demonstration of Blake's aphorism, "if a fool would persist in his folly he would become wise."

The stories in *The Magic Barrel* and *Idiots First* (1963) operate on the edges of magic and mysticism. Malamud puts his mysticism in so real a setting that when his characters accept the supernatural, his reader does also. The stories are populated by angels and devils and dybbuks and talking blackbirds, but in context the reader shrugs his shoulders and says, "of course, they were there." These stories also take up the themes of folly as love and foolish love as wisdom, but their focus is around the central event in Malamud's historical consciousness, the Nazi Holocaust. None of the stories tell directly of the Holocaust but rather tell of the altered consciousness of those who have survived. In "The Loan" coldness of heart by a survivor of the Holocaust turns the loaves in her bakery oven into the charred corpses of Auschwitz, and in "The Lady of the Lake," when the hero denies his Jewishness to get close to a woman he takes to be Italian, she turns out to be a Holocaust survivor who is turned into a marble statue because of his denial. Hardness of heart can never be a minor crime in Malamud's fiction.

Three of the novels, *The Assistant, A New Life* (1961), and *Dubin's Lives* (1979), are set in places that have had an important influence on Malamud's life. Though none is autobiographical, each is built out of his experiences and attitudes. *The Assistant* reflects life in his family's less than successful mom-and-pop grocery; *A New Life* is a fictional version of his early teaching career at Oregon State University; and *Dubin's Lives* is set in rural Vermont where Malamud spent the last third of his life.

Malamud's days behind the counter in his parent's store in Brooklyn are the source of the milieu in *The Assistant*, but he has expanded the events in this tiny world into a moral struggle of immense dimensions. The protagonists, Morris Bober and Frank Alpine, begin almost as ethnic stereotypes of the Jewish-American and the Italian-American but come to stand for important moral positions. As is often the case, Malamud uses the characters' names to suggest allegorical values that become part of, but do not replace, their lives. Bober, as a Jew, reflects the philosophy of the existential Jewish philosopher, Martin Buber, whose philosophy of the I-Thou relationship requires that a man take responsibility for and love one other human being. In such a relationship there is no place to shirk responsibility. When one man says to another, "I am responsible for you," he takes on a much tougher task than a group that says "we are responsible for them," and when a man says to God, "I am responsible to YOU," he leaves himself, the "I," no place to hide. Frank, the Assistant, becomes an incarnation of St. Francis of Assisi and learns the perfect nonselfish love of the medieval saint. In Malamud's paradox the more Frank becomes St. Francis, the more he becomes a Jew, so that he celebrates his perfect sainthood by becoming *bar mitzvah*. Conversely, Morris's Jewish suffering for Frank's guilt makes him Christ-like. While the spirit of the novel is medieval, and biblical, and Talmudic, the characters never leave the Brooklyn of Malamud's childhood.

During the time he was helping in his father's store, Malamud wrote fiction for the literary magazine in Brooklyn's Erasmus Hall High School. He graduated in 1932, at the height of the Depression, and went on to receive his B.A. from the City College of New York four years later. He moved toward an academic career with a master's degree in English from Columbia University, and, after teaching English in several high schools, Malamud went to Oregon State University (1949-1961), where he taught literature and composition. Malamud records a version of his early academic days in *A New Life*, whose hero, S. Levin, is, like Malamud, an easterner among westerners, a liberal among conservatives, a Jew among gentiles, and, most importantly for this novel, an intellectual among philistines. The novel contains the most biting satire in Malamud's work, although, as always, much of this satire is reflexive, with the intellectually pompous Levin almost as guilty as his socially and morally pompous superiors.

Dubin's Lives might be considered the third of a trilogy of novels which look, respectively, at the artist at the beginning, middle, and end of his career. *Pictures of Fidelman* (1969) is a story of beginnings, in which a young painter learns commitment to both art and life. A picaresque novel, it was built out of a number of short stories based on Malamud's visit to Italy. The story tells of the transformation of Fidelman from someone who just "fiddles around" as a would-be artist and would-be romantic lover into a man of faith (fidelity) who is a real artisan and a true lover. The new Fidelman is more real and less exalted than he expected his life and art to make him. *The Tenants* (1971), though ostensibly a novel of race relationships, offers a hero at early midcareer, when his work has been critically acclaimed but before he has finished the novel that will make him a major literary figure. Unfortunately, Harry Lesser's masterpiece, *The Promised End*, as its name implies, will never be finished. If it is, there will be no more to do, and his life as an artist will be over.

In *Dubin's Lives* Malamud offers a reflective look at the twilight of a literary man's career. Dubin is a biographer—a student of lives—who tries to make sense of the relation of his art to his life. Dubin finds himself entangled in a biography of D. H. Lawrence, whose passionate novels do not reflect the uncertain sexual nature of their author. The question is whether the book or the man is more important and more real. For the setting of the novel, an isolated house near a liberated woman's college in Vermont, Malamud drew on his own circumstances: for the last half of his academic career Malamud taught full- and later part-time at Bennington College. At almost the same time as this novel appeared, Malamud's friend and rival, Philip Roth, wrote *The Ghost Writer* (1979), which also tells of the secret life of a revered novelist who lives with his wife in seclusion near a woman's college in New England. Roth's hero, E. I. Lonoff, is, like Malamud, a perfectionist and a constant reviser who often drives his editors crazy by pursuing his manuscripts to press and changing things in proof.

Though Malamud often writes in a realistic mode, two of his novels, *The Natural* and *God's Grace*, are overtly allegorical. *The Natural*, a novel based on a number of baseball legends (Casey at the Bat, The Black Sox Scandal of 1919, and Babe Ruth's exploits), is at the same time a modern retelling of the Grail Quest complete with magic bat/lance, wasteland/ball field, and a team called the

New York Knights. It was made into a fairly successful movie, but Robert Redford would be no Casey, and, instead of striking out as the novel requires, he hits the home run that wins the pennant.

In *God's Grace,* where the last man on earth becomes the patriarch of a tribe of literate and verbal monkeys, Malamud restates all of the major themes of his novels. In this novel a man living on the past, a paleontologist, has a chance to influence the future. He is capable of transforming, by his knowledge and ultimately by his seed, the future of the race, but he fails because he cannot love. In every case his personal and racial ego prevails. He tells his intended, a beautiful chimp, the story of Romeo and Juliet without the tragic ending because he is afraid it might sour her on romantic love. He refuses to tell her he loves her because she is, after all, a monkey (though she is bearing his child). He refuses to allow freedom of religion when the apes want to become Christians but will not offer a valid Judaism to replace it. Instead he offers an agnostic "faith" that is all ritual and no belief. Finally, though he has seen man destroy the world and discovers that the apes are intellectual and morally his equal, he refuses to let them make decisions and ultimately makes the wrong final decision himself.

Malamud's place as a major American novelist seems secure, although he seems destined to bear the cross of hyphenation and be bracketed with Roth and Bellow as Jewish-American novelists. Almost certainly he will be seen in the tradition of Russian writers like Chekhov, Gogol, and Dostoyevski and Yiddish writers like I. L. Peretz and Sholom Aleichem, rather than as a starter of his own tradition. Nonetheless, he was an original—wise, comic, and moral—who looks at the story of Cain and Abel and concludes that a man who denies he is his brother's keeper is as contemptible as a man who murders his brother.

A TRIBUTE
from E. M. BRONER

I saw Bern two days before he died. He was stiffer and slower in movement than usual—but still delighting in conversation, in the beautiful woman next to him. He rose to leave saying, "I used to write six hours a day. Now it's three. But so it goes, on and on and on." But it didn't.

And yet it does—as we whom he influenced go on.

The Magic Barrel helped me gain my own

voice—humor and mysticism—mischievousness, the unexpected, a kvetch—all this I learned from Malamud. The accent became my accent. In *The Fixer* I was again given permission to use our ethnic myths, to shape them to ourselves.

My work has my shape—women are the magical ones—but I am never far from the kind of sense of concentration, of elimination of everything but the essential which marked Bern's earlier works, like *The Assistant*. The smell of the store, the taste of poverty was first his life and then his art.

So, dear Bern, we writers hold your hand even though you go out the door.

A TRIBUTE
from IRVIN FAUST

Nice guys, thank *goodness*, can and do finish first. Bernard Malamud is a luminous case in point. I say "is" because the work, so informed by his caring and his decency, will always be with us.

A TRIBUTE
from LESLIE FIEDLER

From the moment I discovered *The Natural,* I was convinced that Bernard Malamud was one of the most gifted of the then young American writers. As a matter of fact, from that point on I devoted a lot of time trying to establish his reputation. It provided me real satisfaction, therefore, to see his talent widely acknowledged before his death. I have a hunch that he is one of the few writers of his generation who will be read and appreciated a hundred years from now. This gives me special satisfaction because in many ways I identify with him, not just as a Jewish-American writer, but as a pioneer in the second great trek Westward.

Malamud and I made similar moves from the urban East where we had grown up to the (to us) mythological Northwest even before the better advertised migration of the Beats. During our years of exile we were neighbors and became friends. It is not for his resemblance, however, to me or to anyone else that I remember and revere Malamud, but for his differences. He had a unique voice and a unique vision. That voice continues to ring in my head, and when I pick up one of his books I can still share that vision; which is, I suppose, what all writers desire and few achieve.

A TRIBUTE

from CHAIM POTOK

His sentences were what got to me first—the way the words made visible a familiar, musty, and yet somehow strange world of crushed people. I entered his world through "The Magic Barrel," and I remember thinking, while reading that story, that there was something wrong about the way he was presenting the people and their values (I lived inside that world then): none of it was *quite* the way he pictured it; it was all somewhat askew, a vaguely surreal rendering. And yet there were truths there that went beyond the mere surface of the page; truths the words and rhythms of the prose were reaching for: a private vision of a crippled world; a sharp look into the dark side of the American dream; and a view of suffering that raised it to the dimension of the mythic. And the sentences—those carefully crafted amalgams of old-fashioned tale and modern story, of cool literary English and cadenced New York street Yiddishisms—gripped and held and vibrated. I was enchanted by "The Magic Barrel."

I liked *A New Life, The Fixer,* and *The Tenants* a lot when I first read them and less when I read them again. *The Natural* and *The Assistant* remain in memory for their writing, their deep probing into the dark regions of the soul, and their relentless, uncompromising integrity. But it is the short stories, those boldly hued canvases of language and imagination, that linger longest, that grow richer and more resonant with each rereading, and that will be permanent in our literature.

UPDATED ENTRIES

Joan Didion
(5 December 1934-   )

Mary Doll

See also the Didion entries in *DLB 2, American Novelists Since World War II,* and *DLB Yearbook: 1981.*

NEW BOOKS: *Salvador* (New York: Simon & Schuster, 1983);

Democracy (New York: Simon & Schuster, 1984; London: Chatto & Windus, 1984).

Joan Didion continues to produce major works and to excite differing, often exasperated, reactions from the critics. In *Salvador* (1983), an example of reportage or new journalism, and *Democracy* (1984), a novel "that tries to tell the truth," she has maintained her stance as a writer in both the fiction and nonfiction modes, blending the two into new forms. A first collection of writings about Didion, *Essays and Conversations* (1984), contains scholarly criticism of her work culled from such journals as *Modern Fiction Studies, Contemporary Literature, Critique: Studies in Modern Fiction, Commentary,* and the *New York Times Book Review.* That she should be the subject of serious scholarship is a credit not only to her technique but to her vision. With her latest work Didion raises basic questions about the concepts of democracy, narration, motherhood, and memory.

It is not Didion's intention to provide solutions for the problems she sees in modern life. Solutions, and the salve they bring to a reader's mind, are, in Didion's view, the province of the narrative tradition. According to her, narration has historical significance and "makes" sense. It assumes that time contains recognizable segments of past, present, and future which, because they connect, can provide coherence. It has enabled writers to write about heroes who move through plot, accomplishing goals and solutions. But as Didion's work reveals, often with biting nostalgia, the narrative tradition is no longer adequate to the stories of today.

Nevertheless, Didion is firmly rooted in the very tradition she challenges. Her reportorial drive for "getting it right" and her novelist's ear for the way conversation fleshes scene reflect her deep ap-

Dust jacket for Didion's account of her 1982 trip to El Salvador

preciation for such literary predecessors as Hawthorne, Orwell, Hemingway, and Conrad. Being rooted in a culture that gives one despair is among the many fascinating contradictions she feels between romantic yearning and existential angst, detachment and intimacy, desire for fiction in a world of fact, despair in fact's truth power. But perhaps because of these and other tensions, because she has made her private questions public, Didion compels attention.

Salvador was originally published serially in the *New York Review of Books* in November and December 1982. The essays are an account of a two-week trip taken by Didion and her husband, John Gregory Dunne, to El Salvador in June 1982. On a fact-finding mission to the revolution-torn republic of El Salvador, Didion finds that there are no facts sufficient to describe the place; there are only details. Salvador is to reality what Boca Grande was, in *A Book of Common Prayer* (1977), to fiction: a landscape of the equatorial zone "suited for its irrationality, meanness, disease, and unrest." As the final political frontier, it is the logical place where Didion's sensibility could go to work. There the writer cannot make sense; she can only evoke it.

In the *New York Times Book Review*, Warren Hoge remarked: "No one in El Salvador has interpreted the place better. 'Salvador' shines with enlightening observation. . . . [Didion's] novelist's eye examines policy on a plane seldom reached in Congressional hearings or State Department briefings." Paul Stuewe in *Quill Quire* said it was "overwhelmingly effective . . . a timely and timeless work of creation." And Frederick Kiley, in a scholarly essay entitled "Beyond Words: Narrative Art in Joan Didion's *Salvador*," compared it to Picasso's "Guérnica" for the way both shape observations as metaphors.

Other critics tended to dismiss *Salvador* for what Mark Falcoff described in *Commentary* as the book's "two big problems. One has to do with the facts, the other with Joan Didion. There are some serious inaccuracies in the text, and many, many more half-truths. . . . What is even more disturbing about 'Salvador' . . . is the way in which she makes the tiny republic of El Salvador into a mirror reflecting her own basic contempt for liberal democracy and—why not say it?—the American way of life." As Gene Lyons commented in *Newsweek*, "Most readers will not get very far in this short book without wondering whether she visited that sad and tortured place less to report than to validate the Didion world view."

Clearly, with her rejection of the narrative tradition's assumptions about history, Didion has tapped a deep emotional core. She does so ironically, acknowledging her indebtedness to Joseph Conrad, master narrator. *Salvador*'s epigraph, taken from Conrad's *Heart of Darkness*, contrasts the naive political observations of Marlow with hidden political realities. Marlow is so taken by the "burn-

ing noble words" written by Kurtz for the historical record that he hardly notices a postscript. Scrawled in pencil at the end of the report is the phrase "Exterminate all the brutes!" Conrad's point is Didion's. Good language distorts bad truth.

Didion expresses a simmering rage, in *Salvador*, at the rhetorical tricks of the history makers. Her tone represents a shift from the detachment she showed (with the exception of "Bureaucrats") in *The White Album* (1979). Now she views linguistic distortion as nothing short of obscene. Killing, she observes, is made into an abstraction by the phrase "to be disappeared." Numbers, as in body counts, can be obscured to hide the fact that they relate to human beings. Corpses and mutilated bodies are reported and counted by the Salvador government "in a kind of tortured code." As reporter, Didion must attempt the impossible task of penetrating the code in a climate where, because words do not signify, facts do not apply.

She catalogues documents, speeches, reports, and communiques, as well as firsthand observable accounts by herself and others, in this decoding attempt. Code is pervasive on "both sides of the imperialist mirror," used as if "a linguistic deal had been cut." On the side of the Salvadoreans are such terms as improvement, perfection, and pacification which express not reality, but wish. She cites the work of Gabriel García Márquez, whose fiction illuminates a prevailing social realism of "wishful thinking," but which in the present situation has become a perverted habit of mind. "Language as it is now used in El Salvador is the language of advertising, of persuasion, the product of being one or another of the *soluciones* crafted in Washington or Panama or Mexico, which is part of the place's obscenity."

Those on the other side—the American president, the ambassadors, the State Department—use code words as well. Phrases like "democratic turbulence," to describe political disaster, and "birth pangs of nascent democratic institutions," to describe nighttime killing raids, illustrate an absurd connection between language and truth. Didion juxtaposes rhetoric with coincidental detail to undercut the seriousness of the policymakers. The effect is always ironic, often appalling, sometimes hilarious. An example of the latter is a juxtaposition of President Reagan, political actor, with Ronald Reagan, movie actor. She cites a description from his 1982 speech before both houses of the British Parliament, "brave freedom fighters battling oppressive government forces on behalf of the silent, suffering people of that tortured country." Next to this in her text she places a description of a movie she happened to be watching while reviewing the speech, a 1952 film with Doris Day called *The Winning Team*. Its phrase "Play ball!" acts as the hidden metaphoric connector between the two media. Burning noble words, she indicates, are just showmanship to be tossed around, to keep the ball rolling.

Didion is serious about games. For her, evil is the lack of seriousness. Tawdry ritual, frivolous rhetoric, banal expression are all surface beneath which lies bad truth. Not being able to find facts on the surface, she writes to uncover them in metaphor. Government spokesmen are "players" who take part in "performances"; local events have the feel of "opera" with even extras like herself seeming to live "onstage"; a local general is a "main player" perceived by some as "a wild card"; and symbolic action is a pretense for "playing the game," "playing ball." By exposing the metaphor of gaming, mirroring it in her own sentences, she turns language against itself; she cracks the code.

Didion's thesis is problematic. "That we had been drawn, both by a misapprehension of the local rhetoric and by the manipulation of our own rhetorical weakness, into a game we did not understand, a play of power in a political tropic alien to us, seemed apparent, and yet there we remained." Seeing the appearances of things does not mean finding solutions. But she does discover this: in a place of "cultural zero" language is debased, human life is worthless, rituals are only "moves." And so, in a telling passage, she comments on a new way to read the signs of landscape. The place is Puerta del Diablo, where bodies are dumped "or what is left of the bodies, pecked and maggoty masses of flesh, bone, hair." It is a place that— in "an older and distinctly literary tradition"—would have been described in words of pathos: "the sky 'broods,' the stones 'weep,' a constant seepage of water weighting the ferns and moss." Without a depth dimension, however, and in the absence of meaning, one is forced to reapply the old words, literalizing them. Indeed, the only kind of truth available to her reporter's eyes are the truths of a convention turned upside down, metaphors becoming real and reality metaphorical.

Democracy (1984) continues Didion's critique of language and society. Its title alludes to Henry Adams's paean on the idea of democracy in his 1880 work of the same name. What Adams envisioned as promise—democracy, Christianity, moral victory—is seen a century later darkly, through the glass of Didion's mirror. Speaking in fiction through the voice of Inez Christian Victor, she also intrudes her own voice onto the text, showing that she unites her identity with her female character, not with Adams.

The novel describes one post-Vietnam year (1975) as it affects the private life of the main character Inez and the public lives of her senator-husband Harry and her businessman-lover Jack Lovett. The husband is a member of the Alliance for Democratic Institution, funded to keep a particular framework of "democratic" ideals operative. His public image is undermined, however, by the women in his family. Inez carries on an adulterous relationship with Jack Lovett and eventually flees the country; Jessie, his daughter, runs away to find a job in Saigon at the exact time of massive troop evacuation; and Janet, his sister-in-law, is murdered by his demented father-in-law. That the plot is the stuff of which soap opera is made is deliberate. Didion's point is that public scandal of the magnitude of Vietnam has a convulsive effect, infiltrating and making scandalous the lives of private citizens. *Democracy* thus continues *Salvador*'s critique of the inappropriateness of abstract ideals in a world gone crazy. But here her critique is specifically feminist. She implies that America's democratic heritage was founded by men whose patriarchal ideals excluded women.

Reviews of the novel were mixed. Phoebe-Lou Adams in the *Atlantic* called it "striking, provocative, and brilliantly written." Walter Clemons commented in *Newsweek,* "Didion's latest novel is very chic, knowing and romantic. Reading 'Democracy' is like spending a privileged weekend with the great. . . . I had a swell time." And Francis Marnell, writing for the *National Review,* called it "an intelligent and engaging work well worth reading." In a longer review in *Commentary* Joseph Epstein compared Didion with Renata Adler. Epstein wrote that *Democracy* is "her richest novel since *Run River,*" with "lively details, sharp observations, risky but always interesting generalizations, real information." He argued, however, that Didion's vision offers only "plain" pessimism, unrelieved by heroism.

Negative criticism focused partly on tone, partly on style. It was felt she was either too feminist or too pessimistic, and the critics were further bothered by the intrusion of author Joan Didion into the novelistic form, as when Didion would complain, "This is a hard story to tell," or "I am resisting narrative here." Janet Wiehe in *Library Journal* said, "As ever-present narrator and minor character in her own novel, Didion achieves the immediacy of journalism at the expense of emotional depth."

Dust jacket for Joan Didion's 1984 novel treating marriage and politics in the post-Vietnam era

And Paul Stuewe of *Quill Quire* remarked that the book was more like a "glittering mosaic than a coherent novel."

These criticisms ignore Didion's challenge to storytelling as a way of presenting truth. Her concern is like that of Susan Sontag: to raise basic questions about interpretation and evaluation; to avoid the sense of "final" meaning imposed by an omniscient author. Commenting on the shape the novel was taking in her mind, she said in an interview: "I was going to Honolulu because I wanted to see life expanded to a novel. . . . I wanted room for flowers, and reef fish, and people who may or may not be driving one another to murder but in any case are not impelled, by the demands of narrative convention, to say so out loud." What she has in fact done is write a novel that challenges narrative convention. By not assuming an all-knowing pose of the author's authority, she presents a different perspective on telling stories.

The seeds of *Democracy* were sown in *Angel Visits*, the working title of a novel never completed. What Didion had in mind was to write about a dark journey, explored beneath the glamorous surface of an extended dinner party in the glittering setting of Hawaii. Throughout *Democracy* reference is made to the aborted work. Didion writes, " 'Imagine my mother dancing' that novel began in the first person. The first person was Inez, and was later abandoned in favor of the third. 'Inez imagined her mother dancing.' " Here Didion's challenge is to the authority of the *I*. The switch from first- to third-person narration exchanges the omniscient *I* narrator for a more limited third-person viewpoint. In *Democracy*, the first person becomes Joan Didion, who writes in chapter three, "You see the shards of the novel I am no longer writing, the island, the family, the situation. I lost patience with it. I lost nerve." These disclaimers serve several functions. One is to unsettle the reader; another is to imply a certain instability on the part of the author. A third and most important function of these intrusions into form is to suggest that abandonment and aborted effort are female rites. The dark journey beneath the glittering surface is ritually undertaken by women, even by authors, in a male-dominated world.

The men in *Democracy* are thrivers and survivors. They have survived the Vietnam War unwounded and can thrive on its aftermath. Jack

Lovett is typical of male heroics in the post-Vietnam age. As a successful "actor" in the field of international business, Jack is "less interested in laser mirrors than in M-16s, AK-47s, FN-FALs, the everyday implements of short-view power." Jack's sense of reality is shaped according to the "information" he receives. Didion writes about him, "It would be accurate only to say that he regarded the country on whose passport he travelled as an abstraction, a state actor, one of several to be factored into any given play." Dwight Christian, the uncle of Inez, is also a successful image-maker, who builds himself up as a culturally astute person by quoting philosophy from the pages of *Forbes.* And Billy Dillon, whose last name evokes the essence of Western heroics, is Harry Victor's PR man who understands, absolutely, the "moves" of "the game." He is to *Democracy* what the State Department briefings are to *Salvador:* knowing "the moves" he calls the shots.

These male caricatures are part of the reason that *Democracy* is Didion's most devastating feminist work to date. The other reason is the women. They become refugees inside their own country, their own homes, their own beds. Didion shows that women, the targets of sexual and international schemes, are deluded by old ideals and new promises. Inez is the latest in a series of Didion women—Maria in *Play It As It Lays,* Lily in *Run River* (1964), Charlotte in *A Book of Common Prayer*—all of whom are white, Anglo-Saxon socialites: unstable, sexually compelling, enmeshed in a web of violence spun by men. The battleground becomes the female psyche, which turns mothers and daughters against each other. Inez tries to salvage her relationship with her heroin-addicted daughter Jessie. But the strands of that relationship were woven by Inez's relationship with *her* mother, a woman who left home to find a more attractive career in modeling.

Such misapprehension reverberates on the feminine consciousness, making women the victims, not the victors, in their world. Didion's point is that women have been molded by men. Inez, for example, carries the names of the two men in her life: Christian and Victor. To pretend that she embodies either Christianity or Victory is to place her on a too-abstract plane. Whatever Christian or heroic motives she displays are a confused substitute for her roles as mother and wife. In bringing female darkness to light, Didion exposes a gulf between public and private, high and low, male and female images.

Didion's theme in *Democracy,* physical and spiritual abandonment of the homeland, applies a feminist response to the forefathers. It seems that women are refugees in the foreign land of their homes, and so they flee to establish their otherness. Inez's mother abandons her children for a more glamorous life in San Francisco. Inez abandons her children to do good works in Kuala Lumpur. Jessie abandons her mother to get a job in Saigon. These women are all cut off from mothering and so from the real source of nourishment within themselves. In citing a Wallace Stevens poem, Didion makes a statement about the artificiality of the female soul, "without human feeling, a foreign song." Even Didion feels this disconnectedness, able, she says, only to tell (not to write) her story.

Two metaphors establish a sense of the disintegrating female world. One is the metaphor of dance. Women dance, and so give romantic images of themselves—as in the recurrent film clip of Inez dancing on the St. Regis roof. Jack Lovett's first image of Inez is of her at a ballet. These romantic images stand in sharp contrast to the events which surround them. Didion makes a similar point in *Salvador* with a dance ceremony performed by a local Indian tribe. Their costumes of crinkled foil and their downcast eyes are potent metaphors for the impotence of culture. Dance, as celebration of life and grace, has lost meaning.

A second metaphor is that of memory. To be able to say "I remember" is to establish one's self in a particular place at a particular time, to remove one's self from history. When Inez confesses to a loss of memory, she is suggesting that female connectedness to the deep past, to myth, to the roots of culture, has all gone. In a stunning scene Inez is interviewed. It is the height of her husband's political career; public image is at stake. Inez is asked what she believes to be the major cost of her husband's political success: " 'Memory, mainly,' Inez said . . . 'something like shock treatment . . . I mean you lose track. *As if* you'd had shock treatment.' "

Didion's women are detached, cut off even from memory, the ground of being. In *A Book of Common Prayer,* Charlotte "forgets" the details of her daughter's revolutionary activities, leading her to sustain certain fictions about her daughter. Here Inez presents herself as such a fragmented person that "even the most straightforward details of place and date were intrinsically unknowable, open to various readings." Cut off from self, cut off from country, cut into by abortion or by sex or by flash-cut images, what are women left with?

"Colors, moisture, enough blue in the air." This phrase explains why Inez seeks refuge in India. Women must reclaim their senses of sight, sound, and touch in new settings. Removed from the old paradise, from the great American male myth of the frontier, women have to regenerate *themselves*. They have to find another time sense, until the phrase "Every day is all there is" contains ritualistic meaning.

Perhaps this phrase is the closest Didion comes to finding *la verdad*. The meaning of truth is deeper than fact or history or narration. It lies deep within culture—in dance—and within nature. A recent study of Didion by Katherine Henderson concludes that despite her pessimism, Didion is convinced that truth exists and can be approached. Her vision contains the shards of broken dreams, but it also contains the redemption of style. Style is character, revealed in a rhythm of sentences spoken and written, in metaphor, and in the rituals of the day. Didion's work will continue to excite comment as she continues to write about contemporary frontiers, whether they be cultural, psychological, political, or geographical.

References:

Samuel Coale, "Didion's Disorder: An American Romancer's Art," *Critique*, 25 (Spring 1984): 160-170;

Joseph Epstein, "The Sunshine Girls," *Commentary*, 77 (June 1984): 62-67;

Ellen Friedman, ed., *Essays and Conversations* (Princeton, N. J.: Ontario Review Press, 1984);

Lynne T. Hanley, "To El Salvador," *Massachusetts Review*, 24 (Spring 1983): 13-29;

Katherine Usher Henderson, *Joan Didion* (New York: Ungar, 1981).

William Faulkner
(25 September 1897-6 July 1962)

David Krause
Northwestern University

This entry covers the years 1980-1986.

See also the Faulkner entries in *DLB 9: American Novelists, 1910-1945; DLB 11: American Humorists, 1800-1950; DLB 44: American Screenwriters;* and *DLB Documentary Series*, volume two.

NEW BOOKS: *Mayday* (Notre Dame: University of Notre Dame Press, 1980);

Helen: A Courtship and Mississippi Poems, with introductions by Carvel Collins and Joseph Blotner (Oxford, Miss.: Yoknapatawpha Press/New Orleans: Tulane University Press, 1981);

Sanctuary: The Original Text, edited by Noel Polk (New York: Random House, 1981);

Faulkner's MGM Screenplays, edited by Bruce F. Kawin (Knoxville: University of Tennessee Press, 1982);

Father Abraham, edited by James B. Meriwether (New York: Random House, 1984);

The Sound and the Fury: New, Corrected Edition, edited by Polk (New York: Random House, 1984);

Vision in Spring, edited by Judith L. Sensibar (Austin: University of Texas Press, 1984).

OTHER: *Faulkner: A Comprehensive Guide to the Brodsky Collection*, edited by Louis Daniel Brodsky and Robert W. Hamblin, four volumes (Jackson: University Press of Mississippi, 1982-1985)—*Volume I: The Biobibliography* (1982); *Volume II: The Letters* (1984); *Volume III: The De Gaulle Story* (1984); *Volume IV: Battle Cry* (1985).

PERIODICAL PUBLICATIONS: *Elmer*, edited by James B. Meriwether, *Mississippi Quarterly*, 36 (1983): 337-460;

"Never Done No Weeping When You Wanted to Laugh," *Mississippi Quarterly*, 36 (1983): 461-474.

William Faulkner published his most ambitious and stunning novel, *Absalom, Absalom!*, in 1936; fifty years later we are still only beginning to learn how and why to read it. In 1986 it has probably become easier to recognize *Absalom*—along with the rest of Faulkner's large canon, especially *The Sound and the Fury* (1929), *As I Lay Dying* (1930), *Light in August* (1932), *The Hamlet* (1940), and *Go Down, Moses and Other Stories* (1942)—as the troubling work of a man "trying to write down the heart's truth out of the heart's driving complexity, for all the complex and troubled hearts which would beat after" (*Go Down, Moses*). And it has certainly become much more respectable—even academically and culturally *necessary*—to attend to Faulkner's "miragy antics of men and women . . . called honor, principle, marriage, love, bereavement, death," to "his fabulous immeasurable Camelots and Carcassones," to his profoundly "trashy myth of reality's escape" (*Absalom*). Faulkner's best books, however, still refuse to settle comfortably into place "among dusty shelves of ordered certitudes long divorced from reality, desiccating peacefully" (*The Sound and the Fury*). Even when, like *Absalom*, a Faulkner text almost makes us certain "that most of the deeds, good and bad both, incurring opprobrium or plaudits or reward either, within the scope of man's abilities, had already been performed and were to be learned about only from books," that same text, like *As I Lay Dying*, also exposes us to "the old terrors, the old lusts, the old despairs" which cannot be ordered, cannot be written or read. All of Faulkner's works, from *Soldier's Pay* (1927) to *The Reivers* (1962), confront "the immitigable chasm between all life and all print" (*The Unvanquished*, 1938). And all of Faulkner's novels address their readers in the way Horace Benbow addresses his sister Narcissa in a letter near the end of *Flags in the Dust:* "I daresay you cannot read this as usual, or reading it, it will not mean anything to you."

Faulkner's professional readers, the critics, have tried so variously and so relentlessly during the past fifty years or so to make Faulkner readable and meaningful—to make something *usual* of him—that it is tempting to borrow Mr. Compson's cynical words about physicians to describe them: "they make their livings advising people to do whatever they are not doing at the time, which is the extent of anyone's knowledge of the degenerate ape" (*The Sound and the Fury*). Richard Brodhead and André Bleikasten have recently called upon both new and experienced readers of Faulkner to (re)learn how to read him. Reminding us that "the

Faulkner we possess . . . is always and necessarily one his readers have helped to make," Brodhead encourages continued rethinking, reimagining, and remaking—continued repossessing—of Faulkner's texts: "there is still as great a need as ever for Faulkner to be known anew." Bleikasten redefines and reaffirms (in the spirit of Roland Barthes) an erotics of reading Faulkner, celebrating the bursts of ideas and feelings, desires and delights, oppressions and repressions that constitute the work of reading ("Reading Faulkner"). In "For/Against an Ideological Reading of Faulkner's Novels," Bleikasten begins the complex process of articulating not only a poetics, but also a politics and an ethics of reading Faulkner. "The real question," Bleikasten writes, "is whether Faulkner's work ever manages to gain distance from ideology or whether it simply mirrors the perplexities and confusions of a disaffiliated bourgeois intellectual."

Michel Gresset adumbrates one approach to this difficult question in his introduction to *Faulkner in Intertextuality* (1985): situate Faulkner's texts within the vast network of texts articulating the literary and cultural repertoire. Karl Zender suggests a more modest but potentially more helpful approach to questions of Faulknerian reading, representation, and ideology in his essay, "Reading in 'The Bear.' " Zender shows that "the image of the reader in relation to the text becomes a means of exploring the larger matter of the relation of the mind to the world." According to Zender, "Faulkner saw two basic problems in the reader-text (or mind-world) relationship. The one occurs when a reader is not adequate to the demands of a text, the other when a text is not adequate to the needs of a reader." Zender helps raise some intriguing questions about Faulkner's representation of reading, despite his tendency to impose excessively neat critical paradigms on the messy business of reading.

Reading Faulkner, as Zender notes, we often find ourselves reading about someone reading. Narcissa Benbow, for example, "took her book to bed, where she again held her consciousness submerged as you hold a puppy under water until its body ceases to resist" (*Flags in the Dust*, 1973). Rev. Gail Hightower, in *Light in August*, reads Tennyson because "it is better than praying without having to bother to think aloud. It is like listening in a cathedral to a eunuch chanting in a language which he does not even need to not understand." Joe Christmas, in the same novel, reads a lurid magazine from cover to cover, "apparently arrested and held immobile by a single word which had perhaps not yet impacted, his whole being suspended by the single trivial combination of letters in quiet and sunny space." In *The Wild Palms* (1939), the tall convict "followed his printed (and false) authority to the letter; he had saved the paper-backs for two years, reading and rereading them, memorizing them, comparing and weighing story and method against story and method, taking the good from each and discarding the dross as his workable plan emerged." Meanwhile, Harry Wilbourne, in the same novel, speculates that *"it's all exactly backward. It should be the books, the people in the books inventing and reading about us,"* and finds it oddly disturbing that "the four-legged animal gains all its information through smelling and seeing and hearing and distrusts all else while the two-legged one believes only what it reads." Labove, Eula Varner's schoolteacher in *The Hamlet*, sits over "books which he did not love so much as he believed that he must read, compare and absorb and wring dry with something of that same contemptuous intensity with which he chopped firewood, measuring the turned pages against the fleeing seconds of irrevocable time."

Narcissa Benbow, Gail Hightower, Joe Christmas, the tall convict, Harry Wilbourne, and Labove—all these readers (and many more) seem to fail: none of them seem to know how or why to read. And each failure or misreading seems to result from ceasing to resist, from submitting too easily to the authority of the written text, from not thinking enough. If, then, we want to learn how and why to read Faulkner successfully, his own texts must continually be allowed to teach us how to rethink, to reimagine, and to refeel them, and must prepare us to acknowledge but never accept our inevitable failures and frustrations. It will not be enough to "re-read, tedious and intent, poring," as Mr. Compson rereads Charles Bon's letter in *Absalom*. Nor will it be enough to ask of Faulkner's professional readers what the young Thomas Sutpen asks his easily intimidated teacher: "How do I know that what you read was in the book?"

Nevertheless, in order to keep deepening our understanding of Faulkner's achievements, we must continue to reread his books and continue to question each other's rereadings. This essay, then, surveys the most important scholarly contributions made between 1980 and 1986 to the understanding of how and why to read and reread the works of William Faulkner. No attempt is made to duplicate the comprehensive annotated bibliographies published annually by *American Literary Scholarship* and the *Mississippi Quarterly*. This survey, rather, makes every attempt to identify and evaluate that schol-

arship which has already had, or seems destined to have, or deserves to have a significant impact on Faulkner's readers beyond 1986.

Several previously unpublished texts by Faulkner became available between 1980 and 1986. *Mayday* (1980) and *Helen: A Courtship* (1981) were both gift books made personally by Faulkner for Helen Baird in early 1926. *Mayday* allegorizes and ironizes romance, borrowing freely from Arthurian legends, *Don Quixote*, and James Branch Cabell's *Jurgen*, while anticipating the quests of Quentin Compson in *The Sound and the Fury*. Faulkner, who always cared about the way his books looked, illustrated *Mayday* with watercolors (adequately reproduced in this new trade edition). *Helen* is a short sonnet sequence obviously designed to impress and seduce. These sonnets have been published along with twelve additional poems, and valuable introductory essays by Carvel Collins and Joseph Blotner.

Elmer (1983) and *Father Abraham* (1984) both represent fragments of abandoned manuscripts. *Elmer*, written in Europe during August and September of 1925, has been aptly described by David Minter as "a portrait of the artist Faulkner did *not* wish to become: the artist who reduces his gift to a flair for romantic living, and so surrenders his chance to live in and out of the world of creation." Perhaps because the entwined erotic and aesthetic themes remained uncomfortably autobiographical, Faulkner could not sustain distance and control. *Father Abraham*, written in late 1926 and early 1927, also lacks control, but retains great significance because it dramatically records Faulkner's discovery of the irrepressible Snopes family.

Faulkner's MGM Screenplays (1982) conveniently contains all the treatments and scripts Faulkner wrote during his first year as a professional screenwriter (1932-1933) along with extensive notes and commentaries by Bruce F. Kawin. Written soon after *Light in August*, these scripts offer fascinating and valuable glimpses into Faulkner's characteristic modes of imagining and reimagining, composing and recomposing. In *War Birds*, for example, Faulkner reconceives and rewrites the story of John and Bayard Sartoris he had told a few years earlier in *Flags in the Dust*. And in "Turn About," released as *Today We Live*, Faulkner reworks his short story of the same name, while integrating material from *The Sound and the Fury*.

The 1984 edition of *The Sound and the Fury* cannot be definitive, despite Noel Polk's admirable intention of preserving and reproducing Faulkner's "final intentions"; some helpful corrections have been made, however.

Sanctuary: The Original Text (1981) and Vision in Spring (1984) (a poem sequence presented by Faulkner in 1921 to his future wife Estelle Oldham Franklin) have understandably attracted more critical attention than any of the other previously unpublished works by Faulkner released since 1980. In "The Space between Sanctuary," Polk explores Faulkner's writing and rewriting of what he called his "most horrific tale," as well as the extraordinary significance of Faulkner's literary accomplishments in the eighteen months (1929-1930) between the two versions of Sanctuary. Polk makes a persuasive case "that the first Sanctuary is, at least for the time being, in so many ways a more interesting book than the second, and that taken together, in their inter- and intratextual relationships with each other and with the other novels and stories in the space between, the two versions form a single literary text that is far more significant than either of the versions taken singly. We cannot now pretend to understand either Sanctuary without also coming to terms with the other." Polk also makes use of Freud, especially the "Wolf Man" case history to help explain how and why Sanctuary was originally about Horace Benbow rather than about Temple Drake. In a companion essay, "Law in Faulkner's Sanctuary," Polk again uses Freud, demonstrating the centrality of the Oedipus complex to Sanctuary's representations of authority, sexuality, and guilt.

John T. Matthews's "The Elliptical Nature of Sanctuary," accepts Polk's judgment that the two versions should be treated as a single text. Matthews, in perhaps the most original and impressive new study of the novel, discloses that "the figure of ellipsis pervades the rhetorical, psychological, narrative, and thematic structures of Sanctuary." He generates his dense, highly theoretical argument through close textual analysis, powerfully sustaining his thesis that "the text's elliptical texture indicates the unrepresentability of the passage from nature to culture, from mating to the family, from lawlessness to social organization." Matthews nicely explains just how "Temple's story is an elaborate transmogrification of Horace's story," and just how "the two plots of the story, like the two versions of the novel, are more intimately related than earlier criticism has granted." Two essays by André Bleikasten on Sanctuary also deserve to be read carefully. One illuminates the shadowy presence of "Emma Bovary's Ghost in Sanctuary"; the other studies language of the body in the novel and re-

veals "terror and nausea exorcised in the very act of writing."

Vision in Spring has not yet been assimilated into the Faulkner canon as interestingly as Sanctuary: The Original Text; it has not yet provoked—and may never provoke—the same unusually intense level of analysis from critics. Yet its publication demands notice, if only because Faulkner wanted to be a great poet before he wanted to be a great novelist. Judith L. Sensibar, both in her introduction to Vision in Spring and in her companion study, The Origins of Faulkner's Art (1984), unfortunately exaggerates the importance of this modest fourteen-poem sequence in Faulkner's development. According to Sensibar, studying the forms and voice of Vision in Spring can resolve questions of authorial intention in much of Faulkner's

Dust jacket for Judith Sensibar's seminal 1984 study of Faulkner's development as a writer based on an investigation of his attempt to become a poet

fiction." Despite her conscientious attention to Faulkner's poetry, Sensibar cannot persuade that it could or should be so. "What we discern" in Faulkner's poetry, according to David Minter, "is not the source of Faulkner's originality but the direction of his self-education." In its best moments, then, Sensibar's study can reveal something about the beginnings of Faulkner's writing, but little if anything about the genuine origins of his art. Nonetheless, Sensibar has earned the gratitude of Faulknerians for her responsible editing of *Vision in Spring*. And it should be noted that *The Origins of Faulkner's Art* contains several intriguing remarks about Faulkner's personal life made by his daughter Jill Faulkner Summers during a series of interviews with Sensibar between 1979 and 1983.

The years under review in this essay were graced by two major biographies of William Faulkner. David Minter's 1980 account "of deep reciprocities, of relations and revisions, between Faulkner's flawed life and his great art," offered an elegant, engaging, and welcome alternative to Joseph Blotner's plodding and yet necessary two-volume *Faulkner: A Biography* (1974). In *William Faulkner: His Life and Work*, Minter succeeded admirably in presenting Faulkner's "life as a life of writing and his art as a writing or reconstituting of his life." Minter, as he generously acknowledges throughout his book, could not have written his persuasive interpretation of Faulkner's life and work without carefully reading Blotner's monumental record of that life and work. Now it seems likely, or at least plausible, that Blotner, in turn, could not (or would not) have written his superb new one-volume biography of Faulkner without having read Minter. Although it need not (should not) replace Minter's fine book, the one-volume edition of *Faulkner: A Biography* (1984) irrefutably (re)establishes Joseph Blotner's role as the preeminent authority on Faulkner's life. Blotner, making responsible use of scholarly developments between 1974 and 1984, and still scrupulously tactful and deferential toward Faulkner, demonstrates that he has continued to reexamine, to rethink, and—most impressively—to reimagine Faulkner's life and work. Blotner's new biography—and it *is* new and wonderfully readable—tells much more about Faulkner's personal life and risks asking questions and drawing inferences that were suppressed in 1974. More than anyone else, for example, Blotner helps the reader to understand Faulkner's troubled marriage to Estelle; and yet he never pretends to write as if he were a psychoanalyst. At least for now, the one-volume edition of *Faulkner: A Biog-*

raphy: stands alone as authoritative and indispensable.

Future accounts of Faulkner's life and work will owe a major debt to Louis Daniel Brodsky's tireless and scrupulous collecting of letters, manuscripts, first editions, and other documentary evidence. The first volume of *Faulkner: A Comprehensive Guide to the Brodsky Collection* is *The Biobibliography* (1982) which offers an impressive, detailed, and tantalizing descriptive catalogue of a superb private collection. *Volume II: The Letters* (nicely introduced by Robert W. Hamblin) publishes almost 500 letters, including 129 by Faulkner (about 100 first printed here), and about 50 letters by Estelle Faulkner (most to Saxe and/or Dorothy Commins). None of these letters substantially alters our sense of Faulkner's career, but many provide new glimpses, and a few are disconcertingly personal. In February 1954, for example, Estelle writes what she characterizes as a "shocking letter" to Saxe Commins (Faulkner's editor and confidant): "*Nothing* can alter my love and devotion—nor upset my faith in Bill's actual love for me—although right now, he swears he doesn't care.... All I want is Billy's good—and to prove it, I'll do *anything* that is best—The only thing that I shudder at and might try to evade, is a divorce—and *that*, only on Jill's account." If we find this kind of letter more poignant and painful than shocking, if it makes us uncomfortable to confront such intimacies, we might well note Faulkner's own restrained observation to Commins (in a letter reporting that Estelle had read Joan Williams's letters to Faulkner): "people who will open and read another's private and personal letters, do deserve exactly what they get."

We get a great deal from Brodsky, whose collection is graced by other kinds of letters. Jun Takami, for example, writes with a desperate eloquence to Faulkner about his Stockholm address and Japanese fears about the atomic bomb: "What can or should a Japanese writer do with this anguish of the heart?" (25 September 1954). Lawrance Thompson confides to Commins that he finds *A Fable* "bastard-baroque" and that he fears "you and Random House are stuck with a dud" (4 July 1954). And in an alternately amusing, insightful, and self-aggrandizing letter to Carvel Collins, Phil Stone (Faulkner's life-long associate) patiently insists that "Freud and Macbeth had no more to do with the conscious writing of [*The South and the Fury*] . . . than you did and you didn't even know Faulkner then" (16 August 1954). Stone's insistence has all the more bite coming at the end of a lengthy letter in which, among other things, he claims to have been with Faulkner throughout the composition of the novel, teaching him (or trying to teach him) about Joyce and Freud. Stone also tells Collins, "I suggested, since it was a tale told by an idiot that we call it *The Sound and the Fury*," and that "Jason did not come from Freud but from my own brother James Stone, Jr."

The third and fourth volumes of the Brodsky Collection, *The De Gaulle Story* (1984) and *Battle Cry* (1985), make available a substantial new body of Faulkner's work on two aborted screenplays for Warner Bros. For several intense weeks during the summer of 1942 Faulkner wrote and rewrote a script about Charles De Gaulle and the French Resistance. For reasons beyond Faulkner's control the project was abandoned, but not before—under pressure from Hollywood, Washington, and De Gaulle's representative to produce a conventional patriotic tribute—Faulkner came to the characteristically Faulknerian conclusion that De Gaulle himself should not be portrayed in the film about him: "Let's dispense," Faulkner proposed to his producer, "with General De Gaulle as a living character in the story." In the summer of 1943 Faulkner worked with Howard Hawks on an even more ambitious epic of patriotism, "Battle Cry." Like "The De Gaulle Story" the year before, this new project absorbed Faulkner's energies and imagination to no avail. Both anticipate the Stockholm address and *A Fable* in striking and important ways. In an early version of "The De Gaulle Story," for example, a priest tells the young hero (not De Gaulle): "Oppression and suffering come upon mankind and even destroy him as individuals. But they cannot destroy his immortal spirit. That endures." Faulkner's writing in Hollywood deserves more attention than it has yet received. By making significant texts available to a wider audience, Brodsky and Hamblin have made a major contribution to potential understanding of a complex phase of Faulkner's life and work.

Although this essay intends to report major developments in Faulkner scholarship between 1980 and 1986, three studies published in 1979 deserve continued and renewed attention today. Each articulates a compelling strategy for reading Faulkner; none have yet been fully reckoned with by subsequent critics. Donald Kartiganer's chapters on *The Sound and the Fury* and *Absalom, Absalom!* have already had considerable influence, but many critics seem to have ignored, misunderstood, or resisted the theoretical and practical implications of his perceptive analyses of fragmentariness in Faulkner's novels. In *The Fragile Thread: The Mean-*

ing of Form in Faulkner's Novels (1979), Kartiganer demonstrates that "fragmentary structure is the core of Faulkner's novelistic vision, describing a world of broken orders, a world in which meetings of men and words need to be imagined again." Kartiganer does not argue, as some critics have mistakenly claimed he does, that Faulkner's novels fail as narratives but argues rather that each novel tends in one way or another to address the problems of narration and failure. Since Kartiganer so intelligently explores "the larger questions of what a Faulkner novel is and what its structure implies about consciousness, reality, and moral value," it is especially unfortunate that his explorations have sometimes been trivialized as mere deconstructions. *The Fragile Thread* deserves to be reread and reevaluated in 1986.

So does Gary Lee Stonum's *Faulkner's Career: An Internal Literary History* (1979), which claims that the "trajectory of Faulkner's career is . . . shaped by three interrelated things: a practice of challenging the inadequacies of previous texts, a duty to change and advance, and a need to keep future possibilities open." Michael Millgate has cautioned against the necessarily reductive tendencies of Stonum's self-styled "internal literary history," and emphasized the need to remain sensitive to unpredictable pressures, processes, and dynamics within Faulkner's development as a writer. Others have objected that Stonum does not adequately accommodate Faulkner's *southernness*, even though he acknowledges that "some of the phases of Faulkner's career can be roughly defined by changes in the pressure exerted on him by tradition, locality, and also language." Whatever its limitations, however, *Faulkner's Career* raises significant theoretical questions about how and why Faulkner continued to write; moreover, Stonum generates an unusually suggestive reading of Faulkner's visionary poetry, as well as striking revisionary readings of key passages in some major novels, notably *Absalom, Absalom!*

Wesley A. Morris begins *Friday's Footprint: Structuralism and the Articulated Text* (1979) with a strikingly sophisticated essay on *Go Down, Moses* called "The Pilgrimage of Being." Although he uses Faulkner's text in order to illustrate his own theory of language and culture, a theory of "literature's socio-historical involvement," Morris remains keenly responsive to the complex formal, stylistic, and thematic integrities of *Go Down, Moses*. He effectively engages the "startling disjuncture of section four" of "The Bear," for example; and he explains better than anyone else why "we must separate Sam from the romanticized version of him fostered by Ike McCaslin," why Ike "finds himself . . . excluded from the true benefits of belonging yet not free from the genealogical myth's heavy burden of responsibility"—why "Ike can neither move forward into history nor backward into the old myth." Some readers may (upon casual perusal) be intimidated by the density of Morris's argument and by his appropriation of theoretical vocabulary from Roland Barthes, Michel Foucault, Jacques Derrida, and other foreigners in Yoknapatawpha. But when it matters most, Morris thinks for himself (and helps us think for ourselves), articulating his resonant insights with unusual grace and precision. Defining myth as "the *expression* of a cognitive strategy that defines man's sense of belonging to his world," Morris generates a reading of *Go Down, Moses* that ought to stimulate major rereadings of the rest of Faulkner's canon. Though his methodology differs radically from Kartiganer's, Morris pushes toward a richly complementary understanding of Faulkner's enterprise: "the fragmentation of human society into a plurality of epistemological, moral, and political systems, many of which are enslaving and exploitative, reflects not Faulkner's failure to construct in this novel an exemplary, idealized aesthetic order, but his vivid articulation of the failure of misguided romantic humanism." More generally, Morris demonstrates through his analysis of *Go Down, Moses* "that it is not *a* structure but the *potentiality* of structure that is universal."

Since 1980 the three most important book-length studies of Faulkner have been Cleanth Brooks's *William Faulkner: First Encounters* (1983), John T. Matthews's *The Play of Faulkner's Language* (1982), and Eric Sundquist's *Faulkner: The House Divided* (1983).

First Encounters, though "not intended for the Faulkner specialist," demands serious consideration because it distills more than twenty years of Cleanth Brooks's distinguished scholarship into readings of the major works which will influence another generation of new Faulkner readers. Faulkner's current and future readers must remain grateful to Brooks for being among the first to open up the strange world of Yoknapatawpha to the public; yet, some may be legitimately disappointed that at this juncture in his long and generous career, Brooks has not risked reseeing, rethinking, reimagining, has not risked remapping any corner of the topography of Faulkner's imagination. In *First Encounters* Brooks shows no inclination to question any of his old New Critical assumptions

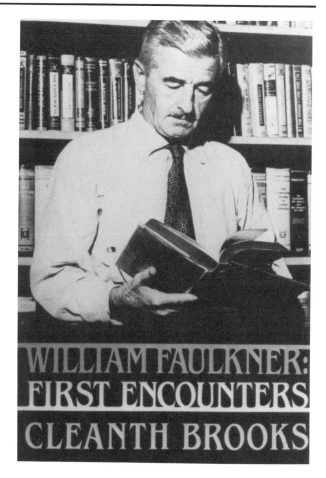

Dust jacket for Cleanth Brooks's introduction to Faulkner's best-known short stories and major novels

about how and why to read Faulkner. He remains surprisingly defensive about Faulkner's southernness. And he remains satisfied to describe themes, characters, and plot—in his own words "undistracted by too much critical apparatus." Alternately disarming and disconcerting, Brooks tends to rely on his own intuitive way of making sense of Faulkner, when instead he might teach readers something about how to make sense (and how to stop making sense?) of Faulkner for themselves. Brooks's (dis-)ingenuous dismissal of any need for a theory, poetics, or at least methodology of reading reveals the very ideological biases and limitations it intends to conceal or displace. Despite obvious good intentions, Brooks unfortunately tries to compromise, simplify, stabilize, and normalize encounters with texts written by Faulkner to resist compromise, simplification, stabilization, and—above all—normalization.

In *The Play of Faulkner's Language*, John T. Matthews pays extraordinary attention to significant excesses, blurs, breaks, leaks, remainders, and holes in Faulkner's writings. Matthews deftly uses language about language to write about Faulkner writing and to engage precisely those moments in Faulkner's texts which have until now proven most resistant to theory and to reading. With sophistication and tact, Matthews appropriates the deconstructive theories of Derrida; his fundamental strategy, however, depends on sensitive, close readings of Faulkner's language. Matthews, it turns out, employs New Critical strategies of textual analysis to reopen the texts, to reopen the work of reading, and to reopen theoretical assumptions about textuality, reading, and theory. Not since John T. Irwin's *Doubling and Incest/Repetition and Revenge: A Speculative Reading of Faulkner* (1975) has a critical book about Faulkner had such an impressive effect. And because Matthews *reads* rather than speculates (unlike Irwin, who speculates rather than reads), *The Play of Faulkner's Language* has been at once more widely influential and less controversial than Irwin's book.

In a lucid introductory chapter—"How to Approach Language"—Matthews summarizes Derrida's position that "disappearance, absence, and articulation all obtain within presence or speech." And, by locating Faulkner within the contexts of modernism articulated by Nietzsche, Freud, and Heidegger, Matthews also explains patiently and persuasively just how and why Derrida can help with language and play in Yoknapatawpha. Matthews borrows the *play* of his title and critical method from Derrida's essay, "Structure, Sign, and Play" (*Writing and Difference*, 1978). According to Derrida, "Play is the disruption of presence . . . Play is always play of absence and presence, but if it is to be thought radically, play must be conceived of before the alternative of presence and absence." Thinking radically and reading disruptively, and yet with scrupulous respect for Faulkner's structures of language, Matthews generates compelling, sometimes startling, commentaries on *The Sound and the Fury*, *Absalom, Absalom!*, *The Hamlet*, and *Go Down, Moses*.

Each of Matthews's rich commentaries offers its own pleasures and rewards, and each eludes easy summary. In his central and representative chapter on *Absalom*, for example, Matthews argues that "in several respects marriage is one of the chief figures for storytelling in *Absalom*, and . . . that a peculiar, perhaps even parodic version of marriage embodies the intimacy and pleasure of narration, and also suggests how fiction makes its meanings." Some readers may remain uncomfortable with Mat-

thews's emphasis on Faulknerian makings rather than Faulknerian meanings, on Faulknerian poetics rather than mimetics. Matthews argues that "Faulkner's major fiction elevates fabrication over representation, confronts the loss of the original idea and subject, makes writing a kind of mourning (as it produces the very insufficiencies it seeks to overcome), and celebrates the playfulness of writing in the space (or play) between the written and the written about." Even those who fail to recognize in Faulkner exactly the kind of elevations, confrontations, grievings, and celebrations of (and in) language disclosed by Matthews, must acknowledge the brilliance and power of his elegant argument. *The Play of Faulkner's Language* clearly emerges as the most original and important study of Faulkner's writing in at least ten years. It also stands as one of the best recent books on *any* American author, and represents the kind of humane and generous literary criticism that may encourage a sustained reevaluation of the possibilities of poststructuralist theory.

If Matthews helps readers to resee Faulkner's language and its play, Eric J. Sundquist helps them to reconceive the place of language and the play of art within cultural and political structure. In *Faulkner: The House Divided*, Sundquist presents an unusually intense meditation on writing and race, writing and difference. According to Sundquist, Faulkner managed to make something great of his writing only by reassociating himself with the color of his skin, only became an important writer when he admitted within his fictions the burdensome worries and pressures of being white, male, and from Mississippi. "Faulkner's best work," Sundquist claims, "reflects a turbulent search for fictional forms in which to contain and express the ambivalent feelings and projected passions that were his as an author and as an American in the South." Sundquist's thesis that "Faulkner's career up to *Light in August* might well be considered an extended repression of the *figure* of the Negro" at times seems needlessly reductive, even if allowing, as Sundquist seems to intend, for the full metaphorical implications of the word 'figure.' Sundquist never really persuades us that Faulkner's only genuine subject is always (or should always have been) miscegenation. Always literate and provocative, Sundquist's chapters on *The Sound and the Fury* and *Sanctuary* remain only marginally relevant to his thesis and only partially successful as coherent readings of the novels. Sundquist's reading of *As I Lay Dying*, simply by making an eloquent case for the novel's greatness, paradoxically subverts his thesis that genuinely great writing only followed Faulkner's discovery of the theme of miscegenation.

For Sundquist, Faulkner discovers the horrors and possibilities of miscegenation in *Light in August*. He cites Mark Twain's *Pudd'nhead Wilson* (1894)—"And why this awful difference made between white and black?"—to illuminate how *Light in August* "begins Faulkner's stunning exploration of that question." *Pudd'nhead Wilson* and Charles Carroll's *Negro as Beast* (1900), now seem, in light of Sundquist's disclosures, necessary reading for anyone trying to come to terms with the strange career of Joe Christmas. If we want that kind of criticism that can respond to "the interplay between . . . fictions and categories that are said to partake of reality, such as the self, man, society, 'the artist, his culture, and the human community,'" then we must welcome Sundquist's unsettling book. More intelligently and responsibly than almost any other critic of Faulkner, Sundquist "strives to reconcile the internal, formal, private structures of literary language with their external, referential and public effects" (Paul De Man, "Semiology and Rhetoric"). His reconciliations remain provisional and reversible; no easy accommodations are allowed.

Sundquist "reconstruct[s] a context for Faulkner's fiction out of historical experience, contemporary literature, [and] political and sociological documents." But working within this fluidly defined cultural context, Sundquist attends very nicely to matters of Faulknerian style and structure; he never moves casually or far beyond the kinds of readings made possible by formalist principles of textuality, but he presents textuality in new and surprising ways. He explicates splendidly, for example, this metaphor in *Light in August* which captures Joe Christmas naked in the headlights of a car: "He watched his body grow white out of the darkness like a kodak print emerging from the liquid." Sundquist sees that "What it offers is a figure of simultaneous concealment and revelation, a figure that marks with explosive precision, at a point of passing from one to the other, the ambiguity of Joe Christmas, who—like Jim Crow, yet with doubled ironic pressure of already appearing to be what he must but cannot become—virtually is a figure rather than a person." With this kind of analytic precision Sundquist neatly negotiates the resonant space between Joe and Jim, between literature and politics. Along with his chapter on *Light in August*, Sundquist's chapters on *Absalom, Absalom!* and *Go Down, Moses* make *Faulkner: The*

House Divided a formidable and distinguished contribution to Faulkner studies.

Three other recent books also contribute significantly to the understanding of Faulkner and race, although none presents an argument of comparable subtlety and rigor, and none remains as committed to a coherent poetics, politics, and ethics of reading as Sundquist's. Writing in 1946, Ralph Ellison suggested that Faulkner "explored perhaps more successfully than anyone else, either white or black, certain forms of Negro humanity," and then went on to propose that Faulkner might be "the example for our writers to follow, for in his work technique has been put once more to the task of creating value" (*Shadow and Act*). In *Faulkner's "Negro": Art and the Southern Context* (1983), Thadious M. Davis stimulates a responsible and necessary reconsideration of the complex dialectic between verbal strategies and moral imperatives, between techniques and values, in Faulkner's best novels. Davis sees Faulkner's art as an "effort to transcend the tensions and divisions emanating from his cultural heritage, as well as from his position as artist in that culture, that divided world." Looking at the Southern context, she observes that "for the southerner of either race, there is usually present the alternative side and the opposite point of view, or simply put, another way of seeing, doing, living, being, or thinking." Looking at Faulkner's art, Davis tries to discover "what the Negro reveals about the novels and the process of creating them." Her balanced point of view works both to accommodate and to explain the kind of tensions and divisions between art and its contexts that empower Faulkner's techniques and values.

Writing firmly within the conventions of orthodox New Criticism, Davis wants to resee and to rethink "how 'Negro' operates within and contributes to the entire novel—its narrative structure, thematic design, character development, or other applicable aspects of the fiction." She tries to keep her focus on the fictions, the art, acknowledging from the start that "Faulkner is neither social historian nor philosopher, particularly in regard to black people," and that his "fiction is neither photographic realism nor journalistic writing," *not* "a mimetic treatment of 'southern' reality." What Davis sees, especially in *The Sound and the Fury* and *Absalom, Absalom!*, frequently startles, if only because earlier critics do not seem to have noticed what her focus makes so obvious and significant. Her rereading of *The Sound and the Fury*, for example, reveals how the entire Gibson family, not just Dilsey, "serve[s] structural, thematic, and symbolic functions." It revoices Faulkner's text, making the Gibsons, especially Luster, much more audible (that is, more visible and legible, more meaningful) than they may have been for many readers—at least many *white* readers—until now. If at first Davis's claim that "Clytie reveals the most about Faulkner's art and the Negro" in *Absalom* seems excessive, her rereading of the novel movingly shows that, although Charles Bon "becomes, like the Negro in general, the metaphorical embodiment of all that is invisible in southern life," it is Clytie who deserves most urgently to be seen in her invisibility, heard in her silences.

Davis's project—to reinvent Faulkner's Yoknapatawpha through a reimagining and revoicing of Faulkner's "Negro"—cannot be accomplished radically or persuasively enough within the margins of New Critical discourse set by Cleanth

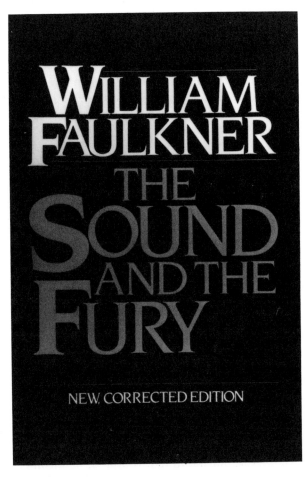

Dust jacket for the first corrected version of Faulkner's fourth novel. This 1984 edition is based on a comparison of Faulkner's holograph manuscript and the carbon typescript in the Faulkner Collection of the Alderman Library, University of Virginia, and the 1929 Cape & Smith first edition.

Brooks. Although Davis insists that she does "not attempt to isolate Faulkner's attitude toward Negro characters and to glean from this his attitude toward black people outside his fiction," she repeatedly evaluates the quality of Faulkner's representations of black experience and "the South's irresponsible and selective morality." Davis wants more realism and more sociology than her critical assumptions and methodology can admit or handle. Nothing in the exegetical procedures of New Criticism really authorizes leaps back and forth between texts and contexts: Art *and* the Southern Context. Davis writes with genuine insight about Faulkner's art, and she writes thoughtfully about the Southern context; but that conjunction gives her more trouble than she acknowledges.

Walter Taylor's *Faulkner's Search for a South* (1983) and Lee Jenkins' *Faulkner and Black-White Relations: A Psychoanalytic Approach* (1981) both contribute to the important task of reevaluating Faulkner's representations of racial difference. Taylor and Jenkins, however, both lack Davis's gifts as a sensitive reader, both have troublesome axes to grind, and both want even more realism and sociology than does Davis. Since, as Irving Howe long ago pointed out, "whoever wants a precise platform or a coherent sociology for the Negroes had better look elsewhere. Faulkner's triumph is of another kind, the novelist's triumph" (*William Faulkner: A Critical Study,* 1952, revised 1975), both Taylor and Jenkins find considerably less to say about Faulkner's art than Davis. And both express impatience and frustration at not finding what they think they ought to find in Faulkner's black and white fictions. Taylor has written a more interesting account of his frustrations with Faulkner than has Jenkins. Taylor asserts that "the image of 'perfection' Faulkner was seeking was usually—perhaps always—something that could be described as 'the South': some cluster of images, experiences, and fantasies inherited from the world of his youth." Taylor's thesis, however, is not simply that an obsessive search for a South motivates and shapes virtually everything about Faulkner's life and work. He argues, rather, that because the South that Faulkner desires can exist only in imaginings and fantasies about the past, Faulkner refused any unmediated dealings with the *real* South (real, as perceived—but never defined—by Taylor himself), and consequently dooms himself to "a kind of social schizophrenia" and a compulsive pattern of failure (artistic *and* moral).

Taylor tries to write an exposé of what he calls Faulkner's "lifelong psychodrama" in black and white, but suppresses an explicitly psychoanalytic method and vocabulary. Lee Jenkins, as his subtitle announces, intends to take "a psychoanalytic approach" to what he perceives as Faulkner's "fundamental sense of the otherness of blacks." Claiming that "the problem is not one of holding Faulkner to a mimetic representation of reality when such is not his intention," Jenkins admits that he has serious problems with Faulkner's "intention, his narrative technique, and the kind of knowledge it yields." Jenkins would require of Faulkner's imaginative creation a "faithfulness to social and historical reality," at least whenever Jenkins determines that Faulkner should have intended such faithfulness. His contention that Faulkner "distort[s] the reality of black life for his own aesthetic effects," insofar as it insinuates racism, results mostly from his confusion about Faulknerian mimesis and intentionality. Faulkner aptly describes his work as "sublimating the actual into apocrypha," adding, "I created a cosmos of my own." Readers like Jenkins and Taylor—and sometimes Davis—remain suspicious of the mysteries of sublimation and creation; they do not like to grant Faulkner his world elsewhere because they cannot quite imagine it. So they look only for whatever actuality they can recognize in Faulkner's apocrypha.

Jenkins hopes to legitimate and substantiate his thesis that Faulkner "misrepresents the meaning and significance of black life, in relation to that of whites, and diminishes and demeans the blacks in comparison" by approaching Faulkner psychoanalytically. Unfortunately, he demonstrates at best a second-hand notion of Freud and Rank. Jenkins offers mostly his own impressions of "Faulkner's racism," his own sense that Faulkner never gets himself "sufficiently liberated." However, he also expresses a somewhat contradictory respect for Faulkner's "uncompromising integrity" and a belief in the "vision of decency and humanity that presides over all his work." If he is right to suggest that "Faulkner gradually revealed himself, on racial matters, to be an artist of more humane and enlightened views," then *Faulkner and Black-White Relations* might ultimately have been a more useful and persuasive account if Jenkins had pursued a chronological and developmental analysis of Faulkner's writing.

Craig Werner's essay, "Tell Old Pharaoh: The Afro-American Response to Faulkner" (1983), rereads Faulkner through the dark and skeptical eyes of Richard Wright, James Baldwin, Toni Morrison, Alice Walker, and several other black writers. Werner finds that "Faulkner is one of the few white writers who adapts aspects of the Afro-American voice, rather than expecting the common language to be essentially Euro-American in structure and content." With careful attention to narrative structures, Werner demonstrates that, "in his most profound moments, Faulkner . . . revoices standard Afro-American scenes in terms of Euro-American experience." Werner's essay represents a tactful and important effort to increase our sensitivities about Faulkner's conviction "that no individual voice can express anything other than a partial truth. . . . the need for both black and white voices for any approach to such truth." Acknowledging Faulkner's "limited understanding of Afro-American culture," Werner hears in Faulkner's voice as well as in those of Afro-American writers responding to Faulkner "a profound statement of the need for a common black-white vocabulary in American literature."

Sundquist, Davis, Taylor, Jenkins, and Werner participate, individually and collectively, in one of the most valuable projects facing Faulkner studies: accommodating racial difference within our readings of Faulkner's writings, listening to marginalized, suppressed, and repressed voices within the texts. In Faulkner's "Pantaloon in Black," perhaps the most powerful chapter in *Go Down, Moses*, he writes of "shards of pottery and broken bottles and old brick and other objects insignificant to sight but actually of a profound meaning and fatal to touch, which no white man could have read." And at the end of the chapter, Gavin Stevens resists publishing Samuel Worsham Beauchamp's obituary, telling Mollie Worsham Beauchamp: "Why, you couldn't read it, Aunty." The question of how and why whites and blacks not only can but must learn to read each other's texts haunts much of Faulkner's best writing. It is especially encouraging, then, that the annual conference on Faulkner and Yoknapatawpha held in Oxford, Mississippi addressed the question of Faulkner and Race in 1986. (Papers from the proceedings should be published during 1987.)

In 1985 the Oxford Faulkner Conference focused on the topic of Faulkner and Women; the papers were not published in time to be included in this survey, but one hopes that they will help provoke a sustained interrogation and reimagining of the representations of sexual difference in Faulkner's fiction. Sophisticated and exciting trends in feminist theory during the past ten years or so, as well as new biographical information, make the time especially ripe for fresh analyses of problems of gender and sexuality in Yoknapatawpha. The aim of such criticism, however, should not be either to recruit Faulkner for feminism or to refuel old but still-smoldering arguments about misogyny. Rather, an effort should now be made to reopen questions of how (and why) Faulkner's texts represent both male and female sexuality, while accommodating (or failing to accommodate) the presence, absence, and difference of the feminine within their masculine structures. How and why is the experience of reading Faulkner necessarily different for men and women? And how and why should readers/critics—especially those who happen to be male and white—recognize such differences?

Not much published Faulkner criticism during the past six or seven years has explicitly raised questions of sexual difference. *Faulkner's Rhetoric of Loss: A Study in Perception and Meaning* (1983), by Gail L. Mortimer, does so in intelligent and interesting ways. Her well-conceived purpose is "to draw connections among various rhetorical choices that Faulkner makes—choices that we refer to collectively and recognize instinctively as his style—and to show how these choices reflect Faulkner's unique ways of organizing experience." Because Mortimer recognizes that Faulkner's "rhetorical choices, as forms of self-expression, have psychological import," she inevitably explores the borders between rhetoric and psychology, between art and life, and between male and female expressions of selfhood. If the results of her explorations remain uneven, it is largely because she has somewhat derivative and ambivalent conceptions of both rhetoric and psychology. Mortimer, however, especially in her pivotal chapter, "Significant Absences," impressively establishes that "Faulkner's world is a world sustained among tensions about loss: loss of the self, loss of control, loss of desired objects through the passage of time." She also explains "how Faulkner's structuring of his narrators' and characters' perceptions expresses a particular way of being in the world and a particular set of expectations about that world." In Faulkner's world as in ours men and women exist, perceive, and expect differently. Mortimer's final chapter presents a moderately feminist account of Faulkner's masculine representations of "ontological and psychological anxiety." According to Mortimer, "women themselves, when they are felt to be sexual beings, evoke in Faulkner's males, as they appear to have done in Faulkner himself, a profound and powerful ambivalence."

One might wish that her methodology had been sophisticated and supple enough to confront this ambivalence about female sexuality without slipping back and forth between Faulkner's art and his life quite so casually. She may not substantiate with adequate textual analysis her thesis that "the ambivalence that we find in Faulkner's fictive presentations of women characters seems a basic component of the perceptual habits this study has attempted to elucidate." Nevertheless, Mortimer does begin anew—and importantly—the difficult process of reseeing and revoicing Faulknerian perceptions and representations of sexual difference, a process equally as necessary as the roughly analogous process of reseeing and revoicing Faulknerian perceptions and representations of *racial* difference.

Several other recent critics might reasonably have borrowed Mortimer's subtitle, *A Study in Perception and Meaning.* Hugh M. Ruppersburg's *Voice and Eye in Faulkner's Fiction* (1983), Carolyn Porter's *Seeing and Being: The Plight of the Participant-Observer in Emerson, James, Adams, and Faulkner* (1981), Michel Gresset's *Faulkner ou la Fascination: Poétique du Regard* (1982), and Karl Zender's "Faulkner and the Power of Sound" (1984), all in one way or another study problems of perception and meaning. Collectively, these five critics make possible continued reevaluation of how we know what's in Faulkner's books, of how we see and hear what Faulkner represents his characters (and sometimes himself, at least as narrator) as seeing and hearing.

Ruppersburg takes a modest but clear-sighted and revealing look at Faulknerian strategies of point of view, employing a relatively old-fashioned critical vocabulary—narrative, perspective, audience, distance—to present a very sensible and readable account of how point of view determines (or makes indeterminate) a novel's themes and meanings. In 1986 some readers will have trouble accepting Ruppersburg's assertion that the "key to [Faulkner's] meanings resides in the minds of his characters, and the minds of his characters compose the foundation of his fiction." But with his problematic "key" in hand, Ruppersburg opens up *Pylon* (1935) and *Requiem for a Nun* (1951) in unusually worthwhile ways. (He is less successful with the more familiar *Light in August* and *Absalom.*) In the end Ruppersburg's conventional analysis leads him to a troubled conclusion familiar to and shared by more avant-garde critics: "What the reader realizes is that there is no discernible ideal; that the world, along with human nature, is imperfect; that while aspects of it can be rationally explained, other aspects remain forever unknowable."

In *Seeing and Being* Carolyn Porter articulates a moderate Marxist strategy for seeing what can be known through the history of writing and the writing of history. She balances the structures of society against the structures of language, fusing ideological and semiotic analysis. Porter's two chapters about Faulkner—"Faulkner's America" and "The Reified Reader"—demonstrate her power as a close reader of both Faulkner's writings and its historical situation. She often reads the margins between political, philosophical, and literary economies, exposing Faulkner's own exposures (and concealments) of contradictions inherent within American capitalism. Her analysis of *Absalom*, for example, convincingly insists on understanding Thomas Sutpen as "a register of American history," specifically, the history of capitalism's complicity with slave-holding. Even more importantly, Porter explains how Faulkner disrupts his own and his readers' most cherished ideological preconceptions and perceptions.

This survey has restricted itself to Faulkner scholarship published in English; but Michel Gresset's *Faulkner ou la Fascination: Poétique du Regard* makes such an important contribution that its publication in France must be called to the attention of all serious students of Faulkner. The conscientous or curious English-speaking reader should at least consult "The 'God' of Faulkner's Fiction" (1985), in which Gresset rehearses some of the central concerns of his book: "Indeed, *the glance*, by putting the object of desire into a focus, leads to the confusion of the real and the imaginary; it creates a conjunction of desire and want: a sign of all power and powerlessness. As a consequence, it is bound to be the geometric place of that rarest of contradictions which must be called an absolute relationship, and, which, in Faulkner's works, is clearly exemplified by the overbearing importance assumed by the phenomenon of fascination. Not the all-too-well-known last sentence, but this, to me, is the highlight of André Malraux's preface to the French version of *Sanctuary:* 'It is a psychological state upon which rests most of tragic art, and which has never been studied because it does not belong to aesthetics; its name is fascination." Gresset's innovative book establishes him as among the very best readers (not just one of the best *French* readers) of Faulkner. Two recent collections of essays attest to the fact that Faulkner continues to attract an important international readership: *Faulkner: International Perspectives* (1984) and *Faulkner Studies in Japan* (1985).

Karl Zender's ambitious essay on the power of sound—and *silence*—in Faulkner also deserves a wide audience. In Faulkner's frequent representations of sound Zender hears "a sustained meditation on the artist's power." Zender writes with real insight about Quentin Compson in *The Sound and the Fury*, Linda Snopes Kohl in *The Mansion* (1959), and "The Jail" section of *Requiem for a Nun*. "For Quentin," Zender demonstrates, "the voices of his memory are the internal symbols of his alienation, as the smells and sounds of nature are the external ones. In his unequal struggle with these voices, smells, and sounds, we see his inability to defend himself against the invasive power of his culture." Zender writes even more interestingly about *The Mansion*, explaining how, "by deafening Linda, Faulkner forces the world to abandon its allegiance to sound and to resume its dependence on reading." "Faulkner and the Power of Sound," then, suggests a great deal about Faulkner's conception of the relative powers of writing and reading, his conceptions about the power of art. Zender argues that Faulkner's confidence both in sound and in his art fluctuates during the course of his career.

Four additional books published since 1980 deserve notice. Martin Kreiswirth's *William Faulkner: The Making of a Novelist* (1983) argues—perhaps overargues—that *The Sound and the Fury* "makes the crucial point in Faulkner's career at which he revisited his past, saw it afresh, and reworked it into his future." Kreiswirth writes with considerable specificity and assurance about Faulkner's first three novels, especially about *Soldiers' Pay*. Economically and reasonably, Kreiswirth shows that *Soldiers' Pay* "more clearly and closely anticipates the structural organization and formal adventurousness of *The Sound and the Fury* than any of the books written in between." He then, somewhat less successfully, treats *Mosquitoes* (1927) "as a kind of compendium or anthology of [Faulkner's] past" and *Flags in the Dust* as "in effect a prospectus for his future." Kreiswirth probably has more to say about the beginnings of Faulkner's career than does Judith Sensibar, but he encounters at least as much trouble as she does accounting for the mysterious origins of Faulkner's art. Conceding (repeatedly) "that the appearance of *The Sound and the Fury* was not only unpredictable but, at bottom, inexplicable," Kreiswirth nevertheless tries to predict and explain the event retrospectively, insisting on characterizing it as "not so much a mysterious leap as an initiation." *William Faulkner: The Making of a Novelist* should be read, but not with any unrealistic expectations that it can finally account for the mysteries of how Faulkner helped make himself into a great novelist. Kreiswirth's observations about Faulkner's compositional habits in his essay, "Centers, Openings, and Endings," are also instructive.

In *Three American Originals: John Ford, William Faulkner, and Charles Ives* (1984), Joseph W. Reed begins with big questions: "what does America do to its artists? what does being American mean to an artist?" His eccentric and suggestive answers emerge through fascinating experiments in comparative biography and cultural history. The films of John Ford, the fiction of William Faulkner, and the music of Charles Ives all—according to Reed—engage common values of originality and community, and common structures of genre and canon. At the center of all three artists' work, Reed finds what he calls *suspension* (not noting that *suspension* happens to be one of Faulkner's favorite words): "the Americans swing between any two qualities, any adjectival epithets, and the suspension in that tethered movement allows for uncertainty of identity." Reed's own thought-provoking essays themselves constitute not so much an argument or even a sustained meditation on suspension and originality, but rather an original and suspended meditation on the place (and displacement) of the artist in America.

Robert Dale Parker begins *Faulkner and the Novelistic Imagination* (1985) asking: "What is it like to read a Faulkner novel?" Parker does especially well in explaining what it is like to read *Sanctuary*, and he also writes with welcome common sense about the fragmented experience of reading *As I Lay Dying*. According to Parker, "radical ignorance . . . is the distinctive problem Faulkner imposes on his readers," and "Faulkner's subject . . . is the ethical dilemma that arises from the problematic . . . status of knowledge." Although he never quite says so, the novelistic imagination referred to in his title must be that of the reader, who must recognize and cope with Faulkner's elusive and evasive narrative strategies: "the main thing we know reading Faulkner is that we don't know the main thing." This refreshingly sane book should somehow reassure both new and seasoned travelers in Yoknapatawpha that reading a Faulkner novel is often like crossing unfamiliar borders without a map.

Finally, the publication in 1985 of *William Faulkner's Short Stories*, by James B. Carothers, reminds us of Faulkner's many superb accomplishments in the short story, of his respect for it as "the most demanding form after poetry," and of his belief that "in the novel you can be careless but in the short story you can't." Carothers advances two general arguments: first, that the short stories retain an essential integrity independent of the novels; and second that the stories document Faulkner's "development from pessimism to optimism," from "ironic determinism to a thoroughly comic artistic vision." Although he does not quite manage to develop either argument satisfactorily in this brief book, Carothers *does* demonstrate that he knows enough about how the short stories work (and about how they were composed and recomposed) to write another more ambitious book. Carothers's next book should substantiate his own very credible claim that Faulkner's "short stories deserve the same close reading given his novels." Noel Polk's 1984 "William Faulkner's 'Carcassonne'" offers a superb example of what remains to be learned from close readings of the short stories.

Although several important articles have been included throughout this survey, it does not seem necessary here to identify all the interesting essay-length work on Faulkner that has been published between 1980-1986. However, it does seem appropriate to recognize publication of the new *Faulkner Journal* and to conclude this essay about reading Faulkner by calling attention to two sets of articles: the first representing brilliant new work by one of Faulkner's earliest and still best serious readers, Michael Millgate; and the second representing what is being written these days about Faulkner's most characteristic novel, *Absalom, Absalom!*, fifty years after its publication in 1936.

The Faulkner Journal, coedited by James B. Carothers and John T. Matthews, began publication in the fall of 1985. Its appearance now testifies to the current healthy level of scholarly interest in all aspects of the Faulkner canon.

Michael Millgate, ever since the publication of his masterful *The Achievement of William Faulkner* (1966), has stood among the most respected and influential of Faulkner scholars. He consistently brings to his discussions of Faulkner's work an uncanny—perhaps unmatched—balance of critical qualities: a wise understanding of Faulkner's literary, cultural, and personal backgrounds; an intimate knowledge of Faulkner's manuscripts and their composition; and shrewd, humane instincts for both analysis and synthesis. When writing about Faulkner, Millgate is always engaged, alert, confident, and disciplined. Twenty years after his *The Achievement of William Faulkner*, Millgate never seems satisfied with merely reiterating or repackaging what he has said before but always seems willing to risk rediscovering and reimagining the the contours of Faulkner's worlds.

The four essays by Millgate covered by this survey demonstrate, moreover, an impressive power of generalization. Sometimes Millgate asserts or suggests somewhat more than he can fully substantiate or illustrate within the compass of an article; but he always does so with such obvious authority and tact that one tends to trust him. In "'A Cosmos of my Own': The Evolution of Yoknapatawpha," for example, Millgate offers the intriguing speculation "that Faulkner at some point had the idea of Quentin as a dying narrator before whose eyes his whole world would pass in almost instantaneous review." The same essay also proposes two crucial moments of discovery for Faulkner: the first, when he perceived the possibility of his own fictional cosmos; the second, when he perceived the endless possibilities for experimenting with fictional techniques to represent Yoknapatawpha. Millgate argues in "Faulkner's First Trilogy" not only that there are complex patterns connecting *Sartoris* (1929), *Sanctuary* (1931), and *Requiem for a Nun* (1951), but also—even more vigorously—that "each Faulkner text must be considered a unique, independent, and self-sufficient work of art, not only capable of being read and contemplated in isolation but actually demanding such treatment." In "William Faulkner: The Shape of a Career," Millgate responds to the implications of Gary Lee Stonum's work. And in "William Faulkner: The Two Voices," he responds to those who, along with Walter Slatoff, have found debilitating oppositions, contradictions, and ambivalences in Faulkner's work: "I would . . . see that kind of patterning as conscious and controlled rather than simply obsessive or schizoid. And I would argue that it operated for Faulkner as a kind of exploratory device, directed toward the expression or (better, perhaps) the exposition of complexities that he believed to be inherent in his own experience as a human being who happened to inhabit a particular society and region." Each of Millgate's essays emerges as a model of superbly imaginative scholarship, and collectively they represent a continuity and originality of purpose (both aesthetic and ethical) all too rare in contemporary criticism.

More critics continue to write about *Absalom, Absalom!* than any other single Faulkner text, no doubt largely because "this novel questions what few do, the sources of the discursive power that not only allows narrators to talk but also allows a novel to dramatize narrators narrating" (Ross,

"The Evocation of Voice in *Absalom, Absalom!*"). *Absalom* asks: why tell (and retell) stories? why listen to stories over and over again? and *how* should we tell and listen to stories? Of the seventy-five or more essays on *Absalom* published within the last half-dozen years, Elisabeth Muhlenfeld's scrupulous and lucid account of the novel's genesis and development, the history of its composition and recomposition, will almost certainly be valued most by future scholars. Muhlenfeld meticulously and interestingly situates *Absalom*'s writing and rewriting within the biographical patterns of a particularly intense two and a half years of Faulkner's life (early 1934 to mid 1936). She also unfolds the extraordinary process through which Faulkner struggled to make decisions about his book's structure, design, and modes of telling.

Among the many compelling observations about how the tale of *Absalom* finally got itself told is Muhlenfeld's discovery that "Faulkner considered beginning his novel with a draft of Mr. Compson's complete letter, the text of which varies only slightly from the printed text in *Absalom, Absalom!* bracketing Chapters VI through IX." This compositional fact would seem to support David Krause's argument, presented in three interrelated essays, that letters within the text—Compson's letter, Bon's letter, as well as several invented by Shreve—provoke characters to read them in ways that significantly help determine (or make indeterminate) how and why to read *Absalom*. Krause appropriates and tests some theoretical conceptions of the reading process from Derrida, Foucault, and—most helpfully—Barthes.

Other critics have found other interesting ways to reread Faulkner's *Absalom* through lenses afforded by contemporary literary theory. Stephen Ross, for example, uses Derridean notions of presence to examine Faulknerian voices. Ross argues that in *Absalom* "voice's power of evocation becomes the text's presumed and unquestioned discursive origin," affirming the novel's "mimetic faith in the power of and escape from voice, a faith in the created presence which the escape from voice produces." In "Incredulous Narration," Peter Brooks reads *Absalom* through the "concept of narrative as a coded activity," articulated by Barthes in *S/Z*. For Brooks, the novel "becomes a kind of detective story where the object of investigation—the mystery—is the narrative design, or plot, itself." He does not intend to reduce *Absalom* to a novel about novels, "but rather to contend that narrating is an urgent function in itself, that in the absence of pattern and structure, patterning and structuration remain necessary projects, dynamic intentions." Brooks makes an interesting case that "the attempted recovery of the past makes known the continuing history of past desire as it persists in the present, shaping the project of telling."

J. Hillis Miller, Jr., in "The Two Relativisms: Point of View and Indeterminacy in the Novel *Absalom, Absalom!*," presents a restrained and unthreatening deconstructive reading of the novel. He focuses "on the relationship between relation as storytelling and relations as the network of family and community ties" and reaches the relatively predictable conclusion that "failure of a narration is, for Faulkner, the evidence of its validity, since only the failed narration, which exposes its loose ends and inconsistencies, can be an adequate representation, figure for what has no literal name, of that unnameable 'it.'" Faulknerians should welcome Miller's thoughtful theoretical discussion but may wish that he (and Peter Brooks as well) showed more familiarity with the history and current state of Faulkner scholarship.

"The Gothicism of *Absalom, Absalom!*: Rosa Coldfield Revisited," an unconventional essay by François L. Pitavy, has much of interest to say about Faulkner's gothic themes, images, structures, and strategies. Pitavy writes especially well about closed doors and dark houses, and the reader's need for intelligence and imagination.

As the present survey of scholarship should have indicated, William Faulkner probably has more intelligent and imaginative readers than ever before as a cumulative result of more than fifty years of critical scrutiny and rereading. But much more obviously remains to be recovered and discovered about the origins and ends, about the power and value, of Faulkner's unparalleled art. Beyond 1986, through "all the old accumulated rubbish years which we call memory, the recognizable I," William Faulkner will continue to be reread and reinvented by men and women who continue to value "that speech sight hearing taste and being which we call human man" (*Absalom, Absalom!*).

Bibliography:

John Earl Bassett, *Faulkner: An Annotated Checklist of Recent Criticism* (Kent, Ohio: Kent State University Press, 1983).

Biographies:

David Minter, *William Faulkner: His Life and Work* (Baltimore & London: Johns Hopkins University Press, 1980);

Joseph Blotner, *Faulkner: A Biography*, revised one-volume edition (New York: Random House, 1984).

References:

André Bleikasten, "'Cet affreux goût d'encore': Emma Bovary's Ghost in *Sanctuary*," in *Intertextuality in Faulkner*, edited by Michel Gresset and Noel Polk (Jackson: University Press of Mississippi, 1985), pp. 36-56;

Bleikasten, "For/Against an Ideological Reading of Faulkner's Novels," in *Faulkner and Idealism: Perspectives from Paris*, edited by Gresset and Patrick Samway, S. J. (Jackson: University Press of Mississippi, 1983), pp. 27-50;

Bleikasten, "Reading Faulkner," in *New Directions in Faulkner Studies: Faulkner and Yoknapatawpha, 1983*, edited by Doreen Fowler and Ann J. Abadie (Jackson: University Press of Mississippi, 1984), pp. 1-17;

Bleikasten, "Terror and Nausea: Bodies in *Sanctuary*," *Faulkner Journal*, 1 (1985): 17-29;

Richard Brodhead, "Introduction: Faulkner and the Logic of Remaking," in his *Faulkner: New Perspectives* (Englewood Cliffs, N.J.: Prentice-Hall, 1983), pp. 1-19;

Cleanth Brooks, *William Faulkner: First Encounters* (New Haven & London: Yale University Press, 1983);

Peter Brooks, "Incredulous Narration: *Absalom, Absalom!*," in his *Reading for the Plot: Design and Intention in Narrative* (New York: Knopf, 1984), pp. 286-312;

James B. Carothers, *William Faulkner's Short Stories* (Ann Arbor: UMI Research Press, 1985);

Thadious M. Davis, *Faulkner's "Negro": Art and the Southern Context* (Baton Rouge & London: Louisiana State University Press, 1983);

Doreen Fowler and Ann J. Abadie, eds., *Faulkner: International Perspectives: Faulkner and Yoknapatawpha, 1982* (Jackson: University Press of Mississippi, 1984);

Michel Gresset, *Faulkner ou la Fascination: Poétique du Regard* (Paris: Klincksieck, 1982);

Gresset, "The 'God' of Faulkner's Fiction," in *Faulkner and Idealism*, pp. 51-70;

Gresset, "Introduction: Faulkner between the Texts," in *Intertextuality in Faulkner*, pp. 3-15;

Lee Jenkins, *Faulkner and Black-White Relations: A Psychoanalytic Approach* (New York: Columbia University Press, 1981);

Donald M. Kartiganer, *The Fragile Thread: The Meaning of Form in Faulkner's Novels* (Amherst: University of Massachusetts Press, 1979);

David Krause, "Opening Pandora's Box: Re-reading Compson's Letter and Faulkner's *Absalom, Absalom!*," *Centennial Review,* 30 (Summer 1986): 358-382;

Krause, "Reading Bon's Letter and Faulkner's *Absalom, Absalom!*," *PMLA,* 99 (March 1984): 225-241;

Krause, "Reading Shreve's Letters and Faulkner's *Absalom, Absalom!*," *Studies in American Fiction,* 11 (1983): 153-169;

Martin Kreiswirth, "Centers, Openings, and Endings: Some Faulknerian Constants," *American Literature,* 56 (1984): 38-50;

Kreiswirth, *William Faulkner: The Making of a Novelist* (Athens: University of Georgia Press, 1983);

John T. Matthews, "The Elliptical Nature of *Sanctuary*," *Novel,* 17 (Spring 1984): 246-265;

Matthews, *The Play of Faulkner's Language* (Ithaca & London: Cornell University Press, 1982);

Thomas L. McHaney, ed., *Faulkner Studies in Japan,* compiled by Kiyoyuki Ono (Athens: University of Georgia Press, 1985);

J. Hillis Miller, Jr., "The Two Relativisms: Point of View and Indeterminacy in the Novel *Absalom, Absalom!*," in *Relativism in the Arts,* edited by Betty Jean Craige (Athens: University of Georgia Press, 1983), pp. 148-170;

Michael Millgate, "'A Cosmos of My Own': The Evolution of Yoknapatawpha," in *Fifty Years of Yoknapatawpha: Faulkner and Yoknapatawpha, 1979,* edited by Fowler and Abadie (Jackson: University Press of Mississippi, 1980), pp. 23-43;

Millgate, "Faulkner's First Trilogy: *Sartoris, Sanctuary,* and *Requiem for a Nun,*" in *Fifty Years of Yoknapatawpha,* pp. 90-109;

Millgate, "William Faulkner: The Shape of a Career," in *New Directions in Faulkner Studies,* pp. 18-36;

Millgate, "William Faulkner: The Two Voices," in *Southern Literature in Transition: Heritage and Promise,* edited by Philip Castille and William Osborne (Memphis: Memphis State University Press, 1983), pp. 73-85;

Wesley A. Morris, *Friday's Footprint: Structuralism and the Articulated Text* (Columbus: Ohio State University Press, 1979);

Gail M. Mortimer, *Faulkner's Rhetoric of Loss: A Study in Perception and Meaning* (Austin: University of Texas Press, 1983);

Elisabeth Muhlenfeld, "Introduction," in her *William Faulkner's Absalom, Absalom!: A Critical Casebook* (New York: Garland, 1984), pp. xi-xxxix;

Robert Dale Parker, *Faulkner and the Novelistic Imagination* (Urbana & Chicago: University of Illinois Press, 1985);

François L. Pitavy, "The Gothicism of *Absalom, Absalom!*: Rosa Coldfield Revisited," in *"A Cosmos of My Own": Faulkner and Yoknapatawpha 1980,* edited by Fowler and Abadie (Jackson: University Press of Mississippi, 1981), pp. 199-226;

Noel Polk, "Law in Faulkner's *Sanctuary*," *Mississippi College Law Review,* 4 (Spring 1984): 246-265;

Polk, "The Space between *Sanctuary*," in *Intertextuality in Faulkner,* pp. 16-35;

Polk, "William Faulkner's 'Carcassone,'" *Studies in American Fiction,* 12 (Spring 1984): 29-43;

Carolyn Porter, *Seeing and Being: The Plight of the Participant-Observer in Emerson, James, Adams, and Faulkner* (Middletown, Conn.: Wesleyan University Press, 1981);

Joseph W. Reed, *Three American Originals: John Ford, William Faulkner, and Charles Ives* (Middletown, Conn.: Wesleyan University Press, 1984);

Stephen M. Ross, "The Evocation of Voice in *Absalom, Absalom!*," *Essays in Literature,* 8 (1981): 135-149;

Ross, "Oratory and the Dialogical in *Absalom, Absalom!*," in *Intertextuality in Faulkner,* pp. 73-86;

Hugh M. Ruppersburg, *Voice and Eye in Faulkner's Fiction* (Athens: University of Georgia Press, 1983);

Judith L. Sensibar, *The Origins of Faulkner's Art* (Austin: University of Texas Press, 1984);

Gary Lee Stonum, *Faulkner's Career: An Internal Literary History* (Ithaca & London: Cornell University Press, 1979);

Eric J. Sundquist, *Faulkner: The House Divided* (Baltimore & London: Johns Hopkins University Press, 1983);

Walter Taylor, *Faulkner's Search for a South* (Urbana, Chicago & London: University of Illinois Press, 1983);

Craig Werner, "Tell Old Pharaoh: The Afro-American Response to Faulkner," *Southern Review,* 19 (1983): 711-735;

Karl F. Zender, "Faulkner and the Power of Sound," *PMLA,* 99 (January 1984): 89-107;

Zender, "Reading in 'The Bear,'" *Faulkner Studies,* 1 (1980): 89-107.

NEW ENTRIES

Alice Adams
(14 August 1926-   )

William L. Stull
University of Hartford

BOOKS: *Careless Love* (New York: New American Library, 1966); republished as *The Fall of Daisy Duke* (London: Constable, 1967);

Families and Survivors (New York: Knopf, 1974; London: Constable, 1976);

Listening to Billie (New York: Knopf, 1978; London: Constable, 1978);

Beautiful Girl (New York: Knopf, 1979);

Rich Rewards (New York: Knopf, 1980);

To See You Again (New York: Knopf, 1982);

Molly's Dog (Concord, N.H.: Ewert, 1983);

Superior Women (New York: Knopf, 1984; London: Heinemann, 1985);

Return Trips (New York: Knopf, 1985).

PERIODICAL PUBLICATIONS:

FICTION

"Sea Gulls Are Happier Here," *Cosmopolitan,* 147 (January 1967): 108-111;

"Young Couple with Class," *Redbook,* 129 (September 1967): 72ff;

"Henry and the Pale-Faced Redskin," *Cosmopolitan,* 163 (October 1967): 146ff;

"A Propitiation of Witches," *Redbook,* 134 (February 1970): 60ff;

"Afternoons at the Beach," *McCall's,* 100 (November 1972): 84ff;

"The Nice Girl," *McCall's,* 101 (August 1974): 94ff;

"A Week in Venice," *McCall's,* 102 (November 1974): 112ff;

"Learning to Be Happy," *Redbook,* 147 (September 1976): 100ff;

"The Polar Route," *Mademoiselle,* 84 (March 1978): 92ff;

"The Last Married Man," *Virginia Quarterly Review,* 54 (Spring 1978): 289-296;

"A Change of Season," *Redbook,* 153 (September 1979): 41ff;

"The Chase," *Cosmopolitan,* 191 (August 1981): 252ff;

"Lovers and Friends," *McCall's,* 109 (August 1982): 94ff;

"A Legendary Lover," *McCall's,* 112 (November 1984): 90;

"Against All Odds," *Redbook,* 165 (August 1985): 52ff.

NONFICTION

"A Talk with the Biographers," *New York Times Book Review,* 20 April 1980, pp. 29-31;

"On Turning Fifty," *Vogue,* 173 (December 1983): 230ff;

"The Wild Coasts of Portugal," *Geo,* 6 (November 1984): 56ff.

Alice Adams is a West Coast writer deeply influenced by a southern childhood, an eastern education, and extensive travels. Her fiction deals with women in transit and transition: careless lovers, beautiful girls, and superior women on the move. When she published her first story in 1959, she described herself as writing "mostly about people who live in strange places." Since then, in five novels and three story collections, she has shown that familiar territory often proves strangest of all.

Adams's parents were Virginians. Her father, Nicholson Barney Adams, taught Spanish at the University of North Carolina at Chapel Hill. In 1924 he and his wife, the former Agatha Erskine Boyd, moved to what their only child has since recalled as "My First and Only House." It was situated just south of Chapel Hill, and she lived there from shortly after her birth in Fredericksburg, Virginia, until she was sixteen. Adams feels she may have been "imprinted" by the house. "What I most remember," she has said, "is flowers—everywhere." Two of these lend their names to her prizewinning story "Roses, Rhododendron," in which an insecure girl much like the author grows up to discover the "terrible emotions" beneath the "genteel and opaque" surface of her adopted family—and to see at last her own part in the family romance.

"My mother wanted to be a writer and was a failed one," Adams told *StoryQuarterly* in a 1980 interview; "she was depressed, unhappy, and peripherally involved with the literary world." In these traits she closely resembles the Jessica Todd of Adams's story "Are You in Love?" Elsewhere Adams recalls, "For hours, almost every night, she

Dust jacket for Adams's fourth novel, a book which, says her mentor William Abrahams, "manages the difficult feat of being at once romantic and truthful"

read poems aloud to me. . . . Long sad Scottish ballads were what we both liked best."

To the Chapel Hill farmhouse Adams's parents added a new wing, a tennis court, even a swimming pool that figures prominently in the first pages of *Families and Survivors* (1974). One fact about the house remained unalterable: its location on the road to humble Pittsboro rather than fashionable Durham. "Although our house became rather grand too in its way, there was always the Pittsboro connotation." Despite the tennis, the swimming, and the parties ("my parents entertained a lot"), Alice Adams and her parents remained "three difficult, isolated people."

This "first and only house" and its domestic disharmonies left lasting imprints on her life and art. Clear evidence of this is "The Todds," a trilogy of separately published stories ("Verlie I Say Unto You," "Are You in Love?," and "Alternatives") gathered under a single heading in *Beautiful Girl* (1979). "Those stories are as close to home as I've come," Adams allows. There and in related pieces like "A Southern Spelling Bee," the Chapel Hill of

her first sixteen years fades into Hilton—"the seat of a distinguished university, in the middle South" ("Truth or Consequences"). Tom and Jessica Todd live in Hilton with their daughter Avery, her shadowy brother Devlin, and their black maid, Verlie Jones. It is also to Hilton that Avery's adult counterpart Claire Williston unwittingly homes in "An Unscheduled Stop." Brief as it is, that stop brings back memories of "her on the whole painful upbringing there" and of a more recent though no less painful summer affair. Versions of Hilton recur as well in "Home Is Where," "New Best Friends," and *Families and Survivors.*

In 1983 Adams made her own return trip to Hilton/Chapel Hill. "I went to see the house, 'my house,' which I had not seen for twenty-five years, not since my father died and my stepmother, who had inherited it outright, put it up for sale (a serious trauma, that . . .)." Overcoming just such feelings of disinheritance is the subject of her story "Berkeley House," in which Charlotte O'Mara is tempted to buy back from her stepmother the "absolutely empty, echoing house" of her childhood. After revisiting it, she chooses instead to start a new painting and pursue a promising love affair—smart choices, Adams suggests.

In "A Southern Spelling Bee" Adams describes Avery Todd as "a dark, sharply skinny child, with large melancholy eyes and a staggering vocabulary." The author herself was "one of those rotten little kids who write poetry. I grew up in a semi-intellectual atmosphere and I was encouraged." Such precocity did not accord with southern traditions. "I was bright in school and ran into trouble because of that Southern thing that women are supposed to be stupid." It was partly for this reason that Adams left Chapel Hill some forty years ago. San Francisco became her adopted home, and her Carolina accent faded; yet as a writer and as a woman, she remains a child of the South.

At sixteen, Adams moved north to Cambridge, where like her "superior women" she entered Radcliffe College. Until then her only creative writing had been poetry, but she got into a short story course. "That seemed fun. Except that the professor—a male teacher from Harvard [Kenneth Kempton]—said to me at the end of the course, 'Miss Adams, you're really an awfully nice girl. Why don't you get married and forget all this writing?'" In her second writing course, taken at Chapel Hill during the summer, Phillips Russell taught Adams a story outline that she has used ever since. "He thought that stories were either three or five acts and the formula for the five acts was ABDCE: action, background, development, climax, ending." (In her *StoryQuarterly* interview Adams shows how "The Swastika on Our Door" follows this pattern.)

After graduating from Radcliffe in 1946, Adams moved to New York and worked briefly in publishing. During that time she had the luck to see Billie Holiday perform at a Manhattan nightclub, singing "Strange Fruit" and "Gloomy Sunday" in her "beautiful, rich and lonely voice." The impression lasted and suggested the leitmotif of Adams's third novel, *Listening to Billie* (1978). In 1947 Adams married Mark Linenthal, Jr., and the couple went to France, where he did graduate work at the Sorbonne. Adams's first published story, "Winter Rain" (*Charm*, July 1959), recalls that "crowded, wild, excited year."

After returning to the United States, Linenthal and Adams moved to California, where he studied and taught English, joining the faculty at San Francisco State University in 1954 and completing his Ph.D. at Stanford in 1957. Adams's only child, Peter Adams Linenthal, was born in San Francisco in 1951. He shares the dedication of *Families and Survivors*, a book that reveals how difficult the 1950s were for his mother as a woman and an artist. During this period Adams continued to write stories and tried her hand at novels, but without success. Nor was her marriage successful. After a separation, she and Linenthal divorced in 1958. Adams's personal and financial dependencies weighed heavily on her, and she went through a difficult period in her writing.

"Success came late," she says. "I wasn't even earning a living at writing until I was over forty. I always had some kind of part-time job, the sort only available to women, which is to say secretarial." Not surprisingly, each of her novels concerns a woman's search for satisfying work as a means to economic, artistic, and finally political independence. Like Adams, Daisy Duke Fabbri, the heretofore male-dependent protagonist of *Careless Love* (1966), attains a measure of freedom through part-time office jobs. Louisa Calloway and Eliza Quarles, the heroines of *Families and Survivors* and *Listening to Billie*, go farther, coming into their own as artist and poet respectively. Daphne Matthiessen, an interior designer, is wholly self-supporting in *Rich Rewards* (1980), as is Megan Greene in *Superior Women* (1984). Indeed, with the help of her friend Peg, an early civil-rights activist, Megan eventually forsakes private enterprise for a higher calling, establishing a shelter for homeless women—"but sometimes men too."

During and after her marriage Adams received encouragement from William Abrahams, since 1967 the editor of the distinguished short-story annual *Prize Stories: The O. Henry Awards*. The two had met in 1948, when Abrahams was a writing fellow at Stanford. From 1971 to 1982 he included an Adams story in every *O. Henry* collection. At least equally important was Adams's meeting with Robert K. McNie, the interior designer with whom she has lived since the mid 1960s. McNie shares the dedication of *Families and Survivors* with Peter Adams Linenthal; the dedication of *Superior Women* is to him alone.

Adams was not pleased with the title of her first novel, *Careless Love*. In England it was published under the title she wanted, *The Fall of Daisy Duke*, "because I was trying to be funny," she explains. "And interestingly, it really bombed in this country and did terribly well in England. A lot of people were put off by the title. They thought, oh Christ, one more sexy divorcee story." That was exactly the reaction of most American reviewers, for whom Daisy's "amorous odyssey" from bad marriage to worse affairs and finally to a psychiatrist's couch was as familiar as the title song. What all but a few Americans missed was the intermittent but unmistakable irony the author highlighted in a prepublication blurb: "This novel is an on-the-whole amused look at San Francisco, specifically at an enormous blonde divorcee . . . loosed in the city's social-sexual jungle. I was also interested in the city's rather kitsch social mores, its very aberrant weather, and its staggering rates of divorce and suicide."

An unsigned "Reader's Report" in the *New York Times* praised the novel's "wry anatomizing" of its protagonist: "The mixture includes a small income, a liberal education and an unreasoning desire to be loved. Emancipated but sentimental Daisy has rejected her husband (too weak) and her diligent lover (too mundane), and she eventually gets what she deserves: a visiting romeo with a line unchanged since Valentino." It is a tribute to Adams's verisimilitude that like Daisy so many readers took Pablo at his word. ("You are so young, always so fresh. You restore me—you remove all pain from my life.") When the retitled English edition appeared the next year, British readers savored the ironies that Adams's fellow Americans, too used to Daisy's kind of downfall to notice the satire, had missed.

The American misreading of *Careless Love* is worth considering because it points to a nagging ambiguity reviewers have sensed in Adams's later work. It is sometimes hard to determine whether her overall attitude toward her characters is sympathetic or satirical. At times, in her five novels and in many uncollected stories, Adams seems to render her characters' lives, no matter how unexamined, without irony. The result is what one reviewer aptly terms "literature soap opera." Elsewhere, notably in her collected stories but often in her novels as well, Adams wields a subtle irony tempered by empathy, and the result is literature. In her "big book," *Superior Women,* her intention seems deeply divided, a have-your-romance-and-mock-it-too attitude that leaves the reader uncertain whether to smirk or sympathize.

During the late 1960s Adams broke into the slick "women's magazines" *Cosmopolitan, Redbook,* and *McCall's,* and she has published many stories, mostly formula romances, in their pages since. Few of them are included in her three collections. In November 1969 she made her debut in the *New Yorker,* and more than a dozen of her best stories have appeared there since. The first was "Gift of Grass," also the first Adams story to be included in

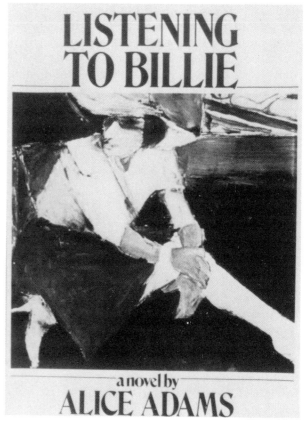

Dust jacket for Adams's third novel, inspired by a Billie Holiday performance

an *O. Henry* annual, where it took a third prize in 1971. Most readers know Adams for her incisive stories of women over thirty: Ardis Bascombe, the aging alcoholic whose furious self-description becomes the title of her story and of Adams's first collection, *Beautiful Girl;* Carol, the thirty-five-year-old florist who finally owns up to her age and experience in "Snow," the opening story in *To See You Again* (1982); and any of a dozen older and wiser women revisiting "strange places" in *Return Trips* (1985). "Gift of Grass" demonstrates that Adams writes with equal insight into young women. Here sixteen-year-old Cathy, herself deeply troubled, senses her stepfather's chronic despair and surreptitiously leaves him the only consolation she knows, two joints of marijuana.

In 1978, explaining what most satisfies her as a writer, Adams used the phrase "steady productivity." During the early 1970s she steadily produced prizewinning stories while working on a second novel. The two projects were closely connected, she found. "*Families and Survivors* came about because I wrote a lot of short stories, and then began to realize I was writing about the same people in a kind of serial way." Central among these people is Louisa Calloway, the titular survivor of a self-destructive southern family, daughter of a "complicated, contradictory" father and a "pained, languid" mother. Into her life, which Adams chronicles from 1941 to New Year's 1970-1971, come a good friend, a bad husband, a promising daughter, and a full cast of men and women caught up with Louisa on the mid-century marriage-go-round.

"*Families and Survivors* is, it seems to me, a personal and—in a sense— social history," Adams says. "It is about what it was like for certain kinds of people—a rather limited kind—to survive the fifties. It makes a rather simplistic point, really, which is that the fifties were horrible and things got better in the sixties. And that, in general, second marriages beat first ones." Over the course of the novel, Louisa forsakes her native Virginia for San Francisco. After her divorce she experiments with various lovers, including a memorable sadist. In the mid 1960s she makes a return trip for her father's funeral and encounters John Jeffreys, once "the most truly desirable boy" known to the Sub-Deb club, of which years before she was a charter member. By the novel's end Louisa and John are married (*happily*, Adams insists in a nervous parenthesis). What's more, Louisa has found her calling as a painter. In the final chapter, as the new decade begins, corks pop, whales spout off the Mendocino coast, and Louisa and her hippie daughter Maude lead their men off to bed.

Reviews were mixed. Adams admitted that her point had been simplistic, and some readers agreed. "Every social convulsion eventually spawns its own set of clichés and oversimplifications," Anatole Broyard lamented. "On the social level Alice Adams has reduced the emergent woman of the 1970s to a formula; on the literary level, she does as much for, or to, certain innovations in the novel form." Those innovations, largely absent from *Careless Love*, include "cinematic cutting and cubistic overlappings" in structure and point of view as well as short, fragmentary paragraphs of prismatic description. Broyard's deeper concern was with the "point," however. "We are all simply survivors—it has a nice contemporary ring. Survivors from what? Why families, of course—what else? Unless you have a better idea." Novelist Anne Bernays concurred: "this novel appears to pose questions it never quite gets around to answering."

Others praised the novel's equally conspicuous strengths. The *New Yorker* called it a "beauti-

fully written, generous book." Writing for the *Washington Post*, Jill Robinson found it to be "a you-can't-put-it-down book, but unlike many of those it belongs to our permanent literature." Peter S. Prescott of *Newsweek* argued that Adams had rescued "feminine sensibility" in fiction from its (mostly feminist) detractors. "Her economical narrative, written in the present tense with constant parenthetical glimpses into the future, has a kind of floating quality entirely suited to the insecurity of these people's lives."

In 1975 *Families and Survivors* was nominated for a National Book Critics Circle Award, and the next year Adams received a National Endowment for the Arts Fiction Grant. Her stories continued to appear in respected magazines—not only the *New Yorker* but also the *Paris Review* and the *Virginia Quarterly Review*—as well as the *O. Henry* collections. ("Roses, Rhododendron" took third prize there in 1976 and appeared as well in *Best American Short Stories 1976*.)

Listening to Billie was published in January 1978 and dedicated to Victoria Wilson, Adams's editor at Knopf. Adams felt that the new book marked a departure from her previous work, particularly in the character of the protagonist, Eliza Hamilton Quarles. "In *Listening to Billie*, I was trying for something very different. I was spurred by a remark by Elizabeth Hardwick, that most women writers tend to write about women who are much less interesting than they. So it occurred to me to try to write about someone much more interesting than I am—which was the character Eliza. So there you are, not really writing about your own experience. So you idealize. You create a sort of myth." Over the three decades since she had heard Billie Holiday, she explained, "Lady Day" had become for her " a tragic figure in the classical sense, a queen brought to disaster by fatal flaws in herself and in society." Eliza also hears Billie sing in a New York club, but at the time she is unable to listen. "She has serious and obsessive problems of her own: is she pregnant? . . . Should she marry Evan Quarles?" She is and does. Shortly thereafter her husband discovers himself "obsessionally in love" with "the most beautiful boy in the world" and commits suicide. Thus, unlike Louisa Calloway, who waits years before ending her bad marriage, Eliza is early thrust on her own in San Francisco.

Like Evan before her, Eliza finds herself in an addictive, all-consuming affair with the "beautiful boy" Reed Ashford, as does her younger stepsister Daria, whose search for selfhood in her marriage to wealthy Smith Worthington makes a compelling subplot. Reed eventually follows Evan (and Eliza's father, Caleb) into suicide, undone by his own narcissism. Once again it is the women who emerge as survivors—not only Daria, Eliza, and their thrice-married mother, Josephine (a successful writer), but Eliza's daughter Catherine as well. As the book ends, some twenty years after listening to Billie, Eliza is finally listening to herself. She has found a lover who is also a friend, wry and supportive Harry Argent (one of Adams's few good men), and she has found her own voice as a poet. Adams never quotes from Eliza's poetry, but her writing is far more credible than Louisa Calloway's barely mentioned art in *Families and Survivors*.

Using classic omniscient narration along with the experimental crosscutting techniques she developed in *Families and Survivors*, Adams deftly interweaves multiple viewpoints and subplots. The book includes memorable set pieces—portions were published separately in the *Atlantic Monthly*, the *Paris Review*, and *Redbook*— but its overall unity is strong.

Writers especially liked *Listening to Billie*. Novelist Anne Tyler called the tone "quick, deft, precise, the plot as seductive as gossip." Poet Helen Chasin found the "myth" of Billie compelling and praised the "interplay of history and current events." Comparing the book with *Families and Survivors*, short story writer Mary Gray Hughes noted that "the same style is used, and the reader again has difficulty becoming strongly involved. But because the book is more centrally focused and comes closer to the characters, the novel is both deeper and more moving." Most dissenters gently faulted Adams for taking on too much in short space or for insufficiently developing her protagonist. Daphne Merkin, of the *New Leader*, raised deeper questions. Beneath the stylish surface of Adams's novel, she argued, lay a plot "laughably Gothic in its intertwining liaisons and coincidence-riddled design." Such a book might serve for entertainment, but no one could take it seriously as "a portrait of the artist as a not-so-young woman." Compounding the damage was the faint praise that *Billie* had brought Adams as a "woman writer," a label that Merkin, following Mary McCarthy, found contemptible.

As 1980 approached, Adams's career redoubled its momentum. In 1978 she received a John Simon Guggenheim Memorial Fellowship, and in January 1979 Knopf published *Beautiful Girl*, a collection of sixteen stories originally published between 1959 and 1977, dedicated to William Abrahams and his collaborator Peter Stansky. Half

of these, including the title story, had been *O. Henry* prizewinners. As the collection reveals, love had long been the abiding theme of Adams's short fiction: "affection between friends, passion between lovers, and the gentle caring between parents and children," as the *Saturday Evening Post* described it. Reviewers compared Adams favorably with past masters—Katherine Mansfield, John O'Hara, and F. Scott Fitzgerald. "Although the times may not call for characters on the scale of a Jay Gatsby or a Dick Diver," wrote Susan Wood, "the search for love, for the self in others, goes on, and the characters in *Beautiful Girl* have not given up the search." Like Fitzgerald, Adams charts the currents of romantic longing that run beneath the surface of modern life. "I am a beautiful girl," bloated, bleary-eyed Ardis Bascombe rasps out at the end of the title story, demanding her due as an erstwhile southern belle. Again and again what Wood calls Adams's "extraordinary ordinary people" cling to what they know they cannot hold. In "Ripped Off," insecure Deborah, certain that freewheeling Philip will be stolen from her, hugs his sleeping form "tightly with her arms, as though she could keep him there." Men, too, love what vanishes. In "A Pale and Perfectly Oval Moon," after the "malingering" death of his wife, Van Moore marries the woman dying Penelope reviled as his "floozy." But late at night, "all alone, over a final brandy," he reads his dead wife's favorite novels and addresses her with conviction: "You're the most remarkable and interesting woman I've ever known. I've never really loved anyone but you." Not every tale ends in loss or longing, however. "Her most striking stories," James N. Baker observed in *Newsweek*, "tell of more offbeat relationships in which help comes unexpectedly." Just such surprising and satisfying turns come in "A Jealous Husband," "Home Is Where," and "For Good," the last piece in the collection. There twelve-year-old Nell finds her intuitive affinity for her father's former mistress confirmed. "Things seem to fit, or to have sorted themselves out, after all."

Reviewers responded warmly to *Beautiful Girl*. "The typical Alice Adams short story announces itself in the very first sentence as a thing of edgy wit and compressed narrative power," wrote Katha Pollitt. She found the author of *Beautiful Girl* "a consummately pleasing writer," but she also noted liabilities in Adams's typical subject matter. "Too many of these stories are about a certain type of woman. She is married to someone prosperous, a little stolid, and not much in evidence; she has an independent income or a little part-time job, and no serious interests; she is romantic, prone to love at first sight, and she establishes her claim to sensitivity by rereading Jane Austen every summer." Likewise L. M. Rosenberg criticized two mannerisms of Adams's style: "one-word sentence fragments that gain emphasis without earning it" and "the parenthetical statement that explains away complicated emotions and ideas." ("A wicked person could do an awfully easy parody of that," Adams has said of her trademark parentheses.) Dean Flower put both sides of the matter well. "At their best these stories explore complex relationships in a quick, deceptively offhand manner," he wrote. "What's too often missing is a final criticism."

Adams's next book, *Rich Rewards*, was dedicated to Diane Johnson, John Murray, and Richard Poirier. It differs from her previous novels in subject and treatment alike. Although it is set in San Francisco, "that spoiled and lovely city," it focuses on a visitor from the East, Daphne Matthiessen. Unlike any Adams novel before or since, the story is told in the first person, exclusively from Daphne's point of view. Fortyish, long divorced, and self-supporting as "a decorator, of sorts," Daphne comes west to help her friend Agatha renovate a house bought with a questionable inheritance. At the same time she is fleeing "a bad love affair in Boston." Sensitive, intelligent, and tough-minded, she has "made a career out of personal relationships" and knows herself to be "addicted to even the most miserable forms of love." Daphne's physical and temperamental displacement makes her an incisive observer of the San Francisco scene, particularly of the Houston family, the beautiful and damned "California nucleus" of the novel. Early on we learn that some twenty years before Daphne had a memorable affair in Paris. Her idealistic young lover, Jean-Paul, has since become a prominent Euro-Socialist. In a happy ending at once hard-won and well deserved, the older, wiser lovers meet again, this time with the possibility of rich rewards.

"You either have to like Daphne and go along with her or the book will fall on its face," Adams said when *Rich Rewards* appeared. Although some reviewers managed to resist Daphne, most sided with novelist Anne Tyler, who called her "one of the most admirable female characters in recent fiction." Comparing her with the protagonists of Adams's earlier novels, Tyler found in Daphne "a true Alice Adams heroine," more mature than Daisy Duke, more complex and self-reliant than either Louisa Calloway or Eliza Quarles. "Unattached, she has made her way through any number of lovers, some of them extremely ill-chosen, but her genuine friendships tend to be with other women." This solidarity in no way hinders Daphne's libido in *Rich Rewards*, which Adams has called her most "directly sexual" book. In both personal and political terms, as novelist Lynn Sharon Schwartz noted, Adams offers "a stringent story elegantly told, and enhanced by a keen moral judgment." Its scope extends well beyond the trendy slopes of San Francisco, to Watergate and Allende's Chile. It is finally Daphne's voice, forthright yet nuanced, wry but unjaded, civilized above all, that allows Adams to tell her story both ways, as romance and satire, without the self-division that has plagued her work from *Careless Love* to *Superior Women*. As her long-time supporter William Abrahams concluded, *Rich Rewards* is "a novel that manages the difficult feat of being at once romantic and truthful."

With the turn of the decade, Adams moved in new directions as she continued to produce prizewinning fiction. In 1980 she taught a writing course at the University of California at Davis (she has since taught at Stanford as well), and it was commuting there from San Francisco that suggested her story "Greyhound People." A signal honor came in 1982, when with her twelfth consecutive appearance in the *O. Henry* collection Adams received a "Special Award for Continuing Achievement." The prize had been given only twice before, to Joyce Carol Oates in 1970 and to John Updike in 1976. "A writer of uncommon excellence whose stories have gained her deserved esteem over the past decade," editor Abrahams wrote, "Miss Adams has become increasingly accomplished—hers is the art that conceals itself in a deceptive effortlessness—secure alike in what she does and in what she chooses not to do."

In 1982 Knopf published *To See You Again*, a collection of nineteen stories. Adams dedicated the book to Francis Kiernan, her editor at the *New Yorker*, where nine of the pieces had originally appeared. Sight and insight are the leitmotifs of *To See You Again*, as the title story suggests. In it a middle-aged teacher dreads the "absolute loss" of her "most brilliant and beautiful student." For her, red-haired Seth has become the West Coast counterpart of dazzling Tadzio in Thomas Mann's *Death in Venice*. Alone in her bed, idly watching television, she feels her burden of memory and desire unexpectedly lightened when she sees Seth again—and anew. In "Greyhound People" an anxious divorcee learns to negotiate the commuter bus to Sacramento. By the story's end she has bought herself a California Pass, a ticket to freedom. "These events can be trivial," Linda Pastan wrote: "the loss of a suitcase, an unscheduled stop by an airplane near a character's home town, the glimpse of a woman across a restaurant who looks like some other woman, long forgotten. But in each case the event leads to a small epiphany, in which at least the possibility of change is opened."

As in *Beautiful Girl,* Adams concentrates on extraordinary ordinary women. Fellow novelist Carolyn See praised her for creating characters who are "like most women, neither slave nor feminist, but something in between." Thus, to the chagrin of her with-it friends in "The Party-Givers," Clover Baskerville refuses to become angst ridden or mellowed out. Instead, in body and soul Clover remains "generous," and her generosity brings her love. Adams richly rewards characters who grow and change, whatever their ages: lusty survivor Maud in "True Colors," the elegant Farquhars in "At the Beach," brave Felicia Lord in "A Wonderful Woman." Hard-won happiness is possible for these romantic realists, only a few of whom, like wary Dylan Ballentyne in "By the Sea," refuse to take chances.

Almost unanimously reviewers agreed that Adams's work had matured in her second collection. Rhonda Brammer, in *Saturday Review,* found the new book "more delicately complex" than *Beautiful Girl,* and Robert Phillips wrote in *Commonwealth* that *To See You Again* shows "a widening of range and subjects, and an admirable ability to shift point-of-view from character to character." Beneath the placid surface of Adams's graceful sentences run turbulent currents of love, loss, and longing. "These stories only pretend to be refined," Carolyn See cautioned. "Actually, they are hard and sharp and unbearably concrete—a hammer on the carpenter's thumb."

"A concept I really object to, which is rampant among publishers and reviewers, is the 'big breakthrough novel,' " Adams said when *Listening to Billie* appeared in 1978. Indeed, at just over 200 pages, *Billie* was the biggest of her typically thin, rich books—until Knopf published *Superior Women* in September 1984. At close to twice the length of her earlier novels, *Superior Women* is big in size and scope alike. Covering forty years, 1943 to 1983, it chronicles the lives of four friends, all members of the Radcliffe class of 1946.

Although Adams returns to omniscient narration in *Superior Women,* her central character is displaced Californian Megan Greene. Plump, pretty, and ingenuous, Megan manages to sidestep marriage as she pursues a series of increasingly demanding jobs and unconventional love affairs. Cool Lavinia, a sharp-tongued southern WASP, engineers herself a "good" marriage that drives her to infidelity and despair. Hearty Peg, the least glamorous of the group, becomes the first to marry. But after four children and a nervous breakdown, she finds herself increasingly drawn to women, both as a lover and as a civil-rights activist. (At the end of the book it is Peg and Megan who establish "a temporary shelter, a way-station hospitality house for the homeless, musty women" of Atlanta.) Cathy, the fourth friend, remains shadowy. Like Maggie in Adams's story "What Should I Have Done?" Cathy languishes in a long affair with a Catholic priest. She is the first of the friends to die. On the edge of the group is a fifth woman, Janet, a Jewish premed who nearly sacrifices her career for marriage to Adam Marr, a wild Irish playwright loosely modeled on Norman Mailer.

Into this ethnic and religious mix of superior women Adams sends an equally mixed cast of men, from black jazzman Jackson Clay to pedigreed leftist Henry Stuyvesant. Her themes include not only women's friendships but also racial/sexual discrimination and the American class system. All these issues bear on the book's central question, voiced by Megan: "Are some men put off by extremes of intelligence or even attractiveness in women—by superior women?" Clearly the answer is yes. But just what constitutes the women's much-discussed superiority is far less clear. Beneath its Proustian veneer, Lavinia's superiority is mostly hauteur; Cathy's is next to nonexistent. Only long-suffering Peg and liberated Megan emerge with anything like moral superiority, and even that is diminished by the book's tidy utopian wrap-up. As Adams herself admitted, "a lot of the end is almost too unreal. It is a longed-for condition."

As in the case of *Careless Love,* what was at issue for the reviewers of *Superior Women* was the author's intention and the novel's genre. Was the book a serious, satiric novel of women's education, written in the tradition of Jane Austen's *Emma* and Mary McCarthy's *The Group?* Or was it lighter, spicier fare, a romance in the manner of June Singer's *The Debutantes* or Rona Jaffe's *Class Reunion?* Was it somehow both at once? At the end of *Superior Women* Megan recalls a conversation with Cathy. "It was about those old boarding school books, where there were always four friends. You know, Grace Harlow, all those?" As John Updike noted, this is but one of many references Adams makes to the schoolgirl novels of Jessie Graham Flower.

Reviewer Lois Gould also discussed Adams's "tricky" variation on the schoolgirl genre, arguing for it as the counterpart of the male writer's coming-of-age book, the bildungsroman. "For the woman writer, 'the group' is a kind of interior quest, a portrait of the artist as several different young selves." But how does the author assess those selves, the four friends whose superiority she more often mentions than illustrates? For much of the novel, certainly at the end, what Peter S. Prescott concluded rings true: "Adams has nothing to say about her women except what they, in often girlish terms, say about themselves." This lack of consistent irony—a staple in Austen and McCarthy—makes it hard to know Adams's final intention. As Francis Taliaferro concluded, it appears that the author wanted things both ways, romantic and realistic at once, thus creating an unstable compound of sugar, spice, and satire. "It's hard not to think that Alice Adams, lapsing from her usual finesse, yielded either to the temptation of parodying the Four Friends formula or to the possibility that Hollywood might gobble up this readable, but artistically disappointing novel." So far, Hollywood has not bitten, but Adams's "five-pound novel," repackaged with a glossy cover, has become a paperback best-seller.

Return Trips, Adams's latest collection of stories, was published in September 1985. The title is apt in every way, from the dedication (*"To Peter Adams Linenthal again, with love"*) to the travel motifs that link these fifteen accounts of women recalling or revisiting people and places that shaped their lives. In the title story Emma, a writer, remembers a summer she spent years before in Yugoslavia with her lover. "Together," she explains, "we suffered the most excruciating romantic agonies" before Paul's early death. Thence, via a dream from that agonized time, she travels farther back to her childhood in Adams's familiar Hilton, "a magic, enchanted place." On her return trip to the present she recalls her mother, her father, and Popsie Hooker—the three leading characters in her family romance. Along the way, like the heroine of "Roses, Rhododendron," she comes to see them and herself anew.

Even more than *Listening to Billie*, beneath its realistic surface *Return Trips* is a mythic book. Underlying the fourteen stories and the memoir "My First and Only House" is what Mircea Eliade has called "the myth of the eternal return," a ceaseless cycle of archetypal repetition and creative rebirth. For Adams as for Eliade, "Everything begins over again at its commencement every instant. The past

is but a prefiguration of the future. No event is irreversible and no transformation is final." Again and again, the women in these stories remake themselves as they travel through time and space, whether their destination is as close as Carmel ("Mollie's Dog") or as far off as Ixtapa ("Mexican Dust"), Fairbanks ("Alaska"), or Yugoslavia ("Return Trips").

Without Freudian fanfare, Adams illustrates the persistence of memory and the return of the repressed, death and distance notwithstanding. "A very wise woman who is considerably older than I am once told me that in her view relationships with people to whom we have been very close can continue to change even after the deaths of those people," Emma observes. Thus, in "Waiting for Stella," characters young and old cluster around the memory of "Stella, the first of them to die," taking their bearings by her dark star. In "Mexican Dust," try as she will to accommodate her "large, fair-haired" husband and in-laws, small, dark Miriam dreams of violence: "Eric's body washed up on a beach, blond hair spread against cold sand and long pale legs crookedly stretched down to the murky, turbulent sea." The titular dog that Molly fails to retrieve becomes the emblem of all she has lost "in a lifetime of dark mistakes"—her youth, her long-ago lover, "something of infinite value."

In most of these stories Adams, like her characters, returns to familiar settings, subjects, and styles. Several point in new directions, however. At six feet and 185 pounds, "oversize" Maxine, the lonely long-distance swimmer in "A Public Pool," is hardly the typical Alice Adams heroine, yet her voice rings true. The rich American discussed in "La Señora" never appears; instead, as in "Verlie I Say Unto You," Adams focuses on the lady's maid. Similarly, in the much-reprinted "Alaska," she charts the crossing paths of Miss Goldstein's two housekeepers: aging black Mrs. Lawson, haunted by her past; young white Gloria, anxious about her future.

Slim and unprepossessing as it appears, Adams's third collection shows a master writer at the height of her powers. Like the women in *Return Trips*, she continues to look back even as she moves forward, writing, "at least in part, about the vagaries of memory and about the house that in dreams I permanently inhabit—or, it might be more accurate to say, the house that inhabits me." She views her life and work with equanimity, and her fifties she considers "the best years of my life, so far." Of the calling that has taken her from Chapel Hill to Cambridge, San Francisco, and the wild coasts of Portugal, Adams observes, "I think too much has been said about the lonely agonies of writing. It isn't that lonely and there isn't that much agony. At least not for me."

Interviews:

Patricia Holt, "PW Interviews: Alice Adams," *Publishers Weekly*, 213 (16 January 1978): 8-9;

Nancy Faber, "Out of the Pages," *People*, 9 (3 April 1978): 48ff;

Sandy Boucher, "Alice Adams—A San Francisco Novelist Who is into Her Third Book," *San Francisco*, 20 (October 1978): 130-133;

Wayne Warga, "A Sophisticated Author Gets by With Help from Her Friends," *Los Angeles Times Book Review*, 16 November 1980, p. 3;

Neil Feinemann, "An Interview with Alice Adams," *StoryQuarterly*, no. 11 (1980): 27-37;

Alix Madrigal, "The Breaking of a Mold," *San Francisco Chronicle Review*, 9 September 1984, p. 11.

References:

William Abrahams, "Introduction," *Prize Stories 1982: The O. Henry Awards* (Garden City: Doubleday, 1982), pp. ix-xi;

Abrahams, "A Tribute to Alice Adams," *San Francisco Chronicle Review*, 11 April 1982, pp. 1, 11;

Abrahams, "Wanting More—And More—In 'That Spoiled and Lovely City,'" *San Francisco Chronicle Review*, 5 October 1980, p. 9;

Anatole Broyard, "Surviving the Novel," *New York Times*, 30 January 1975, p. 33;

Helen Chasin, "Listening to Billie," *Village Voice*, 9 January 1978, pp. 59, 61;

Mircea Eliade, *Cosmos and History: The Myth of the Eternal Return*, translated by Willard R. Trask (New York: Harper & Row, 1959), pp. 89-90;

Dean Flower, "Fiction Chronicle," *Hudson Review*, 32 (Summer 1979): 295-296;

Annie Gottlieb, "They Stumbled Blindly into Marriage," *New York Times Book Review*, 16 March 1975, pp. 28-29;

Lois Gould, "Life After Radcliffe," *New York Times Book Review*, 23 September 1984, p. 9;

Daphne Merkin, "Tale of a Woman Writer," *New Leader*, 61 (27 March 1978): 21-23;

Linda Pastan, *"To See You Again,"* *American Book Review*, 5 (July 1983): 4;

Robert Phillips, "Missed Opportunities, Endless Possibilities," *Commonweal*, 110 (25 March 1983): 188-190;

Katha Pollitt, "Good Old Boys and Wistful Hopes," *New York Times Book Review*, 14 January 1979, pp. 14, 27;

Jill Robinson, "A New Place, a Chillier Season," *Washington Post Book World*, 23 February 1975, p. 3;

Carolyn See, "23 Stories from the Necklace of Thought," *Los Angeles Times*, 13 April 1982, V: 1;

Anne Tyler, "An Honorable Heroine," *New York Times Book Review*, 14 September 1980, pp. 13, 20;

Tyler, *"Listening to Billie,"* *Quest*, 2 (March/April 1978): 84-85;

John Updike, "No More Mr. Knightly," *New Yorker*, 60 (5 November 1984): 161ff;

Susan Wood, "Stories of Love and Loss," *Washington Post Book World*, 21 January 1979, p. 3.

T. Coraghessan Boyle

(1948-)

Michael Adams

BOOKS: *Descent of Man: Stories* (Boston: Little, Brown/Atlantic Monthly Press, 1979; London: Gollancz, 1979);

Water Music (Boston: Little, Brown, 1981; London: Gollancz, 1982);

Budding Prospects: A Pastoral (New York: Viking, 1984; London: Gollancz, 1984);

Greasy Lake & Other Stories (New York: Viking, 1985).

TRANSLATION: Urbina Leandro, "Our Father Who Art in Heaven," trans. by Boyle and Roz Frank, *TriQuarterly*, 35 (Winter 1976): 65.

SELECTED PERIODICAL PUBLICATIONS: "The OD & Hepatitis RR or Bust," *North American Review*, 257 (Fall 1972): 78-81;

"Rock and Roll Star," *North American Review*, 258 (Spring 1973): 52-55;

"The See," *TriQuarterly*, 35 (Winter 1976): 82-84;

"Mise en scene," *North American Review*, 261 (Spring 1976): 68;

"Crossings," *North American Review*, 262 (Summer 1977): 45;

"Hostages," *Antioch Review*, 36 (Spring 1978): 154-160;

"The Zoo," *Texas Quarterly*, 21 (Spring 1978): 143-151;

"Naif," *North American Review*, 264 (Spring 1979): 26-29;

"I Dated Jane Austen," *Georgia Review*, 33 (Summer 1979): 416-420;

"Hit Man," *North American Review*, 265 (June 1980): 50-51.

With the publication of two novels and two collections of short stories in six years, T. Coraghessan Boyle has quickly established a reputation as a distinctive and entertaining writer. His examinations of the banality and bestiality of contemporary life have placed him in the absurdist, experimental, self-conscious tradition of such writers as John Barth and Thomas Pynchon. Boyle's lyrical, bawdy, anarchic tales have earned him comparisons with

James Joyce, Franz Kafka, Evelyn Waugh, Thomas Berger, and Tom Robbins. But for all Boyle's similarities to other artists, no Americans in the 1980s write about the diverse subjects he does in the way he does.

Born in Peekskill, New York, to Irish immigrant parents, Boyle says he never read a book until he was eighteen. He went to college as a music major and then taught high school in Garrison, New York, "to stay out of Vietnam." His main preoccupation during this time "was just hanging out, taking a lot of drugs." After he began reading seriously, he was very much influenced by Barth's *The Sot-Weed Factor* (1960), Pynchon's *V.* (1963), Gabriel García Márquez's *One Hundred Years of Solitude* (1968), and the plays of Eugene Ionesco and Jean Genet.

As "a way out of a dead end," Boyle entered the Iowa Writers' Workshop in 1972. He studied creative writing under Vance Bourjaily and John Irving and eventually earned a Ph.D. in 1977 with a collection of his stories as his dissertation. At the same time, Boyle began publishing short stories and was a fiction editor of the *Iowa Review*. His stories won the Coordinating Council of Literary Magazines Award for Fiction and a Creative Writing Fellowship from the National Endowment for the Arts in 1977. *Descent of Man* (1979), his first collection of stories, received the St. Lawrence Award for Short Fiction in 1980, and *Paris Review* excerpts from his first novel, *Water Music* (1981), won the Aga Khan Award. Boyle lives in Los Angeles with his wife and two children, teaches creative writing at the University of Southern California, and plays saxophone with a rockabilly band.

The seventeen stories in *Descent of Man* depict concerns which run throughout Boyle's fiction: paranoia, violence, sexuality, men's inability to understand women, the similarities of animals and humans, primitive societies, primitivism in supposedly modern civilizations, the refuse of affluent societies, the clichés of popular culture, language, myths, and bodily functions. The subjects of these

Dust jacket for Boyle's first book

usually satirical stories range from a collector of exotic beer cans to a group of Norsemen who discover America and pillage Ireland to a woman scientist who leaves her male roommate for an intellectual chimpanzee who has translated Darwin, Nietzsche, and Noam Chomsky into Yerkish.

"Heart of a Champion" satirizes the banalities of popular culture while showing their absurdities and dangers as wonder-dog Lassie leaves her master Timmy for a coyote. Communism and Christianity are satirized simultaneously in "The Second Swimming," in which Mao Tse-tung exults in his power: "Tell me," he asks an aide as they look down over an admiring crowd, "did the Beatles ever have it this good?" The best two stories are "Bloodfall" and "The Big Garage." In the former, a group of young people is so benumbed by drugs, television, and rock 'n' roll that they are merely irritated by an inexplicable endless rain of blood. One is more concerned with getting blood on the seats of his BMW than with the possibility of survival. "The Big Garage" is a hilarious and horrifying account of what is portrayed as the most terrifying experience known to modern man: taking one's car to be serviced. This story captures society's indiffer-

ence to the individual as well as anything by Kafka.

Descent of Man, like all of Boyle's fiction, is sometimes clever for the sake of being clever; the irony is occasionally too easy, the satire too obvious. But, as Max Apple pointed out in the *New York Times Book Review*, "the failures are the honest failures of an energetic writer who is willing to try anything."

Water Music is loosely based on the exploits of Mungo Park (1771-1806), the Scottish explorer who became, in 1796, the first white man to see the Niger River; returned to Britain to write a best-selling account of his adventures, *Travels in the Interior Districts of Africa* (1797); went back to Africa to lead a larger expedition; and drowned in the rapids of the Niger during an attack by natives. Boyle alternates real and imagined events from Park's life with those involving London criminal Ned Rise, a member of Park's party, to create a large-scale picaresque satire in the vein of *The Sot-Weed Factor*, Thomas Berger's *Little Big Man* (1964), and George Macdonald Fraser's Flashman novels.

Boyle got the inspiration for a book about Mungo Park while reading John Ruskin for his Ph.D. orals. "Ruskin took him to task for deserting his wife and pursuing those crazy dreams," says Boyle. "That interested me . . . and I began toying with the idea of a novel." Boyle visited Park's hometown of Selkirk about that time but has no firsthand knowledge of Africa: "At the time I was writing *Water Music*, a friend went to Nigeria to live and in letters he described what it was like there—flora, fauna, and local color that I incorporated into the novel. If I had had the money to go to Africa, it would've been a very different book."

Boyle's Mungo Park is hardly a heroic figure. Ned Rise sees him as "conceited, mad with ambition, selfish, blind, incompetent, fatuous." Park is racist in his attitudes toward Africans, thinking he has had experiences no other man has because he does not recognize the humanity of the inhabitants of the Dark Continent. Yet he would never have reached the Niger without the aid of several non-whites, especially Johnson, born Katunga Oyo, former slave, ex-valet, worshipper of Alexander Pope, translator of Henry Fielding's *Amelia* (1752) into Mandingo. Park sees this extremely sophisticated man only as a "nigger." Park shamefully neglects Ailie, his long-suffering fiancée and later wife. Without any didacticism, Boyle presents Ailie as a woman of great potential restrained by her roles as wife and mother.

Park is also a liar, giving his readers a distorted, romanticized version of his exploits. He tries to justify his subverting the truth to Johnson: "The good citizens of London and Edinburgh don't want to read about misery and wretchedness and thirty-seven slaves disemboweled, old boy—their lives are grim enough as it is." Johnson considers Park "no better than Herodotus or Desceliers or any of them other armchair heroes that charted out the interior of Africa from behind the four walls of their book-lined studies." Mungo Park is representative of the kind of men who built the British Empire and whose moral blindness led to its inevitable collapse.

Boyle's Park is not, however, a villain. He is a typical picaro, as much victim as victimizer. He is beaten, robbed, shot at, stabbed, urinated on, engulfed in excrement, bitten by a pig, captured again and again by savages. When he returns to civilized England, he is greeted by being struck by a cane. Yet through it all, he remains true to his quest "to know the unknowable." Even Ned Rise admires him for that.

Boyle's other protagonist is even more of a victim: "Not Twist, not Copperfield, not Fagin himself had a childhood to compare with Ned Rise's." He is stolen from his mother at birth and forced to become a beggar at seven; he has his right hand mutilated by a cleaver, is nearly drowned, is robbed of all his money after getting rich off fake caviar, is imprisoned wrongfully and hanged—coming to life as he is about to be dissected—loses Fanny Brunch, his only true love, is imprisoned again, spends two months in a well, is shipped to Africa, and becomes part of Park's disastrous second expedition. His enemies pursue him, yet he survives them all, survives even Park's foolishly fatal leadership, and emerges as a clarinet-playing messiah.

The stories of Mungo Park and Ned Rise, the latter of whom Boyle's agent and publisher suggested he cut from the book, are presented in ironic juxtaposition. Park's Britain is "a society where the forms are observed and love of culture is a way of life, a society that nurtures Shakespeares, Wrens, Miltons and Cooks." Ned's East End of London might as well be on another planet: "Soot hung in the air. Children were begging on the streetcorners, women lay drunk in the alleys. Two pigs gorged on the offal in the gutter, a madman was selling invisible Bibles, a woman with cancer of the throat offered to drink a gallon of water and vomit it up for a penny."

Water Music is a vastly entertaining comic adventure, but it is also a black comedy. It is a portrait of a hostile universe in which "Whenever things start to look up, whenever fantasy begins to jell into possibility, the Hand of Fate intercedes to slap you back to your senses." This is the kind of world in which even an optimistic rationalist like Mungo Park must ask, "What am I doing? . . . What in God's name am I doing?"

Like most black humor, *Water Music* is a self-conscious narrative, constantly calling attention to and mocking its form and style: "The sun scorches the sky as if it were newly created, as if it were flexing its muscle, hammering out the first link in a chain of megatonic nuclear events, flaring up with all the confidence of youth and all the promise of eternal combustion. Which is to say it is hot. Damnably hot." The novel is anachronistic and heavily allusive with echoes of Cervantes, Swift, Dickens, Hardy, Conrad, John Fowles, Kurt Vonnegut, Luis Buñuel, *Alice's Restaurant*, *Apocalypse Now*, and "Days of Our Lives." Boyle's delight in the act of creation is infectious.

Several reviewers resisted the self-conscious pleasures of *Water Music*. In the *New York Times Book Review*, Alan Friedman dismissed the novel as "an extended occasion for comic-strip pathos," but it was appreciated elsewhere. William Cole of *Saturday Review* called it the "most rompish historical novel I've ever seen." In the *Times Literary Supplement*, Thomas Sutcliffe said that it "is occasionally sloppy and often self-indulgent, but it is also compendious, funny and compelling, a hymn to the human debris and detritus of history." George Kearns, in the *Hudson Review*, described *Water Music* as "a historical novel unlike any other," an "astonishing performance." According to Kearns, "Boyle's manner of giving us the late eighteenth century of Mungo Park with reminders that the tale is being told by an American in the 1980s may be a stunt, but it's a stunt so well performed that it never tires." Kearns adds that Boyle "plays English the way Rachmaninoff played Rachmaninoff."

Budding Prospects: A Pastoral (1984) has the same satirical, slapstick, scatalogical tone as *Water Music* but is written in a less ornate style and presents fewer heroic adventures. Felix Nasmyth, thirty-one, divorced, depressed, and restless, has quit everything he has ever started. The mysterious Vogelsang, a Vietnam veteran with a "Charlie Manson stare," gives Felix another chance at success: growing marijuana in an isolated location in Northern California. Vogelsang promises that Felix will earn $500,000 and will have the expert technical guidance of Boyd Dowst, Yale M.S. in botany.

Felix is attracted to the project not just for the money but for the risk involved. He hires his friends Phil and Gesh to help him raise the crop, but they soon discover that Willits, California, is not the perfect spot for growing illegal substances. It is the kind of place where the vehicles parked outside the local bar sport bumper stickers proclaiming, "I'M MORAL." Their neighbors include Marlon Sapers, a 320-pound alumnus of the violent ward of the state mental hospital. Officer John Jerpbak, who takes a special dislike to Felix even before he vomits into the lap of the policeman's mother, declares war on the local pot growers. Felix is told that everyone in Willits knows what he and his friends are doing. All in all, Mendocino County is almost as bizarre for Felix as Africa is for Mungo Park. Rain, fire, a hungry bear, and other disasters reduce the size of the crop to almost nothing, but they persevere, as Felix, an unreliable narrator, says, like "Tess cutting sheaves at Flintcombe-Ash, Job staggering under the burden of calamity."

As epigraphs from Benjamin Franklin's *Poor Richard's Almanac* (1732-1758) and Arthur Miller's *Death of a Salesman* (1947) and an allusion to B. Traven's *The Treasure of the Sierra Madre* (1935) indicate, *Budding Prospects* is a satire of American greed, of simplistic belief in and cynical perversion of the free-enterprise system. Felix and his cohorts want to get rich quick and give little thought to the legality or morality of their scheme: "We knew what counted: money. Money, and nothing else."

Felix convinces himself that what they are doing is in the great American tradition: "We would subdue the land, make it produce, squeeze the dollars from it through sacrifice, sheer force of will and Yankee gumption. It was the dream of the pioneers themselves." Their failure would prove that "the society itself was bankrupt, the pioneers a fraud, true grit, enterprise and daring as vestigial as adenoids or appendixes. We believed in Ragged Dick, P. T. Barnum, Diamond Jim Brady, in Andrew Carnegie, D. B. Cooper, Jackie Robinson. . . . We never doubted that we would make it, that one day we would be the fat cats in the mansion on the hill. Never. Not for a moment. After all, what else was there?" Such comic hyperbole is a key element in Boyle's style and is very appropriate here since self-delusion is another target of his satire.

Dust jacket for Boyle's 1984 satirical novel about a scheme to grow marijuana

The irony of Felix's endeavors is that he, Phil, and Gesh work harder—and under more dangerous conditions—and make less than they would have at any legal manual labor. Felix naively believes in work, any work, as a means of imposing order on chaos without realizing that it is simply a way of ignoring the disorder around him. Felix's friend Dwight Dunn has attempted to make some sense of his life by keeping detailed records of all his experiences only to lose them in a fire: "It was as if he'd never lived." The comic hopelessness of such efforts is another theme of *Budding Prospects*. Like Mungo Park, Felix summarizes the absurd-pathetic condition of his life by asking, "What am I doing?"

Budding Prospects is also notable for Boyle's insight into both California's posthippie world of cynical aimlessness and the violent redneck culture of that state's rural environs. The not-so-quiet desperation of late-twentieth-century man is captured perfectly. Making the exploits of this cast of whiners and zombies entertaining and enlightening is no small achievement.

The novel received decidedly mixed reviews with almost every critic liking and disliking something about Boyle's tale. John Clute, in the *Times Literary Supplement,* approved of Boyle's style but not his protagonist, whom he saw as mean-spirited: "Beneath the chilly high-jinks of its telling, *Budding Prospects* is a palinode, and a quite astonishingly bitter one. It is also, at heart, without humour." In *USA Today,* David Guy said that he "admired its verbal pyrotechnics and comic skills, but found its characters . . . rather boring, the way your favorite hippie finally loses his charm when you realize he really isn't ever going to do anything." Michael Gorra, in the *New York Times Book Review,* objected to Boyle's "settling for one-liners like small fire-crackers, rather than working toward a more sustained comic display." Yet he praised Boyle's "irreverent brio" as being "a refreshing antidote to the attenuated self-pity with which the 'Big Chill' generation tends to see itself in print."

Like Boyle's first collection of stories, *Greasy Lake & Other Stories* (1985) offers diverse subjects and styles. The subjects of the fifteen stories include a husband who falls in love with the surrogate mother of his child, a love affair between President Eisenhower and the wife of Nikita Khrushchev, survivalist paranoia, the mating of whales, construction of a new moon, the final performance of blues musician Robert Johnson, an Elvis Presley imitator, and the importation of starlings into the United States.

There is also "Rupert Beersley and the Beggar Master of Sivani-Hoota," a Sherlock Holmes parody in which "the most brilliant detective in all of Anglo-India" goes berserk and accuses everyone of guilt in the crime he is investigating. "The Overcoat II" updates Nikolai Gogol's classic 1842 tale to the contemporary Soviet Union. This time the timid clerk dies as much from losing faith in the Soviet socialist system as from losing his perfect new overcoat. The most typical Boyle story is "Two Ships," an exploration of paranoia and friendship similar to the treatments of those themes in his novels. The best story in the collection is "The Hector Quesadilla Story," about an aging pinch hitter for the Los Angeles Dodgers who gets a second and then a third chance at glory during the longest game in baseball history. Not just another look at the mythic qualities of the most mythic of sports, "The Hector Quesadilla Story" explains how baseball is a metaphor for life and for art: "it's a game of infinite surprises." This may be taken as the credo for Boyle's approach to fiction. As Larry McCaffery said in reviewing this collection in the *New York Times Book Review,* "Boyle's control of a wide range of narrative styles and voices insures that nothing ever really seems predictable here."

Boyle's favorite stylistic devices are unusual, often comic, seemingly incongruous metaphors and similes. (He frequently uses similes to excess, especially in *Budding Prospects.*) In "All Shook Up," a van is "the color of cough syrup." In "Green Hell," a spider is "the size of a two-egg omelet," and a jungle sound is "like a hundred bums spitting in the gutter." In *Water Music,* Mungo Park's "pubic hair is the color of mashed turnips," and an African rain arrives "like an explosion in a glass factory." In *Budding Prospects,* "Phil looked like a man being strapped into the electric chair while his wife French-kisses the D. A. in the hallway," and Felix is "incontinent, unreliable, about as trustworthy as a shaggy-legged satyr at a Girl Scout jamboree." The relations between Boyle's style, his distinctive humor, and his view of the world are inseparable when he is at his best. The narrator of "Two Ships" observes that "humor resides in exaggeration, and humor is a quick cover for alarm and bewilderment."

Boyle is at work on "World's End," a novel about the intertwined destinies of three families in the Hudson River Valley over 300 years. It will almost certainly bear little resemblance to any other family saga. As Boyle says, "I'm still a wise guy from New York. . . . I've always felt that I would never compromise. I'd do exactly what I wanted and still get my audience."

References:
William Stage, "Tom Boyle: A Writer's Writer," *St.*

Louis Post-Dispatch, 8 June 1984, pp. E3, E11;
"T. Coraghessan Boyle," *Esquire*, 103 (February 1985): 136-144.

Len Fulton
(15 May 1934-   )

Keith Kroll
Kalamazoo Valley Community College

Dan Pearce
University of California, Riverside

BOOKS: *Two Short Stories* (Paradise, Cal.: Dustbooks, 1969);
The Grassman (Berkeley: Thorp Springs Press, 1974);
American Odyssey: A Bookselling Travelogue, with Ellen Ferber (Paradise, Cal.: Dustbooks, 1975);
Dark Other Adam Dreaming (Paradise, Cal.: Dustbooks, 1976);
The Psychologique of Small Press Publishing (New Brunswick, N.J.: Rutgers University Graduate School of Library Service, 1976).

PLAY PRODUCTION: *Dark Other Adam Dreaming*, Paradise, Cal., Theatre on the Ridge, December 1984.

OTHER: *Directory of Little Magazines*, edited by Fulton (Berkeley: Dustbooks, 1965);
International Directory of Little Magazines and Small Presses, edited by Fulton (Berkeley: Dustbooks, 1966-   );
The Small Press Review, edited by Fulton (Berkeley: Dustbooks, 1967-   );
Small Press Record of Books In Print, edited by Fulton, (Paradise, Cal.: Dustbooks, 1969-   );
Directory of Small Magazine/Press Editors and Publishers, edited by Fulton (Paradise, Cal.: Dustbooks, 1970-   );
"Tracking the Small Presses," in *The Publish-It-Yourself Handbook*, edited by Bill Henderson (New York: Pushcart Press, 1973), pp. 103-116;

"Dust: A Trial Seed," in *The Little Magazine in America*, edited by Elliot Anderson and Mary Kinzie (New York: Pushcart Press, 1978), pp. 423-437;
"Piecework," in *The Art of Literary Publishing*, edited by Henderson (New York: Pushcart Press, 1980), pp. 163-178;
Directory of Poetry Publishers, 1985-86, edited by Fulton and Ellen Ferber (Paradise, Cal.: Dustbooks, 1985-   );
"*Dust* and Dustbooks," in *Green Isle in the Sea: An Informal History of the Alternative Press, 1960-85*, edited by Diane Kurchkow and Curt Johnson (Highland Park, Ill.: December Press, 1986), pp. 43-52.

PERIODICAL PUBLICATIONS: "Against the Octopus," *Small Press Review*, 1 (Spring 1967): 2;
"Anima Rising: Little Magazines in the Sixties," *American Libraries*, 2 (January 1971): 25-47;
"Lifenotes of a Small Pressman/I: Moonthoughts," *Small Press Review*, 3 (1972);
"Laboring Long and Dreaming High: Dustbooks," *Small Press*, 1 (March/April 1984): 23-26.

As a writer, editor, and publisher, Len Fulton has been involved with small press publishing since the mid 1960s. Fulton cofounded the literary magazine *Dust* in 1963 and became its sole publisher shortly thereafter. By 1965 he had become "self-consciously interested in the whole process of the

Len Fulton

production of literature" and thus founded his publishing imprint, Dustbooks, with an editorial commitment "to modern, contemporary literature by *living* writers," and to tracking the renaissance of small press publishing. Over the past twenty-one years he has published a variety of poetry collections, novels, how-to books, volumes about bookselling, and the annual reference works that comprise the Small Press Information Library.

Fulton was born on 15 May 1934 in Lowell, Massachusetts (also the birthplace of Jack Kerouac), to Claude E. Fulton, a Canadian Scot, and Louise Vaillant Fulton. After serving two years in the U.S. Army, from 1953-1955, Fulton attended Portland Junior College (now the University of Southern Maine) from 1955 to 1957, where he edited the school newspaper, and also shoveled snow, parked cars, and did a variety of odd jobs. From 1957 to 1959 he and a partner, Bob Fay, published a string of successful and unsuccessful small-town newspapers in Maine. It was during 1958 and 1959, while working as an advertising agent in New York State for the *Middletown Daily Record*, that Fulton was overcome by a "geographic imperative to head west": "In the fall of '58 I was working for one of the world's first offset dailies just outside New York, and I made one last trip to the Maine wilderness. In one night I got my life clean again: found an accountant in a dim storefront to do my income tax, paid off a lawyer for a divorce, drove

my car back to Commercial Credit Corp. and left it as a final balloon payment, signed over every interest I possessed in newspapers, and shook hands with a man who held a note against me for five thousand dollars. Goodbye, Maine, and a year later the East, forever. I would be a professor; I could write and read and teach—let someone else sweat the publishing, the presses, the ads, the linotype operators" ("Tracking the Small Presses").

Fulton enrolled at the University of Wyoming, where he studied English and psychology and received his Bachelor of Arts degree in 1961. After graduation he entered the graduate program in psychology at the University of California at Berkeley. Fulton planned to write a Ph.D. dissertation on Freud's literary roots, but he left the university after two years when the department denied him the opportunity to develop his dissertation topic. Although out of the university, he remained in Berkeley. He had remarried, and in order to support his wife and his son Timothy, and to help finance *Dust* and Dustbooks, Fulton made use of a class in research statistics that he had enjoyed at Wyoming and landed a job as a statistician with the California State Department of Public Health, a position that he held until 1968.

Fulton and five others, including his old newspaper partner Bob Fay, started *Dust* in 1963. Fulton writes that "the name Dust emerged from the polite but mistaken notion that we could maintain an open posture which would not violate any of our editorial proclivities." Fulton says "mistaken" because one by one four of the original editors quit due to disagreements over the contents of the magazine. After six issues only Andrew Curry, an original founder, and Fulton were editing *Dust*. By issue twelve, Fulton, now the sole publisher of *Dust*, had turned the editorial duties over to Curry. In 1970 Wally Depew, a small press writer and publisher, assumed Curry's position. Up until its demise in 1972, *Dust* continued to publish and interview many of the small press writers of the day.

Publishing *Dust* amid the turbulent, antiestablishment atmosphere of Berkeley brought Fulton into close contact with avant-garde literature, and the influence that the experimental forms of literature had on him can be clearly seen in his two short stories, "The Line" and "The Ellipsoid." He has acknowledged that his reading of Samuel Beckett had an important influence on these early efforts, and these two stories are reminiscent of the absurdist-philosophical fiction of Beckett or John Barth. Like so much avant-garde literature, both stories are purposely difficult and elusive. "The

Line" is a rather oblique narrative which attempts to dramatize the birth trauma, while the even more enigmatic "The Ellipsoid" is, according to Fulton, a "satire" on the need or wish for social conformity: "The last line, 'I am the same!,' is the final victory. What you have is the monotony of the Ellipsoids—the monotony of sameness." In 1969 Fulton published "The Line" and "The Ellipsoid," along with an abstruse essay on Samuel Beckett, under his Dustbooks imprint as *Two Short Stories.*

Once he had become the sole publisher of *Dust,* Fulton realized "that a small press [was] essentially a one-man life-style, the essence of that private world of the individual, just as the single work of art is. . . ." By 1965 Fulton had become interested in the "whole production of literature"; thus, he set out to compile and edit a list of all the little magazines and small presses that were in operation at that time.

The first "list" to be published under the Dustbooks imprint was the *Directory of Little Magazines;* it contained forty pages, 250 listings, was printed in 500 copies, and sold for one dollar. By the following year, 1966, Fulton got help from Cavan McCarthy of Locations Press in England and the directory became international. The *International Directory of Little Magazines and Small Presses,* twenty-first edition, published in 1985, lists over 4,000 magazines and small presses, runs over 700 pages, and includes subject and regional indexes. It lists small press publishers from Ampersand Press to Zyga Multimedia Research, and each listing gives information such as editor, type of material published, and production method. Since the very first edition, the directory has been Dustbooks' central title and has been widely acclaimed. Writer and publisher Robert Fox, of Carpenter Press, calls it "the most comprehensive reference book of its kind," and the *Wall Street Journal* has referred to the directory as "the Bible of the business."

In 1967, in order to get even closer to the actual production of small press titles, Fulton began publishing the *Small Press Review.* In the first issue, which was dedicated to the memory of Alan Swallow, of Swallow Press, he wrote, "*SPR* is designed to serve the small-press/little magazine business; but also to go out from the center of that business to a world NEEDING small presses, which may be, with their attendant psycho-politico-literary ramification, our last edge against modern man's cold invasive impersonality." Since its first issue, the *Small Press Review* has published reviews, essays, and interviews, "all calculated to track the energies of the small-press world."

Fulton not only wanted to list as many of the small press publishers as possible but he also desired to gather them together. In 1967 Fulton and Jerry Burns, another small press publisher, began planning for the first conference of small-pressmen. The first conference took place in Berkeley in May 1968, and it was from that conference that the Committee of Small Magazine Editors and Publishers (COSMEP) emerged, with Fulton elected as its first chairman.

In January of 1968, five months before the first COSMEP conference, Fulton became seriously ill while in Los Angeles: the toll of planning the conference, publishing *Dust* and Dustbooks, and working full-time as a statistician simply became too much for him to handle. After a short period of recuperation, Fulton and his wife, Joanne, decided that changes in his life had to be made. He quit his job as a statistician, left Berkeley, and moved in January 1969 with his wife and son to Paradise, California, where he would devote his full time to writing and publishing.

Renewed emotionally and physically by the rustic environment of his new surroundings, Fulton was soon back at work editing and publishing poetry and prose by a variety of authors and compiling, editing, and publishing new small press reference titles. From the beginning of the *Small Press Review,* he had included a section that recorded books published by the small presses, books often overlooked in other reference books. As this "record" began to grow, he realized that the information needed its own forum, and so he compiled, edited, and published the *Small Press Record of Books In Print,* which first appeared in late 1969. A year later, in 1970, he compiled, edited, and published the *Directory of Small Magazine/Press Editors and Publishers,* which was designed to allow readers to connect small press editors with their respective presses. It was also during 1970 that Fulton experienced the death of his wife, Joanne, who was killed in an automobile accident on Mother's Day.

It was not until 1974 that Fulton's first novel, *The Grassman,* was published; it was not, however, published by Dustbooks but rather by Thorp Springs Press in Berkeley. After "The Line" and "The Ellipsoid," one would have hardly expected something as traditional as a western from a writer who seemed committed to the avant-garde. The differences between the novel and the two short stories are easier to understand, however, when one realizes that Fulton started the "western saga" back in the late 1950s and had sporadically, but carefully, been nurturing the novel along throughout the 1960s.

The Grassman concerns a young man's journey away from the repressive "law and manners" of Boston to the free, windswept plains of Wyoming. The novel opens in the spring of 1886, with Andrew Finn heading west to visit his mysterious Uncle Ben, owner of the Blacktail cattle ranch. On the train out to Wyoming, Andrew meets and falls in love with Holly Taft, a young woman who is running away from her family in St. Louis to play the piano in a cattle-town saloon. Andrew arrives in Wyoming to find himself in the middle of a range war over water rights, which pits the Blacktail against the Lazy M ranch, run by a Frenchman named Vitalis Marquand.

Though full of gripping, memorable scenes—the charge of a wild longhorn, a rope fight between ranch hands, and a barroom massacre—*The Grassman* is not a formulaic western in which good triumphs over evil. Among other things, the novel powerfully evokes the *Orestia* myth. Andrew Finn's visit to his uncle's Wyoming ranch is not a stroll on the high plains with a group of cowboys. For like Orestes, Andrew's journey leads him to endure tremendous suffering in order to expiate a family curse.

In keeping with his belief that "nothing is more important for the small publisher than the author's energy" to promote his own book, Fulton set out in June of 1974 with his colleague Ellen Ferber on a 10,000-mile trip across America to sell *The Grassman* (and a few other titles) to bookstores. Fulton chronicled this modern "colportage" in *American Odyssey: A Bookselling Travelogue*, which he published in 1975 as part of the "American Dust Series," started in order to celebrate the upcoming United States Bicentennial. Although he and Ferber lost roughly $700 on the trip, *American Odyssey* remains a consistent seller for Fulton and Dustbooks.

American Odyssey's continued success might at first seem strange considering that its annotated list of bookstores was soon outdated—small, independent bookstores, like the kind Fulton most often visited, seem to come and go with an alarming regularity. But *American Odyssey* is as much about Fulton's life, West versus East, urban life versus country life, and Fulton's feelings about protecting the environment as it is about selling *The Grassman*.

Only a year after the publication of *American Odyssey*, Fulton, with the help of a grant from the National Endowment for the Arts, published as number four in the "American Dust Series" his second novel, *Dark Other Adam Dreaming*, which he describes as "a somewhat autobiographical story of the sexual-intellectual maturation of a Vermont farm boy" (though born in Massachusetts, Fulton had grown up in Vermont). Like *The Grassman*, Fulton wrote and rewrote the manuscript for several years before finally publishing the novel.

Dark Other Adam Dreaming is set on a small dairy farm in northern Vermont in 1947 and centers on a sixteen-year-old boy named Quentin Jensen. The difficult and tedious farm work begins every morning before 5:00 A.M. under the supervision of Quentin's father, Big Sam. Quentin, who is sensitive and meditative and possesses a poetic bent, stands in sharp contrast to his older brother, Sam'l, who is both a basketball star and a ruffian. Quentin seeks respite from both the farm work and his father by taking long evening rides on his beautiful chestnut mare and by reading Keats. Out riding one day, he meets a new girl in town, Nina Van Tyne. Though they fall in love, the romance they both long for is cut cruelly short, as both are inextricably caught in a web of brutal violence, jealousy, alcoholism, and prejudice.

In *Dark Other Adam Dreaming*, the reader will not find any of the sentimentalizing or idealizing of adolescence so commonly found in current fiction and film. The novel is a poignant reminder of the tough side of surviving high school, where how good one is at playing ball, fighting, or drinking determines one's peer status.

The central theme running throughout *Dark Other Adam Dreaming*—a theme also present in *The Grassman*—concerns the influence of place, of even the land itself, on the characteristics of its inhabitants. In *Dark Other Adam Dreaming* the progression of the seasons correlates naturally with the development of the characters. As the novel's skillfully rendered landscapes change from late summer to fall to winter, the mood of the whole community also changes, becoming colder, more bitter, and cruel. Quentin Jensen himself is caught up in this subtle seasonal change and is torn and perplexed by it. For though he longs, in Keats's words, to soar on "the viewless wings of Poesy" above all "the weariness, the fever, and the fret" of his dreary farm life, he also finds himself stirred by darker, more primitive emotions.

Dark Other Adam Dreaming received generally favorable reviews. Several reviewers commented on Fulton's use of place in the novel. The *New York Times Book Review* commented that *Dark Other Adam Dreaming* "develops a fine counterpoint between the rough country environment and the even rougher business of growing up."

From the very beginning, Fulton has maintained his editing and publishing work—he most recently edited with Ellen Ferber the *Directory of Poetry Publishers,* the newest edition to the Small Press Information Library, and he continues to publish work by other authors. His own writing career, however, became a casualty of his editing and publishing work and his involvement in local government. For the past several years, Fulton has served in a variety of public positions, ranging from chairing the local irrigation district to serving on the Butte County Board of Supervisors to campaigning (unsuccessfully) for the California State Assembly. Now soon to be free of his remaining political commitments, he might finally turn his attention once more to writing.

Interviews:
Noel Peattie, "Life, Death, and Resurrection of the Little Mag," *SIPAPU,* 3 (July 1972): 11-15;
Hugh Fox, "Ten Years in the Saddle," *Margins,* 13 (August-September 1974): 24-33.

AN INTERVIEW ————————
with LEN FULTON

DLB: When you first started Dustbooks in 1965, did you think you would still be in publishing twenty-one years later?

FULTON: No. I had no idea.

DLB: Were you surprised at what you found when you compiled the first *Directory of Little Magazines and Small Presses?*

FULTON: I was surprised with that first directory. We sold it for a dollar. I was first of all surprised on the number of listings that ended up in there. I thought it was a lot, over 200. But, second of all, I was surprised at the number of dollars that came in. One-dollar bills one at a time kept rolling in. I had brains enough to know there was something going on there commercially.

DLB: Doesn't the 1985-1986 *International Directory of Little Magazines and Small Presses* have over 4,000 entries?

FULTON: Yes, and the 1986-1987 edition almost 4,200 entries.

DLB: It is safe to say then that small press publishing keeps rolling along?

FULTON: Yes. It has not gone downhill every year. Also, our methods of digging them up has gotten better—more efficient and more routine.

DLB: You said in the paper you delivered at Rutgers in 1976 that you thought in the future most of the so-called literary work that is artistically successful would be published by the small presses and that the major publishing houses would cater more and more to popular demand. Do you think that is what has happened in the last ten years?

FULTON: Yes. I don't think there is any question about it. Some things slip through now and then. We get them here, a few copies at a time. Every now and then there is a big novel done by a major publishing company. They know they are going to lose their shirt, and we know that they did it to maintain their literary posture. The thing that I might not have figured at the time I said that was the ability of the larger publishers—some of them—to throw a bone now and then to literary history. The thing is, they usually discover these authors through the small presses. Small presses, however, have done more than just find authors. They've made publishing itself a kind of art. Just look at the stuff from the small presses. It is more creative than you are going to find coming out of a big publisher.

DLB: Some college and university literary scholars argue that there is currently a lack of great literary talent. Do you think this absence of literary talent could be due to the fact that the small presses and not the major publishers are publishing the best literary work?

FULTON: I don't agree that there is an absence. I think maybe academically. You don't say the same thing you said in the 1930s. You don't have anyone like Henry James anymore. Meanwhile, you have Hemingway and Faulkner and Fitzgerald. Also you have writers like Huxley and Nathaniel West. Then all of a sudden in the 1950s and 1960s they discover these guys. Academe didn't discover them, but they have a very sneaky way of making you think that by the time they started taking them seriously that they've always known them—that they helped make them. In fact, the guy in the first, best part of his life—is youth—when he had the creative energy and no obligations and no kids was ignored. Now all of a sudden when everyone else has discovered him, the university runs across him and suddenly he starts appearing in literature classes. Academe is always that way. It is nothing new. I used to worry a lot about it.

DLB: Do you ever worry that Dustbooks could become a "large" publisher?

FULTON: No. I would have to audit my income tax if it did. We have fallen into reference material; that is our mainstay.

DLB: Hasn't it always been important to you that you were a writer and publisher and not a printer?

FULTON: Oh, yes. Being a printer is a trade and a craft. I was never particularly good at it. When I printed, I wasn't good at it.

DLB: During the early part of your writing career, you were very involved with avant-garde literature, experimental poetry, fiction, and criticism. You even wrote some yourself. Looking back, what do you think of those pieces now?

FULTON: Well, when I read them over, I am a little embarrassed by some of the stuff. What stimulated the essay on Beckett was a book I found by him. It was a study of Proust. It was more esoteric than my essay by a long shot. What I was trying to do was to get into the same flow of thought as Beckett—his inklings and urges. If Beckett would write an essay on his *Trilogy* that's the kind of thing he might write.

DLB: Literary critic Irving Howe has written that he feels experimental literature is basically dead; that it has reached its saturation point, and that not much more can be done with it. Do you think Howe is correct?

FULTON: It's probably true. I think anything phases like that. But the good stuff doesn't pay any attention to the fads.

DLB: You once thought of writing your Ph.D. dissertation on Freud's literary roots. Do you still want to develop this topic?

FULTON: No. I don't have any notion of writing on the topic, but I love the idea.

DLB: They wouldn't let you write about Freud's literary roots at Berkeley?

FULTON: Berkeley was more interested in monkeys and rats. They were very big into experimental stuff. Somewhere in my files I've got a draft of my dissertation. It is focused on artistic roles and models. I loved that stuff. I've got to tell you that one side of my brain is very word oriented, but the other side is very mathematically oriented. I was a good statistician. I was imaginative.

DLB: You have mentioned Samuel Beckett. What other literary figures influenced your writing?

FULTON: My major literary heroes, in terms of literature, include the classical writers like Aeschylus and Euripides. I studied Russian for a few years and got real interested in the Russian writers, Dostoyevski and Tolstoy, and some of the modern Russian poets. I guess in terms of the American West—Americana—I would include Frederick Manfred. When I first met him, he was carrying a copy of *The Grassman.* One of those highs you don't often get. Also, Clay Fisher, Ernest Haycox, Walter Van Tillburg Clark, Jack Schaefer, and Hamlin Garland. And of course Hemingway.

DLB: Your first novel, *The Grassman,* was published by Thorp Springs Press and not by Dustbooks. Can you explain *The Grassman*'s publication history?

FULTON: Well, there was something like five editions. The two original hardbacks and the two original quality paperbacks were all by Thorp. Thorp has had them all except for the Penguin edition. It was originally Penguin Australia. I sold the rights except for the U.S. I've never issued one under the Dustbooks imprint.

DLB: Several years ago you wrote that at one time you actually feared publishing *The Grassman.* Why was that?

FULTON: I guess that's a pretty esoteric and arcane statement. Probably what I meant was that what you do is you cook up this whole different world in your brain. I remember I used to talk about this with my dad. He used to sit in front of his typewriter making over the world, which at that time the real world was a Vermont winter. Everything was dead. I somehow knew what he was doing. He was re-creating the world—probably a warm one and so on. What you do is create a world. The characters become real to you. They become tormentors because they do what they want to do whether you want them to or not. The only way to get out of it is by packaging it up and sending it to a publisher. So what I meant, being flippant, was letting that particular world slide from private to public life. It's like selling public stock in your company. I sit around and wonder when they are starting to develop my meanings out there. The counterpart is the fear that they will start getting the meanings different than what I intended them for.

DLB: Didn't you sell *The Grassman* to Hollywood?

FULTON: Yes, and I wrote the first script. Hal Ashby, who had the option, loved the book but hated my script. They took my script back and wrote one themselves. They butchered the novel, but I wasn't going to complain. They were going to give me $50,000 for the option. But they never did. I was a couple of years getting extensions, options, whatever. I also had a deal with Pocket Books for the distribution of *The Grassman* in the U.S. That happened almost exactly at the same time as I sold the movie rights. But I didn't think Pocket was giving me enough money, so I turned down the contract. They threatened to sue me for not giving them a contract, a contract which most authors would find to be ideal. I did at the time too, in a way. But I still felt I needed to get more money from them. Pocket finally became disinterested in the novel. I blew that one.

DLB: Can you explain how you make use of sound in *The Grassman*?

FULTON: The Grassman has three sounds. It is another way of characterizing once you get done with your Orestes and House of Atreus. It's an argument between three kinds of music: the classical music, which is what Holly played on the piano and used as a weapon; the popular music of the time, which was characterized by the guitar. Popular music told stories, ballads; then there was the natural music, which was the wind. I remember when Holly first sat down at the piano and started to play. The way she got everybody's attention was by seizing their ears with sounds which she commanded. Whenever I do a public reading, I read that section of *The Grassman*. Ultimately you control the mind only while you control the sound. When Holly's sounds stop, she hears the wind again and knows

she has lost their attention. The ultimate ruler was the wind.

DLB: Do you prefer *The Grassman* over *Dark Other Adam Dreaming*?

FULTON: Yes, as a piece of work.

DLB: Dark Other Adam Dreaming has been a better title for you, hasn't it?

FULTON: I haven't made more money if that's what you mean. I don't know how to measure these things anymore. You probably shouldn't measure them.

DLB: You said that *Dark Other Adam Dreaming* was semiautobiographical. Is it closer to autobiography or semiautobiography?

FULTON: More semi.

DLB: Did you use your own experiences in the novel?

FULTON: My early fantasies and some of the events in the novel actually happened. I never had a brother to fight so I took those two characters apart. That's the other part of me I guess. The Sam'l character—that's the one I wanted to be. It's obviously not the one I'm most proud of.

DLB: The psychological implications in *Dark Other Adam Dreaming* are fascinating. Did your training in psychology have any effect on your writing the novel?

FULTON: You can't help but think about it. When you do, however, some of the things you learn in academic psychology are real burdens. In *The Grassman* I went through five different drafts. In each one I changed a lot of stuff. In the final draft I discovered a line that said "the height of a hill enhanced visual perception." I missed it four times.

DLB: In the creative process, then, for example, in writing *The Grassman* did you see the Orestia parallel before you began writing or after you had written the novel?

FULTON: Unfortunately and fortunately, I had maps and genealogical charts of the Orestia trilogy and of The House of Finn. It was a terrible mistake. In fact, I think I made an effort after that to verge from using them. I had all kinds of characters with matching names. I would tell myself, "Don't do this to yourself—don't try to rewrite the Orestia." That's what you really want to do here, but don't have that up front and center. Then you are going to destroy the novel as a modern novel. The characters don't want to be the House of Atreus. Just set it up in the novel and be done with it. If the characters act that way, okay; but if they don't want to act that way, follow them. That's what you have to do in writing—follow the characters in order to create a successful character or a real character.

DLB: The Grassman is much more optimistic than *Dark Other Adam Dreaming.* Readers expect characters to get killed in a western, but a story about brutal adolescence is a bit more shocking. One reviewer said that *Dark Other Adam Dreaming* has absolutely no sentimentality in it. Do you agree?

FULTON: Yes, as against romanticism. There is an insipient violence in the novel, but nobody gets killed. In *The Grassman* there is death by the dozens.

DLB: Another reviewer remarked that *Dark Other Adam Dreaming* had too much symbolical baggage. Do you agree with that statement?

FULTON: Oh, I knew I was doing Cain and Abel. I don't know what else I was doing. I was doing the dark side, the Yin and Yang sort of thing.

DLB: Many writers, especially younger writers, seem to be too much caught up in sending a message rather than getting a story down. When you write, then, is the story itself the most essential aspect of the work?

FULTON: Someone once said that the first novel by a young person—they probably said young man—is as if he is trying to move all his belongings across a river on a raft. He tries to get them all on the raft at once. He may end up sinking the raft. That's one of the things a writer wants to be careful of—trying to accomplish too much in one novel. I don't want to read another Michener novel because it's bound to be 800 pages. But I guess I would like to write a definitive piece of work, and it would be that long I suppose. On the other hand, if someone sends me a book, or comes in and talks to me about a book, I'll say this.

DLB: What advice would you give to someone who wants to be a writer?

FULTON: I still talk to classes when they ask me. I tell the kids that the thing you want to do if you are in a creative mood is to hang it in your ear. That is my main theme. First, it has to sound good. You are not just piling one word on top of another. You are really making some music. That's what is going to carry the story. Then go back and examine it ultimately for meaning. Don't go for the meaning first and the music second. Get this part of it. Then the rest usually tends to take care of itself. That is the poetic view of reading prose. That is the way I looked at Hemingway in the early days.

DLB: Do you get a lot of submissions to Dustbooks?

FULTON: Yes, a lot of walk-throughs. Their main question is how do I get published. I tell them, I'll give you fifteen minutes of advice free and the rest at fifty dollars an hour.

DLB: What advice do you give them?

FULTON: I just give them a policy. In fact, I'm trying to write one now. There are so many and just in this little place. I'd hate to be in New York City. It would be terrible. The first thing I try to do is to discourage them from publishing their book. Most people only want half a dozen copies—to their mother, their father, and their aunt. A thousand copies on their living room floor is going to be a burden to them.

DLB: Would you discourage someone, then, from trying to start their own small press?

FULTON: No, I wouldn't. But I would definitely say that they need to have a niche, an area of expertise, poetry, cookbooks, whatever. Any niche that they are good at or an expert in.

DLB: Is *American Odyssey* still a good seller for Dustbooks?

FULTON: Yes. I lost money on the trip, but *American Odyssey* turned around and made money for us. It has all that bookstore information in it, yet it is still a popular seller. It's trying to do a whole lot of things. It probably ended up trying to be too many things. It's trying to be a trip. It's trying to be an odyssey.

DLB: Do you still feel uncomfortable east of the Mississippi?

FULTON: I like to visit the coast of New England and eat lobster. But once you experience the drama of the West, this landscape, I don't know how you could go back. I would really have to talk to myself to go back.

DLB: What titles has Dustbooks published lately?

FULTON: We do those four annuals—the *International Directory*, the *Directory of Small Magazine/Press Editors and Publishers*, the *Small Press Record*, and the poetry directory. Those four are done

every year. Before we even get started on anything else in the year, we have to do those four. Then, I've got myself down to where I am doing only one maybe two books other than that a year. It's a tough business to make any money in; it's speculation. We did *Words in Our Pockets* the first part of this year. It's a feminist guide to writing and publishing.

DLB: Are you working on anything now?

FULTON: No, but I am getting neurotic and depressed, so maybe.

Laura Furman
(19 November 1945-   )

William J. Scheick
University of Texas at Austin

BOOKS: *The Glass House: A Novella and Stories* (New York: Viking, 1980);
The Shadow Line (New York: Viking, 1982);
Watch Time Fly: Stories (New York: Viking, 1983);
Tuxedo Park (New York: Summit, 1986).

PERIODICAL PUBLICATIONS: "'A House Is Not a Home': Women in Publishing," in *Sisterhood Is Powerful*, edited by Robin Morgan (New York: Random House, 1970), pp. 66-70;
"Last Winter," *New Yorker,* 52 (1 March 1976): 29-36;
"Free and Clear," *New Yorker,* 53 (7 March 1977): 28-32;
"The Kindness of Strangers," *New Yorker,* 53 (11 April 1977): 34-39;
"Real Estate," *New Yorker,* 53 (5 September 1977): 28-32;
"Seesaw," *Redbook,* 148 (October 1977): 134, 250-258;
"Quiet with Belinda," *Fiction,* 5 (January 1978): 63-74;
"Listening to Married Friends," *Mademoiselle,* 84 (February 1978): 70-78;
"For Scale," *New Yorker,* 55 (19 March 1979): 36-37;

"Shazam," *Mississippi Review,* 8 (Winter/Spring 1979): 49-58;
"Arlene," *Vision,* 2 (July 1979): 45-48;
"Sweethearts," *New Yorker,* 55 (12 November 1979): 48-49;
"Atlanta's Jews," *Atlanta Journal and Constitution Sunday Magazine,* 13 April 1980, pp. 26-29, 36-41;
"Buried Treasure," *New Yorker,* 56 (25 August 1980): 27-33;
"Nothing Like It," *New Yorker,* 58 (17 May 1982): 38-45;
"Bulldozing a Refuge," *Texas Humanist,* 6 (January/February 1983): 20-23;
"Zen and the Art of Duck Lasagne," *House and Garden,* 155 (August 1983): 42-44;
"Buddy," *New Yorker,* 60 (9 April 1984): 42-49;
"Tuxedo Park," *House and Garden,* 156 (May 1984): 98-109;
"One Cal: Forever Single at the Health Mart," *Vanity Fair,* 47 (October 1984): 32;
"Sunny," *New Yorker,* 60 (28 January 1985): 29-34;
"Notes from the Rural Underground," *House and Garden,* 157 (August 1985): 26-30;
"Finished," *Writer,* 99 (March 1986): 5.

Born in Brooklyn on 19 November 1945 and raised in Manhattan, Laura Furman attended

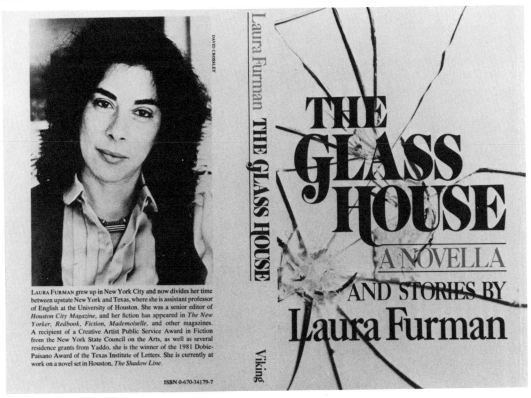

LAURA FURMAN grew up in New York City and now divides her time between upstate New York and Texas, where she is assistant professor of English at the University of Houston. She was a senior editor of *Houston City Magazine*, and her fiction has appeared in *The New Yorker, Redbook, Fiction, Mademoiselle*, and other magazines. A recipient of a Creative Artist Public Service Award in Fiction from the New York State Council on the Arts, as well as several residence grants from Yaddo, she is the winner of the 1981 Dobie-Paisano Award of the Texas Institute of Letters. She is currently at work on a novel set in Houston, *The Shadow Line*.

ISBN 0-670-34179-7

Dust jacket for Laura Furman's first book

Hunter College High School and, later, Bennington College in Vermont, which in 1968 awarded her a B.A. degree with a major in literature. From 1973 to 1978, she lived alone in an old farmhouse in upstate New York, where she devoted herself to writing fiction, though she also worked during this period as an editor for the Menil Foundation. In 1975, at the age of twenty-nine, she had her first story accepted for publication by the *New Yorker,* which would subsequently publish much of Furman's short fiction.

In 1977 she was writer in residence at Wilkes College in Wilkes-Barre, Pennsylvania, and in October 1978 she moved to Texas, where she served for almost a year as a senior editor for *Houston City Magazine*. The following year she was appointed as a visiting assistant professor of English at the University of Houston, and in 1981 and 1982 she was employed as a lecturer at Southern Methodist University. Since 1983 she has been a member of the English department of the University of Texas at Austin, where she is currently an assistant professor teaching creative writing. She resides in a small town near Austin with her husband, Joel Warren Barna, a journalist and editor whom she married in 1981.

Her work has appeared in several anthologies. She has received the Creative Artists Public Service Award in Fiction from the New York State Council on the Arts (1976); residence grants from Yaddo (1972-1978, 1984); the Short Story Award from the Texas Institute of Letters (1980); the Jesse Jones Award for the best book of fiction from the Texas Institute of Letters (1981); the Dobie Paisano Grant from the Texas Institute of Letters and the University of Texas (1981); and a Guggenheim Fellowship (1982-1983). Recognition of her work is also evident in the reprinting of her fiction in several anthologies.

The most difficult part of writing, Furman admits, is to decide how much or how little to say. In practice she manages to reveal much through a careful, restrained style. Perhaps the most useful statement Furman has made about her work occurred during an interview published in the *Houston Chronicle*, where she commented on one of her characters as someone who is searching for "the courage to break off what was not going to work" and who is "trying to rebuild herself."

This need to refurbish the self after one or more major disappointments in life is a prominent trait of the characters in Furman's first book, *The*

Glass House: A Novella and Stories (1980). "The Glass House," the remarkable novella after which the book is titled, concerns Arla Stein, who lives in her deceased mother's country house and works in a small museum. The house and museum comprise Arla's abiding interests in her solitary life until Joseph Bird, an architect, arrives to plan the expansion of the museum to accommodate a valuable glass collection. Arla and Joseph develop a relationship, but Arla is not satisfied with it and Joseph is not fully committed to it. Joseph ends the affair with his revelation that he has terminal cancer. Besides the emotional wounding Arla has received due to this assault on her hope, she is also angered by the damage done to her property during road repair, and she worries also over the possible loss of her job to a new curator when the expansion of the museum is completed. Thinking that she could strengthen her position at the museum by securing the loan of a rare glass house, she fails to get permission and then impulsively steals the art work. Because it is flawed, the glass house is damaged by her theft; and with a sense of loss (the art object, her job, her property, her love) she dashes the glass house to pieces and drives away "without looking back."

At this climactic moment Arla refuses to look back, but the reader is left to wonder if she will be able to escape the past. Furman carefully leaves open the possibility of such freedom for Arla, but the fate of Furman's other characters in the book, whose personalities are rather similar to Arla's, suggests that Arla's release is only a temporary experience; indeed the epigraph of *The Glass House* derives from a poem by Rainer Maria Rilke:

Ah, nostalgia for places not loved
well enough in the passing hour,
how I long to make good from afar
the forgotten gesture, the additional act.

Arla has always been a conservator of the past. She lingers over the past in the museum, in her mother's house, and in her mind.

Haunted by the past, memories provide the very essence of Arla's sense of self. She is good at "caring for things, . . . keeping track, preserving, cleaning, correcting." She savors the "feeling of return" in her home not "because she had been happy there with her mother, but because her mother had been there," whom she recalls in painful memories. Arla's effort to make improvements in this house is a symbolic projection of her sense of constructing a self, a slow and tedious construction which (like

her home) "she would never finish": "Its completion would remain for her, as for her mother, always a little ahead, just out of reach."

Arla's sense of self is as fragile as the glass house she steals, and this fragility leaves Arla vulnerable to emotional devastation. She finds as much security as she can among frangible memories in the museum, her home, and her mind. She especially appreciates the winter months for their image of frozen solidity so appealing to her, for she lacks a firm sense of self in spite of the fact that she, like the lonely widow in "Eldorado," keeps "things going in a certain way" through a ritualistic, repetitive patterning of her life. But the appearance of Joseph in her structured glacial life is like the arrival of spring in the story, a time of melting, of digging up, of coming out. Arla's frozen, yet fragile self, which never "felt free," is as vulnerable to these changes as it was years ago when another "affair began and ended out of her control and beyond her understanding." She falls in love with Joseph and even criticizes herself because she "never appreciated things as they happened"; but he is always aloof and finally, after revealing his illness, tells her, "There isn't anything in me for you."

Joseph remains as much a mystery to Arla as does her father, "an oblique man" like the enigmatic parent in "My Father's Car," another story in *The Glass House*. Similar to most of Furman's lonely female protagonists, Arla finds men to be emotionally different from women. Typical of Furman's males, Joseph is not haunted by the past. Just as Arla's "father never liked remembering," Joseph does not talk of his past. Consequently, when Arla wanders through her house in search of "a sign that he'd been there," she finds nothing to preserve in her museumlike mind; "he'd left nothing behind," no remnant of anything like a memory or an artifact of the past.

At an unconscious level Joseph seems to accept separateness, the isolation of each self. Arla resists this sense of restriction. Arla, who has for a time tried to accept being lonely and trapped, is tempted by Joseph to wish for "sure things in her life," especially someone who would "help her with the house" and "who would fix everything," including her desire to cross the boundary of her imprisoned self by freeing her to commit and care for someone else. The more Joseph seems to resist this intimacy, the more Arla strives for it: "She wanted to bring them closer together." Arla is like Corinne (in "The Smallest Loss"), whose meetings with Penelope leave her "waiting for more, an intimate conversation, a quiet moment that never came." Arla fails because in Furman's fiction the barriers between her characters remain unbroken. Although the self is as fragile as a glass house, it is not as transparent; in Arla's fantasy about exhibiting the glass house "the only thing not transparent would be the people." People in Furman's stories are isolated within themselves—lonely and trapped like Arla, and inaccessible and distant like Joseph.

This isolation is a condition in which Furman's women, like the narrator of "Last Winter," find "relief edged with dread." Arla feels this ambivalence, a simultaneous feeling of pleasure in and fear of solitude. Before Joseph, Arla managed her frangible solitary self through the conservation of memories; after Joseph, she tries to keep that self intact by maintaining an uncertain skepticism about relationships, but the flaw in her delicate self (like the defect in the glass house) makes its feared destruction inevitable. With Joseph's desertion, with her job's likely end, with her yard torn up, with all her money gone toward a new roof rather than a refurbished room, Arla's self, with its last "corner of hope," is inevitably dashed to pieces. Although in actively destroying the glass house Arla seems to conspire willfully with the inescapable, in fact everything, as in her first affair, remains out of her control and beyond her understanding. The effect of Joseph has been like the arrival of spring: "spring came slowly and took hold fast. Before she could see what was happening, everything would be out." Arla is now at the stage described by Furman in her interview: the point where she has broken away from what has not worked and now needs once again to *try* to rebuild a sense of self, a precarious solitary self defined by "relief edged with dread."

Critical response to *The Glass House* included praise for Furman's intense, clear characterization managed through careful authorial tact and discretion, her deft use of symbolism, and her precise style, the muted tone of which does not obscure her characters' longing for permanence. For most reviewers, Furman's disciplined control of tone allows her characters to come to life and permits her stories to bring to focus subtle feelings. As Lynne Sharon Schwartz wrote in the *New York Times Book Review* (9 November 1980), "Furman plays out her glass house metaphor with delicate composure, like a musician dallying with a motif, and leaves the reader entranced."

Memorable characters, complex and credible, were also praised by reviewers of Furman's second work, *The Shadow Line* (1982). Many critics thought this novel to be finely crafted and pleasantly un-

predictable. One of these reviewers, Michele M. Leber, wrote in the *Library Journal* (107: July 1982) that Furman adeptly weaves flashbacks and builds a sense of foreboding in her "memorable, remarkably finished first novel." But a few critics noted that its plot is too contrived and its several levels become snarled. There were suggestions that Furman was more adept at the short story than at the novel, and complaints surfaced concerning stylistic torpor and narrative sluggishness. Most reviewers, however, appreciated Furman's accurate eye and the cool precision of her understated prose.

The Shadow Line is the story of Liz Gold, a journalist living in Houston, Texas. Her good friend, Cal Dayton, gay editor of *Spindletop*, has given her an assignment: to probe into the mystery of the twenty-year-old unsolved murder of Carolyn Sylvan and her four-year-old daughter in Galveston in 1959. Liz's investigation reveals not only who the murderer is but also that Cal has uncaringly endangered her life. Cal has used her (as if their close friendship over the years has meant nothing) to manipulate the murderer (chief financial backer of *Spindletop* and Cal's lover) into retaining Cal as editor, even though everyone else on the staff has been fired.

Liz's betrayal by Cal emphasizes the fundamental isolation of self experienced by Furman's characters. Liz learned something of this reality during her marriage to Willy, and haunting memories of this failed relationship as well as thoughts about the divorce of her lover, David Muse, make Liz skittish about marrying David, her lover of the last seven months. Memories (flashbacks in the novel) undercut her hope for an induring bond with David. Liz needs him—it would be "a body blow if she'd never seen David again"—but she remains tentative, imprisoned within herself, because "if she lost David, she would be losing everything again, leaving the biggest hole in her life." Liz is unable to commit herself totally (unconsciously she is already committed) because her constrictive memories encourage a protective detachment from others, who (her experience has taught her) always disappoint one's desire for something durable.

Liz's fear of devastating disappointment is realized at the end of the novel, when Cal's betrayal becomes evident to her. She has loved Cal as a dear friend, but he has not cared about her, has always mistrusted affection, and has thought of her friendship as merely "a luxury" that he willingly foregoes. This explosive revelation of the impermanence of relationships is worse for Liz than the fact that her life is now threatened unless she keeps to herself the knowledge of who murdered the Sylvans, this latter matter suggesting that death is the ultimate dissolver of the illusion of stability in life. The final words of the novel—"she would fly to David"—suggest the intensification of Liz's need for some permanence in a relationship, and maybe now out of desperation she will be less tentative in her hope in her union with David. But for Liz to "fly to David" so desperately suggests finally the need to "flee" to David, and in this sense the reader cannot be hopeful; for the thrust of the novel has emphasized that neither David nor anyone else can release Liz's self from its essential isolation.

David cannot provide a means for her "to find a way to live with what she knew"—what she knew about betrayal, murder, death—because this is work for the self, and each self is isolated from every other self. This separation of selves prevents one from truly knowing another; hence Liz does not really know Willy or Cal or David. Between Liz and Willy there was a barrier: "herself outside a window, nose pressed to the glass, looking in on Willy." Between Liz and David there is a barrier: "there were complicated moments when she saw him as a stranger." The best she can hope for is some self-knowledge.

These realizations comprise the reality Liz must face, the shadow line she must cross between a childish hope for something stable and a mature acceptance of the impermanence of everything, including life itself. Liz must try to live with the truth of her statement to Cal near the end of the novel: "You think you know a person, everything about them, and then you find out they've changed on you." In Liz's experience people do not share an Emersonian sympathy between selves; each self is phenomenologically isolated, imprisoned. That Liz has not fully accepted this fact is suggested in her resolution to fly (to flee) to David. Although she has seen the shadow line and its dark truth, she as yet refuses to cross that line and still tries to depend on David, as she had on Willy, "to be her guide."

Not that Liz should withdraw from her relationship with David: sometimes, like the narrator of "Last Winter" (in *The Glass House*), Liz thinks that "it seem[s] simpler to be alone"; but like that narrator, Liz finds the idea of solitude a "relief edged with dread" and feels "afraid . . . as if she were standing alone in the world without a friend." Ideally Liz must accept the reality of isolation of self in a world where "people expect security out of the very thing that's the most insecure" and at the same time the reality of the self's need for others, who nonetheless remain separate, strange

entities capable of betraying the closest of friends. To cross the shadow line, ideally Liz must use her memories to manage a precarious balance between her sad isolation from and her happy union with David. Though she does not know it yet, "her real life would finally begin" only with the mature maintenance of this insecure balance of loss and comfort.

Some of the women in *Watch Time Fly* (1983) manage this memory-engendered uncertain balance—accepting their essential aloneness, yet still awaiting some sort of attachment to another. These women usually respond to their isolation with the same paradoxical relief and dread felt by Liz in *The Shadow Line*. Arla, in "Listening to Married Friends," is typical in liking to think "that in one or two weeks her solitude would end"; but "she was used to her life as her married friends were used to theirs, and she made as many adjustments to herself as they had to each other." Arla knows that marriage is only an illusion of togetherness, and she knows the benefits of living alone; nevertheless, she misses something: "She didn't want Carl and Harriet's marriage nor any other she could think of. She wanted a companion and an entrapment of her own, though she had no faith that she would do any better with hers." Arla maintains a tentative balance between the equivocal consolations of solitude and the expectation of the equally equivocal comforts of attachment to another.

The men in these stories are generally different. Warren, in "Watch Time Fly," for example, does not linger over memories of his life with Anna, as she does in her thoughts of him. He admits that at first he had thought he would not be able to get through the first month without her, "but it got better more quickly than he would have imagined." Warren already has a new lover, and Anna pertinently recalls that "he'd always had an enviable ability to forget everything around him." Anna, however, is haunted by memories, from which she derives a contradictory sense of loss and comfort, of old vulnerability and new strength.

This difference between men and women is also evident in "Buried Treasure," in which Nessa, living alone in the country, is suddenly visited by Vance, who left her three years ago. During these years Nessa has struggled to develop an inner strength and a sense of self from her loneliness. Vance, who has returned to retrieve some valuable pre-Columbian Peruvian beads which he buried years ago, has not been haunted by memories of his relationship with Nessa. He misses objects, not people from his past.

When Vance fails to locate the beads, Nessa is quietly pleased. Unconsciously she is angry that he values things more than her, that seeing her again did not awaken in him feelings, memories, and longings similar to hers. Nessa is, however, willing to let him disappear again, as she returns her attention to her garden and her house, symbols of her painstaking, meticulous effort to manage her solitary self balanced precariously between loss and comfort. Her treasure is buried within herself, whence her ability to value the present, where she keeps the smallest (the best) zucchini squash for herself and where, aptly, light falling "from the window into the evening look[s] as though it were made of gold." If for Nessa, as for Kathy in "Sweethearts," there is nothing definite, no rest from the maintenance of an uncertain equilibrium of self, at least there are small treasures to be cherished within that lonely self.

This abiding isolation of every self is a central concern in "Nothing Like It," in which Alice at times pretends that she and Alan will "stay together always." Alan, a typical Furman male, tells Alice that "people just live" day to day. Alan's face remains "masklike" to Alice, and he is as aloof and inaccessible as is Joseph in "The Glass House."

This un-Emersonian separateness of each self from another is, in "Arlene," as true of interaction between women as of interaction between men and women. In this story Marianne, the narrator, is bothered by memories of Arlene, who committed suicide by jumping out of a window. Arlene was Marianne's downstairs neighbor, and although their behavioral patterns differed, they were alike in "not leading a normal family life by neighborhood standards." When Arlene's sister asks, "Who are her friends? I can't seem to find anyone who knew her," Marianne's unconscious sense of relation to Arlene deepens. In spite of such implied similarity between them, Arlene remains an impenetrable mystery to Marianne.

Marianne was asleep when Arlene jumped out the window, and in the back of her mind Marianne worries that just as she had been, as it were, asleep in her encounters with Arlene and did not see the act of suicide looming, perhaps too she is equally unawake regarding herself, so like Arlene in her lonely isolation. Like Arlene, Marianne might be "cracked" and awaiting "just a little tap in the right spot." Marianne is preoccupied with thoughts about Arlene, but despite their similarity, Arlene's self remains mysteriously opaque.

Ironically, the haunting presence of memories of Arlene does nothing to alleviate Marianne's sense of isolation from others. At the end of her narrative, Marianne looks at herself in a mirror, a symbolic act suggesting that her pursuit of the mystery of Arlene has been an inquiry into the mystery of herself. In the mirror Marianne looks beyond her own reflection in search of some movement that would indicate she is not alone. There is no movement, nor is there any answer when she subsequently stands by an open window and asks Arlene what she should do. No motion, no answer: Marianne is utterly alone. Like other of Furman's female protagonists, Marianne will not commit suicide, but will stoically get on with living by using memory to manage a tentative balance between vulnerability and strength within her isolated self.

The quiet, plotless stories of *Watch Time Fly* were lauded by reviewers for their precise detail, their in-depth characterization, and even their strong evocation of place; this last characteristic, according to Lynette Friesen in the *Library Journal* (108: July 1983), is evoked so vividly that it "functions in the reader's imagination almost as a second protagonist." A complaint about a droning similarity between narrators and protagonists did surface, as did some dissatisfaction with the lack of foreward movement or drama and with the author's self-conscious use of elements of chic in the stories. More prevalent, however, was praise for Furman's pared prose, the cadence of which was for many critics a pleasure to read. As Wendy Lesser remarked in the *New York Times Book Review* (9 October 1983), "Furman's facility with words turns the mundane into the slightly eerie, the cliché of common experience into the bizarrely particular tale. . . . Furman manages to combine apparent artlessness with a moving and very sophisticated esthetic sensibility."

Lesser suggests that the style of Furman's fiction is only apparently artless. It draws no attention to itself, as if it were transparent. This transparency is important to remark because her style achieves through its artistry what Furman's fiction indicates cannot be experienced in actual life: a breakdown of the imprisoning barriers which prevents any self from knowing another. The "utopian" style of Furman's fiction satisfies in the reader the same longing for connection between selves that remains unsatisfied in Furman's protagonists.

Of all of Furman's women characters, the one who most resists the fact of this fundamental solitariness of the self is Sadie Ash, the protagonist of *Tuxedo Park* (1986). Orphaned at the age of twelve, Sadie felt from that event as if time had stopped, until she meets Willard Weaver seven years later

Dust jacket for Furman's novel of romantic obsession

in 1945. Although she senses some fear of losing herself to him, she falls deeply in love with Willard, who is fascinated by her devotion to him. Although confused in his own feelings, Willard decides to marry Sadie after she tells him of her pregnancy. About five years and two daughters later, and after the death of his emotionally remote father, Willard moves his family to a home he inherited in Tuxedo Park, New York, an old-fashioned, elite community separated from the outside world by psychological, economic, and physical barriers. Suddenly Willard announces that he wants a divorce; Sadie objects, and so Willard disappears with Cherry Wilde, a rootless, failed painter like himself. Ten years pass as Sadie and her daughters (especially Louise) await the return of Willard, who has remained inaccessible but who has from time to time communicated in letters to Sadie. When Louise discovers that her mother's stubbornness (it is really Sadie's romantic faith) has kept her father away from his daughters—she does not focus on his equivalent obdurateness—she attempts suicide, and the shock of

this failed attempt moves Sadie to accept the inevitable divorce. In a restrained but powerful final chapter, Willard (with Cherry), looking haggard, enters the house in Tuxedo Park for a sad, uncomfortable, essentially silent reunion that will not dissolve the emotional barriers which have separated him from his family.

Willard, whose mother died when he was five and whose father showed him not a trace of affection, is as unstable in his emotions as he is unsettled in his occupation of writing a monograph on the artist Whistler. Emotional attachments make him feel trapped, and so he prefers "exile and restlessness" in an undefined companionship with Cherry (who seems to live "in a fugue, free from time, free from him") to a structured marriage to Sadie. Like other Furman males, Willard not only differs from women emotionally, he also seems to escape haunting memory: "He shared with [his father] his ability to turn from people and strike them from memory." His attraction to Sadie is identical to his attraction to art—a "sudden apprehension of beauty"—and significantly he is most sexually ardent when Sadie wears a white kimono which makes her resemble a painting by Whistler. His desire for Sadie diminishes after the birth of his first daughter because Sadie's body has become heavier and she has "lost her resemblance to the Little White Girl." Willard relates to Sadie as if she were an object, a possession, rather than a person.

Sadie, in contrast, wishes to end her orphan condition. At nineteen she is in fact too dependent, even at one point longing for Reuben, her brother, to tell her what to do. She seeks human connections, attachments which would (she thinks) contribute to the firming up and stabilization of her sense of identity. She desires to merge with Willard and early in their relationship even believes that he knows her "better than anyone else ever has," that "already he was a part of her as no one else would ever be." Armed with these notions, Sadie combats the reality of the fact that neither Willard knows her nor she him, that a "borderless love" is impossible. After five years of marriage reality makes inroads into her resistance when, for example, she realizes that "she had never been able to predict the smallest thing about Willard." But she romantically persists in seeking a love with him that will merge her self with his, as if (to apply an image from the mind of their four-year-old daughter Marilyn and later from the suicidal, drugged mind of their sixteen-year-old daughter Louise) they would become "transparent, no more skin and bones, all light and sound." Even after Willard deserts his family, Sadie idealistically persists in hoping for ten years: "the girls and me, we wait for you to love us."

In Willard's absence Sadie projects her needs for stability and identity onto her husband's home in Tuxedo Park, even though a friend there tells her that the residents of this community "are no more safe and secure than you. It's one of your fairy tales, believing that they are." Like Louise, Sadie thinks of Tuxedo Park "as having around it not only its fence (now untraceable among the trees) and its gate, but an invisible shell." In fact, Tuxedo Park is no longer the haven it once seemed to be; everything there is changing, both plants and people, as the world outside the community steadily invades it and as the "remarkable, adventurous" "generation of the eighties" gives way to the nouveau riche.

Sadie can no more live inside her childish dream of a safe haven for her self than she can maintain her mistaken hope in merging identities with Willard. And after the shock of Louise's attempted suicide makes her realize how she has even failed to know her daughter, she recognizes that her life has not been as fated as she had thought, she ceases her "stubborn waiting for a miracle," she gives up her dream as if it were "one of the last beautiful days of summer," and she faces the reality of life's insecurity (most evident in death) and of the irremediable loneliness of each self. For her now it is as if "a wind had come along and blown a circle away." She now somewhat relaxes her hold on the memories she has been conserving—significantly it is Sadie's old Packard that strikes drugged Louise—and she better understands how her self is like her garden at Tuxedo Park, both fenced-in areas nonetheless pervious to natural forces such as people and death. Presumably a more mature Sadie will give up her childish desire for something stable and discover an adult acceptance of impermanence; presumably she will manage a compromise, a precarious balance between the real loneliness of the fenced-in self and the equally real incursions upon that self from the outside world.

In the novel Louise reads Tolstoy's *Anna Karenina*, and Anna's suicide as a result of frustrated love doubtless influences Louise's attempt to kill herself. But the allusion to Tolstoy's novel more importantly suggests that just as the generation of the 1880s at Tuxedo Park has given away to the parvenu and just as Sadie's naive, romantic dreams have given way to a more mature acceptance of reality, so too the novel as a form has changed from the emphatic, romantically heightened sense of tragedy of the kind conveyed by Tolstoy at the end of the nineteenth century to a more muted sense of tragedy of the kind conveyed by Furman at the end of the twentieth century. The premises for tragedy have mutated during the century between these two writers; and chief among them is the disappearance of Tolstoy's notion of the tragic consequences of insensitive social restrictions expressed in a grand, self-conscious language and the appearance of Furman's idea of the tragic consequences of human limitations expressed in a restrained, even muted prose of near transparency. Perhaps, finally, the tragedy dramatized in *Tuxedo Park* is greater than that of *Anna Karenina,* for Tolstoy could at least suggest the possibility of a change in social reality that could remedy the sort of blight that dooms Anna, whereas Furman can offer no hope in a metamorphosis of the human self that would enable it to transcend the phenomenological boundaries which keep it essentially and tragically isolated. It is Furman's gift, conveyed in her writings, to present this sense of tragedy quietly and subtly so that her readers can merge with the self of Furman's protagonists and thereby gain profound insight into the limitations of their shared human condition.

Indeed, Furman's brilliance in characterization emerges as a refrain in most reviews of *Tuxedo Park.* A somewhat dissenting view, however, was voiced by Frances Taliaferro in the *New York Times Book Review* (28 September 1986), where she complained that Furman's characters display no autonomy and generate little heat, although Taliaferro concedes that overall the novel is well crafted. Perhaps the book received its strongest endorsement from novelist Anne Tyler in *USA Today* (12 September 1986): "This is a book that first catches your eye and then grabs your heart." Although the verdict on Furman's standing among great American writers is still undecided, she is certainly a novelist worthy of attention. It will be interesting to see whether she will eventually range philosophically, structurally, and aesthetically beyond the narrow region she has so far mapped out as her own, especially the region of the lonely heart and separate self. She evinces a wealth of talent that might take some artistically surprising and rewarding excursions in her future work.

References:
George Christian, "Throwing the Watch Overboard," *Houston Chronicle,* 23 October 1983, pp. 20, 24;

John Gardner, *The Art of Fiction: Notes on Craft for Young Writers* (New York: Vintage Books, 1985), pp. 135-136;

Wendy Lesser, "Free and Clear," *New York Times*

Book Review, 9 October 1983, pp. 15, 37;

Susan Wood, "Talking with Laura Furman," *Washington Post Book World*, 19 September 1982, p. 5.

Beth Henley

(8 May 1952-   )

Lucia Tarbox

BOOKS: *Am I Blue* (New York: Dramatists Play Service, 1982);

Crimes of the Heart: A Play (New York: Viking/Penguin, 1982);

The Wake of Jamey Foster (New York: Dramatists Play Service, 1983);

The Miss Firecracker Contest (New York: Dramatists Play Service, 1985).

PLAY PRODUCTIONS: *Am I Blue,* Dallas, Southern Methodist University, 1973;

Crimes of the Heart, Louisville, Kentucky, Actors Theatre, 18 February 1979;

The Miss Firecracker Contest, Los Angeles, Victory Theatre, Spring 1980;

The Wake of Jamey Foster, Hartford, Connecticut, Hartford Stage Theater, 1 January 1982;

The Debutante Ball, Costa Mesa, California, South Coast Repertory, Spring 1985;

The Lucky Spot, Williamstown Theatre Festival, Summer 1986.

SCREENPLAYS: *Nobody's Fool,* Island Pictures, 1986;

True Stories, by Henley, David Byrne, and Stephen Tobolowsky, Warner Bros., 1986;

Crimes of the Heart, De Laurentiis Entertainment Group, 1986.

TELEVISION SCRIPTS: *Morgan's Daughters,* pilot, Paramount, 1979;

Survival Guides, pilot by Henley and Budge Threlkeld, PBS, 1985.

Hazlehurst, Mississippi, Virgil, Texas, and Buckeye Basin, Arizona, are a few of the many small towns which provide settings for Beth Henley's writing. A product of the small-town southern environment which she often portrays, Beth Henley has been compared to such prominent writers as Flannery O'Connor, Tennessee Williams, and Eudora Welty. She uses a special blend of the sympathetic and the absurd to create unique characters and situations, prompting Scot Haller of the *Saturday Review* (November 1981) to state: "Like Flannery O'Connor, Henley creates ridiculous characters but doesn't ridicule them. Like Lanford Wilson, she examines ordinary people with extraordinary compassion."

Elizabeth Becker Henley was born on 8 May 1952 in Jackson, Mississippi, to Charles Boyle Henley, an attorney, and Elizabeth Josephine Becker Henley, an actress. Her southern upbringing had a great influence on her writing as she explains, "In my house, people were more inclined to sit around the kitchen table and talk than to watch TV." Though acting was Henley's original career interest, she had written her first play and had it produced before receiving her B.F.A. in 1974 from Southern Methodist University. *Am I Blue*, a one-act, was staged in the fall of 1973 and was just the beginning of a varied writing career.

After undergraduate school, Henley undertook a year of graduate work and teaching at the University of Illinois at Champaign, in addition to participating in summer stock at New Salem State

Beth Henley (courtesy of William Morris Agency)

beth Mackay on Broadway), has just turned thirty; Meg, the middle sister (Mary Beth Hurt), has failed in her California singing career; and Babe (Mia Dillon), the youngest, has just shot her husband, Zackery.

During the course of the three-act play, the audience is introduced to the sisters and the other three characters: Doc Porter (Raymond Baker), Meg's former flame; Chick Boyle (Sharon Ullrick), the sisters' nosy cousin; and Barnette Lloyd (Peter MacNicol), Babe's young lawyer. The personalities of these characters are well illustrated by Henley's use of realistic dialogue and portrayal of the human situation. A superb example occurs when Chick demands to know what reason Babe will give her lawyer for shooting Zackery. Babe reacts, "That I didn't like his looks! I just didn't like his stinking looks! And I don't like yours much, either. . . ."

The play was praised by many critics and gained Henley immediate recognition; however, other critics did have their complaints. Some felt that the play was a patronizing attempt at southern humor and others claimed that the drama accomplished nothing. For instance, Michael Feingold of the *Village Voice* (18-24 November 1981) was openly berating both of the dramatic work and of its setting: "Perhaps the play supplies a kind of sordid nostalgia for Southerners who, behind the façade of their new double-knit suits and non-union factories, like to think they are still pea-pickin', baccy-chewin', inbreedin', illiterate cretins at heart— Snopeses who have been taught, painstakingly, to sign their names and clip coupons. Or perhaps they still are exactly that, and the South is in desperate need of either cultural mercy missions from New York, or fire and brimstone from Heaven."

Comments such as Feingold's prove that Henley's humor is so blatantly straightforward that it is sometimes misunderstood. For instance, when the three sisters discuss their mother's suicide, they do it honestly. When Meg comments, "She had a bad day. A real bad day. You know how it feels on a real bad day," a bit of humor cannot help but creep in. Her suggestion may not be much of an explanation, but it is the truth, and the play succeeds because the truth often carries a special poignant wit that a more elaborately orchestrated comedy sometimes lacks.

The conflicts among the sisters are portrayed realistically also. For instance, as Lenny raves about a half-eaten box of birthday candy, the audience can easily see that her frustration with Meg has nothing to do with chocolate; instead, the argument reveals Lenny's years of frustration and feelings of

Park. Nevertheless, unconfident in her acting abilities and unsure as to whether she possessed the necessary qualities to be a writer, in 1976—depressed and discouraged—Henley moved to Los Angeles to be with director-actor Stephen Tobolowsky, with whom she still lives. Encouraged, however, by her S.M.U. friends, especially Tobolowsky and director Frederick Bailey, Henley soon turned again to writing. To date her plays include *The Miss Firecracker Contest* (1980), *The Wake of Jamey Foster* (1982), and *The Debutante Ball* (1985), but her best-known drama is *Crimes of the Heart* (1979).

Her first full-length attempt, *Crimes of the Heart* was submitted by Bailey in the Great American Play Contest sponsored by the Actors Theatre of Louisville. It won and was produced there in 1979, before moving to Broadway in 1981. The work eventually won Henley a Pulitzer Prize, marking the first time in twenty-three years that a woman had won the prize for drama. Further recognition for the play included a New York Drama Critics Circle Award, a Guggenheim Award, and a Tony nomination.

Set in Hazlehurst, Mississippi, the play tells the story of the three MaGrath sisters and their individual crises. The eldest, Lenny (played by Liz-

self-inadequacy. While Meg has been surrounded by adoring men, Lenny has feared rejection and thus became withdrawn. She feels repressed, and the demise of her only birthday present gives her an opportunity to explode.

In spite of her overreactions, Lenny's character is an appealing one. Obviously she and her sisters are very close, and Henley presents their relationships with integrity. It is important, however, for the audience to get past the surface of their arguments and discussions. Much occurs in the subtext of Henley's dialogue.

Following her first success, Henley continued to write. Four additional plays have been produced, though none has received the acclaim of *Crimes of the Heart*. Published in *The Ten Best Plays of 1983-1984*, *The Miss Firecracker Contest* had been staged in regional theaters before moving to the Manhattan Theatre Club and enjoying an extended run Off-Broadway. *The Wake of Jamey Foster* was first presented by the Hartford Stage Company in 1982, and it then was directed by Ulu Grosbard on Broadway. Three years later *The Debutante Ball* was staged

in Costa Mesa, California; the next year *The Lucky Spot* was part of the Williamstown Theatre Festival. In the spring of 1987 *The Lucky Spot* will begin a run at the Manhattan Theatre Club.

Henley's talent, however, is not limited to play writing. For instance, she teamed up with Budge Threlkeld in 1985 to write the pilot of *Survival Guides* for PBS. The half-hour episode was directed by Jonathan Demme. Henley explained to Beverly Walker in *American Film* (December 1986), "It was my first collaboration. Budge wanted to help me out of a depression I'd lapsed into after my play [*The Wake of Jamey Foster*] had bombed on Broadway. We wrote it on chocolate bars and vodka!" Appearing in this segment were David Byrne and Rosanna Arquette, both of whom Henley worked with again.

In 1986 Henley was involved in three major motion picture projects. She wrote the screenplay for what was to become *Nobody's Fool* under the original title "The Moonwatcher" in 1977, and it was finally produced in 1986 under the direction of Evelyn Purcell. The story concerns a small-town

Jessica Lange, Sissy Spacek, and Diane Keaton in a publicity still from the 1986 film adaptation of Henley's Crimes of the Heart
(courtesy of the De Laurentiis Entertainment Group)

girl (Rosanna Arquette) who follows a set designer (Eric Roberts) to Los Angeles for a new way of life.

Cassie (Arquette) is a waitress who finds life in her hometown of Buckeye Basin, Arizona, to be terribly dull. When her best friend (Mare Winningham) convinces her to attend a Shakespearean play, everything changes: she meets Riley (Roberts), the theater's set designer, and she is lured into the world of drama. The film was written while Henley herself was experiencing the excitement and pressures of acting, and this firsthand knowledge is evident in Cassie's feelings and in her final decision to follow Riley.

The next screenplay, *True Stories*, written by Henley, Tobolowsky, and musician David Byrne, depicts the day-to-day occurrences of Virgil, Texas. Byrne, the movie's director and narrator, says that much of the script was inspired by articles found in grocery-store tabloids—accounts of incredulous, yet supposedly "true," stories. Henley actually claims to have done very little, for as she explained in the Walker interview, "I am very honored to have a credit, but all I really did was help David organize his ideas."

Henley's final screen project in 1986 was *Crimes of the Heart*, a film adaptation of her play. Starring Diane Keaton as Lenny, Jessica Lange as Meg, and Sissy Spacek as Babe, the movie was directed by the Australian Bruce Beresford. Critical response was respectable, but, again, a few critics found the humor ambiguous and the dialogue inane. Nevertheless, the cast—also including Tess Harper as Chick and Sam Shepard as Doc—strengthened the film and gave spark to the script's situations. Most memorable are the scenes of Lenny chasing the pesky Chick with a broom, Meg lying to her grandfather about her many successes, and Babe naively offering the just-shot Zackery a glass of lemonade.

As Babe, Sissy Spacek portrays an innocence which, though appealing, is a bit nerve-racking to the ones around her. She chews bubble gum while in the jail cell, she tries to hang herself from a precarious chandelier, and she makes lemonade in times of crisis. Jessica Lange portrays an equally appealing Meg who, talented as she is, realizes that

Hollywood is not the answer. Though still able to attract Doc, Meg has acquired a flippant take-me-as-I-am attitude symbolized by her wardrobe—she wears the same clothes throughout the entire movie. And finally Diane Keaton gives the character of Lenny all the worry and anxiety that she requires. For years she has taken care of the family and tolerated cousin Chick, her next-door neighbor. Lenny has a compassion which is often present in older siblings, yet during the film she seems to reach her breaking point. As a trio, these actresses give a great deal to Henley's script. Not only do they attain credibility but they add individuality to their characters, which are major contributions to the film's success. The dry, honest comedy which was created in the play survived the transition to the screen, and, as a result, *Crimes of the Heart* was one of the most acclaimed films of the year, earning Henley an Oscar nomination for best screenplay adaptation.

It is not often that a girl from Jackson, Mississippi, can accomplish so much in what might be called a "big city" world of film and theater. However, Beth Henley has managed to succeed by bringing her southern small-town past with her. She has experienced both the success of a Pulitzer Prize-winning play and the failure of a bomb on Broadway, yet she does not allow the negative to overcome that which is positive. She says of her work: "Something I'm sure has to do with the South's defeat in the Civil War, which is that you should never take yourself too seriously. You may be beaten and defeated, but your spirit cannot be conquered. The South has the gall to still be able to say we have our pride, but as a human characteristic it is admirable."

Interview:

Beverly Walker, "Beth Henley," *American Film*, 12 (December 1986): 30-31.

Reference:

Scot Haller, "Her First Play, Her First Pulitzer Prize," *Saturday Review*, 8 (November 1981): 40, 42, 44.

Janet Kauffman
(10 June 1945-   )

Mark C. Harris
Jackson Community College

BOOKS: *The Weather Book* (Lubbock: Texas Tech Press, 1981);
Places in the World a Woman Could Walk (New York: Knopf, 1983);
Collaborators (New York: Knopf, 1986).

Janet Kauffman was born in Lancaster, Pennsylvania, to parents who worked a tobacco farm in nearby Landisville. She received her B.A. from Juniata College and the M.A. and Ph.D. from the University of Chicago, where she wrote her dissertation on "A Study of Style in the Poetry of Theodore Roethke" (1972).

Kauffman began writing poems in 1972, about the time she moved to Michigan. Her strengths as a poet have carried over to her prose fiction as well. Because many of her poems and stories are in rural settings, and many of the settings are named for towns, villages, and roads near Hudson, Michigan, where Kauffman lives with her husband, James Borland, and two sons, readers may consider her a regional writer. But as Bob Shacochis suggested in *Saturday Review* (January-February 1984), only writers with a strong sense of place earn the label "regional." Although she is not strictly a regional writer—her stories are set in Pennsylvania and Delaware as well as Michigan and Ohio—a strong concern with detail in the settings for her works, both verse and prose, is one of Kauffman's distinguishing characteristics.

This concern with place is very evident in *The Weather Book* (1981), Kauffman's collection of verse first published in various magazines, including the *Beloit Poetry Journal,* the *Nation, Poetry Now,* and the *Chicago Review.* Excerpts from "Working Tobacco," as well as "Watercress" and "The Volunteers," appeared in *The Third Coast,* an anthology of work by Michigan poets edited by Herbert Scott, Conrad Hilberry, and James Tipton.

Kauffman's best poetry is lyrical, fully given to the moment and its spectrum of sensations. "Mennonite Farm Wife," for example, a poem singled out for praise by many reviewers of *The Weather Book,* typifies Kauffman's sense of place.

The poem appears in the first section of the book, "Match." Any figurative value of the farm wife's white sheets takes second place to their existence as tangible reality, hung on Kauffman's smoothly metered line: "by sunrise the sheets were ice./They swung all day on the line,/creaking, never a flutter." The creases the farm wife places in the frozen sheets when she removes them from the line at dusk are a powerful statement about the structure of her world. The narrator muses, "I never doubted they thawed/perfectly dry, crisp,/the corners like thorn." The simple story of laundry drying on the line in Kauffman's skilled hands evokes the outline of a life, precise, ordered, unconsciously or at least implicitly cruel (the edges of the sheets are like thorns).

In Kauffman's poetry a vividly described physical object is often the mechanism for the theme of the poem. "The Womb in the World" transforms the earth into living flesh: "white-rooted clumps of witch grass/kicked up, nerves/tangled through huge red clots." Through this incarnation the narrator revives the ancient image of the earth mother and reforges it for modern readers. Cultivation exploits the earth, metal violating the "ancient crusty garden," unearthing "an inhuman territory." This process, says the narrator, is "No place for worms or feeling/one's way; no place for seeds,/infiltrators, redeemers." The narrator, who *is* perhaps the womb in the world, invites the cultivator to "Meet me machine/. . . that we might engender/anomaly."

Images like these are seen by some readers as evidence of Kauffman's feminism. In fact, although Kauffman is a feminist, such an interpretation mistakes the lines. Plows bear no malice toward the earth; the furrows are simply the natural consequence and end of tillage. Similarly the poem strives for understanding of the issues and roles of masculinity as well as femininity.

The eight-poem series "Working Tobacco" is the best example of Kauffman's ability to render in verse the texture of life. These poems capture the yearly cycle of raising tobacco—which Kauffman learned well as a child—in simple, elegant verse. The series begins with an eleven-line poem titled "Topping, As Preface." Topping, the act of removing the flower buds and auxiliary shoots (known as suckers), increases the size of remaining leaves and thereby improves yield. In many respects topping is the essential act of working tobacco.

The next four poems treat various aspects of the cycle of tobacco farming: "Steamer on the Seedbed" is a detailed account of using steam to rid the seedbeds of organisms or spores that could otherwise damage or destroy the tiny tobacco seeds; "Cultivating" recounts "long rose evenings" spent on a two-seat cultivator, breathing blue exhaust fumes and watching the young tobacco plants pass in endless procession beneath the tractor; "Leaf" is a lyrical meditation on the ripening plant, green changing to gold, an early reminder of autumn; "Cutting" tells of the harvest, "Tobacco hung like dollar bills."

Beyond the beauty of the verse in these poems, Kauffman accomplishes a bending of linear time. The imagery in each suggests both the present moment—the early April of steaming seedbeds, the dry August of cutting—and the end product

of this process, the cured and smokeable tobacco. In "Steamer on the Seedbed" the final lines, "Somewhere inside the steamer's belly/roared fire," are a reminder of the flame used to kindle the cured leaf. The "blue monoxide/cloud of summer" wafting from the tractor as it pulls the cultivator over the rows looks ahead to blue smoke drifting above burning cigarettes or cigars. Together the eight poems present a complex portrait of tobacco agriculture that remains fully aware of the irony of making one's living from a crop that, literally, disappears in smoke: *Tobacco's but an Indian weed,/ Grows green in the Morn, cut down at Eve.*

The second section of *The Weather Book* is one long poem in nine numbered segments, some titled and others not. The title of the whole poem, "Hitching the Americas," suggests both the literal content of the poem (a trip by foot and thumb through Central and South America), and the thematic content, the unification of American (hemisphere-wide) culture.

The third section of *The Weather Book* is called "Rally." Here Kauffman reveals a variety of tones and voices that display her range. With the exception of "Penelope Unwinding" and "December: Drying Corn," the poems in this section are short.

Dust jacket for Kauffman's first volume of fiction, a story collection

Despite their brevity they possess an extraordinary ability to startle the reader out of everyday perception into the rapture that is the product of the best lyric poetry. Certain images recur throughout these poems: trees (catalpa especially), birds, weaving. Two poems about catalpas epitomize Kauffman's ability to alter the reader's perception. One is "Denial," on one level a simple description of the growth of the catalpa seed pod, a long, brown (when ripe) tube favored by children as a mock cigar. After the trees flower toward the end of June, the pods form in early July, grow to long curves resembling fat string beans by mid July, and reach full size by the end of the month. This natural process becomes threatening in the poem, an image of all that is dangerous or harmful.

The early pods are "claws," "blunt/hand-hammered nails." Curving catalpa beans, like knives, "can sever/the thick horizon at dusk." Full-grown catalpa pods "halt in mid-air/as green velveted swords." The poem suggests further that the beans are an emblem of all life's betrayals: "Lovers warn: whatever happens/it is not true." The terse final line, "Blame the trees, blame them," plunges the reader even more deeply into the threatening reality of the catalpa by insisting that the trees, despite their denial, are responsible for the betrayals.

"Catalpas," the second poem, reveals still another aspect of the tree. Though less sinister than "Denial," the poem sees the catalpa as an embodiment of Sisyphean futility. After an intense growing, from the time the tree flowers in late June until the pods are full-grown in July, comes the "sudden brown collapse" of the tree: the pods dry and darken and the leaves fall. The final stanza focuses attention on the recurrence of events:

> Raked into heaps, ashy
> veins splinter,
> the huge heart of the leaf
> in ruins. And so we begin
> again, again.

No brief discussion of Kauffman's poetry can suggest the range of voices she attains. At times she is playful, as in "Appetizer, For You," rhyming *pickle* and *fickle*. Other times she is somber, as in "Recurrent" or "Milkweed." Still other poems evoke a sensuality as passionate as it is understated, "The End of March" being perhaps the best example in this collection:

> The darknesses as we talk
> gather towards love, simply,
>
> follow the narrowing lengths
> like the run of limb
>
> through the same spring rained on
> fruitfulness of maple fringe
>
> tips, the red puffed
> filled ones. Tap that tree.

Although Kauffman recently has worked almost exclusively in prose, the lyricism of her fiction suggests that poetry is never far from her.

Because it is difficult to sustain the reader's attention without some modulation of intensity, Kauffman often divides her longer poems into sections, and many of her most effective poems are short ones. For this same reason, her stories present the fullest realization of her talents to date because the short story form can sustain the intensity which characterizes her truest voice while employing the shifting focus of a plot—however minimal it may be—to modulate this intensity for the reader.

The title story in her collection *Places in the World a Woman Could Walk* (1983) typifies this use of plot. From the opening sentence, which reviewers commented about, the story uses plot to direct the reader's attention *away* from the themes the story develops: "The day the tornado hit Morenci was the day Lady Fretts finally put her mind to the slaughter of Susie Hey Susie and her Babies." This matter-of-fact discussion about the proposed slaughter continues through the first paragraph. The narrator, a young woman named Molly, who is Lady Fretts's sister-in-law, remains nonplussed: "I said good. I said do. Enough of holdover, mournful faces." Not until the final sentence in the paragraph does the reader discover that Susie Hey Susie is a cow. The shock value of this opening is considerable, and Kauffman uses it to prepare the reader for the real action of the story: the change which takes place in Lady Fretts after Susie Hey Susie is killed.

"Susie Hey Susie's prolonged and monotonous life," the narrator tells us, "was Lady's concoction of bliss: sweet timothy hay in the morning, aquamarine and tufted . . . slow stomping; sleep in simple shade"— the measured cadence evokes a bovine paradise. But nurturing the cows "for nobody's benefit" has cost Lady Fretts more than hay and water. Since the death of her husband, Molly's brother Wil-Johnny, who was struck by a lightning bolt, Lady Fretts has done little but feed Susie Hey Susie and her babies. "She *loved* Wil-Johnny," the narrator notes; "she loved Susie Hey Susie, his Jersey cow." These twin loves are the pillars of Lady Fretts's life but they also bind her "to stuff of the world with multiple tendrils. Not much escaped." Lady Fretts's law of love states that love manifests itself "in expansive forms, and in weight, and in hefty creatures of the world." Susie Hey Susie and her twin babies weigh more than a thousand pounds each.

Killing the cows releases Lady Fretts. For years she "rode a sofa" on her porch—very nearly immobilized. "Oh she was my Buddha," the narrator explains, "a plunked-down legitimate deity who knew that walking could give the appearance of too great an involvement with the earth." After the slaughter Lady Fretts regains her ability to act. She plans to sculpt a tribute to Susie Hey Susie and her babies and begins by taking a trip to Greece "to see how sculpting is done." The narrator, left behind in the small unnamed midwestern town, observes, "A woman makes up her mind these days, and life turns right around, pulls out like cartoon knitting."

Exactly what motivates Lady Fretts to destroy the cows is never clear. Susie Hey Susie's twin babies were born on the evening of Wil-Johnny's funeral, and their growth into massive heifers is a measure of her grief. "I can stand it," Lady Fretts three times tells the narrator. "They want better now!" she says of the cows, shouting over the storm that will bring the tornado to Morenci. "They've taken a grief and groaned with it. It's been my pleasure to fatten them." Whatever Lady Fretts's motivation for killing her cows—sacrifice to grief, end to mourning, fiscal expedient—the slaughter is a true liberation, not only for Lady Fretts but for Molly as well, as the final sentence of the story indicates: "I might have known there were places in the world that woman could walk, sure-footed, and look powerful." A woman's place is not only riding a sofa, but riding continents like Colossus.

The strong sense of place Kauffman's poetry reveals also appears in her stories. "At First It Looks Like Nothing" captures winter in Michigan. The cold is palpable, pushing at the windows, creeping in through the metal frames. The pipes freeze in the basement; when the narrator goes downstairs to plug in the heat tape that will thaw them, she finds "two dried-out mice," which she tosses out into the snow. "The state's a significant factor in weather," she comments.

The story also contains an excellent description of Michigan men: Durango, who is not, the narrator comments gratefully, a cowboy, "doesn't resemble Michigan men, who run their lives on motors, like twenty-first-century jet-shooting backpackers, bodies in mechanized flight. Michigan men have to move. They gather their gear and go. They can't reminisce."

The title refers ostensibly to a three-dimensional card the narrator and Durango look at on an old wooden viewer which belonged to the narrator's grandmother. It depicts a quail's nest hidden in tall grass so that the camouflaged hen and her chicks are barely visible. "At first," the narrator observes, "it looks like nothing." This comment resonates through the entire story. Michigan in winter is a study in grays. On cloudy days the sky, ground, and trees are one field, shades of black and white mixed. Objects lose their distinctness. Relationships in the story seem to absorb a fuzziness from the landscape.

Durango can't manage to keep his wives. No matter, says the narrator. "I haven't kept anybody either. But in Michigan, that doesn't matter." The landscape, relationships, the 3-D photo—at first all look like nothing. Closer scrutiny reveals a pattern, one that may contain tenderness, concern, perhaps even love:

> Durango and I are good for each other, no question about it. We walk; we make the slowest and longest love in the state. It's a love like the care of the dead, like the last wash—full of pity.

Part of the appeal of Kauffman's stories for readers is the nature of her characters. They are ordinary people. Some are attractive, though not unusually so; some are unattractive, but even these are not grotesques. The territory of Kauffman's stories is the territory of her readers' everyday lives. Consequently, readers respond well to her portraits of people. The portraits are simple; however, the characters often are not. Reviewers have commented, for example, that the young man, Floyd, in "Patriotic" has "innocence and wonder" but is not portrayed as "a dope." When the narrator of the story, who has hired Floyd to help her harvest hay, removes her blouse at Floyd's suggestion because of the heat, she sees that his "downright factual face" holds no hint of guile. Women for Floyd are "as weird as hors d'oeuvres. Should he use a fork or his fingers?" Despite his simplicity, Floyd is not held up as an object of ridicule. Instead the story stresses his sweetness and resurrects the idea of purity as something other than ironic.

Sherry, in "Harmony," likes sex. "She's fairly general about it," the narrator, Vicki, tells the reader, "but enthusiastic." Sherry is a self-appointed expert on many things, Vicki notes. "No matter what she's got hold of, Sherry acts as if she experiences some kind of special pleasures." Vicki wishes she could take Sherry at her word without suspecting her of lying.

Sherry has made up a song "for the sake of women everywhere in the world. . . . Like we are all poor souls, starting over at A-B-C." Vicki has learned to sing harmony, which she is good at—the source for the story's title. Despite all her advice for Vicki, who is younger and seeks to learn about men from Sherry, Sherry is no expert on romance. Her current partner is Jeff, a semimute ceramicist whose mother still does his laundry. Sherry has been married twice, has two kids and few prospects. Together Sherry and Vicki spend each Saturday "hunting up 'Beautiful Views of Jackson,' " a variation on the theme of "At First It Looks Like Nothing."

Although Sherry has tremendous potential as a satiric portrait of a hopelessly confused woman who nevertheless continues to dispense advice, Kauffman refuses to use her this way. Instead the reader is made to share Vicki's feelings for Sherry, which mix admiration with exasperation and incomprehension. There *are* things Sherry can teach Vicki. Possibly she can prevent Vicki from ending up with "one handsome bastard after another." Kauffman is careful to make clear that Vicki herself is unaware of the most important lesson Sherry has to teach. But the reader cannot miss it. Sherry, says Vicki, would "love a body for thumblessness, Jackson for a swamp, and probably the rest of life for that." Sherry loves the world for its less attractive features.

All but two of the stories in *Places in the World a Woman Could Walk* are narrated in the first person. One token of Kauffman's skill as a writer is that no two of the voices sound alike. Robert, the narrator of "The Mechanics of Good Times," and Bobby-Boo of "At Odds" are male. Some are middle-aged, like the narrator of "Patriotic"; others are young women, like Molly in the title story and Vicki in "Harmony." The unnamed narrator of "My Mother Has Me Surrounded" is perhaps the most interesting in the volume: a grown woman telling a story from her viewpoint as a child.

The story opens on Rehoboth Beach. The narrator, as a child, is lying literally in her mother's shadow. All of a child's ambivalence toward a parent—terrible dependence, guarded resentment—appears in the narrator's repeated comment that she is "invisible," a "ghost" to her mother: "Lightweight, I hover, physically apparent since birth, but not yet fully attached to the world, not weighted with the bodily form she values: working thighs, an emphatic pelvis."

The child's sense of the mother as a Brobdingnagian—a woman who fills the sky—is interspersed with the grown narrator's sense of her mother as merely another human being. "My mother is not a beauty," she comments, "but what child knows?" The child, a "footed farm child," fears the ocean; water is the mother's natural element. "Get your feet wet," the mother commands, and the daughter responds. "My mother has me surrounded. I must be hers. Anyway, I am her daredevil."

"My Mother Has Me Surrounded" appears, slightly altered, as the second chapter in Kauffman's first novel, *Collaborators*, published by Knopf

Dust jacket for Kauffman's novel, expanded from "My Mother Has Me Surrounded," which appeared in her collection of stories

in 1986. The novel extrapolates the relatively simple story of a mother-daughter relationship into a lyric meditation on intergenerational conflict. It is a daring experiment in densely imaged prose, which resembles poetry in its graceful complexity. Indeed Kauffman's skill as a poet is apparent on every page of the manuscript. The book demands a great deal of the reader: concentration, attention to detail. Still, the effort is worth it, for from the clusters of images emerges a complex portrait of a woman whose strength allows her to indulge her weaknesses. The narrator, Andrea Doria, becomes the prototype of all daughters, anxiously scrutinizing their mothers for clues about how to be women. Like her twentieth-century namesake, the ill-fated ship *Andrea Doria,* Andrea (her mother always calls her Dovie) is on a collision course; like the sixteenth-century Italian admiral, one of the last great condottieri, or mercenaries, she is one of the "lucky" ones, although her mother will not tell her so.

As the title suggests, the novel attempts to explain the mechanism through which mothers conspire with their daughters, both consciously and unconsciously, to make women of them. The narrator remembers a series of things her mother told her, some of which—like the grandfather, father, and son the mother says were her lovers—are never fully explained. Together these memories construct a panorama of woman's life. Menstruation, love, the threat of rape—the mother shares with the narrator the nuances of her life.

While the reader never sees in the daughter's behavior the effect of her mother's teaching, the book traces Andrea's growth from a girl totally dependent on her mother's favor, to an angry young woman who rejects her mother (the first line of the book is "My mother lied to me about everything"), to a mature woman who will school her own daughter in her mother's ways. Indeed the final scene of the novel, in which Andrea describes her mother swimming through the fires of hell to her own unbelieving daughter, suggests that Andrea will repeat the cycle with her daughter.

Although Kauffman is not a feminist author any more than a regional author—though she is a feminist and prefers rural life to urban—her work is very much concerned with the roles and fate of women. Her women characters are strong, willful, capable of taking life on its own terms without losing the capacity to care.

Her work, especially her fiction, systematically rejects the conventions of most literature. Her stories and her novel focus on one or two characters. Often there is only the barest hint of plot. Similar in some respects to the fiction of Djuna Barnes (especially *Nightwood*), Kauffman's work makes its point through patterns of imagery and tone. The simple lives of her characters—stripped of the trappings that we know as life in the twentieth century—become a background against which the weighty issues of her themes can be revealed in silhouette—the graceful arc of a hand moving to cover the mouth or wipe the brow.

Kauffman's career is just reaching full stride. Poetry was her apprenticeship, where she crafted a style and found her truest voice, clear and powerful. The short story form provided her a means of modulating her powerful tone to create even more various effects. Her novel extends her technique to the creation of a fictional world.

Sandra McPherson

(2 August 1943-   )

Caroline Cherry
Eastern College

BOOKS: *Elegies for the Hot Season* (Bloomington: Indiana University Press, 1970);

Radiation, American Poetry Series, volume 1 (New York: Ecco Press, 1973);

The Year of Our Birth, American Poetry Series, volume 15 (New York: Ecco Press, 1978);

Sensing (San Francisco: Meadow Press, 1980);

Patron Happiness, American Poetry Series, volume 24 (New York: Ecco Press, 1983);

Responsibility for Blue (Denton, Tex.: Trilobite Press, 1985);

Pheasant Flower (Missoula, Mont.: Owl Creek Press, 1985);

Botanical (Portland, Oreg.: Trace Editions, 1985);

Floralia (Portland, Oreg.: Trace Editions, 1985).

OTHER: *Journey from Essex: Poems for John Clare,* edited by McPherson (Port Townsend, Wash.: Graywolf Press, 1981).

Born in San Jose, California, Sandra McPherson was adopted at birth by Walter James McPherson, basketball coach and professor of physical education at San Jose State University, and Frances Gibson McPherson. She was educated in the San Jose public schools and early developed a love of nature (encouraged by family camping trips), of music, both classical and jazz (she plays the piano), of painting, of languages (Spanish, German, and French), and of writing.

McPherson attended Westmont College (1961-1963) and San Jose State College (now San Jose State University), where she studied with Roberta Holloway and from which she received her B.A. in 1965 (and a Distinguished Alumna award in 1982). She then did graduate study at the University of Washington at Seattle (1965-1966) under David Wagoner and Elizabeth Bishop. It was in Bishop's class that she met the poet Henry Carlile, whom she married on 22 July 1966. At this time she was working as a technical writer at Honeywell, Inc., where she was fascinated by the technical language but felt ill at ease in the defense industry. The following year Henry Carlile began teaching

at Portland State University and their daughter Phoebe was born. McPherson lived primarily in Portland, Oregon, until 1985, when she was divorced and moved to Davis, California.

Since 1966 McPherson's work experience has been in writing, teaching, and editing. She has been guest editor of *Poetry Northwest* (1971), poetry editor of the *Iowa Review* (1974-1975) and the *Antioch Review* (1979-1981), and editor of the *California Quarterly* (1985-1986). She has been on the faculty or teaching staff of many writers' programs, including University of Iowa Writers Workshop (1974-1976, 1978-1980) and the Oregon Writers' Workshop at Pacific Northwest College of Art (1981-1985). Since 1985 she has been an associate professor at the University of California at Davis.

As a writer, Sandra McPherson has won respect from the beginning for her technical proficiency and her gift for careful observation; by the age of thirty she was publishing in journals such as *Poetry*, the *New Yorker*, the *New Republic, Antaeus, Poetry Northwest,* and *Field*. One of her poems, "View from Observatory Hill," was included in the Borestone Mountain Poetry Awards *Best Poems of 1968,* the first of more than forty anthology publications, and in the same year she won the Helen Bullis Prize from *Poetry Northwest*. Her work is distinguished by her affinity for nature, both animate and inanimate, and her ability to capture it in all its concrete detail. Drawn to things not by their abstract significance but by their concrete reality, she resists obtrusive symbolizing and philosophizing; in "Sonnet for Joe" she advises a student, "I would rather you describe a clock than time." This respect for her subject is reflected in her affection for poet John Clare, whose detailed and nonjudgmental descriptions of nature—"simply what happens"—she admires; she has written about him and edited *Journey from Essex: Poems for John Clare* (1981). Similarly, she acknowledges the early influences of Pablo Neruda because of his "love for things."

There is a strong visual priority in her poetry, reinforced by her exposure to Elizabeth Bishop's

Dust jacket for McPherson's fourth poetry collection

work: the images seek to be well etched as well as incandescent. Her love for things influences the precision of her language; she is sensitive to exact descriptions and to color and enriches her diction, as does Marianne Moore, with scientific and technical terms: *caltrop, cucurbits, mycelium, plectrum, geasters.* Her best poems are reticent; she does not reveal too much or jump to conclusions, but makes intuitive links among images in a manner similar to that of poet Laura Jensen, who is her friend. Her images seem vivid because they are put in striking juxtaposition; at her best she avoids conventional associations and shocks the reader into awareness with reversals of expectations. For instance, in "Collapsars" she visually relates an account of a neighbor killed in a fire and information about black holes taken from *Natural History.* Particularly effective is her analogy between the collapsed body in a bag and collapsed space:

> The matter
> in such stars
> has been squashed together
>
> like a victim
> of a fire
> carried down in a bag,

half size,
but then again and again,
fire after fire,

> into forms
> Unknown on earth. . . .

She credits Theolonius Monk as an influence on her poems, particularly in the individuality of his technique of hitting two unexpected notes simultaneously in a way that is ultimately satisfying.

Sandra McPherson's experience as a workshop teacher has imposed on her writing, if not a rigid discipline, at least a characteristic way of happening, a process that is a manner. Many of her poems were begun as exercises, some in response to assignments she has set for her students. More generally she often conceives a poem as a visual and spiritual space to be filled, not as an expression of some prior concept or theme, so that the poem proceeds under its own autonomous associative energy. In "A Coconut for Katerina," for instance, McPherson piles image on image in a technical tour de force to suggest the mingled sadness and hope of pregnancy and miscarriage: "Lappings and gurglings of living hollows half filled,/half with room/

for more empty and hopeful boats and their sails."

The total range of McPherson's subject matter is wide, but there is a handful of topics to which she returns repeatedly: domestic events, relations with family and friends, and above all nature. Although she disclaims closeness to the Romantic poets, she has a Keatsian ability to immerse herself in a creature; however, the nature she records is not always benign and owes more to Baudelaire than to the Romantics. It is always positive, nonetheless, in placing human events in a larger context, one rather easier to contemplate than our own painful and confused lives. Nature gives McPherson a set of objective correlatives which evoke precisely a human thought, emotion, or the impact of an event. It is a way of making private emotions public.

She has said that the poem "helps me to get unbearable emotional pressures into concrete form that other people can use." This is true of "In the Columbia River Gorge, After a Death":

When I come too close,
Earth shuts up its tongues,
But I hear what it means

In the idling motor, in the note
Child-held until the breath runs out,
In the unwinding

Music of the spawning fish,
Playing against the current
Into some longsuffering water.

Here feelings associated with the recent death of an uncle and birth of a daughter are mediated in the exactly calibrated description of traveling through a resonant landscape, likened to salmon driving upstream both to spawn and die. The technique is typical of McPherson's work; she has traded metric and artificial rhythm for the cadences of natural speech but can use syntactical repetition and variation, as with the "in the" formula above, to set up an apparently natural recurrence and rhythm. It is, like the act of mind in the poem, loose, cumulative, and associative. Also typical is the surprise of *longsuffering* applied to *water*.

Death and loss are prominent themes, particularly in McPherson's early poetry, but love and creation are there as well; she is by no means morbid but is often energetic, hopeful, even humorous. She is, moreover, alert to the spiritual dimension of human and natural life; indeed she could be called a religious poet in a nontraditional sense. Brought up as a Presbyterian, she no longer sub-

scribes to a specific doctrinal belief, but she frequently uses biblical imagery—Jacob's ladder ("Extract"), "that sailor" Noah who "started the world over with deuces" ("Studies in the Imaginary"), "sad grapes . . . weighted with the very press/of holy tradition" ("Three from the Market")—or references taken from a religious context, such as the new householders who "brought our own light/Like missionaries" ("Selling the House"). Such religious imagery has a number of uses in her poetry, but most significantly it is connected with childhood memories and with a sense, associated with childhood but continuing into adulthood, of something just glimpsed, something about to be, some mysterious world on the edge of consciousness. This impalpable world of imaginative richness is difficult to find in adult life, but McPherson evokes it in her poetry:

To pray was like living on the road
that goes on to someone else's house
even when it is too far to walk.
Now I'm too far away from hometown streets
to know any listener, being among strangers approaches
being among the imaginary.
                            "Studies in the Imaginary"

In "Poem Whose First Stanza is Martin Heidegger on Georg Trakl" McPherson speaks of a "twilight zone" in which she can recall the mood of childhood stories where "a white road bobbed over low hills/and leaned up in the distance/so that the early days seem/in rural sunshine/like an afterlife." There is a Wordsworthian flavor in her ability to suggest the spiritual world through landscape and childhood.

These themes are evident in McPherson's first volume, *Elegies for the Hot Season* (1970), which won the Association of American University Presses' award for the National Council on the Arts Selection in poetry and which was widely reviewed as the work of a "talented young poet." It was republished in 1982 as volume twenty-three of the American Poetry series. A well-crafted collection, the poems form a rough cycle divided into four sections. The first centers on death in nature and loss in life; the second on human activities imbued with threat; the third, subtitled "A Season of Change," on home and homemaking; and the fourth on family—marriage, childbirth, husband, child.

The title of the volume reminds the reader of the traditional elegy in which death is seen in relation to the cycle of the seasons, and which encompasses not only mourning but affirmation and celebration. Many of the poems juxtapose birth and death, painstaking creation and inexorable destruction: in "Losing Ground," "An Easter hat/Of pink and white flowers resurrects there/Each spring. But the ground it grows on/Is sinking." The complex vision of the poems captures both despair and hope. *Elegies* is aware that "one should never feel safe/Because almost always there is something one can't see" ("Lions"); a shard of glass brought home by a roof rat (that "aristocrat, penthouse Pete") to decorate its nest concentrates the sun's rays and ignites his funeral pyre ("Roof Rat"). But Easter is a recurrent possibility. "Keeping House" describes a world chaotic and decaying as if demonically possessed, but in spite of destruction:

> So spring breaks—breaks in!
> ....
> The house is brimful.
> Eden, pure Eden is chasing us.
> The baby is pounding her bars
> To get out.

What has changed is not circumstance but vision, a vision that sees an ordinary domestic scene in "Balm" as "this city of refuge, this day of rest" or a filthy fraternity house as "our next heaven" ("Succeeding a Fraternity into an Old House"). Death is balanced by a fearsome rebirth in the cycle of life. The "slow-brained" snails, squashed to death, "forgave and fragilely claimed the garden/The next hot season, like old friends, or avengers" ("Elegies for the Hot Season: The Killing of the Snails").

The speaker lives in an animated world: a house is alive, for example, as its "bedrooms stretch and yawn" ("Selling the House"). Accordingly she uses verbs heavily, sometimes quirkily (an old woman "occults" in "Balm"), always kinetically: in dissecting a "Foetal Pig" she "Snapped off nose,/Snipped a quick canal through the eyes."

Among the finest of these poems is "Amanitas," which uses deadly mushrooms, caught in a few deft strokes, to encapsulate an ambiguous psychological moment. The mushrooms are "Yellow-slickered, orange warning Wet Paint if not/Caution, warted and Christmas knicknack/Red." The poet is attracted by their beauty as she picks them for a still life, even though she knows their danger: "You can tell/Centuries later a dead-of-mushrooms mummy—the pinched/Nose, the unbearable skin over pain, pain/A growing thing with a season and a harvest." This still life is a true *nature mort*. The poem holds the beauty and deadliness in tension; it embodies the ambivalence of any fatal attraction:

> I trade only the emptiness of my hands
>
> And eyes for this modern and American generation
> That mockingly doffs its enamelled cap and which
>
> I love for its fight for my heart
> And which I must fight to love.

Love in McPherson's poetry is never an easy sentiment.

Several of these poems show the influence of Sylvia Plath in theme and technique. "Pregnancy" ends:

> The heart sloshes through the microphone
> Like falls in a box canyon.
>
> The queen's only a figurehead.
> Nine months pulled by nine
>
> Planets, the moon slooping
> Through its amnion sea,
>
> Trapped, stone-mad . . . and three
> Beings' lives gel in my womb.

McPherson has said in an interview that this is "awfully derivative of Plath, although I was writing in a style similar to hers just before I read her work." The influence shows itself "in the density of metaphor, the sentence structure, those dry sounding techniques combined with real desperation and an attention-getting tone." It is interesting to watch in subsequent volumes her development toward a style more distinctively her own.

Soon after publishing *Elegies*, McPherson won an Ingram Merrill Foundation grant (1972), the Bess Hokin Prize from *Poetry* (1972), and the Emily Dickinson Prize from the Poetry Society of America (1973). In 1973 she published her second collection, *Radiation*, which was received as warmly as the first had been. Chosen to inaugurate Ecco Press's American Poetry Series, it won the Pacific Northwest Booksellers prize for the best book of poetry published that year by a Northwest poet. David Bromwich and Valerie Trueblood both compared it with Elizabeth Bishop's work, and Bishop herself wrote a jacket blurb commenting: "It's like turning the light switch off, and there in the dark—reality: all kinds of likely and unlikely things, incandescent on their own, beginning to stir and breathe."

The collection extends and intensifies the direction of *Elegies:* familiar fruits and vegetables (provoking some of the best poems), landscape and seascape, and the homely activities of a modern woman coexist with stories of human desperation, murder, and exile. There are experiments with form, including six untraditional sonnets. What McPherson says of grapefruit could be said of this poetry: "34% rind, membrane, seeds;/the rest is light" ("Three from the Market"). The metaphor of light is underlined in the apt title, *Radiation,* which has particular relevance to "Collapsars" and is implicit in the prefatory quotation from Paul Valéry: "If you are good, it is because you retain your evil. If you blaze, hurling off sparkles and lightnings, your sorrow, gloom, and stupidity keep house within you." This suggests, among other things, a deepening of interest in the ambiguity of good and evil, of the paradox of simultaneous attraction and repulsion; one may be an emanation of the other. The complacent reader perhaps has no cause to feel superior to the tormented murderer of "Marlow and Nancy," who feels, "I am the river bottom between debris/And depths. . . ."

Several of the poems are concerned with isolation, distance, separation from the heart's homeland. The ocean is an insistent image; in remote "Siberia" "It feels as if the ocean is near./One stares into the possibility/of its expanse./You are a small boat cut loose./Wherever you go/is deep." The shortening sentences and lines seem to diminish the reach and scope of language appropriately before that immensity. Her images resist reduction to philosophical analysis, a process she protests against in "Sonnet for Joe," where she insists on observing specifics: "the sea/and its marketable herring, its common tuna, and starfish/always losing their legs." What the specifics convey is two poles of human experience: a sense of belonging or of home, set against a sense of isolation, sometimes mild and sometimes amounting to stark terror. This is not cause for protest, however; it is simply part of the natural economy. In "Seaweeds," a beautifully controlled poem, the poet understands the plants, plucked from the ocean floor and "stranded," because she has shared their experience:

> But I
> Have eaten nori and dulse, and to have gone deep
> Before being cast out leaves hardly a taste of loneliness.
> And I take in their iodine.

Ultimately the poem itself is a means of overcoming isolation. The first poem in *Radiation* begins with the lines: "Poetry is a way of counting,/sisters,/it is

acquisitive./I try to find something to hold on to,/laid up in heaven."

Soon after *Radiation,* McPherson won the Blumenthal-Leviton-Blonder Prize from *Poetry* (1975) and received grants from the National Endowment for the Arts (1974-1975) and the Guggenheim Foundation (1976-1977) which enabled her to work on the poems collected in *The Year of Our Birth* (1978), the fifteenth volume in the American Poetry Series and a nominee for the National Book Award in Poetry. Some reviewers, Joyce Carol Oates and David Bromwich among them, found it less sharp and less deeply felt than the earlier volumes, but the majority of critics found much to admire; even Oates commented on some "beautifully-rendered poems with the lucidity of parables." McPherson's command of form continues here to mature, as seen in the energetic long lines and tumbling metaphors of "A Coconut for Katerina," the successful sestina "In a Garden," and the integration of prose poetry in "January Apples."

To a greater extent than *Radiation,* this volume is centered on the human cycle though still finding its correlatives in nature; McPherson has said she shaped the collection to treat "birth through love, marriage, childbirth, death, and out the other side." "Studies in the Imaginary," the title of one sequence, might well apply to the whole. The poems are pervaded by memories of childhood, parents, and ancestors. There are, accordingly, accumulated layers of meaning; the imaginative as well as the literal past color and shape the present as they are re-created in the mind. There is a dynamic interaction among generations; in "Children" the daughter "hangs my picture/forever in her head. So that she always/sees to me when I am down/and thinks the way to raise me is/to climb aboard me toe for toe. . . ."

The aching mystery of love is at the center of this collection: how it is learned, rejected, fought for and against, and how it persists in people and things.

> They were always telling us
> the importance of love
> and how there is an animal in it
> . . . .
> not noble as a bear
> maybe low like a badger
> or hot like red fox fur . . .
>
> how it is human supernatural and animal
> because it is the birthplace
> of likeness

and the embodiment
of reasoning

"The Heredity of Systems"

In a manner reminiscent of William Carlos Williams, the simple prose syntax and apparently commonplace similes form a necessary balance to the complex, multifaceted understanding of love. McPherson alternates between the direct gaze and the fleeting glimpse, the prosaic statement and the compressed metaphor.

Among the best poems are those which find their metaphors in nature, such as "The Bittern," which evokes the attempt to capture an elusive joy, the glimpse of mystery or meaning just beyond the fringe of sight. Though doomed to frustration, the search itself is a sign of hope:

> Because I have turned my head for years
> in order to see the bittern
> I won't mind not finding
> what I am looking for
> as long as I know it could be there . . .
>
> In the end I see
>   nothing
> but how I go blindly on loving
> a life from which something is missing.
>
> Clouds rushing across the sun,
> gold blowing down on the reeds—
>
> nothings like these. . . .

These lines, which conclude *The Year of Our Birth*, circle back to "Childish Landscape" near the beginning: This is the proof of God, they said./The present. Because you see."

A second National Endowment for the Arts grant in 1980 helped McPherson complete *Sensing* (1980), a chapbook of eight poems beautifully printed and decorated with a woodcut by Leigh McLellan, a former student of McPherson's who runs Meadow Press. Various images of communication repeat and connect these poems: telephone calls, conversations, letters, and even quotations from the letters of McPherson's Aunt Ida, a missionary to Peru. Several of the poems are strongly narrative; McPherson is edging away from the more lyrical and subjective early poems toward a more public utterance. "Lifesaving," which describes the setting of a rescue in a motel swimming pool and is apparently a fragment of autobiography, is absolutely straightforward, never self-absorbed yet densely textured and resonant: a poignant moment caught in intense clarity.

Once again McPherson evokes the complex ambiguities of life: pain and fear, callousness and inhumanity, terrifying change, all held in tension with love, tact, concern, the magical richness and variety of nature, an awareness of mystery. In "Writing to a Prisoner" the speaker says, "Of course I am afraid to correspond with you": afraid of getting involved, of being vulnerable, of being intrusive, of the responsibility of having to translate the world for him. Yet the poem overcomes the fears and captures the world for the prisoner and for us; the poem itself makes the relationship.

> This morning the blue inlet shines in fog
> Unbroken by horizon,
> Only the noiseless dives of black and white buffle-
>   heads,
> No splash as they surface,
> The limp long neck of a dead grebe,
> Each khaki foot like a spray of buckeye leaves,
> Its skewery beak, clamped on a kelp strand,
> Pointing toward one boat going out;
> The bird has no eye
> And a gull, probably, has pecked right through the
>   breastbone
> To the heart. . . .

The Washington shore is an effective correlative for her ambivalent feelings about a world which she must fight to love.

McPherson's fourth major collection, *Patron Happiness*, was published in 1983. By this time she had been widely recognized as an established poet of stature; *Publishers Weekly* in reviewing this volume termed her "very fine and unusual. . . . Her poems are bright, crisp and spare; her perceptions intimate and precise." William Logan, writing in the *Times Literary Supplement*, pronounced her "a gorgeous impressionist, whose inventions are a kind of rapture." Such judgments could be applied to parts of the earlier volumes as well; these poems are characteristic in theme, image, and technique, though there are significant shifts in emphasis and a continuing development toward more objective forms despite several personal lyrics in her earlier style. McPherson continues in this collection to explore the painful complexities of human relationships; the poems are peopled with, among others, a dead grandmother, a regained mother, an unfaithful husband, respected teachers, and a much-loved daughter. Some of the poems express a "longing to escape from those I hurt" ("Living Glass"), or a feeling of precarious balance "anxious as fuel/In a dory tank on the ocean" ("The Jet Engine"). Loneliness seems to be the human condition: "Loneliness/Used to feed a lot of us" ("Urban Ode"). But the title of the volume is thematic: happiness can be chosen.

A couple of years before the publication of this volume, when McPherson was in her late thirties, she met her birth parents for the first time and was pleased to discover a mutual affinity for nature and for mathematics. This meeting colors several poems, perhaps the most interesting of which is "Last Week of Winter," which appeared in *Sensing* in an earlier version. In the first version a friend discloses that she has given up a child for adoption, and the poet remarks, "Such instinct: to tell a child given away/You gave your own away." In the second version these lines become "she gave away a child instinctively/So her own life could begin." Compassionate understanding born of experience marks this volume.

The desperation of Plath is still evident in some poems, but a new influence can be seen in the three odes that conclude the collection: the public voice of Horace. This form allows McPherson to deal more freely with large, abstract themes in clean, uncluttered lines. The last of the three, "Urban Ode," concludes with an image of a child running circles around a jay in a bush:

And the girl who made that möbius
Was never separate from the jay again,
    Never objective, never
    Maunderingly subjective, she

Who had seen many.
In all her running, she'd run out of loneliness.
    What do you think? Can such
    Riches fall into our lives?

What do you think, Patron Happiness? ·

The thought is competently embodied in the verbal play of *loneliness* and *happiness,* the repetition of "What do you think?," and the balance maintained in the image between objective observation and subjective identification.

In the years following *Patron Happiness* McPherson won an Ingram Merrill Foundation grant (1984), an Oregon Arts Commission grant (1984-1985), and her third National Endowment for the Arts grant (1985). These enabled her to work on four chapbooks, all published in 1985: *Responsibility for Blue, Pheasant Flower,* and *Floralia.*

In her recent work she has retained what is best in her earlier poetry and has refined it with disciplined experiments in form and a mature understanding of life. This is evident in the sustained, high colloquy of "The Feather" (*New Yorker,* 10 June 1985):

I accept its descent, a trace
Of a good soul taken in the rapture,
Its barbs zipped
Like the slacks of men at church.
Through quick and violent beating against air,
The vane holds, rays determine its outline, run out
To the curve and wait. There is no perimeter. The
    boundary
Is the ends of rays. End after end.

Here are the sharp details, the surprising metaphors, the quirky wit, the controlled rhythm, the unobtrusive play of vowels, the unsentimental empathy with nature, the spiritual concern, and the hard-won optimism that have won Sandra McPherson a respected place among contemporary poets.

References:

John Cooke and Jeanie Thompson, "Three Poets on the Teaching of Poetry," *College English,* 42 (October 1980): 133-140;

Cecelia Hagen, "Dialogue with Sandra McPherson," *Northwest Review,* 20, nos. 2-3 (1982): 29-55;

Karla Hammond, "An Interview with Sandra McPherson," *American Poetry Review* (September/October 1981): 15-20.

Anne Redmon

(13 December 1943-   )

Catherine Rainwater
St. Edward's University

BOOKS: *Emily Stone* (London: Secker & Warburg, 1974);

Music and Silence (London: Secker & Warburg, 1979; New York: Holt, Rinehart & Winston, 1979).

OTHER: "Bat Time," *Bananas* (London), 8 (Summer 1977): 8-12.

In a 1983 interview, Anne Redmon states that she has "great chests full" of rejected plots. Perhaps among such personal documents and unfinished or unpublished writings there is evidence of a neophyte phase in Redmon's literary career, which otherwise appears to have begun with *Emily Stone* (1974) at an already high level of artistic maturity. Moreover, since 1974 Redmon has published two more works which reveal versatility in her management of narrative technique, architectonic arrangement, and characterization. Although her works exhibit an interesting continuity of philosophical and thematic concerns, each one constitutes a significant departure from its predecessor. To read Anne Redmon's works in chronological sequence is to witness the evolution of an authorial consciousness as well as to observe successful experimentation with increasingly complex narrative forms.

Born Anne Bryan Redmon in Stamford, Connecticut, 13 December 1943, to Bryan Collins Redmon and Elizabeth Howe Redmon, the author lived until the age of twenty-one in the northeastern region of the United States. She graduated in 1962 from the Shipley School in Bryn Mawr, Pennsylvania, and from 1962 to 1964 she attended the University of Pennsylvania. In 1964 Redmon married Benedict Nightingale, a well-known drama critic, broadcaster, and free-lance writer, and moved to England, where the couple still resides with their three children, Christopher, Magdalen, and Piers. During her early years in England, 1965-1966, Redmon worked as a researcher at Granada Television in Manchester. Later, from 1977-1978, she was employed in London as a book reviewer

Anne Redmon (photo by Peter O'Rourke)

for the *Sunday Times.* After the publication of *Emily Stone* Redmon won the *Yorkshire Post* prize for a first work, and following the appearance of *Music and Silence* (1979) she was elected Fellow of the Royal Society of Literature (1980). *Music and Silence* has been translated into Japanese, Italian, Finnish, and Swedish. Redmon enjoys traveling and has visited Greece, Russia, Hungary, and parts of Northern and Central Asia. She delivered a lecture on Flannery O'Connor in Budapest in 1980 and has reviewed fiction in various BBC broadcasts. Among her interests are classical music, religion, ancient civilization, and education, especially of her own three children.

Many of these personal interests appear as a part of the content of Redmon's fiction. *Emily Stone* is the story of a lifelong but troubled friendship between two women—Sasha Courtney, an aspiring actress and a devout Catholic, and Emily, an embittered woman who turns to writing in her search for the peace of mind she lacks because of her spiritual emptiness. Emily envies Sasha's spiritual contentment even as she denies its validity. Before Sasha's death from a lingering disease, Sasha befriends Emily's husband, Peter, whose infatuation with the saintly woman continues even beyond her death. Emily's narrative is written as a part of her effort to exorcise Sasha's power over herself and Peter.

"Bat Time" (1977), Redmon's short story, also reveals the author's interest in art, artists, and spirituality. In this work, Mrs. Madden and a dubiously "psychic" friend cast a kind of manipulative spell over Mrs. Madden's daughter, Augusta. The narrator of this story, an artist, observes from a passive yet curiously involved perspective as the daughter's life is managed by the mother's will. Finally, *Music and Silence*, Redmon's latest work, exhibits the author's interest in classical music and in some of the ways in which all the arts can serve human needs. The protagonist, Maud Eustace, is a cellist, but a deep depression renders her unable to play. Like *Emily Stone*, *Music and Silence* is a story of a difficult friendship between two women: Maud is befriended by Beatrice Pazzi, who also becomes a mother-figure for the unhappy young woman. Beatrice tries to shield Maud from the violence of a religious fanatic who waits in the shadows outside their apartment building; she also suggests that Maud should write a journal if she cannot play music. Maud's journal serves a therapeutic purpose as she works her way toward mental health and spiritual contentment.

Redmon's two novels and her short story, "Bat Time," share some thematic and philosophical concerns. These concerns center primarily around matters of free will and fate that, perhaps especially as a Roman Catholic convert, Redmon finds both troublesome and fascinating. In *Emily Stone*, Emily's life crisis involves her own inadvertent submission to fate. Skeptically, she denies any notion of human destiny, yet through default in the exercise of free will she shapes her existence in ways which duplicate the patterns of her mother's unhappy life. In "Bat Time," a charlatan psychic predicts a miserable future for a young couple, whose life begins

uncannily to take on the foretold pattern; their bleak future transpires not so much through any prevailing force of destiny, but because of their own passive acceptance of the gloomy prognostication into which even the young man's past suddenly, eerily, seems to fit. This suggestion that people in various ways make their lives conform to patterns is also put forth in *Music and Silence*, a novel which perhaps most complexly and optimistically of all Redmon's works examines the role of free will. Within an ostensibly predestined pattern of human entanglements, five major characters discover or fail to discover the power of free will to extricate themselves from the destruction and loneliness which result from unquestioned acceptance of patterns established in the past.

Redmon's works explore other issues tangentially related to her concern with freedom and fate. As an author Redmon is preoccupied with various psychological states of being which directly or indirectly contribute to a character's imprisonment within limiting or "fated" patterns. Emily in *Emily Stone* is obsessed with the memory of her dead friend, Sasha Courtney, who before dying became a quite saintly person. Spiritually deficient, Emily tries rationally to decipher and dispel the mystery of Sasha's spirituality, which continues even beyond death to exert force over Emily's and her husband's lives. Her obsession, however, leads only to her increased isolation, and her life becomes a replica of her mother's. In "Bat Time," a young woman's insecurity and anxiety, fueled by the so-called psychic's predictions, contribute to her psychological and spiritual withdrawal from her husband. Her withdrawal leads in turn to the fulfillment of the psychic's prophecy. Finally, in *Music and Silence*, Maud Eustace's depression, Beatrice Pazzi's excessive self-discipline, and Arthur Marsdan's Christian fanaticism are all states of mind which, untranscended, perpetuate old, destructive patterns of the past.

In Redmon's fiction, transcending such destructive patterns requires not only a spiritually informed exercise of free will but also participation in human community. Perhaps the most emphatic message to emerge from Redmon's works is that in a damaged universe, a human can nevertheless achieve an elevated state of being through contact with the sacred self of another. However, Redmon never fails to acknowledge the perverse and shadowy aspects of human nature: aspiration toward a state of grace can become fanatical zeal; free will can be expressed corruptly as power over others;

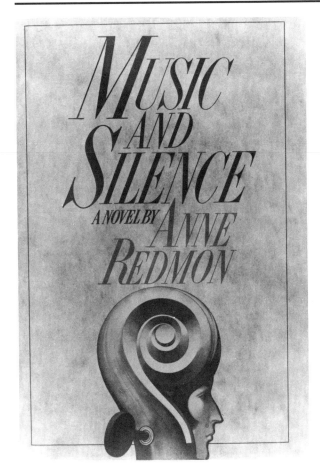

Dust jacket for Redmon's story of a difficult friendship between two women

and a sense of mystical connection with another can become an isolating delusion.

Working through and against the patterns of their lives, Redmon's characters are complex individuals. Even so, they are simultaneously developed in constellations in which each character suggests some component of human consciousness. Rarely is an author able to achieve such a successful balance between "flat" or allegorical characters and "rounded" ones. In *Music and Silence,* for example, the maniacal Arthur is one-dimensional in his religious madness, but Redmon develops his personal background in ways which make him seem fully human; furthermore, his characteristics are orchestrated to echo in twisted fashion the "normal" traits of other people. Consequently, Arthur appears as a three-dimensional man whose unhealthy state of mind has transformed him into a kind of caricature. All of Redmon's works strongly suggest that anyone who does not or cannot participate in human community risks becoming a caricature.

Redmon emphasizes community not only in the subject matter of her works but also in her own sense of herself as an artist in a cultural and historical community. If her characters are aware of the force of the past upon their lives, so is Redmon the artist aware of her literary and philosophical precursors. She writes with a strong sense of tradition. Her works reveal her declared fascination with mythology and Christian mysticism and perhaps reflect in subtle ways her knowledge of the works of such figures as Thomas Merton, Tielhard de Chardin, Julian of Norwich, and Gerard Manley Hopkins. A careful reader also senses within *Music and Silence* Redmon's affinities with Flannery O'Connor, whose works Redmon knows and whose grotesque characters such as the Bible salesman in "Good Country People" perhaps figure in the creation of Redmon's Arthur Marsdan. Appealing to Redmon's literary as well as religious interests is Dante's *Inferno,* and Elizabeth Ammons has noted some similarities between this work and *Music and Silence.* Other writers whom Redmon admires and who have influenced her thought and possibly her art are Emily Dickinson, Henry James, and William Faulkner. Among her contemporaries she admires Patrick White, Joyce Carol Oates, Wilson Harris, and Milan Kundera.

Perhaps the most intricately developed feature of Redmon's art is her management of diverse narrative voices. Each of her three published works exhibits a unique narrative voice; indeed, *Music and Silence* contains two distinctive voices complexly intertwined in a composition approximating the musical fugue. *Emily Stone* is narrated in first person by the title character, Emily, whose main point in telling her story is to "crack [the] bones" of Sasha Courtney, to decipher through the art of narrative what her reason alone cannot discover. Emily tells a story which is chronologically fragmented to follow the pattern of her musings. Chapters intersect to reveal to the reader insights which ultimately elude Emily herself. Her nemesis is her exaggerated pragmatic approach to life as well as her failure or inability to love owing to an atrophied or absent spiritual dimension. To such facts she remains blind even as the reader discovers within the interstices between narrative segments the essential mystery which Emily pursues. In *Music and Silence,* Redmon further develops this use of narrative silence—the use of interstices or gaps in which the reader must draw together fragments or strands of narrative—in ways which *Emily Stone* only begins to anticipate. Held together like the separate but harmonious melodies of a fugue, the voices of *Mu-*

sic and Silence are arranged in a manner which demands from the reader a highly developed ability to "listen" to narrative voices and the silences between them, just as the fugue requires from its audience a finely tuned ear for hearing the relationships between melodies.

Redmon's treatment of narrative voice in her short story, "Bat Time," also merits attention. This narrator's subtle, morally ambivalent presence recalls that of Hawthorne's Miles Coverdale in *The Blithedale Romance*, or of some of James's narrators whose psychology sometimes belies their apparent detachment or good faith. The title of Redmon's story bears important implications about this narrator, whose motives are understated like the references to the bats in the story. Morally inert, the narrator and her husband, like vampire bats, thrive on the energy of other beings: their young college students and the young woman protagonist, Augusta Madden. In the latter's case, even when they witness injustice or cruelty they seem strangely unable to take action. They merely observe, for they are artists for whom life is raw material. The narrator is as subtly ominous as the bat, named "Dracula," which takes up residence in Augusta's room. Indeed, during "bat time" when Augusta's mother and the "psychic" succeed in blighting Augusta's future with dire predictions, the narrator knows how she should defend the girl, whom she says she loves as a daughter. However, she sits still with a "consuming interest" in Augusta's fate and watches Mrs. Madden's "cold artistic eye" as it arranges life according to its vision.

Each of Redmon's works likewise shows that its author is conscious of its status as art and of her role as artist. Redmon apparently sees art as one of the foremost vehicles of human power. Like all human endeavor, art carries with it the potential for good or for destruction; art can unite people, bridge loneliness, and even awaken higher sensibilities, as Maud's cello playing seems to do for Beatrice. But the artist can also "consume" life with a "cold eye" and thus use art for destructive purposes. A consummate but ultimately evil artist is Ilse Alba in *Music and Silence*. Like Mrs. Madden in "Bat Time," she ruins lives just for the pleasure of orchestrating them according to her misguided, selfish but powerful will.

Sensing the profound power of art, Redmon believes that the artist always has a responsibility to humanity. In an interview she declares that to "scandalize" or "shock" a reader without leading that person to "constructive" thought could never be her purpose. Instead, she feels her duty as an artist is to enhance the personal awareness of the reader: "I believe that reading is a creative activity. . . . My most earnest desire is to create a bond between myself and my reader"; "I want people to find . . . the means of meeting their own inner source."

Currently at work on a third novel, Anne Redmon promises to enhance further her status as an important contemporary American author. Owing to its thematic, philosophical, and aesthetic range and depth, her fiction invites inquiry from a number of critical perspectives. Although she cannot be described primarily as a feminist author, her works are also of much interest to scholars of women's studies, for they represent experience from a variety of traditionally and nontraditionally female points of view. Redmon's strong sense of literary tradition places her works clearly within the mainstream of American fiction; her unique management of characterization, architectonic structure, and narrative voice defines her works as some of the most original and distinctive recently to appear.

References:

Elizabeth Ammons, "Infanticide and Other Ways of Mothering in Anne Redmon's *Music and Silence*," *Texas Studies in Literature and Language*, 25 (1983): 343-363;

Catherine Rainwater, "A Bibliography of Writings by Anne Redmon," *Texas Studies in Literature and Language*, 25 (1983): 364-366;

Rainwater, "The Fugal Procedure of Anne Redmon's *Music and Silence*," *Contemporary American Women Writers: Narrative Strategies*, edited by Rainwater and William J. Scheick (Lexington: University Press of Kentucky, 1985), pp. 69-86;

Rainwater and William J. Scheick, "An Interview With Anne Redmon," *Texas Studies in Literature and Language*, 25 (1983): 323-342;

Rainwater and Scheick, " 'Some Godlike Grammar': An Introduction to the Writings of Hazzard, Ozick, and Redmon," *Texas Studies in Literature and Language*, 25 (1983): 181-211.

Erich Segal
(16 June 1937-   )

Mary S. Dye

BOOKS: *Roman Laughter: The Comedy of Plautus* (Cambridge: Harvard University Press, 1968; revised and enlarged, London: Oxford University Press, 1987);

Love Story (New York: Harper & Row, 1970);

Fairy Tale (New York: Harper & Row, 1973);

Oliver's Story (New York: Harper & Row, 1977);

Man, Woman and Child (New York: Harper & Row, 1980);

The Class (Toronto & New York: Bantam, 1985).

SCREENPLAYS: *Yellow Submarine*, by Segal, Lee Minoff, Al Brodax, and Jack Mendelsohn, United Artists, 1968;

The Games, 20th Century-Fox, 1969;

Love Story, Paramount Pictures, 1970;

R.P.M., Stanley Kramer-Columbia Pictures, 1971;

Jennifer On My Mind, United Artists, 1971;

Oliver's Story, Paramount Pictures, 1978;

A Change of Seasons, Ransohoff-Columbia, 1980;

Man, Woman and Child, Paramount Pictures, 1983.

OTHER: *Euripides: A Collection of Critical Essays*, edited by Segal (Englewood Cliffs, N.J.: Prentice-Hall, 1968);

Plautus: Three Comedies, edited and translated by Segal (New York: Harper & Row, 1969);

The Oxford Readings in Greek Tragedy, edited by Segal (New York: Harper & Row, 1983; Oxford: Oxford University Press, 1983);

Caesar Augustus: Seven Aspects, edited by Segal and Fergus Millar (Oxford: Oxford University Press, 1984);

The Dialogues of Plato, edited with an introduction by Segal (New York: Bantam, 1986).

After twenty-five years in the academic profession, novelist and Yale classics scholar Erich Segal has four best-selling novels, a children's book, five critical works, and over fifty scholarly articles and reviews to his credit, and a fifth novel in progress. Ironically, Segal is best known for *Love Story* (1970), his first attempt at fiction, and he has never completely escaped the stigma of being largely identified as a pop writer.

Born 16 June 1937, in Brooklyn, New York, to Rabbi Samuel Michael Segal and Cynthia Shapiro Segal, Erich Wolf Segal traces his beginnings as a writer to the age of two when he dictated "endless biblical and historical" pageants to his mother. Segal was also interested in music at an early age, and his first real writing was for the stage. He wrote the book, music, and lyrics for *Voulez-Vous?*, a revue that played in Boston in 1960. Segal composed the orchestral music for the production that inaugurated the Jewett Art Center of Wellesley College in 1959. The play was Shakespeare's *All's Well That Ends Well* in which Segal costarred with Ali MacGraw.

He then wrote the book and lyrics for *Sing Muse!*, an Off-Broadway play spoofing the Trojan War that premiered in 1960. Although his first royalties were earned for *Sing Muse!*, Segal classifies himself as a "failed musical-comedy playwright:" *Sing Muse!* ran for only thirty-nine performances. Segal also wrote the lyrics to "Odyssey," a musical which was produced at the Kennedy Center in Washington, D.C., in 1974 and starred Yul Brynner.

Segal graduated from Harvard University in 1958 with a bachelor of arts degree and was named class poet as well as Latin salutatorian, the only time in Harvard's 350-year history that one man received both honors. He went on to receive his M.A. in 1959 and Ph.D. in 1965 from Harvard. While an undergraduate, he was on the varsity track team, an activity the former Boston marathoner has only recently given up for daily swimming. He served as a visiting lecturer at Yale University from 1964 to 1965; as an assistant professor from 1965 to 1968; and as an associate professor of classics and comparative literature from 1968 to 1972. Segal was a Guggenheim Fellow in 1968. He has also taught at the University of Munich, Princeton University, Dartmouth College, and was a visiting fellow at Wolfson College in Oxford in 1978, 1979, and 1980. He has been a full professor of classics

Dust jacket for Erich Segal's first and most successful novel

at Yale University since 1981, although he is not teaching there currently. Segal decided to take two years off from Yale to help promote *The Class* (1985), his latest novel. He has made his base in England, where he is now a regular fellow of Wolfson College, Oxford.

A brilliant student at Harvard, he was influenced by classics professor Cedric Whitman and comparative literature professor Harry Levin, whose scholarship provided the foundation for Segal's dissertation. When it was subsequently published as *Roman Laughter: The Comedy of Plautus* (1968), the book was regarded as a scholarly breakthrough. It was the first book on Plautus in English as well as the first book to explain what made the Romans laugh. Segal broadened his study to appeal to the layman by providing translations (which J. N. Hough in the December 1968 *Classical World* considered "excellent") to passages excerpted in the original Latin. Hough also said "it is refreshing to find Plautus examined for what he undeniably was—a theatrical phenomenon."

Segal's next scholarly endeavor was to serve as editor of *Euripides: A Collection of Critical Essays* (1968), which featured nine studies of some of Eu-

ripides better known plays including "Medea", "Hippolytus", "Alcestis", and the "Bacchae". The volume was praised by *Choice* in their March 1969 review, for it's "high quality of style and content," and was recommended as an extremely useful source for both the beginning classics student and the more advanced scholar.

Euripides: A Collection of Critical Essays was followed by *Plautus: Three Comedies* (1969) for which Segal served as editor and translator. It too was fairly well received, though in this instance, Segal's abilities as a translator were not singled out. *Book World* noted that "the introduction and notes are straightforward, helpful and fairly jazzy, but the translations themselves are not much better than, or different from, the other modern translations of Plautus, all of which have some areas of felicity and some pretty lumpy passages here and there."

Segal has continued his interest in academic writing, despite his success as a novelist. In 1984 he co-edited *Caesar Augustus: Seven Aspects,* with Fergus Millar. In a letter to Segal published in Edmund Wilson's *Letters on Literature and Politics: 1912-1972* (1977) Wilson commented that Segal had been extremely successful in "catching the sense and following the meter," and had "managed to avoid Gilbert and Sullivan, to which the translators of Aristophanes had found it difficult not to succumb."

Curiously, for a man with an academic background, Segal began his career as a commercial author writing for the screen. In 1967 during a summer break from Yale, he collaborated on the Beatles's popular cartoon film, *Yellow Submarine* (1968). In 1969 he wrote *The Games*, a multiple-character film about runners who meet in the Olympic marathon, and *R.P.M.*, which focused on a college campus revolution. In 1971 Segal wrote the script for *Jennifer On My Mind*, a black comedy about drug abuse among the New York rich. Segal has continued writing for the screen, though mostly limiting himself to adaptations of his own work.

It was while at Yale as an associate professor that Segal wrote an original screenplay based on a girl he had once dated and on a conversation between two students that he overheard. "I sat down and started writing immediately," Segal told Phil Casey in a 1971 interview with the *Washington Post*. "The story poured out of me. I changed everything except the girl's death and the fact that she supports her husband through graduate school."

When there were no offers to produce *Love Story* as a film, Segal rewrote it as a novel, which he completed in six weeks. Published in February 1970, the 131-page volume made nationwide best-seller lists almost immediately and remained number one for over a year. A Gallup poll showed in 1971 that one out of every five Americans had read the book. There had been twenty-one hardcover printings of *Love Story* by the end of April 1971, totaling 500,000 copies. The first paperback edition run by the New American Library (which sold for ninety-five cents each) had been 4,325,000 copies, the largest single printing in the history of movable type. An article in the 21 December 1970 issue of *Time* magazine noted that booksellers' orders were so frantic that within twenty-four hours a second printing of 650,000 paperback copies was ordered. By the time it reached its fifth printing it was selling at 1,200 copies a day. *Love Story* was translated into over twenty foreign languages, some supervised by Segal, and was simultaneously a best-seller in the United States, England, France, Italy, Brazil, Japan, and Germany. It was also published in India and (without the author's permission) in Communist China.

The essence of this record-breaking story is the old-fashioned, tried-and-true formula of young love opposed by elders, but with a twist: boy meets girl, boy gets girl, girl dies. The boy is Oliver Barrett IV, a wealthy Harvard jock who meets Jennifer Cavelleri, a poor Radcliffe student, in the fall of their senior year. After smart-talking their way into each other's hearts, the pair are off and running towards an endearing and sentimental romance. The dialogue is clean, crisp, and witty throughout the fast-paced melodrama. According to Segal, it intimately reflected the attitudes of college students in the early 1960s prior to the social rebellion that occurred over the violent reaction to the Vietnam War. "*Love Story*," Segal told *Publisher's Weekly* in a February 1970 interview, "is based on what I have observed among my students, living as I do right on campus. It deals with today's personal commitment of one to one and the quest for a permanent relationship which begins much younger than it used to. The old mindless football-game dating is gone. The question of sexual morality is irrelevant, but there is much less 'swinging' among young people now than in the old days."

Oliver and Jennifer are premature yuppies: they are extremely conventional, hard-working, goal-oriented students whom any parent would be delighted to claim. Despite the vast differences in their social and family backgrounds, it seems natural that they be together. They are married in a touching, Unitarian ceremony presided over by the college chaplain during which they quote vows each have selected for the other.

Jenny good-naturedly forsakes her ambitions and teaches music to elementary school students to put Oliver through law school, after they are cut off—emotionally and financially—by Oliver's family. When Oliver graduates third in his class and is employed by a "very prestigious and civil-liberties oriented" firm in New York, they relax and begin planning a family. It is when their attempts to have a baby fail that they consult the physician who eventually diagnoses Jenny's leukemia.

The conclusion comes quickly after this shattering revelation, and it is difficult for even the most casual reader not to shed a tear at Jenny's deathbed scene. Through Segal's use of Oliver as the first-person narrator, the reader empathizes with Oliver standing in Jenny's hospital room, joking up to the last minute, promising he'll take care of her father and himself, and telling her (without telling her) good-bye.

An often overlooked aspect of *Love Story* is that the subject matter is as much about parent-child relationships as it is about husband-wife relationships. From the beginning of the novel Segal, through Oliver Barrett III, is constantly reminding the reader of the parallels between Oliver III and Oliver IV. There is an unconscious competition between the two men, academically and athletically, even if Oliver IV is only competing with his father's past accomplishments in those areas. Oliver is never outwardly disobedient or rude until his father expresses extreme reservations about Jenny. At that point, Oliver walks out of his father's life, determined to be free of the perceived albatross of his father's high expectations which he had carried throughout his life but which he nonetheless lived up to.

On the other hand, Jenny and her father, Phil Cavelleri, a baker from Cranston, Rhode Island, share an intense devotion to one another from the novel's inception to its tearful conclusion, and they are bewildered by the constant bickering between Oliver and his father. Phil has strong (if simple) values and expectations from life. He is the sole source of parental support for the struggling couple; the only one who is wise enough to not only allow them to make their own decisions but to respect them as well.

Segal's "universal message" seems to be that money can't buy happiness. Not particularly original, but apparently one that the reading public identified with, since *Love Story* was a phenomenal success. Moreover, Segal's novel was a refreshing change from the sexually explicit books that had become the literary norm. "My God, nobody can believe the success of this book," Segal told *Newsday* in a 1970 interview. "It smashes all precedents. It's going to reverse the whole 'Portnoy's Complaint,' 'I am Curious (Yellow)' syndrome!"

There were several positive reviews; particularly Barbara Bannon's for the 2 February 1970 issue of *Publisher's Weekly*. Bannon calls the novel "a very simple, immensely appealing love story, with memorable characterizations that haunt you long after you've finished the book." But the novel was critically panned on a large scale. S. K. Oberbeck, reviewing the novel in *Newsweek* (9 March 1970), declared, "*Love Story* makes 'Peyton Place' look like 'Swann's Way' as it skips from cliche to cliche with an abandon that would chill even the blood of a True Romance editor." Writing *Love Story* even had a damaging effect on Segal's academic career. "I came within a year of getting tenure at Yale," he told Wendy Smith of the *Chicago Tribune*, "but unfortunately in that one year, as was said jokingly to me, although I didn't laugh, I published one book too many. Really, it's human. They were hostile, they were deprecating, they were implying—and sometimes saying explicitly—that I

had sold out, that I had vulgarized myself, or that in fact I was always vulgar, and had shown my true colors." Segal told *People* magazine in a 1985 interview that he had apologized to his elders in the academic world, hoping to appease them. "But am I really sorry I wrote *Love Story?*," he said. "Bull----. I'm overjoyed I did." A decade after being denied tenure, Segal was invited back as full professor of classics at Yale.

In 1973 Segal published *Fairy Tale*, his first and only book for children. The story features a hero named Jake Kertuffel from Poop's Peak Mountain, who embarks on a journey to the Big City to trade the family's "old-fangled model T-4-2" for a new "coupe" and along the way encounters a greedy villain, named Happy Humphrey, the Used Car Dealer. The pace of the tale is snappy and the tone often amusing, though much of Segal's witticisms are probably too sophisticated for many children to appreciate.

In 1974 Segal met his future wife, Karen Marianne James, an editor, on a blind date. The couple was married a year later and have a daughter, Francesca, born in August 1980. Segal's wife is always his first reader.

In 1977 Segal wrote *Oliver's Story*, the obligatory sequel to *Love Story*. According to a 1980 interview in the *New York Times*, *Oliver's Story* was "written under the duress of self-doubt, writer's block and the curse of being called a one-off writer." Nevertheless, it rose to the top of the bestseller list, yet it did not enjoy the popularity of its predecessor. In *Oliver's Story* Segal has Oliver, two years after Jenny's death, still grieving and feeling guilty over his loss. He sees a psychologist—who can't help him—and after a brief whirlwind romance with Marcie Binnendale, the love interest in this story, decides that total love only comes along once in a lifetime. Segal portrays Marcie as the opposite of Jenny. As the owner of a chain of upscale department stores, she has the social position that Jenny lacked, but she is lacking in the natural emotional warmth that was at the core of Jenny's character. Also, as an advocate of such things as physical fitness and women's liberation, Marcie is representative of the time in which she lived (mid 1970s), unlike Jenny, who was ahead of hers in the sense that she was an intelligent woman who was willing to support her husband through law school as a means to an end.

The two fathers who were key figures in *Love Story* are also prominent in *Oliver's Story,* though both have changed. Oliver and his father have made peace, and Oliver eventually inherits his father's partnership in the Boston investment banking firm of Barrett, Ward and Seymour. Jenny's father, while still caring and supportive, is perhaps a bit too understanding of Oliver's acceptance of his daughter's death, in that he encourages the romance with Marcie.

By the novel's conclusion, Oliver is still a grieving widower, though wiser since he has come to terms with his life and values. Segal gives *Oliver's Story* a "let's wrap-it-up" finality that was missing from *Love Story,* while allowing that *Oliver's Story* is infinitely sadder than *Love Story* due to Oliver's profound and mature realizations about life.

Oliver's Story, though not a critical success, did receive better reviews than *Love Story.* H. T. Anderson, in his June 1977 review for *Best Sellers,* said, "The book is filled with right-on issues and right-on people, bright people (legal and energetic and concerned) who punctuate with four letter words and are covered with youth and honesty."

Segal followed *Oliver's Story* with *Man, Woman and Child* in 1980. His third novel, also set in New England, is in the same genre as his two previous efforts, but features a new hero, Bob Beckwith, a professor of statistics at M.I.T. and a father with a guilty conscience. He and his wife, Sheila, an editor for the Harvard University Press, had what everyone thought was the perfect marriage until a past infidelity which suddenly disrupts their home comes to light. Bob reveals to an appropriately shocked Sheila that he was involved in a brief affair ten years earlier when in France delivering a lecture at the Sorbonne. The result of this affair is his son, Jean-Claude, who has been orphaned and has nowhere to go. After hearing the entire story—and banishing Bob to sleep on the couch—Sheila allows the child to come live with them for the summer. The Beckwiths' two young daughters, Jessica and Paula, ultimately learn the truth about Jean-Claude's parentage but surprisingly there is little lasting resentment or sibling rivalry between them. And Sheila, the wounded victim, is sympathetic and maternally comforting to Jean-Claude. By the end of the novel, after much hurt and growing and understanding has taken place between the family members, the Beckwiths ask Jean-Claude to stay as part of the family. But he decides to return to France and attend St. Malo, a school for boys that his mother had planned on him attending as soon as he was old enough. On his departure, though promising to visit, it is clear they will never see one another again.

The central problem with this novel, as the critics were quick to point out, is that the family's reactions to Jean-Claude's existence and presence in their home are simply not realistic. When reviewing the novel, Janet Maslin, in the *New York Times* (4 April 1983), said, "*Man, Woman and Child* which bears the unmistakable stamp of its author, Erich Segal, is about wonderful people coping wonderfully with a situation that would seriously frazzle just about anybody else." The movie version fared no better. Gary Arnold, in his review for the *Washington Post* (4 April 1983), blasted Segal for creating a third "Weepie Lit" story and felt that the whole notion of the "perfect marriage" was preposterous to begin with. "Segal may be one of the last educated persons on Earth who still finds it appropriate to blubber about abstractions as fundamentally ridiculous and unattainable as 'the perfect marriage,' " he said. "No one outside the willfully naive confines of heartache fiction would dare to take such a term seriously or even desire the cosmetic, placid sort of relationship it implies."

Nonetheless, Segal appears determined to write novels that deal with the traditional ideals of love and marriage, and oddly enough, he places his male characters in positions that are inferior to women. Arnold attributes this to "Segal's awestruck conception of women [which] is as grossly sentimentalized and cliched as his poor-dears conception of men."

The dialogue for *Man, Woman and Child* was apparently written with the idea that it would be adapted into a screenplay, which it was. Segal attributes this style, which places emphasis on sparse dialogue as opposed to setting, to his experiences as a screenwriter in Hollywood and noted that it is a device that has been successful for him.

Segal, the academician, once labeled his writing of light fiction for the public his hobby, noting that the only similarity between his novels and his scholarly writings was that they were both bound and set on shelves. That was prior to writing *The Class,* which Segal considers a major turning point in his life. *The Class,* which has more plot and a larger number of central characters than his previous works, is about five men looking back at their lives after a twenty-five-year separation, which Segal was inspired to write after attending his own twenty-fifth Harvard reunion. He identifies with each character and admits that each character is based partly on himself.

Bantam Books paid Segal over $1,000,000 for *The Class.* He did extensive research on generations of Harvard alumni to get a true feeling for the college's history and traditions. Segal focuses on five characters, all men: Ted Lambros, a Greek of humble beginnings who becomes a classics scholar; Jason Gilbert, a popular jock who becomes a Zionist and dies a hero in the raid on Entebbe (in which Segal's own mother had been a hostage); Danny Rossi, an extremely gifted pianist, composer, and conductor who sacrifices personal relationships for fame and fortune; Andrew Eliot, the narrator, who is a "Boston Brahmin" descended from generations of Harvard alumni and who is drawn as probably the most levelheaded of the group; and George Keller, a Hungarian refugee who excels in political propaganda and becomes famous as Henry Kissinger's protégé. Each has successes; each has failures. Each takes stock of his life over the twenty-five-year period and comes to terms with what they have become by the time of the reunion.

One must give Segal his due and admit that he knows his Harvard. The story embodies the stereotypical perception of an Ivy League college, while at the same time offering insight into the more sensitive and sensible side of many of its students. Yet Segal has said that *The Class* isn't really a Harvard novel, although nearly one-third of the story takes place in the Harvard setting. Segal is apparently referring to the message that money isn't everything, and success can't buy you happiness, which runs parallel to the Harvard theme.

The Class, at over five hundred pages, is longer than his first three novels put together, and Segal desperately wanted it to be taken seriously. The 21 April 1985 *New York Times* review, while neither wholeheartedly positive or negative, was better than expected. "He is a good enough storyteller that despite the dead language, the reader still wants to find out what happens to his characters," said Susan Isaacs. "If the writing were better, the reader would probably stay up the entire night turning pages. As it is, he can wait until the next day, or, indeed, the day after that, to find out what happened to the members of Harvard's class of '58." Isaacs also noted that Segal's writing relied too heavily on clichés—a device that had caused less than enthusiastic reception by the critics of his previous works—and that he opted to summarize rather than develop in detail the story and the lives of the characters, a sometimes frustrating tactic. *The Class* spent seventeen weeks on the *New York Times* best-seller list and has recently been purchased as a television miniseries. It received the Premio Selezione Bancarella award in Italy (best novel of the year), and it received the Prix Deauville at the 1986 Deauville Film Festival. The prize is awarded annually by the film festival for the best American book published in France; its previous winners include Norman Mailer, Elie Wiesel, and Gore Vidal.

When asked what his long-term goals for writing are, Segal's response seems downhearted. "I have this quixotic dream that some day I'll get a little critical recognition for my novels," he said in a 1986 interview with *Contemporary Authors*. "No one would nominate me for anything in America, except hack of the month. Success poisons the possibility of objective critical appraisal. Maybe when I've been dead two hundred years. . . . I know only too well from my particular studies of classical antiquity that some of the greatest authors, now masters, were considered 'just fun' by their contemporaries—whether it be Aristophanes or Plautus or even Shakespeare. (I hasten to say that I don't compare myself with any of those giants.) Shakespeare was the most popular thing going in the theatre in his time, but he was mercilessly panned by the 'serious' critics. He had to die to become a classic." Segal's sixth novel, *Doctors*, is scheduled for publication in 1988.

Interviews:

Barbara A. Bannon, "Authors and Editors," *Publisher's Weekly*, 197 (2 February 1970): 51-53;

Phil Casey, "Erich Segal: The Loved One-Poor Little Kitsch Boy," *Washington Post*, 11 February 1971, C1;

Wendy Smith, "Segal: 'Class' Author Comes Down to Earth," *Chicago Tribune*, 5 May 1985, pp. 14-15.

Scott Spencer
(1 September 1945-   )

Michael Mullen
Indian Hills Community College

BOOKS: *Last Night at the Brain Thieves' Ball* (Boston: Houghton Mifflin, 1973);
Preservation Hall (New York: Knopf, 1976; London: Hutchinson, 1978);
Endless Love (New York: Knopf, 1979; London: Cape, 1980);
Waking the Dead (New York: Knopf, 1986).

SCREENPLAY: *Act of Vengeance*, HBO, 1985.

PERIODICAL PUBLICATIONS: "Three Finished First Novels," *New York Times Book Review*, 7 September 1980, pp. 13, 30;
"How is Fiction Doing?," *New York Times Book Review*, 14 December 1980, pp. 3, 30.
"John Lennon," *Rolling Stone* (22 January 1981): 12-13;
"Guilty Pleasures," *Film Comment*, 17 (September/October 1981): 21-23;
"Updike Delux," *Esquire*, 100 (November 1983): 197-198.

Scott Spencer has said, "There is really nothing interesting about my life of a biographical nature—born, raised, educated, etc., etc., or, if it would make it more interesting for you, nothing I care to divulge. . . ." After maintaining a very low profile through the publication of his novels, he finally spoke of his life and work for *Conversations with American Writers* (1985) by Charles Ruas.

Spencer was born in Washington, D.C., and grew up in Chicago. His father was a steelworker and a CIO organizer. His mother was also politically active—Spencer described her as "a radical in the thirties and forties"—and both parents were interested in art. Spencer remembers that there were always books around the house and his father had dreams of being a writer—*Blue Collar*, a book about his experiences as a steelworker, was published in 1977. In the interview with Charles Ruas, Spencer says, "There is no question that a part of me wanted to be a writer because they wanted me to. I don't see how I can escape it." Whatever his motivation, Spencer started early:

I think I wrote my first novel when I was eight. I remember it quite well. I wrote a novel about a horse that was captured by the Nazis in Tunisia, and he was picked up and rescued and rehabilitated by an American film crew filming a Buster Crabbe desert epic. Then I wrote a novel about separated twins. *The Prince and the Pauper* had a tremendous influence on my imagination.

Spencer spent a lot of time writing until he was fifteen, when he began devoting his energy to reading and political activities. Before being expelled from the Socialist Party because of a document he wrote that insulted International Social Democracy, he had become executive secretary of the Illinois Socialist Party. At about the time he was curtailing his political activities, Spencer started college and resumed writing. Though he has never said that his declining involvement in things political affected his desire to write, he has stated that there was a direct relationship between his going to college and writing:

College was really my first time away from home. I think that's really what it was, being completely on my own. That's when I started writing again, but I had really no voice. It was so filled with fanatical flourishes and complete insecurities. I felt certain that if I were to endure the scrutiny of others at a time like that, it would have had a demoralizing effect on me. It was very hard for me to tell people that I even *was* a writer. In college I never worked on the literary magazines or took a writing course, and I would hang around with people who wanted to be writers and they all talked about who is a genius and what it felt like to be a genius, and I don't think that six of them knew that I ever put pen to paper, and I wrote all the time.

Two of the writers who influenced Spencer most were Nabokov and Hemingway. From Nabokov, he says, he "learned a large portion of what

Dust jacket for Spencer's second novel, published in 1976

I know about writing." Reading Hemingway taught him how to keep information from the reader, "and that wonderful lesson of how to seduce the reader into accepting your frame of reference. . . ."

Though he attended the University of Illinois for a period, he transferred to the University of Wisconsin at Madison and graduated in 1969. In a recent letter answering a question about his publications before his first novel, Spencer wrote that there was nothing in print before the publication of *Last Night at the Brain Thieves' Ball* in 1973. The introductory material preceding Ruas's interview with Spencer states that Spencer's earliest works were articles written for the *Chicago Tribune*, *Harper's*, and *Redbook*, and that Spencer published short stories under a pseudonym. These have not been located. Michiko Kakutani, in his article "Portrait of the Artist as a First Novelist" in the *New York Times Book Review*, also referred to this early work, noting that one of the things Spencer did to support himself was ghostwrite short stories for women's magazines.

On a more modest scale, Spencer's career parallels that of John Irving. His first two novels met with critical success, but financial success was not forthcoming. Because Spencer had always known

that he wanted to be a writer, he did not take up teaching as a career, which would, he claimed, only have increased his avenues of escape..He therefore did not return to college after completing his B.A. Among the jobs he held before the success of *Endless Love* (1979), which gave him the freedom to devote all his time to writing, were working in an employment agency and being an evaluator for education programs financed by the federal government.

Last Night at the Brain Thieves' Ball, Spencer said, taught him "how to get from the beginning to the end of a novel." The idea for the novel came from "a friend who, after living a completely bohemian, ragtag Lower East Side experience, suddenly felt that it was time for him to take some realistic steps, so he got a job at IBM. He showed me around one day, and I saw these crazy-looking geniuses sitting in their cubicles, staring off into space with these printouts around them."

Paul Galambos, the central figure, is a young psychology professor whose thirst for power motivates him to apply for a position with NESTER (New England Sensory Testing and Engineering Research), a secret company interested in controlling people's desires through the use of implants in the brain. He soon becomes dissatisfied and starts writing a journal (the novel) which will expose NESTER. In a conclusion some reviewers disliked, Galambos finally manages to escape, an action he'd long been contemplating, but he is captured and returned to the NESTER complex. His supervisor, Mr. Worthington, releases him from his contract and explains, during the ride to Boston where Galambos will be released, that he was their first recruit to be rehabilitated. Worthington tells Galambos that he had been accepted because he was a danger to society, that the experiments he'd done for NESTER were fake, and that all the data he'd been given was fabricated. Before he is released, in front of a Boston city hospital, Galambos's hand is cut off by Worthington, who tells him, "... you cannot altogether escape your punishment."

Spencer has said that he writes one book at a time; so, while his books do have elements in common, most notably characters whose desires place them in opposition to society, each is unique. *Last Night at the Brain Thieves' Ball* is Spencer's only comic novel, though it has not always been seen as such. No one at Houghton Mifflin, which published the novel, considered it comic, reading it instead, Spencer said, "as a serious cautionary tale." Spencer was unconcerned about the misinterpretation since he believed it would be corrected by reviewers. The first review of the book he saw was in *Library Journal*. Reacting to the reviewer's comparison of the book to Orwell's *Nineteen Eighty-Four*, Spencer said: "God, I'm sunk. No one's getting it."

He was not sunk. Whether or not reviewers understood the comic intent of the novel, the book was generally well received. The *Publishers Weekly* reviewer, who felt the book fell flat at the end, said, "For much of the way this first novel is a clever and witty satire on the kind of electronic snooping and secret manipulation of people's lives that lies behind Watergate." More enthusiastic was the anonymous *Psychology Today* reviewer: "The obvious comparison for Spencer is Kurt Vonnegut; although their styles differ, both writers deftly mix comedy, social comment and science fiction. But read Spencer for himself; within a few years we may be comparing other writers to him."

About his first novel, Spencer later said: "I was learning how to write, and I think in an accountant sense I didn't want to disturb my store of personal vision for a novel written with the skills I possessed at that time. I have always been shy about being a writer. I wasn't ready to commit the double audaciousness of trying to publish a novel and also

having a subject that I cared deeply about. I needed the ironic remove of writing what I considered essentially a dark entertainment." *Preservation Hall*, published three years later, in 1976, marked an increase in both his confidence and his skill as a writer. It is approximately a third longer than *Last Night at the Brain Thieves' Ball*, and deals with a more complex theme.

Spencer's main concern in *Preservation Hall* is "the man who fundamentally does not know if he's bad or good," and this, he believes, connects the novel with *Last Night at the Brain Thieves' Ball*. Like Paul Galambos, the main character in *Preservation Hall*, Virgil Morgan, is not sure who he is or what his place in the world is, and to learn these things, he must pay a price for them. Virgil sees himself as autonomous (his mother ran away when he was five and he has, since he was a child, despised and been embarrassed by his father, an eccentric composer) and buys a country house in Maine, Preservation Hall, where he and his wife go to spend the New Year's holiday. They are visited by Virgil's stepbrother and his stepbrother's girlfriend, and while the four of them are snowed in, an accident occurs that ultimately disrupts the order of Virgil's life. While smashing a dresser they intend to burn in the fireplace, Virgil kills his stepbrother with a poker. Not certain what role his dislike for his stepbrother played in causing the fatal accident, Virgil is forced to come to terms with what is good and bad in himself. This eventually leads him to reevaluate his relationship with his father in an attempt to expiate the guilt he still feels about killing his stepbrother.

As with his first novel, *Preservation Hall* was not widely reviewed, but again the reception was favorable. *Publishers Weekly* called *Preservation Hall* an "about-face" from his first novel and said, " 'Preservation Hall,' with its deeply personal passion and anguish, is in fact in the province of a first novel, yet it's written with such expert control that one is glad the author waited to tackle its larger theme." The reviewer added that "the novel stings at our age-old fears and makes the pain seem fresh and revelatory."

Preservation Hall was reviewed in the *New York Times Book Review* by Katha Pollitt, who described the novel as "readable and swiftly paced." She felt it triumphed over its weaknesses, most apparent of which was a predictable plot. On the strengths of the novel she called attention to the characterizations of Earl, Virgil's father, "a complex, original figure," and closed by saying: "It's a mark of Spencer's skill that although we hear the whole story

Scott Spencer

DLB Yearbook 1986

*Dust jacket for Spencer's 1979 breakthrough novel which was
warmly received by reviewers and readers*

from Virgil's point of view, ultimately Earl's resentment of his son's success seems less mean-spirited than Virgil's shame at his father's failure. Since the first-person in fiction nowadays is all too often the voice of sheer self-justification on the part of the author-as-hero, Spencer deserves a good deal of praise for having the imagination to know more about his characters than they do themselves."

Spencer's breakthrough novel was *Endless Love*, published in September of 1979. When he began *Endless Love*, Spencer moved to Vermont with his wife and lived on unemployment compensation, what he called "my version of the National Endowment for the Arts grant." Two years later he was out of money and they moved back to New York, where he took a job and completed the novel. The novel as published is the third attempt at the story of David Axelrod's obsessive love for Jade Butterfield. What Spencer always had, he said, "was the title, *Endless Love*, from the Delmore Schwartz poem, and that was the feeling I wanted to convey

in the book." What was not clear was how to present that feeling.

The first version of the novel began with David and Jade's first meeting and was told in third person. About the various drafts of the novel, Spencer told Ruas: "I would always write about a hundred fifty pages and then get that nauseous feeling that I was going in the wrong direction. You can tell because when you begin your day's work it doesn't seem ready, you have to shake it loose, and when I get the narrative right everything's alert and waiting for me the next day."

His second attempt was also a false start. This version, which stretched to three hundred pages before he abandoned it, had the characters sharing narrative duties. He found that he had presented a lot of detail, but not much action. Finally he decided to open with the fire David sets on the porch of Jade's parents' house, and let David narrate. "It wasn't easy to write," Spencer said, "but that draft went all the way through. That was the first time that I could end the book."

The purpose of the fire that David starts at the beginning of the novel is an attempt to prove his value to the Butterfield family. As a result of that fire the house is destroyed. David confesses to the crime and is institutionalized for two years and barred from any contact with the Butterfields. After he is released, he discovers that Ann, Jade's mother, is living in New York, and goes to visit her. While there he is seen by Hugh, Jade's father, who is struck by a taxi and killed while crossing the street against the light in his attempt to reach David. His death brings Jade to New York, where David is reunited with her, and they go to Stoughton, Vermont, where she is finishing college. She discovers his role in her father's death and locks him out, finally turning him in to the police. He is again institutionalized, during which time Jade marries. At the end of the novel David is living with another woman, but he writes Jade telling her that his love for her has not diminished.

In his interview with Ruas, Spencer said that Virgil Morgan "was raised by unrealized people, and these people used him as a mirror." This element links *Preservation Hall* and *Endless Love*, since Spencer also said that David, "once he enters the Butterfield family, acts as a reflection of all its missing, unfulfilled needs for different members of the family—and in that sense shows up all the cracks in that structure." What distinguishes *Endless Love* from Spencer's previous books is that the question of retribution loses some of its significance, because David's belief that his desire is good for Jade and

332

for himself makes him willing to pay forever for it.

Spencer also told Ruas that "all my writing life I've been trying to write in the third person. I feel it's an idea of the dignity of the novel that makes me think it ought to be in third person." His statement is surprising because Spencer handles first-person narration so effectively. As Katha Pollitt noted in her review of *Preservation Hall*, Spencer had presented Virgil Morgan in such a way that the reader could see both his strengths and weaknesses even though the story was told by Virgil. In *Endless Love*, Spencer avoids the similar problem of unreliable first-person narration by peopling the novel with enough clear-headed and well-drawn counterparts to David so that his psychological disorder does not hinder his credibility as the narrator.

If critics had reservations about Spencer before, or if he had been only "a writer of promise," *Endless Love* changed that. As Larry Swindell said in his *Village Voice* review, "Hearts on Fire," the novel is "Spencer's very fulfillment. He has shown just what he can do." The reviews are littered with superlatives. Swindell called the novel "courageous" and Spencer's technique "provocative"; "*Endless Love* is triumphantly a novel of character and action," he wrote. He closed his review by saying, "*Endless Love* is remarkable for being an urgently compassionate novel that never becomes a sentimental one. Sentimentality is a net for emotional trapeze artists in prose. Spencer soars with no net below, and catches the bar every time."

Also excited by the novel was Edward Rothstein, whose review appeared in the *New York Times Book Review*. Spencer, he said, "has achieved something quite remarkable in this unabashedly romantic and often harrowing novel." In addition he noted that "Spencer has an acute grasp of character and situation," "great sympathy for his characters, and the skill to arouse our feelings for them." He called the novel "compelling," and "exceptionally powerful."

An indication of the novel's success is the wide range of periodicals that reviewed it. *Endless Love* was reviewed in *Mother Jones* ("The book seems to get teen-age desire down as well as anything since *Romeo and Juliet*") and *Penthouse* ("a remarkable and disturbing work of fiction"), *English Journal* ("an unusually powerful love story") and *New Republic* ("Scott Spencer is a magnificent writer, and *Endless Love* is his finest novel"). Further indication of the success of *Endless Love* was Spencer's inclusion in Kakutani's "Portrait of the Artist as a First Novel-

ist," and his being asked, along with John Barth, Norman Mailer, Joyce Carol Oates, and others, questions for an article entitled "How is Fiction Doing?," both in the *New York Times Book Review*. Also, since the publication of *Endless Love*, Spencer has reviewed books for the *New York Times Book Review* and *Esquire*, written about movies he remembered from his childhood for *Film Comment*, and written a tribute to John Lennon for *Rolling Stone*.

In July of 1981 the movie version of *Endless Love* was released. Franco Zefferelli directed the Judith Rosco screenplay starring Brooke Shields and Martin Hewett. Most reviewers agreed that the movie was a poor adaptation of the book. Calling it "a cotton-candy rendition of Scott Spencer's powerful novel," the reviewer for *Variety* described it as "a manipulative tale of a doomed romance which careens repeatedly between the credible and the ridiculous . . . tailor-made for the 'Blue Lagoon' crowd. . . ." The reviewer complained that the screenplay straitened the book's structure and made the sex bland, that the filmmakers did not establish a clear point of view and there was confusion about when the story takes place.

Spencer was not particularly troubled by what Hollywood did to his novel, saying "I think that *Endless Love*'s becoming a film cut me off from the work." Though over three pages of his interview with Ruas is a discussion of the film, and much of it is interesting, what is most important is how the success of *Endless Love*, both as a book and as a movie, affected his writing. "The public reaction to *Endless Love*," he told Ruas, "immediately put me into competition with myself—'I sure hope the next one meets with that kind of success.' And with that bald-faced utterance, I ripped the pen from my fingers, broke it in half, and basically didn't work for about a year."

What would come to trouble him was what Hollywood did to him. For nearly five years after the publication of *Endless Love*, Spencer wrote screenplays, a decision that grew out of his struggle with *Endless Love*: working in Hollywood seemed easier than working on another novel. It was a decision he came to regret, saying, "The movie business is a lot like playing the slot machines. It doesn't take your money, but it takes some little piece of your feelings. You stay at the machine because you feel it owes you, and you play it again thinking, 'If the next one works, it will take away the bad feeling of the one before.' Finally, one day, you realize that you have been at it quite a while. It dawned on me that I'd misused my small success to create more problems than I had before the success."

Spencer's first project was *Split Image* (1982), and if seeing the way Hollywood worked was interesting, the writing was not. Dissatisfied with the way things were going, he went to see the producer. "I blew them out of the water," he said. "They had no answers to my arguments. The next day I was fired."

He then worked on *Act of Vengeance*, directed by Brian DePalma. Spencer enjoyed working with him, and liked the script, "But then nobody would make it." Made for Home Box Office, with a different director, and a smaller budget, the story of the killing of Jock Yablonski was aired in 1985.

Even a screenwriting job he enjoyed, that based on Jan Hassler's novel, *The Love Hunter* (1981), a story about a man with multiple sclerosis whose best friend falls in love with his wife, was as Spencer said, "a real experience in frustration." At first, Robert Redford, who asked Spencer to write it, said he wanted to play the MS victim. Later, after Spencer had completed the screenplay, Redford asked if he would rewrite it so Redford could be the victim's best friend. Spencer did so, but Redford, though he liked Spencer's work, was no less reluctant to make the movie.

Spencer continued his own work, but when he had problems with his novel, he came to realize the effect Hollywood was having on his writing. "In retrospect," he said, "I wasn't prepared for the price that you eventually pay as a screenwriter. The price is that you become sort of unconsciously attuned to the fact that what you write isn't going to make a difference. That can make you a little cynical, which is just death for a novelist. In order to sustain the huge improbable enterprise of writing a novel, you have to think that it does make a difference, that what you are doing is important."

The novel he was working on, *Waking the Dead*, was published in May of 1986. It tells the story of a lawyer who begins to realize some of his goals in politics at the same time as his personal life is strained by his belief that his girlfriend, whom he thought was killed in a car bombing, is alive.

The trap of sentimentality Spencer played with in *Endless Love* was replaced by melodrama in *Waking the Dead*, though fewer reviewers believed it was a trap he successfully avoided, and the critical response was generally cool. Most reviewers recognized that with *Waking the Dead*, in spire of some similarities to *Endless Love*, Spencer was attempting

something even more difficult than what he'd done in his previous book. Part of the problem seemed to be that the first person narration, which Spencer used so well in *Endless Love*, failed him here. Michiko Kakutani, in a *New York Times* review, said: "Whereas the reader was inclined to write off a lot of David's lush descriptions as the projections of a moony-eyed teen-age boy, similar passages here—spoken by Fielding, a politician verging on middle age—tend to come across as simple-minded or phony digressions."

Others felt the novel's main character, Fielding Pierce, was the cause of failure. Leading the attack was Jerold Pace, who stated in his *Chicago Tribune* review, "Character Flaws Loud Enough to Wake the Dead," that "Pierce is one of the most unlikeable characters to appear in recent American fiction." Though few faulted Spencer's writing—most would agree with Fay Weldon, in the *New York Times Book Review*, who said, "Scott Spencer is a master of the verbally intense"—this was not enough to sustain the novel.

Relatively unknown at the time of publication of *Endless Love*, Spencer now finds himself on a tightrope. New the end of her *New Republic* review of *Waking the Dead*, Dorothy Wickenden said that "Spencer tries too hard both to sustain his reputation as a popular novelist and to earn recognition as a serious writer." While this leaves many people wondering which way he will fall, Spencer himself seems both untroubled and unconcerned: "It's very easy to buy into a system of judgments and rewards that have nothing to do with what really sustains the spirit of true work and art. I don't want my own sense of myself to rise and fall on the size of my last paperback sale, or what other people are saying. I've always believed that my best work comes from keeping pretty close to my own counsel. It's just a stupid, tragic waste to forget that what really gives me pleasure is to feel I've put in a good day's work."

References:

Michiko Kakutani, "Portrait of the Artist as a First Novelist," *New York Times Book Review*, 8 June 1980, pp. 7, 38-39;

Charles Ruas, *Conversations with American Writers* (New York: Knopf, 1985), pp. 295-324;

Tony Schwartz, "Scott Spencer Comes Home," *New York* (2 June 1986): 50-59.

Susan Allen Toth
(24 June 1940-   )

Patricia L. Skarda
Smith College

BOOKS: *Blooming: A Small-Town Girlhood* (Boston: Little, Brown, 1981);

Ivy Days: Making My Way Out East (Boston: Little, Brown, 1984).

PERIODICAL PUBLICATIONS: "Fantasies," *Redbook,* 149 (August 1977): 64-66;

"Poetry: Fresh Air in the Garret: A Visit with Maxine Kumin," *Ms.,* 6 (June 1978): 32;

"On Picking Raspberries," *Redbook,* 151 (August 1979);

"Going to the Movies," *Harper's,* 260 (May 1980): 99-100;

"The Cut-Glass Christmas," *Redbook,* 156 (December 1980): 84-85;

"Alarms," *Redbook,* 158 (April 1982): 38;

"Sounds," *North American Review,* 268 (March 1983): 4-5.

Susan Allen Toth (photo by Melissa Martina)

When *Blooming* was identified by the *New York Times Book Review* as a "Notable Book of the Year" in 1981, this rich memoir attracted attention to both Susan Allen Toth's life as well as her manner of telling her own story. Her evocative use of detail universalizes her particular experiences as a girl in Ames, Iowa, and in *Ivy Days* as an undergraduate at Smith College. Ames is distinguished from other small towns by being the home of Iowa State University; high school basketball games, Christmas dances, and the community swimming pool make it representative of other midwestern towns with a 1950s population of about ten thousand. In *Ivy Days* undergraduates, past or present, recognize the anxiety and exhilaration of making new male and female friends, answering old academic and moral questions, and coping with the fear of failure and the joy of success. As Susan Toth tells her story, she encourages her many readers to reflect on their own. Since both *Blooming* and *Ivy Days* are now available in Ballantine paperbacks, Toth's coming of age will have a wide audience.

The books are more nearly a series of essays than a chronological account of her girlhood and undergraduate career, for each chapter has its own

unity and each book its own character. The cross-section of her memories richly expresses the rings of time as well as the growth of her determined independence and fertile intelligence. Like E. B. White, Susan Toth is "self-liberated" from conventions of form and simple moral judgments. In italicized prefaces to each chapter, she often admits to an ambivalence about the possible limitations of her background and the quality of the decisions she made or let be made for her. She reflects maturely on her own motherhood and career as she alternately endorses and criticizes Ames, Smith, her peers, and herself within the context of place and community.

Now a full professor of English at Macalester College in St. Paul, Minnesota, Toth has more to teach through her essays than the value of a secure childhood or a liberal arts education. Repeatedly she reminds us that recent events or queries often have a beginning in the past. Her daughter Jennifer's question, "What was it like in the old days, Mommy?" precipitates her retrieval of her own past in the first chapter of *Blooming;* being asked to an adult slumber party results in a chapter in *Ivy Days* called "Learning to Live with Women"; visiting the Palace of Minos at Knossos inspires a chapter on academic life, "Intellectual Butterfly"; and Jennie's refusal to make her bed triggers an essay on the jobs Susan Toth had as "Preparation for Life." The extensive catalogue—baby-sitting, clearing dishes, assisting the Playground Drama Director, selling Camp Fire candy door-to-door and baked goods in a supermarket, detasseling corn, acting as courier and receptionist at a radio and television station, filling vacation spots at the newspaper office—all taught her something. Leading restless children in a "Bear Hunt" by sounds and gestures prepared her for some aspects of college teaching: "the ability to perform under unfavorable conditions, the instant tailoring of material to fit the audience, the necessity to keep going no matter what." Tenacity, imagination, and perseverance undoubtedly characterize the best college professors, but few have the ironic sense Toth cultivated during her summers of work for the *Ames Daily Tribune* where she "was exposed to overwhelming trivia inflated to importance and overwhelming importance reduced to trivia."

Between the summers at the paper and age thirty-six, when she began to write more nonfiction than literary criticism, Toth developed her ironic sense in graduate English classes at Berkeley and the University of Minnesota and by her own teaching at San Francisco State and Macalester. But her academic work was never far distant from her imaginative musing. She vividly recalls, for example, her first notice that "important things in women's lives have not been treated with the dignity and importance they really have." As a child she read a short story in a book from her mother's bookshelf by Mary Wilkins Freeman (1852-1930), one of the three New England local colorists who later became the focus of her doctoral dissertation. The story, "A Gala Dress," tells of two old women, "the Babcock girls," who own only one good dress between them and take turns wearing it, disguised with different trimmings. The one dress recalls the "faint savor of gentility and aristocracy" of their past and the pride in their present social standing. When jealous Matilda ruins the dress by setting off a firecracker beneath it, their sense of self burns

too. The dress itself had held off the hopelessness of their poverty. The dress, Toth says, has a "luminous significance," a symbolic power that resonates beyond its context. It and other details from such writers as Rose Terry Cooke (1827-1892), Alice Brown (1857-1948), and Sarah Orne Jewett (1849-1909) suggest the use of apparently slight details to epitomize and often symbolize a dramatic moment, memorable event, or a particular realization in her own life. Susan Toth's attention to particulars combines scholarship with her own sensitivity as to what went on around her at home in Ames and at school at Smith.

In *Ivy Days*, apples in a bag lunch for the long train ride back to Iowa for her freshman Christmas signify "health, vacation, and freedom." Once she is home, "a worn spot on the rug" suggests something of the changes in a house that seems "a little more cluttered, just a bit smaller" than it had the summer before. From Smith she remembers "Aunt Ted's quilt" as a "totem" of peace and safety. Domestic details accrue significance from the context of place and memory.

In both books Toth focuses often on clothes worn or desired. Although she lacked the appropriate blazers, knee socks, kilts, and Bermuda shorts that gave other college girls "a kind of truncated efficiency," such collegiate apparel did not suit Sue Allen from Ames, Iowa. With wry self-deprecation, she writes: "Wool crew-neck sweaters itched at the back of my neck; knee socks slowly crept to my ankles and collapsed; pleated skirts pulled over my hips. They didn't belong to me." After four years at Smith, she felt "absolutely authentic" only once—dressed in sophisticated jeans, sweatshirt, threadbare sneakers, and a trenchcoat "soiled to a satisfactory gray," she received the coveted Victoria Louise Schrager prize for leadership and academic excellence. On leaving Smith, she gave away an expensive black cocktail dress bought in Iowa to prepare her for an imagined life at Smith; the unworn dress had once been her "key to the East."

Sincerity is everywhere present in her prose. Whether telling of her likes or dislikes, successes or failures, connections and disconnections to her current life, Toth outlines honestly the truth of the issues or the facts of events. Although one childhood friend insisted that Susan Allen was not present at the movie *The Barefoot Contessa* when a girlfriend had to be told the facts of life to understand why a war wound prevented Rossano Brazzi from sleeping with Ava Gardner, Susan Toth the writer believed she was there. She is as faithful to the record as memory can make her. She notes her deliberate transfer of "a rhythmic chant from one memory to another" in her distortion of the Ames high basketball record, but she looks keenly enough on her past not to have to manufacture details. She wrote exactly what it was like to grow up in Ames or to graduate from Smith precisely because no one had told the story before.

As a scholar, Toth knows that bildungsromans for women are rare or limited to the lives of women very different from herself. Men have Horatio Alger, Mark Twain, James Joyce, and John Knowles to tell their stories, but women have had only the relatively foreign and recent renditions by Erica Jong, Eudora Welty, or Alice Walker. The more than 300 letters from readers of *Blooming* told Toth that "women have been led to believe that unless they lead lives as public as men's their lives have no importance." *Blooming* tells the story of hundreds of women who thought they had no story. Toth's memoir proves to these women that "what they did and what they felt and what they cared about does have meaning."

In Ames, Susan Allen grew up "gradually" and "quietly" as one of two daughters of an industrious young widow. Her father, a promising economist at Iowa State, died when she was seven. Her mother packed up Susan and her older sister and drove to California for a year at Claremont Graduate School where she earned the M.A. in English that qualified her to teach English at Iowa State. Without a present father, Toth's reflections focus more on her mother and her friends' mothers than on fathers and their responsibility. Her mother, always surrounded by books and student essays, gave Toth an early and abiding interest in language and literature.

From the perspective of a modern feminist in her late thirties, *Blooming* tells of an emergent self amid what Toth can see now as "provincial smugness," hypocrisy, and prejudice of a hometown with comfortable securities and with both significant and senseless rituals. When the Ames High School basketball team won the state championship, the mayor ordered out the two fire engines for a midnight reception on Main Street complete with snake-dances and speeches; free movies filled a holiday from school the next day. Swimming at Blaine's Pool brought "stinging bits of intense physical sensation" from the blinding light of the sun as well as from the titillations of being dunked by a favorite boy. When Doug Boynton, a seventh-grade boyfriend, moved to Alaska, he sent Toth a pair of wooden kissing dolls whose touching faces

superstitiously implied for years that "everything would be all right." Boyfriends came and went, but "the steady hum of girlfriends, punctuated by laughter and whispers, was a reassuring continuo" throughout childhood, adolescence, and beyond.

On the periphery of Ames were one prostitute, one attempted suicide, one divorce, and only a few memorable deaths. Outside a tight circle of associates lurked cloudy compensations for geographical isolation and cultural deficiencies. Occasional shopping sprees in Des Moines, summer holidays at Lake Carlos in Minnesota, one quick excursion to New York City, and a year in Southern California were all Susan Toth saw of the larger world until she boarded a train for the trip east to Smith College. But her imagination leaped beyond Iowa and America to country inns and English cathedral towns, through fairy tales and fantasies, fiction and nonfiction borrowed weekly from the imposing Ames Public Library where Miss Jepson ruled imperiously over her locked glass case of books "whose literary or scholarly worth was unquestioned but whose text or illustrations she deemed obscene."

Toth was embarrassed at being called a bookworm, but the precision of her style reflects her wide reading and concentrated study of such masters as E. B. White, her admitted model. Like White, Toth varies her sentence patterns and laces her prose with appropriate images and surprising analogies. When ballroom dancing, she remarks, "a girl was supposed to be as finely tuned into her partner's touch as a thoroughbred horse to the gentle press of a rein." Without embarrassment, she continues after a pause, "I strained my nerves trying to read the secret messages being tapped into my back, but I never succeeded." The paragraph concludes with a mix of sentence patterns that reveal her own tight reins on her prose structure and rhythm. Controlling her re-creations, Susan Toth describes the sophistication of a local television personality: "Beauty, polish, and self-confidence floated around Liz like an expensive perfume." Liz's discarded powder blue cashmere skirt-and-sweater set recalls the cast-off "mystique of television." Robert Wagner's impersonal response to her one fan letter pushed Hollywood and its products outside her verifiable Iowa reality where stars were almost exclusively in the sky and appearances were usually what they seemed.

Toth often focuses on a single object or a specific image to make her point. A "shower-cap printed with pink flamingoes" rather than a popular puffy curler-cap "like a boudoir pillow" explains why Emily Harris hung back from the door when boys visited a slumber party. Expensive corsages of orchids for the Christmas Dance were worn by lucky girls "like medals of honor." One year Toth made herself a bright red velveteen gown "with a V-neck that plunged almost four inches below [her] collarbone," making her feel "gloriously like a scarlet woman" though, she admits humbly, she probably looked more "like an overripe apple." Late in the evening, when eye shadow smeared and nylons itched and "the little white foam-rubber cups peeped over the edge" of the red bodice, Toth had every reason to ask if all the preparations had been worth the effort and expense. Perhaps they weren't, she implies, but abiding by the unwritten rules of her social circle often made anticipation greater than realization.

The most painful chapter of *Ivy Days*, "Summa," suggests that Smith promised her more success than it could award. A migraine headache and its attendant illness so diminished the quality of her performance on her Honors examination that she earned a magna cum laude degree rather than the expected "summa." Reviewers have detected more bitterness in this chapter than insight, but Toth's reliable reporting of her own pain proves beyond a doubt her refusal to justify the past in light of present success. The "Summa voice" Susan Toth still hears pushes her toward excellence in her teaching, her mothering, and her writing.

Ivy Days improves on *Blooming* by its more extended metaphors and its more relaxed syntactic control. To an Iowan fond of wide open spaces, the New England topography seemed constrictive; claustrophobic images recur in almost every chapter of *Ivy Days*. The Connecticut Valley does not open up for Sue Allen, not even on geology field trips, and the "monastic cell" of Lawrence House, her college residence, seems equally closed. But the tight circumstances of room, house, college, town, valley, and state produced expansive adventures of mind in art history, history, and finally in her major—English literature. Travel images abound amid allusions to art and literature, guaranteeing transmission of the mystery and mastery of course after course. "Isolated in Lawrence House, on a campus that seemed like a remote island, I loved to escape to the Yorkshire moors, the Castle of Chillon, or Walden Pond." But her response is not only affective: "I began to realize how much I loved the sound of speech, the shape of sentences, and the rhythms of paragraphs." By appreciating how Carlyle resounds, Susan Allen learned more about how to write than any creative writing course could

Dust jacket for Toth's memoir of life at Smith College

teach her. In fact, a fiction-writing course at Smith kept her from writing another short story for eighteen years.

To her credit, Toth does not indulge in clever witticisms about the boors and bores she encountered in the classroom or in her reading. She judges her professors sympathetically, appreciating now their positions in their respective departments or their place in the larger intellectual community. Nothing she heard or read seemed stupid or wrong to her when she was a student, and no professor or author merits unqualified criticism now. Yet her peers come up for indictment again and again through her exposé of college mixers and dormitory life.

Swimming in the social life of Smith created experiences as "ineradicable" as lipstick stains on a white shirt or sweater. Blind dates were often as dull as adult mixers in today's social swim for single parents. Even now dates remind Toth of the truly blind tapping with white canes, "gingerly exploring the unknown territory," looking for "open space" between boundaries of barbed wire. Her boundaries are clearer now than they were, but social circuits can still short out.

Being an Iowan of Protestant principles made Toth a likely candidate for dates with "roommates, brothers, and old-friends-from-highschool who were shy, haltingly conversational, or just plain silent." She fights off a Princeton man in the back seat of a bar-equipped hearse; she longs for another date with an Amherst pre-med; she lets herself in for a dreadfully dull weekend at Yale; and she lets herself go with a seminary student she scarcely knew. She learns what and how to drink, when and why to smoke—"to lighten tedious moments, relax tension, and interrupt routine." Smoking becomes "a defensive weapon" at mixers or on dates she neither sought nor enjoyed, and talking, she explains, successfully fends off advances she unwittingly encouraged. Since sex was rarely discussed even among the initiated women at Smith, Susan Allen, as chairman of the Student Curriculum Committee, arranged for a guest lecture from a family physician at Columbia. From the presentation she hoped to "learn something safely" about the specifics of courtship and sexual consummation. Unfortunately, the visiting speaker avoided direct answers by fumbling analogies . . . intercourse is like helping a boyfriend change the tires on a car. Then and even more now his male chauvinism is laughable.

Somehow, though, Susan Allen learned enough from her undergraduate social life at Smith to find and marry Louis E. Toth, then a graduate student in metallurgy at Berkeley, now at the National Science Foundation in Washington. Anticipating separation and divorce in *Ivy Days*, she admits her "fallible judgment in the men I chose to love." Her marriage lasted eleven years (1963-1974); the privacy of the relationship is breached only in *Blooming* in a brief description of a failed experiment on the random diffusion of atoms, done with small steel balls in pans of jello.

Toth went directly from Smith to Berkeley, completing her master's degree in the required three semesters. She started on her Ph.D. and was ready to go on, but she married instead and decided to take off a year to teach. After her first year of teaching in the classroom at San Francisco State, her husband got a job at Minnesota, and "of course" she went with him. She completed her Ph.D. at Minnesota and assumed a full life as a professor of English at Macalester before having Jennifer, her only child. She did regular book reviews for the *Minneapolis Star* and *Tribune*, but her scholarly work focused principally on the work of New England women writers, writers who deal with the "texture of women's lives." For a time after Jennifer was born, she became interested in women writers who are mothers. In London she interviewed Margaret Drabble, Beryl Bainbridge, and Fay Weldon in anticipation of writing a book on women writers and their views on maternity. Inspired by the example of these British women, Toth began writing about her own life, rather than complete the proposed book.

Her first attempt deals with the complicated tensions between motherhood and a full-time career. She sent "Notes of a Would-be Liberated Mother" to *Cosmopolitan* first and then on to the *Smith Alumnae Quarterly* (November 1975). In 1977, however, *Cosmopolitan* bought her story about a severe emotional upset and gave her a wide audience for the first time. Readers of essays on Alice Brown, she admits, would number but a few, but hundreds of thousands of women would read a story in *Cosmopolitan, Redbook,* or *Harper's*. One publication followed by another encouraged Susan Toth to tell more of her own story in a series of essays sometimes regarded as fiction. The major magazines were reluctant to publish her memoirs about swimming pools, science, girlfriends, or boyfriends, but Toth remained committed to her style and form until the essays coalesced into a book, "much more sensed than planned." When Anne Mollegen Smith, then fiction editor at *Redbook* and a college classmate, announced in an editorial squib at the end of "On Picking Raspberries" that Susan Toth was writing a memoir of her childhood in Ames, a wise editor at Little, Brown asked to see it, and *Blooming* was born.

Susan Toth works extremely hard on her style. She "loves to revise." Sarah Orne Jewett taught her to trust her own writer's instinct as to the apt detail to convey emotion or sensory appeal, and her own sensitive reflections led her to treat with dignity the most ephemeral object, the domestic detail. From E. B. White she learned to say what she means subtly without underlining or shouting her theme or her resolution. One editor called her style "no hands showing," meaning that she doesn't show off or pound out her message. The style seems effortless, simple, but the polish requires buffing. For Toth, whose writing voice is much like her talking voice, the buffing is her pleasure and ours.

References:

Susan Bolotin, "Growing Up in Ames," review of *Blooming, New York Times Book Review,* 24 May 1981, pp. 4, 18;

Barbara Creaturo, "An Innocent from Iowa," review of *Ivy Days, New York Times Book Review,* 17 June 1984, p. 31.

AN INTERVIEW —————— *with SUSAN ALLEN TOTH*

DLB: Are you glad now that you went to Smith?

TOTH: I still do not have an answer to that. In many ways it was a disastrous place for someone of my temperament. The high expectations and the kinds of pressures I talk about in the chapter "Summa" were disastrous for me psychically. On the other hand, it introduced me to an incredibly exciting intellectual life; my horizons were broadened; I was given all kinds of other gifts. I cannot say flatly it would have been better if I had gone, for example, to Stanford. I'll never know because I chose to go to Smith. My ambivalence resembles the ethos of the New England women writers who are both fond of people they write about and critical of the narrowness of their lives. In Jewett, though, even the narrowness is often strength.

DLB: Would you recommend that your students take time off before beginning their graduate work?

TOTH: Absolutely. In fact, the academic market is now so grueling, I feel that, in English, unless a student is incredibly bright and would enjoy teaching, there is no point in getting a Ph.D. For the last five years, I have not strongly recommended that one of my students go on to the Ph.D.

DLB: Given the alumnae audiences in the openings of both books, how does Smith College now figure in your life?

TOTH: I just returned from our annual Minnesota Smith Club extravaganza called "Smith Days in the Country," a fund-raiser run like a bazaar. Two or three hundred women from all over the state show up. Although I see these women only once or twice a year, I look forward to these events because the women are so interesting. I always feel very nurtured by them. These alumnae friends are always very pleased with my progress. They keep up with

my work by reading of what I'm doing, and they have intelligent questions to ask. In 1985 I attended my twenty-fifth reunion and was moved and exhilarated by the stories of some of my classmates. I also saw the college for the first time somewhat objectively, not as That Mythical Place.

DLB: How did you get started writing nonfiction?

TOTH: It's a complex story, but I think an interesting one. I often tell it in an abridged version when I give talks to women who want to be writers because I want them to know that they can begin to do memoirs, essays, fiction, writing of their own at an age when they think the chance for doing it has passed. And they can begin a writing career from a mailbox in St. Paul. I began writing nonfiction to make sense of a major emotional pain. I tried all the things I'd been trained to do: baked bread, talked to all my friends until they no longer wanted to hear my phone calls, went for long walks, went to movies, but I couldn't get rid of the upset. Finally I decided that I would have to write it out. I knew that if I could put words on it that it would help. Being tired and harassed then as the mother of a very young daughter, I thought I didn't have the luxury of sitting down and writing something unless I was going to get paid or get academic credit for it. No one was going to give me academic credit for writing about a broken heart, so I thought I'd have to sell this to someone. This first story, published under a pseudonym, was bought by *Cosmopolitan* for $500, more money than I ever received for any scholarly writing. I sent this over the transom without any entreé, with just a self-addressed stamped envelope, and the editor called me up to say she wanted to buy it. I later learned that if I had had an agent, they would have paid a thousand or more. Now, of course, I have an agent: first Charlotte Sheedy, now Molly Friedrich, the cousin of a former student. I changed agents when Charlotte suggested that I read Lillian Hellman and model my work on hers; by her own admission, she was not as sure as I was about my style.

DLB: How do you now balance your academic, domestic, and creative lives?

TOTH: I don't. I'll share an example of my day. I had thought this morning I would be able to go over a couple of manuscripts that I was going to send to a competition for short stories. In fact, I was so exhausted by my first week of teaching that I took one of the pills I take to avoid a migraine headache so I felt a bit groggy. As I went up to my study to try to get something done for school, the phone rang. It was one of my friends who needed to talk with me before she went away for the weekend. She came over while my daughter, who was preparing to go to a soccer game, needed me to find her knee guards and her leg warmers. When my friend and Jennifer left, I made a list of what I thought I might do today when I wasn't writing. I was going to pay bills, make pesto, make some beef vegetable soup for the winter, get my bicycle fixed, go to the dry cleaner. I was just laughing thinking that my original idea was to work on my word processor this morning.

DLB: What word processor do you use?

TOTH: I use a Morrow Microdecision, a standard CPM-80 machine. I use Wordstar on it. I have become so dependent on the speed and easy revision possible on a word processor that I now own a small laptop computer and a portable printer. I take the laptop with me to our Wisconsin cabin or even on trips when I'm in the middle of writing something. I really love how easy it is to erase. I always put off sitting at the typewriter or word processor as long as possible. My mind goes too quickly for a pencil and paper, and it is essential to get everything out fast. At the MacDowell Colony in the summer of 1984, I had to lug along my electric typewriter as my critical item of baggage. There was no way I was going to use a manual or do without a typewriter. I use an Adler, a small but solid machine.

DLB: What is your next work?

TOTH: It's in such a beginning stage, it may in fact die. But what I think it may be is a story about my grandmother, my mother's mother, about whom I know almost nothing. On my way to MacDowell, I was thinking that I needed a grandmother to talk to. The one thing I did know about this grandmother is that she had agoraphobia, something I sensed in anxiety attacks a few years ago. My grandmother, I learned from my mother, had been "nervous" and in later life was unable even to go to church though she was very religious. That is a classic symptom of agoraphobia. My grandfather was a kind of classically tight-lipped Scandinavian. I began to create a grandmother for myself that is a composite of what I know and have imagined about my grandmother. I began picturing my grandmother on the porch of her house at Lake Carlos, Minnesota, and I began writing about what

she might say to me. I began to imagine what life might have been like for her. I began to think what it would be like to know nothing about agoraphobia and to assume that you had some terrible disease, or to have people tell you all the time that you had "female nerves." What would it be like to have a minister discover that you weren't in church, and he came to call on you? What would it be like when you had the male doctor in town come to visit you and examine you? What would your husband, who was somewhat closed and taciturn, think of all this? I began to think that I would like to tell my grandmother's story, which, of course, I am really inventing. Next winter, when I'm off from teaching, I'll go around and visit my aunts and uncles to gather "real stuff" about Grandmother, who to them has been canonized by time. Then I'll create my grandmother from fact and fiction. I'm also writing travel pieces for the *New York Times*, and I do a regular column for a local magazine, *Twin Cities*.

DLB: Have you ever thought of writing something about your current life or the demands of teaching and writing?

TOTH: I do write about my current life, a very happy one with my second husband, but I do not think I will ever try to cover the years between *Ivy Days* and the present day in any systematic way. I would have to draw in material about my ex-husband and other people close to me which I couldn't sufficiently disguise and which would cause pain and embarrassment to people that I have cared a good deal about. I don't have the right to do that. I have never been able to understand the memoirists who, for the sake of posterity or money or their own concessions, will expose, in that kind of public way, people whom at one point they loved very dearly. I remember once reading a moving memoir of a widow raising two teenage children. It was very explicit about her love affairs, her mistakes. I remember thinking as I read it, how are those twelve- and thirteen-year-old kids going to be handling a best-seller exposure of their mother's sex life? Even now my daughter in seventh grade was very embarrassed by one little section in *Blooming* reporting that she asked me about penises. *Blooming* was put on the reading list of her private school for incoming junior high. Many kids read it, and Jennifer was teased about her question. I feel badly about it. I didn't think about her having to confront her contemporaries at thirteen for something she said when she was six or seven. A few years ago she said, "If you ever write about me again, Mommy, I want to see it first." I said, "I think that's fair." And I will do that.

DLB: How has your life changed with the publication of *Blooming* and *Ivy Days?*

TOTH: I've used the money from both books to buy time off from teaching to get started on another writing project. So, in fact, my financial situation is exactly as it was. I still haven't paid off my four-year-old Toyota, but I have had a year off to finish *Ivy Days,* and I had the spring semester of 1985 off. That's what I really need. The other change is that I am more of a public figure, not in an overwhelming sense and especially not in comparison with Garrison Keillor, who is St. Paul's most noted writer, but I am invited out of academe more. I move in wider circles now. All of us academics need that, and that is a pleasant change. The biggest change in my life, my marriage to James Stageberg, a Minneapolis architect, came about directly because of *Blooming.* He read about the book, came to hear me give a talk, and then called up to ask me for a date. He is from a small town in Minnesota, and we have a great deal in common. With his encouragement, I am now teaching less—about half-time, one course each semester—and trying to write more. We were married in February 1984, and the subsequent move from St. Paul to Minneapolis, and the whole resettling process, has taken a lot of time and energy, but my new life is absolutely worth any temporary slow-down in my writing.

DLB: What do you teach now?

TOTH: I teach a variety of courses in American literature, modern and historical fiction, creative writing, women's literature, as well as my share of service courses. In 1986, for example, I taught a course in the British nineteenth-century novel one semester and jointly taught a seminar in "Geography and Literature" with a geographer the second semester. I have a great deal of freedom to choose what I'm going to teach. But I am not sure how long I'll be in the classroom. I've been teaching since 1969, and it doesn't get easier. I come home after a half-day at Macalester quite wrung out and not feeling like sitting down at a typewriter. For me, teaching demands an intense personal expense of energy. Even with a half-time assignment, I find my commitment to Macalester tends to dominate my life. One of these days I may cut the academic umbilical cord—I've been in academe all my life—and see what happens when I swing loose and free.

DLB: What advice would you give to new writers?

TOTH: Keep writing and don't give up. Have confidence in yourselves and know that you don't have to grow up in New York, you don't have to belong to a writer's group, you don't have to do all the conventional things you think writers do or live in the places writers live, or have the kinds of lives you think writers have to be a successful writer. You do have to trust your own experience even if it doesn't correspond to the experience you think of writers as having.

Frank Waters
(25 July 1902-   )

Alexander Blackburn
University of Colorado, Colorado Springs

BOOKS: *Fever Pitch* (New York: Liveright, 1930); republished as *The Lizard Woman* (Austin, Tex.: Thorpe Springs Press, 1984);

The Wild Earth's Nobility (New York: Liveright, 1935);

Midas of the Rockies: The Story of Stratton and Cripple Creek (New York: Covici-Friede, 1937);

Below Grass Roots (New York: Liveright, 1937);

The Dust Within the Rock (New York: Liveright, 1940);

People of the Valley (New York & Toronto: Farrar & Rinehart, 1941);

River Lady, by Waters and Houston Branch (New York & Toronto: Farrar & Rinehart, 1942);

The Man Who Killed the Deer (New York & Toronto: Farrar & Rinehart, 1942);

The Colorado (New York & Toronto: Rinehart, Rivers of Americas Series, 1946);

The Yogi of Cockroach Court (New York & Toronto: Rinehart, 1947);

Diamond Head, by Waters and Branch (New York: Farrar, Straus, 1948);

Masked Gods: Navaho and Pueblo Ceremonialism (Albuquerque: University of New Mexico Press, 1950);

The Earp Brothers of Tombstone (New York: Clarkson N. Potter, 1960);

Book of the Hopi (New York: Viking, 1963);

Robert Gilruth (Chicago: Encyclopaedia Britannica Press, 1963);

Leon Gaspard (Flagstaff, Ariz.: Northland Press, 1964);

The Woman at Otowi Crossing (Denver: Swallow Press, 1966; revised, 1987);

Pumpkin Seed Point (Chicago: Swallow Press/Sage Books, 1969);

Pike's Peak (Chicago: Swallow Press/Sage Books, 1971);

To Possess the Land: A Biography of Arthur Rochford Manby (Chicago: Swallow Press/Sage Books, 1974);

Mexico Mystique: The Coming Sixth World of Consciousness (Chicago: Swallow Press/Sage Books, 1975);

Mountain Dialogues (Athens, Ohio: Swallow Press/ Ohio University Press, 1981);

Flight from Fiesta (Athens, Ohio: Swallow Press/ Ohio University Press, 1987).

OTHER: *El Crepúsculo* (Taos, N.M.), edited by Waters, 8 September 1949-6 December 1951;

"The Western Novel: A Symposium," *South Dakota Review,* 2 (Autumn 1964): 10-16;

Conversations with Frank Waters, edited by John R. Milton (Chicago: Swallow Press/Sage Books, 1972);

"The Writer's Sense of Place: A Symposium," *South Dakota Review,* 13 (Autumn 1975): 6-9;

"A Discussion with Frank Waters," *Puerto del Sol,* 16 (Spring 1981): 82-86;

"Frank Waters' 'Prelude to Change,' " edited by Charles L. Adams, *Nevada Historical Society Quarterly,* 24 (Fall 1981): 250-254;

Cuchama and Sacred Mountains, edited by Waters and Adams, text by W. Y. Evans-Wentz (Athens, Ohio: Swallow Press/Ohio University Press, 1982);

Frank Waters: A Retrospective Anthology, edited by Adams (Athens, Ohio: Swallow Press/Ohio University Press, 1985).

PERIODICAL PUBLICATIONS: "Relationships and the Novel," *Writer,* 56 (April 1943): 105-107;

"Indian Influence on Taos Art," *New Mexico Quarterly Review,* 21 (Summer 1951): 173-180;

"The Roaring Colorado," *Holiday,* 16 (August 1954): 90-97, 115-116;

"The Mystery of Mesa Verde," *Holiday,* 18 (September 1955): 44-45, 67, 69-71;

"Tucson," *Holiday,* 18 (October 1955): 38-41, 114-118;

"Notes on Alan Swallow," *Denver Quarterly,* 2 (Spring 1967): 16-25;

"Quetzalcoatl versus D. H. Lawrence's *Plumed Serpent,*" *Western American Literature,* 3 (Summer 1968): 103-113;

"Words," *Western American Literature,* 3 (Autumn 1968): 227-234;

"*The Man Who Killed the Deer:* 30 Years Later," *New Mexico Magazine,* 50 (January 1972): 16-23, 49-50;

"Crossroads: Indians and Whites," *South Dakota Review,* 11 (Autumn 1973): 28-38;

"Man and Nature: An Indivisible Unity," *New Mexico Magazine,* 52 (May 1974): 16-21;

"Neihardt and the Vision of Black Elk," in *A Sender of Words: Essays in Memory of John G. Neihardt,* edited by Vine Deloria, Jr. (Salt Lake City: Howe Brothers, 1984).

"Next time, by hook or crook, make sure you're born with a mountain in the front yard," Frank Waters writes in *The Colorado* (1946). "It comes in mighty handy all the way round."

Waters, a 1985 and 1986 nominee for the Nobel Prize in Literature, was born with a mountain in the front yard—in Colorado Springs at the base of Pike's Peak, at 435 East Bijou Street, the large clapboard house of his mother's father, Joseph Dozier. After his own father's death in 1914, the boy and his mother, May Ione Dozier Waters, lived in that house and were daily under the influence of Dozier, one of the first residents of Colorado Springs (founded 1874), a builder of some of the city's most impressive early buildings such as Cutler Hall of Colorado College, and a man of such granitelike will that he would be remembered in Waters's great American epic, *Pike's Peak* (1971), as of a substance with the mountain itself. His grandfather provided Waters with a strong idea of the relationship of man to nature; his mother, also of strong will and mind, provided him with an idea of human relationships and a sense, southern in origin, of family honor and tradition. Both Doziers helped to endow Waters with idealism—"specifically," Thomas J. Lyon, editor of *Western American Literature* at Utah State University, observed in a book about Waters, "an awe for intellectual excellence." Yet it was the mountain in the front yard that most stirred the boy's spirit: Pike's Peak would come to symbolize for him the sacred and the eternal in nature and in man. In a chapter titled "The Sacred Mountains of the World" in his recent *Mountain Dialogues* (1981), Waters declares, "If there does exist for each of us a psychological archetype, or a Guru, manifested as a physical mountain, Pike's Peak is mine. I grew up with it, nurtured by its constant living presence."

In more than twenty published books, including twelve novels, five biographies, five collections

Cover for the announcement of a 1985 celebration at Tutt Library, Colorado College

of philosophical and historical studies, and an objectively created Indian scripture based upon oral narratives and nonverbal ceremonies (*Book of the Hopi,* 1963), he transcends the gulf between subject and object which characterizes the writings of sentimental regionalists and of fantasts who cater to the popular craving for sagebrush-and-six-gun romances.

There is a hard-earned authenticity to Waters's voice as he writes of the peoples and cultures of the American West. Pike's Peak, in fact, early taught Waters some difficult lessons in life. Grandfather Dozier, having accumulated considerable wealth, succumbed to gold fever, perhaps because one of his hired hands, Winfield Scott Stratton, discovered the Cripple Creek gold camp and became known as the "Midas of the Rockies." Dozier poured his wealth into a mine in Cripple Creek, the Sylvanite, which never paid off ("our family folly," Waters terms it). Its failure contributed to the illness and death of the boy's part-Cheyenne Indian father and placed the family in straitened circumstances. Waters grew up with misgivings about the obsessional materialism of New Westerners and Euro-Americans. Their troubled psyches, as he later realized, were leading them to plunder and profane the very land which, if rightly used, could restore their spirits.

On a visit to Colorado Springs in 1981, Waters stared at the bare gravel pit that now scars the slopes of the Pike's Peak Range. "How this was allowed to happen by a city which still boasts of its scenery, I don't know," he remarked ruefully. "Only in the United States have we desecrated and exploited these mountains held sacred by our Indians. In exploiting them for their physical energy, we have deprived ourselves of their psychical energy so necessary for us as a spiritually healthy commonwealth." He recalled the beauty of the city of his childhood, the small town of 30,000 people, the bold blue mountains, clean air, and fresh running streams. He had hunted rabbits on what is now the urban sprawl of Austin Bluffs and had gathered watercress in Shooks Run, once a clear stream, now a polluted one in the neglected downtown area of a city of almost 400,000 people.

Words, like the great mountain in the front yard, spoke to Frank Waters with the mystery of divine origin. At grammar school, where his first published piece appeared in *Columbia Sayings and Doings* in October 1916, he was inspired by an English teacher, Ruth Wattles (named Miss Ruth Watrous in the semi-autobiographical novel *The Dust Within the Rock*, 1940). She rewarded her pupils by reading aloud from books of mythology, and Waters recalls the enchantment he felt: "Pike's Peak rose high, more majestic, into Mount Olympus. The great Labyrinth yawned blacker than the deepest level of the Sylvanite. . . . Thus he [Waters in the persona of March Cable] was baptised in the living mystery. Mythology, the only true history of the soul of man!" The words told him he was not lost in a western wilderness, and in the presence of the timeless mountain he discerned that "the whine of the aimless ancient winds is the voice of America that all the world shall hear, [for] we, its children, are the feather, the drum and the mirror of the old gods who will not die."

Waters found himself deeply perplexed by his dual white and Indian heritage. On the one hand his mother and grandfather represented "white" ideals and failings—male dominance, patriarchy, individualism, rationalism, materialism, even rac-

ism—while on the other his father, Frank Jonathan Waters, embodied gifts of intuitive perception and of passive acceptance of living with the earth. Waters's father and mother came from different worlds. "It has been the life quest of their son," Lyon wrote, "to unite those worlds." Accordingly, Waters "speaks with authority and with depth on the tortured racial and cultural questions of Western civilization."

There is a telling scene between father and son in the nonfictional *Masked Gods* (1950). "Daddy, did you ever kill Indians?" asked the son, having just seen a movie version of "the American morality play" at the age of ten and not yet realizing the duality of his background.

> Father did not answer. Under the pale streetlamp, his swarthy brown face set. His big Indian nose jutted out like Pike's Peak. His large black eyes, usually so soft and compassionate and sick with some strange sadness, seemed hard and shiny as flint. He strode to the buckboard with that sinewy lithe walk so seldom seen now.
>
> "Get in."
>
> He drove silently out of town to the encampment along the creek where Mother never liked him to go. The smoke-grey lodges loomed up palely in the moonlight. Somewhere there sounded the soft beat of a drum. A dog barked. At the end of the lane a fire was burning. Some dirty Utes were sitting around it, wrapped in torn blankets. . . .
>
> They sat down. Father cross-legged as they on his equally small feet. He took off his bowler hat, smoothed back his coarse, straight black hair with a delicate brown hand. They smoked.

The mountain in the front yard became associated, not to the Euro-American pole of Waters's consciousness, which in the personage of Dozier had presumed to possess the land, but to the Indian pole, the mystic sense of life, his father's passively celebrating and ritualistic oneness with the land and with the people so attuned for thousands of years to the spirit of place.

Frank Waters has maintained allegiance to both white and Indian races, a fact often overlooked by readers so entranced by his 1942 book *The Man Who Killed the Deer* (which Stephen Vincent Benét perceived as "the finest novel of American Indian life") that they mistakenly believe Waters has left modern society for a picnic with primitives. In *The Woman at Otowi Crossing* (1966), a white protagonist unifies the best of both Indian and scientific reality, rejecting only the Monster Slayer built at Los Alamos and released at Alamagordo and Hiroshima. Waters's three-year stay with Hopi Indians in Arizona was difficult, as he confesses in *Pumpkin Seed Point* (1969):

> I, like many others, owe allegiance not to one race and people, but to two. One part of me is inherently attuned to that masculine, mental, Euro-American world whose monuments of rational materialism rise higher and higher every year. The other part of me is forever polarized to the feminine realm of instinct, the dark unconscious. Thus, every so often I find myself helplessly drawn back into still-living, ancient America; into the sub-world of continental Indian America; into the Hopi village of New Oraibi, immune, as it always has been, to change and progress.

Waters left Colorado Springs in 1924, seldom to return save for brief visits. He had been encouraged in 1921 to attend Colorado College; there, under sway of the Dozier side of himself, he pursued a curriculum in engineering. But suddenly, disillusioned with the narrow intellectual foundations of his studies, he left college and took up work in the dangerous Salt Creek oil fields of Wyoming, drifted south to the Imperial Valley, where he worked as an engineer for the Southern California Telephone Company, and began writing, with Joseph Conrad a pronounced early influence. At the age of twenty-four he wrote his first novel, *The Lizard Woman*, published as *Fever Pitch* in 1930 by Horace Liveright. While stockpiling manuscripts, Waters continued to wander for many years in the West and in Mexico, driven by an exuberant love for experience, by abiding intellectual curiosity, and by a desire to think things through to the root until he could give in words some fusing not only of his own dual nature but also that of a modern world psychically split between science and myth, reason and intuition, and conscious and unconscious forces. The turning point came in 1931 when he traveled alone on horseback for a thousand miles down the length of the Mexican hinterland. Then he first became aware of the subterranean quality of land and people, of what he called "the mythological content of the unconscious, that one great pool of life and time." By the mid 1930s Waters had settled in New Mexico. Now for almost fifty years he has lived, writing, on a small ranch overlooking from 8,000 feet the Taos Valley, long regarded as peculiarly magnetic and

powerful by such people of vision as D. H. Lawrence and the Pueblo Indians whose ancient home it is.

James Joyce's dictum that an artist needs silence, exile, and cunning in order to form his vision seems particularly apt when one considers the artist as westerner. Where Faulkner could find his little postage stamp of Mississippi sufficient to supply imagination with historical contexts and universal truths, Waters did not belong to a community with established continuities or a fixed sense of order and values. Consequently, his quest for meaning has taken him more deeply into the past than Faulkner's. Like other western artists, Waters has had to go back to the land to explain a continuity between past and present, and he has had to confront the tragedy of the past in order to map out the territory ahead. A tragic awareness of western history opens up on two fronts: that of the attempt of New Westerners to comprehend the land psychically, that attempt failing, they subdue it to Euro-American patterns; and that of the encounter with the Indian, whose near-annihilation in the romanticized "heroic" past is an enduring, ghostly presence. Even though there is epic grandeur in the story of western settlement, its history examined in the full light of tragic consciousness reveals a still living, ancient American heartland that mocks the presence of New Westerners. Even though some of the best serious western writers, such as Walter Van Tilburg Clark in *The City of Trembling Leaves* and Wallace Stegner in *Angle of Repose*, have written novels that bridge past and present, Frank Waters has been especially adequate to the historical task. The reason is plain: his "exile" has taken him all the way back to ancient Mesoamerican civilization, there to take his cultural and spiritual bearings.

The result of Waters's quest can be seen as more remarkable than that of other American artists of this century, including Faulkner. Where Faulkner was consumed by fury and despair over disintegration of an older community of values, Waters finds in Ancient America a way of redemption for New America. That way is expressed by the Myth of Emergence, an Indian story of mankind's slow evolving from lower to higher stages of being. Combining this myth with the discoveries of modern science, the Jungian psychology of self-fulfillment, and some of the tenets of Buddhism, Waters has given artistic form to a new creative mythology, namely the emergence among modern individuals of a wholemindedness fusing reason and intuition to a higher level of consciousness and of world understanding. Having found America's true past—neither Plymouth Rock nor the ante-bellum South—Waters has linked that past to the future of the human species.

In *The Waste Land,* T. S. Eliot's seeker fails in his quest for a revitalizing mythology. He cannot render the modern world spiritually significant. The quest of Frank Waters has fulfilled the prime task of mythology, which is to carry the human spirit forward. His books light a way from the Waste Land to the Heart Land. In the geograph-ical-historical-mythic continental Heart Land, like the seeker in all mythologies (see Joseph Campbell, *The Hero With a Thousand Faces),* he has come under protection of the Cosmic Mother—of the Arche-typal Feminine or the forces of the unconscious—and found in the depths of fathomless being that man's body is but a microcosmic replica of the ma-crocosmic body of all creation. Departing from a doomed and tragic culture, returning to archaic depths, and then surfacing to teach the lesson of life renewed: this, the pattern of quest, is evident from the works of Frank Waters.

The mountain appears in almost all of Waters's major fiction and nonfiction. It is literally the quiet center of *Pike's Peak.* Transformed into human shape as the protagonists of *The Yogi of Cockroach Court* (1947), *People of the Valley* (1941), *The Man Who Killed the Deer,* and *The Woman of Otowi Crossing,* it towers over the horizontal plane of social history; and we see that the fictional characters Ro-gier, Tai Ling, María del Valle, Martiniano, and, above all, Helen Chalmers are embodied myths that waken us to timeless mystery. In *The Colorado* the archetypal mountain becomes the Colorado Pyra-mid with fifty or more peaks protruding above 14,000 feet, "the myriad-pointed apex of this con-tinental pyramid" with a lower section "composed of terraced plateaus." Waters finds the pyramidal pattern of the New World both a living form and the basic symbolic form for the Mayan, Toltec, and Aztec civilizations, as in the Pyramid of the Sun and Moon at Teotihuacán and the great Pyramid of Quetzalcoatl near Cholula. "It is wholly appro-priate," he declares, "that the symbol on one side of the Great Seal of the United States is a pyramid," for "the Colorado Pyramid, carved out of the con-tinent, might well be the mother shape, the ancient and eternal prototype."

In *Masked Gods* Waters explains Pueblo and Navajo ceremonialism as based upon cosmic forces for which the two great polarities are the Encircled Mountain which extends invincibly upward toward the Sun Father and the Grand Canyon's *sipapu* which leads back down into the depths of Mother

Dust jacket for the anthropological study based on the explica-tions by the thirty-two Hopi elders of their religious rituals and ceremonies

Earth. Now the archetypal mountain is called the Rock, the "encircled" Four Corners region of the Southwest. In the collection of essays titled *Moun-tain Dialogues,* he calls himself a mountain man, one akin to that strange breed of men who in the first half of the last century trailed into the Rocky Moun-tains to trap beaver but unconsciously sought not profits but spiritual renewal in "the inimical and unknown heartland of America."

For "as the great bulks of the mountains heaved up inside them as around them, the rivers ran wild in their blood, and the mighty canyons and abysmal gorges shaped the dark depths within them, they knew unconsciously they had found it, whatever it was." If a mountain is an upheaving of enormous physical energies locked into patterns of geological evolution, so humans are locked into pat-terns of psychic evolution. From this evolutionary perspective, people, like a mountain, are always in a process of becoming and of ascending. Thus a mountain yields the myth of an enlargement of consciousness that coincides "with the cyclic changes dictated by the one cosmic power that governs the indivisible life of all mankind, all nature, the universe itself."

Written over a twenty-year span, *The Yogi of Cockroach Court* can be considered as both an early and a mature novel. It begins with stormy, brutish melodrama reminiscent of Conrad and Jack London and ends on a note of sophisticated satire in the manner of Aldous Huxley; in between there are slashes of slangy dialogue and old B-movie, cardboard plot devices. *Yogi* is, nonetheless, a brilliant tour de force featuring four memorably drawn characters within the tawdry confines of a Mexican border town (mainly Mexicali but doubtless with touches of Tijuana, Juárez, and even of Nevada's Las Vegas, all places familiar to Waters from his wanderings and all sharing in common the sleazy atmosphere of transience, violence, cheap degradation, and brutal opportunism). *Yogi* is obviously two books, or rather a dark and passionate extravaganza of youthful writing overlaid by the intellectual and creative audacity of a mature writer who knows exactly how large a stone he is casting in the shallow pool of modern civilization. The reason for the discrepancy is that Waters wrote the first version of this novel in 1927, submitting the manuscript (then titled "Barby" after the mestizo boy of that name who is a tormented neophyte Hitler in the plot) to Liveright in 1930; Liveright rejected the manuscript, but twenty years after the first version Rinehart published a revised version in 1947, thus rounding out Waters's Dark-Skin Trilogy about indigenous types in the Southwest, *People of the Valley* and *The Man Who Killed the Deer* having already appeared under a Farrar and Rinehart imprint. As Waters wrote to John Selby of Rinehart on 16 August 1946, *Yogi* "is at once a universal and realistic 'love-story,' and yet for the first time I'm aware of it presents in novel form the Eastern yogic ideology opposed to Western sociology and psychological method. . . . Its paradox is that it is at once a 'Western' yarn and a novel of strictly modern ideas . . . concerned with basic patterns of religious thought as well as with sociological surface action."

In *The Yogi of Cockroach Court,* Waters not only draws the reader into a swamp of pimps, prostitutes, drunks, smugglers, and slavers but he also does something extraordinarily daring for its day: he depicts with tolerant compassion the lesbianism

of a beautiful half-breed Indian girl. That the portrait of Guadalupe was ahead of its time is indicated by the fact that no English publisher would touch the book. In 1947, let alone in 1927, lesbianism was to be treated solemnly if at all. To his credit, Waters never loses sight of something ludicrous in the proceedings. When Guadalupe surrenders to what (for Waters) is a perverse passion for another woman, Waters writes with understated drollery, "She flung over on Peña, threw both arms about her, gripped her closer and ever closer, wanting her but not knowing how." Tai Ling, the nonviolent Chinese shopkeeper at the center of the book, is completely out of place in Cockroach Court. With Tai Ling, Waters subtly transforms a quixotic situation into one of tender and compelling syncretism. Painfully brought down to earth, Tai Ling achieves his goal of ego-transcendence and of full humanity ironically moments before he is murdered:

> And suddenly his own sense of guilt and his intolerable sadness were made plain. How could he have separated life from the principles which guided it; ignored the fusion that already existed if one could only see it? He forgot himself entirely. . . . He thought of all the poor little fish and human cucarachas, the blind beggar at the corner, all the men betrayed, the mothers who had lost their sons, all the misery and sadness, ignorance and loneliness throughout the world. The old man wept. He wept because he no longer felt separate; because he too was a part of all the misery that ever had existed. . . . And now suddenly in the unfathomable darkness, the quintessential silence of the illimitable void, there exploded light. An explosion of silent, radiant light. An explosion of transcendental bliss.

This description of the death and transfiguration of Tai Ling is worthy of the pen of Tolstoy.

Although Tai Ling is juxtaposed against the world of Cockroach Court, which can be compared with Eliot's Waste Land, desolating undercurrents flowing beneath the surface action make the dominant impression. Tai Ling is out of place, whereas opportunistic materialism, distorted sexuality, and egocentric asceticism are in place—in a symbolically sterile desert with its conglomerate cross-breed underworld where characters are negatively polarized to the instinctive life of fear and desire. Guadalupe, as her name signifies, is the Dark Madonna of the Tepeyac, the ancient Indian Mother of the Gods canonized by the Church, but at the moment when she could make revitalizing identification with mountains "covered with a dark blue mantle and dotted with specks of light, like toasted maize grains, by the bright morning sun," she succumbs to the temporal illusions of sensual pleasure and manipulative power. And Tai Ling's experience of expanded consciousness seems exotic. A death-in-life motif dominates *The Yogi of Cockroach Court*. It can be viewed as largely, if by no means entirely, an expression of an early phase in the quest of Frank Waters.

The epic consisting of *The Wild Earth's Nobility* (1935), the impressive *Below Grass Roots* (1937), and the slightly unfocused *The Dust Within the Rock* (1940) consists of 1,500 pages that Waters compressed by half as *Pike's Peak* in 1971. It is a story of pioneer settlement and gold-mining enterprises in the Pike's Peak region between the 1870s and 1920s. As regionalist literature the epic is original in subject matter and in realism, discarding romantic notions of western history and giving scope to actual family life over three generations. But Waters is a regionalist with universal themes, so the epic's myth is death and rebirth. As an inquiry into the dark side of the American soul, it invites comparison with Herman Melville's *Moby-Dick* (1851), from which the original edition of *Below Grass Roots* in 1937 offers an epigraph—"The subterranean miner that works in us all, how can we tell whither leads his shaft by the ever shifting, muffled sound of his pick?"

The Great White Peak, like the Great White Whale, is a symbol of the mystery of life, of the cosmic principle of creation. The mad white hero, Rogier, like the mad Captain Ahab, attempts to strike through the masks of nature and tear out her heart. Rogier, like Ahab, has his humanities and Americanness: self-reliance, pragmatism, family devotion, constructive work, cultivated sensibility, and will to power. But when he sails the prairie seas and confronts the Peak, he knows himself for a deracinated exile terrified by the secret of nature that recoils from his soul's grasp. Instead of allying himself with nature's invisible forces, "to attain to self-fulfillment, the only true success," Rogier pits his will against the mountain and thus against his own inner nature. The resulting psychic fission, exploding in a western wilderness that is a figurative Waste Land for this Anglo-American prototype, destroys Rogier and ruins not a few of his crew.

In repeated failures to strike gold at Cripple Creek, Rogier is aware that it is not gold itself he seeks so much as mastery of primal energy in the mountain's heart. Therein, for Waters, lies Rogier's strength, his heroic mentality; but therein also lies his madness: the quest for Self has been projected spatially upon the Peak instead of temporally to the ancient past of an alien heartland and psychologically to the depths of his own repressed instincts. It is Rogier's tragic fate, as it is Ahab's, that he cannot bring his psyche into affinity with nature or to enduring intuition of the living moment. Moreover—and Waters's epic is more emphatic about this than Melville's—Rogier's monomania is to a large extent racially and culturally preordained, the components of his heritage including materialism (the attitude that living entities such as mountains are but objects to be used), rationalism (the polarization of the mind toward purely conscious mentation and neglect or repression of unconscious, intuitive wellsprings of thought), and racism (the white man's psychotic fear of dark-skinned peoples). Thus culturally conditioned to an atomic individualism so familiarly disguised behind the American dream of success and progress, Rogier is a Waste Land figure whose quest is doomed to the hell of death-in-life.

Woven through the warp and woof of the epic are Indians and the Navajo country (where Waters's father had taken him for a visit in 1911). The Indians' rightness with the land is set in contrast to Rogier's incapacity for finding that relationship, and the beauty, breadth, music, and ceremony of Indian country become the motif of contrast to the closed-in world of "Little London."

The whole narrative is foreshadowed in its first scene. "HEE-YAH!" cries an Arapaho riding past Rogier's new house in Colorado Springs. Rogier has been lounging on his porch in the evening, studying the mountain that has lured him to the wilderness. But he cannot fit himself into some recognizable pattern of meaning in the new West: the nonverbal natives and the wild nobility of the land are just out of the immigrant's reach and will remain so.

However, Rogier's Ishmael-like grandson, the part-Indian March Cable, fuses the duality of his heritage into "the new American—a continent-soul reborn"—and has a mystical experience which brings him a feeling of unity with the land. This moment of revelation—in *The Dust Within the Rock* but excluded from *Pike's Peak*, presumably on the grounds of its autobiographical nature—occurs on a stormy spring day when March is swimming in a hot spring high in the Pike's Peak Range. Afterward he feels "cleansed, fused, made whole, happy and joyously alive.... How naked and alone he was—gloriously alone, sublimely naked to the lashing of the storm. But a part of it, an inalienable part of the moaning pines reeking water, the sturdy mountains, the foaming stream far below him, the profundity of the aroused heavens." March Cable's emergence from the Waste Land, as a spiritual fact founded upon a quite ordinary psychic experience, prefigures by more than twenty years the emergence of Helen Chalmers in *The Woman at Otowi Crossing* and is thus an indication of what will become the most significant leitmotiv in all of Waters's major fiction.

While he was working on his epic in the mid 1930s, Waters lived in the remote town of Mora, New Mexico, in the Sangre de Cristo Mountains, where simple Spanish-speaking people had been isolated for centuries. Out of this experience he created the pastoral novel *People of the Valley*. In this book the way of life of deeply rooted Hispanic-Americans is threatened by construction of a dam which will protect their valley from floods but will also uproot the people from it. Missing the irony, the people sell their land and communal water rights. Only María del Valle, a shrewd and independent Indian crone, has the wisdom and authority to rescue her people from the Machine of Progress and provide for their exodus to another valley.

The problem faced by Waters in this symphonic novel is to indicate more of the truth about María than she might be expected to know. He solves it omnisciently by defining her against a convincing background of communal code and ceremony, by giving her a force of will behind her words and acts so that she wears a mask larger than life, and by consistently seeing his material as mythical. María, coexistent and identified with the valley and a personification of the Cosmic Mother, timelessly incorporates into herself what is passing and gives it meaning. She relates humankind to history and the cosmos by means of faith "in the one living mystery of ever-flowing life . . . renewed as life itself is ever renewed." With her earth-brown skin and valley-blue spirituality, María del Valle incarnates what Erich Neumann, in *The Great Mother*, has called the "feminine power of the unconscious." But she also significantly adds to her power the generative masculine power of the Sun Father, symbolized by a burnt-orange blanket with which she wraps herself on all ceremonial occasions, thus combining the dualities of nature and mind in a new stage of consciousness. In this respect, *People of the Valley* dramatizes Waters's Myth of Emergence.

If there is a dramatic flaw in the novel, it is that Waters consciously summons the incarnate unconscious to humanity's aid, whereas by contrast the symbol of the deer in *The Man Who Killed the Deer* comes unsummoned to the protagonist, Martiniano, makes his character subject to inner conflict, and earns for his story the force of spiritual combat. Like the Fisher King in Eliot's *The Waste Land*, Martiniano is both physically and psychically wounded after violation of generative power—in his case, the killing of a deer without regard to the animal as part of the living whole of life. He has been to the white man's "away school" and acquired an egocentric, waking consciousness which alienates him from his pueblo and from its myths and rituals. Having rejected the old values, he has not found new ones, but slowly he becomes healed when the power of the Cosmic Mother is revealed to him in the familiar yet transfigured forms of animals and humans, the deer additionally being the constellation of the Pleiades, and his wife, Flowers Playing, enacting the role of Deer Mother in tribal ritual. Martiniano becomes integrated to the collective matriarchy of the Heart Land.

It would be a mistake to infer, however, that Waters is a cultist like D. H. Lawrence recommending that modern civilization return to Dark Gods. Waters does not believe there is any turning back from the evolutionary Road of Life. Here, it is not a matter of nostalgia but of survival. Here also the wisdom of Waters's outlook becomes apparent: via increased awareness reconciling eternal dualities of consciousness and the unconscious, of Sun Father and Cosmic Earth Mother, we are to anticipate human evolution to a new world of balanced perceptiveness, returning to the Cosmic Mother but as a means of releasing beneficent psychical energy for the journey ahead.

Martiniano's return to tribal ways is actually not Waters's recommendation for Anglo culture. The relevance of *The Man Who Killed the Deer* is this: like Tai Ling, Martiniano has to learn not to sever his humanity from society; when he does understand old tribal myth as a new sacred world order, he is not abandoning the modern world but becoming the very type of the truly free modern individual.

In writing *The Man Who Killed the Deer*, Waters faced the difficult problem of remaining faithful to the meaning of the collective society of Pueblo Indians while showing to our noncollective society that what seems ancient and esoteric is actually at the forefront of contemporary ethics. If it could speak, the soul of the Heart Land would say something poetical and mythical. Waters solved the problem by having the chiefs and initiates "speak" collectively in italicized passages to the guilt-haunted and alienated mind of Martiniano. The meaning of the passages is Waters's own, namely that in full consciousness only is there freedom, the ethic of fullness demanding an organic relation whereby an individual is dependent upon the existence of other persons and of all living things, "*breathing mountains, the living stones, each blade of grass, the clouds, the rain, each star, the beasts, the birds and the invisible spirits of the air,*" for all which the metonymical figure is the deer of the book's title. In this novel whose main characters are Martiniano and Palemon, names suggestive of medieval allegories about the soul's quest for beatitude, such as Palamon of "The Knight's Tale" in Chaucer's *Canterbury Tales,* Waters affirms that the modern world is spiritually significant, the answer to the quest of such modernist, self-exiled poets as Eliot having surfaced from the American Heart Land.

This Heart Land is not a geopolitical Lebensraum but a space-time continuum, the geographical heart of the continent, the historical heart of ancient American civilization, and the mythical heart, like Faulkner's Yoknapatawpha County, of a self-subsistent universe wherein the values of human choice and action can be asserted. These three-fold dimensions of geography, history, and myth are, in Waters's nonfiction as well as fiction, a stage upon which world crises may be resolved beyond the narrow confines of politics and economics.

The geographical Heart Land emerges from Pike's Peak and New Mexico, expands to include the vast region drained by the Colorado River, and finally encompasses an area stretching from the Rockies down the spine of the Sierra Madres to Middle and Central America. Throughout the Heart Land beats the living pulse of the past, so historical orientation locates the true heart in pre-Columbian Mexico among Mayan and Aztec cultures, the center being the sacred city of Teotihuacán at the mythic heart of which lies the temple of Quetzalcoatl, symbol of the union of heaven and earth, matter and spirit, a self-sacrificing God-Redeemer who taught that the Road of Life is within man himself. It is this teaching that gives the Heart Land its creative mythology of Emergence. According to the Indian version of myth, there have been four successive underworlds, all embodied within the Cosmic Mother of creation, from which man has been successively reborn. The fire element of the first world gave man his life heat. The air

element of the second world gave him breath of life. From the third world of water man derived his blood and other bodily constituents. The waters subsided and the earth arose, and upon it man emerged as we know him today, for the earth element gave man his flesh. The Road of Life is not individual man's brief diurnity but mankind's evolution, which, more than a mechanical process of geological and biological change, takes place on psychical levels as well and can, in Waters's words, be "hastened or retarded by man's perception of his responsibility in the cosmic plan." The Road of Life is an ethic based upon regard for all forms of life, and it is a psychological affirmation of another world to emerge where dualitites are transcended by an "enlargement and unification of personality" to a new stage of human awareness. Finally, according to Indian prophecy elaborately explained in Waters's *Mexico Mystique* (1975), the time of mankind's latest emergence is our own, and we stand on the threshold of a new epoch.

Waters has brought a lifetime of scientific training to bear upon the Myth of Emergence, and from 1952 to 1956 he served as information director for Los Alamos Scientific Laboratory. He is therefore well informed to write a novel that directly confronts the apocalyptic premise to all thought in our time—the possibility of the destruction of planetary life as we know it confronted by the archetypal promise of the Myth of Emergence. That novel is *The Woman at Otowi Crossing*, the first version of which was completed in 1957 after five years of work, though the published version did not appear until 1966; a new, revised edition containing restored chapters and passages appeared in 1987.

The Woman at Otowi Crossing dramatizes the emergence to a higher level of consciousness through the experiences of a prototypical modern American named Helen Chalmers. She lives in a place called Otowi in New Mexico at the symbolic "crossing" or point of synthesis between the destructive and constructive forces of our world, between counterpointed territories (the Secret City of Los Alamos vs. the Indian pueblo of San Ildefonso), cultures, realities, gender codes, and rituals. Neither modern nor "primitive" world will suffice: polarization to overrationalism leads to Alamagordo, Hiroshima, and the Marshall Islands, whereas polarization to the ascetic collective poses its own kind of tyranny. Obviously, polarities must be transcended in a new creative synthesis, Emergence, and this myth is personified in Helen Chalmers as she grows through totally unexpected but normal stages of shamanistic crisis away from modern society and toward vision of sacred world order consonant with the full radiance of eternity. Waters expresses his theme not only through complex counterpointing but also through complex relationships of characters and happenings that are the past, present, and future of America's life span in the midst of which, like a mountain, a mandala, or the hub of a revolving wheel stands the Woman. Waters's dramatic technique is to give Helen precognitive psychic experiences of fission and fusion that are noncausally synchronized with A-Bomb-to-H-Bomb development and go beyond this to a vision of cosmic cataclysm that could result from further destructive utilization of solar energy locked in the atom. As her spiritual awakening is first dynamited by growth of a malignant cancer in her breast, so the malignant growth of nuclear technology can either waken mankind to fulfillment of civilization's role on the Road of Life or lead to destruction of all life. Helen's awakening is the beneficent one marked by awareness of time as the fourth dimension.

In one of the most powerful passages in the novel, Helen moves through three-dimensional time of past, present, and future to atonement with eternity. She has unearthed a piece of pottery upon which is the thumb print of a Navawi'i woman at the same time that wild geese in a V-formation fly overhead. A psychic experience results:

> At that instant it happened again: the strange sensation as of a cataclysmic faulting of her body, a fissioning of her spirit, and with it the instantaneous fusion of everything about her into one undivided, living whole. In unbroken continuity the microscopic life-patterns in the seeds of fallen cones unfolded into great pines. Her fingers closed over the splotch of clay on the bowl in her arms as the Navawi'i woman released her own, without their separation of centuries. She could feel the enduring mist cooling and moistening a thousand dry summers. The mountain peaks stood firm against time. Eternity flowed in the river below.... And all this jelling of life and time into a composite *now* took place in that single instant when the wedge of wild geese hurtled past her—hurtled so swiftly that centuries of southward migrations, generations of flocks, were condensed into a single plumed serpent with its flat reptilian head outstretched, feet drawn back up, and a solitary feather displaced by the wind, which seemed to be hanging im-

mobile above her against the gray palimpsest of the sky.

The centuries of migrating geese imaginatively transformed in this passage into the redemptive god, the plumed serpent Quetzalcoatl, become symbolic of expanded consciousness, the past of the Navawi'i woman, the future of the trees growing from fallen seeds, and Helen's present time henceforth blessed not only by previous worlds of elements but also by the feather that is arriving to announce a new world.

There is more to Helen's other psychic experiences than precognition about nuclear weaponry. She is a savior figure, a redeeming and liberating human being, not the avatar of some known divinity or model. In this regard, one of the novel's most interesting characters is Dr. Gaylord, a physicist who has suffered from hubristic science. When Emily, Helen's daughter, aborts his child just

Dust jacket for Waters's 1974 biography of a man who spent more than twenty years trying to build an empire on land that belonged to others

before he is sterilized by radioactivity, he becomes a kind of Fisher King of the atomic Waste Land until Helen's death and transfiguration grant him saving spiritual insight. Although at the precise moment of her death Gaylord is thousands of miles away in the Pacific witnessing the light of a thermonuclear explosion, the light of her Emergence transcends all else, so that later, looking back in love and awe, he recognizes it as "perhaps the only true myth of these modern times."

The character of Helen Chalmers is not odd or singular or captivating but, like Hamlet, Don Quixote, and Milton's Satan, truly original, a rarity implying, as Herman Melville declares in *The Confidence-Man*, "original instincts." Everything is lit by the original character, Melville affirms; "everything starts up to it." Although Helen Chalmers's mythic character has been partially prefigured by other characters such as Tai Ling, María del Valle, and Martiniano, she more than these engenders a feeling of possibility for modern mankind, a sense of new and authentic beginnings, the chaos of the Waste Land confronted and contained by a poetic writer's compassion and wisdom.

Waters has probed in both his fiction and nonfiction the ages-old problem of the reconciliation of the opposite polarities which separate us from one another in race, culture, religion, and nationality, yet the simplest expression of reconciliation, that of compassion between persons of opposite gender, has not been selected for emphasis until publication of *Flight from Fiesta* (1987), the story of a lovable but delinquent ten-year-old white girl and an old alcoholic Indian who flee from themselves only to reach an emotional and spiritual union beneath their conflicting personalities. Set in New Mexico in the mid 1950s, the story begins when Elsie, a little, rich tourist girl, maneuvers old Inocencio into running away with her during the annual Santa Fe Fiesta. In the wake of their disappearance, a posse is organized, partly convinced that Inocencio has kidnapped and probably molested Elsie. The odyssey of the fleeing "outcasts" takes them into the realistic world of squalid slum districts, remote Indian trading posts, ancient ruins, and finally into the high mountains and refuge in cave-dwellings thousands of years old. Against this backdrop of time, the girl-man relationship is ageless and purified. Although he could abandon the girl and save himself, Inocencio elects to give her the security she needs and sacrifices his life for the sake of the "common humanness" that has come to be acknowledged in their "secret and essential selves."

Flight from Fiesta is a short and deceptively simple novel rooted in the myth of love (sans passion). The "great forest cathedral" in which "two happy children" share, we are told, "an idyllic interlude" of "sympathy and trust" recalls the chapel in the heart of nature which European poets in the twelfth and thirteenth centuries symbolized as the ground of one's own and the world's true being, surrounded by symbolic wilderness and threatened by conventional society. It also recalls Mark Twain's Huck and Jim on their raft, William Faulkner's Ike McCaslin and Sam Fathers in the woods—whiteboy-and-dark-man stories aimed at compassion. Waters's pairing of a white *girl* with an Indian, a drunken one at that, leads him to part company with the typically American literary romance (boyman, with sexual taboo skirted in depiction of race relations) and to align himself with European literary tradition, namely, love as a dying to the world in order to come to birth from within, the mystery of sex being the given in what Waters calls in this novel "transcendental experience."

As to the validity of the Myth of Emergence, there is an increasing amount of evidence from social history and from science that what Waters has long foreseen as a "coming world of consciousness" is already either coming to pass or is making itself known as the true and verifiable potentiality of the human mind. The free culture of the United States has actually been exhibiting for some time a shift to new philosophical foundations in which intuitive, indeterminate knowledge is complementing rational, determinate knowledge, both forms united by a common base. According to F. S. C. Northrop, Western civilization has begun to learn that intuitional and emotional knowledge is "as primary and hence as justified a criterion of trustworthy knowledge and of the good and the divine in culture" as rational knowledge, thus affirming the basic insight of Eastern civilization (*The Meeting of East and West*). Some process of consciousness is currently changing our notions of "feminine" and "masculine" behavior even as we cling to old sex stereotypes. Some process must be awakening us to the notion of Earth as our nurturing Mother who must be preserved, even as we cling to stereotypes of Earth as exploitable matter. Similarly, some process has been at work in changing racial and international stereotypes. The list could go on to include areas of increased awareness wherein Waters himself has furthered acceptance: Indian history (for example, Dee Brown's *Bury My Heart at Wounded Knee*), Jungian psychology as more holistic than Freudian (Arthur Koestler's *The Act of*

Creation), myths and religions as projections of the unconscious (Joseph Campbell's four-volume *The Masks of God)*.

But evidence from psychology and neurophysiology is most persuasive. Psychologist Robert Ornstein in *The Psychology of Consciousness* has shown the implications of Roger W. Sperry's Nobel Prize-winning experiments on "split-brain" patients: consciousness is constructed from the filtered input of dual brain hemispheres with their somewhat separated rationalistic and intuitive modes; through exercises in attentional deployment we can cease to screen out constancies in the external environment and discover time as a dimension of consciousness, existing in itself, not in how it relates to hours. Neurophysiologist Alberta Gilinsky declares in *Mind and Brain* (1984) that there is a virtual revolution, comparable to the Darwinian and Einsteinian ones, in our conception of the nature of intelligence. Comparing the brain's architecture to a smoothly functioning football team, she concludes: "Our heterarchical brain is a dynamically organized, interconnected set of systems and subsystems that can pass control from one to another in many different directions. Earlier units in a heterarchy can be modified by the activity of later ones, later units can undo mistakes, and units at any point can forestall adverse contingencies. This is the power of intelligence responsible for the higher reaches of human thought." The role of consciousness, as now perceived through clinical tests rather than through introspective philosophy, is to carry out the survival function of the nervous system, so that, when we are confronted with increasingly complex, changing environments, we have a unifying, holistic consciousness freed to concentrate on the priorities of the moment and by selective emphasis direct our behavior to our self-selected ends.

These conclusions validate the essential truth of Frank Waters's creative mythology, a truth to which he has brought also the beauty of great art. More than any other American novelist of our time he has perceived the possibilities of which our minds, operating in society, are capable. Here, from *Mountain Dialogues*, is his description of a personal ritual wherein thought dissolves into an apperception of and acquiescence in the mystery of being: "And so it is this deep silence, this white silence, that I experience during my moment of meditative stillness in the sagebrush at sunrise. All the sensual morning sounds seem to merge into one sound, the steady ringing in my own ears which merges into the steady hum of silence itself, the

voice of the living land, or perhaps the sound of the moving universe itself."

Joe Gordon, Director of Southwest Studies at Colorado College, writes of Waters's reputation: "Frank Waters' literary reputation continues to grow, slowly and steadily, like the ascent of a great mountain, which, in a way, his work most resembles. His books are read by ever widening audiences—both in America and abroad. A growing body of scholarship elucidates the man and his art. Now, serious students of our literature describe him as America's greatest living writer." Whether Frank Waters is recognized with a Nobel Prize or not, there is reason to believe that he is not just America's but one of the world's greatest living writers, for his vision of hope and peace includes all peoples in an hour of peril for mankind.

References:

Charles L. Adams, "Frank Waters: Western Mystic," *Studies in Frank Waters*, 5 (December 1982): 1-11;

Adams, "Teaching *Yogi* in Las Vegas," *South Dakota Review*, 15 (Autumn 1977): 37-42;

Alexander Blackburn, "Archetypal Promise from Apocalyptic Premise: The Art of Frank Waters' *The Woman at Otowi Crossing*," *Studies in Frank Waters*, 6 (October 1984): 48-63;

Blackburn, "Peace Stars: Is There a Coming World of Consciousness?," *Studies in Frank Waters*, 8 (October 1986): 68-98;

Blackburn, ed., "Frank Waters: The Colorado College Symposium," *Writers' Forum*, 11 (Fall 1985): 164-221;

Inés Dölz Blackburn, "Imagery and Motifs in Frank Waters' *People of the Valley*," *Studies in Frank Waters*, 7 (October 1985): 57-75;

Martin Bucco, *Frank Waters* (Austin, Tex.: Steck-Vaughn, 1969);

Jack L. Davis, "Frank Waters' *Mexico Mystique:* The Ontology of the Occult," *South Dakota Review*, 15 (Autumn 1977): 17-24;

Davis, "Frank Waters' Psychology of Consciousness: From Split Brain to Whole Mind," *Studies in Frank Waters*, 5 (December 1982): 56-73;

Davis and June H. Davis, "Frank Waters and the Native American Consciousness," *Western American Literature*, 9 (May 1974): 33-44;

James A. Gonzales, "Like Eyes of Gold: The Images that Define Maria dell Valle," *Studies in Frank Waters*, 7 (October 1985): 77-97;

Quay Grigg, "Frank Waters and the Mountain Spirit," *South Dakota Review*, 15 (Autumn 1977): 45-49;

Grigg, "The Kachina Characters of Frank Waters' Novels," *South Dakota Review*, 11 (Spring 1973): 6-16;

Grigg, "The Sounds of Silence in Frank Waters' Novels," *Studies in Frank Waters*, 7 (October 1985): 27-44;

Christopher Hoy, "The Archetypal Transformations of Martiniano in *The Man Who Killed the Deer*," *South Dakota Review*, 13 (Winter 1975): 43-56;

Hoy, "The Conflict in *The Man Who Killed the Deer*," *South Dakota Review*, 15 (Autumn 1977): 51-57;

Robert Kostka, "Frank Waters and the Visual Sense," *South Dakota Review*, 15 (Autumn 1977): 27-30;

Michael Loudon, "Mountain Talk: Frank Waters as Shaman-Writer," *Studies in Frank Waters*, 5 (December 1982): 74-88;

Thomas J. Lyon, *Frank Waters* (New York: Twayne, 1973);

Lyon, "Frank Waters," in *Fifty Western Writers: A Bio-Bibliographical Sourcebook*, edited by Fred Erisman and Richard W. Etulain (Westport, Conn. & London: Greenwood Press, 1982), pp. 509-518;

Lyon, "Frank Waters and Small-'b' Buddhism," *Studies in Frank Waters*, 5 (December 1982): 89-99;

Lyon, "Frank Waters and the Concept of 'Nothing Special,'" *South Dakota Review*, 15 (Autumn 1977): 31-35;

Lyon, "An Ignored Meaning of the West," *Western American Literature*, 3 (Spring 1968): 51-59;

Frances M. Malpazzi, "The Emergence of Helen Chalmers," in *Women in Western American Literature*, edited by Helen Stauffer (Troy, N.Y.: Whitson Publishing Company, 1982), pp. 100-113;

Malpazzi, "A Study of the Female Protagonist in Frank Waters' *People of the Valley* and Rudolfo Anaya's *Bless Me, Ultima*," *South Dakota Review*, 14 (Summer 1976): 102-110;

Mary McBride, "A Sunrise Brighter Still: Frank Waters and the Concept of Enduring Reality," *Studies in Frank Waters*, 5 (December 1982): 30-41;

John R. Milton, "Intuition and the Dance of Life: Frank Waters," in *The Novel of the American West* (Lincoln: University of Nebraska Press, 1980), pp. 264-297;

Milton, "The Land as Form in Frank Waters and William Eastlake," *Kansas Quarterly*, 2 (Spring 1970): 104-109;

Milton, "The Sound of Space," *South Dakota Review*, 15 (Autumn 1977): 11-15;

Milton, "Symbolic Space and Mysticism in the Novels of Frank Waters," *Studies in Frank Waters*, 5 (December 1982): 12-29;

William T. Pilkington, "Character and Landscape: Frank Waters' Colorado Trilogy," *Western American Literature*, 2 (Fall 1967): 183-193;

Lawrence Clark Powell, "A Writer's Landscape," *Westways*, 66 (January 1974): 24-27, 70-72;

Terence A. Tanner, *Frank Waters : A Bibliography with Relevant Selections from His Correspondence* (Glenwood, Ill.: Meyerbooks, 1983).

Sylvia Wilkinson
(3 April 1940-   )

Katherine Kearns
Louisiana School for Math, Science and the Arts

BOOKS: *Moss on the North Side* (Boston: Houghton Mifflin, 1966; London: Rupert Hart-Davis, 1967);
A Killing Frost (Boston: Houghton Mifflin, 1967);
Cale (Boston: Houghton Mifflin, 1970; revised edition, Chapel Hill: Algonquin, 1986);
Change, A Handbook for the Teaching of English and Social Studies in the Secondary Schools (Durham, N.C.: LINC Press, 1971);
The Stainless Steel Carrot, An Auto Racing Odyssey (Boston: Houghton Mifflin, 1973);
Shadow of the Mountain (Boston: Houghton Mifflin, 1977);
Can-Am (Chicago: Children's Press, 1981);
Endurance Racing (Chicago: Children's Press, 1981);
Stock Cars (Chicago: Children's Press, 1981);
Super Vee (Chicago: Children's Press, 1981);
Formula One (Chicago: Children's Press, 1981);
Formula Atlantic (Chicago: Children's Press, 1981);
Sprint Cars (Chicago: Children's Press, 1981);
Bone of My Bones (New York: Putnam's, 1982);
Champ Cars (Chicago: Children's Press, 1982);
The True Book of Automobiles (Chicago: Children's Press, 1982);
Dirt Tracks To Glory, The Early Days of Stock Car Racing as Told by the Participants (Chapel Hill, N.C.: Algonquin, 1983);
Trans-Am (Chicago: Children's Press, 1983).

PERIODICAL PUBLICATIONS:
FICTION
"Jimson," *Red Clay Reader #3* (1966): 102-106;
"Patch in the Dutch Boy's Britches," *TriQuarterly*, 10 (1967): 182-189;
"A Maypop from Merton," *Red Clay Reader #6* (1969).

NONFICTION
"A Time to Live, A Time to Write," *Writer*, 81 (July 1968): 9-11, 44;
"Growing Up in the South," *Mademoiselle*, 68 (April 1969): 208, 298-302;
"The Machine," *Red Clay Reader #7* (1970): 22-26;

"American Road Race of Champions," *Carolina Sportsman* (November-December 1970);
"To Be King of the Mountain," *Sports Illustrated*, 34 (19 April 1971): 64-71;
"The ARRC, 1970," *Southern Living*, 6 (November 1971): 64-71;
"Publicizing a Solo I Event," *Sports Car* (June 1973);
"The Chimney Rock Hillclimb," *Sports Car* (August 1973);
" John Morton, Driver Profile," *Sports Car* (September 1973).

Sylvia Wilkinson began writing down stories in a Blue Horse notebook when she was twelve. Her instincts dictated a fictional world that was not, at least to her seventh-grade teacher and first critic, prettified: "I had my grandmother picking ticks off a dog. . . . She picked the ticks and scratched his back and he knew he could come to her and get the ticks taken off. Well, I thought this was very nice and worthy of a place in fiction but my teacher was appalled." Wilkinson sees this experience as having been formative: "Negative reinforcement is crucial," she argues, in that it enforces the artist's responsibility to write, alone and without approval, not for someone else, but for herself. By spending the first eight years "up in her room doing her book, writing bad things, terrible writing," Wilkinson learned not how to please others, but how to master her own acute storytelling instincts.

When she emerged from artistic confinement at twenty, it was with a draft of *Moss on the North Side*, which was published in 1966 to consistently favorable reviews. Despite a relative lack of national recognition, Wilkinson has inspired critical confidence. In 1966 she won a *Mademoiselle* Merit Award in Literature. *Moss on the North Side* was completed under a Eugene Saxton Memorial Trust Grant, and in 1965-1966 she was awarded a Wallace Stegner Creative Writing Fellowship at Stanford University, during which time she wrote *A Killing Frost* (1967). A National Endowment for the Arts Creative Writing Fellowship in 1973-1974 produced

Sylvia Wilkinson

Shadow of the Mountain (1977), and a Guggenheim Fellowship in 1977-1978 resulted in *Bone of My Bones* (1982). Wilkinson won, for *A Killing Frost* and *Shadow of the Mountain*, two Sir Walter Raleigh Awards for North Carolina Fiction.

Like most writers, Wilkinson does not live on the proceeds from her books, but her nonwriting life is no mere subordination of art to economic necessity. Her other passion besides writing has long been stock car racing. She has two carefully researched books to document her interest and expertise; she has been a member of racing teams and of a sprint pit crew. Currently she makes a large part of her living as a timer on the racing circuit. One of two women in the United States to do this work, she is proud of her status as an undisputed expert in a very difficult and demanding job.

To write about Wilkinson the novelist without including, from the beginning, this other side

would be to ignore the dual energies that have formed her as an artist. She is both an observer and a participant; her interviews and her novels reiterate the dynamic tension of intense physical energy forced, during the writing process, into reflection. Her sister, Margot Wilkinson, described Wilkinson at a race. Calmly, and without missing a beat, she recorded the lap time of a car that came hurtling into the wall a few feet from where she sat. This scene bears some relationship to Wilkinson as a writer. Her novels are filled with motion; Fred Chappell, in the *Hollins Critic*, has called her worlds "unpeaceable kingdoms" where "everything is alive. Every page bristles, quivers, stammers with the forces of organic change." Yet Wilkinson remains in control, a quiet center in a swirl of activity. Meticulous in her observations, she is unintimidated by characters careening through initiation into adulthood. Her best novels are Bildungsroman, filled with the stuff of her own active life.

Wilkinson was born 3 April 1940 in Durham, North Carolina. Her father, Thomas Noell Wilkinson, is a retired employee of Duke Hospital, and her mother, Peggy (George) Wilkinson, is a painter. As a youngster Wilkinson rode her horse, worked on cars with her brother, and played tennis. She early learned that to discipline herself to sit still and write she had to get rid of some of her physical energy first. Having become eastern North Carolina's women's tennis champion in 1959, she fell during a match and tore the tendons in both ankles. Were it not for this accident, her energies might well have been challenged away from writing and into sports. As it happened, the congenital weakness in her tendons fostered her other unquestioned ambition: to be a writer.

She had a model to follow, her maternal grandmother, Mama George, who was largely responsible for Wilkinson's motivation to write. Wilkinson has described her as "a farm woman with a third grade education from Sunday School who listened to soap operas, read newspapers and comic books. But she was a storyteller with a natural sense of form and drama. . . . I became a writer out of an oral tradition, knowing I could never equal her standards. She would start rocking in her iron porch chair and start talking." Wilkinson was not raised on books, but on these stories, and on cowboy movies.

In 1962 Wilkinson received her B.A. in painting and writing from the University of North Carolina at Greensboro. She studied writing there with Randall Jarrell, who called her "the best prose writer I ever got to teach." In 1963 she received her M.A. in English and writing from Hollins College, where she had studied under Louis D. Rubin, Jr., and Howard Nemerov. Wilkinson was, from 1963-1965, an instructor of English, drama, and art at Asheville-Biltmore College in Asheville, North Carolina. She spent 1965-1966 as a Special Fellow at Stanford University, California, during which time *Moss on the North Side* was published. After leaving California she taught English and creative writing at the College of William and Mary from 1966-1967. More noteworthy, to her mind, than the teaching were a trip to Europe, reflected later in Jean Fitzgerald's travels in *Shadow of the Mountain*, and the purchase of a new Porsche 911. She was beginning by this time to feel that teaching was basically incompatible with writing.

Wilkinson held, from 1967-1970, a position as lecturer and visiting writer at the University of North Carolina at Chapel Hill, where her friend and mentor Louis Rubin also taught. During the three years she taught at UNC, Wilkinson saw the publication of *A Killing Frost* and produced short stories, two essays on writing, and her longest novel, *Cale* (1972). She also began, in 1968, to serve as a public relations agent for several racers and racing associations. She worked in a Special Ford Foundation Workshop for Appalachian Teachers at King College, Tennessee (another reference point for *Shadow of the Mountain*), participated in the Learning Institute of North Carolina, and served as a consultant for Project Change in the North Carolina Public Schools.

It is hard to see Wilkinson's exit from teaching in 1970 as a necessity to her writing, particularly given her current grueling schedule on the racing circuit. She gave a more political reason in the *Washington College Review* in 1975: "I resigned in 1970 from the teaching staff at the University of North Carolina at Chapel Hill because I was miserably paid and I felt that my being a woman had a great deal to do with it." It would be an oversimplification to see Wilkinson's abandoning teaching in merely feminist terms. She had just sold *Cale* and had enough money to be at least temporarily independent. The question of her position as a feminist is inevitable, nonetheless, particularly given her many strong, matriarchal characters: the grandmother in *Moss on the North Side*, the dimly remembered Indian grandmother in *A Killing Frost*, Cale's obsessively maternal Falissa, whose son is her life and whose desperate love for him drives Cale away, Mrs. Higgins in *Bone of My Bones*, whose relationship over her daughter Ella Ruth has the elemental force of the moon over the tides. Yet Wilkinson's answers to questions about her political stance are typically straightforward. She feels that she was affected by sexual prejudices, but she is not active in any feminist organizations and does not like to generalize about "the women's movement" and its effects.

Wilkinson's strength comes, instead, from essentially personal sources; she believes that "the true power of imagination is hidden in the unwritten . . . in memory." Her setting is rural North Carolina, and her characters are absolutely dependent on their sense of place, geographically and seasonally. She believes that knowing place will determine direction, and, in finding direction, the writer will come to know her characters. Each of her novels is predicated on a young person who attempts, through conscious or unconscious artistry, to order his surroundings to fit his personal vision. It does not matter if the raw material is unheroic and sometimes ugly, made of illegitimacy, poverty, and prejudice, set in the farmed-out soil of the tobacco belt. As long as her characters are rooted, they grow; only when Wilkinson withholds the past, as she does from Jean Fitzgerald in *Shadow of the Mountain*, do they fail to transmute memory into meaning. Wilkinson believes that "the true power of the imagination is hidden in the unwritten . . . in memory." Her setting is rural North Carolina, and her characters are absolutely dependent on their sense of place, geographically and seasonally. Wilkinson believes that knowing place will determine direction, and, in finding direction, the writer will come to know her characters. Each of her novels is predicated on a young person who attempts, through conscious or unconscious artistry, to order his surroundings to fit his personal vision.

Moss on the North Side, fourteen years and at least eleven drafts in the making, is about a half-Indian girl named Cary. Cary's name through the first ten or so drafts was "Starrie." It was changed at the suggestion of Louis Rubin, who said it sounded like a dream name conceived by a romantic child. Starrie reappears in *Bone of My Bones* as Ella Ruth Higgins's fantasy character, another half-Indian heroine who is allowed "the cowboys and Indians and melodrama" that Wilkinson eventually revised out of *Moss on the North Side*. But Cary, after Wilkinson pared away her childhood daydreams, is quite essentially the young Sylvia Wilkinson.

Moss on the North Side takes Cary from the death of her beloved father, through a reunion with a mother she hates, and back, after a bitter struggle against her past and her present, to a positive love for a boy named Johnny Strawbright. Cary's movement from isolation to love is tentative. She does not move with the misguided directness which often characterizes the male Bildungsroman figure (Wilkinson's Cale, for example), who is allowed, at the very least, sexual mistakes on the way to maturity. Instead, Cary holds herself back from the intensity of her feelings, and when they become unbearable she purges herself through self-inflicted pain: she runs out into a night storm; she bangs her fist into a splintery fence post.

She directs her emotions into damaged things, a rabbit crippled by the hay bailer, an albino black child who epitomizes fragile helplessness. She clearly identifies with these crippled creatures (in her incarnation as Starrie in *Bone of My Bones* she is actually crippled) and chooses to give to things that can give her nothing back. Jasper, the albino child, is an outsider in his own race—like Cary (the product of an Indian man and a white woman) he is neither black nor white. But, ironically, his mother sees Cary as a white girl and resents her interest in Jasper. The attraction is as one-sided as her passion for the wounded rabbit and in this case is actively repelled by the hostile mother. Jasper's mother can reduce Cary to a strange white girl and thus exclude her, but Cary sees herself as a half-breed in every sense of the term. Her parents were only half-married, common-law partners at best, so that she calls herself a bastard. Sent to an orphanage for two years by a father who wanted her to be better educated than he could make her, she was only a half-orphan; the others resented her because she had living parents. She sees herself as damaged, and as long as she gravitates to other, more damaged creatures she will be isolated. Only when she can perceive herself as something other than "half" will the fragments of her intense emotions allow her to love a whole person like Johnny Strawbright. Like all of Wilkinson's protagonists, Cary is not forced into self-evaluation and change from the outside, but by her own intensely felt need for clarity and beauty.

Her vision of the world seems different from those around her—she picks up bottles for money, but not to save or spend. She puts the coins on the railroad tracks, where they are flattened. She is assembling a necklace, making the nearly useless pennies and dimes "worth keeping" by transforming them. As a young child she gathered autumn leaves and arranged them in fans of ascending shape and variation of color; she instinctively rearranges and orders her world, and this artistic instinct alters her ability to accept a life that is characterized by disorder and a failure of beauty. She watches her handsome father die slowly of a disfiguring fever. The doctor does not arrive in time because he is with a woman in labor, whose baby is finally stillborn. The woman, it turns out, is her mother; the child was probably fathered by the half-black, half-Indian Maurice. Wilkinson sets the stage for Cary's growth and change by asking her to transform this particularly nasty irony into something less ugly.

Sex and death are the fundamental issues in *Moss on the North Side*, and for a long time Cary cannot disassociate one from the other. She cannot purify her father's death, despite her burning of the corpse by igniting the bed and the small tenant house with gasoline. (Wilkinson clearly means to associate Cary's instinctive gesture of despair and anger with the ritual of Indian burial.) And she cannot disassociate sex from her mother's infidelity and promiscuity. She is hard pressed to turn such worthless coin into something worth saving.

She has earlier been in tune with the sounds and movements of her surroundings, with an Indian awareness taught her by her father. But Wilkinson removes Cary from her natural environment after her father's death and puts her with her mother. Before her father dies, her sexuality is parodic—a stolen watermelon under her shirt, she tells a shocked passerby that this baby will be her second, that she gave the first one away. In her new surroundings she becomes sexually self-conscious, no longer able to joke or to ask questions without embarrassment. *Moss on the North Side* teems with sexual imagery, from the prurient to the healthy, from the unnatural to the natural. Maurice and Cary's mother lie at one end of the spectrum and Johnny Strawbright at the other, and Cary must move from her preoccupation with infidelity and lust to the natural love symbolized by Johnny, astride his beautiful white stallion.

Cary emerges having come to terms with both her mother and father. She has decided, at the end, where her heritage lies by returning to her Indian grandmother's abandoned cabin and bringing away books of Indian lore. She has chosen not just to love Johnny but to accept his love for her. Wilkinson gives to Cary an implied "happy ending" in the most traditional sense by affirming her integration into society through love for Johnny Strawbright. If *Moss on the North Side* has a flaw, it lies in the neatness of its romantic resolution, which seems inadequate to contain Cary's powerful energy. Wilkinson does not make this mistake again: the universal human conditions remain constant in her work, but the simple resolution of shared affection fails to suffice.

Time magazine called *Moss on the North Side* "[one of] the season's most flagrantly gifted first novels. . . ." Wilma Dykeman, in the *New York Times Book Review*, pronounced it "a work of high quality," and the *Chicago Daily News* found it "a superior first novel that sets an exciting new writer firmly on her way." Its sales were respectable, beginning a trend of appealing to what Wilkinson calls "a small but select group of loyal readers." (All five of her novels have sold equally well, between 6,000 to 11,000 copies in hardback and from 25,000 to 35,000 in paperback. Pocket Books reprinted all of Wilkinson's adult novels except *Cale* in 1978.)

A Killing Frost retreats from the issue of awakened sexuality raised in *Moss on the North Side* and thus seems markedly different in tone and intensity from Wilkinson's first novel. Its central character,

Ramie Hopkins, is just thirteen, and untormented by desire or hatred. Her story (unlike Cary's, which begins in mid August) takes place over late fall and winter when "everything is just before being dead completely." The primary relationship is between Ramie and her maternal grandmother, Mama Liz; her mother and father are dead. Ramie is more an observer than a participant—it is significant that she tells her own story in the first person—and the symbolic link between nature and character is reflected in Mama Liz's movement toward death.

Yet the fundamental questions remain the same as in *Moss on the North Side*. Ramie, like Cary, is plagued by her ambiguous family status. She knows nothing of her mother and father and discovers very little as the novel progresses. Like Cary, she thinks of herself as a bastard. She finds that she was born of a slow-witted girl and a man despised by Mama Liz and her Aunt Cece; she learns that her mother drowned herself and that her father was killed overseas in the war. Hoping for something of beauty in her parentage, she finds that her father, in Mama Liz's and Cece's eyes, was simply no-account—not evil, but bad enough, not heroically handsome or majestically ugly, but merely pockmarked and greasy looking. The only way she can imagine her parents as beautiful is to place them, with her artist's vision, way off, two tiny romantic figures in a distant field.

Ramie is more literally an artist than Cary. She goes to a private girls' school, takes lessons, and makes *A*s in art. She experiments with techniques and media, rolling a fish in paints to make prints, carving figures out of Mama Liz's lye soap. Ramie is more distanced from nature than Cary and sees it metaphorically, so that the morning glories "are bright as colors in a paint tube," a cedar post has bark "peeling off like old skin," a man's teeth "lean and slant about like a bunch of tombstones." Ramie's thoughts seem consciously poetic, taking perception into a complex system of analogies. She is genuinely an artist, despite her relative self-consciousness, and it is through her artist's vision that she orders her own past and present.

Because she is younger than Cary and less preoccupied with her immediate circumstances, Ramie's vision is multilayered. She looks into the past through the window of Miss Liz's experience, and while searching for the keys to her own existence explores the ways that men and women love and hate. Mama Liz is Ramie's only link to her mother and father; she must rely on her grandmother's memories for any sense of her past. At one point, having been frightened by a spider, Ramie buries her face in Mama Liz's lap and is transported into the dimmest of childhood memories: "Her voice is slow now and I feel small like a child. . . . Her heartbeat is very slow and steady, and as I shut my eyes and press my face deeper, I remember once when I felt a heartbeat against my ear. It was a little hammer beating at me. I couldn't see anything; it was very dark and I was very small, so small that all of me was in my mother's lap and we were inside the dark closet under the steps." Mama Liz's heartbeat—her blood—is the unbroken thread to Ramie's real mama.

In the beginning of the novel Miss Liz seems almost completely positive: strong, wise, maternal, she dominates the action and the dialogue. Her character gains in complexity as it loses its physical dominance, however. For as Ramie learns to see her as human and therefore fallible, and as she begins to realize that Miss Liz will die, she begins to think of her as a woman, no longer simply the grandmother. She begins to discover another side to her grandmother's great strength as she reconstructs the past, finding that her dominance was sometimes ruthless selfishness, both toward her long-mourned husband and her youngest daughter. As Ramie's perspective shifts and readjusts she is forced to question Miss Liz's view of her mother and father.

Wilkinson further grounds the novel to past and present through the character of Dummy, an old, mute man who is about Miss Liz's age. He has grown old in close proximity to Miss Liz, who for not entirely explained reasons hates him. Dummy is very much like a child and acts as a touchstone for innocence. Ramie is quickly convinced of his simplicity, his genuine and honest love of his young playmates, and his desire to make them happy. The young children who play with him accept him absolutely. Dummy acts as the proving ground of Miss Liz's judgment, and she is shown to be prejudiced and wrong.

In the beginning of the novel Ramie paints and carves Miss Liz obsessively. She begins to work and a figure emerges in wood or on canvas. She does not paint landscapes, but faces; she cannot make backgrounds, and when her teacher tells her to fill in around a face she just puts a color there. Miss Liz in particular resists context: "I try to think of something that she would have behind her, but I never can paint it. Not after I already have her face," she says. *A Killing Frost* is Ramie's gathering of context, a filling in of background. In the end, when her grandmother is bedridden and Dummy is dead, Ramie writes Dummy's name in the family

Dust jacket for Wilkinson's 1972 novel tracing the alienation of a young man from his family

Bible, thus creating a context for him.

She also reaches a context for Miss Liz, a balance between love and anger. She holds her grandmother accountable for a list of lost men and boys—her dead brother Gregory, killed by a black widow spider at three after Miss Liz left him alone to play, Dummy, Papa, her own father. She senses a maternal power that has left Miss Liz alive in the wake of all these dead males. Yet her perceptions of the complexities of love and power, submission and dominance, resistance and compliance are qualified by the whole context of her own and her grandmother's lives. She learns to blame without hating and to love without worshipping and thus reaches a growth belied by the dead season around her.

Reviewers saw *A Killing Frost* as fulfilling the promise shown in *Moss on the North Side*. The *Christian Science Monitor* reviewer, Marilyn Gardner, wrote, "[Wilkinson's] second novel, richly detailing a warm grandmother-granddaughter relationship, is credible but not contrived, sensitive but never sentimental. . . . [Her] descriptions of the backwater countryside are often sheer poetry, as integral a part of the book's strength as her portraits of the two women. . . . [The novelist is] gifted with an uncommon eye and ear for the customs and dialects of everyday Southern life." The *American Scholar* reviewer, Roberta Farr, qualified her enthusiasm, seeing *A Killing Frost* as "a more interesting and shapely novel than . . . *Moss on the North Side*," but citing them both for "the same technical problem with weaving in too many memories." The novel was also reviewed by, among others, Martin Levin in the *New York Times Book Review* and in *Saturday Review* and the *Virginia Quarterly Review*.

Cale (1970) is Wilkinson's longest novel and her only novel to depart from a young female protagonist; knowing her character Cale and helping him to manhood clearly demanded a novel with greater scope. Instead of a season or a single turn of the seasons as in her first two novels, *Cale* takes its protagonist from his birth in 1940 until a month before his high-school graduation. He is surrounded by family and caught in a web of old hostilities—his father, Jerome, and mother, Falissa, grate on each other; the constant irritations are complicated by Falissa's father, Papa Lonza, her dying mother, Jerome's wayward brother, Roe, and his vicious, stingy father, Willy. The novel documents Cale's birth, his growth, and his alienation from family. In the last lines he plots to leave home: "I can stay and work and get what I need until I got it planned out where I'm going. Then I can get together what I want to take and tell them I'll be back for visits and go down to the bus station and go. I don't know where but it won't matter as long as nobody knows me."

If Wilkinson's first two novels were Bildungsroman, where positive growth and change left Cary and Ramie ready to proceed with their lives, *Cale* seems less conclusive. Cale moves from a simple acceptance of Falissa's and Papa Lonza's doting over him to resentment of their desire to hold on to him. He goes through the requisite anger at both his father and his mother and at the end of the novel finally raises his hand against Jerome's badgering, pushing him to the ground. He turns from the "respectable" behavior Falissa demands to drinking, gambling, and whoring with his reprobate uncle, Roe. At the end of the novel, Cale has just reached the point of alienation that precedes the male Bildungsroman hero's departure from home, established education, and accepted social values.

The novel is rich in social and familial detail, and the narrative technique contributes to its multifaceted vision. The voice constantly modulates; sometimes the story is being told in Falissa's words, sometimes in Papa Lonza's or Jerome's or Cale's, or even Roe's. Papa Lonza extends the story backwards into the past through memories of his own immigrant father and the circumstances of his voyage from Holland and his settling in America. Wilkinson introduces a black family and Floyd, a black foil for Cale's rebellious nature; unlike Cary and Ramie, who inherit racial ambiguities, Cale is white and thus must by definition participate in racism as part of his growing up.

The seed of the novel lies in Floyd's shooting of a great blue heron. Wilkinson describes the actual event from which she wrote this scene:

> *Cale* was started because I was hurt and angry when a cousin had killed a great blue heron that came to our farm every year. The bird came alone and fed around our pond, thinking it was not threatened. I saw it dead, shot at close range. I wrote about it over and over in my journal because I had to. . . . I couldn't separate my own anger to fictionalize until I changed the characters. They were no longer my cousin and myself, but Cale, a white boy, and Floyd, a black boy. I had to see the incident from the killer's viewpoint too. My cousin had killed the bird out of anger at his father who whipped him. . . . Floyd killed the bird in anger over Cale's humiliation of him. It was Floyd saying I could have aimed the gun from the same woods, moving the barrel a few feet and killed you, Cale. The pain of the real incident will never go away. . . . But writing about it through characters has given it multiple dimensions and multiple viewpoints.

Cale was, like Wilkinson's two previous books, considered a success by critics who read it as a faithful rendering of the South. *Booklist*'s reviewer wrote, "The author of *A Killing Frost* has again captured rural Southern life and family universals in an appealing novel that does not skimp the dark side of that life. . . ." A long review by James W. Clark in the *Carolina Quarterly* was negative, seeing Cale, his family, and his surroundings as stereotypes; but the *Virginia Quarterly Review* acknowledged Wilkinson's excellence—"Within her genre," it said, "Miss Wilkinson would appear to have few present peers."

The novel was, like Wilkinson's others, moderately successful financially, and soon after the publication of *Cale* Wilkinson began writing children's books. She is the author of ten nonfiction books for children on racing. Her children's books have been more lucrative than her novels.

Algonquin Press of Chapel Hill, North Carolina, has reissued a revised version of *Cale* (1986) with an introduction by the press's founder and Wilkinson's mentor, Louis Rubin. This shortened version pares away many of Falissa's long monologues, where, Rubin admits, Wilkinson had allowed herself to become "so caught up in Falissa's voice that she had indulged herself, allowing Falissa to meditate, speculate, remember, moralize, and otherwise express herself interminably." The revised *Cale* thus attempts to intensify Cale himself by undermining Falissa's powerfully maternal presence so that now he occupies, according to Rubin, "the centrally prominent role he was meant to fill."

Shadow of the Mountain (1977) is about Jean Fitzgerald, a young woman searching for something of value in her life. Her particular effort is to find significant work, and ultimately she is given a government job in a small, very poor North Carolina mountain town. The time frame of the novel is a little over a year, from the winter day when Jean finds the frozen corpse of a young mountain woman sitting at the deserted top of Mount Le Conte, to the following March, when she sits, in imminent danger of her life, alone in an isolated mountain cabin. The novel is divided into four parts: the first takes place during her final months of college; the second, during her summer European tour; the third, beginning in August, encompassing the early fall and the first months of her job in the Appalachian Corp.; and the fourth, from November until March, when she is facing increasingly dangerous hostility from the mountain people around her.

There is very little continuity to these stages, for Jean is an isolated character who has no sustained interaction with anyone else. She is a writer and seems more preoccupied with translating her past and present into language than in the immediate experiences themselves. At the end of the novel, as she becomes progressively more isolated, she does not go to her parents or to her friend Clara, nor do they come to her, and her only communication, again, is through letters. Jean Fitzgerald is Wilkinson's most threatened character, because she has no bonds—natural, familial, or romantic—strong enough to keep her safe. Most of what she writes she drops into a hidden box; she

is attempting to reorder her own life but senses that mere words won't change anything: "Maybe I already am what I am now and can't change it or figure out why by going backwards," she writes.

It turns out that her fears are correct, for Jean Fitzgerald is a woman Wilkinson designates as a victim. According to Wilkinson, Jean's story is loosely based on a Vista worker who went into the North Carolina mountains and was murdered. Wilkinson's choice of a predetermined victim to be her main character was problematic. Given Wilkinson's belief in fiction as organic process, where the characters dictate their own development after a point, this choice seems contrary to her instincts as a writer.

Indeed *Shadow of the Mountain* suffers from Wilkinson's knowledge of Jean's inevitable fate. Unlike Cary, Ramie, and Cale, Jean Fitzgerald never seems entirely whole, perhaps because Wilkinson did not want to become too attached to her doomed character. Jean is not, like the earlier characters and Wilkinson herself, rooted to nature, and she is essentially unreconciled to inevitable and uncontrollable natural cycles. She struggles to become part of her natural surroundings, but she is always an alien—whether hiking in the winter in the North Carolina mountains, or in Europe, or in her job in the Appalachian Corp. She has gone through Outward Bound programs, and she is skillful at endurance tests, but she is not a survivor because she is not part of, and does not understand, the natural forces around her.

The result is a fragmented, troubled character who seems to be struggling toward suicide rather than life. Because Jean is an outsider among people she doesn't really understand, the other characters in *Shadow of the Mountain* remain caricatures. Mollie Burcham, an old mountain woman and an outcast among her own people, is the only developed character with any potential for grace; her bitterly hard life and her instinctive will to survive make her a more likeable character than the rest. Ugly, ancient, toothless, nearly bald, Mollie likes Jean in part because Jean listens to stories about her past. She has no pithy mountain wisdom or strong maternal force or warm compassion, but she is the antithesis to Jane Boey, the suicide of the opening pages, to whom Jean directly compares her. She is what Jean is not, a survivor, without illusions. Jean has retained the illusion that she can affect and change others—teach the mountain ladies a powder-puff mechanics course or open their minds to literature. She clearly likes Mollie, but there is an undercurrent of patronage in her friendship, as when she takes Mollie to the ocean as if it will somehow change Mollie's life. She accomplishes nothing during her mountain stay; the forces of hostility, resentment, suspicion, and stupidity are too strong. Yet she mistakenly perceives this as one more survival test, and in the end she sits waiting for her own murder. She does not understand nature and the natural forces that dominate the mountain people around her, and she commits suicide as surely as if she had, like Jane Boey, walked to the top of a mountain in the dead of winter only lightly clothed.

Shadow of the Mountain seems a less reviewed book than Wilkinson's previous novels. *Choice* reviewed *Shadow of the Mountain* negatively, saying, "Although the opening pages of this novel . . . are interesting, Wilkinson jerks the reader from past to present, from consciousness to consciousness so arbitrarily that it is difficult if not impossible for a reader to be engaged with it." The review ended with the terse comment, "Not recommended."

Bone of My Bones (1982) is, in part, a reaction to *Shadow of the Mountain*. Wilkinson says of her main character, "I see Ella Ruth as a survivor not a victim and for now I must have a character to write about who is strong and can fight in order to hold my interest. . . . The pathetic, crushed woman can't come from my imagination right now, though I know Ella Ruth's strength is not universal and not common for a girl with her background." *Bone of My Bones* is Wilkinson's portrait of a girl whose artistic instincts refuse to capitulate to the forces that work to pull her down. Ella Ruth Higgins has, to the world's eyes, all the disadvantages—poor white-trash parents, delinquent and insensitive companions, indifferent schooling. She is raped by a group of boys who have grown up with her. She cannot afford to go to college, despite a partial scholarship, and stays to work as an aide in the hospital so that she can take care of her alcoholic father. Yet Ella Ruth does not see with the world's eyes; most particularly she does not see her father, and especially her mother, as the world sees them. She is so genuinely an artist that she can remake her world, not to some external standard of beauty but to her own wholeness.

The novel takes Ella Ruth from 1950, when she is ten (like Cale, Ella Ruth is born the same year as Wilkinson), through 1958. Wilkinson divides the book into sections, titled "1950," "1954," "1956," and "1958." The first section is interspersed with the "Starrie" stories, which Ella Ruth keeps in a special box. Like *A Killing Frost, Bone of My Bones* is in first person, but Ella Ruth's voice has

a resonance and complexity that Ramie's lacks. Wilkinson is not creating an ordinary woman in *Bone of My Bones*, but one who rejects conventional avenues to fulfillment. Ella Ruth is not interested in sex as she grows older, to the confusion of her friend Al. He says, "Why do you pretend you're an old maid school teacher or something? . . . I mean you dress like a normal person, a girl. You don't paint your nails or nothing, but you fix up like a girl." She looks like the people Al knows, but clearly is quite different: she is, like Cary—and Cary's reincarnation, Starrie—an outcast despite her appearance. She does not react to circumstances in an ordinary way either. When Al shoots her in the leg with his twenty-two, she gets mad, but she doesn't tell and gets Al's precious Phantom ring. Five years later, when Al's group of friends rapes her, she doesn't tell, although she is aware of what has been destroyed in herself. She says, "That night before I went to sleep, I decided I might marry Al Sawyer someday. . . . That is the day I think I became a little crazy for good."

Bone of My Bones is a novel of development, but its goal is not to integrate Ella Ruth into society; a *Kunstlerroman* more than a *Bildungsroman*, it is concerned with her transformation from the artist who wrote the Starrie stories to the artist who writes the long, intricate, and highly personal play at the end of the novel. The last section of the novel represents a form of disintegration but promises the forging of the artistic imagination. Ella Ruth feels herself losing control and imagines herself writing on a hospital admission form for her father, "One daughter, Ella Ruth Higgins. Ruth's OK but Ella's crazy." She begins to assume other voices, becoming Ella Ruth Darwin, anthropologist of the imagination, or the women she cares for in the hospital, Katherine Hinshawe and Elisa Simpson.

Wilkinson sees this final breakdown of narrative conventions as a positive step. She says,

> In the end Ella Ruth weaves her own life up to that point into her imaginery outburst, a play so personal that it can't be read with total understanding out of context. Through it comes something more complex than working out her own confusion about her experience. Through it she makes something that comes out of that mysterious place that inspired writing comes from, something so mysterious that even the creator must stretch and stand on tiptoes to reach it. This creation slides in and out of the artist's reach until she admits it has its own life and that she gave it that life.

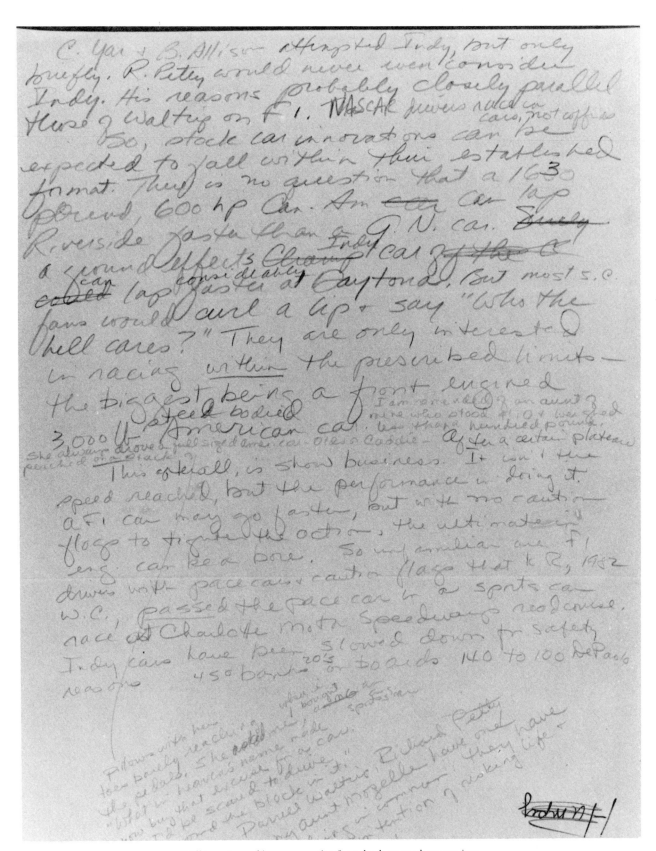

Wilkinson's working manuscript for a book on stock car racing

Ella Ruth's sense of her madness is also proof of her ability to go beyond her own identity into other lives. Wilkinson implies here her possession of a sort of divine schizophrenia, an empathetic power denied to those who see in ordinary ways. Ella Ruth's relationship to her parents is a crucial part of her development. Wilkinson says, "Ella Ruth has pathetic parents to outside eyes, yet they nurture her so strongly, she even finds it difficult to have two parents at once." Her father is a scrawny, ridiculous little man, a racist who agrees with Hitler about Jews and blacks. But he has an extraordinary resilience and moments of comic grace; Wilkinson manages to make the reader care what happens to Maynard Higgins, thus reflecting Ella Ruth's saving vision of her father. Ella Ruth's mother is a complex character, a grossly fat caterer who wastes away to absolute fragility and dies when Ella Ruth is seventeen. Her mother is gentle but slightly foolish and a little bit stupid. She becomes, however, an entirely memorable character; Wilkinson makes her so real and important as a mother to Ella that her death is devastating. In the last pages of the novel, Ella Ruth turns back to memories of her mother, and the final words of the book are her mother's answer to the saving of the Luna moth: "Ella Ruth, all you have to do is cut off the light."

The reviews of *Bone of My Bones* were enthusiastic. David Quammer, in the *New York Times Book Review*, said, "Ella Ruth's voice is an effective voice, graced with humor, richly raucous language and illuminations of the travail of female adolescence." The *Washington Post* reviewer wrote, "Because Sylvia Wilkinson is herself an uncommonly talented writer, and because she knows her territory so well, her work always commands a serious and respectful hearing. An appealing story of a tough, resourceful, determined young woman." Lisa Mitchell said in the *Los Angeles Times*, "Sylvia Wilkinson is a marvel of subtle skill. . . . Everything Wilkinson has laid before us falls into literary and psychological place. Not a word is false."

Sylvia Wilkinson is a skilled and talented writer whose work has become richer and more complex over time. She brings to her fiction an essential optimism, a belief in the value of human experience and in the value of the artist's role in clarifying that experience. Her novels, from the very beginning, show a commitment to craftsmanship: she might just as easily be fitting the parts of a racing engine together. She wants her characters to learn, and she seems to learn from them. There is a sameness in her concerns in these novels, but the novels are never the same. Each moves toward its end with an inevitability born of its particular time, place, character, and form, but there has been a broadening of scope since *Moss on the North Side*. The texture, always rich, has gradually intensified; Fred Chappell has said that Wilkinson "fills up the page" as a painter might, that "every inch is filled up with an organism going about its own purposes, and yet fretfully entangled with the lives about it." She has not lessened this density, and seems to have become more and more three-dimensional, so that in *Bone of My Bones* the characters come alive. They do not live because they are familiar and attractive—they are strange, and rather ugly, in fact— but because Wilkinson crafts them so lovingly that they become quite human.

Wilkinson lives in El Segundo, California. She has spent the time since the publication of *Bone of My Bones* working a grueling schedule on the racing circuit. She has plans for a sixth novel and will soon be taking time off from racing to write full-time.

Interviews:

"Interview: Sylvia Wilkinson," *Washington College Review* (January 1975);

Jane Vance, "An Interview with Sylvia Wilkinson," *Kentucky Review*, 2 (1981): 75-88.

References:

Fred Chappell, "Unpeaceable Kingdoms: The Novels of Sylvia Wilkinson," *Hollins Critic*, 8 (April 1971): 1-10;

Frank N. Magill, "Sylvia Wilkinson," in *Critical Survey of Long Fiction*, edited by Magill (Englewood Cliffs, N.J.: Salem Press, 1983), pp. 2889-2896;

Jane Gentry Vance, "Fat Like Mama/Mean Like Daddy: The Fiction of Sylvia Wilkinson," in *Southern Literary Journal*, 15 (Fall 1982): 22-36.

Literary Awards and Honors Announced in 1986

ACADEMY OF AMERICAN POETS AWARDS

Howard Moss.

LAMONT SELECTION
James Shore, for *The Minute Hand* (University of Massachusetts Press).

IVAN YOUNGER POETS AWARD
Rita Dove, Rodney Jones, Timothy Steele.

WHITMAN AWARD
Chris Llewellyn, for *Fragments from the Fire* (Viking Penguin).

AMERICAN ACADEMY AND INSTITUTE OF ARTS AND LETTERS AWARDS

AWARDS IN LITERATURE
Russell Banks, Frederick Busch, Robert A. Caro, Robert Kelly, Barry Lopez, David Mamet, Marsha Norman, and Lore Segal.

AWARD OF MERIT MEDAL FOR POETRY
Kenneth Koch.

HAROLD D. VURSELL MEMORIAL AWARD
Gretel Ehrlich, for *The Solace of Open Spaces* (Viking).

JEAN STEIN AWARD
Gregory Corso.

MORTON DAUWEN ZABEL AWARD
Philip Whalen.

RICHARD AND HINDA ROSENTHAL FOUNDATION AWARD
Richard Powers, for *Three Farmers on Their Way to a Dance* (Morrow).

ROME FELLOWSHIP IN LITERATURE
Richard Kenney.

SUE KAUFMAN PRIZE FOR FIRST FICTION
Cecile Pineda, for *Face* (Viking).

WITTER BYNNER PRIZE FOR POETRY
C. D. Wright.

E. M. FORSTER AWARD
Julian Barnes.

AMERICAN BOOK AWARDS

FICTION
E. L. Doctorow, for *World's Fair* (Random House).

NONFICTION
Barry Lopez, for *Arctic Dreams* (Scribners).

BENNETT AWARD

Nadine Gordimer.

BOOKER PRIZE

Kingsley Amis, for *The Old Devils* (Hutchinson).

CALDECOTT MEDAL

Chris Van Allsburg, for *The Polar Express* (Houghton Mifflin).

COMMON WEALTH AWARD

John Ashbery.

CURTIS G. BENJAMIN AWARD

Simon Michael Bessie.

DELMORE SCHWARTZ MEMORIAL POETRY AWARD

Brenda Hillman.

DRUE HEINZ LITERATURE PRIZE

Rick DeMarines, for *Under the Wheat* (University of Pittsburgh Press).

EDGAR ALLAN POE AWARDS

GRAND MASTER AWARD
  Ed McBain (Evan Hunter).

NOVEL
  L. R. Wright, for *The Suspect* (Viking Penguin).

FIRST NOVEL
  Jonathan Kellerman, for *When the Bough Breaks* (Atheneum).

FACT CRIME
  Natalie Robins and Steven M. L. Aronson, for *Savage Grace* (Morrow).

CRITICAL/BIOGRAPHICAL STUDY
  Peter Lewis, for *John le Carré* (Ungar).

ORIGINAL SOFTCOVER NOVEL
  Warren Murphy, for *Pigs Get Fat* (New American Library).

JUVENILE NOVEL
  Patricia Windsor, for *The Sandman's Eyes* (Delacorte).

SHORT STORY
  John Lutz, for "Ride the Lightning" (*Alfred Hitchcock's Mystery Magazine*).

MOTION PICTURE
  Earl W. Wallace and William Kelley, for *Witness* (Paramount), from a story by William Kelley, Pamela Wallace, and Earl W. Wallace.

SPECIAL EDGAR
  Walter Albert, for *Detective and Mystery Fiction: An International Bibliography of Secondary Sources* (Brownstone Books).

SPECIAL PLAY AWARD
  Rupert Holmes, for *The Mystery of Edwin Drood* (New York Shakespeare Festival).

READER OF THE YEAR
  New York State Senator Suzi Oppenheimer.

ROBERT L. FISH MEMORIAL AWARD
  Doug Allyn, for "Final Rites" (*Alfred Hitchcock's Mystery Magazine*).

GOVERNOR GENERAL'S LITERARY AWARDS (ENGLISH LANGUAGE)

FICTION
  Margaret Atwood, for *The Handmaid's Tale* (McClelland and Stewart).

POETRY
  Fred Wah, for *Waiting for Saskatchewan* (Turnstone Press).

DRAMA
  George F. Walker, for *Criminals in Love* (Playwrights Canada).

NONFICTION
  Ramsay Cook, for *The Regenerators: Social Criticism in Late Victorian Canada* (University of Toronto Press).

HUGO AWARDS

NOVEL
  Orson Scott Card, for *Ender's Game* (TOR Books).

NOVELLA
  Roger Zelazny, for *Twenty-Four Views of Mount Fuji by Hokusai* (*Isaac Asimov's Science Fiction Magazine*, July 1985).

NOVELETTE
  Harlan Ellison, for *Palladin of the Lost Hour* (*Twilight Zone Magazine*, December 1985).

SHORT STORY
  Frederik Pohl, for "Fermi and Frost" (*Isaac Asimov's Science Fiction Magazine*, January 1985).

JOHN W. CAMPBELL AWARD FOR BEST NEW WRITER
  Melissa Scott.

INGERSOLL PRIZES

T. S. ELIOT AWARD FOR CREATIVE WRITING
V. S. Naipaul.

RICHARD M. WEAVER AWARD FOR SCHOLARLY LETTERS
Andrew Lytle.

IRITA VAN DOREN AWARD

RIF (Reading Is Fundamental), Washington, D.C.

IRMA SIMONTON BLACK AWARD

Sandra Boynton, for *Chloe and Maude* (Little, Brown).

JANET HEIDINGER KAFKA PRIZE FOR FICTION

Ursula LeGuin, for *Always Coming Home* (Harper & Row).

JERUSALEM PRIZE

Luis Alberto Monge, Per Ahlmark, and Rabbi Eliahu Essas.

JOHN D. AND CATHERINE T. MACARTHUR FOUNDATION AWARD

Daryl Hine and Jay Wright.

LAURA INGALLS WILDER AWARD

Jean Fritz.

LOS ANGELES TIMES BOOK AWARDS

FICTION
Margaret Atwood, for *The Handmaid's Tale* (Houghton Mifflin).

HISTORY
Geoffrey Hosking, for *The First Socialist Society: A History of the Soviet Union from Within* (Harvard University Press).

CURRENT INTEREST
Joseph Lelyveld, for *Move Your Shadow: South Africa, Black and White* (Times Books).

BIOGRAPHY
Maynard Mack, for *Alexander Pope: A Life* (Norton).

POETRY
Derek Walcott, for *Collected Poems, 1948-1984* (Farrar, Straus & Giroux).

ROBERT KIRSCH AWARD
Kay Boyle.

MEDAL OF HONOR FOR LITERATURE

Marguerite Yourcenar.

NATIONAL BOOK CRITICS CIRCLE AWARDS

FICTION
Anne Tyler, for *The Accidental Tourist* (Knopf).

POETRY
Louise Glück, for *The Triumph of Achilles* (Ecco Press).

CRITICISM
William Gass, for *Habitations of the Word* (Simon & Schuster).

BIOGRAPHY/AUTOBIOGRAPHY
Leon Edel, for *Henry James: A Life* (Harper & Row).

NATIONAL JEWISH BOOK AWARDS

BIOGRAPHY
Jehuda Reinharz, for *Chaim Weizmann: The Making of a Zionist Leader* (Oxford University Press).

CHILDREN'S LITERATURE
Linda Atkinson, for *In Kindling Flame, The*

Story of Hannah Senesh, 1921-1944 (Lothrop, Lee & Shepard).

FICTION
Arnost Lustig, for *The Unloved: From the Diary of Perla S.* (Arbor House), translated by Vera Kalina Levine.

HOLOCAUST
Raul Hilberg, for *The Destruction of the European Jews: Revised and Definitive Edition* (Holmes and Meier).

ILLUSTRATED CHILDREN'S BOOKS
Florence B. Freedman, for *Brothers*, illustrated by Robert Andrew Parker (Harper & Row).

ISRAEL
Steven Spiegel, for *The Other Arab-Israeli Conflict: Making America's Middle East Policy from Truman to Reagan* (University of Chicago Press).

JEWISH HISTORY
Robert Liberles, for *Religious Conflict in Social Context: The Resurgence of Orthodox Judaism in Frankfurt Am Main, 1839-1877* (Greenwood Press).

JEWISH THOUGHT
David Hartman, for *A Living Covenant: The Innovative Spirit in Traditional Judaism* (Free Press/Macmillan).

SCHOLARSHIP
Michael Fishbane, for *Biblical Interpretation in Ancient Israel* (Oxford University Press).

VISUAL ARTS
Carol Herselle Krinsky, for *Synagogues of Europe: Architecture, History, Meaning* (Architectural History Foundation/MIT Press).

NEBULA AWARDS

NOVEL
Orson Scott Card, for *Ender's Game* (TOR Books).

NOVELLA
Robert Silverberg, for *Sailing to Byzantium*

(*Isaac Asimov's Science Fiction Magazine,* February 1985).

NOVELETTE
George R. R. Martin, for *Portraits of His Children* (*Isaac Asimov's Science Fiction Magazine,* November 1985).

SHORT STORY
Nancy Kress, for "Out of All Them Bright Stars" (*Magazine of Fantasy and Science Fiction,* March 1985).

GRAND MASTER AWARD
Arthur C. Clarke.

NEUSTADT INTERNATIONAL PRIZE FOR LITERATURE

Max Frisch.

NEWBERY MEDAL

Patricia MacLachlan, for *Sarah, Plain and Tall* (Harper & Row).

NOBEL PRIZE IN LITERATURE

Wole Soyinka.

O. HENRY AWARDS

Alice Walker, for "Kindred Spirits" (*Esquire,* August 1985).

SPECIAL AWARD FOR CONTINUING ACHIEVEMENT

Joyce Carol Oates.

PEN AWARDS

PEN/FAULKNER AWARD
Peter Taylor, for *The Old Forest and Other Stories* (Doubleday).

ERNEST HEMINGWAY FOUNDATION AWARD

Alan V. Hewat, for *Lady's Time* (Harper & Row).

PEN MEDAL FOR TRANSLATION OF PROSE

Barbara Bray, for Marguerite Duras's *The Lover* (Pantheon).

PEN MEDAL FOR TRANSLATION OF POETRY

Denis Tedlock, for *Popol Vul: The Mayan Book of the Dawn of Life* (Simon & Schuster).

RENATO POGGIOLI TRANSLATION AWARD FOR A WORK IN PROGRESS

Ned Condini, for a projected anthology of modern Italian poets.

PEN/NELSON ALGREN FICTION AWARD FOR A WORK IN PROGRESS

Mary La Chappelle, for a collection of short fiction.

PRESENT TENSE/JOEL H. CAVIOR LITERARY AWARDS

FICTION

William Herrick, for *That's Life* (New Directions).

HISTORY

Michael R. Marrus, for *The Unwanted: European Refugees in the Twentieth Century* (Oxford University Press).

BIOGRAPHY/AUTOBIOGRAPHY

Jehuda Reinharz, for *Chaim Weizmann: The Making of a Zionist Leader* (Oxford University Press).

RELIGIOUS THOUGHT

Robert Alter, for *The Art of Biblical Poetry* (Basic Books).

GENERAL NONFICTION

Charles E. Silberman, for *A Certain People: American Jews and Their Lives Today* (Summit).

CITATION FOR LIFETIME ACHIEVEMENT

Irving Howe.

PULITZER PRIZES

FICTION

Larry McMurtry, for *Lonesome Dove* (Simon & Schuster).

GENERAL NONFICTION

Joseph Lelyveld, for *Move Your Shadow: South Africa, Black and White* (Times Books); and J. Anthony Lukas, for *Common Ground* (Knopf).

HISTORY

Walter A. McDougall, for *The Heavens and the Earth: A Political History of the Space Age* (Basic Books).

BIOGRAPHY

Elizabeth Frank, for *Louise Bogan: A Portrait* (Knopf).

POETRY

Henry Taylor, for *The Flying Change* (Louisiana State University Press).

REA AWARD FOR THE SHORT STORY

Cynthia Ozick.

REGINA MEDAL

Lloyd Alexander.

RITZ PARIS HEMINGWAY AWARD

Marguerite Duras, for *The Lover* (Pantheon).

ROBERT F. KENNEDY MEMORIAL BOOK AWARDS

J. Anthony Lukas, for *Common Ground* (Knopf); and Robert Norrell, for *Reaping the Whirlwind* (Knopf).

SCOTT O'DELL AWARD FOR HISTORICAL FICTION

Scott O'Dell, for *Streams to the River, River to the Sea* (Houghton Mifflin).

WESTERN STATES BOOK AWARDS

FICTION
Clarence Major, for *My Amputations* (Fiction Collective).

POETRY
Mary Barnard, for *Time and the Tigress* (Breitenbush Books).

CREATIVE NONFICTION
Anita Sullivan, for *The Seventh Dragon: The Riddle of Equal Temperament* (Metamorphous Press).

CITATION FOR EXCELLENCE
Kim Stafford, for *Having Everything Right: Essays of Place* (Confluence Press).

WHITBREAD AWARDS

FICTION
Douglas Dunn, for *Elegies* (Faber).

BIOGRAPHY
Richard Mabey, for *Gilbert White* (Century).

WHITING AWARDS

John Ash, Hayden Carruth, Kent Haruf, Denis Johnson, Darryl Pinckney, Padgett Powell, Mona Simpson, Frank Stewart, Ruth Stone, and August Wilson.

W. H. SMITH AWARD

Doris Lessing, for *The Good Terrorist* (Cape).

Checklist: Contributions to Literary History and Biography, 1986

This checklist is a selection of new books on various aspects and periods of literary and cultural history; biographies, memoirs, and correspondence of literary people and their associates; and primary bibliographies. Not included are volumes in general reference series, literary criticism, and bibliographies of criticism.

Abt, Samuel, ed. *The Paris Edition: The Autobiography of Waverly Root, 1927-1934.* Berkeley, Cal.: North Point, 1986.

Ahearn, Barry, ed. *Selected Letters of Ezra Pound and Louis Zukofsky.* New York: New Directions, 1986.

Alderson, Brian. *Sing a Song of Sixpence: The English Picture Book Tradition and Randolph Caldecott.* New York: Cambridge University Press, 1986.

Barbera, Jack, and William McBrien. *Stevie Smith: A Biography.* New York: Oxford University Press, 1986.

Beer, Gillian. *George Eliot.* Bloomington: Indiana University Press, 1986.

Branch, Edgar Marquess, and others, eds. *Mark Twain's Collected Letters: Volume I (1853-1866).* Berkeley: University of California, 1986.

Brown, E. K. *Willa Cather: A Critical Biography.* Lincoln: University of Nebraska Press, 1986.

Brown, J. D. *Henry Miller.* New York: Ungar, 1986.

Bruccoli, Matthew J. *The Fortunes of Mitchell Kennerley, Bookman.* New York & San Diego: Harcourt Brace Jovanovich, 1986.

Burgess, Anthony. *Little Wilson and Big God.* New York: Weidenfeld & Nicolson, 1986.

Burnshaw, Stanley. *Robert Frost Himself.* New York: Braziller, 1986.

Caldwell, Erskine. *With All My Might: An Autobiography.* Atlanta: Peachtree, 1986.

Campbell, Will D. *Forty Acres and a Goat: A Memoir.* Atlanta: Peachtree, 1986.

Charters, Ann. *Beats & Company.* Garden City: Doubleday/Dolphin, 1986.

Cooper, Wayne F. *Claude McKay: Rebel Sojourner in the Harlem Renaissance.* Baton Rouge: Louisiana State University Press, 1986.

Devlin, Albert J. *Conversations With Tennessee Williams.* Jackson: University Press of Mississippi, 1986.

Donald, David Herbert. *Look Homeward: A Life of Thomas Wolfe.* Boston: Little, Brown, 1986.

DuPlessis, Rachel Blau. *H. D.: The Career of That Struggle.* Bloomington: Indiana University Press, 1986.

Edel, Leon. *Henry James: A Life.* Revised and abridged edition. New York: Harper & Row, 1986.

Ewell, Barbara. *Kate Chopin.* New York: Ungar, 1986.

Feinstein, Elaine. *A Captive Lion: The Life of Marina Tsvetayeva.* Garden City: Doubleday, 1986.

Ffinch, Michael. *G. K. Chesterton: A Life.* New York: Weidenfeld & Nicolson, 1986.

Ford, Hugh. *Four Lives in Paris.* Berkeley: North Point Press, 1986.

Francis, Claude, and Fernande Gontier. *Simone de Beauvoir: A Life, A Love Story.* New York: St. Martin's, 1986.

Frank, Joseph. *Dostoevsky: The Stir of Liberation, 1860-1865.* Princeton: Princeton University Press, 1986.

Fullbrook, Kate. *Katherine Mansfield.* Bloomington: Indiana University Press, 1986.

Gibbs, James, Ketu H. Katrak, and Henry Louis Gates, Jr., comps. *Wole Soyinka: A Bibliography of Primary and Secondary Sources.* Westport, Conn. & London: Greenwood, 1986.

Givner, Joan, ed. *Katherine Anne Porter: Conversations.* Jackson: University Press of Mississippi, 1986.

Gordon, Lyndall. *Virginia Woolf: A Writer's Life.* New York: Norton, 1986.

Hayman, Ronald. *Sartre.* New York: Simon & Schuster, 1986.

James, Henry. *The Complete Notebooks of Henry James.* Edited by Leon Edel and Lyall H. Powers. New York: Oxford University Press, 1986.

Joyce, James. *James Joyce's Letters to Sylvia Beach, 1921-1940.* Edited by Melissa Banta and Oscar A. Silverman. Bloomington: Indiana University Press, 1986.

King, James. *William Cowper: A Biography.* Durham: Duke University Press, 1986.

Koon, Helene. *Colley Cibber: A Biography.* Lexington: University Press of Kentucky, 1986.

L'Engle, Madeleine. *The Irrational Season.* New York: Farrar, Straus & Giroux, 1986.

Lingeman, Richard. *Theodore Dreiser: At The Gates of the City 1871-1907.* New York: Putnam's, 1986.

Lowell, Robert. *The Collected Prose.* Edited by Robert Giroux. New York: Farrar, Straus & Giroux, 1986.

Mack, Maynard. *Alexander Pope.* New York: Norton, 1986.

Magee, Rosemary M., ed. *Conversations With Flannery O'Connor.* Jackson: University Press of Mississippi, 1986.

Marx, Sam. *A Gaudy Spree: Literary Hollywood When the West Was Fun.* Danbury, Conn.: Franklin Watts, 1986.

McCarthy, Mary. *How I Grew.* New York & San Diego: Harcourt Brace Jovanovich, 1986.

Merwin, W. S. *Regions of Memory: Uncollected Prose, 1949-82.* Champaign: University of Illinois Press, 1986.

O'Brien, Sharon. *Willa Cather: The Emerging Voice.* New York: Oxford University Press, 1986.

Orton, Joe. *The Orton Diaries.* New York: Harper & Row, 1986.

Rampersad, Arnold. *The Life of Langston Hughes, Volume I: I, Too, Sing America.* New York: Oxford University Press, 1986.

Richardson, Joan. *Wallace Stevens: The Early Years, 1879-1923.* New York: Beech Tree/Morrow, 1986.

Richardson, Robert D. *Henry Thoreau: A Life of the Mind.* Berkeley: University of California Press, 1986.

Rodgers, Marion Elizabeth. *Mencken and Sara: A Life in Letters.* New York: McGraw-Hill, 1986.

Sarton, May. *May Sarton: A Self-Portrait.* New York: Norton, 1986.

Sartre, Jean-Paul. *Thoughtful Passions: Jean-Paul Sartre's Intimate Letters to Simone de Beauvoir, 1926-1939.* Translated by Matthew Ward with Irene Ilton. New York: Macmilllan, 1986.

Sendak, Maurice. *On Books and Pictures.* New York: Farrar, Straus & Giroux, 1986.

Smith, David. *H. G. Wells, Desperately Mortal: A Biography.* New Haven & London: Yale University Press, 1986.

Spark, Muriel. *Mary Shelley.* New York: Dutton/William Abrahams, 1986.

Stannard, Martin. *Evelyn Waugh: The Early Years, 1903-1939.* New York: Norton, 1986.

Stuart, David. *O. Henry: A Biography of William Sydney Porter.* New York: Stein & Day, 1986.

Tolstoy, Sophia. *The Diaries of Sophia Tolstoy.* Edited by O. A. Golinenko, S. A. Rozanova, B. M. Shumova, I. A. Pokrovskaya and N. I. Azarova. Translated by Cathy Porter. New York. Random House, 1986.

Troyat, Henri. *Chekov.* Translated by Michael Henry Heim. New York: Dutton, 1986.

Weidman, Jerome. *Praying For Rain.* New York: Harper & Row, 1986.

Wilson, Edmund. *The Fifties: From Notebooks and Diaries of the Period.* Edited by Leon Edel. New York: Farrar, Straus & Giroux, 1986.

Winslow, Kathryn. *Henry Miller: Full of Life.* Los Angeles: Jeremy P. Tarcher, 1986.

Wolff, Cynthia Griffin. *Emily Dickinson.* New York: Knopf, 1986.

Wright, William. *Lillian Hellman: The Image, the Woman.* New York: Simon & Schuster, 1986.

Necrology

V. C. Andrews—19 December 1986
Harriette Arnow—22 March 1986
Mel Arrighi—16 September 1986
William E. Barrett—14 September 1986
Simone de Beauvoir—14 April 1986
Jorge Luis Borges—14 June 1986
John Braine—28 October 1986
Michael Braude—29 November 1986
Harry Brown—2 November 1986
Cass Canfield—27 March 1986
John Ciardi—30 March 1986
Arthur A. Cohen—31 October 1986
George Dangerfield—27 December 1986
Judy-Lynn del Rey—20 February 1986
Stanley Ellin—31 July 1986
Lyle Kenyon Engle—10 August 1986
Francis Fergusson—19 December 1986
Rudolph Flesch—5 October 1986

Dame Helen Gardner—4 June 1986
Jean Genet—15 April 1986
Rosamond Gilder—5 September 1986
Peter Heggie—31 March 1986
Mary Hemingway—26 November 1986
L. Ron Hubbard—24 January 1986
Christopher Isherwood—4 January 1986
Storm Jameson—30 September 1986
Donald Klopfer—30 May 1986
John D. MacDonald—28 December 1986
Bernard Malamud—18 March 1986
Dumas Malone—27 December 1986
Merle Miller—10 June 1986
Vrest Orton—2 December 1986
Gordon Norton Ray—15 December 1986
Brother Jonathan Ringkamp—19 September 1986
Helen Hooven Santmyer—21 February 1986
Dwight Taylor—31 December 1986
Era Bell Thompson—30 December 1986

Contributors

Michael Adams .... *Syracuse, New York*
Jaime Alazraki .... *Harvard University*
Ronald Baughman ....*University of South Carolina*
Alexander Blackburn ....*University of Colorado, Colorado Springs*
John C. Broderick... *Library of Congress*
Matthew J. Bruccoli ....*University of South Carolina*
Caroline Cherry ....*Eastern College*
Thorne Compton...*University of South Carolina*
Dame Felicitas Corrigan, O.S.B. ....*Stanbrook Abbey*
Peter Davison .... *London, England*
Mary Doll .... *Fulton, New York*
Mary S. Dye..*Columbia, South Carolina*
Stuart S. Elenko .... *Holocaust Studies Center,*
Bronx High School of Science
Stuart Evans .... *London, England*
Wallace Fowlie.. *Duke University*
George Garrett ....*University of Virginia*
Alex Gildzen...*Kent State University Libraries*
Martyn Goff .... *London, England*
Daniel Haberman ....*New York, New York*
Mark C. Harris ....*Jackson Community College*
Thomas Hayes...*University of South Carolina*
Carolyn Heilbrun...*Columbia University*
Jeffrey Helterman...*University of South Carolina*
Edgar W. Hirshberg .... *University of South Florida*
Katherine Kearns...*Louisiana School for Math,*
Science and the Arts
David Krause ....*Northwestern University*
Keith Kroll..*Kalamazoo Valley Community College*
Liliane Lazar...*New York, New York*
John Letts.. *The Folio Society*
Michael Mullen .... *Indian Hills Community College*
Yolanda Astarita Patterson ....*California State University, Hayward*
Dan Pearce....................................... *University of California, Riverside*
Felix Pryor .... *London, England*
Catherine Rainwater .... *St. Edward's University*
Jean W. Ross...*Columbia, South Carolina*
William J. Scheick .... *University of Texas at Austin*
Gay Sibley...*University of Hawaii*
Judy Simons ....*Sheffield City Polytechnic*
Patricia L. Skarda .... *Smith College*
William L. Stull.. *University of Hartford*
Lucia Tarbox ....*Columbia, South Carolina*
John Tebbel...*Southbury, Connecticut*
Lewis Turco.. *Oswego, New York*
Miller Williams .... *University of Arkansas Press*

Cumulative Index

Dictionary of Literary Biography, Volumes 1-56
Dictionary of Literary Biography Yearbook, 1980-1986
Dictionary of Literary Biography Documentary Series, Volumes 1-4

Cumulative Index

DLB before number: *Dictionary of Literary Biography,* Volumes 1-56
Y before number: *Dictionary of Literary Biography Yearbook,* 1980-1986
DS before number: *Dictionary of Literary Biography Documentary Series,* Volumes 1-4

A

Heyward, Dorothy 1890-1961 and
    Heyward, DuBose 1885-1940 ....DLB-7

Heyward, DuBose 1885-1940............ DLB-7, 9, 45

Higgins, Aidan 1927- DLB-14

Higgins, Colin 1941- DLB-26

Higgins, George V. 1939- DLB-2; Y-81

Higginson, Thomas Wentworth 1822-1911......DLB-1

Highwater, Jamake 1942?- DLB-52; Y-85

Hildreth, Richard 1807-1865 ....DLB-1, 30

Hill, Geoffrey 1932- DLB-40

Hill, George M., Company DLB-49

Hill, "Sir" John 1714?-1775................... DLB-39

Hill, Lawrence, and Company, Publishers DLB-46

Hill, Leslie 1880-1960 .... DLB-51

Hill, Susan 1942- DLB-14

Hill, Walter 1942- DLB-44

Hill and Wang................................ DLB-46

Hilliard, Gray and Company DLB-49

Hillyer, Robert 1895-1961 .... DLB-54

Hilton, James 1900-1954 .... DLB-34

Hilton and Company DLB-49

Himes, Chester 1909-1984.....................DLB-2

The History of the Adventures of Joseph Andrews
    (1742), by Henry Fielding [excerpt]....... DLB-39

Hoagland, Edward 1932- DLB-6

Hoagland, Everett H. III 1942- DLB-41

Hoban, Russell 1925- DLB-52

Hobsbaum, Philip 1932- DLB-40

Hobson, Laura Z. 1900- DLB-28

Hochman, Sandra 1936- DLB-5

Hodgman, Helen 1945- DLB-14

Hodgson, Ralph 1871-1962.................... DLB-19

Hoffenstein, Samuel 1890-1947 .... DLB-11

Hoffman, Charles Fenno 1806-1884.............DLB-3

Hoffman, Daniel 1923- DLB-5

Hofmann, Michael 1957- DLB-40

Hofstadter, Richard 1916-1970............... DLB-17

Hogan, Desmond 1950- DLB-14

Hogan and Thompson DLB-49

Hohl, Ludwig 1904-1980 .... DLB-56

Holbrook, David 1923- DLB-14, 40

Holcroft, Thomas 1745-1809 .... DLB-39

Holden, Molly 1927-1981..................... DLB-40

Holiday House DLB-46

Hollander, John 1929- DLB-5

Holley, Marietta 1836-1926................... DLB-11

Hollo, Anselm 1934- DLB-40

Holloway, John 1920- DLB-27

Holloway House Publishing Company........ DLB-46

Holme, Constance 1880-1955.................. DLB-34

Holmes, Oliver Wendell 1809-1894.............DLB-1

Holmes, John Clellon 1926- DLB-16

Holst, Hermann E. von 1841-1904 .... DLB-47

Holt, Henry, and Company DLB-49

Holt, John 1721-1784 .... DLB-43

Holt, Rinehart and Winston DLB-46

Home, Henry, Lord Kames 1696-1782........ DLB-31

Home Publishing Company DLB-49

Home, William Douglas 1912- DLB-13

Homes, Geoffrey (see Mainwaring, Daniel)

Honig, Edwin 1919- DLB-5

Hood, Hugh 1928- DLB-53

Hooker, Jeremy 1941- DLB-40

Hooker, Thomas 1586-1647................... DLB-24

Hooper, Johnson Jones 1815-1862 ....DLB-3, 11

Hopkins, Gerard Manley 1844-1889........... DLB-35

Hopkins, John H., and Son................... DLB-46

Hopkins, Lemuel 1750-1801................... DLB-37

Hopkins, Pauline Elizabeth 1859-1930........ DLB-50

Hopkins, Samuel 1721-1803................... DLB-31

Hopkinson, Francis 1737-1791 .... DLB-31

Horgan, Paul 1903- Y-85

Horizon Press DLB-46

Horne, Frank 1899-1974 .... DLB-51

Horne, Richard Henry (Hengist) 1802
    or 1803-1884............................ DLB-32

Horovitz, Israel 1939- DLB-7

Horton, George Moses 1797?-1883?.......... DLB-50

Hosford, E. and E. [publishing house]........ DLB-49

Hotchkiss and Company....................... DLB-49

Hough, Emerson 1857-1923....................DLB-9

Cumulative Index

L

Cumulative Index

O

P

Y